ACCA

PAPER P2

CORPORATE REPORTING
(INTERNATIONAL AND UK STREAM)

BPP Learning Media is the **sole ACCA Platinum Approved Learning Partner – content** for the ACCA qualification. In this, **the only Paper P2 Practice and Revision Kit to be reviewed by the examiner**:

- We discuss the **best strategies** for revising and taking your ACCA exams

- We show you how to be **well prepared** for your exam

- We give you **lots of great guidance** on tackling questions

- We show you how you can **build your own exams**

- We provide you with **three** mock exams including the **December 2012 exam**

- We provide the **ACCA examiner's answers** as well as our own to the June and December 2012 exams as an additional revision aid

Our **Passcard** and **i-pass** products also support this paper.

FOR EXAMS UP TO JUNE 2014

BPP
LEARNING MEDIA

PRACTICE & REVISION KIT

First edition 2007
Eighth edition January 2013

ISBN 9781 4453 6652 4
(previous ISBN 9781 4453 8001 8)

e-ISBN 9781 4453 6955 6

British Library Cataloguing-in-Publication Data
A catalogue record for this book
is available from the British Library

Published by

BPP Learning Media Ltd
BPP House, Aldine Place
London W12 8AA

www.bpp.com/learningmedia

Printed in the United Kingdom by Polestar Wheatons

Hennock Road
Marsh Barton
Exeter
EX2 8RP

We are grateful to the Association of Chartered Certified Accountants for permission to reproduce past examination questions. The suggested answers have been prepared by BPP Learning Media Ltd, except where otherwise stated.

Contents

A note about copyright

Dear Customer

What does the little © mean and why does it matter?

Your market-leading BPP books, course materials and e-learning materials do not write and update themselves. People write them: on their own behalf or as employees of an organisation that invests in this activity. Copyright law protects their livelihoods. It does so by creating rights over the use of the content.

Breach of copyright is a form of theft – as well as being a criminal offence in some jurisdictions, it is potentially a serious breach of professional ethics.

With current technology, things might seem a bit hazy but, basically, without the express permission of BPP Learning Media:

- Photocopying our materials is a breach of copyright
- Scanning, ripcasting or conversion of our digital materials into different file formats, uploading them to facebook or emailing them to your friends is a breach of copyright

You can, of course, sell your books, in the form in which you have bought them – once you have finished with them. (Is this fair to your fellow students? We update for a reason.) Please note the e-products are sold on a single user licence basis: we do not supply 'unlock' codes to people who have bought them second-hand.

And what about outside the UK? BPP Learning Media strives to make our materials available at prices students can afford by local printing arrangements, pricing policies and partnerships which are clearly listed on our website. A tiny minority ignore this and indulge in criminal activity by illegally photocopying our material or supporting organisations that do. If they act illegally and unethically in one area, can you really trust them?

Using your BPP Learning Media products

This Kit gives you the question practice and guidance you need in the exam. Our other products can also help you pass:

- **Learning to Learn Accountancy** gives further valuable advice on revision
- **Passcards** provide you with clear topic summaries and exam tips
- **Success CDs** help you revise on the move
- **i-Pass CDs** offer tests of knowledge against the clock
- **Underlying knowledge CD** offers guidance on assumed knowledge for Options papers P4, P5, P6, P7

You can purchase these products by visiting http://www.bpp.com/acca

Question index

The headings in this checklist/index indicate the main topics of questions, but questions often cover several different topics.

Questions set under the old syllabus *Advanced Corporate Reporting* paper are included because their style and content are similar to those which appear in the P2 exam. The questions have been amended to reflect the current exam format.

Planning your question practice

Our guidance from page xxv shows you how to organise your question practice, either by attempting questions from each syllabus area or **by building your own exams** – tackling questions as a series of practice exams.

June and December 2013 exams

BPP's answers for these exams will be available for free after the exams on http://www.bpp.com/acca

BPP
LEARNING MEDIA

Topic index

Listed below are the key Paper P2 syllabus topics and the numbers of the questions in this Kit covering those topics.

If you need to concentrate your practice and revision on certain topics or if you want to attempt all available questions that refer to a particular subject, you will find this index useful.

Syllabus topic	Question numbers
Associates	33
Complex groups	34 – 37
Consolidated statement of financial position	41
Consolidated statement of profit or loss and other comprehensive income	37
Consolidated statement of cash flows	50 – 52
Corporate citizenship	71
Disposals	38 – 44
Employee benefits	9 – 12
Environmental issues	4
Ethics	41 – 43
Financial instruments	16 – 20
Foreign currency	44 – 48
IAS 1 (revised)	Throughout
Impairment	57, 59
International issues	59, 60, 74, 78
IFRS 2	21 – 23
IFRS 3	32 – 52
IFRS 9	16 – 20
IFRS 10 to 11	32 – 52
IFRS 13	59, throughout
Joint ventures	37, 59
Measurement of performance	53 – 60
Non-current assets	5 – 7
Provisions	24 – 26
Related party transactions	27, 28
Reporting performance	54, 76
Revenue recognition	3, 7, 55
Share-based payment	21 – 23
Small and medium-sized entities	69, 70
Taxation	13 – 15

Helping you with your revision – the ONLY P2 Practice and Revision Kit to be reviewed by the examiner!

BPP Learning Media – the sole Platinum Approved Learning Partner – content

As ACCA's **sole Platinum Approved Learning Partner – content**, BPP Learning Media gives you the **unique opportunity** to use **examiner-reviewed** revision materials for the exams up to June 2014. By incorporating the examiner's comments and suggestions regarding syllabus coverage, the BPP Learning Media Practice and Revision Kit provides excellent, **ACCA-approved** support for your revision.

Tackling revision and the exam

Using feedback obtained from ACCA examiners as part of their review:

- We look at the dos and don'ts of revising for, and taking, ACCA exams

- We focus on Paper P2; we discuss revising the syllabus, what to do (and what not to do) in the exam, how to approach different types of question and ways of obtaining easy marks

Selecting questions

We provide signposts to help you plan your revision.

- A full **question index**

- A **topic index** listing all the questions that cover key topics, so that you can locate the questions that provide practice on these topics, and see the different ways in which they might be examined

- **BPP's question plan** highlighting the most important questions and explaining why you should attempt them

- **Build your own exams**, showing how you can practise questions in a series of exams

Making the most of question practice

At BPP Learning Media we realise that you need more than just questions and model answers to get the most from your question practice.

- Our **Top tips** included for certain questions provide essential advice on tackling questions, presenting answers and the key points that answers need to include

- We show you how you can pick up **Easy marks** on some questions, as we know that picking up all readily available marks often can make the difference between passing and failing

- We include **marking guides** to show you what the examiner rewards

- We include **examiners' comments** to show you where students struggled or performed well in the actual exam

- We refer to the **2012 BPP Study Text** (for exams up to June 2014) for detailed coverage of the topics covered in questions

- In a bank at the end of this Kit we include the **examiner's answers** to the June and December 2012 papers. Used in conjunction with our answers they provide an indication of all possible points that could be made, issues that could be covered and approaches to adopt.

Attempting mock exams

There are three mock exams that provide practice at coping with the pressures of the exam day. We strongly recommend that you attempt them under exam conditions. **Mock exams 1 and 2** reflect the question styles and syllabus coverage of the exam; **Mock exam 3** is the December 2012 paper.

Revising P2

Topics to revise

P2 has the reputation of being a difficult paper. However its pass rate is usually quite high. Although the examiner, Graham Holt, sets challenging questions, the styles of question he uses are now familiar because he has been the examiner for many years. He has also provided a great deal of feedback in his examiner's reports and in the very detailed published marking schemes, many of which are included in this Kit.

Graham Holt has warned very strongly against question-spotting and trying to predict the topics that will be included in the exam. He has on occasions examined the same topic in two successive sittings. He regards few areas as off-limits for questions, and nearly all of the major areas of the syllabus can and have been tested.

That said, exams over the years have shown that the following areas of the syllabus are very important, and your revision therefore needs to cover them particularly well.

- **Group accounts.** You should not omit any aspect of group accounts, as they come up every sitting. We would advise against question spotting, but if a statement of cash flows, say, has not come up for a few sittings, it might be a good bet. Group accounts will always be examined as part of the 50 mark case study question, in which you may also expect a question on some aspect of **ethics**

- **Emerging issues.** The impact of a change in accounting standards on the financial statements is often examined. Look on the IASB website for details: www.iasb.org

- **Share based payment** usually comes up as part of a question.

- **Financial instruments** was the subject of regular *Student Accountant* articles, and it is regularly tested. Questions will be set in terms of IFRS 9 as far as it applies.

- **Developments in financial reporting**, for example, IFRS 10 to 13 and the revised IAS 19.

Question practice

Question practice under timed conditions is essential, so that you can get used to the pressures of answering exam questions in **limited time** and practise not only the key techniques but allocating your time between different requirements in each question. Our list of recommended questions includes compulsory Section A and optional Section B questions; it's particularly important to do all the Section A case-study-style questions in full as a case study involving group accounts will always come up.

Passing the P2 exam

What to expect on the paper

Of course you cannot know in advance what questions are going to come up, but you can have a fair idea of what kind of questions.

Question 1

This will always be a case study, with half or a little more than half on group accounts. It will often involve high speed number crunching. Easy marks, it cannot be said too often, will always be available for basic consolidation techniques. You cannot pass the groups part on these alone, but it can give you a foothold. Question 1 usually has a bit of a twist, for example financial instruments or pensions. This question will also contain an element of written explanation and a question on ethics or corporate social accounting. For example, the December 2010 paper had a statement of cash flows; then you were asked to explain whether a change of method of preparing such a statement was ethical.

The examiner has stressed the importance of answering the written parts of question 1. Many students ignore parts (b) and (c), but marks can be gained for common sense.

Question 1 will always have more than half the marks allocated to the computational part. Generally, it will be in the order of 35 marks.

Questions 2 and 3

These each cover several IFRSs and are very often – although not always – mini-case-studies, involving you in giving advice to the directors on accounting treatment, possibly where the directors have followed the wrong treatment. Being multi-standard, you may be able to answer parts, but not all of a question, so it makes sense to look through the paper to select a question where you can answer most of it. If Part (a) is on an area you are not confident about, do not dismiss the question out of hand.

The examiner is testing whether you can identify the issues. Even if you don't get the accounting treatment exactly right, you will still gain some credit for showing that you have seen what the problem is about. So do not be afraid to have a stab at something, even if you are not sure of the details.

These questions can be on a single standard or theme. One of these questions will be the specialised industry question.

Question 4

This question is generally on developments in financial reporting. It may cover an aspect of reporting financial performance – for example the Management Commentary, but it can also be set on just one standard if this standard is undergoing revision.

While you certainly cannot bluff your way through Question 4, if you know your material it is a good way of earning marks without high speed number crunching.

Question 4 may now include a computational aspect illustrating the topic you have just discussed. Usually these are fairly straightforward.

> **Remember!**
>
> The examiner stresses that it is important to learn principles rather than rote-learning techniques. He has also said on a number of occasions that candidates should use the information in the scenario. For example, in June 2012:
>
> 'Often the content of the scenario will help students answer the question as the scenario gives candidates direction in terms of their answers.'
>
> The examiner has stated that students need to have a basic/good understanding of all standards and the capability of applying them. They should always give an explanation of the IFRSs which underpin their answer.

Exam technique for P2

Do not be needlessly intimidated

There is no shortcut to passing this exam. It looks very difficult indeed, and many students wonder if they will ever pass. But most students generally do. Why is this?

Easy marks

All the questions are demanding, but there are many easy marks to be gained. Suppose, for example, you had a consolidated statement of cash flows with a disposal, a pension complication and a financial instruments calculation. There will be easy marks available simply for the basic cash flow aspects, setting out the proforma, setting up your workings, presenting your work neatly. If you recognise, as you should, that the disposal needs to be taken into account, of course you will get marks for that, even if you make a mistake in the arithmetic. If you get the pension bit right, so much the better, but you could pass the question comfortably while omitting this altogether. If you're short of time, this is what you should do.

Be ruthless in ignoring the complications

Look at the question. Within reason, if there are complications – often only worth a few marks – that you know you will not have time or knowledge to do, cross them out. It will make you feel better. Than tackle the bits you can do. This is how people pass a seemingly impossible paper.

Be ruthless in allocating your time

At BPP, we have seen how very intelligent students do two almost perfect questions, one averagely good and one sketchy. The first eight to ten marks are the easiest to get. Then you have to push it up to what you think is fifteen (thirty for the case study question), to get yourself a pass.

Do your best question either first or second, and the compulsory question either first or second. The compulsory question, being on groups, will always have some easy marks available for consolidation techniques.

Exam information

Format of the exam

Section A will consist of one scenario based question worth 50 marks. It will deal with the preparation of consolidated financial statements including group statements of cash flow and with issues in financial reporting.

Students will be required to answer two out of three questions in Section B, which will normally comprise two questions which will be scenario or case-study based and one question which will be an essay. Section B could deal with any aspects of the syllabus.

Additional information

The Study Guide provides more detailed guidance on the syllabus.

December 2012

Section A

1   Consolidated statement of financial position with sub-subsidiary, associate and disposal group; discussion on IFRS 5; ethical considerations of accounting treatment

Section B

2   Government grant; foreign exchange and cash flows; IFRS 10 and control; taxation and prior period adjustment
3   Investment property; leasing (substance of transaction); provision; impairment
4   IFRS 13 *Fair value measurement:* principles, three-level hierarchy; IFRS 13 fair valuing of asset and liability with computations

The December 2012 Paper is Mock Exam 3 in this Kit.

June 2012

Section A   *Question in this Kit*

1   42
     Consolidated statement of financial position with business combination achieved in stages and joint operation; de-recognition of financial asset ; ethics

Section B

2   Sale and leaseback, defined benefit pension plan, cash-settled share-based payment and contingent liability in the context of a business combination   31
3   Measuring fair value, impairment of goodwill, deferred tax liabilities and the fair value option for an accounting mismatch; shares as financial liability or equity   64
4   Changing rules on provisions (discussion and calculation)   25

Examiner's comments

Generally candidates performed well on this paper, with Questions 1 and 2 being answered better than Questions 3 and 4.

Candidates approached the examination well and did not appear too time-pressured, but some failed to produce answers of sufficient length and appear to be spending too much time on question 1. Question 1(a) is designed to test candidates' computational skills and very brief explanations may be useful to the marker but many candidates entered into detailed discussion of the relevant standard, which costs time in the examination, and it is important for candidates to use their time effectively. Very few marks are allocated in question 1(a) for detailed discussion.

Candidates often wasted time discussing a standard in detail when an application of the standard was required. Candidates should read the question and formulate an answer in their mind. The answer should be based upon the detail of the question. Simply reading the requirement without application to the scenario does not gain marks.

This examination focussed on application of knowledge and it was application, which often let candidates down. Candidates often do not use the information in the scenario in order to develop their answers. Often the content of the scenario will help students answer the question as the scenario gives candidates direction in terms of their answers. This was particularly true of Question 4.

December 2011

Section A   *Question in this Kit*

1   Consolidated statement of financial position with business combination achieved in   41
      stages; segment reporting; ethics

Section B

2   Internal reconstruction   68
3   Specialised industry question: intangible assets and impairment testing rules   8
4   Revenue recognition: current problems and proposed changes   3

Examiner's comments

The standard of answers varied. Many candidates passed the examination because of strong performance on question 1 and the questions answered best by candidates were Question 1a, Questions 3(a/c), and Question 4(a)(i).

Answers to Section B questions are often very general in nature with no relationship to the facts given in the scenario. This can involve just repeating information given in the question without explaining how it impacts on the financial statements or just quoting facts from standards without reference to the question. This can result in long answers that often don't address the issues in a scenario and may leave candidates bemused as to why they have failed when they have written so much. Often these scripts bordered on illegibility, which makes marking difficult. It is often better to explain a few points well than trying to regurgitate all the knowledge that the candidate possesses. There were however many excellent scripts, particularly in answering the technical aspects of group accounting and the issues surrounding intangible assets.

Too many candidates let themselves down by failing to attempt all parts of the questions chosen, or in some cases by answering all four questions.

June 2011

Section A

Examiner's comments

The examination consisted of four questions (Question 1 for 50 marks and three further questions of 25 marks each of which candidates had to choose two to answer) The performance of candidates was quite pleasing with good marks being achieved in all aspects of the paper. The approach to the examination is good with little evidence of time pressure although some candidates are still failing to produce answers of sufficient length and appear to be spending too much time on a single question. Candidates do not use the information in the scenario in order to develop their answers.

Question 1 is designed to test candidates' computational skills and brief explanations are often useful to the marker but detailed discussion of the relevant standard is not normally required. Candidates often wasted time discussing a standard in detail when an application of the standard was required. It is important also to make sure that the answer is relevant to the question. In this exam there was evidence of students discussing standards at length that were not relevant to the question.

December 2010

June 2010

Section A		Question in this Kit
1	SPLOC1 with two disposals and adjustments relating to other topics	44
Section B		
2	Deferred tax; impairments; deemed disposal / discontinuation; retirement benefits	57
3	Specialised industry: derivatives and hedging; brands; purchase of retail outlets through companies	63
4	Flaws in accounting for leasing; numerical adjustments on sale and leaseback	30

December 2009

Examiner's comments The paper dealt with a wide range of issues and accounting standards. The examiner said that the paper was quite testing but that candidates responded well resulting in a pleasing pass rate. Candidates had benefited from reading articles in *Student Accountant* on specific topics and had built on their knowledge, particularly of the revised IFRS 3 and financial instruments. Candidates also seem to have applied good examination techniques in answering the paper. In particular, candidates were not making the mistake of missing out questions or parts of questions.

June 2009

Examiner's comments. This was the first sitting where the technical aspects of IFRS 3 (Revised) 'Business Combinations' were examined in question 1. It seemed as though many candidates were not adequately prepared for the question even though several articles had appeared in the student accountant. The results overall were disappointing. The main reasons for this appeared to be lack of a thorough understanding of IFRS 3 (Revised), poor time management and difficulty in applying knowledge to questions. An important aspect of the paper is the current issues question. Generally speaking current issues would comprise those issues being discussed in the accountancy press or those issues being dealt with by the IASB in its current work programme or very recent accounting standards. Candidates do not perform well on current issues questions and in order to improve their performance in this area, they should make sure that they manage their own learning by reading wider than just course notes and manuals. The IASB work programme for example is open for everyone to view and web sites such as www.iasplus.com are available for candidates to read around subjects that are on the programme.

December 2008

June 2008

Section A   *Question in this Kit*

1   Groups with a foreign subsidiary, other adjustments and the remainder on ethical issues   47

Section B

2   Segment reporting and revenue recognition in a specialised industry   65
3   Retirement benefits and financial instruments   72
4   Transition to IFRS   78

December 2007

Section A   *Question in this Kit*

1   Business combination achieved in stages; factored receivables; environmental provision
    and report; ethical and social altitudes   75

Section B

2   Retirement benefits; provisions   11
3   Discontinued operations; deferred tax; impairment; lease   56
4   Conceptual framework   1

Pilot paper

Exam update

Examinable documents

The following documents are examinable up to and including the June 2014 sitting.

Knowledge of new examinable regulations issued by 30 September will be required in examination sessions being held in the following calendar year. Documents may be examinable even if the effective date is in the future.

The documents listed as being examinable are the latest that were issued prior to 30 September 2012 and will be examinable in June and December 2013, and June 2014 examination sessions.

[For sittings beyond June 2014, the exam year will run from 1 September to the following 31 August. The cut off relating to examinable documents will be set 12 months prior to the start of the year. The first exam year that will use this new cycle is the 12 months that commences 1 September 2014, in other words the December 2014 exams onwards.]

The study guide offers more detailed guidance on the depth and level at which the examinable documents will be examined. The study guide should be read in conjunction with the examinable documents list.

	Title
	International Accounting Standards (IASs)/International Financial Reporting Standards (IFRSs)
IAS 1	Presentation of financial statements
IAS 2	Inventories
IAS 7	Statement of cash flows
IAS 8	Accounting policies, changes in accounting estimates and errors
IAS 10	Events after the reporting period
IAS 12	Income taxes
IAS 16	Property, plant and equipment
IAS 17	Leases
IAS 18	Revenue
IAS 19	Employee benefits
IAS 20	Accounting for government grants and disclosure of government assistance
IAS 21	The effects of changes in foreign exchange rates
IAS 23	Borrowing costs
IAS 24	Related party disclosures
IAS 27	Separate financial statements
IAS 28	Investments in associates and joint ventures
IAS 32	Financial Instruments: presentation
IAS 33	Earnings per share
IAS 34	Interim financial reporting
IAS 36	Impairment of assets
IAS 37	Provisions, contingent liabilities and contingent assets
IAS 38	Intangible assets
IAS 39	Financial Instruments: recognition and measurement
IAS 40	Investment property
IFRS 1	First-time adoption of international financial reporting standards
IFRS 2	Share-based payment
IFRS 3	Business combinations (revised Jan 2008)
IFRS 5	Non-current assets held for sale and discontinued operations
IFRS 7	Financial instruments: disclosures
IFRS 8	Operating segments
IFRS 9	Financial instruments

	Title
IFRS 11	Joint arrangements
IFRS 12	Disclosure of interests in other entities
IFRS 13	Fair value measurement
IFRS	For Small and Medium-sized Entities
	Other Statements
	Conceptual Framework for Financial reporting
	Management Commentary
	EDs, Discussion Papers and Other Documents
ED	Revenue from contracts with customers
ED	Leases
ED	Financial instruments: amortised cost and impairment (including expected loss approach)
ED/Draft IFRS	IFRS 9 Chapter 6 Hedge accounting
ED	Offsetting financial assets and liabilities
ED	Improvements to IFRS
ED	Investment entities

Note. The accounting of financial assets and financial liabilities is accounted for in accordance with IFRS 9 to the extent that this standard was in issue as at 30 September 2012. For any elements of the study guide deemed as examinable and not covered by IFRS 9, these elements should be dealt with by studying IAS 39.

Important!

For any updates on documents and other matters relating to P2 (International or UK), please see our BPP Learning Media ACCA Platinum micro site. This site can be accessed by following the link below and using your unique login details that are given at the front of this kit.

http://accaresources.bpp.com/student/login/index.php

For the UK Stream Supplement, visit http:///www.bpp.com/acca

Useful websites

The websites below provide additional sources of information of relevance to your studies for *Corporate Reporting*.

•	ACCA	www.accaglobal.com
•	BPP	www.bpp.com
•	IASB	www.iasb.org
•	Financial Times	www.ft.com
•	Accountancy Foundation	www.accountancyfoundation.com
•	International Federation of Accountants (IFAC)	www.ifac.org
•	IAS Plus	www.IASPlus.com

Planning your question practice

We have already stressed that question practice should be right at the centre of your revision. Whilst you will spend some time looking at your notes and Paper P2 Passcards, you should spend the majority of your revision time practising questions.

We recommend two ways in which you can practise questions.

- Use **BPP's question plan** to work systematically through the syllabus and attempt key and other questions on a section-by-section basis

- **Build your own exams** – attempt questions as a series of practice exams

These ways are suggestions and simply following them is no guarantee of success. You or your college may prefer an alternative but equally valid approach.

BPP's question plan

The BPP plan below requires you to devote a **minimum of 50 hours** to revision of Paper P2. Any time you can spend over and above this should only increase your chances of success.

Step 1   **Review your notes** and the chapter summaries in the Paper P2 **Passcards** for each section of the syllabus.

Step 2   **Answer the key questions** for that section. These questions have boxes round the question number in the table below and you should answer them in full. Even if you are short of time you must attempt these questions if you want to pass the exam. You should complete your answers without referring to our solutions.

Step 3   **Attempt the other questions** in that section. For some questions we have suggested that you prepare **answer plans or do the calculations** rather than full solutions. Planning an answer means that you should spend about 40% of the time allowance for the questions brainstorming the question and drawing up a list of points to be included in the answer.

Step 4   Attempt **Mock exams 1, 2 and 3** under strict exam conditions.

Syllabus section	2012 Passcards chapters	Questions in this Kit	Comments	Done ☑
Conceptual framework	1	1	Learn our answer. Covers most aspects of this topic that are likely to come up.	☐
Environmental, social and cultural issues	2, 3	4	Comes up regularly. This question covers most topics you're likely to need.	☐
Non-current assets	4	5	Key. A question that requires you to think clearly about the issues. Do in full.	☐
Taxation	6	15	A demanding question from the pilot paper. Answer in full.	☐
Employee benefits	5	10	Accounting for employee benefits. Do in full. Make sure that you understand how the calculation 'works'.	☐
Leasing contracts	10	30	Leasing will come up as part of a longer question.	☐
Financial instruments	7	19	Granger. Do in full. Very topical.	☐
Mixed bag	11	25	Royan. Typical 'mixed tag' question from theJune 2012 paper.	☐
Measurement of performance	18	55	Carpart. Useful question. Answer plan.	☐
Reporting financial performance	18	57	Cate. Redo if necessary to make sure you have this topic well sorted for the exam.	☐
Share-based payment	16	23	Greenie. A full question on a favourite topic.	☐
Related party disclosures	8	27	Egin Group. Useful question. Prepare an answer plan and make sure you remember the key learning points for exam purposes.	☐
Associates and joint ventures	12, 13	33	Revision question to remind you of IAS 28.	☐
Joint arrangements	13	62	Burley. A recent question, amended to test the IFRS 11 rules on joint arrangements.	
Complex groups	13	37	Rod. A high priority question. Make sure you review your answer thoroughly. Identify areas where you require remedial action.	☐ ☐
		44	Recent complex group case study question. Do in full.	☐
Changes in group structures	14	41	Traveler. Good, recent question.	☐
		43	Grange – case study questions testing changes in group structure. Do in full.	☐
		75	Beth – useful case study with step acquisition.	
Foreign currency transaction	16	47	Memo. A useful question. Have a good stab at it.	☐
		49	Rose – a case study question with FX. Do in full.	

Syllabus section	2012 Passcards chapters	Questions in this Kit	Comments	Done ✓
Statements of cash flows	17	51	Jocatt. Statements of cash flows can yield sure marks. Do and redo till you can complete one quickly and accurately in an exam. This is a case study question. Do in full.	☐
	17	52	Warrburt: question with a group statement of cash flows. Do in full.	☐
Current events	19	58	Useful coverage of range of issues. Do in full.	☐

Build your own exams

Having revised your notes and the BPP Passcards, you can attempt the questions in the Kit as a series of practice exams. You can organise the questions in the following ways.

- Either you can attempt complete past exam papers; recent papers are listed below:

	Dec 08 Question in Kit	June 09 Question in Kit	Dec 09 Question in this Kit	June 10 Question in this Kit	Dec 10 Question in this Kit	June 11 Question in this Kit	Dec 11 Question in this Kit	June 12 Question in this Kit
Section A								
1	52	43	44	44	51	49	41	42
Section B								
2	32	20	5	57	22	62	68	31
3	7	55	62	63	23	50	8	64
4	2	12	17	30	70	19	3	25

- Or you can make up practice exams, either yourself or using the suggestions we have listed below.

	Practice exams						
	1	2	3	4	5	6	7
Section A							
1	37	45	37	52	40	75	52
Section B							
2	12	13	16	17	20	22	19
3	64	61	62	63	54	56	18
4	72	59	65	58	58	59	60

Whichever practice exams you use, you must attempt **Mock exams 1, 2 and 3** at the end of your revision.

Planning your question practice

BPP
LEARNING MEDIA

Questions

REGULATORY AND ETHICAL FRAMEWORK

Questions 1 to 4 cover Regulatory and Ethical Framework, the subject of Part A of the BPP Study Text for Paper P2.

1 Conceptual framework

45 mins

`12/07`

The International Accounting Standards Board (IASB) is working on a joint project with the FASB to revisit its conceptual framework for financial accounting and reporting. The goals of the project are to build on the existing frameworks and converge them into a common framework. The first phase has now been published as the *Conceptual Framework for Financial Reporting*.

Required

(a)   Discuss why there is a need to develop an agreed international conceptual framework and the extent to which an agreed international conceptual framework can be used to resolve practical accounting issues.

(13 marks)

(b)   Discuss the key issues which will need to be addressed in determining the basic components of an internationally agreed conceptual framework.

(10 marks)

Appropriateness and quality of discussion.

(2 marks)

(Total = 25 marks)

2 Accounting standards and disclosure

45 mins

`12/08`

Whilst acknowledging the importance of high quality corporate reporting, the recommendations to improve it are sometimes questioned on the basis that the marketplace for capital can determine the nature and quality of corporate reporting. It could be argued that additional accounting and disclosure standards would only distort a market mechanism that already works well and would add costs to the reporting mechanism, with no apparent benefit. It could be said that accounting standards create costly, inefficient, and unnecessary regulation. It could be argued that increased disclosure reduces risks and offers a degree of protection to users. However, increased disclosure has several costs to the preparer of financial statements.

Required

(a)   Explain why accounting standards are needed to help the market mechanism work effectively for the benefit of preparers and users of corporate reports.

(9 marks)

(b)   Discuss the relative costs to the preparer and benefits to the users of financial statements of increased disclosure of information in financial statements.

(14 marks)

Quality of discussion and reasoning.

(2 marks)

(Total = 25 marks)

3 Venue

45 mins

`12/11`

It is argued that there is limited revenue recognition guidance available from IFRS with many companies following the current provisions of US GAAP. The revenue recognition standard, IAS 18 *Revenue*, has been criticised because an entity applying the standards might recognise amounts in the financial statements that do not faithfully represent the nature of the transactions. It has been further argued that current standards are inconsistent with principles used in other accounting standards, and further that the notion of the risks and rewards of ownership has also been subjectively applied in sale transactions.

Required

(a) (i)   Discuss the main weaknesses in the current standard on revenue recognition.   **(11 marks)**

     (ii) Discuss the reasons why it might be relevant to take into account credit risk and the time value of money in assessing revenue recognition.   **(5 marks)**

           Professional marks will be awarded in part (a) for clarity and expression of your discussion.   **(2 marks)**

(b) (i)   Venue enters into a contract with a customer to provide computers at a value of $1 million. The terms are that payment is due one month after the sale of the goods. On the basis of experience with other contractors with similar characteristics, Venue considers that there is a 5% risk that the customer will not pay the amount due after the goods have been delivered and the property transferred. Venue subsequently felt that the financial condition of the customer has deteriorated and that the trade receivable is further impaired by $100,000.

     (ii) Venue has also sold a computer hardware system to a customer and, because of the current difficulties in the market, Venue has agreed to defer receipt of the selling price of $2 million until two years after the hardware has been transferred to the customer.

           Venue has also been offering discounts to customers if products were sold with terms whereby payment was due now but the transfer of the product was made in one year. A sale had been made under these terms and payment of $3 million had been received.

           A discount rate of 4% should be used in any calculations.

     Required

     Discuss how both of the above transactions would be treated in subsequent financial statements under IAS 18 and also whether there would be difference in treatment if the collectability of the debt and the time value of money were taken into account.   **(7 marks)**

                                                                      (Total = 25 marks)

4 Glowball   **45 mins**

ACR, Pilot paper

The directors of Glowball, a public limited company, had discussed the study by the Institute of Environmental Management which indicated that over 35% of the world's largest 250 corporations are voluntarily releasing green reports to the public to promote corporate environmental performance and to attract customers and investors. They have heard that their main competitors are applying the 'Global Reporting Initiative' (GRI) in an effort to develop a worldwide format for corporate environmental reporting. However, the directors are unsure as to what this initiative actually means. Additionally they require advice as to the nature of any legislation or standards relating to environmental reporting, as they are worried that any environmental report produced by the company may not be of sufficient quality and may detract and not enhance their image if the report does not comply with recognised standards. Glowball has a reputation for ensuring the preservation of the environment in its business activities.

Further the directors have collected information in respect of a series of events which they consider to be important and worthy of note in the environmental report but are not sure as to how they would be incorporated in the environmental report or whether they should be included in the financial statements.

The events are as follows.

(a) Glowball is a company that pipes gas from offshore gas installations to major consumers. The company purchased its main competitor during the year and found that there were environmental liabilities arising out of the restoration of many miles of farmland that had been affected by the laying of a pipeline. There was no legal obligation to carry out the work but the company felt that there would be a cost of around $150 million if the farmland was to be restored.

(b) Most of the offshore gas installations are governed by operating licenses which specify limits to the substances which can be discharged to the air and water. These limits vary according to local legislation and tests are carried out by the regulatory authorities. During the year the company was prosecuted for infringements of an environmental law in the USA when toxic gas escaped into the atmosphere. In 20X2 the company was prosecuted five times and in 20X1 eleven times for infringement of the law. The final amount of the fine/costs to be imposed by the courts has not been determined but is expected to be around $5 million. The escape occurred over the seas and it was considered that there was little threat to human life.

(c)   The company produced statistics that measure their improvement in the handling of emissions of gases which may have an impact on the environment. The statistics deal with:

(i)   Measurement of the release of gases with the potential to form acid rain. The emissions have been reduced by 84% over five years due to the closure of old plants.

(ii)   Measurement of emissions of substances potentially hazardous to human health. The emissions are down by 51% on 20W8 levels.

(iii)   Measurement of emissions to water that removes dissolved oxygen and substances that may have an adverse effect on aquatic life. Accurate measurement of these emissions is not possible but the company is planning to spend $70 million on research in this area.

(d)   The company tries to reduce the environmental impacts associated with the siting and construction of its gas installations. This is done in the way that minimises the impact on wild life and human beings. Additionally when the installations are at the end of their life, they are dismantled and are not sunk into the sea. The current provision for the decommissioning of these installations is $215 million and there are still decommissioning costs of $407 million to be provided as the company's policy is to build up the required provision over the life of the installation.

Required

Prepare a report suitable for presentation to the directors of Glowball in which you discuss the following elements:

(a)   Current reporting requirements and guidelines relating to environmental reporting.   **(10 marks)**

(b)   The nature of any disclosure which would be required in an environmental report and/or the financial statements for the events (a)-(d) above.   **(15 marks)**

(The mark allocation includes four marks for the style and layout of the report.)   **(Total = 25 marks)**

ACCOUNTING STANDARDS

Questions 5 to 31 cover Accounting Standards, the subject of Part B of the BPP Study Text for Paper P2.

5 Key

45 mins

12/09

(a) Key, a public limited company, is concerned about the reduction in the general availability of credit and the sudden tightening of the conditions required to obtain a loan from banks. There has been a reduction in credit availability and a rise in interest rates. It seems as though there has ceased to be a clear relationship between interest rates and credit availability, and lenders and investors are seeking less risky investments. The directors are trying to determine the practical implications for the financial statements particularly because of large write downs of assets in the banking sector, tightening of credit conditions, and falling sales and asset prices. They are particularly concerned about the impairment of assets and the market inputs to be used in impairment testing. They are afraid that they may experience significant impairment charges in the coming financial year. They are unsure as to how they should test for impairment and any considerations which should be taken into account.

Required

Discuss the main considerations that the company should take into account when impairment testing non-current assets in the above economic climate. **(8 marks)**

Professional marks will be awarded in part (a) for clarity and expression. **(2 marks)**

(b) There are specific assets on which the company wishes to seek advice. The company holds certain non-current assets, which are in a development area and carried at cost less depreciation. These assets cost $3 million on 1 June 20X3 and are depreciated on the straight-line basis over their useful life of five years. An impairment review was carried out on 31 May 20X4 and the projected cash flows relating to these assets were as follows:

Year to	31 May 20X5	31 May 20X6	31 May 20X7	31 May 20X8
Cash flows ($'000)	280	450	500	550

The company used a discount rate of 5%. At 30 November 20X4, the directors used the same cash flow projections and noticed that the resultant value in use was above the carrying amount of the assets and wished to reverse any impairment loss calculated at 31 May 20X4. The government has indicated that it may compensate the company for any loss in value of the assets up to 20% of the impairment loss.

Key holds a non-current asset, which was purchased for $10 million on 1 December 20X1 with an expected useful life of 10 years. On 1 December 20X3, it was revalued to $8.8 million. At 30 November 20X4, the asset was reviewed for impairment and written down to its recoverable amount of $5.5 million.

Key committed itself at the beginning of the financial year to selling a property that is being under-utilised following the economic downturn. As a result of the economic downturn, the property was not sold by the end of the year. The asset was actively marketed but there were no reasonable offers to purchase the asset. Key is hoping that the economic downturn will change in the future and therefore has not reduced the price of the asset.

Required

Discuss with suitable computations, how to account for any potential impairment of the above non-current assets in the financial statements for the year ended 30 November 20X4. **(15 marks)**

Note: The following 5% discount factors may be relevant

Year 1	0.9524
Year 2	0.9070
Year 3	0.8638
Year 4	0.8227

(Total = 25 marks)

6 Prochain

Prochain, a public limited company, operates in the fashion industry and has a financial year end of 31 May 20X6. The company sells its products in department stores throughout the world. Prochain insists on creating its own selling areas within the department stores which are called 'model areas'. Prochain is allocated space in the department store where it can display and market its fashion goods. The company feels that this helps to promote its merchandise. Prochain pays for all the costs of the 'model areas' including design, decoration and construction costs. The areas are used for approximately two years after which the company has to dismantle the 'model areas'. The costs of dismantling the 'model areas' are normally 20% of the original construction cost and the elements of the area are worthless when dismantled. The current accounting practice followed by Prochain is to charge the full cost of the 'model areas' against profit or loss in the year when the area is dismantled. The accumulated cost of the 'model areas' shown in the statement of financial position at 31 May 20X6 is $20 million. The company has estimated that the average age of the 'model areas' is eight months at 31 May 20X6. **(7 marks)**

Prochain acquired 100% of a sports goods and clothing manufacturer, Badex, a private limited company, on 1 June 20X5. Prochain intends to develop its own brand of sports clothing which it will sell in the department stores. The shareholders of Badex valued the company at $125 million based upon profit forecasts which assumed significant growth in the demand for the 'Badex' brand name. Prochain had taken a more conservative view of the value of the company and measured the fair value as being in the region of $108 million to $112 million of which $20 million relates to the brand name 'Badex'. Prochain is only prepared to pay the full purchase price if profits from the sale of 'Badex' clothing and sports goods reach the forecast levels. The agreed purchase price was $100 million plus a further payment of $25 million in two years on 31 May 20X7. This further payment will comprise a guaranteed payment of $10 million with no performance conditions and a further payment of $15 million if the actual profits during this two year period from the sale of Badex clothing and goods exceed the forecast profit. The forecast profit on Badex goods and clothing over the two year period is $16 million and the actual profits in the year to 31 May 20X6 were $4 million. Prochain did not feel at any time since acquisition that the actual profits would meet the forecast profit levels. **(8 marks)**

After the acquisition of Badex, Prochain started developing its own sports clothing brand 'Pro'. The expenditure in the period to 31 May 20X6 was as follows:

Period from	Expenditure type	$m
1 June 20X5 – 31 August 20X5	Research as to the extent of the market	3
1 September 20X5 – 30 November 20X5	Prototype clothing and goods design	4
1 December 20X5 – 31 January 20X6	Employee costs in refinement of products	2
1 February 20X6 – 30 April 20X6	Development work undertaken to finalise design of product	5
1 May 20X6 – 31 May 20X6	Production and launch of products	6
		20

The costs of the production and launch of the products include the cost of upgrading the existing machinery ($3 million), market research costs ($2 million) and staff training costs ($1 million). Currently an intangible asset of $20 million is shown in the financial statements for the year ended 31 May 20X6. **(6 marks)**

Prochain owns a number of prestigious apartments which it leases to famous persons who are under a contract of employment to promote its fashion clothing. The apartments are let at below the market rate. The lease terms are short and are normally for six months. The leases terminate when the contracts for promoting the clothing terminate. Prochain wishes to account for the apartments as investment properties with the difference between the market rate and actual rental charged to be recognised as an employee benefit expense. **(4 marks)**

Assume a discount rate of 5·5% where necessary.

Required

Discuss how the above items should be dealt with in the financial statements of Prochain for the year ended 31 May 20X6 under International Financial Reporting Standards.

(Total = 25 marks)

7 Johan

Johan, a public limited company, operates in the telecommunications industry. The industry is capital intensive with heavy investment in licences and network infrastructure. Competition in the sector is fierce and technological advances are a characteristic of the industry. Johan has responded to these factors by offering incentives to customers and, in an attempt to acquire and retain them, Johan purchased a telecom licence on 1 December 20X6 for $120 million. The licence has a term of six years and cannot be used until the network assets and infrastructure are ready for use. The related network assets and infrastructure became ready for use on 1 December 20X7. Johan could not operate in the country without the licence and is not permitted to sell the licence. Johan expects its subscriber base to grow over the period of the licence but is disappointed with its market share for the year to 30 November 20X8. The licence agreement does not deal with the renewal of the licence but there is an expectation that the regulator will grant a single renewal for the same period of time as long as certain criteria regarding network build quality and service quality are met. Johan has no experience of the charge that will be made by the regulator for the renewal but other licences have been renewed at a nominal cost. The licence is currently stated at its original cost of $120 million in the statement of financial position under non-current assets.

Johan is considering extending its network and has carried out a feasibility study during the year to 30 November 20X8. The design and planning department of Johan identified five possible geographical areas for the extension of its network. The internal costs of this study were $150,000 and the external costs were $100,000 during the year to 30 November 20X8. Following the feasibility study, Johan chose a geographical area where it was going to install a base station for the telephone network. The location of the base station was dependent upon getting planning permission. A further independent study has been carried out by third party consultants in an attempt to provide a preferred location in the area, as there is a need for the optimal operation of the network in terms of signal quality and coverage. Johan proposes to build a base station on the recommended site on which planning permission has been obtained. The third party consultants have charged $50,000 for the study. Additionally Johan has paid $300,000 as a single payment together with $60,000 a month to the government of the region for access to the land upon which the base station will be situated. The contract with the government is for a period of 12 years and commenced on 1 November 20X8. There is no right of renewal of the contract and legal title to the land remains with the government.

Johan purchases telephone handsets from a manufacturer for $200 each, and sells the handsets direct to customers for $150 if they purchase call credit (call card) in advance on what is called a prepaid phone. The costs of selling the handset are estimated at $1 per set. The customers using a prepaid phone pay $21 for each call card at the purchase date. Call cards expire six months from the date of first sale. There is an average unused call credit of $3 per card after six months and the card is activated when sold.

Johan also sells handsets to dealers for $150 and invoices the dealers for those handsets. The dealer can return the handset up to a service contract being signed by a customer. When the customer signs a service contract, the customer receives the handset free of charge. Johan allows the dealer a commission of $280 on the connection of a customer and the transaction with the dealer is settled net by a payment of $130 by Johan to the dealer being the cost of the handset to the dealer ($150) deducted from the commission ($280). The handset cannot be sold separately by the dealer and the service contract lasts for a 12 month period. Dealers do not sell prepaid phones, and Johan receives monthly revenue from the service contract.

The chief operating officer, a non-accountant, has asked for an explanation of the accounting principles and practices which should be used to account for the above events.

Required

Discuss the principles and practices which should be used in the financial year to 30 November 20X8 to account for:

(a)	The licences	**(8 marks)**
(b)	The costs incurred in extending the network	**(7 marks)**
(c)	The purchase of handsets and the recognition of revenue from customers and dealers	**(8 marks)**

Appropriateness and quality of discussion. **(2 marks)**

(Total = 25 marks)

8 Scramble

Scramble, a public limited company, is a developer of online computer games.

(a)   At 30 November 20X1, 65% of Scramble's total assets were mainly represented by internally developed intangible assets comprising the capitalised costs of the development and production of online computer games. These games generate all of Scramble's revenue. The costs incurred in relation to maintaining the games at the same standard of performance are expensed to profit or loss for the year. The accounting policy note states that intangible assets are valued at historical cost. Scramble considers the games to have an indefinite useful life, which is reconsidered annually when the intangible assets are tested for impairment. Scramble determines value in use using the estimated future cash flows which include maintenance expenses, capital expenses incurred in developing different versions of the games and the expected increase in turnover resulting from the above mentioned cash outflows. Scramble does not conduct an analysis or investigation of differences between expected and actual cash flows. Tax effects were also taken into account.   **(7 marks)**

(b)   Scramble has two cash generating units (CGU) which hold 90% of the internally developed intangible assets. Scramble reported a consolidated net loss for the period and an impairment charge in respect of the two CGUs representing 63% of the consolidated profit before tax and 29% of the total costs in the period. The recoverable amount of the CGUs is defined, in this case, as value in use. Specific discount rates are not directly available from the market, and Scramble estimates the discount rates, using its weighted average cost of capital. In calculating the cost of debt as an input to the determination of the discount rate, Scramble used the risk-free rate adjusted by the company specific average credit spread of its outstanding debt, which had been raised two years previously. As Scramble did not have any need for additional financing and did not need to repay any of the existing loans before 20X4, Scramble did not see any reason for using a different discount rate. Scramble did not disclose either the events and circumstances that led to the recognition of the impairment loss or the amount of the loss recognised in respect of each cash-generating unit. Scramble felt that the events and circumstances that led to the recognition of a loss in respect of the first CGU were common knowledge in the market and the events and the circumstances that led to the recognition loss of the second CGU were not needed to be disclosed.   **(7 marks)**

(c)   Scramble wished to diversify its operations and purchased a professional football club, Rashing. In Rashing's financial statements for the year ended 30 November 20X1, it was proposed to include significant intangible assets which related to acquired players' registration rights comprising registration and agents' fees. The agents' fees were paid by the club to players' agents either when a player is transferred to the club or when the contract of a player is extended. Scramble believes that the registration rights of the players are intangible assets but that the agents fees do not meet the criteria to be recognised as intangible assets as they are not directly attributable to the costs of players' contracts. Additionally, Rashing has purchased the rights to 25% of the revenue from ticket sales generated by another football club, Santash, in a different league. Rashing does not sell these tickets nor has any discretion over the pricing of the tickets. Rashing wishes to show these rights as intangible assets in its financial statements.   **(9 marks)**

Required

Discuss the validity of the accounting treatments proposed by Scramble in its financial statements for the year ended 30 November 20X1.

The mark allocation is shown against each of the three accounting treatments above.

Professional marks will be awarded for clarity and expression of your discussion.   **(2 marks)**

(Total = 25 marks)

9 Preparation question: Defined benefit plan

> **BPP Note**. In this question, proformas are given to you to help you get used to setting out your answer. You may wish to transfer them to a separate sheet, or alternatively to use a separate sheet for your workings.

Brutus Co operates a defined benefit pension plan for its employees conditional on a minimum employment period of 6 years. The present value of the future benefit obligations and the fair value of its plan assets on 1 January 20X1 were $110 million and $150 million respectively.

The pension plan received contributions of $7m and paid pensions to former employees of $10m during the year.

Extracts from the most recent actuary's report show the following:

Present value of pension plan obligation at 31 December 20X1	$116m
Fair value of plan assets at 31 December 20X1	$140m
Present cost of pensions earned in the period	$11m
Yield on high quality corporate bonds at 1 January 20X1	10%

On 1 January 20X1, the rules of the pension plan were changed to improve benefits for plan members. The actuary has advised that this will cost $10 million.

Required

Produce the extracts for the financial statements for the year ended 31 December 20X1.

Assume contributions and benefits were paid on 31 December.

Statement of profit or loss and other comprehensive income notes

Defined benefit expense recognised in profit or loss

	$m
Current service cost	
Past service cost	
Net interest on the net defined benefit asset	___
	═══

Other comprehensive income (items that will not be reclassified to profit or loss)
 Remeasurement of defined benefit plans

	$m
Actuarial gain on defined benefit obligation	
Return on plan assets (excluding amounts in net interest)	___
	═══

Statement of financial position notes

Net defined benefit asset recognised in the statement of financial position

	31 December 20X1 $m	31 December 20X0 $m
Present value of pension obligation		
Fair value of plan assets		
Net asset	___	___
	═══	═══

Changes in the present value of the defined benefit obligation

	$m
Opening defined benefit obligation	
Interest on obligation	
Current service cost	
Past service cost	
Benefits paid	
Gain on remeasurement of obligation(balancing figure)	_____
Closing defined benefit obligation	_____

Changes in the fair value of plan assets

	$m
Opening fair value of plan assets	
Interest on plan assets	
Contributions	
Benefits paid	
Loss on remeasurement of assets (balancing figure)	_____
Closing fair value of plan assets	_____

10 Macaljoy

45 mins

12/07, amended

Macaljoy, a public limited company, is a leading support services company which focuses on the building industry. The company would like advice on how to treat certain items under IAS 19 *Employee benefits* and IAS 37 *Provisions, contingent liabilities and contingent assets*. The company operates the Macaljoy Pension Plan B which commenced on 1 November 20X6 and the Macaljoy Pension Plan A, which was closed to new entrants from 31 October 20X6, but which was open to future service accrual for the employees already in the scheme. The assets of the schemes are held separately from those of the company in funds under the control of trustees. The following information relates to the two schemes.

Macaljoy Pension Plan A

The terms of the plan are as follows.

(i)   Employees contribute 6% of their salaries to the plan.

(ii)   Macaljoy contributes, currently, the same amount to the plan for the benefit of the employees.

(iii)   On retirement, employees are guaranteed a pension which is based upon the number of years service with the company and their final salary.

The following details relate to the plan in the year to 31 October 20X7:

	$m
Present value of obligation at 1 November 20X6	200
Present value of obligation at 31 October 20X7	240
Fair value of plan assets at 1 November 20X6	190
Fair value of plan assets at 31 October 20X7	225
Current service cost	20
Pension benefits paid	19
Total contributions paid to the scheme for year to 31 October 20X7	17

Remeasurement gains and losses are recognised in accordance with IAS 19 as revised in 2011.

Macaljoy Pension Plan B

Under the terms of the plan, Macaljoy does not guarantee any return on the contributions paid into the fund. The company's legal and constructive obligation is limited to the amount that is contributed to the fund. The following details relate to this scheme:

	$m
Fair value of plan assets at 31 October 20X7	21
Contributions paid by company for year to 31 October 20X7	10
Contributions paid by employees for year to 31 October 20X7	10

The interest rate on high quality corporate bonds for the two plans are:

1 November 20X6   31 October 20X7
   5%   6%

The company would like advice on how to treat the two pension plans, for the year ended 31 October 20X7, together with an explanation of the differences between a defined contribution plan and a defined benefit plan.

Warranties

Additionally the company manufactures and sells building equipment on which it gives a standard one year warranty to all customers. The company has extended the warranty to two years for certain major customers and has insured against the cost of the second year of the warranty. The warranty has been extended at nil cost to the customer. The claims made under the extended warranty are made in the first instance against Macaljoy and then Macaljoy in turn makes a counter claim against the insurance company. Past experience has shown that 80% of the building equipment will not be subject to warranty claims in the first year, 15% will have minor defects and 5% will require major repair. Macaljoy estimates that in the second year of the warranty, 20% of the items sold will have minor defects and 10% will require major repair.

In the year to 31 October 20X7, the following information is relevant.

	Standard warranty (units)	Extended warranty (units)	Selling price per unit (both)($)
Sales	2,000	5,000	1,000

	Major repair $	Minor defect $
Cost of repair (average)	500	100

Assume that sales of equipment are on 31 October 20X7 and any warranty claims are made on 31 October in the year of the claim. Assume a risk adjusted discount rate of 4%.

Required

Draft a report suitable for presentation to the directors of Macaljoy which:

(a)   (i)   Discusses the nature of and differences between a defined contribution plan and a defined benefit plan with specific reference to the company's two schemes.   **(7 marks)**

       (ii)   Shows the accounting treatment for the two Macaljoy pension plans for the year ended 31 October 20X7 under IAS 19 *Employee benefits* (revised 2011).   **(7 marks)**

(b)   (i)   Discusses the principles involved in accounting for claims made under the above warranty provision.   **(6 marks)**

       (ii)   Shows the accounting treatment for the above warranty provision under IAS 37 *Provisions, contingent liabilities and contingent assets* for the year ended 31 October 20X7.   **(3 marks)**

Appropriateness of the format and presentation of the report and communication of advice.   **(2 marks)**

(Total = 25 marks)

11 Savage   45 mins

ACR, 12/05, amended

Savage, a public limited company, operates a funded defined benefit plan for its employees. The plan provides a pension of 1% of the final salary for each year of service. The cost for the year is determined using the projected unit credit method. This reflects service rendered to the dates of valuation of the plan and incorporates actuarial assumptions primarily regarding discount rates, which are based on the market yields of high quality corporate bonds.

The directors have provided the following information about the defined benefit plan for the current year (year ended 31 October 20X5).

(a) The actuarial cost of providing benefits in respect of employees' service for the year to 31 October 20X5 was $40 million. This is the present value of the pension benefits earned by the employees in the year.

(b) The pension benefits paid to former employees in the year were $42 million.

(c) Savage should have paid contributions to the fund of $28 million. Because of cash flow problems $8 million of this amount had not been paid at the financial year end of 31 October 20X5.

(d) The present value of the obligation to provide benefits to current and former employees was $3,000 million at 31 October 20X4 and $3,375 million at 31 October 20X5.

(e) The fair value of the plan assets was $2,900 million at 31 October 20X4 and $3,170 million (including the contributions owed by Savage) at 31 October 20X5.

With effect from 1 November 20X4, the company had amended the plan so that the employees were now provided with an increased pension entitlement. The actuaries computed that the present value of the cost of these benefits at 1 November 20X4 was $125 million. The interest rate on high quality corporate bonds was as follows from the following dates:

	31 October 20X4	31 October 20X5
Interest rate	6%	7%

The company recognises remeasurement gains and losses in 'other comprehensive income (items that will not be reclassified to profit or loss)' in accordance with IAS 19, revised 2011.

Required

(a) Show the amounts which will be recognised in the statement of financial position, in profit or loss and in other comprehensive income' of Savage for the year ended 31 October 20X5 under IAS 19 *Employee benefits* (revised 2011), and the movement in the asset and liability in the statement of financial position. (Your calculations should show the changes in the present value of the obligation and the fair value of the plan assets during the year. Ignore any deferred taxation effects and assume that pension benefits and the contributions paid were settled at 31 October 20X5.) **(21 marks)**

(b) Explain how the non-payment of contributions and the change in the pension benefits should be treated in the financial statements of Savage for the year ended 31 October 20X5. **(4 marks)**

(Total = 25 marks)

12 Smith

45 mins

6/09, amended

(a) Accounting for defined benefit pension schemes is a complex area of great importance. In some cases, the net pension liability even exceeds the market capitalisation of the company. The financial statements of a company must provide investors, analysts and companies with clear, reliable and comparable information on a company's pension obligations and interest on net plan assets/obligations.

Required

(i) Discuss the problems associated with IAS 19 *Employee benefits* prior to its revision in June 2011 regarding the accounting for actuarial gains and losses, setting out the main criticisms of the approach taken under the old version of the standard. **(6 marks)**

(ii) Outline the advantages of immediate recognition of such gains and losses. **(4 marks)**

(iii) Discuss the other main changes to IAS 19 when it was revised in June 2011, explaining how the revised treatment differed from the previous treatment . **(5 marks)**

(iv) Outline the likely consequences of the revision of IAS 19. **(5 marks)**

Professional marks will be awarded in part (a) for clarity and quality of discussion. **(2 marks)**

(b) Smith operates a defined benefit pension plan for its employees. At 1 January 20X2 the fair value of the pension plan assets was $2,600,000 and the present value of the plan liabilities was $2,900,000.

The actuary estimates that the current and past service costs for the year ended 31 December 20X2 is $450,000 and $90,000 respectively. The past service cost is caused by an increase in pension benefits and takes effect from 31 December 20X2. The plan liabilities at 1 January and 31 December 20X2 correctly reflect the impact of this increase.

The interest rate on high quality corporate bonds for the year ended 31 December 20X2 was 8%.

The pension plan paid $240,000 to retired members on 31 December 20X2. On the same date, Smith paid $730,000 in contributions to the pension plan and this included $90,000 in respect of past service costs.

At 31 December 20X2 the fair value of the pension plan assets is $3,400,000 and the present value of the plan liabilities is $3,500,000.

In accordance with the 2011 revision to IAS 19 *Employee benefits*, Smith recognises actuarial gains and losses (now called 'remeasurement gains and losses') in other comprehensive income in the period in which they occur.

Required

Calculate the remeasurement gains or losses on pension plan assets and liabilities that will be included in other comprehensive income for the year ended 31 December 20X2. (Round all figures to the nearest $'000.)

(3 marks)

(Total = 25 marks)

13 Cohort

40 mins

ACR, 6/02, amended

is a private limited company and has two 100% owned subsidiaries, Legion and Air, both themselves private limited companies. Cohort acquired Air on 1 January 20X2 for $5 million when the fair value of the net assets was $4 million, and the tax base of the net assets was $3.5 million. The acquisition of Air and Legion was part of a business strategy whereby Cohort would build up the 'value' of the group over a three year period and then list its existing share capital on the stock exchange.

(a) The following details relate to the acquisition of Air, which manufactures electronic goods.

(i) Air has sold goods worth $3 million to Cohort since acquisition and made a profit of $1 million on the transaction. The inventory of these goods recorded in Cohort's statement of financial position at the year end of 31 May 20X2 was $1.8 million.

(ii) The balance on the retained earnings of Air at acquisition was $2 million. The directors of Cohort have decided that, during the three years to the date that they intend to list the shares of the company, they will realise earnings through future dividend payments from the subsidiary amounting to $500,000 per year. Tax is payable on any remittance or dividends and no dividends have been declared for the current year.

(10 marks)

(b) Legion was acquired on 1 June 20X1 and is a company which undertakes various projects ranging from debt factoring to investing in property and commodities. The following details relate to Legion for the year ending 31 May 20X2.

(i) Legion has a portfolio of readily marketable government securities which are held as current assets. These investments are stated at market value in the statement of financial position with any gain or loss taken to profit or loss for the year. These gains and losses are taxed when the investments are sold. Currently the accumulated unrealised gains are $4 million.

(ii) Legion has calculated that it requires a specific allowance of $2 million against loans in its portfolio. Tax relief is available when the specific loan is written off.

(iii)   When Cohort acquired Legion it had unused tax losses brought forward. At 1 June 20X1, it appeared that Legion would have sufficient taxable profit to realise the deferred tax asset created by these losses but subsequent events have proven that the future taxable profit will not be sufficient to realise all of the unused tax loss.

The current tax rate for Cohort is 30% and for public companies is 35%.   **(12 marks)**

Required

Write a note suitable for presentation to the partner of an accounting firm setting out the deferred tax implications of the above information for the Cohort Group of companies.

(Total = 22 marks)

14 Panel   **45 mins**

ACR, 12/05

The directors of Panel, a public limited company, are reviewing the procedures for the calculation of the deferred tax liability for their company. They are quite surprised at the impact on the liability caused by changes in accounting standards such as IFRS 1 *First time adoption of International Financial Reporting Standards* and IFRS 2 *Share-based payment*. Panel is adopting International Financial Reporting Standards for the first time as at 31 October 20X5 and the directors are unsure how the deferred tax provision will be calculated in its financial statements ended on that date including the opening provision at 1 November 20X3.

Required

(a)   (i)   Explain how changes in accounting standards are likely to have an impact on the deferred tax liability under IAS 12 *Income taxes*.   **(5 marks)**

       (ii)   Describe the basis for the calculation of the deferred taxation liability on first time adoption of IFRS including the provision in the opening IFRS statement of financial position.   **(4 marks)**

Additionally the directors wish to know how the provision for deferred taxation would be calculated in the following situations under IAS 12 *Income taxes*:

(i)   On 1 November 20X3, the company had granted ten million share options worth $40 million subject to a two year vesting period. Local tax law allows a tax deduction at the exercise date of the intrinsic value of the options. The intrinsic value of the ten million share options at 31 October 20X4 was $16 million and at 31 October 20X5 was $46 million. The increase in the share price in the year to 31 October 20X5 could not be foreseen at 31 October 20X4. The options were exercised at 31 October 20X5. The directors are unsure how to account for deferred taxation on this transaction for the years ended 31 October 20X4 and 31 October 20X5.

(ii)   Panel is leasing plant under a finance lease over a five year period. The asset was recorded at the present value of the minimum lease payments of $12 million at the inception of the lease which was 1 November 20X4. The asset is depreciated on a straight line basis over the five years and has no residual value. The annual lease payments are $3 million payable in arrears on 31 October and the effective interest rate is 8% per annum. The directors have not leased an asset under a finance lease before and are unsure as to its treatment for deferred taxation. The company can claim a tax deduction for the annual rental payment as the finance lease does not qualify for tax relief.

(iii) A wholly owned overseas subsidiary, Pins, a limited liability company, sold goods costing $7 million to Panel on 1 September 20X5, and these goods had not been sold by Panel before the year end. Panel had paid $9 million for these goods. The directors do not understand how this transaction should be dealt with in the financial statements of the subsidiary and the group for taxation purposes. Pins pays tax locally at 30%.

(iv)   Nails, a limited liability company, is a wholly owned subsidiary of Panel, and is a cash generating unit in its own right. The value of the property, plant and equipment of Nails at 31 October 20X5 was $6 million and purchased goodwill was $1 million before any impairment loss. The company had no other assets or liabilities. An impairment loss of $1·8 million had occurred at 31 October 20X5. The tax base of the property, plant and equipment of Nails was $4 million as at 31 October 20X5. The directors wish to know how the impairment loss will affect the deferred tax liability for the year. Impairment losses are not an allowable expense for taxation purposes.

Assume a tax rate of 30%.

Required

(b) Discuss, with suitable computations, how the situations (i) to (iv) above will impact on the accounting for deferred tax under IAS 12 *Income taxes* in the group financial statements of Panel. **(16 marks)**

(The situations in (i) to (iv) above carry equal marks) **(Total = 25 marks)**

15 Kesare

45 mins

Pilot paper

The following statement of financial position relates to Kesare Group, a public limited company, at 30 June 20X6.

	$'000
Assets	
Non current assets:	
Property, plant and equipment	10,000
Goodwill	6,000
Other intangible assets	5,000
Financial assets (cost)	9,000
	30,000
Current assets	
Trade receivables	7,000
Other receivables	4,600
Cash and cash equivalents	6,700
	18,300
Total assets	48,300
Equity and liabilities	
Equity	
Share capital	9,000
Other reserves	4,500
Retained earnings	9,130
Total equity	22,630
Non-current liabilities	
Long term borrowings	10,000
Deferred tax liability	3,600
Employee benefit liability	4,000
Total non-current liabilities	17,600
Current liabilities	
Current tax liability	3,070
Trade and other payables	5,000
Total current liabilities	8,070
Total liabilities	25,670
Total equity and liabilities	48,300

The following information is relevant to the above statement of financial position:

(i) The financial assets are classified as 'investments in equity instruments' but are shown in the above statement of financial position at their cost on 1 July 20X5. The market value of the assets is $10.5 million on 30 June 20X6. Taxation is payable on the sale of the assets. As allowed by IFRS 9, an irrevocable election was made for changes in fair value to go through other comprehensive income (not reclassified to profit or loss).

(ii) The stated interest rate for the long term borrowing is 8 per cent. The loan of $10 million represents a convertible bond which has a liability component of $9.6 million and an equity component of $0.4 million. The bond was issued on 30 June 20X6.

(iii) The defined benefit plan had a rule change on 1 July 20X5, giving rise to past service costs of $520,000. The past service costs have not been accounted for.

(iv) The tax bases of the assets and liabilities are the same as their carrying amounts in the draft statement of financial position above as at 30 June 20X6 except for the following:

(1)

	$'000
Property, plant and equipment	2,400
Trade receivables	7,500
Other receivables	5,000
Employee benefits	5,000

(2) Other intangible assets were development costs which were all allowed for tax purposes when the cost was incurred in 20X5.

(3) Trade and other payables includes an accrual for compensation to be paid to employees. This amounts to $1 million and is allowed for taxation when paid.

(v) Goodwill is not allowable for tax purposes in this jurisdiction.

(vi) Assume taxation is payable at 30%.

Required

(a) Discuss the conceptual basis for the recognition of deferred taxation using the temporary difference approach to deferred taxation. **(7 marks)**

(b) Calculate the deferred tax liability at 30 June 20X6 after any necessary adjustments to the financial statements showing how the deferred tax liability would be dealt with in the financial statements. (Assume that any adjustments do not affect current tax. Candidates should briefly discuss the adjustments required to calculate deferred tax liability.) **(18 marks)**

(Total = 25 marks)

Two marks will be awarded for the quality of the discussion of the conceptual basis of deferred taxation in (a).

16 Preparation question: Financial instruments

(a) Graben Co purchases a bond for $441,014 on 1 January 20X1. It will be redeemed on 31 December 20X4 for $600,000. The bond is held at amortised cost and carries no coupon.

Required

Calculate the valuation of the bond for the statement of financial position as at 31 December 20X1 and the finance income for 20X1 shown in profit or loss.

Compound sum of $1: $(1 + r)^n$

Year	2%	4%	6%	8%	10%	12%	14%
1	1.0200	1.0400	1.0600	1.0800	1.1000	1.1200	1.1400
2	1.0404	1.0816	1.1236	1.1664	1.2100	1.2544	1.2996
3	1.0612	1.1249	1.1910	1.2597	1.3310	1.4049	1.4815
4	1.0824	1.1699	1.2625	1.3605	1.4641	1.5735	1.6890
5	1.1041	1.2167	1.3382	1.4693	1.6105	1.7623	1.9254

(b) Baldie Co issues 4,000 convertible bonds on 1 January 20X2 at par. The bond is redeemable 3 years later at its par value of $500 per bond, which is its nominal value.

The bonds pay interest annually in arrears at an interest rate (based on nominal value) of 5%. Each bond can be converted at the maturity date into 30 $1 shares.

The prevailing market interest rate for three year bonds that have no right of conversion is 9%.

Required

Show the statement of financial position valuation at 1 January 20X2.

Cumulative 3 year annuity factors:

5%   2.723
9%   2.531

17 Complexity

The definition of a financial instrument captures a wide variety of assets and liabilities including cash, evidence of an ownership interest in an entity, or a contractual right to receive or deliver cash or another financial instrument. Preparers, auditors and users of financial statements have found the requirements for reporting financial assets and liabilities to be very complex, problematical and sometimes subjective. The result is that there is a need to develop new standards of reporting for financial instruments that are principle-based and significantly less complex than current requirements. It is important that a standard in this area should allow users to understand the economic substance of the transaction and preparers to properly apply generally accepted accounting principles.

Required

(a)   (i)   Discuss how the measurement of financial instruments under International Financial Reporting Standards can create confusion and complexity for preparers and users of financial statements.

(9 marks)

(ii)   Set out the reasons why using fair value to measure all financial instruments may result in less complexity in accounting for financial instruments, but may lead to uncertainty in financial statements.

(9 marks)

Professional marks will be awarded in part (a) for clarity and expression.   **(2 marks)**

(b)   A company borrowed $47 million on 1 December 20X4 when the market and effective interest rate was 5%. On 30 November 20X5, the company borrowed an additional $45 million when the current market and effective interest rate was 7.4%. Both financial liabilities are repayable on 30 November 20X9 and are single payment notes, whereby interest and capital are repaid on that date.

Required

Discuss the accounting for the above financial liabilities under current accounting standards using amortised cost, and additionally using fair value as at 30 November 20X5.   **(5 marks)**

(Total = 25 marks)

18 Ambush

(a)   Ambush loaned $200,000 to Bromwich on 1 December 20X3. The effective and stated interest rate for this loan was 8 per cent. Interest is payable by Bromwich at the end of each year and the loan is repayable on 30 November 20X7. At 30 November 20X5, the directors of Ambush have heard that Bromwich is in financial difficulties and is undergoing a financial reorganisation. The directors feel that it is likely that they will only receive $100,000 on 30 November 20X7 and no future interest payment. Interest for the year ended 30 November 20X5 had been received. The financial year end of Ambush is 30 November 20X5.

Required

(i)   Outline the requirements of IAS 39 as regards the impairment of financial assets.   **(6 marks)**

(ii)   Explain the accounting treatment under IAS 39 of the loan to Bromwich in the financial statements of Ambush for the year ended 30 November 2005.   **(4 marks)**

(b)   The impairment of trade receivables has been calculated using a formulaic approach which is based on a specific percentage of the portfolio of trade receivables. The general provision approach has been used by

the company at 30 November 20X5. At 30 November 20X5, one of the credit customers, Tray, has come to an arrangement with Ambush whereby the amount outstanding of $4 million from Tray will be paid on 30 November 20X6 together with a penalty of $100,000. The total amount of trade receivables outstanding at 30 November 20X5 was $11 million including the amount owed by Tray. The following is the analysis of the trade receivables.

	Balance $m	Cash expected $m	Due date
Tray	4	4.1	30 November 20X6
Milk	2	2.0	31 January 20X5
Other receivables	5	4.6	On average 31 January 20X5
	11	10.7	

Ambush has made an allowance of $520,000 against trade receivables which represents the difference between the cash expected to be received and the balance outstanding plus a 2% general allowance. Milk has a similar credit risk to the 'other receivables'. (Use a discount rate of 5% in any calculations.) **(8 marks)**

(c)   Ambush is reviewing the accounting treatment of its buildings. The company uses the 'revaluation model' for its buildings. The buildings had originally cost $10 million on 1 December 20X3 and had a useful economic life of 20 years. They are being depreciated on a straight line basis to a nil residual value. The buildings were revalued downwards on 30 November 20X4 to $8 million which was the buildings' recoverable amount. At 30 November 20X5 the value of the buildings had risen to $11 million which is to be included in the financial statements. The company is unsure how to treat the above events.   **(7 marks)**

(Total = 25 marks)

19 Grainger

6/11

The publication of IFRS 9, *Financial instruments*, represents the completion of the first stage of a three-part project to replace IAS 39 *Financial instruments: recognition and measurement* with a new standard. The new standard purports to enhance the ability of investors and other users of financial information to understand the accounting of financial assets and reduces complexity.

Required

(a)   (i)   Discuss the approach taken by IFRS 9 in measuring and classifying financial assets and the main effect that IFRS 9 will have on accounting for financial assets.   **(11 marks)**

        (ii)   Grainger, a public limited company, has decided to adopt IFRS 9 prior to January 20X2 and has decided to restate comparative information under IAS 8 *Accounting policies, changes in accounting estimates and errors*. The entity has an investment in a financial asset which was carried at amortised cost under IAS 39 but will be valued at fair value through profit and loss (FVTPL) under IFRS 9. The carrying value of the assets was $105,000 on 30 April 20X0 and $110,400 on 30 April 20X1. The fair value of the asset was $106,500 on 30 April 20X0 and $111,000 on 30 April 20X1. Grainger has determined that the asset will be valued at FVTPL at 30 April 20X1.

                Required

                Discuss how the financial asset will be accounted for in the financial statements of Grainger in the year ended 30 April 20X1.   **(4 marks)**

(b)   Recently, criticisms have been made against the current IFRS impairment model for financial assets (the incurred loss model). The issue with the incurred loss model is that impairment losses (and resulting write-downs in the reported value of financial assets) can only be recognised when there is evidence that they exist and have been incurred. Reporting entities are not allowed currently to consider the effects of expected losses. There is a view that earlier recognition of loan losses could potentially reduce the problems incurred in a credit crisis.

Grainger has a portfolio of loans of $5 million which was initially recognised on 1 May 20X0. The loans mature in 10 years and carry an interest rate of 16%. Grainger estimates that no loans will default in the first two years, but from the third year onwards, loans will default at an annual rate of about 9%. If the loans default as expected, the rate of return from the portfolio will be approximately 9·07%. The number of loans are fixed without any new lending or any other impairment provisions.

Required

(i) Discuss briefly the issues related to considering the effects of expected losses in dealing with impairment of financial assets. **(4 marks)**

(ii) Calculate the impact on the financial statements up to the year ended 30 April 20X3 if Grainger anticipated the expected losses on the loan portfolio in year three. **(4 marks)**

Professional marks will be awarded in this question for clarity and quality of discussion. **(2 marks)**

(Total = 25 marks)

20 Aron

45 mins

6/09, amended

The directors of Aron, a public limited company, are worried about the challenging market conditions which the company is facing. The markets are volatile and illiquid. The central government is injecting liquidity into the economy. The directors are concerned about the significant shift towards the use of fair values in financial statements. IFRS 9 *Financial instruments* in conjunction with IFRS 13 *Fair value measurement* defines fair value and requires the initial measurement of financial instruments to be at fair value. The directors are uncertain of the relevance of fair value measurements in these current market conditions.

Required

(a) Briefly discuss how the fair value of financial instruments is measured, commenting on the relevance of fair value measurements for financial instruments where markets are volatile and illiquid. **(4 marks)**

(b) Further they would like advice on accounting for the following transactions within the financial statements for the year ended 31 May 20X8.

(i) Aron issued one million convertible bonds on 1 June 20X5. The bonds had a term of three years and were issued with a total fair value of $100 million which is also the par value. Interest is paid annually in arrears at a rate of 6% per annum and bonds, without the conversion option, attracted an interest rate of 9% per annum on 1 June 20X5. The company incurred issue costs of $1 million. If the investor did not convert to shares they would have been redeemed at par. At maturity all of the bonds were converted into 25 million ordinary shares of $1 of Aron. No bonds could be converted before that date. The directors are uncertain how the bonds should have been accounted for up to the date of the conversion on 31 May 20X8 and have been told that the impact of the issue costs is to increase the effective interest rate to 9.38%. **(6 marks)**

(ii) Aron held a 3% holding of the shares in Smart, a public limited company, The investment was classified as an investment in equity instruments and at 31 May 20X8 had a carrying value of $5 million (brought forward from the previous period). As permitted by IFRS 9 *Financial instruments*, Aron had made an irrevocable election to recognise all changes in fair value in other comprehensive income (items that will not be reclassified to profit or loss). The cumulative gain to 31 May 20X7 recognised in other comprehensive income relating to the investment was $400,000. On 31 May 20X8, the whole of the share capital of Smart was acquired by Given, a public limited company, and as a result, Aron received shares in Given with a fair value of $5.5 million in exchange for its holding in Smart. The company wishes to know how the exchange of shares in Smart for the shares in Given should be accounted for in its financial records. **(4 marks)**

(iii) The functional and presentation currency of Aron is the dollar ($). Aron has a wholly owned foreign subsidiary, Gao, whose functional currency is the zloti. Gao owns a debt instrument which is held for trading. In Gao's financial statements for the year ended 31 May 20X7, the debt instrument was carried at its fair value of 10 million zloti.

At 31 May 20X8, the fair value of the debt instrument had increased to 12 million zloty. The exchange rates were:

	Zloti to $1
31 May 20X7	3
31 May 20X8	2
Average rate for year to 31 May 20X8	2.5

The company wishes to know how to account for this instrument in Gao's entity financial statements and the consolidated financial statements of the group. **(5 marks)**

(iv) Aron granted interest free loans to its employees on 1 June 20X7 of $10 million. The loans will be paid back on 31 May 20X9 as a single payment by the employees. The market rate of interest for a two year loan on both of the above dates is 6% per annum. The company is unsure how to account for the loan but wishes to hold the loans at amortised cost under IFRS 9 *Financial instruments*

(4 marks)

Required

Discuss, with relevant computations, how the above financial instruments should be accounted for in the financial statements for the year ended 31 May 20X8.

Note 1. The mark allocation is shown against each of the transactions above.

Note 2. The following discount and annuity factors may be of use.

	Discount factors			Annuity factors		
	6%	9%	9.38%	6%	9%	9.38%
1 year	0.9434	0.9174	0.9142	0.9434	0.9174	0.9174
2 years	0.8900	0.8417	0.8358	1.8334	1.7591	1.7500
3 years	0.8396	0.7722	0.7642	2.6730	2.5313	2.5142

Professional marks will be awarded for clarity and quality of discussion. **(2 marks)**

(Total = 25 marks)

21 Leigh

45 mins

ACR, 6/07

(a) Leigh, a public limited company, purchased the whole of the share capital of Hash, a limited company, on 1 June 20X6. The whole of the share capital of Hash was formerly owned by the five directors of Hash and under the terms of the purchase agreement, the five directors were to receive a total of three million ordinary shares of $1 of Leigh on 1 June 20X6 (market value $6 million) and a further 5,000 shares per director on 31 May 20X7, if they were still employed by Leigh on that date. All of the directors were still employed by Leigh at 31 May 20X7.

Leigh granted and issued fully paid shares to its own employees on 31 May 20X7. Normally share options issued to employees would vest over a three year period, but these shares were given as a bonus because of the company's exceptional performance over the period. The shares in Leigh had a market value of $3 million (one million ordinary shares of $1 at $3 per share) on 31 May 20X7 and an average fair value of $2.5 million (one million ordinary shares of $1 at $2.50 per share) for the year ended 31 May 20X7. It is expected that Leigh's share price will rise to $6 per share over the next three years. **(10 marks)**

(b) On 31 May 20X7, Leigh purchased property, plant and equipment for $4 million. The supplier has agreed to accept payment for the property, plant and equipment either in cash or in shares. The supplier can either choose 1.5 million shares of the company to be issued in six months time or to receive a cash payment in three months time equivalent to the market value of 1.3 million shares. It is estimated that the share price will be $3.50 in three months time and $4 in six months time.

Additionally, at 31 May 20X7, one of the directors recently appointed to the board has been granted the right to choose either 50,000 shares of Leigh or receive a cash payment equal to the current value of 40,000 shares at the settlement date. This right has been granted because of the performance of the director during the year and is unconditional at 31 May 20X7. The settlement date is 1 July 20X8 and the company estimates the fair value of the share alternative is $2.50 per share at 31 May 20X7. The share price of Leigh at 31 May 20X7 is $3 per share, and if the director chooses the share alternative, they must be kept for a period of four years. **(9 marks)**

(c)   Leigh acquired 30% of the ordinary share capital of Handy, a public limited company, on 1 April 20X6. The purchase consideration was one million ordinary shares of Leigh which had a market value of $2.50 per share at that date and the fair value of the net assets of Handy was $9 million. The retained earnings of Handy were $4 million and other reserves of Handy were $3 million at that date. Leigh appointed two directors to the Board of Handy, and it intends to hold the investment for a significant period of time. Leigh exerts significant influence over Handy. The summarised statement of financial position of Handy at 31 May 20X7 is as follows.

	$m
Share capital of $1	2
Other reserves	3
Retained earnings	5
	10
Net assets	10

There had been no new issues of shares by Handy since the acquisition by Leigh and the estimated recoverable amount of the net assets of Handy at 31 May 20X7 was $11 million. **(6 marks)**

Required

Discuss with suitable computations how the above share-based transactions should be accounted for in the financial statements of Leigh for the year ended 31 May 20X7.

(Total = 25 marks)

22 Margie   45 mins

12/10

Margie, a public limited company, has entered into several share related transactions during the period and wishes to obtain advice on how to account for the transactions.

(a)   Margie has entered into a contract with a producer to purchase 350 tonnes of wheat. The purchase price will be settled in cash at an amount equal to the value of 2,500 of Margie's shares. Margie may settle the contract at any time by paying the producer an amount equal to the current market value of 2,500 of Margie shares, less the market value of 350 tonnes of wheat. Margie has entered into the contract as part of its hedging strategy and has no intention of taking physical delivery of the wheat. Margie wishes to treat this transaction as a share based payment transaction under IFRS 2 *Share-based payment*. **(7 marks)**

(b)   Margie has acquired 100% of the share capital of Antalya in a business combination on 1 December 20X3. Antalya had previously granted a share-based payment to its employees with a four-year vesting period. Its employees have rendered the required service for the award at the acquisition date but have not yet exercised their options. The fair value of the award at 1 December 20X3 is $20 million and Margie is obliged to replace the share-based payment awards of Antalya with awards of its own.

Margie issues a replacement award that does not require post-combination services. The fair value of the replacement award at the acquisition date is $22 million. Margie does not know how to account for the award on the acquisition of Antalya. **(6 marks)**

(c)   Margie issued shares during the financial year. Some of those shares were subscribed for by employees who were existing shareholders, and some were issued to an entity, Grief, which owned 5% of Margie's share capital. Before the shares were issued, Margie offered to buy a building from Grief and agreed that the purchase price would be settled by the issue of shares. Margie wondered whether these transactions should be accounted for under IFRS 2. **(4 marks)**

(d)   Margie granted 100 options to each of its 4,000 employees at a fair value of $10 each on 1 December 20X1. The options vest upon the company's share price reaching $15, provided the employee has remained in the company's service until that time. The terms and conditions of the options are that the market condition can be met in either year 3, 4 or 5 of the employee's service.

At the grant date, Margie estimated that the expected vesting period would be four years which is consistent with the assumptions used in measuring the fair value of the options granted, and maintained this estimate at 30 November 20X2 and 30 November 20X3. The company's share price reached $15 on 30 November 20X4. **(6 marks)**

Required

Discuss, with suitable computations where applicable, how the above transactions would be dealt with in the financial statements of Margie for the year ending 30 November 20X4.

Professional marks will be awarded for clarity and quality of discussion. **(2 marks)**

(Total = 25 marks)

23 Greenie   45 mins

12/10

(a)   Greenie, a public limited company, builds, develops and operates airports. During the financial year to 30 November 20X0, a section of an airport collapsed and as a result several people were hurt. The accident resulted in the closure of the terminal and legal action against Greenie. When the financial statements for the year ended 30 November 20X0 were being prepared, the investigation into the accident and the reconstruction of the section of the airport damaged were still in progress and no legal action had yet been brought in connection with the accident. The expert report that was to be presented to the civil courts in order to determine the cause of the accident and to assess the respective responsibilities of the various parties involved, was expected in 20X1.

Financial damages arising related to the additional costs and operating losses relating to the unavailability of the building. The nature and extent of the damages, and the details of any compensation payments had yet to be established. The directors of Greenie felt that at present, there was no requirement to record the impact of the accident in the financial statements.

Compensation agreements had been arranged with the victims, and these claims were all covered by Greenie's insurance policy. In each case, compensation paid by the insurance company was subject to a waiver of any judicial proceedings against Greenie and its insurers. If any compensation is eventually payable to third parties, this is expected to be covered by the insurance policies.

The directors of Greenie felt that the conditions for recognising a provision or disclosing a contingent liability had not been met. Therefore, Greenie did not recognise a provision in respect of the accident nor did it disclose any related contingent liability or a note setting out the nature of the accident and potential claims in its financial statements for the year ended 30 November 20X0. **(6 marks)**

(b)   Greenie was one of three shareholders in a regional airport Manair. As at 30 November 20X0, the majority shareholder held 60·1% of voting shares, the second shareholder held 20% of voting shares and Greenie held 19·9% of the voting shares. The board of directors consisted of ten members. The majority shareholder was represented by six of the board members, while Greenie and the other shareholder were represented by two members each. A shareholders' agreement stated that certain board and shareholder resolutions required either unanimous or majority decision. There is no indication that the majority shareholder and the other shareholders act together in a common way. During the financial year, Greenie had provided Manair with maintenance and technical services and had sold the entity a software licence for $5 million. Additionally, Greenie had sent a team of management experts to give business advice to the board of Manair. Greenie did not account for its investment in Manair as an associate, because of a lack of significant influence over the entity. Greenie felt that the majority owner of Manair used its influence as the parent to control and govern its subsidiary. **(10 marks)**

(c)   Greenie has issued 1 million shares of $1 nominal value for the acquisition of franchise rights at a local airport. Similar franchise rights are sold in cash transactions on a regular basis and Greenie has been offered a similar franchise right at another airport for $2·3 million. This price is consistent with other prices given the market conditions. The share price of Greenie was $2·50 at the date of the transaction. Greenie wishes to record the transaction at the nominal value of the shares issued.

Greenie also showed irredeemable preference shares as equity instruments in its statement of financial position. The terms of issue of the instruments give the holders a contractual right to an annual fixed cash dividend and the entitlement to a participating dividend based on any dividends paid on ordinary shares. Greenie felt that the presentation of the preference shares with a liability component in compliance with IAS *32 Financial instruments: presentation* would be so misleading in the circumstances that it would conflict with the objective of financial statements set out in the *IASB's Conceptual Framework.*. The reason given by Greenie for this presentation was that the shares participated in future profits and thus had the characteristics of permanent capital because of the profit participation element of the shares.   **(7 marks)**

Required

Discuss how the above financial transactions should be dealt with in the financial statements of Greenie for the year ended 30 November 20X0.

Professional marks will be awarded in question 3 for clarity and quality of discussion.   **(2 marks)**

(Total = 25 marks)

24 Ryder

45 mins

ACR, 12/05

Ryder, a public limited company, is reviewing certain events which have occurred since its year end of 31 October 20X5. The financial statements were authorised on 12 December 20X5. The following events are relevant to the financial statements for the year ended 31 October 20X5:

(a)   Ryder disposed of a wholly owned subsidiary, Krup, a public limited company, on 10 December 20X5 and made a loss of $9 million on the transaction in the group financial statements. As at 31 October 20X5, Ryder had no intention of selling the subsidiary which was material to the group. The directors of Ryder have stated that there were no significant events which have occurred since 31 October 20X5 which could have resulted in a reduction in the value of Krup. The carrying value of the net assets and purchased goodwill of Krup at 31 October 20X5 were $20 million and $12 million respectively. Krup had made a loss of $2 million in the period 1 November 20X5 to 10 December 20X5.   **(6 marks)**

(b)   Ryder acquired a wholly owned subsidiary, Metalic, a public limited company, on 21 January 20X4. The consideration payable in respect of the acquisition of Metalic was 2 million ordinary shares of $1 of Ryder plus a further 300,000 ordinary shares if the profit of Metalic exceeded $6 million for the year ended 31 October 20X5. The profit for the year of Metalic was $7 million and the ordinary shares were issued on 12 November 20X5. The annual profits of Metalic had averaged $7 million over the last few years and, therefore, Ryder had included an estimate of the contingent consideration in the cost of the acquisition at 21 January 20X4. The fair value used for the ordinary shares of Ryder at this date including the contingent consideration was $10 per share. The fair value of the ordinary shares on 12 November 20X5 was $11 per share. Ryder also made a one for four bonus issue on 13 November 20X5 which was applicable to the contingent shares issued. The directors are unsure of the impact of the above on the accounting for the acquisition.   **(8 marks)**

(c)   The company acquired a property on 1 November 20X4 which it intended to sell. The property was obtained as a result of a default on a loan agreement by a third party and was valued at $20 million on that date for accounting purposes which exactly offset the defaulted loan. The property is in a state of disrepair and Ryder intends to complete the repairs before it sells the property. The repairs were completed on 30 November 20X5. The property was sold after costs for $27 million on 9 December 20X5. The property was classified as 'held for sale' at the year end under IFRS 5 *Non-current assets held for sale and discontinued operations* but shown at the net sale proceeds of $27 million. Property is depreciated at 5% per annum on the straight-line basis and no depreciation has been charged in the year.   **(6 marks)**

(d)   The company granted share appreciation rights (SARs) to its employees on 1 November 20X3 based on ten million shares. The SARs provide employees at the date the rights are exercised with the right to receive cash equal to the appreciation in the company's share price since the grant date. The rights vested on 31 October 20X5 and payment was made on schedule on 1 December 20X5. The fair value of the SARs per share at 31 October 20X4 was $6, at 31 October 2005 was $8 and at 1 December 20X5 was $9. The company has recognised a liability for the SARs as at 31 October 20X4 based upon IFRS 2 *Share-based payment* but the liability was stated at the same amount at 31 October 20X5.   **(5 marks)**

Required

Discuss the accounting treatment of the above events in the financial statements of the Ryder Group for the year ended 31 October 20X5, taking into account the implications of events occurring after the end of the reporting period.

(The mark allocations are set out after each paragraph above.)   **(Total = 25 marks)**

25 Royan

45 mins

6/12

(a)   The existing standard dealing with provisions, IAS 37 *Provisions, contingent liabilities and contingent assets*, has been in place for many years and is sufficiently well understood and consistently applied in most areas. The IASB feels it is time for a fundamental change in the underlying principles for the recognition and measurement of non-financial liabilities. To this end, the Board has issued an Exposure Draft *Measurement of liabilities in IAS 37 – Proposed amendments to IAS 37.*

Required

(i)   Discuss the existing guidance in IAS 37 as regards the recognition and measurement of provisions and why the IASB feels the need to replace this guidance.   **(9 marks)**

(ii)   Describe the new proposals that the IASB has outlined in the Exposure Draft.   **(7 marks)**

(b)   Royan, a public limited company, extracts oil and has a present obligation to dismantle an oil platform at the end of the platform's life, which is ten years. Royan cannot cancel this obligation or transfer it. Royan intends to carry out the dismantling work itself and estimates the cost of the work to be $150 million in ten years' time. The present value of the work is $105 million.

A market exists for the dismantling of an oil platform and Royan could hire a third party contractor to carry out the work. The entity feels that if no risk or probability adjustment were needed then the cost of the external contractor would be $180 million in ten years' time. The present value of this cost is $129 million. If risk and probability are taken into account, then there is a probability of 40% that the present value will be $129 million and 60% probability that it would be $140 million, and there is a risk that the costs may increase by $5 million.

Required

Describe the accounting treatment of the above events under IAS 37 and the possible outcomes under the proposed amendments in the Exposure Draft.   **(7 marks)**

Professional marks will be awarded for the quality of the discussion.   **(2 marks)**

(Total = 25 marks)

26 Electron

45 mins

Pilot paper

Electron, a public limited company, operates in the energy sector. The company has grown significantly over the last few years and is currently preparing its financial statements for the year ended 30 June 20X6.

Electron buys and sells oil and currently has a number of oil trading contracts. The contracts to purchase oil are treated as non-current assets and amortised over the contracts' durations. On acceptance of a contract to sell oil,

fifty per cent of the contract price is recognised immediately with the balance being recognised over the remaining life of the contract. The contracts always result in the delivery of the commodity. **(4 marks)**

Electron has recently constructed an ecologically efficient power station. A condition of being granted the operating licence by the government is that the power station be dismantled at the end of its life which is estimated to be 20 years. The power station cost $100 million and began production on 1 July 20X5. Depreciation is charged on the power station using the straight line method. Electron has estimated at 30 June 20X6 that it will cost $15 million (net present value) to restore the site to its original condition using a discount rate of five per cent. Ninety-five per cent of these costs relate to the removal of the power station and five per cent relates to the damage caused through generating energy. **(7 marks)**

Electron has leased another power station, which was relatively inefficient, to a rival company on 30 June 20X6. The beneficial and legal ownership remains with Electron and in the event of one of Electron's power stations being unable to produce energy, Electron can terminate the agreement. The leased power station is being treated as an operating lease with the net present value of the income of $40 million being recognised in profit or loss. The fair value of the power station is $70 million at 30 June 20X6. A deposit of $10 million was received on 30 June 20X6 and it is included in the net present value calculation. **(5 marks)**

The company has a good relationship with its shareholders and employees. It has adopted a strategy of gradually increasing its dividend payments over the years. On 1 August 20X6, the board proposed a dividend of 5c per share for the year ended 30 June 20X6. The shareholders will approve the dividend along with the financial statements at the general meeting on 1 September 20X6 and the dividend will be paid on 14 September 20X6. The directors feel that the dividend should be accrued in the financial statements for the year ended 30 June 20X6 as a 'valid expectation' has been created. **(3 marks)**

The company granted share options to its employees on 1 July 20X5. The fair value of the options at that date was $3 million. The options vest on 30 June 20X8. The employees have to be employed at the end of the three year period for the options to vest and the following estimates have been made:

Estimated percentage of employees leaving during vesting period at:

Grant date 1 July 20X5	5%	
30 June 20X6	6%	**(4 marks)**
Effective communication to the directors		**(2 marks)**

Required

Draft a report suitable for presentation to the directors of Electron which discusses the accounting treatment of the above transactions in the financial statements for the year ended 30 June 20X6, including relevant calculations.

(Total = 25 marks)

27 Egin Group
45 mins

ACR, 6/06

On 1 June 20X5, Egin, a public limited company, was formed out of the reorganisation of a group of companies with foreign operations. The directors require advice on the disclosure of related party information but are reluctant to disclose information as they feel that such transactions are a normal feature of business and need not be disclosed.

Under the new group structure, Egin owns 80% of Briars, 60% of Doye, and 30% of Eye. Egin exercises significant influence over Eye. The directors of Egin are also directors of Briars and Doye but only one director of Egin sits on the management board of Eye. The management board of Eye comprises five directors. Originally the group comprised five companies but the fifth company, Tang, which was a 70% subsidiary of Egin, was sold on 31 January 20X6. There were no transactions between Tang and the Egin Group during the year to 31 May 20X6. 30% of the shares of Egin are owned by another company, Atomic, which exerts significant influence over Egin. The remaining 40% of the shares of Doye are owned by Spade, which exerts significant influence over Doye.

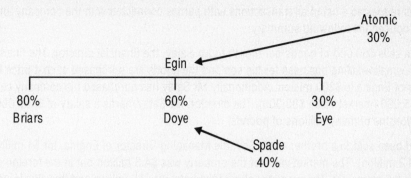

During the current financial year to 31 May 20X6, Doye has sold a significant amount of plant and equipment to Spade at the normal selling price for such items. The directors of Egin have proposed that where related party relationships are determined and sales are at normal selling price, any disclosures will state that prices charged to related parties are made on an arm's length basis.

The directors are unsure how to treat certain transactions relating to their foreign subsidiary, Briars. Egin purchased 80% of the ordinary share capital of Briars on 1 June 20X5 for 50 million euros when its net assets were fair valued at 45 million euros. At 31 May 20X6, it is established that goodwill is impaired by 3 million euros. Additionally, at the date of acquisition, Egin had made an interest free loan to Briars of $10 million. The loan is to be repaid on 31 May 20X7. An equivalent loan would normally carry an interest rate of 6% taking into account Briars' credit rating.

The exchange rates were as follows:

	Euros to $
1 June 20X5	2
31 May 20X6	2·5
Average rate for year	2·3

Financial liabilities of the group are normally measured at amortised cost.

One of the directors of Briars who is not on the management board of Egin owns the whole of the share capital of a company, Blue, that sells goods at market price to Briars. The director is in charge of the production at Briars and also acts as a consultant to the management board of the group.

Required

(a) (i)   Discuss why it is important to disclose related party transactions, explaining the criteria which determine a related party relationship. **(5 marks)**

     (ii) Describe the nature of any related party relationships and transactions which exists:

          (1)   within the Egin Group including Tang   **(5 marks)**
          (2)   between Spade and the Egin Group   **(3 marks)**
          (3)   between Atomic and the Egin Group   **(3 marks)**

          commenting on whether transactions should be described as being at 'arm's length'.

(b)   Describe with suitable calculations how the goodwill arising on the acquisition of Briars will be dealt with in the group financial statements and how the loan to Briars should be treated in the financial statements of Briars for the year ended 31 May 20X6. **(9 marks)**

(Total = 25 marks)

28 Engina

45 mins

ACR, Pilot paper

Engina, a foreign company, has approached a partner in your firm to assist in obtaining a local Stock Exchange listing for the company. Engina is registered in a country where transactions between related parties are considered to be normal but where such transactions are not disclosed. The directors of Engina are reluctant to disclose the nature of their related party transactions as they feel that although they are a normal feature of business in their part of the world, it could cause significant problems politically and culturally to disclose such transactions.

The partner in your firm has requested a list of all transactions with parties connected with the company and the directors of Engina have produced the following summary:

(a) Every month, Engina sells $50,000 of goods per month to Mr Satay, the financial director. The financial director has set up a small retailing business for his son and the goods are purchased at cost price for him. The annual turnover of Engina is $300 million. Additionally Mr Satay has purchased his company car from the company for $45,000 (market value $80,000). The director, Mr Satay, earns a salary of $500,000 a year, and has a personal fortune of many millions of pounds.

(b) A hotel property had been sold to a brother of Mr Soy, the Managing Director of Engina, for $4 million (net of selling cost of $0.2 million). The market value of the property was $4.3 million but in the foreign country, property prices were falling rapidly. The carrying value of the hotel was $5 million and its value in use was $3.6 million. There was an over supply of hotel accommodation due to government subsidies in an attempt to encourage hotel development and the tourist industry.

(c) Mr Satay owns several companies and the structure of the group is as follows.

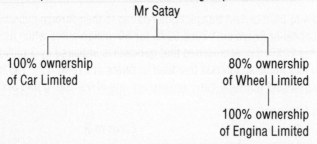

Engina earns 60% of its profits from transactions with Car and 40% of its profits from transactions from Wheel. All the above companies are incorporated in the same country.

Required

Write a report to the directors of Engina setting out the reasons why it is important to disclose related party transactions and the nature of any disclosure required for the above transactions under IAS 24 *Related party disclosures*. **(25 marks)**

The mark allocation will be as follows:

		Mark
Style/layout of report		4
Reasons		8
Transaction	(a)	4
	(b)	5
	(c)	4
		25

29 Preparation question: Leases

Sugar Co leased a machine from Spice Co. The terms of the lease are as follows:

Inception of lease	1 January 20X1
Lease term	4 years at $78,864 per annum payable in arrears
Present value of minimum lease payments	$250,000
Useful life of asset	4 years

Required

(a) Calculate the interest rate implicit in the lease, using the table below.

This table shows the present value of $1 per annum, receivable or payable at the end of each year for n years.

Years (n)	Interest rates		
	6%	8%	10%
1	0.943	0.926	0.909
2	1.833	1.783	1.736
3	2.673	2.577	2.487
4	3.465	3.312	3.170
5	4.212	3.993	3.791

(b) Prepare the extracts from the financial statements of Sugar Co for the year ended 31 December 20X1. Notes to the accounts are not required.

30 Holcombe

45 mins

`6/10`

(a) Leasing is important to Holcombe, a public limited company as a method of financing the business. The Directors feel that it is important that they provide users of financial statements with a complete and understandable picture of the entity's leasing activities. They believe that the current accounting model is inadequate and does not meet the needs of users of financial statements.

Holcombe has leased plant for a fixed term of six years and the useful life of the plant is 12 years. The lease is non-cancellable, and there are no rights to extend the lease term or purchase the machine at the end of the term. There are no guarantees of its value at that point. The lessor does not have the right of access to the plant until the end of the contract or unless permission is granted by Holcombe.

Fixed lease payments are due annually over the lease term after delivery of the plant, which is maintained by Holcombe. Holcombe accounts for the lease as an operating lease but the directors are unsure as to whether the accounting treatment of an operating lease is conceptually correct.

Required

(i) Discuss the reasons why the current lease accounting standards may fail to meet the needs of users and could be said to be conceptually flawed. **(7 marks)**

(ii) Discuss whether the plant operating lease in the financial statements of Holcombe meets the definition of an asset and liability as set out in *Conceptual Framework for Financial Reporting*.

(7 marks)

Professional marks will be awarded in part (a) (i) and (ii) for clarity and quality of discussion. **(2 marks)**

(b) Holcombe also owns an office building with a remaining useful life of 30 years. The carrying amount of the building is $120 million and its fair value is $150 million. On 1 May 20X4, Holcombe sells the building to Brook, a public limited company, for its fair value and leases it back for five years at an annual rental payable in arrears of $16 million on the last day of the financial year (30 April). This is a fair market rental. Holcombe's incremental borrowing rate is 8%.

On 1 May 20X4, Holcombe has also entered into a short operating lease agreement to lease another building. The lease will last for three years and is currently $5 million per annum. However an inflation adjustment will be made at the conclusion of leasing years 1 and 2. Currently inflation is 4% per annum.

The following discount factors are relevant (8%).

	Single cash flow	Annuity
Year 1	0.926	0.926
Year 2	0.857	1.783
Year 3	0.794	2.577
Year 4	0.735	3.312
Year 5	0.681	3.993

Required

(i) Show the accounting entries in the year of the sale and lease back assuming that the operating lease is recognised as an asset in the statement of financial position of Holcombe. **(6 marks)**

(ii) State how the inflation adjustment on the short term operating lease should be dealt with in the financial statements of Holcombe. **(3 marks)**

(Total = 25 marks)

31 William

45 mins

6/12

William is a public limited company and would like advice in relation to the following transactions.

(a) William owned a building on which it raised finance. William sold the building for $5 million to a finance company on 1 June 20X2 when the carrying amount was $3.5 million. The same building was leased back from the finance company for a period of twenty years, which was felt to be equivalent to the majority of the asset's economic life. The lease rentals for the period are $441,000 payable annually in arrears. The interest rate implicit in the lease is 7%. The present value of the minimum lease payments is the same as the sale proceeds.

William wishes to know how to account for the above transaction for the year ended 31 May 20X3.

(7 marks)

(b) William operates a defined benefit pension plan for its employees. Shortly before the year end of 31 May 20X3, William decided to relocate a division from one country to another, where labour and raw material costs are cheaper. The relocation is due to take place in December 20X3. On 13 May 20X3, a detailed formal plan was approved by the board of directors. Half of the affected division's employees will be made redundant in July 20X3, and will accrue no further benefits under William's defined benefit pension plan. The affected employees were informed of this decision on 14 May 20X3. The resulting reduction in the net pension liability due the relocation is estimated to have a present value of $15 million as at 31 May 20X3. Total relocation costs (excluding the impact on the pension plan) are estimated at $50 million.

William requires advice on how to account for the relocation costs and the reduction in the net pension liability for the year ended 31 May 20X3. **(7 marks)**

(c) On 1 June 20X0, William granted 500 share appreciation rights to each of its twenty managers. All of the rights vest after two years' service and they can be exercised during the following two years up to 31 May 20X4. The fair value of the right at the grant date was $20. It was thought that three managers would leave over the initial two-year period and they did so. The fair value of each right was as follows.

Year	Fair value at the year-end ($)
31 May 20X1	23
31 May 20X2	14
31 May 20X3	24

On 31 May 20X3, seven managers exercised their rights when the intrinsic value of the right was $21.

William wishes to know what the liability and expense will be at 31 May 20X3. **(5 marks)**

(d)   William acquired another entity, Chrissy, on 1 May 20X3. At the time of the acquisition, Chrissy was being sued as there is an alleged mis-selling case potentially implicating the entity. The claimants are suing for damages of $10 million. William estimates that the fair value of any contingent liability is $4 million and feels that it is more likely than not that no outflow of funds will occur.

William wishes to know how to account for this potential liability in Chrissy's entity financial statements and whether the treatment would be the same in the consolidated financial statements. **(4 marks)**

Required

Discuss, with suitable computations, the advice that should be given to William in accounting for the above events.

Note. The mark allocation is shown against each of the four events above.

Professional marks will be awarded for the quality of the discussion. **(2 marks)**

(Total = 25 marks)

GROUP FINANCIAL STATEMENTS

Questions 32 to 52 cover Group Financial Statements, the subject of Part C of the BPP Study Text for Paper P2.

32 Marrgrett

45 mins

12/08

Marrgrett, a public limited company, is currently planning to acquire and sell interests in other entities and has asked for advice on the impact of IFRS 3 (Revised) *Business combinations* . The company is particularly concerned about the impact on earnings, net assets and goodwill at the acquisition date and any ongoing earnings impact that the revised standards may have.

The company is considering purchasing additional shares in an associate, Josey, a public limited company. The holding will increase from 30% stake to 70% stake by offering the shareholders of Josey cash and shares in Marrgrett. Marrgrett anticipates that it will pay $5 million in transaction costs to lawyers and bankers. Josey had previously been the subject of a management buyout. In order that the current management shareholders may remain in the business, Marrgrett is going to offer them share options in Josey subject to them remaining in employment for two years after the acquisition. Additionally, Marrgrett will offer the same shareholders, shares in the holding company which are contingent upon a certain level of profitability being achieved by Josey. Each shareholder will receive shares of the holding company up to a value of $50,000, if Josey achieves a pre-determined rate of return on capital employed for the next two years.

Josey has several marketing-related intangible assets that are used primarily in marketing or promotion of its products. These include trade names, internet domain names and non-competition agreements. These are not currently recognised in Josey's financial statements.

Marrgrett does not wish to measure the non-controlling interest in subsidiaries on the basis of the proportionate interest in the identifiable net assets, but wishes to use the 'full goodwill' method on the transaction. Marrgrett is unsure as to whether this method is mandatory, or what the effects are of recognising 'full goodwill'. Additionally the company is unsure as to whether the nature of the consideration would affect the calculation of goodwill.

To finance the acquisition of Josey, Marrgrett intends to dispose of a partial interest in two subsidiaries. Marrgrett will retain control of the first subsidiary but will sell the controlling interest in the second subsidiary which will become an associate. Because of its plans to change the overall structure of the business, Marrgrett wishes to recognise a re-organisation provision at the date of the business combination.

Required

Discuss the principles and the nature of the accounting treatment of the above plans under International Financial Reporting Standards setting out any impact that IFRS 3 (Revised) *Business combinations* might have on the earnings and net assets of the group.

Note: this requirement includes 2 professional marks for the quality of the discussion.   **(25 marks)**

33 Preparation question: Associate

The statements of financial position of J Co and its investee companies, P Co and S Co, at 31 December 20X5 are shown below.

STATEMENTS OF FINANCIAL POSITION AS AT 31 DECEMBER 20X5

	J Co $'000	P Co $'000	S Co $'000
Assets			
Non-current assets			
Freehold property	1,950	1,250	500
Plant and equipment	795	375	285
Investments	1,500	–	–
	4,245	1,625	785
Current assets			
Inventories	575	300	265
Trade receivables	330	290	370
Cash	50	120	20
	955	710	655
	5,200	2,335	1,440
Equity and liabilities			
Equity			
Share capital ($1 ordinary shares)	2,000	1,000	750
Retained earnings	1,460	885	390
	3,460	1,885	1,140
Non-current liabilities			
12% debentures	500	100	–
Current liabilities			
Bank overdraft	560		
Trade payables	680	350	300
	1,240	350	300
	5,200	2,335	1,440

Additional information

(a)   J Co acquired 600,000 ordinary shares in P Co on 1 January 20X0 for $1,000,000 when the accumulated retained earnings of P Co were $200,000.

(b)   At the date of acquisition of P Co, the fair value of its freehold property was considered to be $400,000 greater than its value in P Co's statement of financial position. P Co had acquired the property ten years earlier and the buildings element (comprising 50% of the total value) is depreciated on cost over 50 years.

(c)   J Co acquired 225,000 ordinary shares in S Co on 1 January 20X4 for $500,000 when the retained profits of S Co were $150,000.

(d)   P Co manufactures a component used by J Co only. Transfers are made by P Co at cost plus 25%. J Co held $100,000 of these components in inventories at 31 December 20X5.

(e)   It is the policy of J Co to review goodwill for impairment annually. The goodwill in P Co was written off in full some years ago. An impairment test conducted at the year end revealed impairment losses on the investment in S Co of $92,000.

(f)   It is the group's policy to value the non-controlling interest at acquisition at fair value. The market price of the shares of the non-controlling shareholders just before the acquisition was $1.65.

Required

Prepare, in a format suitable for inclusion in the annual report of the J Group, the consolidated statement of financial position at 31 December 20X5.

34 Preparation question: 'D'-shaped group

> **BPP note**. In this question, a proforma is given to you for Part (a) to help you get used to setting out your answer. You may wish to transfer it to a separate sheet or to use a separate sheet for workings.

Below are the statements of financial position of three companies as at 31 December 20X9.

	Bauble Co $'000	Jewel Co $'000	Gem Co $'000
Non-current assets			
Property, plant and equipment	720	60	70
Investments in group companies	185	100	–
	905	160	70
Current assets	175	95	90
	1,080	255	160
Equity			
Share capital – $1 ordinary shares	400	100	50
Retained earnings	560	90	65
	960	190	115
Current liabilities	120	65	45
	1,080	255	160

You are also given the following information:

(a) Bauble Co acquired 60% of the share capital of Jewel Co on 1 January 20X2 and 10% of Gem on 1 January 20X3. The cost of the combinations were $142,000 and $43,000 respectively. Jewel Co acquired 70% of the share capital of Gem Co on 1 January 20X3.

(b) The retained earnings balances of Jewel Co and Gem Co were:

	1 January 20X2 $'000	1 January 20X3 $'000
Jewel Co	45	60
Gem Co	30	40

(c) No impairment loss adjustments have been necessary to date.

(d) It is the group's policy to value the non-controlling interest at acquisition at its proportionate share of the fair value of the subsidiary's identifiable net assets.

Required

(a) Prepare the consolidated statement of financial position for Bauble Co and its subsidiaries as at 31 December 20X9.

(b) Calculate the total goodwill arising on acquisition if Bauble Co had acquired its investments in Jewel and Gem on 1 January 20X3 at a cost of $142,000 and $43,000 respectively and Jewel Co had acquired its investment in Gem Co on 1 January 20X2.

(a) BAUBLE – CONSOLIDATED STATEMENT OF FINANCIAL POSITION AS AT 31 DECEMBER 20X9

	$'000
Non-current assets	
Property, plant and equipment	
Goodwill	————
	————
Current assets	————
	————
Equity attributable to owners of the parent	
Share capital – $1 ordinary shares	
Retained earnings	————
Non-controlling interest	————
Current liabilities	————
	————

35 Preparation question: Sub-subsidiary

The Exotic Group carries on business as a distributor of warehouse equipment and importer of fruit into the country. Exotic was incorporated in 20X1 to distribute warehouse equipment. It diversified its activities during 20X3 to include the import and distribution of fruit, and expanded its operations by the acquisition of shares in Melon in 20X5 and in Kiwi in 20X7.

Accounts for all companies are made up to 31 December.

The draft statements of profit or loss and other comprehensive income for Exotic, Melon and Kiwi for the year ended 31 December 20X9 are as follows.

	Exotic	Melon	Kiwi
	$'000	$'000	$'000
Revenue	45,600	24,700	22,800
Cost of sales	18,050	5,463	5,320
Gross profit	27,550	19,237	17,480
Distribution costs	(3,325)	(2,137)	(1,900)
Administrative expenses	(3,475)	(950)	(1,900)
Finance costs	(325)	–	–
Profit before tax	20,425	16,150	13,680
Income tax expense	8,300	5,390	4,241
Profit for the year	12,125	10,760	9,439

	Exotic	Melon	Kiwi
	$'000	$'000	$'000
Other comprehensive income for the year			
Items that will not be reclassified to profit or loss			
Revaluation of property	200	100	-
Total comprehensive income for the year	12,325	10,860	9439
Dividends paid and declared for the period	9,500	–	–

The draft statements of financial position as at 31 December 20X9 are as follows.

	Exotic $'000	Melon $'000	Kiwi $'000
Non-current assets			
Property, plant and equipment (at carrying value)	35,483	24,273	13,063
Investments			
Shares in Melon	6,650		
Shares in Kiwi		3,800	
	42,133	28,073	13,063
Current assets	1,568	9,025	8,883
	43,701	37,098	21,946
Equity			
$1 ordinary shares	8,000	3,000	2,000
Reserves (retained earnings and reval'n surplus)	22,638	24,075	19,898
	30,638	27,075	21,898
Current liabilities	13,063	10,023	48
	43,701	37,098	21,946

The following information is available relating to Exotic, Melon and Kiwi.

(a) On 1 January 20X5 Exotic acquired 2,700,000 $1 ordinary shares in Melon for $6,650,000 at which date there was a credit balance on the retained earnings of Melon of $1,425,000. No shares have been issued by Melon since Exotic acquired its interest.

(b) At the date of acquisition, the fair value of the identifiable net assets of Melon was $5m. The excess of the fair value of net assets is due to an increase in the value of non-depreciable land.

(c) On 1 January 20X7 Melon acquired 1,600,000 $1 ordinary shares in Kiwi for $3,800,000 at which date there was a credit balance on the retained earnings of Kiwi of $950,000. No shares have been issued by Kiwi since Melon acquired its interest.

(d) During 20X9, Kiwi had made intragroup sales to Melon of $480,000 making a profit of 25% on cost and $75,000 of these goods were in inventories at 31 December 20X9.

(e) During 20X9, Melon had made intragroup sales to Exotic of $260,000 making a profit of 25% on sales and $60,000 of these goods were in inventories at 31 December 20X9.

(f) Melon charges depreciation on its warehouse equipment at 20% on cost. It is company policy to charge a full year's depreciation in the year of acquisition to be included in the cost of sales.

(g) An impairment test conducted at the year end did not reveal any impairment losses.

(h) It is the group's policy to value the non-controlling interest at fair value at the date of acquisition. The fair value of the non-controlling interests in Melon on 1 January 20X5 was $500,000. The fair value of the 28% non-controlling interest in Kiwi on 1 January 20X7 was $900,000.

Required

Prepare for the Exotic Group:

(a) A consolidated statement of profit or loss and other comprehensive income for the year ended 31 December 20X9

(b) A consolidated statement of financial position as at that date

36 Glove

ACR, 6/07, amended

The following draft statements of financial position relate to Glove, Body and Fit, all public limited companies, as at 31 May 20X7.

	Glove $m	Body $m	Fit $m
Assets			
Non-current assets			
Property, plant and equipment	260	20	26
Investment in Body	60		
Investment in Fit		30	
Investments in equity instruments	10		
Current assets	65	29	20
Total assets	395	79	46
Ordinary shares	150	40	20
Other reserves	30	5	8
Retained earnings	135	25	10
Total equity	315	70	38
Non-current liabilities	45	2	3
Current liabilities	35	7	5
Total liabilities	80	9	8
Total equity and liabilities	395	79	46

The following information is relevant to the preparation of the group financial statements.

(a) Glove acquired 80% of the ordinary shares of Body on 1 June 20X5 when Body's other reserves were $4 million and retained earnings were $10 million. The fair value of the net assets of Body was $60 million at 1 June 20X5. Body acquired 70% of the ordinary shares of Fit on 1 June 20X5 when the other reserves of Fit were $8 million and retained earnings were $6 million. The fair value of the net assets of Fit at that date was $39 million. The excess of the fair value over the net assets of Body and Fit is due to an increase in the value of non-depreciable land of the companies. There have been no issues of ordinary shares in the group since 1 June 20X5.

(b) Body owns several trade names which are highly regarded in the market place. Body has invested a significant amount in marketing these trade names and has expensed the costs. None of the trade names has been acquired externally and, therefore, the costs have not been capitalised in the statement of financial position of Body. On the acquisition of Body by Glove, a firm of valuation experts valued the trade names at $5 million and this valuation had been taken into account by Glove when offering $60 million for the investment in Body. The valuation of the trade names is not included in the fair value of the net assets of Body above. Group policy is to amortise intangible assets over ten years.

(c) On 1 June 20X5, Glove introduced a defined benefit retirement plan. During the year to 31 May 20X7, loss on remeasurement on the defined benefit obligation was $1m, and gain on remeasurement on the plan assets were $900,000. These have not yet been accounted for and need to be treated in accordance with IAS 19, as revised in 2011. The net defined benefit liability is included in non-current liabilities..

(d) Glove has issued 30,000 convertible bonds with a three year term repayable at par. The bonds were issued at par with a face value of $1,000 per bond. Interest is payable annually in arrears at a nominal interest rate of 6%. Each bond can be converted at any time up to maturity into 300 shares of Glove. The bonds were issued on 1 June 20X6 when the market interest rate for similar debt without the conversion option was 8% per annum. Glove does not wish to account for the bonds at fair value through profit or loss. The interest has been paid and accounted for in the financial statements. The bonds have been included in non-current liabilities at their face value of $30 million and no bonds were converted in the current financial year.

(e) On 31 May 20X7, Glove acquired plant with a fair value of $6 million. In exchange for the plant, the supplier received land, which was currently not in use, from Glove. The land had a carrying value of $4 million and an open market value of $7 million. In the financial statements at 31 May 20X7, Glove had made a transfer of $4 million from land to plant in respect of this transaction.

(f) Goodwill has been tested for impairment at 31 May 20X6 and 31 May 20X7 and no impairment loss occurred.

(g) It is the group's policy to value the non-controlling interest at acquisition at its proportionate share of the fair value of the subsidiary's identifiable net assets.

(h) Ignore any taxation effects.

Required

Prepare the consolidated statement of financial position of the Glove Group at 31 May 20X7 in accordance with International Financial Reporting Standards (IFRS). **(25 marks)**

37 Case study question: Rod

90 mins

The following draft statements of financial position relate to Rod, a public limited company, Reel, a public limited company, and Line, a public limited company, as at 30 November 20X3.

	Rod $m	Reel $m	Line $m
Non-current assets			
Property, plant and equipment	1,230	505	256
Investment in Reel	640		
Investment in Line	160	100	
	2,030	605	256
Current assets			
Inventory	300	135	65
Trade receivables	240	105	49
Cash at bank and in hand	90	50	80
	630	290	194
Total assets	2,660	895	450
Equity			
Share capital	1,500	500	200
Share premium account	300	100	50
Revaluation surplus			70
Other components of equity	25		
Retained earnings	600	200	60
	2,425	800	380
Non-current liabilities	135	25	20
Current liabilities	100	70	50
Total equity and liabilities	2,660	895	450

The following information is relevant to the preparation of the group financial statements.

(a) Rod had acquired eighty per cent of the ordinary share capital of Reel on 1 December 20X0 when the retained earnings were $100 million. The fair value of the net assets of Reel was $710 million at 1 December 20X0. Any fair value adjustment related to net current assets and these net current assets had been realised by 30 November 20X3. There had been no new issues of shares in the group since the current group structure was created.

(b) Rod and Reel had acquired their holdings in Line on the same date as part of an attempt to mask the true ownership of Line. Rod acquired forty per cent and Reel acquired twenty-five per cent of the ordinary share capital of Line on 1 December 20X1. The retained earnings of Line on that date were $50 million and those of Reel were $150 million. There was no revaluation surplus in the books of Line on 1 December 20X1. The fair values of the net assets of Line at December 20X1 were not materially different from their carrying values.

(c) The group operates in the pharmaceutical industry and incurs a significant amount of expenditure on the development of products. These costs were formerly written off to profit or loss as incurred but then reinstated when the related products were brought into commercial use. The reinstated costs are shown as 'development inventories'. The costs do not meet the criteria in IAS 38 *Intangible assets* for classification as intangibles and it is unlikely that the net cash inflows from these products will be in excess of the development costs. In the current year, Reel has included $20 million of these costs in inventory. Of these costs $5 million relates to expenditure on a product written off in periods prior to 1 December 20X0. Commercial sales of this product had commenced during the current period. The accountant now wishes to ensure that the financial statements comply strictly with IAS/IFRS as regards this matter.

(d) Reel had purchased a significant amount of new production equipment during the year. The cost before trade discount of this equipment was $50 million. The trade discount of $6 million was taken to profit or loss. Depreciation is charged on the straight line basis over a six year period.

(e) The policy of the group is now to state property, plant and equipment at depreciated historical cost. The group changed from the revaluation model to the cost model under IAS 16 *Property, plant and equipment* in the year ended 30 November 20X3 and restated all of its assets to historical cost in that year except for the property, plant and equipment of Line which had been revalued by the directors of Line 1 December 20X2. The values were incorporated in the financial records creating revaluation surplus of $70 million. The property, plant and equipment of Line were originally purchased on December 20X1 at a cost of $300 million. The assets are depreciated over six years on the straight line basis. The group does not make an annual transfer from revaluation reserves to retained earnings in respect of the excess depreciation charged on revalued property, plant and equipment. There were no additions or disposals of the property, plant and equipment of Line for the two years ended 30 November 20X3.

(f) It is the group's policy to value the non-controlling interest at acquisition at its proportionate share of the subsidiary's identifiable net assets.

(g) During the year the directors of Rod decided to form a defined benefit pension scheme for the employees of the parent and contributed cash to it of $100 million. The following details relate to the scheme at 30 November 20X3.

	$m
Present value of defined benefit obligation	130
Fair value of plan assets	125
Current service cost	110
Interest cost on defined benefit obligation	20
Interest on plan assets	10

The only entry in the financial statements made to date is in respect of the cash contribution which has been included in Rod's trade receivables. The directors have been uncertain as how to deal with the above pension scheme in the consolidated financial statements because of the significance of the potential increase in the charge to the statement of profit or loss and other comprehensive income relating to the pension scheme. Any gain on remeasurement of the asset or obligation will be recognised in accordance with IAS 19 *Employee benefits* as revised in 2011.

Required

(a) Show how the defined benefit pension scheme should be dealt with in the consolidated financial statements.

(5 marks)

(b) Prepare a consolidated statement of financial position of the Rod Group for the year ended 30 November 20X3 in accordance with the standards of the International Accounting Standards Board. **(22 marks)**

(c) You are now advising the financial director of Rod about certain aspects of the financial statements for the year ended 30 November 20X4. The director has summarised these points as follows.

(i) **Restructuring of the group.** A formal announcement for a restructuring of the group was made after the year end on 5 December 20X4. A provision has not been made in the financial statements as a public issue of shares is being planned and the company does not wish to lower the reported profits. Prior to the year end, the company has sold certain plant and issued redundancy notices to some employees in anticipation of the formal commencement of the restructuring. The company prepared a formal plan for the restructuring which was approved by the board and communicated to the trade union representatives prior to the year end. The directors estimate the cost of the restructuring to be $60 million, and it could take up to two years to complete the restructuring. The estimated cost of restructuring includes $10 million for retraining and relocating existing employees, and the directors feel that costs of $20 million (of which $5 million is relocation expenses) will have been incurred by the time the financial statements are approved. **(7 marks)**

(ii) **Fine for illegal receipt of a state subsidy**. The company was fined on 10 October 20X4 for the receipt of state subsidies that were contrary to a supra-national trade agreement. The subsidies were used to offset trading losses in previous years. Rod has to repay to the government $300 million plus interest of $160 million. The total repayment has been treated as an intangible asset which is being amortised over twenty years with a full year's charge in the current year. **(5 marks)**

The financial director wishes to prepare a report for submission to the Board of Directors which discusses the above accounting treatment of the key points in the financial statements.

(d) Rod spends many millions of pounds on research in innovative areas. Often the research and development expenditure does not provide a revenue stream for many years. The company has gained a significant expertise in this field and is frustrated by the fact that the value which is being created is not shown in the statement of financial position, but the cost of the innovation is charged to profit or loss. The knowledge gained by the company is not reported in the financial statements.

Advise the directors on the current problems of reporting financial performance in the case of a 'knowledge led' company such as Rod. **(8 marks)**

(e) In many organisations, bonus payments related to annual profits form a significant part of the total remuneration of all senior managers, not just the top few managers. The directors of Rod feel that the chief internal auditor makes a significant contribution to the company's profitability, and should therefore receive a bonus based on profit.

Advise the directors as to whether this is appropriate. **(3 marks)**

(Total = 50 marks)

38 Preparation question: Part disposal

> **BPP note**. In this question, proformas are given to you to help you get used to setting out your answer. You may wish to transfer them to a separate sheet or to use a separate sheet for your workings.

Angel Co bought 70% of the share capital of Shane Co for $120,000 on 1 January 20X6. At that date Shane Co's retained earnings stood at $10,000.

The statements of financial position at 31 December 20X8, summarised statements of profit or loss and other comprehensive income to that date and movement on retained earnings are given below.

	Angel Co $'000	Shane Co $'000
STATEMENTS OF FINANCIAL POSITION		
Non-current assets		
Property, plant and equipment	200	80
Investment in Shane Co	120	–
	320	80
Current assets	890	140
	1,210	220
Equity		
Share capital – $1 ordinary shares	500	100
Retained reserves	400	90
	900	190
Current liabilities	310	30
	1,210	220
SUMMARISED STATEMENTS OF PROFIT OR LOSS AND OTHER COMPREHENSIVE INCOME		
Profit before interest and tax	100	20
Income tax expense	(40)	(8)
Profit for the year	60	12
Other comprehensive income (not reclassified to P/L) , net of tax	10	6
Total comprehensive income for the year	70	18
MOVEMENT IN RETAINED RESERVES		
Balance at 31 December 20X7	330	72
Total comprehensive income for the year	70	18
Balance at 31 December 20X8	400	90

Angel Co sells one half of its holding in Shane Co for $120,000 on 30 June 20X8. At that date, the fair value of the 35% holding in Shane was slightly more at $130,000 due to a share price rise. The remaining holding is to be dealt with as an associate. This does not represent a discontinued operation.

No entries have been made in the accounts for the above transaction.

Assume that profits accrue evenly throughout the year.

It is the group's policy to value the non-controlling interest at acquisition fair value. The fair value of the non-controlling interest on 1 January 20X6 was $51.4m.

Required

(a) Prepare the consolidated statement of financial position, statement of profit or loss and other comprehensive income and a reconciliation of movement in retained reserves for the year ended 31 December 20X8.

Ignore income taxes on the disposal. No impairment losses have been necessary to date.

PART DISPOSAL PROFORMA

ANGEL GROUP
CONSOLIDATED STATEMENT OF FINANCIAL POSITION
AS AT 31 DECEMBER 20X8 $'000
Non-current assets
Property, plant and equipment
Investment in Shane
                                                                         _____

Current assets
                                                                         _____
                                                                         ══════

Equity attributable to owners of the parent
Share capital
Retained reserves
                                                                         _____

Current liabilities
                                                                         _____
                                                                         ══════

CONSOLIDATED STATEMENT OF PROFIT OR LOSS AND OTHER COMPREHENSIVE INCOME
FOR THE YEAR ENDED 31 DECEMBER 20X8

                                                                         $'000
Profit before interest and tax
Profit on disposal of shares in subsidiary
Share of profit of associate
                                                                         _____
Profit before tax
Income tax expense
                                                                         _____
Profit for the year
                                                                         _____

Other comprehensive income (not reclassified to P/L) net of tax:
Share of other comprehensive income of associate
Other comprehensive income for the year
Total comprehensive income for the year

Profit attributable to:
  Owners of the parent
  Non-controlling interests
                                                                         _____

Total comprehensive income attributable to
  Owners of the parent
  Non-controlling interests
                                                                         _____
                                                                         ══════

CONSOLIDATED RECONCILIATION OF MOVEMENT IN RETAINED RESERVES
                                                                         $'000
Balance at 31 December 20X7
Total comprehensive income for the year
Balance at 31 December 20X8
                                                                         _____
                                                                         ══════

(b)   Explain the accounting treatment that would be required if Angel had disposed of 10% of its holding in
      Shane.

39 Preparation question: Purchase of further interest

RBE owns 70% of the ordinary share capital of DCA. The total group equity as at 31 December 20X1 was $4,000,000, which included $650,000 attributable to non-controlling interest.

RBE purchased a further 20% of the ordinary share capital of DCA on 1 October 20X2 for $540,000.

During the year to 31 December 20X2, RBE issued 2 million $1 ordinary shares, fully paid, at $1.30 per share.

Dividends were paid by both group entities in April 20X2. The dividends paid by RBE and DCA were $200,000 and $100,000, respectively.

Total comprehensive income for the year ended 31 December 20X2 for RBE was $900,000 and for DCA was $600,000. Income is assumed to accrue evenly throughout the year.

Required

(a) Explain the impact of the additional 20% purchase of DCA's ordinary share capital by RBE on the equity of the RBE Group.

(b) Prepare the consolidated statement of changes in equity for the year ended 31 December 20X2 for the RBE Group, showing the total equity attributable to the parent and to the non-controlling interest.

40 Ejoy

54 mins

ACR, 6/06, amended

Ejoy, a public limited company, has acquired two subsidiaries. The details of the acquisitions are as follows:

Company	Date of acquisition	Ordinary share capital of $1 $m	Reserves at acquisition $m	Fair value of net assets at acquisition $m	Cost of investment $m	Ordinary share capital of $1 acquired $m
Zbay	1 June 20X4	200	170	600	520	160
Tbay	1 December 20X5	120	80	310	192	72

Any fair value adjustments relate to non-depreciable land. The draft statements of profit or loss and other comprehensive income for the year ended 31 May 20X6 are:

	Ejoy $m	Zbay $m	Tbay $m
Revenue	2,500	1,500	800
Cost of sales	(1,800)	(1,200)	(600)
Gross profit	700	300	200
Other income	70	10	–
Distribution costs	(130)	(120)	(70)
Administrative expenses	(100)	(90)	(60)
Finance costs	(50)	(40)	(20)
Profit before tax	490	60	50
Income tax expense	(200)	(26)	(20)
Profit for the year	290	34	30
Other comprehensive for the year (not reclassified to profit or loss):			
Gain on property revaluation net of tax	80	10	8
Total comprehensive income for the year	370	44	38
Total comprehensive income for year 31 May 20X5	190	20	15

The following information is relevant to the preparation of the group financial statements.

(a) Tbay was acquired exclusively with a view to sale and at 31 May 20X6 meets the criteria of being a disposal group. The fair value of Tbay at 31 May 20X6 is $344 million and the estimated selling costs of the shareholding in Tbay are $5 million.

(b) Ejoy entered into a joint arrangement with another company on 31 May 20X6, which met the IFRS 11 definition of a joint venture. The joint venture is a limited company and Ejoy has contributed assets at fair value of $20 million (carrying value $14 million). Each party will hold five million ordinary shares of $1 in the joint venture. The gain on the disposal of the assets ($6 million) to the joint venture has been included in 'other income'.

(c) Zbay has a loan asset which was carried at $60 million at 1 June 20X5. The loan's effective interest rate is six per cent. On 1 June 20X5 the company felt that because of the borrower's financial problems, it would receive $20 million in approximately two years time, on 31 May 20X7. At 31 May 20X6, the company still expects to receive the same amount on the same date. The loan asset is held at amortised cost.

(d) On 1 June 20X5, Ejoy purchased a five year bond with a principal amount of $50 million and a fixed interest rate of five per cent which was the current market rate. The bond is classified as at fair value through profit or loss. Because of the size of the investment, Ejoy has entered into a floating interest rate swap. Ejoy has designated the swap as a fair value hedge of the bond. At 31 May 20X6, market interest rates were six per cent. As a result, the fair value of the bond has decreased to $48·3 million. Ejoy has received $0·5 million in net interest payments on the swap at 31 May 20X6 and the fair value hedge has been 100% effective in the period, and you should assume any gain/loss on the hedge is the same as the loss/gain on the bond. No entries have been made in the statement of profit or loss and other comprehensive income to account for the bond or the hedge.

(e) No impairment of the goodwill arising on the acquisition of Zbay had occurred at 1 June 20X5. The recoverable amount of Zbay was $630 million and the value in use of Tbay was $334 million at 31 May 20X6. Impairment losses on goodwill are charged to cost of sales.

(f) Assume that profits accrue evenly throughout the year and ignore any taxation effects.

(g) It is the group's policy to value the non-controlling interest at its proportionate share of the fair value of the subsidiary's identifiable net assets.

Required

Prepare a consolidated statement of profit or loss and other comprehensive income for the Ejoy Group for the year ended 31 May 20X6 in accordance with International Financial Reporting Standards.

(30 marks)

41 Case study question: Traveler

90 mins

`12/11`

Traveler, a public limited company, operates in the manufacturing sector. The draft statements of financial position of the group companies are as follows at 30 November 20X1.

	Traveler $m	Data $m	Captive $m
Assets			
Non-current assets			
Property, plant and equipment	439	810	620
Investment in subsidiaries:			
Data	820		
Captive	541		
Financial assets	108	10	20
	1,908	820	640
Net defined benefit asset	72		
Current assets	995	781	350
Total assets	2,975	1,601	990

	Traveler $m	Data $m	Captive $m
Equity and liabilities			
Share capital	1,120	600	390
Retained earnings	1,066	442	169
Other components of equity	60	37	45
Total equity	2,246	1,079	604
Non-current liabilities	455	323	73
Current liabilities	274	199	313
Total liabilities	729	522	386
Total equity and liabilities	2,975	1,601	990

The following information is relevant to the preparation of the group financial statements.

(i)   On 1 December 20X0, Traveler acquired 60% of the equity interests of Data, a public limited company. The purchase consideration comprised cash of $600 million. At acquisition, the fair value of the non-controlling interest in Data was $395 million. Traveler wishes to use the 'full goodwill' method. On 1 December 20X0, the fair value of the identifiable net assets acquired was $935 million and retained earnings of Data were $299 million and other components of equity were $26 million. The excess in fair value is due to non-depreciable land.

On 30 November 20X1, Traveler acquired a further 20% interest in Data for a cash consideration of $220 million.

(ii)   On 1 December 20X0, Traveler acquired 80% of the equity interests of Captive for a consideration of $541 million. The consideration comprised cash of $477 million and the transfer of non-depreciable land with a fair value of $64 million. The carrying amount of the land at the acquisition date was $56 million. At the year end, this asset was still included in the non-current assets of Traveler and the sale proceeds had been credited to profit or loss.

At the date of acquisition, the identifiable net assets of Captive had a fair value of $526 million, retained earnings were $90 million and other components of equity were $24 million. The excess in fair value is due to non-depreciable land. This acquisition was accounted for using the partial goodwill method in accordance with IFRS 3 (Revised) *Business combinations*.

(iii)   Goodwill was impairment tested after the additional acquisition in Data on 30 November 20X1. The recoverable amount of Data was $1,099 million and that of Captive was $700 million.

(iv)   Included in the financial assets of Traveler is a ten-year 7% loan. At 30 November 20X1, the borrower was in financial difficulties and its credit rating had been downgraded. Traveler has adopted IFRS 9 *Financial instruments* and the loan asset is currently held at amortised cost of $29 million. Traveler now wishes to value the loan at fair value using current market interest rates. Traveler has agreed for the loan to be restructured; there will only be three more annual payments of $8 million starting in one year's time. Current market interest rates are 8%, the original effective interest rate is 6·7% and the effective interest rate under the revised payment schedule is 6·3%.

(v)   Traveler acquired a new factory on 1 December 20X0. The cost of the factory was $50 million and it has a residual value of $2 million. The factory has a flat roof, which needs replacing every five years. The cost of the roof was $5 million. The useful economic life of the factory is 25 years. No depreciation has been charged for the year. Traveler wishes to account for the factory and roof as a single asset and depreciate the whole factory over its economic life. Traveler uses straight-line depreciation.

(vi)   The actuarial value of Traveler's pension plan showed a surplus at 1 December 20X0 of $72 million. Losses of $25 million on remeasurement of the net defined benefit asset are to be recognised in other comprehensive income in accordance with IAS 19 (revised 2011). The aggregate of the current service cost and the net interest cost amounted to a cost of $55 million for the year. After consulting with the actuaries, the company decided to reduce its contributions for the year to $45 million. The contributions were paid on 7 December 20X1. No entries had been made in the financial statements for the above amounts. The present value of available future refunds and reductions in future contributions was $18 million.

Required

(a) Prepare a consolidated statement of financial position for the Traveler Group as at 30 November 20X1.

(35 marks)

(b) Traveler has three distinct business segments. The management has calculated the net assets, turnover and profit before common costs, which are to be allocated to these segments. However, they are unsure as to how they should allocate certain common costs and whether they can exercise judgement in the allocation process. They wish to allocate head office management expenses; pension expense; the cost of managing properties and interest and related interest bearing assets. They also are uncertain as to whether the allocation of costs has to be in conformity with the accounting policies used in the financial statements.

Required

Advise the management of Traveler on the points raised in the above paragraph. **(7 marks)**

(c) Segmental information reported externally is more useful if it conforms to information used by management in making decisions. The information can differ from that reported in the financial statements. Although reconciliations are required, these can be complex and difficult to understand. Additionally, there are other standards where subjectivity is involved and often the profit motive determines which accounting practice to follow. The directors have a responsibility to shareholders in disclosing information to enhance corporate value but this may conflict with their corporate social responsibility.

Required

Discuss how the ethics of corporate social responsibility disclosure are difficult to reconcile with shareholder expectations. **(6 marks)**

Professional marks will be awarded in Part (c) for clarity and expression of your discussion **(2 marks)**

(Total = 50 marks)

42 Case study question: Robby   90 mins

6/12

The following draft statements of financial position relate to Robby, Hail and Zinc, all public limited companies, as at 31 May 20X3

	Robby $m	Hail $m	Zinc $m
Assets			
Non-current assets			
Property, plant and equipment	112	60	26
Investments in subsidiaries:			
Hail	55		
Zinc	19		
Financial assets	9	6	14
Joint operation	6		
Current assets	5	7	12
Total assets	206	73	52
Equity and liabilities			
Ordinary shares	25	20	10
Other components of equity	11	-	-
Retained earnings	70	27	19
Total equity	106	47	29
Non-current liabilities:	53	20	21
Current liabilities	47	6	2
Total equity and liabilities	206	73	52

The following information is relevant to the preparation of the group financial statements of Robby.

(a)   On 1 June 20X1, Robby acquired 80% of the equity interests of Hail. The purchase consideration comprised cash of $50 million. Robby has treated the investment in Hail at fair value through other comprehensive income (OCI).

A dividend received from Hail on 1 January 20X3 of $2 million has similarly been credited to OCI.

It is Robby's policy to measure the non-controlling interest at fair value and this was $15 million on 1 June 20X1.

On 1 June 20X1, the fair value of the identifiable net assets of Hail was $60 million and the retained earnings of Hail were $16 million. The excess of the fair value of the net assets is due to an increase in the value of non-depreciable land.

(b)   On 1 June 20X0, Robby acquired 5% of the ordinary shares of Zinc. Robby had treated this investment at fair value through profit or loss in the financial statements to 31 May 20X2.

On 1 December 20X2, Robby acquired a further 55% of the ordinary shares of Zinc and gained control of the company.

The consideration for the acquisitions was as follows.

	Shareholding	Consideration
		$m
1 June 20X0	5%	2
1 December 20X2	55%	16
	60%	18

At 1 December 20X2, the fair value of the equity interest in Zinc held by Robby before the business combination was $5 million.

It is Robby's policy to measure the non-controlling interest at fair value and this was $9 million on 1 December 20X2.

The fair value of the identifiable net assets at 1 December 20X2 of Zinc was $26 million, and the retained earnings were $15 million. The excess of the fair value of the net assets is due to an increase in the value of property, plant and equipment (PPE), which was provisional pending receipt of the final valuations. These valuations were received on 1 March 20X3 and resulted in an additional increase of $3 million in the fair value of PPE at the date of acquisition. This increase does not affect the fair value of the non-controlling interest at acquisition. PPE is to be depreciated on the straight-line basis over a remaining period of five years.

(c)   Robby has a 40% share of a joint operation, a natural gas station. Assets, liabilities, revenue and costs are apportioned on the basis of shareholding. The following information relates to the joint arrangement activities.

(i)   The natural gas station cost $15 million to construct and was completed on 1 June 20X2 and is to be dismantled at the end of its life of ten years. The present value of this dismantling cost to the joint arrangement at 1 June 20X2, using a discount rate of 5%, was $2 million.

(ii)   In the year, gas with a direct cost of $16 million was sold for $20 million. Additionally, the joint arrangement incurred operating costs of $0·5 million during the year.

Robby has only contributed and accounted for its share of the construction cost, paying $6 million. The revenue and costs are receivable and payable by the other joint operator who settles amounts outstanding with Robby after the year end.

(d)   Robby purchased PPE for $10 million on 1 June 20X0. It has an expected useful life of twenty years and is depreciated on the straight-line method. On 31 May 20X2, the PPE was revalued to $11 million. At 31 May 20X3, impairment indicators triggered an impairment review of the PPE. The recoverable amount of the PPE was $7·8 million. The only accounting entry posted for the year to 31 May 20X3 was to account for the depreciation based on the revalued amount as at 31 May 20X2. Robby's accounting policy is to make a transfer of the excess depreciation arising on the revaluation of PPE.

(e) Robby held a portfolio of trade receivables with a carrying amount of $4 million at 31 May 20X3. At that date, the entity entered into a factoring agreement with a bank, whereby it transfers the receivables in exchange for $3·6 million in cash. Robby has agreed to reimburse the factor for any shortfall between the amount collected and $3·6 million. Once the receivables have been collected, any amounts above $3·6 million, less interest on this amount, will be repaid to Robby. Robby has derecognised the receivables and charged $0·4 million as a loss to profit or loss.

(f) Immediately prior to the year end, Robby sold land to a third party at a price of $16 million with an option to purchase the land back on 1 July 20X3 for $16 million plus a premium of 3%. The market value of the land is $25 million on 31 May 20X3 and the carrying amount was $12 million. Robby accounted for the sale, consequently eliminating the bank overdraft at 31 May 20X3.

Required

(a) Prepare a consolidated statement of financial position of the Robby Group at 31 May 20X3 in accordance with International Financial Reporting Standards. **(35 marks)**

(b) (i) In the above scenario (information point (e)), Robby holds a portfolio of trade receivables and enters into a factoring agreement with a bank, whereby it transfers the receivables in exchange for cash. Robby additionally agreed to other terms with the bank as regards any collection shortfall and repayment of any monies to Robby. Robby derecognised the receivables. This is an example of the type of complex transaction that can arise out of normal terms of trade. The rules regarding derecognition are quite complex and are often not understood by entities.

Describe the rules of IFRS 9 *Financial Instruments* relating to the derecognition of a financial asset and how these rules affect the treatment of the portfolio of trade receivables in Robby's financial statements. **(9 marks)**

(ii) Discuss the legitimacy of Robby selling land just prior to the year end in order to show a better liquidity position for the group and whether this transaction is consistent with an accountant's responsibilities to users of financial statements. **(6 marks)**

Note. Your answer should include reference to the above scenario.

(Total = 50 marks)

43 Case study question: Bravado

90 mins

Bravado, a public limited company, has acquired two subsidiaries and an associate. The draft statements of financial position are as follows at 31 May 20X9.

	Bravado $m	Message $m	Mixted $m
Assets			
Non-current assets			
Property, plant and equipment	265	230	161
Investments in subsidiaries:			
Message	300		
Mixted	133		
Investment in associate: Clarity	20		
Investment in equity instruments	51	6	5
	769	236	166
Current assets			
Inventories	135	55	73
Trade receivables	91	45	32
Cash and cash equivalents	102	100	8
	328	200	113
	1,097	436	279

	Bravado $m	Message $m	Mixted $m
Total assets			
Equity and liabilities			
Share capital	520	220	100
Retained earnings	240	150	80
Other components of equity	17	4	7
Total equity	777	374	187
Non-current liabilities:			
Long-term borrowings	120	15	5
Deferred tax	25	9	3
Total non-current liabilities	145	24	8
Current liabilities			
Trade and other payables	115	30	60
Current tax payable	60	8	24
Total current liabilities	175	38	84
Total liabilities	320	62	92
Total equity and liabilities	1,097	436	279

The following information is relevant to the preparation of the group financial statements.

(a) On 1 June 20X8, Bravado acquired 80% of the equity interests of Message, a private entity. The purchase consideration comprised cash of $300 million. The fair value of the identifiable net assets of Message was $400 million, including any related deferred tax liability arising on acquisition. The owners of Message had to dispose of the entity for tax purposes by a specified date, and therefore sold the entity to the first company to bid for it, which was Bravado. An independent valuer has stated that the fair value of the non-controlling interest in Message was $86 million on 1 June 20X8. Bravado does not wish to measure the non-controlling interest in subsidiaries on the basis of the proportionate interest in the identifiable net assets, but wishes to use the 'full goodwill' method. The retained earnings of Message were $136 million and other components of equity were $4 million at the date of acquisition. There had been no new issue of capital by Message since the date of acquisition and the excess of the fair value of the net assets is due to an increase in the value of non-depreciable land.

(b) On 1 June 20X7, Bravado acquired 6% of the ordinary shares of Mixted. Bravado had treated this as an as investment in equity instruments at fair value in the financial statements to 31 May 20X8, and had made an irrevocable election (see note (d)) to recognise changes in fair value in other comprehensive income. There were no changes in the fair value of Mixted in the year to 31 May 20X9. On 1 June 20X8, Bravado acquired a further 64% of the ordinary shares of Mixted and gained control of the company. The consideration for the acquisitions was as follows.

	Holding	Consideration $m
1 June 20X7	6%	10
1 June 20X8	64%	118
	70%	128

Under the purchase agreement of 1 June 20X8, Bravado is required to pay the former shareholders 30% of the profits of Mixted on 31 May 20Y0 for each of the financial years to 31 May 20X9 and 31 May 20Y0. The fair value of this arrangement was measured at $12 million at 1 June 20X8 and at 31 May 20X9 this value had not changed. This amount has not been included in the financial statements.

At 1 June 20X8, the fair value of the equity interest in Mixted held by Bravado before the business combination was $15 million, and the fair value of the non-controlling interest in Mixted was $53 million. The fair value of the identifiable net assets at 1 June 20X8 of Mixted was $170 million (excluding deferred tax assets and liabilities), and the retained earnings and other components of equity were $55 million and $7 million respectively. There had been no new issue of share capital by Mixted since the date of acquisition and the excess of the fair value of the net assets is due to an increase in the value of property, plant and equipment (PPE).

The fair value of the PPE was provisional pending receipt of the final valuations for these assets. These valuations were received on 1 December 20X8 and they resulted in a further increase of $6 million in the fair

BPP
LEARNING MEDIA

value of the net assets at the date of acquisition. This increase does not affect the fair value of the non-controlling interest. PPE is depreciated on the straight-line basis over seven years. The tax base of the identifiable net assets of Mixted was $166 million at 1 June 20X8. The tax rate of Mixted is 30%.

(c) Bravado acquired a 10% interest in Clarity, a public limited company, on 1 June 20X7 for $8 million. The investment was accounted for as an investment in equity instruments and at 31 May 20X8, its value was $9 million. On 1 June 20X8, Bravado acquired an additional 15% interest in Clarity for $11 million and achieved significant influence. Clarity made profits after dividends of $6 million and $10 million for the years to 31 May 20X8 and 31 May 20X9. An irrevocable election was made to take changes in fair value through other comprehensive income (items that will not be reclassified to profit or loss).

(d) Bravado has made an irrevocable election to hold its investments in Message, Mixted and Clarity at fair value with changes in fair value recognised in other comprehensive income. There were no changes in fair value during the year ended 31 May 20X9.

(e) On 1 June 20X7, Bravado purchased an equity instrument of 11 million dinars which was its fair value. On that date an election was made to hold it at fair value through other comprehensive income. The relevant exchange rates and fair values were as follows:

	$ to dinars	Fair value of instrument – dinars
1 June 20X7	4.5	11
31 May 20X8	5.1	10
31 May 20X9	4.8	7

Bravado has not recorded any change in the value of the instrument since 31 May 20X8. The reduction in fair value as at 31 May 20X9 is deemed to be as a result of impairment.

(f) Bravado manufactures equipment for the retail industry. The inventory is currently valued at cost. There is a market for the part completed product at each stage of production. The cost structure of the equipment is as follows.

	Cost per unit $	Selling price per unit $
Production process: 1st stage	1,000	1,050
Conversion costs: 2nd stage	500	
Finished product	1,500	1,700

The selling costs are $10 per unit, and Bravado has 10,000 units at the first stage of production and 20,000 units of the finished product at 31 May 20X9. Shortly before the year end, a competitor released a new model onto the market which caused the equipment manufactured by Bravado to become less attractive to customers. The result was a reduction in the selling price to $1,450 of the finished product and $950 for 1st stage product.

(g) The directors have included a loan to a director of Bravado in cash and cash equivalents of $1 million. The loan has no specific repayment date on it but is repayable on demand. The directors feel that there is no problem with this accounting entry as there is a choice of accounting policy within International Financial Reporting Standards (IFRS) and that showing the loan as cash is their choice of accounting policy as there is no IFRS which says that this policy cannot be utilised.

(h) There is no impairment of goodwill arising on the acquisitions.

Required

(a) Prepare a consolidated statement of financial position as at 31 May 20X9 for the Bravado Group. **(35 marks)**

(b) Calculate and explain the impact on the calculation of goodwill if the non-controlling interest was calculated on a proportionate basis for Message and Mixted. **(8 marks)**

(c) Discuss the view of the directors that there is no problem with showing a loan to a director as cash and cash equivalents, taking into account their ethical and other responsibilities as directors of the company.
(5 marks)

Professional marks will be awarded in part (c) for clarity and expression of your discussion. **(2 marks)**

(Total = 50 marks)

44 Case study question: Grange

90 mins

Grange, a public limited company, operates in the manufacturing sector. The draft statements of financial position of the group companies are as follows at 30 November 20X9.

	Grange $m	Park $m	Fence $m
Assets			
Non-current assets			
Property, plant and equipment ~8000	257	311	238
Investment in subsidiaries:			
Park	340		
Fence	134		
Investment in Sitin	16		
	747	311	238
Current assets	475	304	141
Total assets	1,222	615	379
Equity and liabilities			
Share capital 430	430	230	150
Retained earnings	410	170	65
Other components of equity	22	14	17
Total equity	862	414	232
Non-current liabilities	172	124	38
Current liabilities			
Trade and other payables	178	71	105
Provisions for liabilities (10+6+4+25)	10	6	4
Total current liabilities	188	77	109
Total liabilities	360	201	147
Total equity and liabilities	1,222	615	379

The following information is relevant to the preparation of the group financial statements.

(i) On 1 June 20X8, Grange acquired 60% of the equity interests of Park, a public limited company. The purchase consideration comprised cash of $250 million. Excluding the franchise referred to below, the fair value of the identifiable net assets was $360 million. The excess of the fair value of the net assets is due to an increase in the value of non-depreciable land.

Park held a franchise right, which at 1 June 20X8 had a fair value of $10 million. This had not been recognised in the financial statements of Park. The franchise agreement had a remaining term of five years to run at that date and is not renewable. Park still holds this franchise at the year-end.

Grange wishes to use the 'full goodwill' method for all acquisitions. The fair value of the non-controlling interest in Park was $150 million on 1 June 20X8. The retained earnings of Park were $115 million and other components of equity were $10 million at the date of acquisition.

Grange acquired a further 20% interest from the non-controlling interests in Park on 30 November 20X9 for a cash consideration of $90 million.

(ii) On 31 July 20X8, Grange acquired 100% of the equity interests of Fence for a cash consideration of $214 million. The identifiable net assets of Fence had a provisional fair value of $202 million, including any contingent liabilities. At the time of the business combination, Fence had a contingent liability with a fair value of $30 million. At 30 November 20X9, the contingent liability met the recognition criteria of IAS 37 *Provisions, contingent liabilities and contingent assets* and the revised estimate of this liability was $25 million. The accountant of Fence is yet to account for this revised liability.

However, Grange had not completed the valuation of an element of property, plant and equipment of Fence at 31 July 20X8 and the valuation was not completed by 30 November 20X8. The valuation was received on 30 June 20X9 and the excess of the fair value over book value at the date of acquisition was measured at $4 million. The asset had a useful economic life of 10 years at 31 July 20X8.

The retained earnings of Fence were $73 million and other components of equity were $9 million at 31 July 20X8 before any adjustment for the contingent liability.

On 30 November 20X9, Grange disposed of 25% of its equity interest in Fence to the non-controlling interest for a consideration of $80 million. The disposal proceeds had been credited to the cost of the investment in the statement of financial position.

(iii)   On 30 June 20X8, Grange had acquired a 100% interest in Sitin, a public limited company, for a cash consideration of $39 million. Sitin's identifiable net assets were fair valued at $32 million.

On 30 November 20X9, Grange disposed of 60% of the equity of Sitin when its identifiable net assets were $36 million. Of the increase in net assets, $3 million had been reported in profit or loss and $1 million had been reported in other comprehensive income as profit on an investment in equity instruments (with irrevocable OCI election). The sale proceeds were $23 million and the remaining equity interest was fair valued at $13 million. Grange could still exert significant influence after the disposal of the interest. The only accounting entry made in Grange's financial statements was to increase cash and reduce the cost of the investment in Sitin.

(iv)   Grange acquired a plot of land on 1 December 20X8 in an area where the land is expected to rise significantly in value if plans for regeneration go ahead in the area. The land is currently held at cost of $6 million in property, plant and equipment until Grange decides what should be done with the land. The market value of the land at 30 November 20X9 was $8 million but as at 15 December 20X9, this had reduced to $7 million as there was some uncertainty surrounding the viability of the regeneration plan.

(v)   Grange anticipates that it will be fined $1 million by the local regulator for environmental pollution. It also anticipates that it will have to pay compensation to local residents of $6 million, although this is only the best estimate of that liability. In addition, the regulator has requested that certain changes be made to the manufacturing process in order to make the process more environmentally friendly. This is anticipated to cost the company $4 million.

(vi)   Grange has a property located in a foreign country, which was acquired at a cost of 8 million dinars on 30 November 20X8 when the exchange rate was $1 = 2 dinars. At 30 November 20X9, the property was revalued to 12 million dinars. The exchange rate at 30 November 20X9 was $1 = 1.5 dinars. The property was being carried at its value as at 30 November 20X8. The company policy is to revalue property, plant and equipment whenever material differences exist between book and fair value. Depreciation on the property can be assumed to be immaterial.

(vii)   Grange has prepared a plan for reorganising the parent company's own operations. The board of directors has discussed the plan but further work has to be carried out before they can approve it. However, Grange has made a public announcement as regards the reorganisation and wishes to make a reorganisation provision at 30 November 20X9 of $30 million. The plan will generate cost savings. The directors have calculated the value in use of the net assets (total equity) of the parent company as being $870 million if the reorganisation takes place and $830 million if the reorganisation does not take place. Grange is concerned that the parent company's property, plant and equipment have lost value during the period because of a decline in property prices in the region and feel that any impairment charge would relate to these assets. There is no reserve within other equity relating to prior revaluation of these non-current assets.

(viii) Grange uses accounting policies, which maximise its return on capital employed. The directors of Grange feel that they are acting ethically in using this approach as they feel that as long as they follow 'professional rules', then there is no problem. They have adopted a similar philosophy in the way they conduct their business affairs. The finance director had recently received information that one of their key customers, Brook, a public limited company, was having serious liquidity problems. This information was received from a close friend who was employed by Brook. However, he also learned that Brook had approached a rival company Field, a public limited company, for credit and knew that if Field granted Brook credit then there was a high probability that the outstanding balance owed by Brook to Grange would be paid. Field had approached the director for an informal credit reference for Brook who until recently had always paid promptly. The director was intending to give Brook a good reference because of its recent prompt payment history, as the director felt that there was no obligation or rule which required him to mention the company's liquidity problems. (There is no change required to the financial statements as a result of the above information.)

Required

(a)   Calculate the consolidated gain or loss arising on the disposal of the equity interest in Sitin.   **(6 marks)**

(b)   Prepare a consolidated statement of financial position of the Grange Group at 30 November 20X9 in accordance with International Financial Reporting Standards.   **(35 marks)**

(c)   Discuss the view that ethical behaviour is simply a matter of compliance with professional rules and whether the finance director should simply consider 'rules' when determining whether to give Brook a good credit reference.   **(7 marks)**

Professional marks will be awarded in part (c) for clarity and expression.   **(2 marks)**

(Total = 50 marks)

45 Case study question: Ashanti

90 mins

6/10, amended

The following financial statements relate to Ashanti, a public limited company.

ASHANTI GROUP: STATEMENTS OF PROFIT OR LOSS AND OTHER COMPREHENSIVE INCOME
FOR THE YEAR ENDED 30 APRIL 20X5

	Ashanti	Bochem	Ceram
	$m	$m	$m
Revenue	810	235	142
Cost of sales	(686)	(137)	(84)
Gross profit	124	98	58
Other income	31	17	12
Distribution costs	(30)	(21)	(26)
Administrative costs	(55)	(29)	(12)
Finance costs	(8)	(6)	(8)
Profit before tax	62	59	24
Income tax expense	(21)	(23)	(10)
Profit for the year	41	36	14
Other comprehensive income for the year, net of tax - Items that will not be reclassified to profit or loss:			
Investment in equity instruments	20	9	6
Gains (net) on PPE revaluation	12	6	–
Actuarial losses on defined benefit plan	(14)	–	–
Other comprehensive income for the year, net of tax	18	15	6
Total comprehensive income and expense for year	59	51	20

The following information is relevant to the preparation of the group statement of profit or loss and other comprehensive income:

(i)   On 1 May 20X3, Ashanti acquired 70% of the equity interests of Bochem, a public limited company. The purchase consideration comprised cash of $150 million and the fair value of the identifiable net assets was $160 million at that date. The fair value of the non-controlling interest in Bochem was $54 million on 1 May 20X3. Ashanti wishes to use the 'full goodwill' method for all acquisitions. The share capital and retained earnings of Bochem were $55 million and $85 million respectively and other components of equity were $10 million at the date of acquisition. The excess of the fair value of the identifiable net assets at acquisition is due to an increase in the value of plant, which is depreciated on the straight-line method and has a five year remaining life at the date of acquisition. Ashanti disposed of a 10% equity interest to the non-controlling interests (NCI) of Bochem on 30 April 20X5 for a cash consideration of $34 million. The carrying value of the net assets of Bochem at 30 April 20X5 was $210 million before any adjustments on consolidation. Goodwill has been impairment tested annually and as at 30 April 20X4 had reduced in value by 15% and at 30 April

20X5 had lost a further 5% of its original value before the sale of the equity interest to the NCI. The goodwill impairment should be allocated between group and NCI on the basis of equity shareholding.

(ii) Bochem acquired 80% of the equity interests of Ceram, a public limited company, on 1 May 20X3. The purchase consideration was cash of $136 million. Ceram's identifiable net assets were fair valued at $115 million and the NCI of Ceram attributable to Ashanti had a fair value of $26 million at that date. On 1 November 20X4, Bochem disposed of 50% of the equity of Ceram for a consideration of $90 million. Ceram's identifiable net assets were $160 million and the consolidated value of the NCI of Ceram attributable to Bochem was $35 million at the date of disposal. The remaining equity interest of Ceram held by Bochem was fair valued at $45 million. After the disposal, Bochem can still exert significant influence. Goodwill had been impairment tested and no impairment had occurred. Ceram's profits are deemed to accrue evenly over the year.

(iii) Ashanti has sold inventory to both Bochem and Ceram in October 20X4. The sale price of the inventory was $10 million and $5 million respectively. Ashanti sells goods at a gross profit margin of 20% to group companies and third parties. At the year-end, half of the inventory sold to Bochem remained unsold but the entire inventory sold to Ceram had been sold to third parties.

(iv) On 1 May 20X2, Ashanti purchased a $20 million five-year bond with semi annual interest of 5% payable on 31 October and 30 April. The purchase price of the bond was $21·62 million. The effective annual interest rate is 8% or 4% on a semi annual basis. The bond is held at amortised cost. At 1 May 20X4 the amortised cost of the bond was $21.046 million. The issuer of the bond did pay the interest due on 31 October 20X4 and 30 April 20X5, but was in financial trouble at 30 April 20X5. Ashanti feels that as at 30 April 20X5, the bond is impaired and that the best estimates of total future cash receipts are $2·34 million on 30 April 20X6 and $8 million on 30 April 20X7. The current interest rate for discounting cash flows as at 30 April 20X5 is 10%. No accounting entries have been made in the financial statements for the above bond since 30 April 20X4. (You should assume the annual compound rate is 8% for discounting the cash flows.)

(v) Ashanti sold $5 million of goods to a customer who recently made an announcement that it is restructuring its debts with its suppliers including Ashanti. It is probable that Ashanti will not recover the amounts outstanding. The goods were sold after the announcement was made although the order was placed prior to the announcement. Ashanti wishes to make an additional allowance of $8 million against the total receivable balance at the year end, of which $5 million relates to this sale.

(vi) Ashanti owned a piece of property, plant and equipment (PPE) which cost $12 million and was purchased on 1 May 20X3. It is being depreciated over 10 years on the straight-line basis with zero residual value. On 30 April 20X4, it was revalued to $13 million and on 30 April 20X5, the PPE was revalued to $8 million. The whole of the revaluation loss had been posted to other comprehensive income and depreciation has been charged for the year. It is Ashanti's company policy to make all necessary transfers for excess depreciation following revaluation.

(vii) The salaried employees of Ashanti are entitled to 25 days paid leave each year. The entitlement accrues evenly over the year and unused leave may be carried forward for one year. The holiday year is the same as the financial year. At 30 April 20X5, Ashanti has 900 salaried employees and the average unused holiday entitlement is three days per employee. 5% of employees leave without taking their entitlement and there is no cash payment when an employee leaves in respect of holiday entitlement. There are 255 working days in the year and the total annual salary cost is $19 million. No adjustment has been made in the financial statements for the above and there was no opening accrual required for holiday entitlement.

(viii) As permitted by IFRS 9 *Financial instruments* all group companies have made an irrevocable election to recognise changes in the fair value of investments in equity instruments in other comprehensive income (items that will not be reclassified to profit or loss).

(ix) Ignore any taxation effects of the above adjustments and the disclosure requirements of IFRS 5 *Non-current assets held for sale and discontinued operations*.

Required

(a) Prepare a consolidated statement of profit or loss and other comprehensive income for the year ended 30 April 20X5 for the Ashanti Group. **(35 marks)**

(b) Explain the factors which provide encouragement to companies to disclose social and environmental information in their financial statements, briefly discussing whether the content of such disclosure should be at the company's discretion. **(7 marks)**

(c) Discuss the nature of and incentives for 'management of earnings' and whether such a process can be deemed to be ethically acceptable. **(6 marks)**

Professional marks will be awarded in question 1(c) for clarity and quality of discussion. **(2 marks)**

(Total = 50 marks)

46 Preparation question: Foreign operation

> **BPP Note.** In this question the proformas are given to you to help you get used to setting out your answer. You may wish to transfer them to a separate sheet, or alternatively use a separate sheet for your workings only.

Standard Co acquired 80% of Odense SA for $520,000 on 1 January 20X4 when the retained reserves of Odense were 2,100,000 Danish Krone.

An impairment test conducted at the year end revealed impairment losses of 168,000 Danish Krone relating to Odense's recognised goodwill. No impairment losses had previously been recognised.

The translation differences in the consolidated financial statements at 31 December 20X5 relating to the translation of the financial statements of Odense (excluding goodwill) were $27,000. Retained reserves of Odense in Odense's separate financial statements in the post-acquisition period to 31 December 20X5 as translated amounted to $138,000. The dividends charged to retained earnings in 20X6 were paid on 31 December 20X6.

It is the group's policy to value the non-controlling interest at acquisition at its proportionate share of the fair value of the subsidiary's net assets.

Exchange rates were as follows:

	Kr to $1
1 January 20X4	9.4
31 December 20X5	8.8
31 December 20X6	8.1
Average 20X6	8.4

Required

Prepare the consolidated statement of financial position, statement of profit or loss and other comprehensive income and statement of changes in equity extract for retained earnings of the Standard Group for the year ended 31 December 20X6.

Set out your answer below, using a separate sheet for workings.

STATEMENTS OF FINANCIAL POSITION AT 31 DECEMBER 20X6

	Standard $'000	Odense Kr'000	Rate	Odense $'000	Consol $'000
Property, plant and equipment	1,285	4,400	8.1	543	
Investment in Odense	520	–		–	
Goodwill	–	–		–	
	1,805	4,400		543	
Current assets	410	2,000	8.1	247	
	2,215	6,400		790	
Share capital	500	1,000	9.4	106	
Retained reserves	1,115				
Pre-acquisition		2,100	9.4	224	
Post-acquisition			Bal	324	
	1,615	5,300		654	
Non-controlling interest					
Loans	200	300	8.1	37	

	Standard $'000	Odense Kr'000	Rate	Odense $'000	Consol $'000
Current liabilities	400	800	8.1	99	
	600	1,100		136	
	2,215	6,400		790	

STATEMENT OF PROFIT OR LOSS AND OTHER COMPREHENSIVE INCOME FOR YEAR ENDED 31 DECEMBER 20X6

	Standard $'000	Odense Kr'000	Rate	Odense $'000	Consol $'000
Revenue	1,125	5,200	8.4	619	
Cost of sales	(410)	(2,300)	8.4	(274)	
Gross profit	715	2,900		345	
Other expenses	(180)	(910)	8.4	(108)	
Impairment loss	–	–		–	
Dividend from Odense	40				
Profit before tax	575	1,990		237	
Income tax expense	(180)	(640)	8.4	(76)	
Profit for the year	395	1,350		161	
Other comprehensive income for the year:					
Items that may be reclassified to profit or loss					
Exchange differences on translation of foreign operation	–	–			
Total comprehensive income for the year	395	1,350			
Profit attributable to:					
Owners of the parent					
Non-controlling interest					
Total comprehensive income attributable to:					
Owners of the parent					
Non-controlling interest					

STATEMENTS OF CHANGES IN EQUITY FOR THE YEAR (EXTRACT FOR RETAINED RESERVES)

	Standard $'000	Odense Kr'000
Balance at 1 January 20X6	915	3,355
Dividends paid	(195)	(405)
Total comprehensive income for the year	395	1,350
Balance at 31 December 20X6	1,115	4,300

CONSOLIDATED STATEMENT OF CHANGES IN EQUITY
FOR YEAR ENDED 31 DECEMBER 20X6 (EXTRACTS)

	Retained Earnings $'000
Balance at 1 January 20X6	1,065
Dividends paid	
Total comprehensive income for the year	
Balance at 31 December 20X6	

47 Memo

58 mins

ACR, 6/04, amended

Memo, a public limited company, owns 75% of the ordinary share capital of Random, a public limited company which is situated in a foreign country. Memo acquired Random on 1 May 20X3 for 120 million crowns (CR) when the retained profits of Random were 80 million crowns. Random has not revalued its assets or issued any share capital since its acquisition by Memo. The following financial statements relate to Memo and Random:

STATEMENTS OF FINANCIAL POSITION AT 30 APRIL 20X4

	Memo $m	Random CRm
Property, plant and equipment	297	146
Investment in Random	48	–
Loan to Random	5	–
Current assets	355	102
	705	248
Equity		
Ordinary shares of $1/1CR	60	32
Share premium account	50	20
Retained earnings	360	95
	470	147
Non current liabilities	30	41
Current liabilities	205	60
	705	248

STATEMENTS OF PROFIT OR LOSS AND OTHER COMPREHENSIVE INCOME FOR YEAR ENDED 30 APRIL 20X4

	Memo $	Random CRm
Revenue	200	142
Cost of sales	(120)	(96)
Gross profit	80	46
Distribution and administrative expenses	(30)	(20)
Profit from operations	50	26
Interest receivable	4	–
Interest payable	–	(2)
Profit before taxation	54	24
Income tax expense	(20)	(9)
Profit/total comprehensive income for the year	34	15

The following information is relevant to the preparation of the consolidated financial statements of Memo.

(a) Goodwill is reviewed for impairment annually. At 30 April 20X4, the impairment loss on recognised goodwill was CR4.2m.

(b) During the financial year Random has purchased raw materials from Memo and denominated the purchase in crowns in its financial records. The details of the transaction are set out below:

	Date of transaction	Purchase price $m	Profit percentage on selling price
Raw materials	1 February 20X4	6	20%

At the year end, half of the raw materials purchased were still in the inventory of Random. The intragroup transactions have not been eliminated from the financial statements and the goods were recorded by Random at the exchange rate ruling on 1 February 20X4. A payment of $6 million was made to Memo when the exchange rate was 2·2 crowns to $1. Any exchange gain or loss arising on the transaction is still held in the current liabilities of Random.

(c) Memo had made an interest free loan to Random of $5 million on 1 May 20X3. The loan was repaid on 30 May 20X4. Random had included the loan in non-current liabilities and had recorded it at the exchange rate at 1 May 20X3.

(d) The fair value of the net assets of Random at the date of acquisition is to be assumed to be the same as the carrying value.

(e) The functional currency of Random is the Crown.

(f) The following exchange rates are relevant to the financial statements:

	Crowns to $
30 April/1 May 20X3	2·5
1 November 20X3	2·6
1 February 20X4	2
30 April 20X4	2·1
Average rate for year to 30 April 20X4	2

(g) Memo has paid a dividend of $8 million during the financial year and this is not included in profit or loss.

It is the group's policy to value the non-controlling interest at acquisition at its proportionate share of the fair value of the subsidiary's identifiable net assets.

Required

Prepare a consolidated statement of profit or loss and other comprehensive income for the year ended 30 April 20X4 and a consolidated statement of financial position at that date in accordance with International Financial Reporting Standards.

(Candidates should round their calculations to the nearest $100,000.) **(32 marks)**

48 Case study question: Ribby
90 mins

6/08, amended

The following draft statements of financial position relate to Ribby, Hall, and Zian, all public limited companies, as at 31 May 20X8.

	Ribby $m	Hall $m	Zian Dinars m
Assets			
Non-current assets:			
Property, plant and equipment	250	120	360
Investment in Hall	98	–	–
Investment in Zian	30	–	–
Financial assets	10	5	148
Current assets	22	17	120
Total assets	410	142	628
Equity			
Ordinary shares	60	40	209
Other components of equity	30	10	–
Retained earnings	120	80	307
Total equity	210	130	516
Non-current liabilities	90	5	40
Current liabilities	110	7	72
Total equity and liabilities	410	142	628

The following information needs to be taken account of in the preparation of the group financial statements of Ribby.

(a) Ribby acquired 70% of the ordinary shares of Hall on 1 June 20X6 when Hall's other components of equity were $10 million and retained earnings were $60 million. The fair value of the net assets of Hall was $120 million at the date of acquisition. Ribby acquired 60% of the ordinary shares of Zian for 330 million dinars on 1 June 20X6 when Zian's retained earnings were 220 million dinars. The fair value of the net assets of Zian on 1 June 20X6 was 495 million dinars. The excess of the fair value over the net assets of Hall and Zian is due to an increase in the value of non-depreciable land. There have been no issues of ordinary shares since acquisition and goodwill on acquisition is not impaired for either Hall or Zian.

(b) Zian is located in a foreign country and imports its raw materials at a price which is normally denominated in dollars. The product is sold locally at selling prices denominated in dinars, and determined by local

competition. All selling and operating expenses are incurred locally and paid in dinars. Distribution of profits is determined by the parent company, Ribby. Zian has financed part of its operations through a $4 million loan from Hall which was raised on 1 June 20X7. This is included in the financial assets of Hall and the non-current liabilities of Zian. Zian's management have a considerable degree of authority and autonomy in carrying out the operations of Zian and other than the loan from Hall, are not dependent upon group companies for finance.

(c) Ribby has a building which it purchased on 1 June 20X7 for 40 million dinars and which is located overseas. The building is carried at cost and has been depreciated on the straight-line basis over its useful life of 20 years. At 31 May 20X8, as a result of an impairment review, the recoverable amount of the building was estimated to be 36 million dinars.

(d) Ribby has a long-term loan of $10 million which is owed to a third party bank. At 31 May 20X8, Ribby decided that it would repay the loan early on 1 July 20X8 and formally agreed this repayment with the bank prior to the year end. The agreement sets out that there will be an early repayment penalty of $1 million.

(e) The directors of Ribby announced on 1 June 20X7 that a bonus of $6 million would be paid to the employees of Ribby if they achieved a certain target production level by 31 May 20X8. The bonus is to be paid partly in cash and partly in share options. Half of the bonus will be paid in cash on 30 November 20X8 whether or not the employees are still working for Ribby. The other half will be given in share options on the same date, provided that the employee is still in service on 30 November 20X8. The exercise price and number of options will be fixed by management on 30 November 20X8. The target production was met and management expect 10% of employees to leave between 31 May 20X8 and 30 November 20X8. No entry has been made in the financial statements of Ribby.

(f) Ribby operates a defined benefit pension plan that provides a pension of 1·2% of the final salary for each year of service, subject to a minimum of four years service. On 1 June 20X7, Ribby improved the pension entitlement so that employees receive 1·4% of their final salary for each year of service. This improvement applied to all prior years service of the employees. As a result, the present value of the defined benefit obligation on 1 June 20X7 increased by $3.5 million as follows:

	$m
Employees with more than four years service	3.0
Employees with less than four years service (average service of two years)	0.5
	3.5

Ribby had not accounted for the improvement in the pension plan.

(g) Ribby is considering selling its subsidiary, Hall. Just prior to the year end, Hall sold inventory to Ribby at a price of $6 million. The carrying value of the inventory in the financial records of Hall was $2 million. The cash was received before the year end, and as a result the bank overdraft of Hall was virtually eliminated at 31 May 20X8. After the year end the transaction was reversed, and it was agreed that this type of transaction would be carried out again when the interim financial statements were produced for Hall, if the company had not been sold by that date.

(h) The following exchange rates are relevant to the preparation of the group financial statements:

	Dinars to $
1 June 20X6	11
1 June 20X7	10
31 May 20X8	12
Average for year to 31 May 20X8	10.5

(i) It is the group's policy to value the non-controlling interest at acquisition at fair value. The fair value of the non-controlling interest in Hall on 1 June 20X6 was $42million. The fair value of the non-controlling interest in Zian on 1 June 20X6 was 220 million dinars.

Required

(a) Discuss and apply the principles set out in IAS 21 *The effects of changes in foreign exchange rates* in order to determine the functional currency of Zian. **(8 marks)**

(b) Prepare a consolidated statement of financial position of the Ribby Group at 31 May 20X8 in accordance with International Financial Reporting Standards. **(35 marks)**

(c)   Discuss how the manipulation of financial statements by company accountants is inconsistent with their responsibilities as members of the accounting profession, setting out the distinguishing features of a profession and the privileges that society gives to a profession. (Your answer should include reference to the above scenario.)   **(7 marks)**

Note: requirement (c) includes 2 marks for the quality of the discussion.

(Total = 50 marks)

49 Case study question: Rose   **90 mins**

Rose, a public limited company, operates in the mining sector. The draft statements of financial position are as follows, at 30 April 20X8.

	Rose $m	Petal $m	Stem Dinars m
Assets			
Non-current assets:			
Property, plant and equipment	370	110	380
Investment in subsidiaries			
Petal	113	–	–
Stem	46	–	–
Financial assets	15	7	50
	544	117	430
Current assets	118	100	330
Total assets	662	217	760
Equity and liabilities			
Share capital	158	38	200
Retained earnings	256	56	300
Other components of equity	7	4	–
Total equity	421	98	500
Non-current liabilities	56	42	160
Current liabilities	185	77	100
Total liabilities	241	119	260
Total equity and liabilities	662	217	760

The following information is relevant to the preparation of the group financial statements.

(a)   On 1 May 20X7, Rose acquired 70% of the equity interests of Petal, a public limited company. The purchase consideration comprised cash of $94 million. The fair value of the identifiable net assets recognised by Petal was $120 million excluding the patent below. The identifiable net assets of Petal at 1 May 20X7 included a patent which had a fair value of $4 million. This had not been recognised in the financial statements of Petal. The patent had a remaining term of four years to run at that date and is not renewable. The retained earnings of Petal were $49 million and other components of equity were $3 million at the date of acquisition. The remaining excess of the fair value of the net assets is due to an increase in the value of land.

Rose wishes to use the 'full goodwill' method. The fair value of the non-controlling interest in Petal was $46 million on 1 May 20X7. There have been no issues of ordinary shares since acquisition and goodwill on acquisition is not impaired.

Rose acquired a further 10% interest from the non-controlling interest in Petal on 30 April 20X8 for a cash consideration of $19 million.

(b)   Rose acquired 52% of the ordinary shares of Stem on 1 May 20X7 when Stem's retained earnings were 220 million dinars. The fair value of the identifiable net assets of Stem on 1 May 20X7 was 495 million dinars. The excess of the fair value over the net assets of Stem is due to an increase in the value of land. The fair value of the non-controlling interest in Stem at 1 May 20X7 was 250 million dinars.

Stem is located in a foreign country and operates a mine. The income of Stem is denominated and settled in dinars. The output of the mine is routinely traded in dinars and its price is determined initially by local supply and demand. Stem pays 40% of its costs and expenses in dollars with the remainder being incurred locally and settled in dinars. Stem's management has a considerable degree of authority and autonomy in carrying out the operations of Stem and is not dependent upon group companies for finance.

Rose wishes to use the 'full goodwill' method to consolidate the financial statements of Stem. There have been no issues of ordinary shares and no impairment of goodwill since acquisition.

The following exchange rates are relevant to the preparation of the group financial statements.

	Dinars to $
1 May 20X7	6
30 April 20X8	5
Average for year to 30 April 20X8	5.8

(c) Rose has a property located in the same country as Stem. The property was acquired on 1 May 20X7 and is carried at a cost of 30 million dinars. The property is depreciated over 20 years on the straight-line method. At 30 April 20X8, the property was revalued to 35 million dinars. Depreciation has been charged for the year but the revaluation has not been taken into account in the preparation of the financial statements as at 30 April 20X8.

(d) Rose commenced a long-term bonus scheme for employees at 1 May 20X7. Under the scheme employees receive a cumulative bonus on the completion of five years service. The bonus is 2% of the total of the annual salary of the employees. The total salary of employees for the year to 30 April 20X8 was $40 million and a discount rate of 8% is assumed. Additionally at 30 April 20X8, it is assumed that all employees will receive the bonus and that salaries will rise by 5% per year.

(e) Rose purchased plant for $20 million on 1 May 20X4 with an estimated useful life of six years. Its estimated residual value at that date was $1·4 million. At 1 May 20X7, the estimated residual value changed to $2·6 million. The change in the residual value has not been taken into account when preparing the financial statements as at 30 April 20X8.

Required

(a) (i) Discuss and apply the principles set out in IAS 21 *The effects of changes in foreign exchange rates* in order to determine the functional currency of Stem. **(7 marks)**

(ii) Prepare a consolidated statement of financial position of the Rose Group at 30 April 20X8 in accordance with International Financial Reporting Standards (IFRS), showing the exchange difference arising on the translation of Stem's net assets. Ignore deferred taxation. **(35 marks)**

(b) Rose was considering acquiring a service company. Rose stated that the acquisition may be made because of the value of the human capital and the opportunity for synergies and cross-selling opportunities. Rose measured the fair value of the assets based on what it was prepared to pay for them. Rose further stated that what it was willing to pay was influenced by its future plans for the business.

The company to be acquired had contract-based customer relationships with well-known domestic and international companies and some mining companies. Rose measured that the fair value of all of these customer relationships at zero because Rose already enjoyed relationships with the majority of those customers.

Required

Discuss the validity of the accounting treatment proposed by Rose and whether such a proposed treatment raises any ethical issues. **(6 marks)**

Professional marks will be awarded in part (b) for clarity and quality of the presentation and discussion

(2 marks)

(Total = 50 marks)

50 Preparation question: Consolidated statement of cash flows

BPP Note. In this question, proformas are given to you to help you get used to setting out your answer. You may wish to transfer them to a separate sheet, or alternatively to use a separate sheet for your workings.

On 1 September 20X5 Swing Co acquired 70% of Slide Co for $5,000,000 comprising $1,000,000 cash and 1,500,000 $1 shares.

The statement of financial position of Slide Co at acquisition was as follows:

	$'000
Property, plant and equipment	2,700
Inventories	1,600
Trade receivables	600
Cash	400
Trade payables	(300)
Income tax payable	(200)
	4,800

The consolidated statement of financial position of Swing Co as at 31 December 20X5 was as follows:

	20X5	20X4
Non-current assets	$'000	$'000
Property, plant and equipment	35,500	25,000
Goodwill	1,400	–
	36,900	25,000
Current assets		
Inventories	16,000	10,000
Trade receivables	9,800	7,500
Cash	2,400	1,500
	28,200	19,000
	65,100	44,000
Equity attributable to owners of the parent		
Share capital	12,300	10,000
Share premium	5,800	2,000
Revaluation surplus	350	–
Retained earnings	32,100	21,900
	50,550	33,900
Non-controlling interest	1,750	–
	52,300	33,900
Current liabilities		
Trade payables	7,600	6,100
Income tax payable	5,200	4,000
	12,800	10,100
	65,100	44,000

The consolidated statement of profit or loss and other comprehensive income of Swing Co for the year ended 31 December 20X5 was as follows:

	20X5
	$'000
Profit before tax	16,500
Income tax expense	(5,200)
Profit for the year	11,300
Other comprehensive income (not reclassified to P/L)	
Revaluation surplus	500
Total comprehensive income for the year	11,800
Profit attributable to:	
Owners of the parent	11,100
Non-controlling interest	200
	11,300
Total comprehensive income for the year attributable to	
Owners of the parent	11,450
Non-controlling interest 200 + (500 × 30%)	350
	11,800

Notes:

1   Depreciation charged for the year was $5,800,000. The group made no disposals of property, plant and equipment.

2   Dividends paid by Swing Co amounted to $900,000.

It is the group's policy to value the non-controlling interest at its proportionate share of the fair value of the subsidiary's identifiable net assets.

Required

Prepare the consolidated statement of cash flows of Swing Co for the year ended 31 December 20X5. No notes are required.

CONSOLIDATED STATEMENT OF CASH FLOWS PROFORMA
STATEMENT OF CASH FLOWS FOR THE YEAR ENDED 31 DECEMBER 20X5

	$'000	$'000
Cash flows from operating activities		
Profit before tax		
Adjustments for:		
Depreciation		
Impairment losses	_____	
Increase in trade receivables		
Increase in inventories		
Increase in trade payables	_____	
Cash generated from operations		
Income taxes paid (W4)	_____	
Net cash from operating activities		
Cash flows from investing activities		
Acquisition of subsidiary, net of cash acquired (Note 1)		
Purchase of property, plant & equipment (W1)	_____	
Net cash used in investing activities		

	$'000	$'000
Cash flows from financing activities		
Proceeds from issue of share capital		
Dividends paid		
Dividends paid to non-controlling interest (W3)	_____	
Net cash used in financing activities		_____
Net decrease in cash and cash equivalents		
Cash and cash equivalents at the beginning of the period		
Cash and cash equivalents at the end of the period		

Workings

1   *Additions to property, plant and equipment*

PROPERTY, PLANT AND EQUIPMENT

$'000	$'000

2   *Goodwill impairment losses*

GOODWILL

$'000	$'000

3   *Dividends paid to non-controlling interest*

NON-CONTROLLING INTEREST

$'000	$'000

4   *Income taxes paid*

INCOME TAX PAYABLE

$'000	$'000

51 Case study question: Jocatt

90 mins

12/10

The following draft group financial statements relate to Jocatt, a public limited company.

JOCATT GROUP
STATEMENT OF FINANCIAL POSITION AS AT 30 NOVEMBER

	20X2 $m	20X1 $m
Assets		
Non-current assets		
Property, plant and equipment	327	254
Investment property	8	6
Goodwill	48	68
Intangible assets	85	72
Investment in associate	54	-
Investments in equity instruments	94	90
	616	490
Current assets		
Inventories	105	128
Trade receivables	62	113
Cash and cash equivalents	232	143
	399	384
	1,015	874
Equity and Liabilities		
Equity attributable to the owners of the parent:		
Share capital	290	275
Retained earnings	351	324
Other components of equity	15	20
	656	619
Non-controlling interest	55	36
Total equity	711	655
Non-current liabilities		
Long-term borrowings	67	71
Deferred tax	35	41
Long-term provisions: pension liability	25	22
Total non-current liabilities	127	134
Current liabilities		
Trade payables	144	55
Current tax payable	33	30
Total current liabilities	177	85
Total liabilities	304	219
Total equity and liabilities	1,015	874

JOCATT GROUP
STATEMENT OF PROFIT OR LOSS AND OTHER COMPREHENSIVE INCOME
FOR THE YEAR ENDED 30 NOVEMBER 20X2

	$m
Revenue	432.0
Cost of sales	(317.0)
Gross profit	115.0
Other income	25.0
Distribution costs	(55.5)
Administrative expenses	(36.0)
Finance costs paid	(6.0)
Gains on property	10.5
Share of profit of associate	6.0
Profit before tax	59.0
Income tax expense	(11.0)
Profit for the year	48.0
Other comprehensive income after tax (items that will not be reclassified to profit or loss)	
Gain on investments in equity instruments (IEI)	2.0
Losses on property revaluation	(7.0)
Remeasurement losses on defined benefit plan	(6.0)
Other comprehensive income for the year, net of tax	(11.0)
Total comprehensive income for the year	37.0
Profit attributable to	
Owners of the parent	38.0
Non-controlling interest	10.0
	48.0
Total comprehensive income attributable to	
Owners of the parent	27.0
Non-controlling interest	10.0
	37.0

JOCATT GROUP
STATEMENT OF CHANGES IN EQUITY FOR THE YEAR ENDED 30 NOVEMBER 20X2

	Share capital	Retained earnings	Investments in equity instruments	Revaluation surplus (PPE)	Total	Non-controlling interest	Total equity
	$m	$m	$m	$m	$m	$m	$m
Balance at 1 December 20X1	275	324	4	16	619	36	655
Share capital issued	15				15		15
Dividends		(5)			(5)	(13)	(18)
Rights issue						2	2
Acquisitions						20	20
Total comprehensive income for the year		32	2	(7)	27	10	37
Balance at 30 November 20X2	290	351	6	9	656	55	711

The following information relates to the financial statements of Jocatt.

(i) On 1 December 20X0, Jocatt acquired 8% of the ordinary shares of Tigret. Jocatt had treated this as an investment in equity instruments in the financial statements to 30 November 20X1 with changes in fair value taken to profit or loss for the year. There were no changes in fair value in the year to 30 November 20X1. On 1 January 20X2, Jocatt acquired a further 52% of the ordinary shares of Tigret and gained control of the company. The consideration for the acquisitions was as follows.

	Holding	Consideration
		$m
1 December 20X0	8%	4
1January 20X2	52%	30
	60%	34

At 1 January 20X2, the fair value of the 8% holding in Tigret held by Jocatt at the time of the business combination was $5 million and the fair value of the non-controlling interest in Tigret was $20 million. The purchase consideration at 1 January 20X2 comprised cash of $15 million and shares of $15 million.

The fair value of the identifiable net assets of Tigret, excluding deferred tax assets and liabilities, at the date of acquisition comprised the following.

	$m
Property, plant and equipment	15
Intangible assets	18
Trade receivables	5
Cash	7

The tax base of the identifiable net assets of Tigret was $40 million at 1 January 20X2. The tax rate of Tigret is 30%.

(ii) On 30 November 20X2,Tigret made a rights issue on a 1 for 4 basis. The issue was fully subscribed and raised $5 million in cash.

(iii) Jocatt purchased a research project from a third party including certain patents on 1 December 20X1 for $8 million and recognised it as an intangible asset. During the year, Jocatt incurred further costs, which included $2 million on completing the research phase, $4 million in developing the product for sale and $1 million for the initial marketing costs. There were no other additions to intangible assets in the period other than those on the acquisition of Tigret.

(iv) Jocatt operates a defined benefit scheme. The current service costs for the year ended 30 November 20X2 are $10 million. Jocatt enhanced the benefits on 1 December 20X1.The total cost of the enhancement is $2 million. The net interest on net plan assets was $8 million for the year and Jocatt recognises remeasurement gains and losses in accordance with IAS 19 as revised in 2011.

(v) Jocatt owns an investment property. During the year, part of the heating system of the property, which had a carrying value of $0·5 million, was replaced by a new system, which cost $1 million. Jocatt uses the fair value model for measuring investment property.

(vi) Jocatt had exchanged surplus land with a carrying value of $10 million for cash of $15 million and plant valued at $4 million. The transaction has commercial substance. Depreciation for the period for property, plant and equipment was $27 million.

(vii) Goodwill relating to all subsidiaries had been impairment tested in the year to 30 November 20X2 and any impairment accounted for. The goodwill impairment related to those subsidiaries which were 100% owned.

(viii) Deferred tax of $1 million arose in the year on the gains on investments in equity in the year where the irrevocable election was made to take changes in fair value through other comprehensive income

(ix) The associate did not pay any dividends in the year.

Required

(a) Prepare a consolidated statement of cash flows for the Jocatt Group using the indirect method under IAS 7 *Statements of cash flows.*

Note: Ignore deferred taxation other than where it is mentioned in the question. **(35 marks)**

(b) Jocatt operates in the energy industry and undertakes complex natural gas trading arrangements, which involve exchanges in resources with other companies in the industry. Jocatt is entering into a long-term contract for the supply of gas and is raising a loan on the strength of this contract. The proceeds of the loan are to be received over the year to 30 November 20X3 and are to be repaid over four years to 30 November 20X7. Jocatt wishes to report the proceeds as operating cash flow because it is related to a long-term purchase contract. The directors of Jocatt receive extra income if the operating cash flow exceeds a predetermined target for the year and feel that the indirect method is more useful and informative to users of financial statements than the direct method.

(i) Comment on the directors' view that the indirect method of preparing statements of cash flow is more useful and informative to users than the direct method. **(7 marks)**

(ii) Discuss the reasons why the directors may wish to report the loan proceeds as an operating cash flow rather than a financing cash flow and whether there are any ethical implications of adopting this treatment **(6 marks)**

Professional marks will be awarded in part (b) for clarity and expression. **(2 marks)**

(Total = 50 marks)

52 Case study question: Warrburt

90 mins

12/08, amended

Note: This question has been amended in accordance with issues raised with the examiner.

The following draft group financial statements relate to Warrburt, a public limited company:

WARRBURT GROUP: STATEMENT OF FINANCIAL POSITION AS AT 30 NOVEMBER 20X8

	30 Nov 20X8	30 Nov 20X7
	$m	$m
Assets		
Non-current assets		
Property, plant and equipment	350	360
Goodwill	80	100
Other intangible assets	228	240
Investment in associate	100	–
Investment in equity instruments	142	150
	900	850
Current assets		
Inventories	135	198
Trade receivables	92	163
Cash and cash equivalents	288	323
	515	684
Total assets	1,415	1,534
Equity and liabilities		
Equity attributable to owners of the parent: to last million		
Share capital	650	595
Retained earnings	367	454
Other components of equity	49	20
	1,066	1,069

	30 Nov 20X8	30 Nov 20X7
	$m	$m
Non-controlling interest	46	53
Total equity	1,112	1,122
Non-current liabilities		
Long-term borrowing	20	64
Deferred tax	28	26
Long-tem provisions	100	96
Total non-current liabilities	148	186
Current liabilities:		
Trade payables	115	180
Current tax payable	35	42
Short-term provisions	5	4
Total current liabilities	155	226
Total liabilities	303	412
Total equity and liabilities	1,415	1,534

WARRBURT GROUP: STATEMENT OF PROFIT OR LOSS AND OTHER COMPREHENSIVE INCOME FOR THE YEAR ENDED 30 NOVEMBER 20X8

	$m
Revenue	910
Cost of sales	(886)
Gross profit	24
Other income	7
Distribution costs	(40)
Administrative expenses	(35)
Finance costs	(9)
Share of profit of associate	6
Loss before tax	(47)
Income tax expense	(29)
Loss for the year from continuing operations	(76)
Loss for the year	(76)
Other comprehensive income for the year (after tax, not reclassified to P/L)	
Investment in equity instruments (IEI)	27
Gains on property revaluation	2
Actuarial losses on defined benefit plan	(4)
Other comprehensive income for the year (after tax)	25
Total comprehensive income for the year	(51)
Profit/loss attributable to:	
Owners of the parent	(74)
Non-controlling interest	(2)
	(76)
Total comprehensive income attributable to:	
Owners of the parent	(49)
Non-controlling interest	(2)
	(51)

WARRBURT GROUP: STATEMENT OF CHANGES IN EQUITY FOR THE YEAR ENDED 30 NOVEMBER 20X8

	Share capital $m	Retained earnings $m	IEI $m	Revaluation surplus $m	Total $m	Non-controlling interest $m	Total equity $m
Balance at 1 December 20X7	595	454	16	4	1,069	53	1,122
Share capital issued	55				55		55
Dividends		(9)			(9)	(5)	(14)
Total comprehensive income for the year		(78)	27	2	(49)	(2)	(51)
Balance at 30 November 20X8	650	367	43	6	1,066	46	1,112

NOTE TO STATEMENT OF CHANGES IN EQUITY:

	$m
Profit/loss attributable to owners of parent	(74)
Actuarial losses on defined benefit plan	(4)
Total comprehensive income for year – retained earnings	(78)

The following information relates to the financial statements of Warrburt.

(i) Warrburt holds investments in equity instruments (IEI) which are owned by the parent company. At 1 December 20X7, the total carrying amount of those investments was $150m. In respect of $112m of this $150m, Warrburt had made an irrevocable election under IFRS 9 for changes in fair value to go through other comprehensive income (items that will not be reclassified to profit or loss). The remaining $38m related to an investment in the shares of Alburt, in respect of which changes in fair value had been taken to profit or loss for the year. During the year, the investment in Alburt was sold for $45m, with the fair value gain shown in 'other income' in the financial statements. The following schedule summarises the changes:

	Alburt $m	Other $m	Total $m
Carrying value at 1 December 20X7	38	112	150
Add gain on derecognition/revaluation of IEI	7	30	37
Less sales of IEI at fair value	(45)	--	(45)
Carrying value at 30 November 20X8	--	142	142

Deferred tax of $3 million arising on the $30m revaluation gain above has been taken into account in 'other comprehensive income' for the year.

(ii) The retirement benefit liability is shown as a long-term provision in the statement of financial position and comprises the following:

	$m
Liability at 1 December 20X7	96
Expense for period	10
Contributions to scheme (paid)	(10)
Actuarial losses	4
Liability at 30 November 20X8	100

Warrburt recognises remeasurement gains and losses in other comprehensive income in the period in which they occur, in accordance with IAS 19 (revised 2011). The benefits paid in the period by the trustees of the scheme were $3 million. There is no tax impact with regards to the retirement benefit liability.

(iii) The property, plant and equipment (PPE) in the statement of financial position comprises the following:

	$m
Carrying value at 1 December 20X7	360
Additions at cost	78
Gains on property revaluation	4
Disposals	(56)
Depreciation	(36)
Carrying value at 30 November 20X8	350

Plant and machinery with a carrying value of $1 million had been destroyed by fire in the year. The asset was replaced by the insurance company with new plant and machinery which was valued at $3 million. The machines were acquired directly by the insurance company and no cash payment was made to Warrburt. The company included the net gain on this transaction in 'additions at cost' and as a deduction from administrative expenses.

The disposal proceeds were $63 million. The gain on disposal is included in administrative expenses. Deferred tax of $2 million has been deducted in arriving at the 'gains on property revaluation' figure in 'other comprehensive income (items that will not be reclassified to profit or loss)'.

The remaining additions of PPE comprised imported plant and equipment from an overseas supplier on 30 June 20X8. The cost of the PPE was 380 million dinars with 280 million dinars being paid on 31 October 20X8 and the balance to be paid on 31 December 20X8.
The rates of exchange were as follows:

	Dinars to $1
30 June 20X8	5
31 October 20X8	4·9
30 November 20X8	4·8

Exchange gains and losses are included in administrative expenses.

(iv) Warrburt purchased a 25% interest in an associate for cash on 1 December 20X7. The net assets of the associate at the date of acquisition were $300 million. The associate made a profit after tax of $24 million and paid a dividend of $8 million out of these profits in the year ended 30 November 20X8.

(v)   An impairment test had been carried out at 30 November 20X8, on goodwill and other intangible assets. The result showed that goodwill was impaired by $20 million and other intangible assets by $12 million.

(vi) The short term provisions relate to finance costs which are payable within six months.

Warrburt's directors are concerned about the results for the year in the statement of profit or loss and other comprehensive income and the subsequent effect on the statement of cash flows. They have suggested that the proceeds of the sale of property, plant and equipment and the sale of investments in equity instruments should be included in 'cash generated from operations'. The directors are afraid of an adverse market reaction to their results and of the importance of meeting targets in order to ensure job security, and feel that the adjustments for the proceeds would enhance the 'cash health' of the business.

Required

(a) Prepare a group statement of cash flows for Warrburt for the year ended 30 November 20X8 in accordance with IAS 7 *Statement of cash flows*, using the indirect method. **(35 marks)**

(b) Discuss the key issues which the statement of cash flows highlights regarding the cash flow of the company. **(10 marks)**

(c) Discuss the ethical responsibility of the company accountant in ensuring that manipulation of the statement of cash flows, such as that suggested by the directors, does not occur. **(5 marks)**

Note: requirements (b) and (c) include 2 professional marks in total for the quality of the discussion.

(Total = 50 marks)

PERFORMANCE REPORTING

Questions 53 to 70 cover Performance Reporting, the subject of Part D of the BPP Study Text for Paper P2.

53 Rockby and Bye

34 mins

ACR, 6/04, amended

Rockby, a public limited company, has committed itself before its year-end of 31 March 20X4 to a plan of action to sell a subsidiary, Bye. The sale is expected to be completed on 1 July 20X4 and the financial statements of the group were signed on 15 May 20X4. The subsidiary, Bye, a public limited company, had net assets at the year end of $5 million and the book value of related goodwill is $1 million. Bye has made a loss of $500,000 from 1 April 20X4 to 15 May 20X4 and is expected to make a further loss up to the date of sale of $600,000. Rockby was, at 15 May 20X4, negotiating the consideration for the sale of Bye but no contract has been signed or public announcement made as of that date.

Rockby expected to receive $4·5 million for the company after selling costs. The value-in-use of Bye at 15 May 20X4 was estimated at $3·9 million.

Further, the non-current assets of Rockby include the following items of plant and head office land and buildings.

(i)   **Property, plant and equipment held for use in operating leases**. At 31 March 20X4 the company has at carrying value $10 million of plant which has recently been leased out on operating leases. These leases have now expired. The company is undecided as to whether to sell the plant or lease it to customers under finance leases. The fair value less selling costs of the plant is $9 million and the value-in-use is estimated at $12 million.

Plant with a carrying value of $5 million at 31 March 20X4 has ceased to be used because of a downturn in the economy. The company had decided at 31 March 20X4 to maintain the plant in workable condition in case of a change in economic conditions. Rockby subsequently sold the plant by auction on 14 May 20X4 for $3 million net of costs.

(ii)   The Board of Rockby approved the relocation of the head office site on 1 March 20X3. The head office land and buildings were renovated and upgraded in the year to 31 March 20X3 with a view to selling the site. During the improvements, subsidence was found in the foundations of the main building. The work to correct the subsidence and the renovations were completed on 1 June 20X3. As at 31 March 20X3 the renovations had cost $2·3 million and the cost of correcting the subsidence was $1 million. The carrying value of the head office land and buildings was $5 million at 31 March 20X3 before accounting for the renovation. Rockby moved its head office to the new site in June 20X3, and at the same time, the old head office property was offered for sale at a price of $10 million.

However, the market for commercial property had deteriorated significantly and as at 31 March 20X4, a buyer for the property had not been found. At that time the company did not wish to reduce the price and hoped that market conditions would improve. On 20 April 20X4, a bid of $8·3 million was received for the property and eventually it was sold (net of costs) for $7·5 million on 1 June 20X4. The carrying value of the head office land and buildings was $7 million at 31 March 20X4.

Non-current assets are shown in the financial statements at historical cost.

Required

(a)   Discuss the way in which the sale of the subsidiary, Bye, would be dealt with in the group financial statements of Rockby at 31 March 20X4.   **(7 marks)**

(b)   Discuss whether the following non-current assets should be classed as 'held for sale'.

(i)   The items of plant in the group financial statements at 31 March 20X4;   **(7 marks)**

(ii)   The head office land and buildings in the group financial statements at 31 March 20X3 and 31 March 20X4.   **(5 marks)**

(Total = 19 marks)

54 Alexandra

Alexandra, a public limited company, designs and manages business solutions and infrastructures.

(a)   In November 20X0, Alexandra defaulted on an interest payment on an issued bond loan of $100 million repayable in 20X5. The loan agreement stipulates that such default leads to an obligation to repay the whole of the loan immediately, including accrued interest and expenses. The bondholders, however, issued a waiver postponing the interest payment until 31 May 20X1. On 17 May 20X1, Alexandra felt that a further waiver was required, so requested a meeting of the bondholders and agreed a further waiver of the interest payment to 5 July 20X1, when Alexandra was confident it could make the payments. Alexandra classified the loan as long-term debt in its statement of financial position at 30 April 20X1 on the basis that the loan was not in default at the end of the reporting period as the bondholders had issued waivers and had not sought redemption.   **(6 marks)**

(b)   Alexandra enters into contracts with both customers and suppliers. The supplier solves system problems and provides new releases and updates for software. Alexandra provides maintenance services for its customers. In previous years, Alexandra recognised revenue and related costs on software maintenance contracts when the customer was invoiced, which was at the beginning of the contract period. Contracts typically run for two years.

During 20X0, Alexandra had acquired Xavier Co, which recognised revenue, derived from a similar type of maintenance contract as Alexandra, on a straight-line basis over the term of the contract. Alexandra considered both its own and the policy of Xavier Co to comply with the requirements of IAS 18 *Revenue* but it decided to adopt the practice of Xavier Co for itself and the group. Alexandra concluded that the two recognition methods did not, in substance, represent two different accounting policies and did not, therefore, consider adoption of the new practice to be a change in policy.

In the year to 30 April 20X1, Alexandra recognised revenue (and the related costs) on a straight-line basis over the contract term, treating this as a change in an accounting estimate. As a result, revenue and cost of sales were adjusted, reducing the year's profits by some $6 million.   **(5 marks)**

(c)   Alexandra has a two-tier board structure consisting of a management and a supervisory board. Alexandra remunerates its board members as follows:

–   Annual base salary
–   Variable annual compensation (bonus)
–   Share options

In the group financial statements, within the related parties note under IAS 24 *Related party disclosures*, Alexandra disclosed the total remuneration paid to directors and non-executive directors and a total for each of these boards. No further breakdown of the remuneration was provided.

The management board comprises both the executive and non-executive directors. The remuneration of the non-executive directors, however, was not included in the key management disclosures. Some members of the supervisory and management boards are of a particular nationality. Alexandra was of the opinion that in that jurisdiction, it is not acceptable to provide information about remuneration that could be traced back to individuals. Consequently, Alexandra explained that it had provided the related party information in the annual accounts in an ambiguous way to prevent users of the financial statements from tracing remuneration information back to specific individuals.   **(5 marks)**

(d)   Alexandra's pension plan was accounted for as a defined benefit plan in 20X0. In the year ended 30 April 20X1, Alexandra changed the accounting method used for the scheme and accounted for it as a defined contribution plan, restating the comparative 20X0 financial information. The effect of the restatement was significant. In the 20X1 financial statements, Alexandra explained that, during the year, the arrangements underlying the retirement benefit plan had been subject to detailed review. Since the pension liabilities are fully insured and indexation of future liabilities can be limited up to and including the funds available in a special trust account set up for the plan, which is not at the disposal of Alexandra, the plan qualifies as a defined contribution plan under IAS 19 *Employee benefits* rather than a defined benefit plan. Furthermore, the trust account is built up by the insurance company from the surplus yield on investments. The pension plan is an average pay plan in respect of which the entity pays insurance premiums to a third party insurance company to fund the plan. Every year 1% of the pension fund is built up and employees pay a contribution of 4% of their salary, with the employer paying the balance of the contribution. If an employee leaves Alexandra and transfers the pension to another fund, Alexandra is liable for, or is refunded the difference between the benefits the employee is entitled to and the insurance premiums paid. **(7 marks)**

Professional marks will be awarded in this question for clarity and quality of discussion. **(2 marks)**

Required

Discuss how the above transactions should be dealt with in the financial statements of Alexandra for the year ended 30 April 20X1. **(Total = 25 marks)**

55 Carpart

29 mins

6/09, amended

Carpart, a public limited company, is a vehicle part manufacturer, and sells vehicles purchased from the manufacturer. Carpart has entered into supply arrangements for the supply of car seats to two local companies, Vehiclex and Autoseat.

(a) **Vehiclex**

This contract will last for five years and Carpart will manufacture seats to a certain specification which will require the construction of machinery for the purpose. The price of each car seat has been agreed so that it includes an amount to cover the cost of constructing the machinery but there is no commitment to a minimum order of seats to guarantee the recovery of the costs of constructing the machinery. Carpart retains the ownership of the machinery and wishes to recognise part of the revenue from the contract in its current financial statements to cover the cost of the machinery which will be constructed over the next year. **(4 marks)**

(b) **Vehicle sales**

Carpart sells vehicles on a contract for their market price (approximately $20,000 each) at a mark-up of 25% on cost. The expected life of each vehicle is five years. After four years, the car is repurchased by Carpart at 20% of its original selling price. This price is expected to be significantly less than its fair value. The car must be maintained and serviced by the customer in accordance with certain guidelines and must be in good condition if Carpart is to repurchase the vehicle.

The same vehicles are also sold with an option that can be exercised by the buyer two years after sale. Under this option, the customer has the right to ask Carpart to repurchase the vehicle for 70% of its original purchase price. It is thought that the buyers will exercise the option. At the end of two years, the fair value of the vehicle is expected to be 55% of the original purchase price. If the option is not exercised, then the buyer keeps the vehicle.

Carpart also uses some of its vehicles for demonstration purposes. These vehicles are normally used for this purpose for an eighteen-month period. After this period, the vehicles are sold at a reduced price based upon their condition and mileage. **(10 marks)**

Professional marks will be awarded for clarity and quality of discussion. **(2 marks)**

Required

Discuss how the above transactions would be accounted for under International Financial Reporting Standards in the financial statements of Carpart.

Note. The mark allocation is shown against both of the arrangements above. **(Total = 16 marks)**

56 Ghorse

Ghorse, a public limited company, operates in the fashion sector and had undertaken a group re-organisation during the current financial year to 30 September 20X7. As a result the following events occurred.

(a) Ghorse identified two manufacturing units, Cee and Gee, which it had decided to dispose of in a single transaction. These units comprised non-current assets only. One of the units, Cee, had been impaired prior to the financial year end on 30 September 20X7 and it had been written down to its recoverable amount of $35 million. The criteria in IFRS 5 *Non-current assets held for sale and discontinued operations*, for classification as held for sale had been met for Cee and Gee at 30 September 20X7. The following information related to the assets of the cash generating units at 30 September 20X7:

	Depreciated historical cost $m	Fair value less costs of disposal and recoverable amount $m	Carrying value under IFRS $m
Cee	50	35	35
Gee	70	90	70
	120	125	105

The fair value less costs of disposal had risen at the year end to $40 million for Cee and $95 million for Gee. The increase in the fair value less costs of disposal had not been taken into account by Ghorse. **(7 marks)**

(b) As a consequence of the re-organisation, and a change in government legislation, the tax authorities have allowed a revaluation of the non-current assets of the holding company for tax purposes to market value at 31 October 20X7. There has been no change in the carrying values of the non-current assets in the financial statements. The tax base and the carrying values after the revaluation are as follows:

	Carrying amount at 31 October 20X7 $m	Tax base at 31 October 20X7 after revaluation $m	Tax base at 31 October 20X7 before revaluation $m
Property	50	65	48
Vehicles	30	35	28

Other taxable temporary differences amounted to $5 million at 31 October 20X7. Assume income tax is paid at 30%. The deferred tax provision at 31 October 20X7 had been calculated using the tax values before revaluation. **(6 marks)**

(c) A subsidiary company had purchased computerised equipment for $4 million on 31 October 20X6 to improve the manufacturing process. Whilst re-organising the group, Ghorse had discovered that the manufacturer of the computerised equipment was now selling the same system for $2·5 million. The projected cash flows from the equipment are:

		Cash flows $
Year ended 31 October	20X8	1.3
	20X9	2.2
	20Y0	2.3

The residual value of the equipment is assumed to be zero. The company uses a discount rate of 10%. The directors think that the fair value less costs of disposal of the equipment is $2 million. The directors of Ghorse propose to write down the non-current asset to the new selling price of $2·5 million. The company's policy is to depreciate its computer equipment by 25% per annum on the straight line basis. **(5 marks)**

(d)   The manufacturing property of the group, other than the head office, was held on an operating lease over eight years. On re-organisation on 31 October 20X7, the lease has been renegotiated and is held for twelve years at a rent of $5 million per annum paid in arrears. The fair value of the property is $35 million and its remaining economic life is thirteen years. The lease relates to the buildings and not the land. The factor to be used for an annuity at 10% for 12 years is 6·8137.   **(5 marks)**

The directors are worried about the impact that the above changes will have on the value of its non-current assets and its key performance indicator which is 'Return on Capital Employed' (ROCE). ROCE is defined as operating profit before interest and tax divided by share capital, other reserves and retained earnings. The directors have calculated ROCE as $30 million divided by $220 million, ie 13·6% before any adjustments required by the above.

Formation of opinion on impact on ROCE.   **(2 marks)**

Required

Discuss the accounting treatment of the above transactions and the impact that the resulting adjustments to the financial statements would have on ROCE.

Note. Your answer should include appropriate calculations where necessary and a discussion of the accounting principles involved.

(Total = 25 marks)

57 Cate
45 mins

6/10

(a)   Cate is an entity in the software industry. Cate had incurred substantial losses in the financial years 31 May 20X0 to 31 May 20X5. In the financial year to 31 May 20X6 Cate made a small profit before tax. This included significant non-operating gains. In 20X5, Cate recognised a material deferred tax asset in respect of carried forward losses, which will expire during 20X8. Cate again recognised the deferred tax asset in 20X6 on the basis of anticipated performance in the years from 20X6 to 20X8, based on budgets prepared in 20X6. The budgets included high growth rates in profitability. Cate argued that the budgets were realistic as there were positive indications from customers about future orders. Cate also had plans to expand sales to new markets and to sell new products whose development would be completed soon. Cate was taking measures to increase sales, implementing new programs to improve both productivity and profitability. Deferred tax assets less deferred tax liabilities represent 25% of shareholders' equity at 31 May 20X6. There are no tax planning opportunities available to Cate that would create taxable profit in the near future.

(5 marks)

(b)   At 31 May 20X6 Cate held an investment in and had a significant influence over Bates, a public limited company. Cate had carried out an impairment test in respect of its investment in accordance with the procedures prescribed in IAS 36, *Impairment of assets*. Cate argued that fair value was the only measure applicable in this case as value-in-use was not determinable as cash flow estimates had not been produced. Cate stated that there were no plans to dispose of the shareholding and hence there was no binding sale agreement. Cate also stated that the quoted share price was not an appropriate measure when considering the fair value of Cate's significant influence on Bates. Therefore, Cate measured the fair value of its interest in Bates through application of two measurement techniques; one based on earnings multiples and the other based on an option–pricing model. Neither of these methods supported the existence of an impairment loss as of 31 May 20X6.   **(5 marks)**

(c)   At 1 April 20X5 Cate had a direct holding of shares giving 70% of the voting rights in Date. In May 20X6, Date issued new shares, which were wholly subscribed for by a new investor. After the increase in capital, Cate retained an interest of 35% of the voting rights in its former subsidiary Date. At the same time, the shareholders of Date signed an agreement providing new governance rules for Date. Based on this new agreement, Cate was no longer to be represented on Date's board or participate in its management. As a consequence Cate considered that its decision not to subscribe to the issue of new shares was equivalent to a decision to disinvest in Date. Cate argued that the decision not to invest clearly showed its new intention not to recover the investment in Date principally through continuing use of the asset and was considering selling the investment. Due to the fact that Date is a separate line of business (with separate cash flows, management and customers), Cate considered that the results of Date for the period to 31 May 20X6 should be presented based on principles provided by IFRS 5 *Non-current assets held for sale and discontinued operations*.   **(8 marks)**

(d)   In its 20X6 financial statements, Cate disclosed the existence of a voluntary fund established in order to provide a post-retirement benefit plan (Plan) to employees. Cate considers its contributions to the Plan to be voluntary, and has not recorded any related liability in its consolidated financial statements. Cate has a history of paying benefits to its former employees, even increasing them to keep pace with inflation since the commencement of the Plan.

The main characteristics of the Plan are as follows:

(i)   The Plan is totally funded by Cate.

(ii)   The contributions for the Plan are made periodically.

(iii)   The post retirement benefit is calculated based on a percentage of the final salaries of Plan participants dependent on the years of service.

(iv)   The annual contributions to the Plan are determined as a function of the fair value of the assets less the liability arising from past services.

Cate argues that it should not have to recognise the Plan because, according to the underlying contract, it can terminate its contributions to the Plan, if and when it wishes. The termination clauses of the contract establish that Cate must immediately purchase lifetime annuities from an insurance company for all the retired employees who are already receiving benefit when the termination of the contribution is communicated.   **(5 marks)**

Required

Discuss whether the accounting treatments proposed by the company are acceptable under International Financial Reporting Standards.

Professional marks will be awarded in this question for clarity and quality of discussion.   **(2 marks)**

The mark allocation is shown against each of the four parts above.

(Total = 25 marks)

58 Preparation question: Current issues

BPP Note. Current developments are mainly covered within individual topics, for example all the questions on employee benefits test the 2011 revised IAS 19.

(a)   IFRS 10 *Consolidated financial statements* was published in 2011. It retains control from its predecessor IAS 27 as the key concept underlying the parent/subsidiary relationship but it has broadened the definition and clarified its application.

(i)   Explain the circumstances in which an investor controls an investee according to IFRS 10

(ii)   Twist holds 40 per cent of the voting rights of Oliver and twelve other investors each hold 5 per cent of the voting rights Oliver. A shareholder agreement grants Twist the right to appoint, remove and set the remuneration of management responsible for directing the relevant activities. To change the agreement, a two-thirds majority vote of the shareholders is required. To date, Twist has not exercised its rights with regard to the management or activities of Oliver.

Required

Explain whether Twist should consolidate Oliver in accordance with IFRS 10.

(iii)   Copperfield holds 45 per cent of the voting rights of Spenlow. Murdstone and Steerforth each hold 26 per cent of the voting rights of Spenlow. The remaining voting rights are held by three other shareholders, each holding 1 per cent. There are no other arrangements that affect decision-making.

Required

Explain whether Copperfield should consolidate Spenlow in accordance with IFRS 10.

(b) Red, a public company, is preparing its financial statements for the year ended 31 December 20X6. The Finance Director of Red has set up a company, Blue, through which Red conducts its investment activities. Red has paid $400 million to Blue during the year and this has been included in dividends paid. The money was invested in a specified portfolio of investments. Ninety five per cent of the profits and one hundred per cent of the losses in the specified portfolio of investments are transferred to Red. An investment manager has charge of the company's investments and owns all of the share capital of Blue. An agreement between the investment manager and Red sets out the operating guidelines and prohibits the investment manager from obtaining access to the investments for the manager's benefit. An annual transfer of the profit/loss will occur on 31 December annually and the capital will be returned in four years' time. The transfer of $400 million cash occurred on 1 July 20X6 but no transfer of profit/loss has yet occurred. The statement of financial position of Blue at 31 December 20X6 is as follows:

BLUE: STATEMENT OF FINANCIAL POSITION AT 31 DECEMBER 20X6

	$m
Investment at fair value through profit or loss	390
	390
Share capital	400
Retained earnings	(10)
	390

Required

Discuss the issues which would determine whether Blue should be consolidated by Red in the group financial statements.

(c) IFRS 12 *Disclosure of interests in other entities* was issued in 2011. It sets out the disclosure requirements for entities that have an interest in a subsidiary, a joint arrangement, an associate or an unconsolidated structured entity. Its objective is to require the disclosure of information which enables users of financial statements to evaluate the nature of, and risks associates with, its interests in other entities, and the effects of those interests on its financial position, financial performance and cash flows.

Required

Summarise the disclosures required by IFRS 12 in order to meet this objective.

(d) In 2010, the IASB issued an Exposure Draft *Hedge accounting,* now a Draft IFRS.

Required

(i) What problems were identified in the current hedging rules?

(ii) Summarise the main proposals of the ED.

(iii) What problems have been identified in the new proposals?

59 Fair values and IFRS 13

45 mins

Financial statements have seen an increasing move towards the use of fair values in accounting. Advocates of 'fair value accounting' believe that fair value is the most relevant measure for financial reporting whilst others believe that historical cost provides a more useful measure. Issues have been raised over the reliability and measurement of fair values, and over the nature of the current level of disclosure in financial statements in this area.

In 2011 the IASB published IFRS 13 *Fair value measurement,* which sets out to sets out to define fair value, set out in a single IFRS a framework for measuring fair value and require disclosure about fair value measurements.

Required

(a)   Discuss the view that fair value is a more relevant measure to use in corporate reporting than historical cost.

(12 marks)

(b)   Discuss the main changes introduced by IRS 13 *Fair value measurement.*

(9 marks)

(c)   Fairview holds shares in Greenfield, which it treats as an equity instrument (a financial asset). Sale of this financial asset is restricted by contract to qualifying investors.

How would the fair value of this instrument be measured?

(4 marks)

(Total = 25 marks)

60 Jones and Cousin

45 mins

ACR,12/06

Jones and Cousin, a public quoted company, operate in twenty seven different countries and earn revenue and incur costs in several currencies. The group develops, manufactures and markets products in the medical sector. The growth of the group has been achieved by investment and acquisition. It is organised into three global business units which manage their sales in international markets, and take full responsibility for strategy and business performance. Only five per cent of the business is in the country of incorporation. Competition in the sector is quite fierce.

The group competes across a wide range of geographic and product markets and encourages its subsidiaries to enhance local communities by reinvestment of profits in local education projects. The group's share of revenue in a market sector is often determined by government policy. The markets contain a number of different competitors including specialised and large international corporations. At present the group is awaiting regulatory approval for a range of new products to grow its market share. The group lodges its patents for products and enters into legal proceedings where necessary to protect patents. The products are sourced from a wide range of suppliers, who, once approved both from a qualitative and ethical perspective, are generally given a long term contract for the supply of goods. Obsolete products are disposed of with concern for the environment and the health of its customers, with reusable materials normally being used. The industry is highly regulated in terms of medical and environmental laws and regulations. The products normally carry a low health risk.

The Group has developed a set of corporate and social responsibility principles during the period, which is the responsibility of the Board of Directors. The Managing Director manages the risks arising from corporate and social responsibility issues. The group wishes to retain and attract employees and follows policies which ensure equal opportunity for all the employees. Employees are informed of management policies, and regularly receive in-house training.

The Group enters into contracts for fixed rate currency swaps and uses floating to fixed rate interest rate swaps. The cash flow effects of these swaps match the cash flows on the underlying financial instruments. All financial instruments are accounted for as cash flow hedges. A significant amount of trading activity is denominated in the Dinar and the Euro. The dollar is its functional currency.

Required

(a)   Describe the principles and objectives behind the Management Commentary, discussing whether the commentary should be made mandatory or whether directors should be free to use their judgement as to what should be included in such a commentary.

(13 marks)

(b)   Draft a report suitable for inclusion in a Management Commentary for Jones and Cousin which deals with:

(i)   The key risks and relationships of the business

(9 marks)

(ii)   The strategy of the business regarding its treasury policies

(3 marks)

(Marks will be awarded in Part (b) for the identification and discussion of relevant points and for the style of the report.)

(Total = 25 marks)

61 Lockfine

6/11

Lockfine, a public limited company, operates in the fishing industry and has recently made the transition to International Financial Reporting Standards (IFRS). Lockfine's reporting date is 30 April 20X9.

(a) In the IFRS opening statement of financial position at 1 May 20X7, Lockfine elected to measure its fishing fleet at fair value and use that fair value as deemed cost in accordance with IFRS 1 *First time adoption of international financial reporting standards*. The fair value was an estimate based on valuations provided by two independent selling agents, both of whom provided a range of values within which the valuation might be considered acceptable. Lockfine calculated fair value at the average of the highest amounts in the two ranges provided. One of the agents' valuations was not supported by any description of the method adopted or the assumptions underlying the calculation. Valuations were principally based on discussions with various potential buyers. Lockfine wished to know the principles behind the use of deemed cost and whether agents' estimates were a reliable form of evidence on which to base the fair value calculation of tangible assets to be then adopted as deemed cost. **(6 marks)**

(b) Lockfine was unsure as to whether it could elect to apply IFRS 3 *Business Combinations* retrospectively to past business combinations on a selective basis, because there was no purchase price allocation available for certain business combinations in its opening IFRS statement of financial position.

As a result of a major business combination, fishing rights of that combination were included as part of goodwill. The rights could not be recognised as a separately identifiable intangible asset at acquisition under the local GAAP because a reliable value was unobtainable for the rights. The fishing rights operated for a specified period of time.

On transition from local GAAP to IFRS, the fishing rights were included in goodwill and not separately identified because they did not meet the qualifying criteria set out in IFRS 1, even though it was known that the fishing rights had a finite life and would be fully impaired or amortised over the period specified by the rights. Lockfine wished to amortise the fishing rights over their useful life and calculate any impairment of goodwill as two separate calculations. **(6 marks)**

(c) Lockfine has internally developed intangible assets comprising the capitalised expenses of the acquisition and production of electronic map data which indicates the main fishing grounds in the world. The intangible assets generate revenue for the company in their use by the fishing fleet and are a material asset in the statement of financial position. Lockfine had constructed a database of the electronic maps. The costs incurred in bringing the information about a certain region of the world to a higher standard of performance are capitalised. The costs related to maintaining the information about a certain region at that same standard of performance are expensed. Lockfine's accounting policy states that intangible assets are valued at historical cost. The company considers the database to have an indefinite useful life which is reconsidered annually when it is tested for impairment. The reasons supporting the assessment of an indefinite useful life were not disclosed in the financial statements and neither did the company disclose how it satisfied the criteria for recognising an intangible asset arising from development. **(6 marks)**

(d) The Lockfine board has agreed two restructuring projects during the year to 30 April 20X9:

Plan A involves selling 50% of its off-shore fleet in one year's time. Additionally, the plan is to make 40% of its seamen redundant. Lockfine will carry out further analysis before deciding which of its fleets and related employees will be affected. In previous announcements to the public, Lockfine has suggested that it may restructure the off-shore fleet in the future.

Plan B involves the reorganisation of the headquarters in 18 months time, and includes the redundancy of 20% of the headquarters' workforce. The company has made announcements before the year end but there was a three month consultation period which ended just after the year end, whereby Lockfine was negotiating with employee representatives. Thus individual employees had not been notified by the year end.

Lockfine proposes recognising a provision in respect of Plan A but not Plan B. **(5 marks)**

Professional marks will be awarded in this question for clarity and quality of discussion. **(2 marks)**

Required

Discuss the principles and practices to be used by Lockfine in accounting for the above valuation and recognition issues.

(Total = 25 marks)

62 Burley

45 mins

12/09, amended

Burley, a public limited company, operates in the energy industry. It has entered into several arrangements with other entities as follows.

(a)   Burley and Slite, a public limited company, jointly control an oilfield. Burley has a 60% interest and Slite a 40% interest and the companies are entitled to extract oil in these proportions. An agreement was signed on 1 December 20X8, which allowed for the net cash settlement of any over/under extraction by one company. The net cash settlement would be at the market price of oil at the date of settlement. Both parties have used this method of settlement before. 200,000 barrels of oil were produced up to 1 October 20X9 but none were produced after this up to 30 November 20X9 due to production difficulties. The oil was all sold to third parties at $100 per barrel. Burley has extracted 10,000 barrels more than the company's quota and Slite has under extracted by the same amount. The market price of oil at the year end of 30 November 20X9 was $105 per barrel. The excess oil extracted by Burley was settled on 12 December 20X9 under the terms of the agreement at $95 per barrel.

Burley had purchased oil from another supplier because of the production difficulties at $98 per barrel and has oil inventory of 5,000 barrels at the year end, purchased from this source. Slite had no inventory of oil. Neither company had oil inventory at 1 December 20X8. Selling costs are $2 per barrel.

Burley wishes to know how to account for the recognition of revenue, the excess oil extracted and the oil inventory at the year end.   **(9 marks)**

(b)   Burley also entered into an agreement with Jorge, a public limited company, on 1 December 20X8. Each of the companies holds one half of the equity in an entity, Wells, a public limited company, which operates offshore oil rigs. The contractual arrangement between Burley and Jorge establishes joint control of the activities that are conducted in Wells. The main feature of Wells's legal form is that Wells, not Burley or Jorge, has rights to the assets, and obligations for the liabilities, relating to the arrangement.

The terms of the contractual arrangement are such that:

(i)   Wells owns the oil rigs. The contractual arrangement does not specify that Burley and Jorge have rights to the oil rigs.

(ii)   Burley and Jorge are not liable in respect of the debts, liabilities or obligations of Wells. If Wells is unable to pay any of its debts or other liabilities or to discharge its obligations to third parties, the liability of each party to any third party will be limited to the unpaid amount of that party's capital contribution.

(iii)   Burley and Jorge have the right to sell or pledge their interests in Wells

(iv)   Each party receives a share of the income from operating the oil rig in accordance with its interest in Wells.

Burley wants to account for the interest in Wells by using the equity method, and wishes for advice on the matter.

The oilrigs of Wells started operating on 1 December 20W8, ie ten years before the agreement was signed, and are measured under the cost model. The useful life of the rigs is 40 years. The initial cost of the rigs was $240 million, which included decommissioning costs (discounted) of $20 million. At 1 December 20X8, the carrying amount of the decommissioning liability has grown to $32.6 million, but the net present value of decommissioning liability has decreased to $18.5 million as a result of the increase in the risk-adjusted discount rate from 5% to 7%. Burley is unsure how to account for the oilrigs in the financial statements of Wells for the year ended 30 November 20X9.

Burley owns a 10% interest in a pipeline, which is used to transport the oil from the offshore oilrig to a refinery on the land. Burley has joint control over the pipeline and has to pay its share of the maintenance costs. Burley has the right to use 10% of the capacity of the pipeline. Burley wishes to show the pipeline as an investment in its financial statements to 30 November 20X9.

(10 marks)

(c) Burley has purchased a transferable interest in an oil exploration licence. Initial surveys of the region designated for exploration indicate that there are substantial oil deposits present, but further surveys will be required in order to establish the nature and extent of the deposits. Burley also has to determine whether the extraction of the oil is commercially viable. Past experience has shown that the licence can increase substantially in value if further information becomes available as to the viability of the extraction of the oil. Burley wishes to capitalise the cost of the licence but is unsure as to whether the accounting policy is compliant with International Financial Reporting Standards. **(4 marks)**

Required

Discuss with suitable computations where necessary, how the above arrangements and events would be accounted for in the financial statements of Burley.

Professional marks will be awarded in this question for clarity and expression. **(2 marks)**

(Total: 25 marks)

63 Seltec

45 mins

6/10

Seltec, a public limited company, processes and sells edible oils and uses several financial instruments to spread the risk of fluctuation in the price of the edible oils. The entity operates in an environment where the transactions are normally denominated in dollars. The functional currency of Seltec is the dollar.

(a) The entity uses forward and futures contracts to protect it against fluctuation in the price of edible oils. Where forwards are used the company often takes delivery of the edible oil and sells it shortly afterwards. The contracts are constructed with future delivery in mind but the contracts also allow net settlement in cash as an alternative. The net settlement is based on the change in the price of the oil since the start of the contract. Seltec uses the proceeds of a net settlement to purchase a different type of oil or purchase from a different supplier. Where futures are used these sometimes relate to edible oils of a different type and market than those of Seltec's own inventory of edible oil. The company intends to apply hedge accounting to these contracts in order to protect itself from earnings volatility. Seltec has also entered into a long-term arrangement to buy oil from a foreign entity whose currency is the dinar. The commitment stipulates that the fixed purchase price will be denominated in pounds sterling.

Seltec is unsure as to the nature of derivatives and hedge accounting techniques and has asked your advice on how the above financial instruments should be dealt with in the financial statements. **(14 marks)**

(b) Seltec has decided to enter the retail market and has recently purchased two well-known brand names in the edible oil industry. One of the brand names has been in existence for many years and has a good reputation for quality. The other brand name is named after a famous film star who has been actively promoting the edible oil as being a healthier option than other brands of oil. This type of oil has only been on the market for a short time. Seltec is finding it difficult to estimate the useful life of the brands and therefore intends to treat the brands as having indefinite lives.

In order to sell the oil, Seltec has purchased two limited liability companies from a company that owns several retail outlets. Each entity owns retail outlets in several shopping complexes. The only assets of each entity are the retail outlets. There is no operational activity and at present the entities have no employees.

Seltec is unclear as to how the purchase of the brands and the entities should be accounted for. **(9 marks)**

Required

Discuss the accounting principles involved in accounting for the above transactions and how the above transactions should be treated in the financial statements of Seltec.

Professional marks will be awarded in this question for clarity and quality of discussion. **(2 marks)**

The mark allocation is shown against each of the two parts above.

(Total = 25 marks)

64 Ethan

Ethan, a public limited company, develops, operates and sells investment properties.

(a) Ethan focuses mainly on acquiring properties where it foresees growth potential, through rental income as well as value appreciation. The acquisition of an investment property is usually realised through the acquisition of the entity, which holds the property.

In Ethan's consolidated financial statements, investment properties acquired through business combinations are recognised at fair value, using a discounted cash flow model as approximation to fair value. There is currently an active market for this type of property. The difference between the fair value of the investment property as determined under the accounting policy, and the value of the investment property for tax purposes results in a deferred tax liability.

Goodwill arising on business combinations is determined using the measurement principles for the investment properties as outlined above. Goodwill is only considered impaired if and when the deferred tax liability is reduced below the amount at which it was first recognised. This reduction can be caused both by a reduction in the value of the real estate or a change in local tax regulations. As long as the deferred tax liability is equal to, or larger than, the prior year, no impairment is charged to goodwill. Ethan explained its accounting treatment by confirming that almost all of its goodwill is due to the deferred tax liability and that it is normal in the industry to account for goodwill in this way.

Since 20X0, Ethan has incurred substantial annual losses except for the year ended 31 May 20X3, when it made a small profit before tax. In year ended 31 May 20X3, most of the profit consisted of income recognised on revaluation of investment properties. Ethan had announced early in its financial year ended 31 May 20X4 that it anticipated substantial growth and profit. Later in the year, however, Ethan announced that the expected profit would not be achieved and that, instead, a substantial loss would be incurred. Ethan had a history of reporting considerable negative variances from its budgeted results. Ethan's recognised deferred tax assets have been increasing year-on-year despite the deferred tax liabilities recognised on business combinations. Ethan's deferred tax assets consist primarily of unused tax losses that can be carried forward which are unlikely to be offset against anticipated future taxable profits. **(11 marks)**

(b) Ethan wishes to apply the fair value option rules of IFRS 9 *Financial instruments* to debt issued to finance its investment properties. Ethan's argument for applying the fair value option is based upon the fact that the recognition of gains and losses on its investment properties and the related debt would otherwise be inconsistent. Ethan argued that there is a specific financial correlation between the factors, such as interest rates, that form the basis for determining the fair value of both Ethan's investment properties and the related debt. **(7 marks)**

(c) Ethan has an operating subsidiary, which has in issue A and B shares, both of which have voting rights. Ethan holds 70% of the A and B shares and the remainder are held by shareholders external to the group. The subsidiary is obliged to pay an annual dividend of 5% on the B shares. The dividend payment is cumulative even if the subsidiary does not have sufficient legally distributable profit at the time the payment is due.

In Ethan's consolidated statement of financial position, the B shares of the subsidiary were accounted for in the same way as equity instruments would be, with the B shares owned by external parties reported as a non-controlling interest. **(5 marks)**

Required

Discuss how the above transactions and events should be recorded in the consolidated financial statements of Ethan.

Note. The mark allocation is shown against each of the three transactions above.

Professional marks will be awarded for the quality of the discussion. **(2 marks)**

(Total = 25 marks)

65 Norman

(a) Norman, a public limited company, has three business segments which are currently reported in its financial statements. Norman is an international hotel group which reports to management on the basis of region. It does not currently report segmental information under IFRS 8 *Operating segments*. The results of the regional segments for the year ended 31 May 20X8 are as follows.

	Revenue		Segment results	Segment	Segment
Region	External	Internal	profit/(loss)	assets	liabilities
	$m	$m	$m	$m	$m
European	200	3	(10)	300	200
South East Asia	300	2	60	800	300
Other regions	500	5	105	2,000	1,400

There were no significant intra-group balances in the segment assets and liabilities. The hotels are located in capital cities in the various regions, and the company sets individual performance indicators for each hotel based on its city location.

Required

Discuss the principles in IFRS 8 *Operating segments* for the determination of a company's reportable operating segments and how these principles would be applied for Norman plc using the information given above. **(11 marks)**

(b) One of the hotels owned by Norman is a hotel complex which includes a theme park, a casino and a golf course, as well as a hotel. The theme park, casino, and hotel were sold in the year ended 31 May 20X8 to Conquest, a public limited company, for $200 million but the sale agreement stated that Norman would continue to operate and manage the three businesses for their remaining useful life of fifteen years. The residual interest in the business reverts back to Norman after the fifteen year period. Norman would receive 75% of the net profit of the businesses as operator fees and Conquest would receive the remaining 25%. Norman has guaranteed to Conquest that the net minimum profit paid to Conquest would not be less than $15 million. **(4 marks)**

Norman has recently started issuing vouchers to customers when they stay in its hotels. The vouchers entitle the customers to a $30 discount on a subsequent room booking within three months of their stay. Historical experience has shown that only one in five vouchers are redeemed by the customer. At the company's year end of 31 May 20X8, it is estimated that there are vouchers worth $20 million which are eligible for discount. The income from room sales for the year is $300 million and Norman is unsure how to report the income from room sales in the financial statements. **(4 marks)**

Norman has obtained a significant amount of grant income for the development of hotels in Europe. The grants have been received from government bodies and relate to the size of the hotel which has been built by the grant assistance. The intention of the grant income was to create jobs in areas where there was significant unemployment. The grants received of $70 million will have to be repaid if the cost of building the hotels is less than $500 million. **(4 marks)**

Appropriateness and quality of discussion **(2 marks)**

Required

Discuss how the above income would be treated in the financial statements of Norman for the year ended 31 May 20X8.

(Total = 25 marks)

66 Preparation question: Reconstruction scheme

Contemplation is a company that carries on business as film processors. For the past few years it has been making losses owing to the low price competition.

The company's statement of financial position as at 30 June 20X2 was as follows.

	$'000
Non-current assets	3,600
Current assets	4,775
	8,375
Equity	
Ordinary shares of $1 each fully paid	10,000
Retained earnings	(9,425)
	575
Non-current liabilities	
8% cumulative preference shares ((2,500,000 shares of $1 each)	3,300
11% Loan notes redeemable 20X9	3,500
Current liabilities	1,000
	8,375

The company has changed its marketing strategy and is now aiming at the specialist portrait print market. It is expected that the company will earn annual profits after tax of $1,500,000 for the next five years; the figure is before an interest charge. Income tax is assumed to be at a rate of 35%.

The directors are proposing to reconstruct the company and have produced the following proposal for discussion.

(a) To cancel the existing ordinary shares.

(b) The 11% loan notes are to be retired and the loan note holders issued in exchange with:

   (i) $3,000,000 14% redeemable loan notes 20Y5; and
   (ii) 2,000,000 ordinary shares of 25c each, fully paid up.

(c) The carrying value of the preference share capital above includes four years of dividends arrears. Assume that the IAS 32 definition of a liability is met. The preference shareholders are to be issued with 2,000,000 ordinary shares of 25c each fully paid up in exchange for the cancellation of these dividends arrears.

(d) The existing ordinary shareholders will be issued with 3,500,000 ordinary shares of 25c each, fully paid up.

In the event of a liquidation, it is estimated that the net realisable value of the assets would be $3,100,000 for the non-current assets and $3,500,000 for the net current assets.

Required

(a) Prepare a statement of financial position as at 1 July 20X2 after the reconstruction has been effected.

(b) Prepare computations to show the effect of the proposed reconstruction scheme on each of the loan note holders, preference shareholders and ordinary shareholders.

(c) Write a brief report to advise a shareholder who owns 10% of the issued ordinary share capital on whether to agree to the reconstruction as proposed. The shareholder has informed you that he feels the proposals are unfair.

(d) In your capacity as adviser to the shareholder, write a brief report to the directors suggesting any amendments you consider advisable.

Guidance notes

1   Layout a proforma statement of financial position for part (a) and fill in numbers as you work them out. Clearly label and cross reference workings.

2   The acceptability of any scheme to the major parties involved will be the main issue in such reconstructions. You must weigh up how much each group has to lose or gain and then reach a compromise.

67 Plans

X, a public limited company, owns 100 per cent of companies Y and Z which are both public limited companies. The X group operates in the telecommunications industry and the directors are considering two different plans to restructure the group. The directors feel that the current group structure is not serving the best interests of the shareholders and wish to explore possible alternative group structures.

The statements of financial position of X and its subsidiaries Y and Z at 31 May 20X7 are as follows:

	X	Y	Z
	$m	$m	$m
Property, plant and equipment	600	200	45
Cost of investment in Y	60		
Cost of investment in Z	70		
Net current assets	160	100	20
	890	300	65
Share capital – ordinary shares of $1	120	60	40
Retained earnings	770	240	25
	890	300	65

X acquired the investment in Z on 1 June 20X1 when the company's retained earnings balance was $20 million. The fair value of the net assets of Z on 1 June 20X1 was $60 million. Company Y was incorporated by X and has always been a 100 per cent owned subsidiary. The fair value of the net assets of Y at 31 May 20X7 is $310 million and of Z is $80 million. The fair values of the net current assets of both Y and Z are approximately the same as their book values.

The directors are unsure as to the impact or implications that the following plans are likely to have on the individual accounts of the companies and the group accounts.

Local companies legislation requires that the amount at which share capital is recorded is dictated by the nominal value of the shares issued and if the value of the consideration received exceeds that amount, the excess is recorded in the share premium account. Shares cannot be issued at a discount. In the case of a share for share exchange, the value of the consideration can be deemed to be the book value of the investment exchanged.

The two different plans to restructure the group are as follows:

Plan 1

Y is to purchase the whole of X's investment in Z. The purchase consideration would be 50 million $1 ordinary shares of Y.

Plan 2

The same scenario as Plan 1, but the purchase consideration would be a cash amount of $75 million.

Required

Discuss the key considerations and the accounting implications of the above plans for the X group. Your answer should show the potential impact on the individual accounts of X, Y and Z and the group accounts after each plan has been implemented.

(Total = 15 marks)

68 Decany

12/11

Decany owns 100% of the ordinary share capital of Ceed and Rant. All three entities are public limited companies. The group operates in the shipbuilding industry, which is currently a depressed market. Rant has made losses for the last three years and its liquidity is poor. The view of the directors is that Rant needs some cash investment. The directors have decided to put forward a restructuring plan as at 30 November 20X1. Under this plan:

(a) Ceed is to purchase the whole of Decany's investment in Rant. The purchase consideration is to be $98 million payable in cash to Decany and this amount will then be loaned on a long-term unsecured basis to Rant.

(b) Ceed will purchase land with a carrying amount of $10 million from Rant for a total purchase consideration of $15 million. The land has a mortgage outstanding on it of $4 million. The total purchase consideration of $15 million comprises both five million $1 nominal value non-voting shares issued by Ceed to Rant and the $4 million mortgage liability which Ceed will assume.

(c) A dividend of $25 million will be paid from Ceed to Decany to reduce the accumulated reserves of Ceed.

The statements of financial position of Decany and its subsidiaries at 30 November 20X1 are summarised below.

	Decany	Ceed	Rant
	$m	$m	$m
Non-current assets			
Property, plant and equipment at cost/valuation	600	170	45
Cost of investment in Ceed	130		
Cost of investment in Rant	95		
Current assets	155	130	20
	980	300	65
Equity and reserves			
Share capital	140	70	35
Retained earnings	750	220	5
	890	290	40
Non-current liabilities			
Long-term loan	5		12
Current liabilities			
Trade payables	85	10	13
	980	300	65

As a result of the restructuring, several of Ceed's employees will be made redundant. According to the detailed plan, the costs of redundancy will be spread over two years with $4 million being payable in one year's time and $6 million in two years' time. The market yield of high quality corporate bonds is 3%. The directors feel that the overall restructure will cost $2 million.

Required

(a) (i) Prepare the individual entity statements of financial position after the proposed restructuring plan.

(13 marks)

(ii) Set out the requirements of IAS 27 (Revised) *Separate financial statements* as regards the reorganisation and payment of dividends between group companies, discussing any implications for the restructuring plan. **(5 marks)**

(b) Discuss the key implications of the proposed plans for the restructuring of the group. **(5 marks)**

Professional marks will be awarded in Part (b) for clarity and expression of your discussion. **(2 marks)**

(Total = 25 marks)

69 IFRSs and SMEs

45 mins

ACR, 6/06, amended

International Financial Reporting Standards (IFRSs) are primarily designed for use by publicly listed companies and in many countries the majority of companies using IFRSs are listed companies. In other countries IFRSs are used as national Generally Accepted Accounting Practices (GAAP) for all companies including unlisted entities. It has been argued that the same IFRSs should be used by all entities or alternatively a different body of standards should apply to small and medium entities (SMEs) and recently the IASB published an IFRS for SMEs.

(a)   Discuss whether it was necessary to develop a set of IFRSs specifically for SMEs.   **(7 marks)**

(b)   Discuss the nature of the following issues in developing IFRSs for SMEs.

    (i)   The purpose of the standards and the type of entity to which they should apply.   **(7 marks)**
    (ii)   How existing standards could be modified to meet the needs of SMEs.   **(6 marks)**
    (iii)   How items not dealt with by an IFRS for SMEs should be treated.   **(5 marks)**

(Total = 25 marks)

70 Whitebirk

40 mins

12/10, amended

(a)   The principal aim when developing accounting standards for small to medium-sized enterprises (SMEs) is to provide a framework that generates relevant, reliable, and useful information which should provide a high quality and understandable set of accounting standards suitable for SMEs. There is no universally agreed definition of an SME and it is difficult for a single definition to capture all the dimensions of a small or medium-sized business. The main argument for separate SME accounting standards is the undue cost burden of reporting, which is proportionately heavier for smaller firms.

Required

    (i)   Comment on the different approaches which could have been taken by the International Accounting Standards Board (IASB) in developing the *IFRS for Small and Medium-sized Entities (IFRS for SMEs),* explaining the approach finally taken by the IASB.   **(6 marks)**

    (ii)   Discuss the main differences and modifications to IFRS which the IASB made to reduce the burden of reporting for SME's, giving specific examples where possible and include in your discussion how the Board has dealt with the problem of defining an SME.   **(8 marks)**

Professional marks will be awarded in part (a) for clarity and quality of discussion.   **(2 marks)**

(b)   Whitebirk has met the definition of a SME in its jurisdiction and wishes to comply with the *IFRS for Small and Medium-sized Entities.* The entity wishes to seek advice on how it will deal with the following accounting issues in its financial statements for the year ended 30 November 20X2. The entity already prepares its financial statements under full IFRS.

    (i)   Whitebirk purchased 90% of Close, a SME, on 1 December 20X1. The purchase consideration was $5·7 million and the value of Close's identifiable assets was $6 million. The value of the non-controlling interest at 1 December 20X1 was measured at $0·7 million. Whitebirk has used the full goodwill method to account for business combinations and the life of goodwill cannot be estimated with any accuracy. Whitebirk wishes to know how to account for goodwill under the *IFRS for SMEs.*

    (ii)   Whitebirk has incurred $1 million of research expenditure to develop a new product in the year to 30 November 20X2. Additionally, it incurred $500,000 of development expenditure to bring another product to a stage where it is ready to be marketed and sold.

Required

Discuss how the above transactions should be dealt with in the financial statements of Whitebirk, with reference to the *IFRS for Small and Medium-sized Entities.*   **(6 marks)**

(Total = 22 marks)

Answers

1 Conceptual framework

Marking scheme

		Marks
(a)	Subjective	13
(b)	Up to 2 marks per key issue	10
	(i) Objectives	
	(ii) Qualitative characteristics	
	(iii) Definitions	
	(iv) Recognition and de-recognition	
	(v) Measurement	
	(vi) Reporting entity	
	(vii) Presentation and disclosure	
	Appropriateness and quality of discussion	2
	Maximum	25

(a) **The need for a conceptual framework**

The financial reporting process is concerned with providing information that is useful in the business and economic decision-making process. Therefore a conceptual framework will form the theoretical basis for determining which events should be accounted for, how they should be measured and how they should be communicated to the user.

Although it is theoretical in nature, a conceptual framework for financial reporting has highly practical final aims.

The **danger of not having a conceptual framework** is demonstrated in the way some countries' standards have developed over recent years; standards tend to be produced in a **haphazard and fire-fighting approach**. Where an agreed framework exists, the standard-setting body act as an architect or designer, rather than a fire-fighter, building accounting rules on the foundation of sound, agreed basic principles.

The lack of a conceptual framework also means that fundamental principles are tackled more than once in different standards, thereby producing contradictions and inconsistencies in basic concepts, such as those of prudence and matching. This leads to ambiguity and it affects the true and fair concept of financial reporting.

Another problem with the lack of a full conceptual framework has become apparent in the USA. The large number of highly detailed standards produced by the Financial Accounting Standards Board (FASB) has created a financial reporting environment governed by specific rules rather than general principles. FASB has 'concept statements' but a full conceptual framework would be better.

A conceptual framework can also bolster standard setters against political pressure from various 'lobby groups' and interested parties. Such pressure would only prevail if it was acceptable under the conceptual framework.

Can it resolve practical accounting issues?

A framework cannot provide all the answers for standard setters. It can provide **basic principles** which can be used when deciding between alternatives, and can narrow the range of alternatives that can be considered. In the UK, the *Statement of Principles* has provided **definitions that have formed the basis of definitions in accounting standards,** as has the IASB's conceptual framework in areas such as financial instruments and provisions. A framework can also provide guidance in the absence of an accounting standard. For example, there is no IFRS dealing specifically with off balance sheet finance, so the IASB *Conceptual Framework* must form the basis for decisions.

However, a conceptual framework is **unlikely**, on past form, to **provide all** the **answers to practical accounting problems**. There are a number of reasons for this:

(i) Financial statements are intended for a variety of users, and it is not certain that a single conceptual framework can be devised which will suit all users.

(ii) Given the diversity of user requirements, there may be a need for a variety of accounting standards, each produced for a different purpose (and with different concepts as a basis).

(iii) It is not clear that a conceptual framework makes the task of preparing and then implementing standards any easier than without a framework.

The IASB's *Conceptual Framework for Financial Reporting* has been criticised by the UK Accounting Standards Board at least partly on grounds of practical utility – it is thought to be **too theoretical,** and also for focusing on **some users (decision makers) at the expense of others (shareholders).** Perhaps it is not possible to satisfy all users.

(b) **Key issues in determining the basic components of an internationally agreed conceptual framework**

(i) Objectives.

There needs to be agreement on the principal users of financial statements. Are the statements produced for shareholders or for other users, and is decision usefulness the main purpose or is it stewardship? The UK Accounting Standards Board has expressed concern that the Conceptual Framework does not resolve these matters.

(ii) Qualitative characteristics

The *Conceptual Framework* sets out the following fundamental characteristics:

(1) **Relevance**: predictive value, confirmatory value

(2) **Faithful representation**: data must be complete, neutral and free from error

And these 'enhancing' characteristics

(1) **Comparability** (including consistency)

(2) **Verifiability** (meaning that different observers could agree that a particular depiction is a faithful representation)

(3) **Timeliness** (information provided in time to influence decisions)

(4) **Understandability** (Information must be classified, characterized and presented clearly and concisely).

There is a cost constraint on financial reporting. The benefits of providing financial information must exceed the costs of providing it.

The ASB is not happy that 'reliability' has been replaced by 'faithful representation', but there was in any case a conflict or trade-off between reliability and relevance. For example, historical cost is more reliable, but fair values are more relevant.

(iii) **Elements of financial statements**

Elements of financial statements are, for example, assets and liabilities. Definitions of these need to be agreed on, as they are particularly important for developing accounting standards. Certain issues are as yet unresolved, for example whether control should be part of the definition of an asset. Some IFRSs contradict the IASB's *Conceptual Framework* regarding elements of financial statements. IAS 12 *Income Taxes,* for example requires recognition of deferred tax liabilities, even though these do not meet the *Conceptual Framework* definition of a liability. It can be argued that goodwill does not meet the *Conceptual Framework* definition of an asset either, but IFRS 3 *Business Combinations* requires that it should be capitalised. Financial instruments can be problematic, in that some, for example obligations settled in shares, could either be equity or liabilities.

(iv) **Recognition and de-recognition**

De-recognition is not addressed by the IASB *Conceptual Framework,* although it is an important matter, particularly as regards financial instruments. Uncertainties remain regarding criteria for recognition, although frameworks do address this. For example, should an asset be recognised subsequent to acquisition, if it does not meet the recognition criteria on acquisition?

(v) **Measurement**

There are unresolved issues about measurement concepts. Consistency and theoretical justification are needed for the use of historical cost, fair value or current cost, and guidance should be given on initial measurement and subsequent measurement (for example impairment and revaluation, and classification of gains or losses arising from impairment or revaluation).

(vi) **Presentation**

Presentation and disclosure are important because they enable users to assess the elements of financial statements. General principles need to be established about what should be disclosed and how the financial statements should be presented.

(vii) **Reporting entity**

The question arises as to what constitutes a reporting entity. Which entities should be consolidated? Is the legal unit more important than the economic unit? This touches on aspects of off balance sheet finance and quasi-subsidiaries.

2 Accounting standards and disclosure

Marking scheme

		Marks
(a)	Common understanding	2
	Neutral, unbiased	2
	Comparability	1
	Credibility	2
	Consistency	2
		9
(b)	Investment process	4
	Risk	2
	Protection	2
	Costs	2
	Competitive disadvantage	2
	Other criteria	2
		14
	Professional marks	2
	Available	25

(a) Accounting standards and the market mechanism

Independently from financial reporting standards, the marketplace for capital encourages entities to invest time and thought into the quality of their reports. Companies have a vested interest in providing quality reports to potential lenders and investors, and if such information is not forthcoming, the cost of capital will be higher. However, **accounting standards play a key role in the effective functioning of the market mechanism** in the following ways.

(i) **Consistency.** Accounting standards are generally developed in accordance with an agreed conceptual framework. For example International Financial Reporting Standards use definitions of assets and liabilities that are found in the IASB's *Conceptual Framework for Financial Reporting,* and UK Financial Reporting Standards use the *Statement of Principles.* In consequence, there is consistency in the presentation of financial information, and a common understanding of terms used for the elements of financial statements. This aids efficiency and decision-making, since users do not need to learn a new set of concepts for each reporting entity.

(ii) **Neutrality.** While companies have an incentive to provide information in order to gain access to capital, they do not necessarily have an incentive to be unbiased. On the contrary, they may wish to portray their performance and financial position in a misleadingly favourable light. Users are aware of the potential bias, but if accounting standards are in place, compelling a company to present the information fairly, they can have more confidence in the financial statements. This increased trust helps decision making and efficiency, while too much scepticism is as bad as too little.

(iii) **Comprehensiveness.** Reports prepared in accordance with, say, International Financial Reporting Standards or UK Financial Reporting Standards, and generally accepted accounting principles, are required to contain certain information. As a minimum, certain financial statements and notes are required, for example a statement of cash flows. Potential lenders and companies are aware of these requirements, and therefore know that reports prepared under accounting standards will meet certain of their information needs. In the absence of accounting standards, lenders would have to request information on an *ad hoc* basis, or speculate as to why certain information was missing.

(iv) **Comparability.** If accounting standards are in force, the financial statements of companies can be compared effectively, which makes the decision-making process more efficient. Without them, companies could use very different bases for the preparation of accounts, and the user would not be comparing like with like. This is particularly important in the context of a global economy, where comparisons cross national borders, and was one of the main reasons why International Financial Reporting Standards were developed.

(v) **Verification.** Auditors verify that financial statements have been prepared in accordance with applicable accounting standards. While an audit report is not a guarantee of a good investment, it lends credibility to the financial statements in a report.

(b) **Costs and benefits of increased disclosure**

Benefits of disclosure

Users of financial statements need **as much relevant information as possible** in order to make or retain wise investments and to avoid less prudent uses of capital. Companies also benefit from providing this information as it means that they do not take on debt that they cannot afford. There are, then, obvious advantages to increased disclosure.

(i) **Lenders** need to know if a company has **liquidity problems**. Disclosure of reasons for a large bank overdraft, or changes in gearing, may help allay any concerns, or alternatively may help the lender avoid a bad decision.

(ii) Users need to know the full extent of **any risk** they are taking on in investing in – or indeed trading with – a company. Risk is not automatically a bad thing, if potential returns are good, and information on both profitability and gearing can help the decision-making process along. A venture capitalist may be more willing to take on risk than a high street bank, but both will need full disclosure of relevant information. A better understanding of risk may lower the cost of capital.

(iii) **Investors** and potential investors will need to know which companies are the most **profitable**, and whether those profits are sustainable. Their job is to maximise returns. It is not in the long-term interests of either companies or potential investors to withhold information.

An article by KPMG's Andrew Vials *(Accountancy,* December 2008) emphasised the **importance of disclosure in a recession,** specifically the 'credit crunch' of 2008. Profits or cash balances may have fallen, but a user needs to know why:

'Now, more than ever, companies in their business review and in the accounts should be providing full disclosures around their business risks and the factors and assumptions that have featured in the going concern assessments.'

Costs of disclosure

Companies are sometimes reluctant to increase the level of disclosure, not because they have anything to hide, but because of the associated costs. These include the following.

(i) **Costs to collate and prepare the required information.** These costs are principally time-costs of senior and junior staff, but may include fees to external consultants or lawyers. Training of staff – for example in moving to IFRS – may be required, or staff may need to be moved from other, revenue generating projects.

(ii) **Costs of disseminating information.** This may simply mean a thicker annual report, or the cost of more time to present the information on the web. The annual report and accounts may not be adequate, and additional reports may be used.

(iii) **Cost of lost competitive advantage**. Extra information on marketing strategies, planned products or locations for expansion can give competitors an advantage that they might not otherwise have. In particular, disclosure of problems, weaknesses and strategies for improvement may give the competitor an idea of areas to target. This disadvantage should not be overstated, however. A company does not need to give away trade secrets, and if the competitor is, for the benefits outlined above, also providing increased disclosure, there is no advantage to either party.

(iv) **Potential litigation.** The additional information disclosed needs to be accurate, as misleading disclosure runs the risk of litigation. Time – and therefore money – needs to be spent checking the information to avoid this risk. That said, there is also a risk of litigation arising from incomplete or inadequate disclosure, so potential litigation should not, in itself be a reason to avoid increased disclosure.

Even in a recession, **enhanced disclosures are arguably worth the extra cost.** Even if the news is bad, it is better that users know, rather than find out later when it gets worse. A company with a reputation for full disclosure will earn the trust of potential investors. There are indeed costs to increased disclosure, but the **cost of non-disclosure may be greater.**

It is noticeable that there has been little opposition to the introduction of the IASB's *Management Commentary,* or, in the UK, the *Operating and Financial Review,* which requires disclosures above and beyond what is in the financial statements. Clearly companies and users are in agreement that the **benefits of disclosure outweigh the costs.**

3 Venue

Text reference. Revenue recognition is covered in Chapter 1 of your Study Text.

Top tips. This is a topical issue and the subject of an Exposure Draft, which is covered in your Study Text. You should not just give the details of the new approach, but explain why it was needed. The examiner has indicated that there will be a computational element in his current issues question. As here, it is not too complex.

Easy marks. Credit will be given for valid arguments in Part (a), which has a generous mark allocation.

Examiner's comment. Part (a) of this question was well answered and discussions were good. However some candidates wrote general comments about recognition criteria for revenue and again these answers did not relate to the requirements of the question and were not in sufficient detail to justify full marks and the length and depth of the answers were often too short given the mark allocation for this question. Part (b) was well answered, except that candidates did not appear to realise that IAS 18 already deems it is necessary to discount the consideration to present value in order to arrive at fair value.

Marking scheme

		Marks
(a)	Main weaknesses of IAS 18	11
	Credit risk/time value	5
	Professional marks	2
(b)	Subjective	7
		25

(a) (i) **Main weaknesses of current standard on revenue recognition**

Under current US GAAP there are more than 100 revenue recognition standards, dealing with specific industries but these are sometimes inconsistent with each other. This has led **to contracts with similar economic effects being treated differently in different industries**. In addition, the amounts recognised under current standards **may not faithfully represent the nature of the transactions.**

IAS 18 *Revenue* has been criticised for being **vague** and this has led to inconsistency in how it has been applied by different entities. IAS 11 *Construction contracts* has also been criticised, and there is sometimes uncertainty about which standard to apply.

Specifically, the weaknesses of the current standard are as follows.

(1) **Timing of revenue recognition.**

Many companies remain uncertain about when they should recognise revenue because there is a lack of clear and comprehensive guidance in IAS 18 and IAS 11. This is particularly the case for goods and services because goods are sold at a point in time whereas services may be provided over time. This means that the revenue recognised does not represent fairly the pattern of transfer to the customer of the goods and services.

(2) **Distinguishing between goods and services**

IFRS does not clearly distinguish between goods and services, so some companies may not be entirely sure whether to account for some transactions under IAS 18 or IAS 11. The standards are very different. Even though construction contracts are effectively the 'sale of goods', IAS 11 uses the 'stage of completion' method, under which, contract revenue and costs are recognised as revenue and expenses in profit or loss in the period in which the work is performed and losses recognised immediately when foreseen. IAS 18, in contrast, revenue from sale of goods is recognised only when the risks and rewards of ownership are transferred to the customer. The revenue reported could vary considerably depending on which standard is applied.

(3) **Conflict with the IASB *Conceptual Framework***

Under the Conceptual Framework, income is recognised when an increase in future economic benefits related to an increase in an asset or a decrease of a liability has arisen that can be measured reliably. This means, in effect, that recognition of income occurs simultaneously with the recognition of increases in assets or decreases in liabilities (for example, the net increase in assets arising on a sale of goods or services or the decrease in liabilities arising from the waiver of a debt payable). It is not clear how this applies in the case of construction contracts.

(4) **Variable consideration**

Some contracts will have variable terms for the consideration paid to company by its customer. However, IAS 18 and IAS 11 do not include comprehensive guidance for measuring how much revenue should be recognised in such cases.

(5) **Multi-element arrangements**

Some transactions, often called multi-element arrangements, involve the delivery of more than one good or service. **IFRS does not give sufficient guidance on dealing with such transactions.** IAS 18 states that in certain circumstances the revenue recognition criteria must be applied to the separately identifiable components of a transaction. However, it does not explain the circumstances when a transaction can be broken down into separate components or the basis for identifying those components. Sometimes all the revenue of in a multi-element arrangement is recognised on delivery of the first item. Alternatively, and inconsistently, sometimes recognition is delayed until delivery of the final item.

Under the standard proposed in the Exposure Draft *Revenue from contracts with customers*, distinct performance obligations would be accounted for separately. Goods or services are

distinct if they are sold separately by the company, or if it provides benefits to the company's customer.

(6) **Disclosures**

Disclosures in current standards on revenue recognition are seen as inadequate when compared to disclosures in other standards.

(ii) **Credit risk and time value of money**

In general a **customer's credit risk** is not considered to be material and revenue is recognised at the invoiced amount, subject to the entity performing its obligations. However, it might be appropriate to take account of the **possibility of default** by a customer or customers. For example, if an entity sells goods to 100 customers, it may consider that three of these customers will default. Other standards, for example IAS 37 in respect of warranties, adopt a **probability-weighted approach**, and it might be considered appropriate to apply this to revenue by calculating an expected value of the amount of consideration to be received.

In many transactions, the **time value of money** is immaterial because the revenue is received soon after the good or service is provided. In other cases, however, it could be appropriate to consider the effects of the time value of money when determining the transaction price – particularly under long-term contracts or those that give rise to customer payments at significantly different times. In such cases a **discount rate** could usefully be applied. This should reflect the timing of receipt and the credit risk – in effect it is treating the receipt as a financing transaction. The use of discount rates involves judgement, and could be viewed as **subjective**. The proposed standard would take account of the time value of money.

(b) (i) **Credit risk**

IAS 18 treatment

Under IAS 18, revenue of $1m would be recognised on the sale of the computers and a trade receivable of $1m set up. The trade receivable would be reviewed periodically for impairment, and the deteriorating financial situation of the customer would be seen as an indicator of impairment. An impairment of $100,000 would be recognised. However, no recognition would be made, under current rules of the 5% risk that the customer would default. This is not 5% of the revenue – if it were, a receivables expense of $50,000 would be required - but a 5% risk that none of the revenue can be collected, for which current standards make no arrangements.

Taking account of credit risk

If credit risk is taken into account in the recognition of revenue, the amount recognised on the sale would be reduced by the 5% likelihood of default, meaning that only 95% of the revenue, ie $950,000 would be recognised. The impairment of $100,000 would still be recognised as an expense, not as a reduction in revenue.

(ii) **Time value of money**

IAS 18 treatment

Under IAS 18, where payment is deferred, **the substance of the arrangement is that there is both a sale and a financing transaction**. The treatment of the £2m deferred receipt is the same whether IAS 18 or the proposed standard is applied, in that the fair value of the consideration is the **consideration discounted to present value.**

Receipt of the selling price of $2m is deferred for two years. Using a 4% discount rate, the present value of the consideration is $2m/1.04^2 = $1.85m. The unwinding of the discount would be charged as an expense over the two year period. **Alternatively**, if Venue sells the same goods to other customers for cash, normally at a discount, the **cash price** of those goods could be used in determining fair value.

Regarding the $3m **payment in advance**, revenue would not be recognised immediately; instead a **deferred income liability** would be set up:

DEBIT	Cash	$3m	
CREDIT	Deferred income		$3m

Then on delivery in a year's time, revenue is recognised:

DEBIT	Deferred income	$3m	
CREDIT	Sales revenue		$3m

Taking account of the time value of money

While the $2m deferred receipt would be treated the same way under the proposed standard, that of $3m payment in advance would differ in having to recognise an interest expense on what is effectively a financing transaction. Venue would recognise a contract liability of $3m:

DEBIT	Cash	$3m	
CREDIT	Contract liability		$3m

During the year to the date of transfer of the product, an interest expense would be recognised of ($3m × 1.04) -- $3m = $120,000, and the liability would be increased to $3.12m:

DEBIT	Interest expense	$120,000	
CREDIT	Contract liability		$120,000

On transfer of the product to the customer, Venue would recognise revenue of $3.12m:

DEBIT	Contract liability	$3.12m	
CREDIT	Sales revenue		$3.12m

4 Glowball

Text reference. Covered in Chapter 3 of your text.

Top tips. This is a comprehensive question covering most aspects of environmental reporting that are likely to come up. Learn our answer and apply it to many questions on this topics

		Marks
(a)	Current reporting requirements	10
(b)	Restoration	5
	Infringement of law	4
	Emissions	4
	Decommissioning activities	4
	Report	4
	Available	31
	Maximum	25

REPORT

To: The Directors   Date: 8 June 20X3
      Glowball

From: Ann Accountant

Environmental Reporting

Introduction

The purpose of this report is to provide information about current reporting requirements and guidelines on the subject of environmental reporting, and to give an indication of the required disclosure in relation to the specific

BPP
LEARNING MEDIA

events which you have brought to my attention. We hope that it will assist you in preparing your environmental report.

Current reporting requirements and guidelines

Most businesses have generally ignored environmental issues in the past. However, the use and **misuse** of **natural resources** all lead to environmental costs generated by businesses, both large and small.

There are very few rules, legal or otherwise, to ensure that companies disclose and report environmental matters. Any **disclosures tend to be voluntary**, unless environmental matters happen to fall under standard accounting principles. Environmental matters may be reported in the accounts of companies in the following areas.

IFRS and environmental reporting

There are **no required disclosures** under IFRS. However, if environmental matters fall within the scope of specific accounting principles they must be dealt with under the relevant standard. In particular:

- IAS 1 (revised) *Presentation of financial statements* requires disclosure of facts material to a proper understanding of financial statements.
- IAS 37 *Provisions, contingent liabilities and contingent assets* requires provisions for environmental damage to be recognised.

National and legal requirements

In the UK, the Companies Act 2006 requires disclosure of environmental matters in the Expanded Business Review, now incorporated into the Operating and Financial Review as best practice in Reporting Statement 1. Other countries require environmental reporting under national law.

Voluntary disclosure: sustainability

Most environmental disclosure is voluntary, although lists of companies in particular are under a great deal of pressure to make such disclosures. There have been a number of **initiatives** in the past (CERES, Friends of the Earth Charter) but the most important of these is the **Global Reporting Initiative (GRI)**.

The GRI is an international not-for-profit organisation, with many stakeholders. Its aim is to develop **Sustainability Reporting Guidelines** for voluntary use. These guidelines cover a number of areas (economic, environmental and social), and the latest guidelines were published in 2006. The GRI specified key performance indicators for each area. For environmental reporting the indicators are: materials; energy; water; biodiversity; emissions; energy and waste; products and services; compliance, transport.

Comments on 'environmental events'

(a) Of relevance to the farmland restoration is IAS 37 *Provisions, contingent liabilities and contingent assets*. Provisions for environmental liabilities should be recognised where there is a **legal or constructive obligation** to rectify environmental damage or perform restorative work. The mere existence of the restorative work does not give rise to an obligation and there is no legal obligation. However, it could be argued that there is a constructive obligation arising from the company's approach in previous years, which may have given rise to an **expectation** that the work would be carried out. If this is the case, a provision of $150m would be required in the financial statements. In addition, this provision and specific examples of restoration of land could be included in the environmental report.

(b) The treatment of the **fine** is straightforward: it is an obligation to transfer economic benefits. An estimate of the fine should be made and a **provision** set up in the financial statements for $5m. This should be mentioned in the environmental report. The report might also **put the fines in context** by stating how many tests have been carried out and how many times the company has passed the tests. The directors may feel that it would do the company's reputation no harm to point out the fact that the number of prosecutions has been falling from year to year.

(c) These statistics are good news and need to be covered in the environmental report. However, the emphasis should be on **accurate factual reporting** rather than boasting. It might be useful to provide target levels for comparison, or an industry average if available. The emissions statistics should be split into three categories:

- Acidity to air and water
- Hazardous substances
- Harmful emissions to water

As regards the aquatic emissions, the $70m planned expenditure on **research** should **be mentioned in the environmental report**. It shows a commitment to benefiting the environment. However, **IAS 37 would not permit a provision** to be made for this amount, since an obligation does not exist and the **expenditure is avoidable**. Nor does it qualify as development expenditure under IAS 38.

(d) The environmental report should mention the steps the company is taking to minimise the harmful impact on the environment in the way it sites and constructs its gas installations. The report should also explain the policy of dismantling the installations rather than sinking them at the end of their useful life.

Currently the company builds up a provision for decommissioning costs over the life of the installation. However, IAS 37 does not allow this. Instead, the **full amount must be provided** as soon as there is an **obligation** arising as a result of **past events**, the **settlement** of which is **expected** to result in an **outflow of resources**. The obligation exists right at the beginning of the installation's life, and so the full $407m must be provided for. A corresponding asset is created.

5 Key

Text reference. Impairment is covered in Chapter 4 of the BPP Study Text.

Top tips. A full question on impairment is unusual, although the topic itself comes up regularly. There are a lot of marks for discussion in Part (a), including 2 professional marks, so don't rush this bit. Part (b) says 'discuss with suitable computations', so do not make the mistake of expecting the calculations to speak for themselves. P2 is a preparation for the accountant's role as advisor – and explanations will be just as important in this role as computations.

Easy marks. These are available for bookwork in Part (a), and for the calculation of value in use in Part (b).

Examiner's comments. The examiner was pleased with candidates' answers to the first part of the question, which asked them to discuss the main considerations which an entity should take into account when impairment testing non-current assets in a climate where there were credit limitations. However, many made the mistake of simply setting out the rules of impairment testing without relating it to the economic climate set out in the question. The second part of the question required candidates to set out how to account for any potential impairment in given circumstances. This was quite well answered. Some candidates had difficulties in discounting future cash flows and the treatment of the impairment loss and revaluation gain. Many did not discuss the key issues in sufficient depth, or simply calculated the accounting adjustments without sufficient discussion of the issues.

(a) The basic principle of IAS 36 *Impairment of assets* is that an asset should be carried at no more than its recoverable amount, that is the amount to be recovered through use or sale of the asset. If an **asset's value** is **higher than its recoverable amount**, an **impairment loss** has occurred. The impairment loss should be **written off** against profit or loss for the year.

Entities must determine, **at each reporting date**, whether there are any indications that impairment has occurred. Indicators of impairment may be internal or external. Where it is not possible to measure impairment for individual assets, the loss should be measured for a **cash generating unit. Internal factors** may apply in any economic climate, and include such matters as physical damage, adverse changes to the methods of use of the asset, management restructuring and over-estimation of cash flows. In an adverse economic climate, additional, **external indicators** of impairment are more likely to be evident. Such factors include:

(i) A **significant decrease** in the **market** value of an asset in excess of **normal passage of time**

(ii) Significant **adverse changes** in the **markets** or **business** in which the asset is used

(iii) Adverse changes to the **technological, economic or legal environment** of the business

(iv) Increase in **market interest rates** likely to affect **the discount rate** used in calculating value in use

(v) Where **interest rates increase**, adversely affecting **recoverable amounts**

(vi) The **carrying amount** of an entity's assets exceeding its **market capitalisation**

The **recoverable amount** is **defined** as the **higher** of:

(i) The **asset's fair value less costs of disposal.** This is the price that would be received to sell the asset in an orderly transaction between market participants at the measurement date under current market conditions, net of costs of disposal.

(ii) The asset's **value in use.** This is the present value of estimated future cash flows (inflows minus outflows) generated by the asset, including its estimated net disposal value (if any) at the end of its useful life. A number of factors must be reflected in the calculation of value in use (variations, estimates of cash flows, uncertainty), but the most important is the **time value of money** as value in use is based on **present value calculations.**

Impairment testing is difficult whether the recoverable amount is based on fair value less costs of disposal, because of the uncertainties surrounding **assumptions** that must be made. IAS 36 requires that these **are 'reasonable and supportable'**. Cash flow projections up to five years should be based on the most recent budgets and financial forecasts, but in a recession, these **should not be overly optimistic**. Longer term cash flow projections should be based on a steady or declining growth rate. Discount rates should reflect the specific risks of the asset or cash generating unit.

In an adverse economic climate, the entity will need to **consider the market** in which it operates in making its assumptions about recoverable amounts, because the market affects recoverable amounts. If **comparable industries** are taking impairment losses, then the entity will need to **explain the absence of such impairment charges**. Industry analysts will expect this. The market also needs to be informed about how the entity is reflecting the economic downturn in its impairment calculations, and what market information is being used in the impairment testing.

Clearly, testing for impairment will be a **time-consuming activity.** Cash flow assumptions may need to be reassessed, and **discount rates** must be scrutinised to see if they are **still valid** in a time of rising risk premiums and poor liquidity. Detailed calculations must be made and revised as necessary. Estimates and calculations may also need to be **revised** in the light of **information** becoming available only **after the end of the reporting period.** Last but not least, **extensive disclosures** will be required of discount rates, long-term growth rate assumptions and the reasons behind such assumptions.

(b) **Impairment loss for year ended 31 May 20X4**

IAS 36 states that if an **asset's value** is **higher than** its **recoverable amount**, an **impairment loss** has occurred. The impairment loss should be written off to profit or loss for the year.

The carrying value of the non-current assets of Key at 31 May 20X4 is cost less depreciation:

$3m – ($3m ÷ 5) = $2.4m.

This needs to be compared to value in use at 31 May 20X4, which, using a discount rate of 5%, is calculated as:

Year ended	31 May 20X5	31 May 20X6	31 May 20X7	31 May 20X8	Total
Cash flows	280	450	500	550	
Discount factors	0.9524	0.9070	0.8638	0.8227	
Discounted cash flows ($'000)	267	408	432	452	1,559

The value in use of $1,559,000 is below the carrying value, so the carrying value must be written down, giving rise to an **impairment loss:**

$2,400,000 - $1,559,000 = $841,000$

Value in use at 30 November 20X4

The directors wish to reverse the impairment loss calculated as at 31 May 20X4, on the grounds that, using the same cash flows, the value in use of the non-current assets is now above the carrying value. However, while IAS 36 requires an assessment at each reporting date of whether an impairment loss has decreased, this does not apply to the unwinding of the discount (or goodwill). Since the **same cash flows** have been used, the increase in value in use is **due to the unwinding of the discount, and so cannot be reversed.**

Government reimbursement

The treatment of compensation received in the form of reimbursements is governed by IAS 37 *Provisions, contingent liabilities and contingent assets.* Reimbursements from governmental indemnities are recorded in profit or loss for the year **when the compensation becomes receivable,** and the receipt is **treated as a separate economic event** from the item it was intended to compensate for. In this particular case, receipt is by no means certain, since the government has merely indicated that it may compensate.

Thus **no credit can be taken** for compensation of 20% of the impairment loss.

Revalued asset

When an **impairment loss occurs** for a **revalued asset**, the **impairment loss** should be first be charged to other comprehensive income (that is, treated as a **revaluation decrease**). Any **excess** is then charged to **profit or loss**.

The revaluation gain and impairment loss will be accounted for as follows:

	Revalued carrying value $m
1 December 20X1	10.0
Depreciation (10 × 2/10)	(2.0)
Revaluation (bal. fig.)	0.8
1 December 20X3	8.8
Depreciation (1 year) (8.8 × 1/8)	(1.1)
Impairment loss (bal. fig.)	(2.2)
Recoverable amount at 30 November 20X4	5.5

The impairment loss of $2.2m is charged to **other comprehensive income** until the revaluation surplus has been eliminated, and the rest is charged to profit or loss. Therefore the impairment **loss charged to other comprehensive income** will be **$0.8m.** The **remainder**, $2.2m – $0.8m = $1.4m will be **charged to profit or loss.**

It is possible that the company would transfer an amount from revaluation surplus to retained earnings to cover the excess depreciation of $0.1m. If so, the impairment loss charged to OCI would be $(0.8 – 0.1m) = $0.7m

Property to be sold

The fact that management plans to sell the property because it is being under-utilised may be an **indicator** of **impairment**. Such assets (or cash generating units) must be tested for impairment when the decision to sell is made.

IFRS 5 *Non-current assets held for sale and discontinued operations* may apply in such cases, but the decision to sell the asset is generally made well before the IFRS 5 criteria are met. IFRS requires an asset or disposal group to be classified as held for sale where it is **available for immediate sale** in its **present condition** subject only to **terms that are usual** and customary and the sale is **highly probable.** For a sale to be highly probable:

- Management must be **committed** to the sale.
- An **active programme to locate a buyer** must have been initiated.
- The **market price** must be **reasonable** in relation to the asset's current fair value.
- The sale must be **expected to be completed within one year** from the date of classification.

An asset (or disposal group) that is held for sale should be measured at the **lower of** its **carrying amount** and **fair value less costs to sell.** Immediately before classification of the asset as held for sale, the entity must update any impairment test carried out. **Once** the asset has been **classified as held for sale**, any **impairment loss** will be based on the **difference between the adjusted carrying amounts and the fair value less cost to sell**. The impairment loss (if any) will be **recognised in profit or loss**.

A **subsequent increase** in fair value less costs of disposal may be **recognised** in profit or loss **only to the extent of any impairment previously recognised**.

In the case of the property held by Key, it is likely that **IFRS 5 would not apply** because **not all the criteria for a highly probable sale** have been met. Management is committed to the sale, and there is an active programme to locate a buyer. However, **Key has not reduced the price of the asset, which is in excess of its market value** – one of the IFRS 5 criteria is that the market price must be reasonable in relation to the asset's current fair value. In addition, the asset has remained unsold for a year, so it **cannot be assumed that the sale will be completed within one year** of classification.

The property does not meet the IFRS 5 criteria, so it **cannot be classified as held for sale**. However, an **impairment** has taken place and, in the circumstances, the **recoverable amount** would be **fair value less costs to sell**.

6 Prochain

Text reference. This topic is covered in Chapters 4 and 1 of your text.

Top tips. This question was a case study that dealt with the accounting issues for an entity engaged in the fashion industry. The areas examined were fundamental areas of the syllabus: non-current assets, intangible assets, determination of the purchase consideration for the subsidiary, and research and development expenditure. Tricky bits to get right were:

(a)   A provision for dismantling the 'model areas' would need to be set up and discounted back to the present.
(b)   Contingent consideration that is not probable would not be included in the cost of acquisition.
(c)   Investment properties do not include properties owned and occupied by the entity.

When discussing the development expenditure, the criteria for capitalisation may be remembered using the mnemonic PIRATE.

Easy marks. Stating the obvious – that the model areas are items of property, plant and equipment and need to be depreciated will earn you easy marks, as will mentioning the basic distinction between research and development expenditure and listing the criteria when talking about the brand.

Examiner's comment. Generally, candidates answered the question quite well, obtaining a pass mark, although accounting for the non-current assets did confuse some candidates.

Marking scheme

	Marks
Model areas	7
Purchase of Badex	8
Research and Development	6
Apartments	4
Maximum/Available	25

Model areas

IAS 16 *Property, plant and equipment* is the relevant standard here. The model areas are held for use in the supply of goods and are used in more than one accounting period. The company should recognise the costs of setting up the model areas as **tangible non-current assets** and should **depreciate** the costs over their useful lives. **Subsequent measurement should be based on cost**. In theory the company could measure the model areas at fair value if the revaluation model of IAS 16 was followed, but it would be difficult to measure their fair value reliably.

IAS 16 states that the initial cost of an asset **should include** the initial estimate of the **costs of dismantling and removing the item and restoring the site** where the entity has an obligation to do so. A **present obligation appears to exist**, as defined by IAS 37 *Provisions, contingent liabilities and contingent assets* and therefore the entity should also **recognise a provision** for that amount. The provision should be **discounted to its present value** and the unwinding of the discount recognised in profit or loss.

At 31 May 20X6, the entity should recognise a non-current asset of $15.7 million (cost of $23.6 million (W) less accumulated depreciation of $7.9 million (W)) and a provision of $3.73 million (W).

Working

	$m
Cost of model areas	20.0
Plus provision ($20 \times 20\% \times \dfrac{1}{1.055^2}$ (= 0.898))	3.6
Cost on initial recognition	23.6
Less accumulated depreciation ($23.6 \times 8/24$)	(7.9)
Net book value at 31 May 20X6	15.7
Provision: on initial recognition ($20 \times 20\% \times 0.898$)	3.6
Plus unwinding of discount ($3.6 \times 5.5\% \times 8/12$)	0.13
Provision at 31 May 20X6	3.73

Purchase of Badex

IFRS 3 *Business Combinations* states that the consideration transferred in a business combination shall be measured at **fair value at the acquisition date**.

The **$100 million cash paid** on the acquisition date, 1 June 20X5 is **recognised as purchase consideration**. The **$25 million payable on 31 May 20X7** (two years after acquisition) should be **split** into the **$10 million deferred consideration** which should be **discounted to its present value** by two years ($10m x $1/1.055^2$ = $8.98m) and the **contingent consideration** of $15 million. The contingent consideration should be measured at its **acquisition-date fair value**. Here, as the profit forecast targets are unlikely to be met, **the fair value would be significantly less than $15 million** but as the percentage chance of the targets being met and other relevant information are not given, it is not possible to establish a fair value.

Prochain should also recognise a corresponding **financial liability for the deferred and contingent consideration** (rather than equity) as they meet the definition of a financial liability in IAS 32 *Financial Instruments: Presentation*. This is because Prochain has a **contractual obligation to deliver cash** on 31 May 20X7 providing the conditions of the contingent consideration are met. At the year end 31 May 20X6, any **changes in the contingent consideration** as a result of changes in expectations of the targets being met will be recognised in **profit or loss** (rather than adjusting goodwill).

Under IFRS 3, any associated **transaction costs** should be **expensed to profit or loss**.

A further issue concerns the valuation and treatment of the 'Badex' brand name. IAS 38 *Intangible Assets* prohibits the recognition of internally generated brands and therefore the brand will not **be recognised in Badex's individual statement of financial position** prior to the acquisition. However, **IFRS 3 requires intangible assets** of an acquiree to be **recognised in a business combination if they meet the identifiability criteria** in IAS 38. For an intangible to be identifiable, the asset must be separable or it must arise from contractual or legal rights. Here, these **criteria appear to have been met** as the brand could be sold separately from the entity. Therefore, the 'Badex' brand should be **recognised as an intangible asset at $20m in the consolidated statement of financial position**.

Development of own brand

IAS 38 *Intangible assets* divides a development project into a research phase and a development phase. In the research phase of a project, an entity cannot yet demonstrate that the expenditure will generate probable future economic benefits. Therefore expenditure on **research** must be **recognised as an expense when it occurs**.

Development expenditure is capitalised when an entity demonstrates **all** the following.

(a)   The **technical feasibility** of completing the project

(b)   Its **intention to complete** the asset and use or sell it

(c)   Its **ability to use or sell** the asset

(d)   That the asset will generate **probable future economic benefits**

(e)   The availability of **adequate technical, financial and other resources** to complete the development and to use or sell it

(f)   Its ability to **reliably measure** the expenditure attributable to the asset.

Assuming that all these criteria are met, the cost of the development should comprise **all directly attributable costs** necessary to **create the asset** and to make it **capable of operating in the manner intended by management**. Directly attributable costs **do not include selling or administrative costs**, or **training costs** or market research. The **cost of upgrading** existing machinery can be recognised as **property, plant and equipment**. Therefore the expenditure on the project should be treated as follows:

	Expense (P/L) $m	Recognised in statement of financial position	
		Intangible Assets $m	Property, plant and equipment $m
Research	3		
Prototype design		4	
Employee costs		2	
Development work		5	
Upgrading machinery			3
Market research	2		
Training	1		
	6	11	3

Prochain should **recognise $11 million** as an intangible asset.

Apartments

The apartments are leased to persons who are under contract to the company. Therefore they **cannot be classified as investment property**. IAS 40 *Investment property* specifically states that **property occupied by employees** is not investment property. The apartments must be treated as **property, plant and equipment**, carried at cost or fair value and depreciated over their useful lives.

Although the rent is below the market rate the difference between the actual rent and the market rate is simply **income foregone** (or an opportunity cost). In order to recognise the difference as an employee benefit cost it would also be necessary to **gross up rental income** to the market rate. The financial statements would **not present fairly** the financial performance of the company. Therefore the company **cannot recognise the difference** as an employee benefit cost.

7 Johan

Marking scheme

		Marks
Intangible assets:	Licence	2
	Amortisation	2
	Impairment	2
	Renewal	2
		8
Tangible fixed assets:	Cost	1
	Feasibility study	1
	Location and condition	1
	Capitalised costs	1
Leases:	Operating lease	2
	Prepayment	1
		7
Inventory		2
IAS 18 Revenue recognition:	Recognition	2
	Agency	2
	Separability	2
		8
Discussion		2
	Available	25

(a) **Licences**

The relevant standard here is IAS 38 *Intangible assets*. An intangible asset may be **recognised if it meets the identifiability criteria** in IAS 38, if it is probable that future economic benefits attributable to the asset will flow to the entity and if its fair value can be **measured reliably**. For an intangible asset to be identifiable the asset must be separable or it must arise from contractual or other legal rights. It appears that these **criteria have been met**. The licence has been acquired separately, and its value can be measured reliably at

$120 million (cost). It is also expected that future economic benefits will flow to Johan. Therefore **the licence will be recognised as an intangible asset at cost.**

Regarding **subsequent valuation,** IAS 38 has two models: the **cost model** and the **revaluation model**. The revaluation model can only be used if intangible assets are traded in an active market. As Johan cannot sell the licence, this is not the case here, so Johan **cannot use the revaluation model.**

Under the **cost model,** intangible assets must be carried at **cost less amortisation and impairment losses.** The depreciable amount of an asset is cost less residual value; since the licence has no residual value, the depreciable amount is the cost. However, an impairment review should have been undertaken at 30 November 20X7, before amortisation commenced, and the licence written down, if necessary to its recoverable amount.

The **depreciable amount** must be **allocated over the useful life of the licence on a systematic basis.** The basis of allocation should reflect the **pattern of consumption** of the asset's benefit, unless this cannot be reliably determined, in which case the straight line basis would be used. The **straight line basis is appropriate**, in any case, for this licence, because the economic benefit is Johan's ability to earn income from the licence which accrues on a time basis and is not affected by wear and tear as some assets would be.

The **amortisation starts on the day that the network is available for use,** that is 1 December 20X7. Although the licence runs for six years from the date of purchase, 1 December 20X6, economic benefits cannot flow to the entity before the network assets and infrastructure are ready for use.

Other licences have been renewed at a nominal cost. It could therefore be argued that the licence should be amortised over two periods totalling eleven years: a period of five years from 1 December 20X7 to the renewal date, followed by six years from the renewal date. However, Johan does not know for certain what charge the regulator will make on renewal, so it would be more **appropriate to amortise the licence over a five year period,** that is $24 million per annum.

For the purposes of any **impairment review**, the licence and network assets should be classified as a single cash generating unit. They cannot be used separately from one another. There are **indications that the licence may be impaired:** disappointing market share, fierce competition and difficulty in retaining customers. Therefore the cash generating unit (licence and network assets) **must be tested for impairment.**

(b) **Costs incurred in extending the network**

The applicable standards here are IAS 16 *Property, plant and equipment,* and IAS 17 *Leases.*

IAS 16 states that the **cost** of an item of property, plant and equipment should be **recognised when two conditions** have been fulfilled:

It is probable that future economic benefits associated with the item will flow to the entity.

The cost of the item can be measured reliably.

The cost, according to IAS 16, includes **directly attributable costs of bringing the asset to the location and condition necessary for it to be capable of operating in a manner intended by management**. Examples of such directly attributable costs are site preparation costs and installation and assembly costs.

Applying the first criterion (probability of economic benefits) would **exclude the costs of the feasibility study**, both internal and external, because by definition, the economic benefits of a feasibility study are uncertain. These costs, $250,000 in total, should be **expensed as incurred.**

Applying the IAS 16 definition of directly attributable costs, the selection of the base station site is critical for the optimal operation of the network, and is part of the process of bringing the network assets to the location and condition necessary for operation. The **$50,000 paid to third party consultants** to find a suitable site is part of the cost of constructing the network, and **may thus be capitalised.**

The other costs – a payment of $300,000 followed by $60,000 a month for twelve years – is a **lease**, and is governed by IAS 17. IAS 17 defines a lease as an agreement whereby the lessor conveys to the lessee, in return for a payment or series of payments, the right to use an asset for an agreed period of time.

The question arises as to whether the payments are to be treated as **a finance lease or as an operating lease**. IAS 17 defines a finance lease as a lease that transfers substantially all the risks and rewards incidental to ownership of the leased asset to the lessee. An operating lease is a lease other than a finance lease.

In the case of the contract with the government for access to the land, there is **no transfer of ownership**. The term of the lease is **not for the major part of the asset's life**, because the land has an indefinite economic life. The lease **cannot therefore be said to transfer substantially all the risks and rewards of ownership** to Johan. Accordingly, the contract should be treated as an operating lease. The initial payment of $300,000 should be treated as a prepayment in the statement of financial position, and charged to profit or loss for the year on a straight line basis over the life of the contract. The monthly payments of $60,000 should be expensed. No value will be shown for the lease contract in the statement of financial position.

(c) **Purchase of handsets and revenue recognition**

The applicable standards in this case are IAS 2 *Inventories* and IAS 18 *Revenue.*

Inventory of handsets

IAS 2 states that inventories must be valued at the lower of cost and net realisable value. The handsets cost $200, and the net realisable value is selling price of $150 less costs to sell of $1, which is $149. All handsets in inventory – whether they are to be sold to prepaid customers or dealers – must be written down to $149 per handset.

Call cards and prepaid phones

Under IAS 18, revenue is recognised by reference to the stage of completion of the transaction at the reporting date. In the case of the call cards, revenue is generated by the provision of services, not the sale of the card itself, and accordingly revenue should be recognised as the services are provided. The $21 received per call card should therefore be treated as deferred revenue at the point of sale. Of this, $18 per card should be recognised over the six month period from the date of the sale. The $3 of unused credit – an average figure may be used rather than the figure for each card – should be recognised when the card expires, that is when Johan has no further obligation to the customer.

Sales to dealers

Johan bears the risk of loss in value of the handset, as the dealer may return any handsets before a service contract is signed with a customer. In addition, Johan sets the price of the handset. Therefore the **dealer, in this case, is acting as an agent for the sale of the handset and service contract.** The handset cannot be sold separately from the service contract, so the two transactions must be taken together because the commercial effect of either transaction cannot be understood in isolation. Johan earns revenue from the service contract with the final customer, not from the sale of the handset to the dealer.

IAS 18 does not deal directly with agency, but implies that revenue for an agent is not the amounts collected on behalf of the principal, but the commission earned for collecting them. From Johan's point of view **revenue is not earned when the handsets are sold to the dealer, so revenue should not be recognised at this point**. Instead the net payment of $130 (commission paid to the agent less cost of the handset) should be recognised as a customer acquisition cost, which may qualify as an intangible asset under IAS 38. If it is so recognised, it will be amortised over the twelve month contract. **Revenue from the service contract will be recognised as the service is rendered.**

8 Scramble

Text reference. Intangible assets and impairment are covered in Chapter 4. IFRS 9 is covered in Chapter 7.

Top tips. Parts (a) and (b) were on impairment testing. You may have found Part (b), requiring determination of the discount rate to be used, rather difficult, and you may have needed to draw on your financial management studies. Part (c) was on intangible assets (agents' fees on transfer of players to the club and extension of players' contracts) and an IFRS 9 financial asset (rights to ticket sales of another football club).

Easy marks. There are no obviously easy marks in this question.

Examiner's commnet. In Part (a) many candidates automatically assumed that the accounting treatments were incorrect but in this case the entity was correctly expensing maintenance costs, as these did not enhance the asset over and above original benefits. Similarly, the decision to keep intangibles at historical cost is a matter of choice and therefore the accounting policy outlined in the question was acceptable. In Part (b), candidates realised that the discount rate was not in accordance with IAS 36, but did not explain why. In Part (c) definition of an intangible asset was well expressed by students and candidates realised in most cases that the players' registration rights met the definition of intangible assets. However very few candidates stated that the agents' fees represented professional fees incurred in bringing the asset into use and therefore could be included in intangibles.

(a)   **Internally developed intangibles**

IAS 38 *Intangible assets* **allows internally developed intangibles such to be capitalised** provided certain criteria (technological feasibility, probable future benefits, intent and ability to use or sell the software, resources to complete the software, and ability to measure cost) are met. It is assumed, in the absence of information to the contrary, that they have; accordingly Scramble's treatment is correct in this respect.

Scramble is also correct in expensing the maintenance costs. These should not be capitalised as they do not enhance the value of the asset over and above the original benefits.

As regards subsequent measurement, IAS 38 requires that **an entity must choose either the cost model or the revaluation** model for each class of intangible asset. Scramble has chosen cost, and this is acceptable as an accounting policy.

Intangible assets **may have a finite or an indefinite useful life**. IAS 38 states that an entity may treat an intangible asset as having an indefinite useful life, when, having regard to all relevant factors there is no foreseeable limit to the period over which the asset is expected to generate net cash inflows for the entity.

'Indefinite' is not the same as 'infinite'. Computer software is mentioned in IAS 38 as an intangible that is prone to technological obsolescence and whose life may therefore be short. Its **useful life should be reviewed each reporting period** to determine whether events and circumstances continue to support an indefinite useful life assessment for that asset. If they do not, the change in the useful life assessment from indefinite to finite should be accounted for as a change in an accounting estimate.

The asset should also be **assessed for impairment in accordance with IAS 36** *Impairment of assets*. Specifically, the entity must test the intangible asset for impairment annually, and whenever there is an indication that the asset may be impaired. The asset is tested by **comparing its recoverable amount with its carrying amount.**

The **cash flows** used by Scramble to determine value in use for the purposes of impairment testing **do not comply with IAS 36**. Scramble does not analyse or investigate the differences between expected and actual cash flows, but this is an important way of testing the reasonableness of assumptions about expected cash flows, and IAS 36 requires such **assumptions to be reasonable and supported by evidence.**

Scramble is also **incorrect** to include in its estimate of future cash flows those **expected to be incurred in improving the games and the expected increase in revenue** resulting from that expense. IAS 36 requires cash flow projections to relate to the asset in its current condition. Nor should cash flow estimates include tax payments or receipts as here.

(b)   **Discount rate for impairment**

While the cash flows used in testing for impairment are specific to the entity, the **discount rate is supposed to appropriately reflect the current market assessment of the time value of money and the risks specific to the asset or cash generating unit.** When a specific rate for an asset or cash generating unit is not directly available from the market, which is usually the case, the discount rate to be used is a surrogate. An estimate should be made of a **pre-tax rate that reflects the current market assessment of the time value of money and the risks specific to the asset** that have **not been adjusted** for in the estimate of future cash flows. According to IAS 36, this rate is the return that the investors would require if they chose an investment that would generate cash flows of amounts, timing and risk profile equivalent to those that the entity expects to derive from the assets.

Rates that should be considered are the entity's weighted average cost of capital, the entity's incremental borrowing rate or other market rates. The objective must be to obtain a rate which is sensible and justifiable. Scramble should not use the risk free rate adjusted by the company specific average credit spread of outstanding debt raised two years ago. Instead the credit spread input applied **should reflect the current market assessment of the credit spread at the time of impairment testing**, even though Scramble does not intend raising any more finance.

Disclosures

With regard to the impairment loss recognised in respect of each cash generating unit, IAS 36 would disclosure of:

- The amount of the loss
- The events and circumstances that led to the loss
- A description of the impairment loss by class of asset

It is **no defence** to maintain that this information was **common knowledge in the market.** The disclosures are still needed. It should be noted that IAS 1 requires disclosure of material items, so this information needs to be disclosed if the loses are **material,** with materiality determined using a suitable measure such as percentage of profit before tax.

(c)   **Recognition of intangible assets**

Registration rights and agents' fees

The relevant standard here is IAS 38 *Intangible assets.* An **intangible asset may be recognised** if it gives control (the power to benefit from the asset), if it meets the identifiability criteria in IAS 38, if it is probable that future economic benefits attributable to the asset will flow to the entity and if its fair value can be measured reliably. For an intangible asset to be identifiable the asset must be separable or it must arise from contractual or other legal rights. It appears that these **criteria have been met**:

(i)   The registration rights are contractual.

(ii)   Scramble has control, because it may transfer or extend the rights.

(iii)   Economic benefits will flow to Scramble in the form of income it can earn when fans come to see the player play.

IAS 38 specifies the items that make up the **cost** of separately acquired assets:

(i)   Its purchase price, including import duties and non-refundable purchase taxes, after deducting trade discounts and rebates, and

(ii)   Any directly attributable cost of preparing the asset for its intended use

IAS 38 specifically mentions, as an example of directly attributable costs, 'professional fees arising directly from bringing the asset to its working condition'. In this business, **the players' registration rights meet the definition of intangible assets**. In addition, **Scramble is incorrect** in believing that the **agents' fees** paid on extension of players' contracts do not meet the criteria to be recognised as intangible assets. The fees are incurred to service the player registration rights, and **should therefore be treated as intangible assets.**

Rights to revenue from ticket sales

Whether Rashing can show these rights as intangible assets depends on whether the IAS 38 criteria have been met. Since Rashing has no discretion over the pricing of the tickets and cannot sell them, it cannot be said to control the asset. Accordingly, the rights **cannot be treated as an intangible asset.**

The entity is only entitled to cash generated from ticket sales, so the issue is one of a **contractual right to receive cash.** The applicable standard is therefore not IAS 38 but IFRS 9 *Financial instruments,* under which the rights to ticket revenue represent a **financial asset.**

IFRS 9 has two classifications for financial assets: amortised cost and fair value. Financial assets are classified as being at **amortised cost** if **both** of the following apply.

(i)   The asset is held within a business model whose objective is to hold the assets to collect the contractual cash flows.

(ii)   The contractual terms of the financial asset give rise, on specified dates, to cash flows that are solely payments of principal and interest on the principal outstanding.

All other financial assets are measured at fair value.

Rashing's receipts are regular cash flows, but they are based on ticket revenues, which are determined by match attendance. Therefore they are not solely payments of principal and interest, and **do not meet the criteria for classification at amortised cost.** Consequently, the financial asset should be classified as being **at fair value** under IFRS 9.

9 Preparation question: Defined benefit plan

Statement of profit or loss and other comprehensive income notes

Defined benefit expense recognised in profit or loss

	$m
Current service cost	11
Past service cost	10
Net interest on the net defined benefit asset $(10\% \times (110 + 10)) - (10\% \times 150)$	(3)
	18

Other comprehensive income (items that will not be reclassified to profit or loss)
Remeasurement of defined benefit plans

	$m
Actuarial gain on defined benefit obligation	17
Return on plan assets (excluding amounts in net interest)	(22)
	(5)

Statement of financial position notes

Net defined benefit asset recognised in the statement of financial position

	31 December 20X1 $m	31 December 20X0 $m
Present value of pension obligation	116	110
Fair value of plan assets	(140)	(150)
Net asset	(24)	(40)

Changes in the present value of the defined benefit obligation

	$m
Opening defined benefit obligation	110
Interest on obligation (10% × (110 + 10))	12
Current service cost	11
Past service cost	10
Benefits paid	(10)
Gain on remeasurement through OCI (balancing figure)	(17)
Closing defined benefit obligation	116

Changes in the fair value of plan assets

	$m
Opening fair value of plan assets	150
Interest on plan assets (10% × 150)	15
Contributions	7
Benefits paid	(10)
Loss on remeasurement through OCI (balancing figure)	(22)
Closing fair value of plan assets	140

10 Macaljoy

Text reference. Pensions are covered in Chapter 5; provisions in Chapter 9.

Top tips. Part (a)(i) is very straightforward, but make sure you relate your answer to the pension schemes of Macaljoy. Similarly in Part (b)(i), you need to write specifically about warranty provisions, as well as more generally about provisions. Note that IAS 19 was revised in 2011. Actuarial gains and losses must now be recognised immediately in other comprehensive income (not reclassified to profit or loss).

Easy marks. Two marks are available for presentation and communication, and would be silly marks to lose. Plus there are marks for straightforward bookwork that you can get even if you don't get all the calculations right.

Examiner's comments. The question was quite well answered and candidates often produced good quality answers. The examiner was surprised to see that several candidates confused defined benefit and defined contribution schemes. Also at this level, it is important that candidates have an in depth knowledge of the differences between the two schemes rather than just a general view of the differences. Professional marks were awarded for the structure of the report and consideration of certain factors, that is:

(a) The intended purpose of the document
(b) Its intended users and their needs
(c) The appropriate type of document
(d) Logical and appropriate structure/format
(e) Nature of background information and technical language
(f) Detail required
(g) Clear, concise and precise presentation

Marking scheme

				Marks
(a)	Pensions	(i)	Explanation	7
		(ii)	Calculation	7
(b)	Provisions	(i)	Explanation	6
		(ii)	Calculation	3
Structure of report				2
Maximum				25

To: The Directors
        Macaljoy

Date: 1 November 20X7

Subject: **Pension plans and warranty claims**

The purpose of this report is to explain the difference between defined benefit and defined contribution pension plans, and to show the accounting treatment of Macaljoy's pension schemes. It also discusses the principles of accounting for warranty claims and shows the accounting treatment of Macaljoy's warranty claims.

(a)   (i)   **Defined contribution plans and defined benefit plans**

With **defined contribution** plans, the employer (and possibly, as here, current employees too) pay regular contributions into the plan of a given or 'defined' amount each year. The contributions are invested, and the size of the post-employment benefits paid to former employees depends on how well or how badly the plan's investments perform. If the investments perform well, the plan will be able to afford higher benefits than if the investments performed less well.

The B scheme is a defined contribution plan. The employer's liability is limited to the contributions paid.

With **defined benefit** plans, the size of the post-employment benefits is determined in advance, ie the benefits are 'defined'. The employer (and possibly, as here, current employees too) pay contributions into the plan, and the contributions are invested. The size of the contributions is set at an amount that is expected to earn enough investment returns to meet the obligation to pay the post-employment benefits. If, however, it becomes apparent that the assets in the fund are insufficient, the employer will be required to make additional contributions into the plan to make up the expected shortfall. On the other hand, if the fund's assets appear to be larger than they need to be, and in excess of what is required to pay the post-employment benefits, the employer may be allowed to take a 'contribution holiday' (ie stop paying in contributions for a while).

The **main difference** between the two types of plans lies in **who bears the risk**: if the employer bears the risk, even in a small way by guaranteeing or specifying the return, the plan is a defined benefit plan. A defined contribution scheme must give a benefit formula based solely on the amount of the contributions.

A defined benefit scheme may be created even if there is no legal obligation, if an employer has a practice of guaranteeing the benefits payable.

The A scheme is a defined benefit scheme. Macaljoy, the employer, guarantees a pension based on the service lives of the employees in the scheme. The company's liability is not limited to the amount of the contributions. This means that the employer bears the investment risk: if the return on the investment is not sufficient to meet the liabilities, the company will need to make good the difference.

(ii)   **Accounting treatment: B scheme**

No assets or liabilities will be recognised for this defined contribution scheme. The **contributions** paid by the company of $10m will be **charged to profit or loss**. The contributions paid by the employees will be part of the wages and salaries cost.

Accounting treatment: A scheme

The accounting treatment is as follows:

Statement of profit or loss and other comprehensive income notes

Expense recognised in profit or loss for the year ended 31 October 20X7

	$m
Current service cost	20.0
Net interest on the net defined benefit liability (10 – 9.5)	0.5
Net expense	20.5

Other comprehensive income: remeasurement of defined benefit plans (for the year ended 31 October 20X7)

	$m
Actuarial loss on defined benefit obligation	(29.0)
Return on plan assets (excluding amounts in net interest)	27.5
Net actuarial loss	(1.5)

STATEMENT OF FINANCIAL POSITION NOTES

Amounts recognised in statement of financial position

	31 October 20X7	1 November 20X6
	$m	$m
Present value of defined benefit obligation	240	200
Fair value of plan assets	(225)	(190)
Net liability	15	10

Change in the present value of the defined benefit obligation

	$m
Present value of obligation at 1 November 20X6	200
Interest on obligation: 5% × 200	10
Current service cost	20
Benefits paid	(19)
Loss on remeasurement through OCI (balancing figure)	29
Present value of obligation at 31 October 20X7	240

Change in the fair value of plan assets

	$m
Fair value of plan assets at 1 November 20X6	190.0
Interest on plan assets: 5% × 190	9.5
Contributions	17.0
Benefits paid	(19.0)
Gain on remeasurement through OCI (balancing figure)	27.5
Fair value of plan assets at 31 October 20X7	225.0

(b) Warranty provisions

(i) Principles

Under IAS 37 *Provisions, contingent liabilities and contingent assets,* provisions must be recognised in the following circumstances.

(1) There is a **legal** or **constructive obligation** to transfer benefits as a result of past events.

(2) It is probably that **an outflow of economic resources** will be required to **settle** the **obligation.**

(3) A **reasonable estimate** of the amount required to settle the obligation can be made.

If the company can **avoid expenditure by its future action, no provision** should be recognised. A legal or constructive obligation is one created by an **obligating event.** Constructive obligations arise when an entity is committed to certain expenditures because of a pattern of behaviour which the public would expect to continue.

IAS 37 states that the amount recognised should be the **best estimate of the expenditure required to settle the obligation at the end of the reporting period.** The estimate should **take the various possible outcomes into account** and should be the **amount that an entity would rationally pay** to settle the obligation at the reporting date or to transfer it to a third party. In the case of warranties, the provision will be made at a probability weighted expected value, taking into account the risks and uncertainties surrounding the underlying events.

The amount of the provision should be **discounted to present value** if the time value of money is material using a **risk adjusted rate.** If some or all of the expenditure is expected to be **reimbursed** by a third party, the reimbursement should be **recognised as a separate asset,** but only if it is virtually certain that the reimbursement will be received.

(ii) **Accounting treatment**

In Macaljoy's case, the past event giving rise to the obligation is the sale of the product with a warranty. A provision for the warranty will be made as follows:

	$
Re year 1 warranty	280,000
Re year 2 warranty	350,000
	630,000

If material, the provisions may be discounted:

	$
Re year 1 warranty	269,000
Re year 2 warranty	323,000
	592,000

Calculations are shown below.

Macaljoy may be able to **recognise the asset and income from the insurance claim,** but only if the insurance company has validated the claim and **receipt is virtually certain**. In general contingent assets are not recognised, but disclosed if an inflow of economic benefits is probable.

Calculations

Year 1: warranty

	Expected value	Discounted expected value (4%)
	$'000	$'000
80% × Nil	0	
15% × 7,000 × $100	105	
5% × 7,000 × $500	175	
	280	$280,000/1.04 = $269,000*

Year 2: extended warranty

	Expected value	Discounted expected value (4%)
	$'000	$'000
70% × Nil	0	
20% × 5,000 × $100	100	
10% × 5,000 × $500	250	
	350	$350,000/(1.04)^2 = $323,000*

* Note. These figures are rounded

11 Savage

(a)   STATEMENT OF PROFIT OR LOSS AND OTHER COMPREHENSIVE INCOME NOTES

Expense recognised in profit or loss for the year ended 31 October 20X5

	$m
Current service cost	40
Net interest on the net defined benefit liability (188 – 174)	14
Past service cost	125
	179

Other comprehensive income: remeasurement of defined benefit plans (for the year ended 31 October 20X5)

	$m
Actuarial loss on defined benefit obligation	(64)
Return on plan assets (excluding amounts in net interest)	110
	46

STATEMENT OF FINANCIAL POSITION NOTE

Amounts recognised in the statement of financial position

	31 October 20X5	31 October 20X4
	$m	$m
Present value of defined benefit obligation	3,375	3,000
Less fair value of plan assets (3,170 – 8)	(3,162)	(2,900)
Net liability	213	100

Changes in the present value of the defined benefit obligation

	$m
Present value of obligation at 1 November 20X4	3,000
Past service cost	125
Interest cost (6% × (3,000 + 125))	188
Current service cost	40
Benefits paid	(42)
Loss on remeasurement through OCI (balancing figure)	64
Present value of obligation at 31 October 20X5	3,375

Note: the past service costs of $125 million are recognised immediately in profit or loss in accordance with IAS 19. They are also included in opening scheme liabilities for the purpose of calculating interest.

Changes in the fair value of plan assets

	$m
Fair value of plan assets at 1 November 20X4	2,900
Interest on plan assets (6% × 2,900)	174
Contributions	20
Benefits paid	(42)
Gain on remeasurement through OCI (balancing figure)	110
Fair value of plan assets at 31 October 20X4 (3,170 – 8)	3,162

(b)   At 31 October 20X5, contributions of $8 million remain unpaid. IAS 19 *Employee benefits* states that **plan assets do not include unpaid contributions**. However, contributions payable of $8 million should be disclosed in the notes to the accounts of Savage at 31 October 20X5. This amount is payable to the Trustees.

IAS 19 also states that where there are changes to a defined benefit plan, **past service costs** should be **recognised immediately in profit or loss**. Therefore past service costs of $125 million should be recognised in profit or loss for the year ended 31 October 20X5.

12 Smith

(a)   (i)   **Problems with the previous version of IAS 19**

An entity's defined benefit pension scheme can be a significant net asset or liability. The size of some schemes, together with the complexity of the accounting, meant that IAS 19 *Employee benefits* (prior to its revision in June 2011) came **in for criticism**.

One area that was particularly problematic was the **treatment of actuarial gains and losses**. The old IAS 19 treatment did not provide clear, full and understandable information to users. Specifically, IAS 19 gave a number of options for recognition of actuarial gains and losses: immediate recognition through profit or loss, immediate recognition through other comprehensive income and delaying recognition using the so-called 'corridor method'. This element of choice meant that the figures in the statement of financial position (and profit or loss for the year) were misleading.

The **main problems with the deferred recognition** model were:

(1)   It was **inconsistent** the treatment of other assets and liabilities.

(2)   It meant that the employer was **not matching** the cost of providing post-employment benefits (as represented by the changes in plan assets and benefit obligations) to the periods in which those changes take place.

(3)   The accounting was **complex** and required complex records to be kept.

(4)   The statement of financial position figure could be **misleading**, for example, the plan might be in surplus and a liability shown in the financial statements or the plan might be in deficit with an asset shown.

(ii) **Immediate recognition** has the following **advantages**:

(1) By eliminating the options it **improves consistency** and comparability between accounting periods between different entities.

(2) It gives a more **faithful representation** of the entity's financial position. A surplus in the pension plan will result in an asset being recognised and a deficit in a liability being recognised.

(3) The financial statements are **easier to understand** and more transparent than if deferred recognition is used.

(4) The income and expense recognised in profit or loss (or in other comprehensive income) **correspond** to changes in the fair value of the plan assets or the defined benefit obligation.

(5) It is **consistent with the IASB** *Conceptual Framework for Financial Reporting*, which requires that 'the effects of transactions and other events are recognised when they occur ... and recorded ... and reported in the financial statements of the periods to which they relate.

(6) It is **consistent with IAS 8** *Accounting policies, changes in accounting estimates and errors* (changes in estimates must be included in the period in which the assets and liabilities change as a result) **and IAS 37** *Provisions, contingent liabilities and contingent assets* (changes in long term liabilities must be recognised in the period in which they occur).

(iii) **Other changes to IAS 19**

(1) **Remeasurements.** The revised standard introduced the term **'remeasurements'**. This is made up of the actuarial gains and losses on the defined benefit obligation, the difference between actual investment returns and the return implied by the net interest cost and the effect of the asset ceiling. Remeasurements are recognised immediately in other comprehensive income and **not** reclassified to profit or loss. This reduces diversity of presentation that was possible under the previous version of the standard.

(2) **Net interest cost.** The revised standard requires interest to be calculated on **both** the plan assets and plan obligation at the same rate and the **net** interest to be recognised in the profit or loss. The rationale for this is the view that the **net** defined benefit liability/(asset) is equivalent to an amount owed by the company to the plan (or vice versa). The difference under the previous version of the standard was that an 'Expected return on assets' was calculated, based on assumptions about the long term rates of return on the particular classes of asset held within the plan.

(3) **Past service costs.** The revised standard requires all past service costs to be recognised in the period of plan amendment. The previous standard made a distinction between past service costs that were **vested** (all past service costs relating to former employees and those relating to current employees that were not subject to any condition relating to further service) and those that were **not vested** (relating to current employees and where the entitlement was subject to further service). Only **vested** past service costs were recognised in profit or loss, and unvested benefits were deferred, and spread over remaining service lives.

(iv) **Likely consequences of the revision to IAS 19**

(1) **Increased comparability but increased volatility.** The new rules on recognition of gains and losses will increase comparability and bring increased transparency to the statement of financial position. However, companies that have the corridor approach may find that the new rules bring increased volatility to the statement of profit or loss and other comprehensive income.

(2) **Pension funds invested differently.** The removal of the corridor method may result in changes in the way in which pension fund assets are invested. Pension companies have been able to take risks by investing in equities in the knowledge that gains and losses could be smoothed over the working lives of employees if the reporting entity chose to do so. Now that this option is no longer available, they may choose to invest in bonds, which are more stable.

(3) **Expenses will be more visible.** Under the previous version of the standard, the cost of running post-employment plans was accounted for either as a reduction to the expected return on plan assets or reserved for as an addition to the present value of the liabilities. Under the revised IAS 19, expenses will be split into those relating to the management of plan assets (charged to other comprehensive income) and those relating to the administration of the scheme (charged to profit or loss).

(4) More extensive disclosures will be required particularly relating to risk.

(5) **Change to the type of assets invested in because of the requirement to use the discount rate as for liabilities.** The replacement of the expected return on plan assets with an interest credit based on the discount rate will affect all companies, as the nature of the assets held in the scheme's investment portfolio will no longer influence the credit to the profit and loss account. This may lead to a reduction in investment risk as companies move to asset classes which tend to provide more stable returns and provide a better correlation with the scheme's liabilities, albeit at a higher expected long-term cost.

(b) **Gains or loss on plan assets**

	$
Fair value of plan assets at 1.1.20X2	2,600
Interest on plan assets (8% × $2,600,000)	208
Contributions	730
Benefits paid	(240)
Gain on remeasurement through OCI (balancing figure)	102
Fair value of plan assets at 31.12.20X2	3,400

Gains or loss on obligation

	$'000
Present value of obligation at 1.1.20X2	2,900
Current service cost	450
Past service cost	90
Interest cost (8% × $2,900,000)	232
Benefits paid	(240)
Loss on remeasurement through OCI (balancing figure)	68
Present value of obligation at 31.12.20X2	3,500

The net gain on remeasurement that will be recognised in other comprehensive income is $34,000 ($102,000 - $68,000).

13 Cohort

Text reference. Taxation is in Chapter 6 of the text.

Top tips. This question required a knowledge of deferred tax (IAS 12). The question focused on the key areas of the Standard and required an understanding of those areas. It did not require detailed computational knowledge but the ability to take a brief outline scenario and advise the client accordingly. Rote knowledge would be of little use in this situation.

Examiner's comment. Some candidates scored quite well on the question but again guessing at the answer was a fruitless exercise. The key areas were intragroup profit in inventory, unremitted earnings of subsidiaries, revaluation of securities, general provisions and tax losses. Basically an appreciation was required of how to deal with each of these areas but unfortunately most candidates struggled to deal with the issues involved.

		Marks
Air	– acquisition	5
	– intra group profit	3
	– unremitted earnings	3
Legion	– long term investments	4
	– loan provision	4
	– deferred tax asset	4
	Maximum	23

Acquisition of the subsidiaries – general

Fair value adjustments have been made for consolidation purposes in both cases and these will **affect the deferred tax charge for the year**. This is because the deferred tax position is viewed **from the perspective of the group** as a whole. For example, it may be possible to recognise deferred tax assets which previously could not be recognised by individual companies, because there are now sufficient tax profits available within the group to utilise unused tax losses. Therefore a **provision** should be made for **temporary differences between fair values of the identifiable net assets acquired and their carrying values** ($4 million less $3.5 million in respect of Air). **No provision should be made for the temporary difference** of $1 million **arising on goodwill** recognised as a result of the combination with Air.

Future listing

Cohort plans to seek a listing in three years time. Therefore it will become a **public company** and will be subject to a **higher rate of tax**. IAS 12 states that deferred tax should be measured at the **average tax rates expected to apply in the periods in which the timing differences are expected to reverse**, based on current enacted tax rates and laws. This means that Cohort may be paying tax at the higher rate when some of its timing differences reverse and this should be taken into account in the calculation.

Acquisition of Air

(a)   The intra-group transaction has resulted in an **unrealised profit** of $0.6 million in the group accounts and this will be **eliminated on consolidation**. The tax charge in group profit or loss includes the tax on this profit, for which **the group will not become liable to tax until the following period. From the perspective of the group, there is a temporary difference.** Because the temporary difference arises in the financial statements of Cohort, **deferred tax should be provided** on this difference (an asset) using the rate of tax payable by Cohort.

(b)   **Deferred tax should be recognised on the unremitted earnings of subsidiaries** unless the parent is able to **control the timing of dividend payments** and it is **unlikely that dividends will be paid for the foreseeable future**. Cohort controls the dividend policy of Air and this means that there would normally be no need to make a provision in respect of unremitted profits. However, the profits of Air **will be distributed** to Cohort over the next few years and **tax will be payable** on the dividends received. Therefore a **deferred tax liability should be shown**.

Acquisition of Legion

(a)   A **temporary difference arises** where non-monetary assets are **revalued upwards** and the **tax treatment of the surplus is different from the accounting treatment**. In this case, the revaluation surplus has been **recognised in profit or loss** for the current period, rather than in equity but no corresponding adjustment has been made to the tax base of the investments because the gains will be taxed in future periods. Therefore the company **should recognise a deferred tax liability on the temporary difference of $4 million**.

(b)   A temporary difference arises when the provision for the loss on the loan portfolio is first recognised. The general allowance is expected to increase and therefore it is unlikely that the temporary difference will reverse in the near future. However, a **deferred tax liability should still be recognised**. The temporary difference gives rise to a **deferred tax asset**. IAS 12 states that **deferred tax assets should not be recognised unless it is probable that taxable profits will be available** against which the taxable profits can be utilised. **This is affected by the situation in point (c) below**.

(c)   In theory, unused tax losses give rise to a deferred tax asset. However, IAS 12 states that **deferred tax assets should only be recognised to the extent that they are regarded as recoverable**. They should be regarded as recoverable to the extent that on the basis of all the evidence available it is **probable that there will be suitable taxable profits against which the losses can be recovered**. The future taxable profit of Legion **will not be sufficient to realise all the unused tax loss. Therefore the deferred tax asset is reduced to the amount that is expected to be recovered**.

This reduction in the deferred tax asset implies that it was **overstated at 1 June 20X1**, when it was acquired by the group. As these are the first post-acquisition financial statements, **goodwill should also be adjusted**.

14 Panel

> **Text reference.** Tax is covered in Chapter 6 of the text.
>
> **Top tips.** This is a single topic question, which is a departure from the examiner's usual mixed standard question. The IFRS 1 aspects are likely to become less frequent over time.
>
> **Easy marks.** Part (b) (iii) and (iv) are easier than (i) and (ii), though they carry the same number of marks.
>
> **Examiner's comment.** Part (a) was quite well answered albeit often in a very general way. Part (b) was answered far better than when this area was tested in June 2005. The other three areas were a leasing transaction, an inter company sale and an impairment of property plant and equipment. These elements of the question were quite well answered although the discussion of the topic areas was generally quite poor whilst the computations were quite good. Deferred tax is a key area and must be understood.

(a)   (i)   **The impact of changes in accounting standards**

IAS 12 *Income taxes* is based on the idea that all **changes in assets and liabilities** have unavoidable **tax consequences**. Where the recognition criteria in IFRS are different from those in tax law, the **carrying amount of an asset or liability in the financial statements is different from the amount at which it is stated for tax purposes (its 'tax base')**. These differences are known as **'temporary differences'**. The practical effect of these differences is that a transaction or event occurs in a different accounting period from its tax consequences. For example, income from interest receivable is recognised in the financial statements in one accounting period but it is only taxable when it is actually received in the following accounting period.

IAS 12 requires a company to make **full provision** for the tax effects of temporary differences. Where a change in an accounting standard results in a change to the carrying value of an asset or liability in the financial statements, the **amount of the temporary difference** between the carrying value and the tax base **also changes**. Therefore the amount of the deferred tax liability is affected.

(ii)   **Calculation of deferred tax on first time adoption of IFRS**

IFRS 1 *First time adoption of International Financial Reporting Standards* requires a company to **prepare an opening IFRS statement of financial position** and to **apply IAS 12 to temporary differences** between the carrying amounts of assets and liabilities and their tax bases at that date. Panel prepares its opening IFRS statement of financial position sheet **at 1 November 20X3**. The carrying values of its assets and liabilities are **measured in accordance with IFRS 1** and other **applicable IFRSs** in force at 31 October 20X5. The deferred tax provision is based on **tax rates that have been enacted or substantially enacted by the end of the reporting period**. Any **adjustments** to the deferred tax liability under previous GAAP are **recognised directly in equity (retained earnings)**.

(b) (i) **Share options**

Under IFRS 2 *Share based payment* the company **recognises an expense** for the employee services received in return for the share options granted over the vesting period. The related tax deduction **does not arise until the share options are exercised**. Therefore a **deferred tax asset arises**, based on the difference between the intrinsic value of the options and their carrying amount (normally zero).

At 31 October 20X4 the tax benefit is as follows:

	$m
Carrying amount of share based payment	–
Less: tax base of share based payment (16 ÷ 2)	(8)
Temporary difference	(8)

The **deferred tax asset is $2.4 million** (30% × 8). This is recognised at 31 October 20X4 provided that taxable profit is available against which it can be utilised. Because the tax effect of the remuneration expense is greater than the tax benefit, the tax benefit is **recognised in profit or loss.** (The tax effect of the remuneration expense is 30% × $40 million ÷ 2 = $6 million.)

At 31 October 20X5 there is **no longer a deferred tax asset** because the options have been exercised. The **tax benefit receivable is $13.8 million** (30% × $46 million). Therefore the deferred tax asset of $2.4 million is no longer required.

(ii) **Leased plant**

An asset leased under a finance lease is **recognised as an asset** owned by the company and the **related obligation** to pay lease rentals is **recognised as a liability**. Each instalment payable is treated partly as interest and partly as repayment of the liability. The **carrying amount** of the plant for accounting purposes is the **net present value of the lease payments less depreciation**.

A **temporary difference** effectively arises between the value of the plant for accounting purposes and the equivalent of the outstanding obligations, as the annual rental payments quality for the relief. The tax base of the asset is the amount deductable for tax in future, which is zero. The tax base of the liability is the carrying amount less any future tax deductible amounts, which will give a **tax base of zero.**

Therefore at 31 October 20X5 a **net temporary difference** will be as follows:

	$m	$m
Carrying value in financial statements:		
Asset:		
Net present value of future lease payments at inception of lease	12	
Less depreciation (12 ÷ 5)	(2.4)	
		9.60
Less finance lease liability		
Liability at inception of lease	12.00	
Interest (8% × 12)	0.96	
Lease rental	(3.00)	
		(9.96)
		0.36
Less tax base		(0.00)
Temporary difference		0.36

A **deferred tax asset of $108,000** (30% × 360,000) arises.

(iii) **Intra-group sale**

Pins has **made a profit of $2 million** on its sale to Panel. Tax is **payable on the profits of individual companies**. Pins is liable for tax on this profit in the current year and will have provided for the related tax in its individual financial statements. However, **from the viewpoint of the group** the profit **will not be realised until the following year**, when the goods are sold to a third party and must be **eliminated** from the consolidated financial statements. Because the group **pays tax before the profit is realised** there is a **temporary difference of $2 million** and a **deferred tax asset of $600,000** (30% × $2 million).

(iv)   **Impairment loss**

The impairment loss in the financial statements of Nails **reduces the carrying value** of property, plant and equipment, but is **not allowable for tax**. Therefore the **tax base** of the property, plant and equipment **is different from its carrying value** and there is a **temporary difference**.

Under IAS 36 *Impairment of assets* the impairment loss is allocated first to goodwill and then to other assets:

	Goodwill $m	Property, plant and equipment $m	Total $m
Carrying value at 31 October 20X5	1	6.0	7.0
Impairment loss	(1)	(0.8)	(1.8)
	–	5.2	5.2

IAS 12 states that **no deferred tax should be recognised on goodwill** and therefore **only the impairment loss relating to the property, plant and equipment affects the deferred tax position**.

The effect of the impairment loss is as follows:

	Before impairment $m	After impairment $m	Difference $m
Carrying value	6	5.2	
Tax base	(4)	(4)	
Temporary difference	2	1.2	0.8
Tax liability (30%)	0.6	0.36	0.24

Therefore the impairment loss reduces deferred the tax liability by $240,000.

15 Kesare

Text reference. Covered in Chapter 6 of the text.

Top tips. To state the obvious, this is a question best avoided unless you like deferred tax. However, if you do, or if you dislike other topics more, the question may be broken down into components where you can get a foothold. Layout is important to avoid getting muddled.

Easy marks. For those not fond of high speed number-crunching, there are some fairly easy marks in Part (a) available for a general discussion about concepts and the framework. In addition there are some easy marks for adjustments to the financial statements, most of which do not relate to the deferred tax aspects. In generally, however, this is not a question that lends itself to easy marks.

Marking scheme

			Marks
(a)	Quality of discussion		2
	Conceptual Framework		1
	Temporary difference		2
	Liability		1
	Weakness		1
			7
(b)	Adjustments:	Investment in equity instruments	2
		Convertible bond	2
		Defined benefit plan	2
		Property, plant and equipment	1
	Deferred tax:	Goodwill	1
		Other intangibles	1

		1
Financial assets		1
Trade receivables		1
Other receivables		1
Long-term borrowings		1
Employee benefits		1
Trade payables		1
Calculation		3
	Maximum	18
	Available	25
Professional communication		2

(a) IAS 12 *Income taxes* is based on the idea that **all changes in assets and liabilities** have **unavoidable tax consequences.** Where the recognition criteria in IFRS are different from those in tax law, **the carrying amount of an asset or liability in the financial statements is different from its tax base** (the amount at which it is stated for tax purposes). These differences are known as **temporary differences.** The practical effect of these differences is that a transaction or event occurs in a different accounting period from its tax consequences. For example, depreciation is recognised in the financial statements in different accounting periods from capital allowances.

IAS 12 requires a company to make **full provision** for the tax effects of temporary differences. Both **deferred tax assets,** and **deferred tax liabilities** can arise in this way.

It may be argued that deferred tax assets and liabilities **do not meet the definition of assets and liabilities** in the IASB *Conceptual Framework for Financial Reporting.* Under the *Conceptual Framework* an asset is the right to receive economic benefits as a result of past events, and a liability is an obligation to transfer economic benefits, again as a result of past events.

Under IAS 12, the tax effect of transactions are recognised in the same period as the transactions themselves, but in practice, tax is paid in accordance with tax legislation when it becomes a legal liability. There is a **conceptual weakness** or inconsistency, in that only one liability, that is tax, is being provided for, and not other costs, such as overhead costs.

(b)

	$'000	Adjustments to financial statements $'000	Adjusted financial statements $'000	Tax base $'000	Temporary difference $'000
Property, plant and equipment	10,000		10,000	2,400	7,600
Goodwill	6,000		6,000	6,000	
Other intangible assets	5,000		5,000	0	5,000
Financial assets (cost)	9,000	1,500	10,500	9,000	1,500
Total non-current assets	30,000		31,500		
Trade receivables	7,000		7,000	7,500	(500)
Other receivables	4,600		4,600	5,000	(400)
Cash and cash-equivalents	6,700		6,700	6,700	–
Total current assets	18,300		18,300		
Total assets	48,300		49,800		
Share capital	(9,000)		(9,000)		
Other reserves	(4,500)	(1,500) (400)	(6,400)		
Retained earnings	(9,130)	520	(8,610)		
Total equity	(22,630)		(24,010)		
Long term borrowings	(10,000)	400	(9,600)	(10,000)	400
Deferred tax liability	(3,600)		(3,600)	(3,600)	–

	$'000	Adjustments to financial statements $'000	Adjusted financial statements $'000	Tax base $'000	Temporary difference $'000
Employee benefits	(4,000)	(520)	(4,520)	(5,000)	480
Current tax liability	(3,070)		(3,070)	(3,070)	–
Trade and other payables	(5,000)		(5,000)	(4,000)	(1,000)
Total liabilities	(25,670)		(25,790)		13,080
Total equity and liabilities	48,300		49,800		

					$'000
Deferred tax liability					
Liability b/fwd (per draft SOFP)					3,600
Charge: OCI ($1,500 × 30%					
(note (i))				450	
P/L (bal. fig)				(126)	
					324
Deferred tax liability c/fwd	14,980 × 30%			4,494	
Deferred tax asset – c/fwd	1,900 × 30%			(570)	
Net deferred tax liability	13,080 × 30%				3,924

Notes on adjustments

(i)   The investments in equity instruments are shown at cost. However, per IFRS 9, they should instead be valued at fair value, with the increase ($10,500 – $9,000 = $1,500) going to other comprehensive income (items that will not be reclassified to profit or loss) as per the irrevocable election.

(ii)   IAS 32 states that convertible bonds must be split into debt and equity components. This involves reducing debt and increasing equity by $400.

(iii)   The defined benefit plan needs to be adjusted to reflect the change. The liability must be increased by $520,000. The same amount is charged to retained earnings.

(iv)   The development costs have already been allowed for tax, so the tax base is nil. No deferred tax is recognised on goodwill.

(v)   The accrual for compensation is to be allowed when paid, ie in a later period. The tax base relating to trade and other payables should be reduced by $1m.

16 Preparation question: Financial instruments

(a)   STATEMENT OF PROFIT OR LOSS AND OTHER COMPREHENSIVE INCOME

	$
Finance income	
(441,014 × (W1) 8%)	35,281

STATEMENT OF FINANCIAL POSITION

Non-current assets	
Financial asset (441,014 + 35,281)	476,295

Working: Effective interest rate

$$\frac{600,000}{441,014} = 1.3605 \therefore \text{from tables interest rate is 8\%}$$

(b) **Compound instrument**

Presentation

	$
Non-current liabilities	
Financial liability component of convertible bond (Working)	1,797,467
Equity	
Equity component of convertible bond (2,000,000 − (Working) 1,797,467)	202,533

Working

	$
Fair value of equivalent non-convertible debt	
Present value of principal payable at end of 3 years	1,544,367

$$(4{,}000 \times \$500 = \$2m \times \frac{1}{(1.09)^3})$$

Present value of interest annuity payable annually in arrears
for 3 years [(5% × $2m) × 2.531]

	253,100
	1,797,467

17 Complexity

Text reference. Financial instruments are covered in Chapter 7 of the BPP Study Text.

Top tips. A regular topic – financial instruments – is examined in a current issues context. Recently the examiner has started to insert a calculation element into his current issues question. On past form, the calculations have not been difficult, but have served to illustrate the impact of a change or proposed change. The 2008 Discussion Paper is not specifically examinable, and some of its arguments have been addressed by IFRS 9. However, IFRS 9 is a work-in-progress, and many of the problems have not yet been solved.

Easy marks. The calculation is a good source of easy marks as it is straightforward. And there are marks for bookwork – listing the problems of complexity and advantages of fair value.

Examiner's comments. This question was quite well answered. In part (a) candidates were asked to discuss the measurement issues relating to financial instruments and how these issues would be alleviated if fair value were used for all financial instruments. However, many candidates simply quoted the measurement rules relating to financial instruments without setting out how these rules created confusion and complexity for users. Some simply set out the advantages and disadvantages of fair value accounting rather than discussing how the use of fair value might result in less complexity in financial statements. The calculations in part (b) of the question were quite well done although very few candidates saw that the although redemption amounts were the same, the carrying amounts were quite different.

Marking scheme

			Marks
(a)	(i)	1 mark per point up to maximum	9
	(ii)	1 mark per point up to maximum	9
		Professional marks	2
(b)		Identical payment	2
		Carrying amount	1
		Fair value	2
			25

(a) (i) Many users and preparers of accounts have found financial instruments to be **complex**. There are a number of reasons for this complexity and resulting confusion, many of which were covered in a Discussion Paper, *Reducing Complexity in Reporting Financial Instruments*, issued by the IASB in 2008.

The main reason for complexity in accounting for financial instruments is the **many different ways in which they can be measured**. The measurement method depends on:

(1) The **applicable financial reporting standard.** A variety of IFRS and IAS apply to the measurement of financial instruments. For example, financial assets may be measured using consolidation for subsidiaries (IFRS 10), the equity method for associates and joint ventures (IAS 28 and IFRS 11) or IFRS 9 for most other financial assets. Currently the situation is made more complicated by the fact that IAS 39 still applies to hedging and impairment.

(2) The **categorisation of the financial instrument**. IAS 39 *Financial instruments: recognition and measurement* had four categories: fair value through profit or loss, available for sale financial assets, loans and receivables and held to maturity.

However, IFRS 9 simplifies these categories so that financial assets are classified as measured at **either amortised cost or fair value**. A financial asset may only be classified as measured at amortised cost if the object of the business model in which it is held is to collect contracted cash flows and its contractual terms give rise on specified dates to cash flows that are solely payments of principal and interest.

(3) Whether **hedge accounting** has been applied. Hedge accounting is **complex**, for example when cash flow hedge accounting is used, gains and losses may be split between profit or loss for the year and other comprehensive income (items that may subsequently be reclassified to profit or loss). In addition, there may be mismatches when hedge accounting applies reflecting the underlying mismatches under the non-hedging rules.

Some measurement methods use an estimate of **current value, and others use historical cost.** Some include impairment losses, others do not.

The different measurement methods for financial instruments creates a number of **problems for preparers and users** of accounts:

(1) The treatment of a particular instrument **may not be the best**, but may be determined by other factors.

(2) Gains or losses resulting from different measurement methods may be combined in the same line item in the statement of profit or loss and other comprehensive income. **Comparability** is therefore compromised.

(3) Comparability is also affected when it is **not clear** what measurement method has been used.

(4) It is **difficult to apply the criteria** for deciding which instrument is to be measured in which way. As new types of instruments are created, the criteria may be applied in ways that are not consistent.

(ii) There is pressure to reduce complexity in accounting for financial instruments. One idea, put forward in the 2008 Discussion Paper, is that **fair value is the only measure that is appropriate for all types of financial instruments**, and that a full fair value model would be much simpler to apply than the current mixed model. A single measurement method would, it is argued:

(1) Significantly **reduce complexity in classification**. There would be no need to classify financial instruments into the four categories of fair value through profit or loss, available for sale financial assets, loans and receivables and held to maturity. This simplification has already been achieved by IFRS 9.

(2) **Reduce complexity in accounting**. There would be no need to account for transfers between the above categories, or to report how impairment losses have been quantified.

(3) **Eliminated measurement mismatches** between financial instruments and reduce the need for fair value hedge accounting.

(4) Eliminate the need to identify and separate **embedded derivatives.**

(5) **Better reflect the cash flows** that would be paid if liabilities were transferred at the re-measurement date.

(6) Make reported information **easier to understand**

(7) **Improve the comparability** of reported information between entities and between periods

However, while fair value has some obvious advantages, it has problems too. **Uncertainty** may be an issue for the following reasons

(1) Markets are not all liquid and transparent.

(2) Many assets and liabilities do not have an active market, and methods for estimating their value are more subjective.

(3) Management must exercise judgement in the valuation process, and may not be entirely objective in doing so.

(4) Because fair value, in the absence of an active market, represents an estimate, additional disclosures are needed to explain and justify the estimates. These disclosures may themselves be subjective.

(5) Independent verification of fair value estimates is difficult for all the above reasons.

(b) Different valuation methods bring comparability problems, as indicated in Part (a), and this can be seen with the examples in this part of the question.

Amortised cost

Using amortised cost, both the initial loan and the new loan result in **single payments that are almost identical** on 30 November 20X9:

Initial loan: $47m × 1.05 for 5 years = $59.98m

New loan: $45m × 1.074 for 4 years = $59.89m

However, the **carrying amounts at 30 November 20X5 will be different:**

Initial loan: $47m + ($47m × 5%) = $49.35m

New loan: $45m

Fair value

If the two loans were carried at fair value, both **the initial loan and the new loan would have the same value,** and be carried at $45m. There would be a net profit of $2m, made up of the interest expense of $47m × 5% = $2.35m and the unrealised gain of $49.35m - $45m = $4.35m.

Arguably, since the obligation on 30 November 20X9 will be the same for both loans, fair value is a more appropriate measure than amortised cost.

18 Ambush

Text reference. Financial instruments are covered in Chapter 7 of your text.

Top tips. As far as impairment is concerned, IAS 39 still applies.

Easy marks. These are available for the discursive aspects, which are most of the question.

(a) (i) **Impairment of financial assets**

IAS 39 states that **at each reporting date**, an entity should **assess** whether there is any **objective evidence that a financial asset or group of assets measured at amortised cost is impaired. Indications** of impairment include **significant financial difficulty** of the issuer; the probability that the borrower will **enter bankruptcy**; or a **default** in interest or principal payments.

Where there is objective evidence of impairment, the entity should **determine the amount** of any impairment loss, which should be **recognised immediately in profit or loss**. Only losses relating to **past events** can be recognised. **Two conditions** must be met before an impairment loss is recognised:

- There is **objective evidence** of impairment as a result of one or more events that **occurred after the initial recognition** of the asset; and
- The **impact on the estimated future cash flows** of the asset can be **reliably estimated**.

For financial assets **carried at amortised cost** the impairment loss is the **difference** between the asset's **carrying amount** and its **recoverable amount**. The asset's recoverable amount is the **present value of estimated future cash flows**, discounted at the financial instrument's **original** effective interest rate.

Assets at **fair value** are **not subject to impairment testing**, because **changes in fair value are automatically recognised immediately** in profit or loss (or other comprehensive income for investments in equity instruments where the election was made to report all gains and losses in other comprehensive income).

(ii) **Loan to Bromwich**

The **financial difficulties** and **reorganisation** of Bromwich are **objective evidence of impairment**. The impairment loss is the **difference** between the **carrying amount** of the loan at 30 November 20X5 and the **present value of the estimated future cash flows**, $100,000 on 30 November 20X7, discounted at the **original effective interest rate of 8%**.

This is **$85,730** (100,000 × 0.8573). Therefore **the impairment loss is $114,270** (200,000 – 85,730) and this is **recognised immediately in profit or loss**.

(b) **Trade receivables**

IFRS 9 *Financial instruments* classifies trade receivables as **financial assets at amortised cost**. This classification is made on the basis of both:

(i) The **entity's business model** for managing the financial assets, and

(ii) The **contractual cash flow** characteristics of the financial asset.

A financial asset is classified as measured at amortised cost where:

(i) The objective of the business model within which the asset is held is to hold assets in order to collect contractual cash flows and

(ii) The contractual terms of the financial asset give rise on specified dates to cash flows that are solely payments of principal and interest on the principal outstanding.

IFRS 9 requires that loans and receivables should be **measured at amortised cost using the effective interest rate method.** This method, which spreads the interest income over the life of the financial asset, may not seem appropriate for short-term trade receivables with no stated interest rate, as they do not normally bring in any interest income. IFRS 9 allows such receivables to be measured at the **original invoiced amount**, if the effect of **discounting is not material**.

As with other financial assets, however, IAS 39 requires an **annual impairment test**, in order to assess, at each reporting date, whether the receivable is impaired. (Note that IAS 39 applies to impairment as IFRS 9 does not yet cover this.) The carrying value of the trade receivable must be compared with the present value of the estimated future cash flows. For other assets, the cash flows would be discounted at the effective interest rate, but this is not normally required for trade receivables. Nevertheless, an estimate is needed of the **cash that will actually be received.**

Ambush has calculated the impairment using a formulaic approach. This is only acceptable if it produces an estimate sufficiently close to that produced by the IAS 39 method. It is not acceptable to use a formula based on possible trends. The **general allowance of two percent is not acceptable**, because it is not based on past experience and is unlikely to be an accurate estimate of the cash flows that will be received.

General allowance

Following the above, the general allowance will not be permitted under IAS 39.

Tray

Where it is probable that payment will not be received in full for a significant balance, an **allowance for impairment** must be made.

It looks as if Tray will pay in full plus a penalty. However, the payment will be in a year's time, and so **discounting should be used** to calculate any impairment.

Milk

Where, as in the case of Milk, there is **no objective evidence of impairment**, the individual asset is **included in a group of assets** with a similar credit risk, and the group as a whole is assessed for impairment. Milk has a similar credit risk to 'other receivables' and so will be grouped in with those.

Allowance for impairment

This is calculated as follows.

	Balance	Cash to be Received
	$m	$m
Tray	4	3.9*
Milk and other receivables	7	6.6
	11	10.5

*$4.1m discounted at 5%

Ambush should **reduce trade receivables** by $11m − $10.5m = $500,000 (or show a balance of $500,000 on the allowance account).

(c) **Buildings**

Under IAS 16 *Property, plant and equipment,* as amended by IAS 1 (revised), an **increase** in the carrying amount of an asset must be **recognised in other comprehensive income (items that will not be reclassified to profit or loss) and accumulated in equity under the heading of revaluation surplus**. The decrease should **be recognised in profit or loss** to the extent that **it reverses a revaluation** decrease of the same asset previously recognised in profit or loss. If an asset's carrying value is decreased as a result of a revaluation, the **decrease must be recognised in profit or loss**. However, the decrease must be recognised in other comprehensive income to the extent of any credit balance existing in the revaluation surplus in respect of that asset. The decrease recognised in other comprehensive income reduces the amount accumulated in equity under the heading of revaluation surplus.

The buildings would be treated as follows:

	Year ended 30 Nov 20X4	Year ended 30 Nov 20X5
	$m	$m
Cost/valuation	10.0	8.00
Depreciation (Note 1)	(0.5)	(0.42)
	9.5	7.58
Impairment charged to profit or loss	(1.5)	–
Reversal of impairment charged to profit or loss (Note 2)	–	1.42
Gain on revaluation to revaluation surplus		2.00
Carrying amount	8.0	11.00

Notes

1 Depreciation charged in the year to 30 November 20X5 is based on the carrying amount at 30 November 20X4 spread over the remaining life of 19 years: $8m ÷ 19 = $421,053 rounded to $420,000.

2 The gain on revaluation in 20X5 is recognised in profit or loss to the extent that it reverses the revaluation loss charged in 20X4. However, this amount ($1.5m) is adjusted for the additionally depreciation that would have been recognised in 20X54had the revaluation loss not been recognised. This is $1.5m ÷ 19 = $0.8m.

19 Grainger

Marking scheme

			Marks
(a)	(i)	1 mark per point, maximum	11
	(ii)	IAS 8	1
		$1,500 credit to equity	1
		$4,500 will be credited to profit or loss	2
			4
(b)	(i)	1 mark per point up to	4
	(ii)	Calculations	4
Professional marks			2
Maximum			25

(a) (i) **IFRS 9 and financial assets**

Many users and preparers of accounts have found financial instruments to be **complex**. One of the reasons for this was **many different ways in which they could be measured**. The **categorisation of the financial instrument** under IAS 39 *Financial instruments: Recognition and measurement* was a contributor to this. Where IAS 39 still applies – IFRS 9 is not in force yet (effective for periods beginning on or after 1 January 2013 although earlier adoption is encouraged) - there are four categories: fair value through profit or loss, available for sale financial assets, loans and receivables and held to maturity.

IFRS 9 *Financial Instruments*, issued in November 2009, replaced parts of IAS 39, with respect to the classification and measurement of financial assets. In October 2010, IFRS 9 was updated to include the classification and measurement of financial liabilities and the derecognition of financial assets and liabilities. This standard is a work in progress and in due course will be developed further to fully replace IAS 39. It will come into force for accounting periods ending in 2013. This is Phase 1 of the project to replace IAS 39.

IFRS 9 simplifies the IAS 39 categories such that, on initial recognition, financial assets are classified as measured at either:

(1) Amortised cost, or

(2) Fair value

A financial asset is classified as measured at amortised cost where:

BPP
LEARNING MEDIA

(1)   The objective of the business model within which the asset is held is to hold assets in order to collect contractual cash flows and

(2)   The contractual terms of the financial asset give rise on specified dates to cash flows that are solely payments of principal and interest on the principal outstanding.

An application of these rules means that **equity investments may not be classified as measured at amortised cost** and must be measured at fair value. This is because contractual cash flows on specified dates are not a characteristic of equity instruments. By default, gains and losses on equity investments within the scope of IFRS 9 are recognised in profit or loss for the year. However, if the equity investment is not held for trading **an irrevocable election can be made at initial recognition to measure it at fair value through other comprehensive income** with only dividend income recognised in profit or loss. The amounts recognised in OCI are not re-classified to profit or loss on disposal of the investment although they may be reclassified in equity.

Assets that are currently classified as held-to-maturity are likely to continue to be measured at amortised cost as they are held to collect the contractual cash flows and often give rise to only payments of principal and interest.

One of the most significant changes will be the ability to measure some debt instruments, for example investments in government and corporate bonds at amortised cost. Many available-for-sale debt instruments currently measured at fair value will qualify for amortised cost accounting.

A **debt instrument** may be classified as measured at either amortised cost or fair value **depending on whether it meets the criteria above.** Even where the criteria are met at initial recognition, a debt instrument may be classified as measured at fair value through profit or loss if doing so eliminates or significantly reduces a measurement or recognition inconsistency (sometimes referred to as an 'accounting mismatch') that would otherwise arise from measuring assets or liabilities or recognising the gains and losses on them on different bases. An example of this may be where an entity holds a fixed rate loan receivable that it hedges with an interest rate swap that swaps the fixed rates for floating rates. Measuring the loan asset at amortised cost would create a measurement mismatch, as the interest rate swap would be held at FVTPL. In this case, the loan receivable could be designated at FVTPL under the fair value option to reduce the accounting mismatch that arises from measuring the loan at amortised cost.

Financial assets are subsequently measured at:

(1)   **Fair value** with changes in value normally recognised in profit or loss, or
(2)   **Amortised cost** with interest recognised in profit or loss

The extent to which IFRS 9 simplifies the IAS 39 definitions can be seen by taking each IAS 39 category in turn.

Old IAS 39 Category	IFRS 9 measurement	Gains and losses
Financial asset at fair value through profit or loss	Fair value	Profit or loss
Available for sale financial asset	Fair value	Profit or loss, unless irrevocable election to recognise in OCI
Financial asset held to maturity	Amortised cost	Profit or loss
Loans and receivables	Amortised cost	Profit or loss

Many loans and receivables and held-to-maturity investments will continue to be measured at amortised cost but some will have to be measured instead at FVTPL. For example some instruments, such as cash-collateralised debt obligations, that may under IAS 39 have been measured entirely at amortised cost or as available-for-sale will more likely be measured at FVTPL.

All **derivatives** are measured at **fair value.** IFRS 9 also simplified the rule on embedded derivatives. Where the host contract is a financial asset within the scope of the standard, the classification and **measurement rules of the standard are applied to the entire hybrid contract**.

This is a simplification of the IAS 39 rules, which required that an embedded derivative be separated from its host **contract** and accounted for as a derivative under certain conditions, although the more complex rule still applies for liabilities and other items that are not assets within the scope of IFRS 9.

IFRS 9 does not directly address impairment, which is currently still covered by IAS 39. However, as IFRS 9 eliminates the available-for-sale category of financial asset, it also eliminates the impairment rules in relation to those assets. Under IAS 39 measuring impairment losses on debt securities in illiquid markets based on fair value often led to reporting **an impairment loss that exceeded the credit loss** that management expected.

So far, it appears that IFRS 9 has simplified the IAS 39 rules. However, as indicated above, this is only the first phase. IFRS 9 is a work in progress, and has been criticised, notably by the European Union, who warned that the new rules could lead to greater volatility in accounts, undermining broader financial stability, and postponed its EU adoption.

(ii) Under IAS 8 *Accounting policies, changes in* accounting *estimates and errors,* Grainger's treatment would be a change in accounting policy, which means that the opening balance of equity must be adjusted as if the new policy has always been applied. The adjustment to equity at 1 May 20X0 will be a credit of $1,500:

	$
Fair value (IFRS 9) at 1 May 20X0	106,500
Carrying value of asset at 1 May 20X0 (amortised cost)	(105,000)
Credit to equity	1,500

Since the financial asset is now at fair value through profit or loss, the increase of in fair value during the year will be taken to profit or loss for the year. The increase is calculated as the fair value at 30 April 20X1 ($111,000) less fair value at 30 April 20X0 ($106,500), that is $4,500.

(b) (i) **Expected loss model**

IFRS 9 has not yet been updated to cover impairment of financial assets, which is still governed by IAS 39. IAS 39 uses an **'incurred loss' model** for the impairment of financial assets. This model assumes that all loans will be repaid until evidence to the contrary, that is until the occurrence of an event that triggers an impairment indicator. Only at this point is the impaired loan written down to a lower value. The global financial crisis has led to criticism of this approach for many reasons, including that it leads to an overstatement of interest revenue in the periods prior to the occurrence of a loss event, and produces deficient information.

Under the proposals in ED *Amortised cost and impairment*, which will update IFRS 9, the 'incurred loss' model would be replaced with an approach **whereby expected losses are recognised throughout the life of the loan** (or other financial asset measured at amortised cost), and not just after a loss event has been identified. This is known as **an expected cash flow (ECF) approach**. Note the following:

(1) The ECF approach uses forward-looking cash flows that incorporate expected future credit losses throughout the term of a financial asset (eg, a loan). In contrast to the existing incurred loss approach, the ECF approach would not require identification of impairment indicators or triggering events and would result in earlier recognition of credit losses.

(2) The effective interest rate will include an initial estimate of any expected credit losses. Credit losses will be held in a separate allowance account. Losses due to changes in cash flow estimates will be disclosed as a separate line item. If the item is considered uncollectable, write-offs will be made directly to the financial asset account.

(3) The expected loss model is more **subjective** in nature compared to the incurred loss model, since it relies significantly on the cash flow estimates prepared by the reporting entity which are inherently subjective. Therefore safeguards are needed to be built into the process such as disclosures of methods applied.

(4)   The proposals represent a **significant change from current practice.** The IASB acknowledges that their application would probably result in significant systems and operational challenges such as developing reliable estimates of cash flows over the expected lives of financial assets. In particularly data collection will be onerous, since data needs to be collected for the whole portfolio of financial assets measured at amortised cost held by a reporting entity. This means that data is not only required for impaired financial assets but it also requires having historical loss data for all financial assets held at amortised cost. Entities do not always have the relevant data.

(ii)   **Incurred loss model**

Date	Loan asset (A)	Interest at 16% (B)	Cash flow	Loss (C)	Loan asset	Return (B – C)/A%
	$'000	$'000	$'000	$'000	$'000	$'000
Y/e 30 April 20X1	5,000	800	(800)	0	5,000	16%
Y/e 30 April 20X2	5,000	800	(800)	0	5,000	16%
Y/e 30 April 20X3	5,000	800	* (728)	(522) (β)	**4,550	5.56%

*Being 0. 8m × 91%
**$5m ×91%

Expected loss model

Date	Loan asset (A)	Interest at 9.07% (B)	Cash flow	Loan asset	Return B /A%
	$'000	$'000	$'000	$'000	$'000
Y/e 30 April 20X1	5,000	453.5	(800)	4,653.5	9.07%
Y/e 30 April 20X2	4,653.5	422.1	(800)	4,275.6	9.07%
Y/e 30 April 20X3	4,275.6	387.8	(728)*	3,935.4	9.07%

*Being 800 ×91%

20 Aron

Text reference. Financial instruments are covered in Chapter 7 of the BPP Study Text.

Top tips. Part (a) required a brief discussion of how the fair value of financial instruments is determined with a comment on the relevance of fair value measurements for financial instruments where markets are volatile and illiquid. Part (b) required you to discuss the accounting for four different financial instruments. The financial instruments ranged from a convertible bond to transfer of shares to a debt instrument in a foreign subsidiary to interest free loans. Bear in mind that you need to discuss the treatment and not just show the accounting entries. And while you may not have come across the specific treatment of interest-free loans before, you can apply the principles of IFRS 9 (what is fair value in this case?) and the *ConceptualFramework*.

Easy marks. These are available for the discussion in Part (a) and the convertible bond.

Examiner's comment. This was the best answered question on the paper. Part (a) was quite well answered although the answers were quite narrow and many candidates simply described the classification of financial instruments in loans and receivables, fair value through profit or loss etc. In Part (b) many candidates simply showed the accounting entries without any discussion. If the accounting entries were incorrect then it was difficult to award significant marks for the attempt. The treatment of the convertible bond was quite well done except for the treatment of the issue costs and the conversion of the bond. This part of the question often gained good marks. Again the treatment of the transfer of shares and interest free loans was well done but the exchange and fair value gains were often combined and not separated in the case of the debt instrument of the foreign subsidiary.

			Marks
(a)	Fair value – subjective		4
(b)	Convertible bond:	explanation	2
		Calculation	4
	Shares in Smart:	explanation	2
		Calculation	2
	Foreign subsidiary:	explanation of principles	2
		accounting treatment	3
	Interest free loan:	explanation of principles	2
		accounting treatment	2
	Quality of explanations		2
		Available/Maximum	25

(a) **Fair value**

The **fair value** of an asset the price that would be received to sell an asset or paid to transfer a liability in an orderly transaction between market participants at the measurement date (IFRS 13 *Fair value measurement*). IFRS 13 states that valuation techniques must be those which are appropriate and for which sufficient data are available. Entities should maximise the use of relevant **observable inputs** and minimise the use of **unobservable inputs**. The standard establishes a three-level hierarchy for the inputs that valuation techniques use to measure fair value.

Level 1 Quoted prices (unadjusted) in active markets for identical assets or liabilities that the reporting entity can access at the measurement date

Level 2 Inputs other than quoted prices included within Level 1 that are observable for the asset or liability, either directly or indirectly, eg quoted prices for similar assets in active markets or for identical or similar assets in non-active markets or use of quoted interest rates for valuation purposes

Level 3 Unobservable inputs for the asset or liability, ie using the entity's own assumptions about market exit value

The IASB believes that fair value is the **most appropriate measure** for most financial instruments because it is the **most relevant**. However, it, may be **less reliable.** There is more scope for manipulation. Particular difficulties arise where quoted prices are unavailable. If this is the case – and it frequently is – there is more reliance on estimates.

Not all markets are liquid and transparent. Where a market is **illiquid**, it is particularly difficult to apply fair value measurement, because the information will not be available. In addition, not all markets are stable; some are volatile. Fair valuing gives a measurement at a particular point in time, but in a **volatile** market this measure may not apply long term. It needs to be considered whether an asset is to be actively traded or held for the long term.

Disclosure is important in helping to deal with some of the problems of fair value, particularly as it provides an indicator of a company's risk profile.

(b) (i) **Convertible bond**

Some financial instruments contain both a liability and an equity element. In such cases, IAS 32 requires the component parts of the instrument to be **classified separately**, according to the substance of the contractual arrangement and the definitions of a financial liability and an equity instrument.

One of the most common types of compound instrument, as here, is **convertible debt**. This creates a primary financial liability of the issuer and grants an option to the holder of the instrument to convert it into an equity instrument (usually ordinary shares) of the issuer. This is the economic equivalent of the issue of conventional debt plus a warrant to acquire shares in the future.

Although in theory there are several possible ways of calculating the split, the following method is recommended:

(1) Calculate the value for the liability component.
(2) Deduct this from the instrument as a whole to leave a residual value for the equity component.

The reasoning behind this approach is that an entity's equity is its residual interest in its assets amount after deducting all its liabilities.

The **sum of the carrying amounts** assigned to liability and equity will always be equal to the carrying amount that would be ascribed to the instrument **as a whole**.

The **equity component is not re-measured.** However, the **liability component** is measured at amortised cost using an **effective interest rate** (here 9.38%).

It is important to note that the issue costs (here $1 million) are allocated in proportion to the value of the liability and equity components when the initial split is calculated.

Step 1 Calculate liability element

A 9% discount rate is used, which is the market rate for similar bonds without the conversion rights:

Present value of interest at end of:	
Year 1 (31 May 20X6) ($100m × 6%) × 0.9174	5,505
Year 2 (31 May 20X7) ($100m × 6%) × 0.8417	5,050
Year 3 (31 May 20X8) ($100m × ($100m × 6%)) × 0.7722	81,852
Total liability component	92,407
Total equity element	7,593
Proceeds of issue	100,000

Step 2 Allocate issue costs

	Liability $'000	Equity $'000	Total $'000
Proceeds	92,407	7,593	100,000
Issue cost	(924)	(76)	(1,000)
	91,483	7,517	99,000

The double entry is:

		$'000	$'000			$'000	$'000
DEBIT	Cash	100,000		CREDIT	Cash		1,000
CREDIT	Liability		92,407	DEBIT	Liability	924	
CREDIT	Equity		7,593	DEBIT	Equity	76	

Step 3 Re-measure liability using effective interest rate

	$'000
Cash – 1.6.20X5 (net of issue costs per Step 2)	91,483
Effective interest to 31.5.20X6 (9.38% × 91,483)	8,581
Coupon paid (6% × $100m)	(6,000)
At 31.5.20X6	94,064
Effective interest to 31.5.20X7 (9.38% × 94,064)	8,823
Coupon paid (6% × $100m)	(6,000)
At 31.5.20X7	96,887
Effective interest to 31.5.20X8 (9.38% × 96,887)	9,088
Coupon paid (6% × $100m)	(6,000)
At 31.5.20X8	100,000*

Step 4   **Conversion of bond**

On conversion of the bond on 31 May 20X8, Aron will issue 25 million ordinary shares. The consideration for these shares will be the original equity component (net of its share of issue costs) together with the balance on the liability.

	$'000
Share capital – 25 million at $1	25,000
Share premium	82,517
Equity and liability components (100,000 + 7,593 – 76)	107,517

(ii)   **Shares in Smart**

Firstly, the carrying value of the investment in shares in Smart of $5m (which is the fair value as at 31 May 20X7) needs updating to the fair value at 31 May 20X8. The fair value of the investment in shares in Smart at 31 May 20X8 is $5.5m – this is because Given are prepared to buy the shares in Smart and pay with consideration in the form of shares in Given with a fair value of $5.5m. IFRS 13 *Fair value measurement* defines fair value as the 'price that would be received to sell an asset...between market participants at the measurement date'. Here the price that Aron receives for shares in Smart is in the form of shares in Given worth $5.5m.

Aron should therefore recognise a gain on remeasurement of the investment in shares in Smart of $0.5m ($5.5m - $5m) in other comprehensive income(items that will not be reclassified to profit or loss):

DEBIT	Financial Asset: Investment in shares in Smart	$0.5m
CREDIT	Remeasurement gain (in OCI: not reclassified to profit or loss)	$0.5m.

The second issue here is whether the investment in shares in Smart should be **derecognised**. Derecognition is the removal of a previously recognised financial instrument from an entity's statement of financial position.

An entity should derecognise a **financial asset** when:

(a)   The **contractual rights** to the cash flows from the financial asset **expire**, or

(b)   The entity **transfers substantially all the risks and rewards of ownership** of the financial asset to another party.

In this case, Aron no longer retains any risks and rewards of ownership in the investment in shares in Smart (instead Aron now has access to the risks and rewards of ownership in the investment in shares in Given). Accordingly the financial asset 'Investment in shares in Smart' should be derecognised and instead a financial asset for the 'Investment in shares in Given' should be recognised. No gain or loss on derecognition will arise.

The investment in shares in Smart of $5.5m is then derecognised and an investment in Shares in Given is recognised instead:

DEBIT	Financial asset: shares in Given	$5.5m	
CREDIT	Financial asset: shares in Smart		$5.5m.

Tutorial note. Both the revaluation gain at the date of derecognition taken to other comprehensive income (not reclassified to profit or loss) of $500,000 and the cumulative gain of $400,000 previously recognised in other comprehensive income (not reclassified to profit or loss), and therefore held in other components of equity may be transferred to retained earnings as a reserves movement.

(iii)   **Foreign subsidiary**

Two International Accounting Standards apply to this transaction:

(1)   The debt instrument in the foreign subsidiary's financial statements is dealt with under IFRS 9 *Financial instruments..*

(2)   The translation of the financial statements of the foreign subsidiary is governed by IAS 21 *The effects of changes in foreign exchange rates.*

Under IAS 21, **all exchange differences resulting from translation are recognised in other comprehensive income (items that may subsequently be reclassified to profit or loss) until the subsidiary is disposed of**. This includes exchange differences that arise on financial instruments carried at fair value through profit or loss and investments in equity instruments. It is important to distinguish gains that result from increases in fair value from gains that result from changes in exchange rates.

The debt instrument owned by Gao is held for trading, and will therefore be carried at **fair value through profit or loss** in Gao's financial statements. At 31 May 20X8, there will be a gain in the financial statements of Gao 12m – 10m = 2 million zloti. In accordance with IFRS 9, this will be credited to profit or loss for the year in Gao's statement of profit or loss and other comprehensive income.

In the consolidated financial statements, the carrying value of the debt at 1 June 20X7 would be calculated using the exchange rate at that date as: 10 million zloti ÷ 3 = $3.3m. By 31 May 20X8, the carrying value will have increased to: 12 million zloti ÷ 2 = $6m. **Part of the increase** in value of $6m - $ 3.3m = $2.7m is attributable to a **change in the exchange rate**, and **part** of it to an **increase in fair value**. Only the latter can be recognised in profit or loss for the year.

Aaron will use the average rate for the year of 2.5 to translate the statement of profit or loss and other comprehensive income, giving a gain of 2 million zloti ÷ 2.5 = $800,000 to be taken to profit or loss for the year. The remaining part of the increase in value, $2.7m - $0.8m = $1.9m will be **classified in other comprehensive income** until Gao is disposed of.

The accounting is as follows:

	$m
Balance at 1 June 20X7	3.3
Increase in year	2.7
Balance at 31 May 20X8	6.0

DEBIT	Debt instrument	$2.7m	
CREDIT	Profit or loss		$0.8m
CREDIT	Equity		$1.9m

(iv) **Interest free loans**

IFRS 9 *Financial instruments* requires financial assets to be measured on initial recognition at **fair value** plus transaction costs. Usually the fair value of the consideration given represents the fair value of the asset. However, this is not necessarily the case with an interest-free loan. An interest free loan to an employee is not costless to the employer, and the **face value may not be the same as the fair value.**

To arrive at the fair value of the loan, Aaron needs to consider **other market transactions** in the same instrument. The market rate of interest for a two year loan on the date of issue (1 June 20X7) and the date of repayment (31 May 20X9) is 6% pa, and this is rate should be used in valuing the instrument. The **fair value** may be measured as the **present value of future receipts using the market interest rate**. There will be a difference between the face value and the fair value of the instrument, calculated as follows:

	$m
Face value of loan at 1 June 20X7	10.0
Fair value of loan at 1 June 20X7: 10 × 0.8900	8.9
Difference	1.1

The **difference** of $1.1m is the extra cost to the employer of not charging a market rate of interest. It will be treated as **employee compensation** under IAS 19 *Employee benefits*. This employee compensation must be charged over the two year period to the statement of profit or loss and other comprehensive income, through profit or loss for the year.

With regard to subsequent measurement Aron wishes to hold the loan at amortised cost. For this to be possible, two criteria must be met under IFRS 9:

(1) **Business model test.** The objective of the entity's business model is to hold the financial asset to collect the contractual cash flows (rather than to sell the instrument prior to its contractual maturity to realise its fair value changes).

(2) **Cash flow characteristics test:** The contractual terms of the financial asset give rise on specified dates to cash flows that are solely payments of principal and interest on the principal outstanding.

These criteria have been met. Accordingly, the loan may be measured at 31 May 20X8 at **amortised cost** using the effective interest method. The **effective interest rate** is 6%, so the value of the loan in the statement of financial position is: $8.9m × 1.06 = $9.43m. Interest will be credited to profit or loss for the year of: $8.9 × 6% = $53m.

The **double entry** is as follows:

At 1 June 20X7

DEBIT	Loan	$8.9m	
DEBIT	Employee compensation	$1.1m	
CREDIT	Cash		$10m

At 31 May 20X8

DEBIT	Loan	$0.53m	
CREDIT	Profit or loss – interest for the year $8.9m × 6%		$0.53m

21 Leigh

Text reference. See Chapters 8 and 12 of the text.

Top tips. This was a difficult question, as all three parts included peripheral areas of the syllabus. This question dealt with several share-based payment transactions. However, not all such transactions were dealt with by a single accounting standard. Part (a) dealt with the cost of a business combination and the issue of shares as purchase consideration. It also dealt with shares given to employees as remuneration. The events are dealt with under the separate accounting standards IFRS 2 and IFRS 3. Part (b) dealt with the purchase of property, plant and equipment, and the grant of rights to a director when there is a choice of settlement.
This part of the question was quite technically demanding. Part (c) dealt with the issue of shares to acquire an associate and the subsequent accounting for the associate.

Easy marks. It is difficult to identify easy marks for this question. Unless share-based payment is your 'pet topic', it would have been best avoided in an exam.

Examiner's comment. The question was poorly answered. Parts (a) and (c) were very straightforward but candidates did not seem to recognise the issues or accounting standards which should be used. The question required an application of some basic knowledge but candidates failed to do this. Part (b) required some detailed knowledge of IFRS 2 and again candidates did not have such knowledge. It appears that unless the examiner details the accounting standard to be used in answering the question, candidates have difficulty in applying knowledge to scenarios.

Marking scheme

		Marks
(a)	Hash	7
	Employees	3
(b)	Property, plant and equipment	5
	Director	4
(c)	Handy	6
	Available/Maximum	25

(a) **Shares issued to the directors**

The three million $1 shares issued to the directors **on 1 June 20X6** as part of the **purchase consideration** for Hash are accounted for under **IFRS 3** *Business combinations* rather than under IFRS 2 *Share-based payment.* This is because they are not remuneration or compensation, but simply part of the purchase price of the company. The cost of the business combination will be the total of the fair values of the consideration given by Leigh plus any attributable costs. The total fair value here is $6m, of which $3m is share capital and $3m is share premium.

The **contingent consideration** – 5,000 shares per director to be received on 31 May 20X7 if the directors are still employed by Leigh – may, however, be seen as compensation and thus fall to be treated under IFRS 2. The fact that the additional payment of shares is **linked to continuing employment** suggests that it is a compensation arrangement, and therefore **IFRS 2 will apply.**

Under IFRS 2, the fair value used is that at the **grant date,** rather than when the shares vest. The market value of each share at that date is $2. (Three million shares are valued at $6m.) So the total value of the compensation is $5 \times 5,000 \times \$2 = \textbf{\$50,000.}$

The $50,000 is charged to profit or loss with a corresponding increase in equity.

Shares issued to employees

These shares are remuneration and are **accounted for under IFRS 2.**

The fair value used is that at the **date of issue,** as the grant date and issue date are the same, **that is $3 per share.** Because the shares are given as a bonus they vest immediately and are presumed to be consideration for past services.

The total of $3m would be changed to profit or loss and included in equity.

(b) **Purchase of property, plant and equipment**

Under IFRS 2, the purchase of property, plant and equipment would be treated as a share-based payment in which the counterparty has a **choice of settlement**, in shares or in cash. Such transactions are **treated as cash-settled** to the extent that the entity has incurred a **liability**. It is treated as the issue of a compound financial instrument, with a debt and an equity element.

Similar to IAS 32 *Financial instruments: presentation,* IFRS 2 requires the **determination of the liability element and the equity element**. The fair value of the equity element is the fair value of the goods or services (in this case the property) less the fair value of the debt element of the instrument. The fair value of the property is $4m (per question). The share price of $3.50 is the expected share price in three months' time (assuming cash settlement). The fair value of the liability component at 31 May 20X7 is its present value: $1.3 \times \$3 = \$3.9$.

The journal entries are:

DEBIT	Property, plant and equipment	$4m	
CREDIT	Liability		$3.9m
CREDIT	Equity		$0.1m

In three months' time, the debt component is remeasured to its fair value. Assuming the estimate of the future share price was correct at $3.50, the liability at that date will be 1.3 million × $3.5 = $4.55. An adjustment must be made as follows:

DEBIT	Expense (4.55 - 3.9)	$0.65m	
CREDIT	Liability		$0.65m

Choice of share or cash settlement

The share-based payment to the new director, which offers a choice of cash or share settlement, is also treated as the issue of a compound instrument. In this case, the **fair value of the services is determined by the fair value of the equity instruments given**. The fair value of the equity alternative is $2.50 × 50,000 = $125,000. The cash alternative is valued at 40,000 × $3 = $120,000. The **difference** between these two values – $5,000 – is deemed to be the **fair value of the equity component**. At the settlement date, the liability element would be measured at fair value and the method of settlement chosen by the director would determine the final accounting treatment.

At 31 May 20X7, the accounting entries would be:

DEBIT	Profit or loss – directors' remuneration	$125,000	
CREDIT	Liability		$120,000
CREDIT	Equity		$5,000

In effect, the director surrenders the right to $120,000 cash in order to obtain equity worth $125,000.

(c) **Investment in Hardy**

The investment in Hardy should be treated as an **associate under** IAS 28 *Investment in associates.* Between 20% and 50% of the share capital has been acquired, and significant influence may be exercised through the right to appoint directors. Associates are accounted for as cost plus post acquisition change in net assets, **generally cost plus share of post-acquisition retained earnings**. The cost is the fair value of the shares in Leigh exchanged for the shares of Handy. However, negative goodwill arises because the fair value of the net assets of Hardy exceeds this. The negative goodwill must be added back to determine the cost to be used for the carrying value, and, following a reassessment, credited to profit or loss. (Dr Cost 0.2, Cr P/L 0.2)

	$m
Cost: 1m × $2.50	2.5
Add back negative goodwill: (2.5 + (9 × 70% 'NCI') − 9)	0.2
	2.7
Post acquisition profits: (5 − 4) × 30%	0.3
Carrying value at 31 May 20X7	3.0

Note. The 0.2 is not part of post acquisition retained earnings. It is adjustment to the original cost to remove the negative goodwill.

Because negative goodwill has arisen, the investment must be **impairment tested**. A comparison must be made with the estimated recoverable amount of Hardy's net assets. The investment must not be carried above the recoverable amount:

Recoverable amount at 31 May 20X7: $11m × 30% = $3.3m

The recoverable amount is above the carrying value, so the investment at 31 May 20X7 will be shown at $3m.

22 Margie

Text reference. Share-based payment is covered in Chapter 8. Derivatives are covered in Chapter 7.

Top tips. This is a multi-part question, set in the context of share-related transactions. However, you should not assume that all transactions should be accounted for under IFRS 2. Part (a), a contract for the purchase of wheat, could be settled in the entity's own shares, but is intended to be settled net in cash, and is therefore a derivative rather than a share-based payment. Part (b) deals with the situation where share-based payment award is exchanged for awards held by the acquiree's employees as part of the business combination, so IFRS 3 is relevant. Part (c) deals with two share issues, one of which is outside the scope of IFRS 2. Part (d) is an equity-settled share-based payment with a variable vesting period based on a market condition.

Easy marks. There aren't any obvious easy marks here, but if you attempt all parts of the question you can gain the first few marks of each part.

Examiner's comment. In Part (a), Many candidates did not recognise the fact that the transaction should be dealt with under IFRS 9.This type of transaction has been examined recently but candidates did not seem to recognise the nature of the transaction. In Part (b), candidates had to understand the interaction of IFRS 2 and IFRS 3 in order to answer the question. The question was not well answered although candidates did seem to realise that there was a post combination expense to be taken into account. In Part (c), candidates often felt that the first transaction was within the scope of IFRS 2 and the second was not. Unfortunately this assumption was incorrect with the correct answer being that the first transaction was outside the scope and the second was within the scope. Part (d) was well answered. Candidates generally seemed to understand the effect of a market condition.

		Marks
(a)	Discussion IFRS 9	5
	Conclusion	2
(b)	Discussion of IFRS 3/IFRS 2	4
	Calculation	2
(c)	Discussion	4
(d)	Discussion	4
	Calculation	2
Professional		2
		25

(a) **Contract for the purchase of wheat**

Although the amount paid to settle the contract will be equal to the value of 2,500 of Margie's shares, this is **not a share-based payment** within the scope of IFRS 2. There are two main reasons for this:

(i) The contract may be **settled net in cash.**

(ii) The contract has **not been entered into be entered into in order to satisfy Margie's normal sales and purchases requirements**. Margie has no intention of taking delivery of the wheat; this is a financial contract to pay or receive a cash amount.

Contracts for purchase or sale of non-financial items that meet certain conditions are accounted for under under IFRS 9 *Financial instruments.* Specifically, contracts to buy or sell non-financial items are within the scope of IFRS 9 if they can be settled net in cash or another financial asset, and are not entered into and held for the purpose of the receipt or delivery of a non-financial item in accordance with the entity's expected purchase, sale, or usage requirements. Contracts to buy or sell non-financial items are inside the scope if **net settlement** occurs.

Any one of the following situations constitutes **net settlement**

(i) The terms of the contract permit either counterparty to settle net.

(ii) There is a past practice of settling similar contracts net.

(iii) There is a past practice, for similar contracts, of taking delivery of the underlying and selling it within a short period after delivery to generate a profit from short-term fluctuations in price, or from a dealer's margin.

(iv) The non-financial item is readily convertible to cash.

Contracts that allow net settlement in cash can be entered into for satisfying the normal sales and purchases requirements of the two parties but this is not such a contract.

The contract to purchase the wheat will be accounted for as a **derivative** and valued at fair value (an **asset or liability at fair value** according to IFRS 9). **On inception the fair value of the contract will be nil** because the value of 350 tonnes of wheat will be equivalent to 2,500 of Margie's shares. This will not be the case at subsequent period ends because factors affecting the market price of wheat will not be the same as those affecting the market price of Margie's shares. Accordingly, differences will arise and there will be a **gain or loss, which must be taken to profit or loss for the year.**

Margie wishes to use this contract as part of its **hedging strategy**. However, **this would not be appropriate**. There is no firm commitment to purchase the wheat (in fact Margie has no intention of purchasing it), and it is not a highly probable forecast transaction.

(b)   **Replacement award**

In a business combination, an acquirer may exchange its share-based payment awards for awards held by employees of the acquiree. This may be termed a **replacement award,** and must be measured using IFRS 2 *Share-based payment.* Part of the fair value of the replacement award may, depending on the circumstances, be treated in accordance with IFRS 3 *Business combinations.*

IFRS 3 provides guidance on whether share-based payment awards in a business combination are part of the consideration transferred to obtain control (accounted for under IFRS 3) or as a post-combination expense (accounted for under IFRS 2**). If the acquirer is obliged to replace the acquiree's award, then all or part of the acquirer's award is part of the consideration transferred. If not, then it is a post-combination expense.**

Margie obliged to replace Antalya's award

If the Margie is obliged to replace Antalya's award, all or a portion of the fair value of Margie's replacement award must be included in the measurement of the consideration transferred by Margie. **The amount included in the consideration transferred is the fair value of Antalya's award at the acquisition date of $20 million.**

The **difference** between the fair value of Margie's replacement award and the fair value of the reward replaced, $22m – $20m = $2m is **recognised as an expense in the post-combination – profit or loss.** This is the case even though no post-combination services are required.

Margie not obliged to replace Antalya's award

If Margie is not obliged to replace Antalya's award, then **Margie should not adjust the consideration**, whether or not it actually does replace Antalya's award. **All** of the fair value of Margie's award would be recognised immediately as a **post-combination expense,** despite the fact that no post-combination services are required.

(c)   **Issue of shares to employees**

Margie's issue of shares to its employees who are already shareholders d**oes not fall within the scope of IFRS 2 *Share-based payment.*** The issue was made to the employees in their capacity as shareholders, not as employees. There are **no service or performance requirements** demanded in exchange for the shares.

The employees are therefore just shareholders like any other, and the issue of shares will be accounted for like any other, with a debit to cash and a credit to share capital and to share premium for any excess over the nominal value.

Issue of shares to Grief

The issue of the shares to Grief does come within the scope of IFRS 2 *Share-based payment.* Share-based payment occurs when an entity purchases goods or services from another party such as a supplier or employee and rather than paying directly in cash, settles the amount owing in shares, share options or future cash amounts linked to the value of shares.

In this case, **Grief is acting as a supplier** (of the building), the payment is in shares, and the purpose of issuing the shares was to buy the building. **In accordance with IFRS 2, the building will be shown at fair value on the statement of financial position, with a corresponding credit to equity.**

(d)   **Share-based payment with variable vesting period**

The grant of the options to employees clearly falls within the scope of IFRS 2. In this case there is a **market condition** which must be met before the shares vest. The vesting period may change as a result of a vesting condition being met. IFRS 2 makes a distinction between the handling of market based performance features from non-market features. Market conditions are those related to the market price of any entity's equity, such as achieving a specified share price or a specified target based on a comparison of the entity's share price with an index of share prices of other entities. Market based performance features should be included in the grant-date fair value measurement. However, the fair value of the equity instruments should not be reduced to take into consideration non-market based performance features or other vesting features.

An entity needs **to estimate, at grant date, the expected vesting period** over which the charge should be spread, on the assumption that services will be rendered by employees over this vesting period in exchange for the equity instruments.

If the vesting period turns out to be **shorter** than estimated, the charge will be **accelerated** in the period in which the entity must fulfil its obligations by delivering shares or cash to the employee or supplier. If the actual vesting period is **longer** than estimated, the expense **is recognised over the original vesting period.**

At the grant date (1 December 20X1), Margie estimated the vesting period to be four years, the assumption being that the market condition would be met four years later in 20X5. Thus the charge over the four years was calculated as (100 × 4,000 × $10) ÷ 4 years = $1m per year.

The market condition was actually **met a year early**, on 30 November 20X4. The **expense therefore needs to be accelerated** and charged in the year ended 30 November 20X4. The charge for the year is calculated as:

	$m
Total charge: 100 × 4,000 × $10	4
Less already charged in the two years to 30.11. 20X3: 2 × $1m	(2)
Charge in the year ended 30.11.20X4	2

23 Greenie

Text reference. Specialised entities are covered in general terms in Chapter 20. The specific issues are covered as follows: share-based payment in Chapter 8, provisions and contingencies in Chapter 9, associates in Chapter 12 and preference shares in Chapter 7.

Top tips. This question is set in the airport industry. In keeping with the examiner's guidance, no specific knowledge of this industry is required. Part (a) covered provisions, contingent liabilities and contingent assets. There is a lot of information, but this part is more straightforward than it looks. In Part (b) you need to consider whether IAS 28 should be applied, that is whether there is significant influence. The percentage holding is not the only determining factor. Part (c) covered purchase of a franchise by issuing shares. This is a form of share-based payment. This part asked for the treatment of irredeemable preference shares with a fixed cash dividend. This meets the definition of a financial liability (in this case a contractual obligation to deliver cash) but also has an equity component, so needs to be accounted for as a compound instrument.

Easy marks. This was a challenging question and required a lot of thought. However, there are some easy marks for textbook learning in explaining what a provision is and what a contingent liability is, and also for listing the ways in which significant influence can be shown.

Examiner's comment. This question dealt with real world scenarios taken from corporate financial statements. Parts (a) of the question was well answered although many candidates came to the incorrect conclusion. Part (b) was also well answered, but many candidates did not use the scenario and in this question it was critical to discuss the facts in the question. Part (c) was not well answered, particularly regarding the irredeemable preference shares.

Marking scheme

		Marks
(a)	Provision discussion	3
	Contingent liability discussion	3
(b)	Significant influence discussion and application	10
(c)	Intangible assets	3
	Preference shares	4
	Professional	2
		25

(a)   **Provision or contingent liability?**

A **provision** is defined by IAS 37 *Provisions, contingent liabilities and contingent assets* as **a liability of uncertain timing or amount.** IAS 37 states that a provision should only be recognised if:

- There is a **present obligation** as the result of a **past event**
- An **outflow of resources embodying economic benefits is probable**, and
- A **reliable estimate** of the amount can be made

If these conditions apply, a provision must be recognised.

The past event that gives rise, under IAS 37, to a present obligation, is known as the **obligating event.** The obligation may be legal, or it may be constructive (as when past practice creates a valid expectation on the part of a third party). The entity must have no realistic alternative but to settle the obligation.

As at 30 November 20X0, Greenie **has no legal obligation to pay compensation** to third parties. No legal action has been brought in respect of the accident. Nor can Greenie be said to have a constructive obligation at the year end, because the investigation has not been concluded, and the expert report will not be presented to the civil courts until 20X1. Therefore under IAS 37 *Provisions, contingent liabilities and contingent assets* no provision would be recognised for this amount.

However, the possible payment does fall within the IAS 37 definition of a **contingent liability,** which is:

- A possible obligation depending on whether some uncertain future event occurs, or
- A present obligation but payment is not probable or the amount cannot be measured reliably

There is uncertainty as to the outcome of the investigation and findings of the report, and the extent of the damages and any compensation arising remain to be confirmed. However, the uncertainty over these details is not so great that the possibility of an outflow of economic benefits is remote.

Therefore as **a contingent liability** the details and, if possible an estimate of the amount payable, would be **disclosed** in the notes to the financial statements.

The question arises as to whether the **possible recovery of the compensation costs from the insurance company** constitutes a contingent asset under IAS 37. A contingent asset is a possible asset that arises from past events, and whose existence will be confirmed only by the occurrence or non-occurrence of one or more uncertain future events not wholly within the control of the entity.

Because any insurance claim will only be made after the courts have determined compensation, and will then need to be assessed on its merits, any payout is one step removed from the potential payment of compensation. In other words it is merely possible rather than probable, and **disclosure of a contingent asset would not be appropriate.**

(b)   **Significant influence**

In accounting for Manair, Greenie needs to have regard to IAS 28 *Investments in associates.* IAS 28 defines an associate as 'an entity, including an unincorporated entity such as a partnership, over which an investor has significant influence and which is neither a subsidiary nor a joint venture of the investor.'

Significant influence is the power to participate in the financial and operating policy decisions of an economic activity but is not control or joint control over those policies.

Significant influence can be determined by the holding of voting rights (usually attached to shares) in the entity. IAS 28 states that if an investor holds **20% or more** of the voting power of the investee, it can be presumed that the investor has significant influence over the investee, *unless* it can be clearly shown that this is not the case.

Significant influence can be presumed *not* to exist if the investor holds **less than 20%** of the voting power of the investee, unless it can be demonstrated otherwise.

The **existence of significant influence** is evidenced in one or more of the following ways.

(i)   Representation on the **board of directors** (or equivalent) of the investee

(ii)   Participation in the **policy making process**

(iii)   **Material transactions** between investor and investee

(iv)   Interchange of management personnel

(v)   Provision of essential technical information

The fact that Greenie holds 19. 9% of the voting shares of Manair suggests that it **wishes to keep just below the threshold** at which significant influence would be presumed in order to avoid accounting for Manair as an associate. The percentage of shares held is only one factor to consider, and the other factors above need to be considered in turn.

(i)   Greenie does have representation on the board of directors.

(ii)   Greenie **can participate in some decisions**. It is not clear whether these are financial and operating decisions, but the fact that the shareholders' agreement requires a unanimous or majority decision suggests that Greenie is more than just an ordinary investor.

(ii)   During the year, Greenie has sold Mainair a software licence for $5m, which is **at least one material transaction**.

(iv)   There is **no evidence** of interchange of management personnel.

(v)   Greenie has provided Manair with **maintenance and technical services**, another indication of significant influence.

The fact that so many indications of significant influence appear to be present, together with the holding of just under the threshold, suggests that Greenie does have significant influence over Manair. Accordingly, IAS 28 applies: **Manair must be treated as an associate and equity accounted** in the financial statements.

Related party

As an associate, Manair is a related party of Greenie under IAS 24 *Related party disclosures.* IAS 24 requires disclosure in the financial statements of Greenie of the **related party relationship** between Greenie and Manair and also of **transactions** between the two companies, the total value of those transactions and outstanding balances and, if applicable, debts deemed irrecoverable.

(c)   **Franchise rights**

The issue of shares for the acquisition of franchise rights falls to be accounted for under IFRS 2 *Share-based payment.* **Share-based payment** occurs when an entity purchases goods or services from another party such as a supplier or employee and rather than paying directly in cash, settles the amount owing in shares (as here), share options or future cash amounts linked to the value of shares.

Greenie's proposal to record the transaction at the **nominal value** of the shares issued, that is $1m, is **incorrect.** IFRS 2 requires that the asset (franchise rights) should be recorded at **the fair value of the rights acquired.** The fair value can be established, according to IFRS 2, **by reference to prices for similar transactions**. In this case a similar franchise was acquired for $2.3m, and this can be taken as the fair value of the asset:

DEBIT   Intangible assets $2.3m
CREDIT   Equity $2.3m

In some cases the fair value of the asset acquired in a share-based payment **cannot be reliably measured.** If so, the **asset is recorded at the fair value of the equity instrument issued.** In this case, the fair value would be $2.5m.

Irredeemable preference shares

IAS 32 *Financial instruments: presentation* **normally treats irredeemable preference shares as equity** because there is normally no obligation to deliver cash or other financial assets to another entity. However, in the case of Greenie there appears to be **both an equity and a liability element:**

(i)   The **right to participate in profits** in the form of a participating dividend based on dividends paid on ordinary shares is an **equity element.**

(ii)   The contractual obligation to pay an **annual fixed cash dividend** is a **liability component.**

IAS 32 required that the preference shares should be treated as **compound instruments,** with both a liability and an equity component. The equity component is determined by deducting the liability component from the fair value of the instrument and taking the residual figure as the equity component.

Greenie has invoked the IASB *Framework* in arguing that compliance with IAS 32 would **not give a fair presentation**. The contention is that the profit participation element of the shares gives them the characteristic of permanent capital.

The motive for wishing the preference shares to be classified solely as equity may be to reduce gearing. This is **not acceptable** under IAS 1 *Presentation of financial statements.* IAS 1 allows **departure from IFRS only in exceptional circumstances** where compliance would not give a fair presentation. This is not one such circumstance. It would be misleading not to present the liability component of the preference shares.

IAS 1 does, however, allow **additional disclosures** where compliance with an IFRS gives insufficient information for a clear understanding of the impact of a transaction on an entity's financial performance or position. The appropriate course of action for Greenie to take would be to **record the preference shares as compound instruments** with an equity and a liability element in accordance with IAS 32, and **to provide disclosures** explaining the participative nature of the shares which make them akin to equity.

24 Ryder

Text reference. IAS 10 is in Chapter 9, IAS 36 in Chapter 4 and IFRS 5 in Chapter 15.

Top tips. This is a mixed standard question, of the kind that the examiner generally likes.

Easy marks. Parts (a) and (b) are fairly straightforward. You should be familiar with IAS 10 and 36, even if you missed the IFRS 5 aspect.

Examiner's comment. This question was generally well answered. The question was quite discriminating as there was in most cases a correct answer rather than an issue to discuss. Surprisingly many candidates did not know how to deal with contingent consideration on the purchase of subsidiary. Candidates dealt well with the property intended for sale but many candidates did not realise that cash settled share based payments (share appreciation rights) are remeasured to fair value at each reporting date. There was some confusion in candidate's answers over what constitutes 'grant date' and 'vesting date' and the importance for the share based payment transactions. The question was quite discriminating as there was in most cases a correct answer rather than an issue to discuss. Surprisingly many candidates did not know how to deal with a proposed dividend or how to deal with contingent consideration on the purchase of subsidiary. Candidates dealt well with the property intended for sale but many candidates did not realise that cash settled share based payments (share appreciation rights) are remeasured to fair value at each reporting date. There was some confusion in candidate's answers over what constitutes 'grant date' and 'vesting date' and the importance for the share based payment transactions.

(a) **Disposal of subsidiary**

The issue here is the value of the subsidiary at 31 October 20X5. The directors have stated that there has been no significant event since the year end which could have resulted in a reduction in its value. This, taken together with the loss on disposal, indicates that the subsidiary had **suffered an impairment at 31 October 20X5.** IAS 10 requires the sale to be treated as an **adjusting event** after the reporting period as it provides **evidence of a condition that existed at the end of the reporting period.**

The assets of Krup should be **written down to their recoverable amount**. In this case this is the eventual sale proceeds. Therefore the value of the net assets and purchased goodwill of Krup should be **reduced by $11 million** (the loss on disposal of $9 million plus the loss of $2 million that occurred between 1 November 2005 and the date of sale). IAS 36 *Impairment of assets* states that an impairment loss should be allocated to goodwill first and therefore the **purchased goodwill of $12 million is reduced to $1 million**. The impairment loss of $11 million is **recognised in profit or loss**.

Because there was no intention to sell the subsidiary at 31 October 20X5, **IFRS 5 *Non current assets held for sale and discontinued operations* does not apply**. The disposal is **disclosed** in the notes to the financial statements in accordance with IAS 10.

(b)   **Issue of shares at fair value**

IFRS 3 *Business combinations* (revised 2008) recognises that, by entering into an acquisition, the acquirer becomes obliged to make additional payments. The revised IFRS 3 **requires recognition of contingent consideration, measured at fair value, at the acquisition date.**

The treatment of **post-acquisition changes** in the fair value of the contingent consideration **depends on the circumstances.**

(i)   If the change is due to **additional information** that affects the position at the acquisition date, **goodwill should be re-measured, as a retrospective adjustment**. The additional information must come to light **within the measurement period,** a maximum of one year after acquisition.

(ii)   If the change is **due to events which took place after the acquisition date,** for example meeting earnings target, an **equity instrument is not re-measured.** Other instruments are re-measured, with changes to total comprehensive income.

Ryder has **correctly included** an estimate of the amount of consideration in the cost of the acquisition on 21 January 20X4. This would have been based on the fair value of the ordinary shares at that date of $10 per share, giving a total of 300,000 × $10 = $3,000,000:

DEBIT Investment $3,000,000
CREDIT Equity $3,000,000

As the consideration is in the form of shares, and the change is due to an event which took place after the acquisition date (the rise in share price), **the consideration is not remeasured.**

The value of the contingent shares should be included in a **separate category of equity** in the statement of financial position at 31 October 20X5. They should be transferred to share capital and share premium after the actual issue of the shares on 12 November 20X5.

IAS 10 requires **disclosure of all material share transactions** or potential share transactions entered into after the reporting period end, excluding the bonus issue. Therefore **details of the issue of the contingent shares should be disclosed** in the notes to the financial statements.

(c)   **Property**

The property appears to have been **incorrectly classified** as 'held for sale'. Although the company had always intended to sell the property, IFRS 5 states that in order to qualify as 'held for sale' an asset must be **available for immediate sale in its present condition**. Because **repairs were needed** before the property could be sold and these were **not completed until after the reporting period end**, this was clearly **not the case at 31 October 20X5**.

In addition, even if the property had been correctly classified, it has been **valued incorrectly**. IFRS 5 requires assets held for sale to be valued at **the lower of their carrying amount or fair value less costs to sell**. The property **should have been valued at its carrying amount of $20 million**, not at the eventual sale proceeds of $27 million.

The property **must be included within property, plant and equipment** and must be **depreciated**. Therefore its **carrying amount at 31 October 20X5 is $19 million** ($20 million less depreciation of $1 million). The **gain of $7 million** that the company has previously recognised **should be reversed**.

Although the property cannot be classified as 'held for sale' in the financial statements for the year ended 31 October 2005, it **will qualify for the classification after the end of the reporting period**. Therefore details of the sale should be **disclosed** in the notes to the financial statements.

(d)   **Share appreciation rights**

The granting of share appreciation rights is a **cash settled share based payment transaction** as defined by IFRS 2 *Share based payment*. IFRS 2 requires these to be **measured at the fair value of the liability** to pay cash. The liability should be **re-measured at each reporting date and at the date of settlement**. Any **changes in fair value** should be **recognised in profit or loss** for the period.

However, the company has **not remeasured the liability since 31 October 20X4**. Because IFRS 2 requires the expense and the related liability to be recognised over the two-year vesting period, the rights should be measured as follows:

	$m
At 31 October 20X4: ($6 × 10 million × ½)	30
At 31 October 20X5 ($8 × 10 million)	80
At 1 December 20X5 (settlement date) ($9 × 10 million)	90

Therefore at 31 October 20X5 the liability **should be re-measured to $80 million** and an **expense of $50 million** should be recognised in profit or loss for the year.

The additional expense of $10 million resulting from the remeasurement at the settlement date is not included in the financial statements for the year ended 31 October 20X5, but is recognised the following year.

25 Royan

Text reference. Provisions and contingent liabilities are covered in Chapter 9 of your Study Text.

Top tips. This is a topical issue and the subject of an Exposure Draft, which is covered in your Study Text. You should not just give the details of the new approach, but explain why it was needed. The examiner has indicated that there will be a computational element in his current issues question. As here, it is not too complex.

Easy marks. As the examiner pointed out,'there were several marks for simply spelling out current guidance, which is rote learning. Secondly; there are basic reasons why the IASB would wish to replace any standard. For example consistency with US standards, fitness for purpose, inappropriateness in the current business climate. Thus, candidates could have answered this part of the question with basic general knowledge of the standard setting process.'

Examiner's comment. There were a number of easy marks (see above). However, the question was not well answered. It is very important to read the scenario carefully as there are clues in the question which are there to help the candidate. Specifically, a reading of Part (b) of the question would have given candidates an insight into the nature of the proposals on provisions, for example, net present value calculations and risk and probability adjustments.

ACCA Examiner's answer. The examiner's answer to this question is included at the back of this kit.

Marking scheme

	Marks
Existing guidance and critique	9
New proposals	7
IAS 37 and ED	7
Communication skills	2
	25

(a) (i) **Existing guidance in IAS 37**

Under IAS 37 *Provisions, contingent liabilities and contingent assets,* provisions must be recognised in the following circumstances.

(1) There is a **legal** or **constructive obligation** to transfer benefits as a result of past events.
(2) It is **probable** that **an outflow of economic resources** will be required to **settle** the **obligation.**
(3) The obligation can be **measured reliably**.

IAS 37 considers an outflow to be probable if the event is **more likely than not** to occur

If the company can **avoid expenditure by its future action, no provision** should be recognised. A legal or constructive obligation is one created by an **obligating event.** Constructive obligations arise when an entity is committed to certain expenditures because of a pattern of behaviour which the public would expect to continue.

IAS 37 states that the amount recognised should be the **best estimate of the expenditure required to settle the obligation at the end of the reporting period.** The estimate should **take the various possible outcomes into account** and should be the **amount that an entity would rationally pay** to settle the obligation at the reporting date or to transfer it to a third party. Where there is **s large population of items,** for example in the case of warranties, the provision will be made at **a probability weighted expected value,** taking into account the risks and uncertainties surrounding the underlying events. Where there is a **single obligation**, **the individual most likely outcome** may be the best estimate of the liability.

The amount of the provision should be **discounted to present value** if the time value of money is material using a **risk adjusted rate.** If some or all of the expenditure is expected to be **reimbursed** by a third party, the reimbursement should be **recognised as a separate asset,** but only if it is virtually certain that the reimbursement will be received.

Why replace IAS 37?

IAS 37 has provided useful guidance over the years that it has been in force, and is generally consistent with the *Conceptual Framework.* However, for the following reasons, it has been considered necessary to replace it.

(1) IAS 37 requires recognition of a liability only if it is **probable,** that is more than 50% likely, that the obligation will result in an outflow of resources from the entity. This is **inconsistent with other standards,** for example IFRS 3 *Business combinations* and IFRS 9 *Financial instruments* which do not apply the probability criterion to liabilities. In addition, probability is not part of the *Conceptual Framework* definition of a liability.

(2) There is **inconsistency with US GAAP** as regards how they treat the **cost of restructuring** a business. US GAAP requires entities to recognise a liability for individual costs of restructuring only when the entity has incurred that particular cost, while IAS 37 requires recognition of the total costs of restructuring when the entity announces or starts to implement a restructuring plan.

(3) The **measurement rules** in IAS 37 are **vague and unclear.** In particular, 'best estimate' could mean a number of things: the mot likely outcome the most likely outcome, the weighted average of all possible outcomes or even the minimum/maximum amount in a range of possible outcomes. IAS 37 does not clarify which costs need to be included in the measurement of a liability, and in practice different entities include different costs. It is also unclear if 'settle' means 'cancel', 'transfer' or 'fulfil' the obligation.

(ii) **New proposals in Exposure Draft**

The IASB intends to replace IAS 37, and issued an Exposure Draft in 2005, supplemented by a 2010 re-exposure of the proposed changes to the measurement rules (ED *Measurement of liabilities in IAS 37).* The main changes are as follows.

(1) The **probability** of outflows criterion is **no longer included.** A liability for which the settlement amount is contingent on one or more uncertain future events is recognised independently of the probability that the event will or will not occur.

(2) The liability will be measured at **the amount an entity would rationally pay to be relieved of the present obligation.** This is defined as the **lower of**:

- The present value of the resources required to **fulfil** the obligation
- The amount that the entity would have to pay to **cancel** the obligation, and
- The amount that the entity would have to pay to **transfer** the obligation to a third party

(3) It is likely that this amount would normally be the **present value** of the resources required to **fulfil** the obligation. This would be a **discounted expected value,** ie a probability-weighted average of outflows for possible outcomes, taking into account the expected outflow of resources, the time value of money and the risk that the outflows might differ from those expected.

(4)   Expected values would be used whether measuring a single obligation or a population of items. If the obligation is to **pay cash to another party,** for example in a legal dispute, the **outflows** would be the **expected cash payments plus any associated costs,** for example legal fees. For **future services,** for example decommissioning, **outflows are based on the amounts the entity estimates it would pay a contractor at the future date** to undertake the services on its behalf. The contractor price is used regardless of whether the entity does in fact pay a contractor or carries out the work itself.

(b)   (i)   **Treatment under IAS 37**

The IAS 37 criteria for recognising a **provision** have been met as there is a present obligation to dismantle the oil platform, of which the present value has been measured at **$105m**. Because Royan cannot operate the oil without incurring an obligation to pay dismantling costs at the end of ten years, the expenditure also enables it to acquire **economic benefits** (income from the oil extracted). Therefore Royan should **recognise an asset of $105m** (added to the 'oil platform' in property, plant and equipment) and this should be **depreciated** over the life of the oil platform, which is ten years. In addition, there will be an adjustment charged in profit or loss each year to the present value of the obligation for the **unwinding of the discount.**

(ii)   **Treatment under new proposals**

If the Exposure Draft treatment is followed, under normal circumstances, Royan's liability will be measured at **the amount the entity would rationally pay to be relieved of the present obligation.** This is defined as the **lower of:**

(1)   The present value of the resources required to **fulfil** the obligation, that is $105m.

(2)   The amount that the entity would have to pay to **cancel** the obligation. This **does not apply here,** since Royan cannot cancel the obligation.

(3)   The amount that the entity would have to pay to **transfer** the obligation to a third party

The amount Royan would pay to transfer the obligation to a third party is calculated using the discounted expected value, with a 40% probability that the present value will be $129m, a 60% probability that it will be $140m and a $5m risk adjustment:

$[(40\% \times 129m) + (60\% \times 140m) + 5m] = \$140.6m$

Therefore, with most obligations the amount provided would be $105m, being the lower of the two. However, the **ED stipulates** that in the case of provisions relating to **service costs** such as decommissioning (as here) **the amount an entity would rationally pay the contractor at the future date to undertake the services on its behalf.** Therefore Royan must make a **provision of $140.6m.**

26 Electron

Text reference. Environmental provisions are covered in Chapter 9; share schemes in Chapter 8.

Top tips. This is a multi-standard question on environmental provisions, leases, proposed dividend and a share option scheme. The question on the power station is similar to one you will have already met in this kit, and you have come across longer, more complicated questions on share-based payment, a favourite topic with this examiner.

Easy marks. The proposed dividend is straightforward, as is the explanation (if not the calculations) for the provision. The treatment of share options provides 4 easy marks for nothing much in the way of complications.

	Marks
Oil contracts	4
Power station	7
Operating leases	5
Proposed dividend	3
Share options	4
Effective communication	2
Available/Maximum	25

REPORT

To: The Directors, Electron
From: Accountant

Date: July 20X6

Accounting treatment of transactions

Oil trading contracts

The first point to note is that the contracts always result in the delivery of the commodity. They are therefore correctly treated as normal sale and purchase contracts, **not financial instruments.**

The adoption of a policy of **deferring recognising revenue and costs is appropriate** in general terms because of the duration of the contracts. Over the life of the contracts, costs and revenues are equally matched. However, there is a mismatch between costs and revenues in the early stages of the contracts.

In the first year of the contract, 50% of revenues are recognised immediately. However, costs, in the form of amortisation, are recognised evenly over the duration of the contract. This means that **in the first year, a higher proportion of the revenue is matched against a smaller proportion of the costs.** It could also be argued that revenue is inflated in the first year.

While there is no detailed guidance on accounting for this kind of contract, IAS 18 *Revenue* and the IASB *Conceptual Framework* give general guidance. IAS 18 states that revenue and expenses that relate to the same transaction or event should be recognised simultaneously, and the *Conceptual Framework* says that the 'measurement and display of the financial effect of like transactions must be carried out in a consistent way'

It would be advisable, therefore, to match revenue and costs, and to **recognise revenue evenly** over the duration of the contract.

Power station

IAS 37 *Provisions, contingent liabilities and contingent assets* states that a provision should be recognised if:

- There is a present obligation as a result of a past transaction or event and
- It is probable that an outflow of resources embodying economic benefits will be required to settle the obligation
- A reliable estimate can be made of the amount of the obligation

In this case, the obligating event is the **installation of the power station**. The **operating licence** has created a **legal obligation** to incur the cost of removal, the expenditure is **probable,** and a **reasonable estimate** of the amount can be made.

Because Electron cannot operate its power station without incurring an obligation to pay for removal, **the expenditure also enables it to acquire economic benefits** (income from the energy generated). Therefore Electron correctly **recognises an asset** as well as a provision, and **depreciates this asset over its useful life of 20 years.**

Electron should recognise a provision for the cost of removing the power station, but should not include the cost of rectifying the damage caused by the generation of electricity until the power is generated. In this case the cost of rectifying the damage would be 5% of the total discounted provision.

The accounting treatment is as follows:

STATEMENT OF FINANCIAL POSITION AT 30 JUNE 20X6 (EXTRACTS)

	$m
Property, plant and equipment	
Power station	100.0
Decommissioning costs (W)	13.6
	113.6
Depreciation (113.6 ÷ 20)	(5.7)
	107.9
Provisions	
Provision for decommissioning at 1 July 20X5	13.6
Plus unwinding of discount (13.6 × 5%)	0.7
	14.3
Provision for damage (0.7(W)÷20)	0.1
	14.4

STATEMENT OF PROFIT OR LOSS AND OTHER COMPREHENSVIE INCOME
FOR THE YEAR ENDED 30 JUNE 20X6 (EXTRACTS)

	$m
Depreciation	5.7
Provision for damage	0.1
Unwinding of discount (finance cost)	0.7

Working

	$m
Provision for removal costs at 1 July 20X5 (95% × (15 ÷ 1.05))	13.6
Provision for damage caused by extraction at 30 June 20X6 (5% (15 ÷ 1.05))	0.7

Operating lease

One issue here is the **substance** of the lease agreement. IAS 17 *Leases* classifies leases as either finance leases or operating leases. A finance lease **transfers substantially all the risks and rewards of ownership to the lessee**, while an operating lease does not. The company **retains legal ownership of the equipment** and also **retains the benefits of ownership** (the equipment remains available for use in its operating activities). In addition, the **present value of the minimum lease payments is only 57.1% of the fair value of the leased assets** ($40 million ÷ $70 million). For a lease to be a finance lease, the present value of the minimum lease payments should be **substantially all** the fair value of the leased assets. Therefore the lease **appears to be correctly classified as an operating lease**.

A further issue is the **treatment of the fee received**. The company has recognised the whole of the net present value of the future income from the lease in profit or loss for the year to 30 June 20X6, despite the fact that only a deposit of $10 million has been received. In addition, the date of inception of the lease is 30 June 20X6, so **the term of the lease does not actually fall within the current period**. IAS 17 states that **income from operating leases should be recognised on a straight line basis over the lease term** unless another basis is more appropriate. IAS 18 *Revenue* applies here. It does not allow revenue to be recognised **before an entity has performed under the contract** and therefore **no revenue should be recognised** in relation to the operating leases for the current period.

Proposed dividend

The dividend was **proposed after the end of the reporting period** and therefore IAS 10 *Events after the reporting period* applies. This **prohibits the recognition of proposed dividends** unless these are declared before the end of the reporting period. The directors **did not have an obligation** to pay the dividend **at 31 October 20X5** and therefore there **cannot be a liability**. The directors seem to be arguing that their past record creates a constructive obligation as defined by IAS 37 *Provisions, contingent liabilities and contingent assets*. A constructive obligation may exist as a result of the proposal of the dividend, but this had **not arisen at the end of the reporting period**.

Although the proposed dividend is not recognised it was **approved before the financial statements were authorised for issue** and should be **disclosed** in the notes to the financial statements.

Share options

The share options granted on 1 July 20X5 are **equity-settled transactions**, and are governed by IFRS 2 *Share based payment*. The aim of this standard is to recognise the cost of share based payment to employees over the period in which the services are rendered. The options are generally **charged to profit or loss** on the basis of their **fair value at the grant date**. If the equity instruments are traded on an active market, market prices must be used. Otherwise an option pricing model would be used.

The conditions attached to the shares state that the share options will vest in three years' time provided that the employees remain in employment with the company. Often there are other conditions such as growth in share price, but here **employment is the only condition**.

The **treatment** is as follows:

- Determine the fair value of the options at grant date.
- Charge this fair value to profit or loss equally over the three year vesting period, making adjustments at each accounting date to reflect the best estimate of the number of options that will eventually vest. This will depend on the estimated percentage of employees leaving during the vesting period.

For the year ended 30 June 20X6, the charge to profit or loss is $3m × 94% × 1/3 = $940,000. Shareholders' equity will be increased by an amount equal to this profit or loss charge.

27 Egin Group

Text reference. Related parties are covered in Chapter 10 of the text.

Top tips. This question dealt with the importance of the disclosure of related party transactions and the criteria determining a related party. Additionally, it required candidates to identify related parties, and to account for goodwill and a loan made to one of the related parties which was a foreign subsidiary. Don't forget, from your group accounting knowledge, that goodwill relating to the foreign subsidiary is treated as a foreign currency asset and translated at the closing rate of exchange.

Easy marks. Part (a) should earn you five very easy marks, as it is basic knowledge. Part (b) is application, but very straightforward. This leaves only nine marks for the more difficult aspects.

Examiner's comment. The importance of related parties and their criteria was quite well answered, although candidates often quoted specific examples rather than the criteria for establishing related parties. The identification of related party relationships was well answered, but the accounting for the goodwill of the foreign subsidiary (and the loan made to it) were poorly answered.

Marking scheme

				Marks
(a)	(i)	Reasons and explanation		5
	(ii)	Egin		5
		Spade		3
		Atomic		3
(b)		Goodwill		5
		Loan		5
			Available	26
			Maximum	25

(a)   (i)   **Why it is important to disclose related party transactions**

The directors of Egin are correct to say that related party transactions are a normal feature of business. However, where entities are members of the same group, for example parent and subsidiary, the **financial performance and position of both entities can be affected**. An obvious instance of this is where one group company sells goods to another at artificially low prices. Even where there are no actual transactions between group companies, **a parent normally influences the way in which a subsidiary operates**. For example, a parent may instruct a subsidiary not to trade with particular customers or suppliers or not to undertake particular activities.

In the absence of other information, users of the financial statements **assume that a company pursues its interests independently** and undertakes transactions on an **arm's length basis** on terms that could have been obtained in a transaction with a third party. Knowledge of related party relationships and transactions affects the way in which users assess a company's operations and the risks and opportunities that it faces. Therefore **details of an entity's controlling party and transactions with related parties should be disclosed.** Even if the company's transactions and operations have not been affected by a related party relationship, **disclosure puts users on notice that they may be affected in future.**

Under IAS 24 *Related party disclosures* a related party is a person or entity that is related to the entity that is preparing its financial statements (the 'reporting entity')

Persons

IAS 24 states that a person or a close member of that person's family is related to a reporting entity if that person:

(1)   has **control** or **joint control** over the reporting entity;

(2)   has **significant influence** over the reporting entity; or

(3)   is a member of the **key management personnel** of the reporting entity or of a parent of the reporting entity.

Entities

An entity is related to a reporting entity if any of the following conditions applies:

(1)   The entity and the reporting entity are **members of the same group** (which means that each parent, subsidiary and fellow subsidiary is related to the others).

(2)   One entity is an **associate* or joint venture*** of the other entity (or an associate or joint venture of a member of a group of which the other entity is a member).

(3)   Both entities are **joint ventures* of the same third party**.

(4)   One entity is a **joint venture* of a third entity** and the other entity is an **associate of the third entity**.

(5)   The entity is a **post-employment benefit plan** for the benefit of employees of either the reporting entity or an entity related to the reporting entity.

(6)   The entity is **controlled** or **jointly controlled** by a person identified in the definition above

(7)   A person identified above as having control or joint control over the reporting entity has **significant influence** over the entity or is a member of the **key management personnel** of the entity (or of a parent of the entity).

*Including subsidiaries of the associate or joint venture.

(ii)   **Nature of related party relationships**

Within the Egin Group

Briars and Doye are related parties of Egin because they are **members of the same group** (both subsidiaries of Egin). For the same reason, as fellow subsidiaries, **Briars and Doye** are also **related parties of each other** . **Eye is also a related party of Egin** because it is an **associate of Egin.** (Egin has **significant influence** over Eye.)

Briars and Doye may be related parties of Eye. There is only one director in common and IAS 24 states that entities are not necessarily related simply because they have a director (or other member of key management personnel) in common, or because a member of key management personnel of one entity has significant influence over the other entity. However, **Eye is an associate of Egin**, and therefore **a member of the group** that Briars and Doye are members of (see (2) under 'Entities' above).

Although Tang was sold several months before the year end it was a **related party of Egin, Briars and Doye until then**. Therefore the related party relationship between Tang and the Egin group **should be disclosed** even though there were no transactions between them during the period.

Blue is a related party of Briars as a **director of Briars controls it**. Because the director is not on the management board of Egin it is **not clear whether Blue is also a related party of Egin group**. This would depend on whether the director is considered key management personnel at a group level. The director's services as a consultant to the group may mean that a related party relationship exists. . The issue would depend on whether this role meant that this person was directing or controlling a major part of the group's activities and resources.

Between Spade and the Egin Group

Spade is a related party of Doye because it exertss **significant influence** over Doye. This means that the **sale** of plant and equipment **to Spade must be disclosed**. **Egin is not necessarily a related party of Spade** simply because both have an investment in Doye. A related party relationship will only exist if one party **exercises influence** over another **in practice.**

The directors have proposed that disclosures should state that prices charged to related parties are set on an **arm's length basis**. Because the transaction took place **between related parties** by definition it **cannot have taken place on an arm's length basis** and this description would be **misleading**. Doye sold plant and equipment to Spade at **normal selling prices** and this is the information that should be disclosed, provided the terms can be substantiated.

Between Atomic and the Egin Group

Atomic is a related party of Egin because it can exercise **significant influence** over it. Atomic's significant influence over Egin gives it **significant influence over Briars and Doye** as they are controlled by Egin. **Eye is not a related party of Atomic** as atomic has no ability to exercise control or significant influence over Eye

(b)   **Goodwill arising on the acquisition of Briars**

IAS 21 *The effect of changes in foreign exchange rates* states that goodwill arising on the acquisition of a foreign subsidiary should be expressed in the functional currency of the foreign operation and **retranslated at the closing rate at each year-end**. Goodwill is calculated and translated as follows:

	Euros m	Rate	$m
Consideration transferred	50		25.0
Non-controlling interests (45 × 20%)	9	2	4.5
Less fair value of identifiable net assets at acquisition	(45)		(22.5)
Goodwill at acquisition	14		7.0
Impairment	(3)	2.5	(1.2)
Exchange loss (balancing figure)			(1.4)
At 31 May 20X6	11	2.5	4.4

Goodwill is measured at **$4.4 million** in the statement of financial position. An impairment loss of **$1.2 million** is **recognised in profit or loss** and an **exchange loss of $1.4 million** is **recognised in other comprehensive income (items that may subsequently be reclassified to profit or loss,** and taken to the translation reserve in equity.

Loan to Briars

The loan is a **financial liability measured at amortised cost**. The loan is measured at **fair value** on initial recognition. Fair value **the price that would be received to sell an asset or paid to transfer a liability in an orderly transaction between market participants at the measurement date**. This would normally be the actual transaction price. However, Egin and Briars are **related parties** and the transaction **has not taken place on normal commercial terms**.

IFRS 9 states that it is necessary to **establish what the transaction price would have been** in an orderly transaction between market participants at the measurement date. The amount that will eventually be repaid to Egin is $10 million and the normal commercial rate of interest is 6%. Therefore the fair value of the loan is its **discounted present value**, which is **retranslated at the closing rate** at each year-end.

Therefore the loan is measured at the following amounts in the statement of financial position:

	$'000	Rate	Euros000
At 1/6/20X5 $(10 \times \frac{1}{1.06^2})$	8,900	2	17,800
Interest (unwinding of discount) $(8,900 \times 6\%)$	534	2.3	1,228
Exchange loss			4,557
At 31/5/20X6 $(10 \times \frac{1}{1.06})$	9,434	2.5	23,585

The **unwinding of the discount** is recognised as a **finance cost** in profit or loss for the year and the **exchange loss** is also **recognised in profit or loss**.

Note. it would also be possible to calculate the finance cost for the year ended 31 May 20X6 at the closing rate. This would increase the exchange loss and the total expense recognised in profit and loss would be the same.

28 Engina

Text reference. Related parties are covered in Chapter 10.

Top tips. A good test of your ability to apply IAS 24 to a practical scenario.

Marking scheme

	Marks
Style of letter/report	4
Reasons	8
Goods to directors	4
Property	5
Group	4
Maximum	25

REPORT

To: The Directors
       Engina Co
       Zenda
       Ruritania
From: Ann Accountant

Date: 12 May 20X3

Related Party Transactions

The purpose of this report is to explain why it is necessary to **disclose related party transactions**. We appreciate that you may regard such disclosure as politically and culturally **sensitive**. However, there are **sound reasons why International Financial Reporting Standards require such disclosures**. It should be emphasised that related party transactions are a **normal part of business** life, and the disclosures are required to give a **fuller picture** to the users of accounts, rather than because they are problematic.

Prior to the issue of IAS 24, disclosures in respect of related parties were concerned with directors and their relationship with the group. The **IASB extends this definition and also the required disclosures**. This reflects the objective of the IASB to provide **useful data for investors**, not merely for companies to report on stewardship activities.

Unless investors know that transactions with related parties have not been carried out at **'arm's length'** between independent parties, they may fail to ascertain the **true financial position**.

Related party transactions typically take place on **terms which are significantly different** from those undertaken on normal commercial terms.

IAS 24 requires all material related party transactions to be disclosed.

It should be noted that related party transactions are not necessarily fraudulent or intended to deceive. Without proper disclosures, investors may be disadvantaged – IAS 24 seeks to remedy this.

Sale of goods to the director

(a) **Disclosure** of related party transactions is only necessary when the transactions are material. For the purposes of IAS 24, however, transactions are material when their disclosure might reasonably be **expected to influence decisions made by users of the financial statements, irrespective of their amount**.

(b) The **materiality** of a related party transaction with an individual, for example a director, must be **judged by reference to that individual** and not just the company. In addition, **disclosure of contracts** of **significance** with **directors** is required by most **Stock Exchanges**.

(c) Mr Satay has purchased $600,000 (12 × $50,000) worth of goods from the company and a car for $45,000, which is just over half its market value.

(d) The transactions are not material to the company, and because Mr Satay has considerable personal wealth, they are not material to him either.

(e) However, IAS 24 confirms that directors are related parties and transactions with directors should be disclosed. In addition, IAS 24 requires disclosure of **compensation** paid to directors. Compensation includes subsidised goods and benefits in kind. **Details of the transaction should be disclosed**, including the amount of the transactions and any outstanding balances.

Hotel property

(a) The hotel property sold to the Managing Director's brother is a **related party transaction**, and it appears to have been undertaken at **below market price**.

(b) IAS 24 envisages disclosure of the substance of the transaction.

(c) IAS 24 requires disclosure of 'information about the **transaction** and **outstanding balances** necessary for an understanding of the **potential effect of the relationship upon the financial statements**'.

(d) Not only must the transaction itself be disclosed, but the question of **impairment** needs to be **considered**. The value of the hotel has become impaired due to the **fall in property prices**, so the **carrying value needs to be adjusted** in accordance with IAS 36 *Impairment of assets*. The hotel should be shown at the lower of carrying value ($5m) and the recoverable amount. The recoverable amount is the higher of fair value less costs of disposal ($4.3m – $0.2m = $4.1m) and value in use ($3.6m). Therefore the hotel should be shown at $4.1m.

The sale of the property was for $100,000 below this impaired value, and it is this amount which needs to be disclosed. This would highlight the nature of the transactions within the existing property market conditions.

Group structure

(a) Local companies legislation and the Stock Exchange often require **disclosure of directors' interests** in a company's share capital. IAS 24 requires disclosure of the 'ultimate controlling party'. Mr Satay controls Engina as a result of his ownership of 80% of the share capital of Wheel.

(b) IAS 24 requires disclosure of the **related party relationship** between Engina and Wheel and also of **transactions** between the two companies, despite the fact that Engina is a wholly owned subsidiary.

(c) Engina's transactions with Car Ltd will also need to be disclosed. IAS 24 states that companies under **common control** are related parties, and the two companies are under the common control of Mr Satay.

29 Preparation question: Leases

(a) Interest rate implicit in the lease

PV = annuity × cumulative discount factor

250,000 = 78,864 × CDF

$$\therefore \text{CDF} \quad = \frac{250,000}{78,864}$$

= 3.170

∴ Interest rate is 10%

(b) *Property, plant and equipment*

Net book value of assets held under finance leases is $187,500.

Non-current liabilities

	$
Finance lease liabilities (W)	136,886

Current liabilities

	$
Finance lease liabilities (W) (196,136 – 136,886)	59,250

Statement of profit or loss and other comprehensive income (profit or loss section)

Depreciation on assets held under finance leases	62,500
Finance charges	25,000

Working

		$
Year ended 31 December 20X1:		
1.1.20X1	Liability b/d	250,000
1.1.20X1 – 31.12.20X1	Interest at 10%	25,000
31.12.20X1	Instalment in arrears	(78,864)
31.12.20X1	Liability c/d	196,136
Year ended 31 December 20X2:		
1.1.20X2 – 31.12.20X2	Interest at 10%	19,614
31.12.20X2	Instalment in arrears	(78,864)
31.12.20X2	Liability c/d	136,886

30 Holcombe

Text reference. Leasing is covered in Chapter 11. The *Conceptual Framework* is covered in Chapter 1.

Top tips. This was an untypical and rather demanding question. It is best to focus on Part (a), where marks are available for reasonable arguments. Make a reasonable attempt at the accounting entries in Part (b)(i), even if you are not sure about all of them. It is best not to worry about Part (b)(ii) which carries only three marks.

Easy marks. The definitions of asset and liability come straight from the *Conceptual Framework*, and should give some easy marks.

Examiner's comment. In discussing the weakness of current accounting standards in Part (a), candidates' answers were often quite narrow. Candidates scored well on the definitions of asset and liability, however. The purpose of Part (b) of the question was to show how a change in the current accounting standards (by recognising operating leases in the statement of financial position) would affect their accounting treatment. The question was well answered and candidates scored well generally on this question.

			Marks
(a)	(i)	Subjective	7
	(ii)	Subjective	7
		Professional marks	2
(b)	(i)	Recognition of gain	1
		Recognition of the leaseback	1
		Recognition of payment of rentals	2
		Recognition of interest expense and deprecation	2
	(ii)	Contingent rentals	3
			25

(a) (i) **Problems with current standards on lease accounting**

The different accounting treatment of finance and operating leases has been **criticised** for a number of reasons.

(1) Many users of financial statements believe that **all lease contracts give rise to assets and liabilities that should be recognised in the financial statements of lessees**. Therefore these users routinely adjust the recognised amounts in the statement of financial position in an attempt to assess the effect of the assets and liabilities resulting from operating lease contracts.

(2) The split between finance leases and operating leases can result in **similar transactions being accounted for very differently,** reducing comparability for users of financial statements.

(3) The difference in the accounting treatment of finance leases and operating leases also provides **opportunities to structure transactions so as to achieve a particular lease classification**.

It is also argued that the current accounting treatment of operating leases is **inconsistent with** the definition of assets and liabilities in the **IASB's** *Conceptual Framework*. An operating lease contract confers a valuable right to use a leased item. This right meets the *Conceptual Framework's* definition of an asset, and the liability of the lessee to pay rentals meets the *Conceptual Framework's* definition of a liability. However, the right and obligation are not recognised for operating leases.

Lease accounting is **scoped out of IAS 32, IAS 39 and IFRS 9,** which means that there are considerable differences in the treatment of leases and other contractual arrangements.

The IASB is addressing this matter. An Exposure Draft *Leases* was issued in 2010 and re-exposed in 2011. The proposed changes would put in place a consistent approach to lease accounting for both lessees and lessors – a '**right-of-use' approach.** Among other changes, this approach would result in the liability for payments arising under the lease contract and the right to use the underlying asset being included in the lessee's statement of financial position, thus providing more complete and useful information to investors and other users of financial statements.

(ii) **Holcombe's lease and framework definitions**

The IASB *Conceptual Framework* defines an **asset** as 'a resource controlled by the entity as a result of past events and from which future economic benefits are expected to flow to the entity'. Holcombe's leased plant would appear to meet this definition:

(1) Holcombe has the right to use the leased plant as an economic resource, that is to generate cash inflows or reduce cash outflows.

(2) Holcombe can be said to control the resource because the lessor does not have the right of access to the plant until the end of the contract without Holcombe's permission.

(3) The control results from past events, that is the signing of the lease contract.

(4)   Future economic benefits are expected to flow to Holcombe during the lease term.

In conclusion, the leased plant meets the *Framework's* definition of an asset.

The *Conceptual Framework* defines a **liability** as 'a present obligation of the entity arising from past events, the settlement of which is expected to result in an outflow from the entity of resources embodying economic benefits'. Applying this to Holcombe's lease of plant:

(1)   There is a present obligation to pay rentals.

(2)   The lessor has no contractual right (unless Holcombe breaches the contract) to take possession of the plant before the end of the contract, and similarly. Holcombe has no contractual right to terminate the contract and avoid paying rentals.

(3)   The obligation to pay rentals arises from a past event, namely the signing of the lease.

(4)   The obligation is expected to result in an outflow of economic benefits in the form of cash payments.

In conclusion, the leased plant meets the *Conceptual Framework's* definition of a liability.

(b)   (i)   **Sale and leaseback**

This is a sale and leaseback transaction involving an operating lease. It is assumed that the operating lease is being treated as an asset, and will therefore be accounted for using the same principles as IAS 17 currently uses for finance leases. It will be accounted for as follows in the financial statements of Holcombe for the year ended 30 April 20X5:

Sale of building on 1 May 20X4

DEBIT	Cash	$150m	
CREDIT	Office building		$120m
CREDIT	Deferred income (SOFP)		$30m

Being recognition of the gain on the sale of the building.

The gain is released over the five year lease period

DEBIT	Deferred income (SOFP) $30m ÷ 5	$6m	
CREDIT	Deferred income (P/L)		$6m

Being release of gain on sale of building.

DEBIT	Operating lease asset		$63.89m
CREDIT	Obligation to pay rentals		$63.89m

Being recognition of the leaseback at net present value of lease payments using 8% discount factor ($16m × 3.993)

First year of leaseback to 30 April 20X5

DEBIT	Lease obligation: rentals	$16m	
CREDIT	Cash		$16m

Being recognition of payment of rentals.

DEBIT	Finance cost	$5.11	
CREDIT	Lease obligation		$5.11

Being recognition of interest expense ($63.89m × 8%)

DEBIT	Depreciation expense	$12.78m	
CREDIT	Operating lease asset		$12.78m

Being recognition of depreciation of operating lease asset over five years ($63.89m ÷ 5)

In Holcombe's statement of financial position, the operating lease asset will be shown at a carrying value of $63.89m (initial recognition) less $12.78m (depreciation) = $51.11.

(ii)   **Inflation adjustment**

Inflation adjustments are not included in the minimum lease payment calculations. Instead they are effectively **contingent rent**, defined in IAS 17 *Leases* as 'that part of the rent that is not fixed in amount, but based on the future amount of a factor that changes other than with the passage of time'. They should be **recognised in the period in which they are incurred.**

Holcombe would recognise operating rentals as follows:

Year 1

$5 million

Year 2
$5 million plus ($5m × 4%) = $5.2m

Year 3
$5.2 million plus ($5.2m × 4%) = $5.408m

31 William

Text reference. Sale and leaseback is covered in Chapter 11 of your BPP Study Text. Employee benefits are in Chapter 5. Share-based payment is covered in Chapter 8 and contingent liabilities in Chapter 9 and Chapter 12 (in the context of business combinations).

Top tips. Part (a), on sale and leaseback, is more straightforward than some of the past exam questions on this subject. We have amended Part (b) on the defined benefit pension plan as it referred to an IAS 19 treatment prior to its 2011 revision, and now only the revised version is examinable. Part (c) deals with a a cash-settled share-based payment, a popular topic with this examiner. Part (d) tested a contingent liability: candidates needed to know that the treatment is different in the individual financial statements of the acquiree and in the consolidated financial statements, where the liability is recognised whether or not it is probable that an outflow of economic benefits will take place.

Easy marks. The structure of the question, which is broken down into manageable chunks, should make it easy to pick up the first few marks on each topic. There are some very easy marks for explaining when a lease is a finance lease in Part (a).

Examiner's comment. In Part (a), candidates generally dealt correctly with the treatment of the finance lease and the nature of the transfer of substantially the entire risks and rewards incident to ownership and understood the situations that would normally lead to a lease being classified as a finance lease. Candidates recognised that the building is derecognised at its carrying amount and then reinstated at its fair value but often took the disposal gain entirely to profit or loss, instead of it being deferred over the new lease term.. Answers to Part (c) were often confused. Part (d) was well answered on the whole, but some candidates were confused over the treatment of the two situations and stated that the treatment was the same in both scenarios.

ACCA Examiner's answer. The Examiner's answer to this question is included at the back of this Kit.

		Marks
(a)	Definition of lease	3
	Leaseback principle	1
	Accounting	3
(b)	Provision for relocation costs	3
	Curtailment (past service cost) of defined benefit pension plan	4
(c)	Cash-settled share-based payments	2
	Calculation	3
(d)	Contingent liability - discussion	4
Communication skills		2
		25

(a)   **Sale and leaseback**

The accounting treatment for this transaction will be depend, in the first instance, on whether it is a finance lease. A finance lease is a lease that **transfers substantially all the risks and rewards incidental to ownership of an asset.** All other leases are classified as operating leases. The classification, which is made at the inception of the lease, depends on the substance rather than the form, and could include the following situations.

(i)   The lease transfers ownership of the asset to the lessee by the end of the lease term.

(ii)   The lessee has the option to purchase the asset at a price which is expected to be sufficiently lower than the fair value at the date the option becomes exercisable for it to be reasonably certain, at the inception of the lease, that the option will be exercised.

(iii)   The lease term is for the major part of the economic life of the asset even if title is not transferred.

(iv)   At the inception of the lease, the present value of the minimum lease payments amounts to at least substantially all of the fair value of the leased asset.

(v)   The leased assets are of such a specialised nature that only the lessee can use them without major modifications.

William's lease of the building is for the **majority of the asset's life,** ie twenty years (criterion (iii) and the **present value of the minimum lease payments amounts to all the fair value** (sales proceeds) of the leased building of $5m. The lease should therefore be accounted for as a **finance lease.**

The **form** of this transaction is a **sale and leaseback,** but **in substance there has been no disposal** because William has **retained the risks and rewards of ownership.** A liability must be set up for the finance lease On 1 June 20X2:

DEBIT   Cash $5m
CREDIT   Finance lease liability $5m

The apparent gain (that is, the difference between the sale price and the previous carrying value) should be deferred and amortised in the financial statements of the seller/lessee over the lease term. It should not be recognised as income immediately:

DEBIT   Property, plant and equipment ($5m – $3.5m) $1.5m
CREDIT   Deferred income   (SOFP) $1.5m

The building is depreciated over the shorter of its useful life and the lease term, both twenty years, $5m ÷ 20 years = $0.25m:

DEBIT   Depreciation expense $0.25m
CREDIT   Accumulated depreciation $0.25m

The finance cost on the lease liability is charged at the implicit rate of 7% to profit or loss for the year ended 31 May 20X3. The amount is calculated as follows:

Finance lease liability

	$m
1 June 20X2 b/f	5.000
Finance cost: 5m × 7%	0.350
Instalment	(0.441)
31 May 20X3 c/f	4.909
Finance cost: 4.909m × 7%	0.344
Instalment	(0.441)
31 May 20X4 c/f	4.812

The finance lease liability at 31 May 20X3 is split between current and non-current:

	$m
Non-current liability (owed at 31 May 20X4)	4.812
Current liability (bal. fig.) = instalment (0.441) less finance cost (0.344)	0.097
Total liability at 31 May 20X3	4.909

The gain on the 'sale' is released over the twenty year period, $1.5m ÷ 20 years = $0.075m:

DEBIT   Deferred income   (SOFP) $0.075m
CREDIT   Deferred income   (P/L) $0.075m

(b)   **Relocation costs and reduction to net pension liability**

A **provision for restructuring** should be recognised in respect of the relocation of the provision during the year ended 31 May 20X3 in accordance with IAS 37 *Provisions, contingent liabilities and contingent assets*. This is because William's board of directors authorised a **detailed formal plan** for the relocation shortly before the year end (13 May 20X3) and William has **raised a valid expectation in affected employees** that it will carry out the restructuring by informing them of the main features of the plan. As the relocation is due to take within two months of the year end (July 20X3), the time value of money is likely to be immaterial. Therefore no discounting is required and a provision should be recognised at the estimated relocation costs of $50 million.

The reduction in the net pension liability as a result of the employees being made redundant and no longer accruing pension benefits is a **curtailment** under IAS 19 *Employee benefits (revised 2011)*. IAS 19 defines a curtailment as occurring when an entity significantly reduces the number of employees covered by a plan. It is **treated as a type of past service costs.** The past service cost may be negative (as is the case here) when the benefits are withdrawn so that the present value of the defined benefit obligation decreases. IAS 19 requires the past service cost to be **recognised in profit or loss** at the earlier of:

- When the plan curtailment occurs, and
- When the entity recognises the related restructuring costs

Here the restructuring costs (and corresponding provision) are recognised in the year ended 31 May 20X3 and the plan curtailment will not take place until after the year end in July 20X3 when the employees are made redundant. Therefore the reduction in the net pension liability and corresponding income in profit or loss should be recognised at the earlier of these two dates, ie when the restructuring costs are recognised in the year ended 31 May 20X3.

Both the relocation costs and income from the reduction in the net pension liability are likely to require **separate disclosure** in the statement of profit or loss and other comprehensive income or in the notes to the accounts per IAS 1 *Presentation of financial statements* due to their materiality.

(c)   **Share-based payment**

Share appreciation rights are **cash-settled share-based-payments.** IFRS 2 *Share-based payment* requires that the entity should measure the goods or services acquired and the liability incurred at the **fair value of the liability**. The fair value of the liability should be **measured at each reporting date** until the liability is settled and at the date of settlement. Any **changes** in fair value are recognised in profit or loss for the period.

	$
1 June 20X2 liability b/f: (20 – 3 (managers)) × 500 SARS × $14 (fair value) × 2/2 (vested)	119,000
Cash paid on exercise: 7 managers × 500 SARS × $21 (intrinsic value)	(73,500)
Expense (balancing figure)	74,500
31 May 20X3 liability c/f: (20 – 3 – 7 (managers)) × 500 SARS × $24 (fair value)	120,000

The expense for the year is accounted for as follows:

DEBIT Expense	(P/L)	$74,500	
CREDIT	Cash		$73,500
CREDIT	Liability		$1,000

(d)   **Contingent liability**

The legal claim against Chrissy will be treated differently in Chrissy's individual financial statements as compared with the consolidated accounts of the William group.

Chrissy's individual financial statements

The legal claim against Chrissy **does not meet the definition of a provision** under IAS 37 *Provisions, contingent liabilities and contingent assets.* One of IAS 37's requirements for a provision is that an outflow of resources embodying economic benefits should be probable, and William believes that it is more likely than not that such an **outflow will not occur.**

However, the possible payment does fall within the IAS 37 definition of a **contingent liability,** which is:

- A possible obligation depending on whether some uncertain future event occurs, or

- A present obligation but payment is not probable or the amount cannot be measured reliably

Therefore as **a contingent liability** the details of the claim and the $4 million estimated fair value of the contingent liability would be **disclosed** in the notes to the financial statements.

Consolidated financial statements

Under IFRS 3 *Business combinations,* an acquirer must allocate the cost of a business combination by recognising the acquiree's identifiable assets, liabilities and contingent liabilities that satisfy the recognition criteria at their **fair values** at the date of the acquisition. Contingent liabilities where there is only a possible obligation which, under IAS 37, depend on the occurrence or non-occurrence of some uncertain future event are not recognised under IFRS 3. However, the **IAS 37 probability criterion does not apply under IFRS 3**: a contingent liability is recognised **whether or not it is probable that an outflow** of economic benefits will take place, where there is a present obligation and its fair value can be measured reliably.

Consequently, William should **recognise the contingent liability as part of the business combination at its fair value** of $4 million. This will reduce net assets at acquisition, and therefore increase goodwill.

32 Marrgrett

Marking scheme

	Marks
Consideration	6
IFRS 3 and consideration	5
Consideration	2
Intangible assets	2
NCI	5
Finalisation and reorganisation provision	2
IFRS 10	3
Professional marks	2
Available	25

Revision of IFRS 3 Business combinations

IFRS 3 Business combinations was extensively revised, and the revised standard issued in 2008. The revised IFRS 3 views **the group as an economic entity.** This means that it treats all providers of equity – including non-controlling interests – as shareholders in the group, even if they are not shareholders of the parent.

All business combinations are accounted for as **acquisitions**. The revisions to IFRS 3 affect both the consideration, and the business acquired. Specifically, **all consideration is now measured at fair value,** and there are implications for the valuation of the non-controlling interest.

Marrgrett is proposing to purchase additional shares in its associate, Josey. An increase from 30% to 70% will **give control,** as the holding passes the all-important 50% threshold. The changes to IFRS 3 have far-reaching implications for various aspects of the acquisition, which is what the standard calls a 'business combination achieved in stages'.

Equity interest already held

Consideration includes cash, assets, contingent consideration, equity instruments, options and warrants. It also includes the **fair value of any equity interest already held**, which marks a departure from the previous version of IFRS 3. This means that **the 30% holding must be re-measured to fair value** at the date of the acquisition of the further 40% holding. The revalued 30% stake, together with the consideration transferred in the form of cash and shares, is compared to the fair value of Josey's net assets at the date control was obtained, in order to arrive at a figure for goodwill.

Any **gain or loss** on the revaluation of the associate is taken to **profit or loss for the year.**

Transaction costs

The original IFRS 3 required fees (legal, accounting, valuation etc) paid in relation to a business acquisition to be included in the cost of the acquisition, which meant that they were measured as part of goodwill.

Under the revised IFRS 3 **costs relating to the acquisition must be recognised as an expense** at the time of the acquisition. They are not regarded as an asset. (Costs of issuing debt or equity are to be accounted for under the rules of IFRS 9.)

Share options

As an incentive to the shareholders and employees of Josey to remain in the business, Marrgrett has offered share options in Josey. These are conditional on them remaining in employment for two years after the acquisition, that is they are contingent on future events. The question arises of whether they are **contingent consideration**, for which the treatment is specified in the revised IFRS 3, **or as compensation** for services after the acquisition, for which the treatment is given in IFRS 2 Share-based payment.

The conditions attached to the share options are employment based, rather than contingent on, say, the performance of the company. Accordingly the options must be treated as **compensation and valued under the rules of IFRS 2. The charge will be to post-acquisition earnings**, since the options are given in exchange for services after the acquisition.

Contingent consideration

The additional shares being offered to Josey's shareholders to the value of $50,000 are contingent on the achievement of a certain level of profitability. These are contingent consideration, defined in IFRS 3 as:

> Usually, an obligation of the acquirer to transfer additional assets or equity interests to the former owners of an acquiree as part of the exchange for control of the acquiree if specified future events occur or conditions are met.

The original IFRS 3 required contingent consideration to be accounted for **only if it was probable that it would become payable** and could be measured reliably. Subsequent changes in the amount of the contingent consideration were accounted for as adjustments to the cost of the business combination, and therefore generally as changes to goodwill.

However, the revised IFRS 3 recognises that, by entering into an acquisition, the acquirer becomes obliged to make additional payments. Not recognising that obligation means that the consideration recognised at the acquisition date is not fairly stated. Accordingly, the revised IFRS 3 **requires recognition of contingent consideration, measured at fair value, at the acquisition date.**

The shares worth up to $50,000 meet the IAS 32 *Financial instruments: presentation* definition of a financial liability. This contingent consideration will be **measured at fair value,** and any **changes** to the fair value on subsequent re-measurement will be taken to **profit or loss for the year.**

Intangible assets

Josey's intangible assets, which include trade names, internet domain names and non-competition agreements, will be **recognised on acquisition** by Marrgrett of a controlling stake. IFRS 3 revised gives more detailed guidance on intangible assets than did the previous version; as a result, more intangibles may be recognised than was formerly the case. The more intangibles are recognised, the lower the figure for goodwill, which is consideration transferred less fair value of assets acquired and liabilities assumed.

Non-controlling interest

As indicated above, the revised IFRS views the group as an economic entity and so non-controlling shareholders are also shareholders in the group. This means that goodwill attributable to the non-controlling interest needs to be recognised.

The non-controlling interest now forms part of the calculation of goodwill. The question now arises as to how it should be valued.

The 'economic entity' principle suggests that the non-controlling interest should be valued at fair value. In fact, IFRS 3 gives a **choice:**

For each business combination, the acquirer shall measure any non-controlling interest in the acquiree **either at fair value or at the non-controlling interest's proportionate share of the acquiree's identifiable net assets**. *(IFRS 3)*

IFRS 3 revised suggests that the closest approximation to fair value will be the market price of the shares held by the non-controlling shareholders just before the acquisition by the parent.

Non-controlling interest at fair value will be different from non-controlling interest at proportionate share of the acquiree's net assets. The difference is goodwill attributable to non-controlling interest, which may be, but often is not, proportionate to goodwill attributable to the parent.

Effect of type of consideration

The nature of the consideration transferred – cash, shares, contingent, and so on – **does not affect the goodwill.** However, the structure of the payments may affect post-acquisition profits. For example if part of the consideration is contingent (as here), changes to the fair value will be reflected in profit or loss for the year in future years.

Partial disposal

Under the revised IFRS 3, the treatment of a partial disposal depends on whether or not control is retained. Generally, control is lost when the holding is decreased to less than 50%.

On disposal of a controlling interest, any retained interest (an associate or trade investment) is measured at fair value on the date that control is lost. This fair value is used in the calculation of the gain or loss on disposal, and also becomes the carrying amount for subsequent accounting for the retained interest.

If the **50%** boundary is **not crossed**, as when the interest in a subsidiary is reduced, the event is treated as a **transaction between owners**.

Whenever the 50% boundary is crossed, the existing interest is revalued, and a gain or loss is reported in profit or loss for the year. If the 50% boundary is not crossed, no gain or loss is reported; instead there is an **adjustment to the parent's equity.**

Margrett intends to **retain control of the first subsidiary**, so in this case there will be no gain or loss, but an adjustment to the Margrett's equity to reflect the increase in non-controlling interest. In the case of the **second subsidiary,** however, **control is lost**. A **gain will be recognised on the portion sold, and also on the portion retained,** being the difference between the fair value and the book value of the interest retained.

Re-organisation provision

IFRS 10 *Consolidated financial statements* explains that a plan to restructure a subsidiary following an acquisition is not a present obligation of the acquiree at the acquisition date, unless it meets the criteria in IAS 37 *Provisions, contingent liabilities and contingent assets*. This is very unlikely to be the case at the acquisition date. Therefore Margrett **should not recognise a liability** for the re-organisation of the group at the date of the acquisition.

This **prevents creative accounting**. An acquirer cannot set up a provision for restructuring or future losses of a subsidiary and then release this to profit or loss in subsequent periods in order to reduce losses or smooth profits.

33 Preparation question: Associate

J GROUP CONSOLIDATED STATEMENT OF FINANCIAL POSITION AS AT 31 DECEMBER 20X5

Assets	$'000
Non-current assets	
Freehold property (1,950 + 1,250 + 370 (W7))	3,570
Plant and equipment (795 + 375)	1,170
Investment in associate (W3)	480
	5,220
Current assets	
Inventories (575 + 300 – 20 (W6))	855
Trade receivables (330 + 290))	620
Cash at bank and in hand (50 + 120)	170
	1,645
	6,865

	$'000
Equity and liabilities	
Equity attributable to owners of the parent	
Issued share capital	2,000
Retained earnings	1,785
	3,785
Non-controlling interests (W5)	890
Total equity	4,675
Non-current liabilities	
12% debentures (500 + 100)	600
Current liabilities	
Bank overdraft	560
Trade payables (680 + 350)	1,030
	1,590
Total liabilities	2,190
	6,865

Workings

1   Group structure

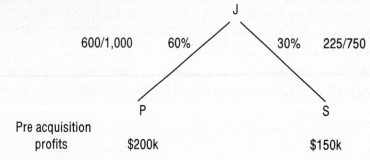

	P	S
Pre acquisition profits	$200k	$150k

2   Goodwill

	$'000	$'000
Consideration transferred		1,000
NCI (at 'full' FV: 400 × $1.65)		660
Net assets acquired:		
Share capital	1,000	
Retained earnings at acquisition	200	
Fair value adjustment (W7)	400	
		(1,600)
		60
Impairments to date		(60)
Year-end value		–

3   *Investment in associate*

	$'000
Cost of associate	500.0
Share of post acquisition retained reserves (W4)	72.0
Less impairment of investment in associate	(92.0)
	480.0

4   *Retained earnings*

	J Co $'000	P Co $'000	S Co $'000
Retained earnings per question	1,460	885	390
Unrealised profit (W6)		(20)	
Fair value adjustment movement (W6)		(30)	
Retained earnings at acquisition		(200)	(150)
		635	240

P Co: share of post acquisition retained earnings
60% × 635   381

S Co: share of post acquisition retained earnings
30% × 240   72

Goodwill impairments to date
P Co: 60 (W2) × 60%   (36)
S Co   (92)
                                                                         1,785

5   *Non-controlling interests*

	$'000
NCI at acquisition (W2)	660
NCI share of post acq'n ret'd earnings ((W4) 635 × 40%)	254
NCI share of impairment losses ((W2) 60 × 40%)	(24)
	890

6   *Unrealised profit on inventories*

P Co ⟶ J Co $100k × 25/125 = $20,000

7   Fair value adjustment table

	At acquisition $'000	Movement $'000	At reporting date $'000
Land	200		200
Buildings	200	(30)	170 (200 × 34/40)
	400	(30)	370

34 Preparation question: 'D'-shaped group

(a) BAUBLE GROUP

CONSOLIDATED STATEMENT OF FINANCIAL POSITION AS AT 31 DECEMBER 20X9

	$'000
Non-current assets	
Property, plant and equipment (720 + 60 + 70)	850
Goodwill (W2)	111
	961
Current assets (175 + 95 + 90)	360
	1,321
Equity attributable to owners of the parent	
Share capital – $1 ordinary shares	400
Retained earnings (W3)	600
	1,000
Non-controlling interest (W4)	91
	1,091
Current liabilities (120 + 65 + 45)	230
	1,321

Workings

1   *Group Structure*

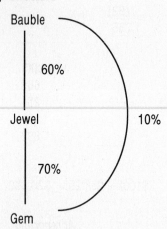

Bauble

60%

Jewel   10%

70%

Gem

Bauble interest in Gem

– direct	10%
– indirect (60% × 70%)	42%
	52%
Non-controlling interest in Gem	48%

2   *Goodwill*

	Jewel		*Gem*	
	$'000	$'000	$'000	$'000
Consideration transferred: Bauble		142		43.0
Consideration transferred: Jewel			(100 × 60%)	60.0
NCI	(145 × 40%)	58	(90 × 48%)	43.2
Net assets at acq'n as represented by:				
Share capital	100		50	
Ret'd earnings	45		40	
		(145)		(90.0)
Goodwill		55		56.2

Total goodwill = $111,200

3   *Consolidated retained earnings*

	B $'000	J $'000	G $'000
Per Q	560	90	65
Less: pre-acquisition ret'd earnings		(45)	(40)
		45	25
J – share of post acquisition ret'd earnings (45 × 60%)	27		
G – share of post acquisition ret'd earnings (25 × 52%)	13		
	600		

4   *Non-controlling interests*

	Jewel $'000	Gem $'000
NCI at acquisition (W2)	58	43.2
NCI share of post acquisition retained earnings:		
Jewel ((W3) 45 × 40%)	18	
Gem ((W3) 25 × 48%)		12
NCI in investment in Gem (100 × 40%)	(40)	
	36	55.2

91.2

(b)   **Goodwill**

	Jewel		Gem	
	$'000	$'000	$'000	$'000
Consideration transferred: Bauble		142		43.0
Consideration transferred: Jewel			(100 × 60%)	60.0
NCI	(160 × 40%)	64	(90 × 48%)	43.2
Net assets at acq'n as represented by:				
Share capital	100		50	
Ret'd earnings	60		40	
		(160)		(90)
Goodwill		46		56.2

102.2

35 Preparation question: Sub-subsidiary

Text reference. Complex groups are covered in Chapter 13.

Top tips. This question is quite straightforward as long as you remember how to calculate the NCI of a sub-subsidiary. Points to watch in this question are the treatment of intragroup transactions and the calculation of non-controlling interest.

Easy marks. With complex groups, remember to sort out the group structure first. There are enough straightforward marks available here if you remember your basic rules for consolidations. The consolidation is quite straightforward as long as you remember how to calculate the NCI of a sub-subsidiary.

(a) EXOTIC GROUP
CONSOLIDATED STATEMENT OF PROFIT OR LOSS AND OTHER COMPREHENSIVE INCOME
FOR THE YEAR ENDED 31 DECEMBER 20X9

	$'000
Revenue: 45,600 + 24,700 + 22,800 – (W6) 740	92,360
Cost of sales: 18,050 + 5,463 + 5,320 – (W6) 740+ (W6) 15 + (W6) 15(W6)	(28,123)
Gross profit	64,237
Distribution costs (3,325 + 2,137 + 1,900)	(7,362)
Administrative expenses (3,475 + 950 + 1,900)	(6,325)
Finance costs	(325)
Profit before tax	50,225
Income tax expense (8,300 + 5,390 + 4,241)	(17,931)
Profit for the year	32,294

Other comprehensive income for the year (items that will not be reclassified to P/L)

	$'000
Revaluation of property (200 + 100)	300
Total comprehensive income	32,594

Profit attributable to:

	$'000
Owners of the parent	28,581
Non-controlling interest (W4)	3,713
	32,294

Total comprehensive income attributable to:

	$'000
Owners of the parent	28,871
Non-controlling interest (W4)	3723
	32,594
Dividends paid and declared for the period	9,500

(b) EXOTIC GROUP
CONSOLIDATED STATEMENT OF FINANCIAL POSITION AS AT 31 DECEMBER 20X9

	$'000
Non-current assets	
Property, plant and equipment: 35,483 + 24,273 + 13,063 + (W7) 575	73,394
Goodwill (W2)	3,520
	76,914
Current assets :1,568 + 9,025 + 8,883 – (W6) 15 – (W6) 15	19,446
	96,360
Equity attributable to owners of the parent	
Share capital	8,000
Retained earnings (W3)	56,642
	64,642
Non-controlling interest (W4)	8,584
	73,226
Current liabilities (13,063 + 10,023 + 48)	23,134
	96,360

Workings

1   *Group structure*

         Exotic
         | 90%
         Melon
         | 80%

Kiwi	Effective interest (90% × 80%)	72%
	∴ Non-controlling interest	28%
		100%

2 Goodwill

	Melon $000		Kiwi $000
Consideration transferred	6,650	3,800 × 90%	3,420
Non-controlling interests (at 'full' fair value)	500		900
FV of identifiable net assets at acq'n:			
Per qu/ 2,000 (SC) + 950 (RE)	(5,000)		(2,950)
	2,150		1,370
		3,520	

3 Retained earnings

	Exotic $'000	Melon $'000	Kiwi $'000
Retained earnings per question	22,638	24,075	19,898
Less: PUP (W6)		(15)	(15)
Pre-acquisition retained earnings		(1,425)	(950)
		22,635	18,933
Share of Melon (22,635 × 90%)	20,372		
Share of Kiwi (18,933 × (W1) 72%)	13,632		
	56,642		

4 Non-controlling interest (SOCI)

	Melon		Kiwi	
	PFY $'000	TCI $'000	PFY $'000	TCI $'000
Per question	10,760	10,860	9,439	9,439
Less intragroup trading (W6)	(15)	(15)	(15)	(15)
	10,745	10,845	9,424	9,424
× 10%	1,074	1,084		
× 28% (W1)			2,639	2,639
		3,713		
			3,723	

5 Non-controlling interests (statement of financial position)

	Melon $000	Kiwi $000
NCI at acquisition (W2)	500	900
NCI share of post acquisition retained earnings:		
Melon ((W3) 22,635 × 10%)	2,263.5	
Kiwi ((W3) 18,933 × (W1) 28%)		5,301.2
NCI in investment in Kiwi (3,800 × 10%)	(380)	
	2,383.5	6,201.2
		8,584.7

6 Intragroup trading

(i) Cancel intragroup sale/purchase:

DEBIT group revenue (260 + 480)	$740,000	
CREDIT group cost of sales		$740,000

(ii)   Unrealised profit

		$'000
Melon (60 × 25/125)		15
Kiwi (75 × 25/125)		15

Adjust in books of seller:

DEBIT Cost of sales/retained earnings
CREDIT Group Inventories

7   *Fair value adjustment*

Melon:

	At acqn 1 Jan 20X5 $'000	Movement $'000	At year end 31 Dec 20X9 $'000
Land: 5,000.000 – (3,000,000 + 1,425,000)	575	–	575

8   *Revenue* *

	$'000
Exotic	45,600
Melon	24,700
Kiwi	22,800
Less intragroup sales (W6)	(740)
	92,360

9   *Cost of sales* *

	$'000
Exotic	18,050
Melon	5,463
Kiwi	5,320
Add PUP (W6): Melon	15
Kiwi	15
	28,123

* **Note**. Workings 8 and 9 are included for completeness. You should do the workings on the face of the SPLOCI.

36 Glove

Text reference. Complex groups are covered in Chapter 13.

Top tips. This question required the preparation of a consolidated statement of financial position of a group which contained a sub-subsidiary. In addition, candidates had to account for brand names, a retirement benefit plan, a convertible bond, and an exchange of plant. The question was a little easier than in previous exams, and you should not have been alarmed at getting both pensions and financial instruments, since only the straightforward aspects were being tested.

Easy marks. There are marks for standard consolidation calculations (goodwill, NCI, retained earnings) which should be familiar to you from your earlier studies, and for setting out the proforma, even if you didn't have time to do the fiddly adjustments. The convertible bond – don't be scared because it is a financial instrument! – is something you have covered at an earlier level.

Examiner's comment. The accounting for the sub-subsidiary was reasonably well answered but candidates found the application of the corridor approach a major problem. The convertible bond element was relatively straight-forward and would have sat quite well in a lower level paper. However, candidates found this element quite difficult.

The parameters of the syllabus in the area of financial instruments have been well documented, but candidates do not seem to be able to grasp the fundamentals of the subject. The treatment of the trade name was again not well answered with the principles of recognition seldom set out correctly. Overall, the consolidation element was quite well answered but the additional technical elements were poorly treated by candidates in their answers.

	Marks
Equity	7
Reserves	6
Non-current liabilities	3

	Marks
Defined benefit plan	4
Convertible bond	4
Plant	2
Trade name	3
Available	29
Maximum	25

GLOVE GROUP
CONSOLIDATED STATEMENT OF FINANCIAL POSITION AS AT 31 MAY 20X7

	$m
Non-current assets	
Property, plant and equipment	
260 + 20 + 26 + 6 (W6) + 5(W6) + 3 (W9)	320.0
Goodwill (W2)	10.1
Other intangibles: trade name (W6)	4.0
Investments in equity instruments	10.0
Current assets: 65 + 29 + 20	344.1
	114.0
Total assets	458.1
Equity and liabilities	
Equity attributable to owners of parent	
Ordinary shares	150.0
Other reserves (W4)	30.7
Retained earnings (W3)	150.9
Equity component of convertible debt (W8)	1.6
	333.2
Non-controlling interests (W5)	28.9
	362.1
Non-current liabilities (W10)	
45 + 2 + 3 + 0.1 (W7) − 30 + 28.9 (W8)	49.0
Current liabilities: 35 + 7 + 5	47.0
	96.0
Total equity and liabilities	458.1

Workings

1   Group structure

	Glove		
1 June 20X5	80%	Retained earnings	$10m
		Other reserves	$4m
	Body		
1 June 20X5	70%	Retained earnings	$6m
		Other reserves	$8m
	Fit		

	%
Effective interest: 80% × 70%	56
∴ Non-controlling interest	44
	100

2 Goodwill

	Glove in Body		Body in Fit	
	$m	$m	$m	$m
Consideration transferred		60	(30 × 80%)	24.00
Non-controlling interests	(65 × 20%)	13	(39 × 44%)	17.16
Fair value of net assets at acq'n:				
Per question	60		39	
Trade name (W6)	5		–	
		(65)		(39.00)
		8		2.16

10.16

3 Retained earnings

	Glove	Body	Fit
	$m	$m	$m
Per question	135.00	25	10
Fair value movement (W6)	–	(1)	–
Convertible bonds (W8) (2.3 – 1.8)	(0.50)		
Assets exchange:			
Adjustment to plant (W9)	3.00		
Less pre-acquisition		(10)	(6)
		14	4
Share of Body			
80% × 14			
	11.20		
Share of Fit			
56% × 4	2.24		
	150.94		

4 Other reserves

	Glove	Body	Fit
	$m	$m	$m
Per question	30.0	5	8
Pension scheme (W7)	(0.1)		
Less pre-acquisition		(4)	(8)
		1	–
Share of body			
80% × 1	0.8		
Share of Fit			
56% × 0	0.0		
	30.7		

5 Non-controlling interests

	Body	Fit
	$m	$m
NCI at acquisition (W2)	13	17.16
NCI share of post acquisition retained earnings:		
Body ((W3) 14 × 20%)	2.8	
Fit ((W3) 4 × 44%)		1.76
NCI share of post acquisition other reserves:		
Body ((W4) 1 × 20%)	0.2	
Fit ((W4) 0 × 44%)		0
NCI in investment in Fit (30 × 20%)	(6)	
	10	18.92

28.92

6   *Fair value adjustments*

	At acquisition $m	Movement (2 years) $m	At reporting date (31 May 20X7) $m
Body			
Land: 60 – (40 + 10 + 4)	6	–	6
Brand name (note)	5	(1)	4
	11	(1)	10
Fit			
Land: 39 – (20 + 8 + 6)	5	–	5

Note. The trade name is an internally generated intangible asset. While these are not normally recognised under IAS 38 *Intangible assets*, IFRS 3 *Business combinations* allows recognition if the fair value can be measured reliably. Thus this Glove should recognise an intangible asset on acquisition (at 1 June 20X5). This will reduce the value of goodwill.

The trade name is amortised over ten years, of which two have elapsed: $5m × 2/10 = $1m.

So the value is $(5 – 1)m = $4m in the consolidated statement of financial position.

7   *Defined benefit pension scheme*

The amount to be recognised is as follows

	$m
Loss on remeasurement through OCI on defined benefit obligation	(1.0)
Gain on remeasurment through OCI on plan assets	0.9
	(0.1)

Accounting entries:

DEBIT	Other comprehensive income	$0.1m	
CREDIT	Net defined benefit liability		$0.1m

8   *Convertible bond*

Under IAS 32, the bond must be split into a liability and an equity component:

	$m	$m
Proceeds: 30,000 × $1,000		30

Present value of principal in three years' time

$$\$30m \times \frac{1}{1.08^3}$$ 23.815

Present value of interest annuity
$30m × 6% = $1,800,000

$$\times \frac{1}{1.08}$$ 1.667

$$\times \frac{1}{(1.08)^2}$$ 1.543

$$\times \frac{1}{(1.08)^3}$$ 1.429

Liability component	(28.454)
∴ Equity component	1.546

Rounded to $1.6m

Balance of liability at 31 May 20X7

	$'000
Balance b/d at 1 June 20X6	28,454
Effective interest at 8%	2,276
Coupon interest paid at 6%	(1,800)
Balance c/d at 31 May 20X7	28,930

9   *Exchange of assets*

The cost of the plant should be measured at the fair value of the asset given up, rather than the carrying value. An adjustment must be made to the value of the plant, and to retained earnings.

	$
Fair value of land	7
Carrying value of land	(4)
∴ Adjustment required	3

DEBIT	Plant	$3m
CREDIT	Retained earnings	$3m

10   *Non-current liabilities*

Note. This working is for additional information. To save time, you should do yours on the face of the consolidated position statement

	$m	$m
Non-current liabilities per question:		
Glove	45	
Body	2	
Fit	3	
		50.0
Unrecognised actuarial losses (W7)		0.1
Proceeds of convertible bond		(30.0)
Value of liability component		28.9
		49.0

37 Case study question: Rod

Text reference. Complex groups are covered in Chapter 13; provisions in Chapter 9; intangibles in Chapter 4; ethics in Chapter 2.

Top tips. This question required candidates to prepare a consolidated statement of financial position of a complex group. Candidates were given a basic set of data – information concerning current accounting practices – which required adjustment in the financial statements, and information about the implementation of 'new' accounting standards. This type of question will appear regularly on this paper (obviously with different group scenarios and different accounting adjustments). Candidates had to deal with adjustments relating to tangible non-current assets, inventory and defined benefit pension schemes. Part (c) is a practical question on key issues. In part (d), do not be tempted to waffle. Part (e) concerns ethics, a topic new to this syllabus.

Examiner's comment. Generally speaking, candidates performed quite well on this question but often struggled with the accounting for the defined benefit pension scheme. Many candidates treated one of the subsidiaries as an associate. In this situation, where the relationship between the companies has been incorrectly determined, marks are awarded for the methodology used in the question.

Marking scheme

			Marks
(a)	Defined benefit pension scheme		5
(b)	Shareholding		3
	Equity – Line		6
	Non current assets – Line		4
	Equity – Reel		8
	Fair value adjustment		2
	Group properties, plant and equipment		2
	Group retained earnings		3
	Trade receivables		1
	Inventory		1
(c)	(i)	Provision: current practice	4
		acceptability	2
	(ii)	Fine: intangible asset	3
		acceptability	2
(d)	1 mark per valid point		10
(e)	For		2
	Against		2
	Conclusion		1
		Available	61
		Maximum	50

(a) Defined benefit pension scheme

The defined benefit pension scheme is treated in accordance with IAS 19 *Employee benefits*.

The pension scheme has a deficit of liabilities over assets:

The statement of financial position includes:

	$m
Present value of pension obligation	(130)
Fair value of plan assets	125
Liability	(5)

The defined benefit expense recognised in profit or loss for the year includes:

	$m
Current service cost	110
Net interest cost (20 – 10)	10
	120

The defined benefit remeasurement included in other comprehensive income for the year (not to be reclassified to profit or loss), in accordance with the revised IAS 19, is a gain of $15m (see below for calculation).

Changes in present value of the defined benefit obligation

	$m
Opening defined benefit obligation	nil
Interest cost on defined benefit obligation	20
Current service cost	110
Gain/loss on remeasurement through OCI (balancing figure)	0
Closing defined benefit obligation	130

Changes in fair value of plan assets

	$m
Opening fair value of plan assets	nil
Interest on plan assets	10
Contributions	100
Gain on remeasurement through OCI (balancing figure)	15
Closing fair value of plan assets	125

..

Adjustment to the group accounts:

	$m	$m
DEBIT Retained earnings	120	
CREDIT Other comprehensive income (other components of equity)		15
CREDIT Trade receivables		100
CREDIT Defined benefit pension liability		5

(b) ROD

CONSOLIDATED STATEMENT OF FINANCIAL POSITION AT 30 NOVEMBER 20X3

	$m
Non-current assets	
Property, plant and equipment (W6)	1,930
Goodwill (W2)	132
	2,062
Current assets	
Inventories (300 + 135 + 65 – 20)	480
Receivables (240 + 105 + 49 – 100(part (a))	294
Cash at bank and in hand	220
	994
	3,056
Equity attributable to owners of the parent	
Share capital	1,500
Share premium	300
Other components of equity (W4)	40
Retained earnings (W3)	546
	2,386
Non-controlling interest (W5)	265
	2,651
Non-current liabilities	
Net pension liability	5
Other	180
Current liabilities	220
	3,056

Workings

1   *Group structure*

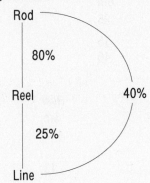

Rod's total holding in Line is 60% (40% direct + 80% × 25% indirect).

2   *Goodwill*

	Reel		Line	
	$m	$m	$m	$m
Consideration transferred – Rod		640		160
Consideration transferred – Reel (100 × 80%)				80
Non-controlling interests (710 × 20%)/(300 × 40%)		142		120
FV of identifiable net assets at acq'n:				
Share capital	500		200	
Share premium	100		50	
Retained earnings	100		50	
Fair value adjustment	10		—	
		(710)		(300)
		72		60
			132	

3   *Retained earnings*

	Rod	Reel	Line
	$m	$m	$m
Per question	600.0	200	60
Fair value adjustment realised		(10)	
Development costs written off		(20)	
Trade discount on tangible assets less depreciation		(5)	
Adjustment for excess depreciation (W6)			14
At acquisition		(100)	(50)
	600.0	65	24
Group share of Reel (80% × 65)	52.0		
Group share of Line (60% × 24)	14.4		
Less defined benefit pension scheme (part (a))	(120.0)		
	546.4		

Note. The development costs do not meet the recognition criteria in IAS 38 and they cannot be treated as inventory because they have previously been written off as incurred. They were reinstated after acquisition, so they must be written off post-acquisition reserves.

4 Other components of equity

	Rod $m
Per question	25
Add benefit pension scheme (part (a))	15
	40

5 Non-controlling interests

	Reel $m	Line $m
NCI at acquisition (W2)	142	120
NCI share of post acquisition retained earnings:		
Reel ((W3) 65 × 20%)	13	
Line ((W3) 24 × 40%)		9.6
NCI in investment in Line (100 × 20%)	(20)	—
	135	129.6

264.6

6 Property, plant and equipment

	$m
Rod	1,230
Reel	505
Line	256
	1,991
Less adjustment to PPE of Line (W7)	(56)
Reel: trade discount net of depreciation (6 × 5/6)	(5)
	1,930

Note. IAS 16 states that the cost of a item of PPE should be measured net of trade discounts. The trade discount must be deducted from Reel's tangible assets.

7 Adjustment to property, plant and equipment of Line

An adjustment must be made to re-state the PPE of Line from their revalued amount to depreciated historical cost, in line with group accounting policies.

The revaluation took place after acquisition, so the adjustment does not affect goodwill.

	Valuation $m	Depreciated historic cost $m
Cost at 1 December 20X1 (date of acquisition by Rod)	300	300
Depreciation (300/6)	(50)	(50)
NBV at 30 November 20X2	250	250
Revaluation	70	–
Revalued amount	320	
Depreciation (320/5)	(64)	(50)
NBV at 30 November 20X3	256	200

Adjustment required to the group accounts:	$m	$m
DEBIT Revaluation surplus	70	
CREDIT Retained earnings (64 – 50)		14
CREDIT Property, plant and equipment (256 – 200)		56

(c) (i) **Restructuring of the group**

IAS 37 *Provisions, contingent liabilities and contingent assets* **contains specific requirements** relating to **restructuring provisions**. The general recognition criteria apply and IAS 37 also states that **a provision should be recognised** if an entity has a **constructive obligation** to carry out a restructuring. A constructive obligation exists where **management has a detailed formal plan** for the restructuring and has also raised a **valid expectation** in those affected that it will carry out the restructuring. In this case, the company made a **public announcement** of the restructuring **after the year end**, but it had actually **drawn up the formal plan and started to implement it before the year end**, by communicating the plan to trade union representatives. Although the plan is **expected to take two years to complete**, it appears that the company **had a constructive obligation to** restructure at the year end. Therefore **a provision should be recognised**.

IAS 37 states that a restructuring provision should include **only the direct expenditure** arising from the restructuring. Costs that relate to the **future conduct of the business**, such as training and relocation costs, **should not be included**. Measuring the provision is likely to be difficult in practice, given that the restructuring will take place over two years. IAS 37 requires the provision to be the **best estimate** of the expenditure required to settle the present obligation at the reporting date, **taking all known risks and uncertainties into account**. There **may be a case for providing $50 million** (total costs of $60 million less relocation costs of $10 million) and the company **should certainly provide at least $15 million** ($20 million incurred by the time the financial statements are approved less $5 million relocation expenses). IAS 37 requires **extensive disclosures** and these **should include an indication of the uncertainties** about the amount or timing of the cash outflows.

(ii) **Fine for illegal receipt of a state subsidy**

IAS 38 *Intangible assets* defines an **intangible asset** as a **resource controlled by the company** as a result of **past events** and **from which economic benefits are expected to flow**. The fine **does not meet this definition**. The subsidy was used to offset trading losses, not to generate future income. The fine should be **charged as an expense** in profit or loss for the year ended 30 November 20X4. As it is **material** it should be **separately disclosed**.

(d) Rod spends considerable amounts of money on research that ultimately creates economic benefits and enhances shareholder value. However, this **research does not meet the criteria for deferral** under IAS 38 *Intangible assets* because of the time lag between the expenditure and the revenue that it generates. Therefore the company's activities **appear to reduce profits, rather than increase them**. The company's expertise is **part of its inherent goodwill** and cannot be valued reliably at a monetary amount. Therefore it is **not recognised** on the statement of financial position.

There is a strong argument that traditional financial reporting is **inadequate to deal with 'knowledge led' companies** such as Rod. It is possible that the capital markets will undervalue the company because the financial statements **do not reflect the 'true' effect of the company's research activities**. The economy is becoming more 'knowledge based' and many companies find themselves in this situation.

The market value of a company is **based on the market's assessment of its future prospects**, based on available information. Analysts have developed **alternative measures of performance such as Economic Value Added (EVA)**. These take factors such as expenditure on research and development expenditure into account, so that they attempt to assess estimated future cash flows. **There is a growing interest in ways of measuring shareholder value as opposed to earnings**.

Analysts and other users of the financial statements now **recognise the importance of non-financial information about a company**. Many Stock Exchanges require companies to present an Operating and Financial Review (sometimes called Management Discussion and Analysis) and some large companies do so voluntarily. This normally includes a description of the business, its objectives and its strategy. It is current best practice to analyse the **main factors and influences that may have an effect on future performance** and to comment on how the directors have sought to **maintain and improve future performance**. In this way the directors of Rod can make the markets aware of its research activities and the way in which they give rise to future income streams and enhance shareholder value.

(e)   **Internal auditor bonus**

For

The chief internal auditor is an employee of Rod, which pays a salary to him or her. As part of the internal control function, he or she is helping to **keep down costs and increase profitability**. It could therefore be argued that the chief internal auditor should have a reward for adding to the profit of the business.

Against

Conversely, the problem remains that, if the chief internal auditor receives a bonus based on results, he or she may be **tempted to allow certain actions, practices or transactions which should be stopped**, but which are increasing the profit of the business, and therefore the bonus.

Conclusion

On balance, it is **not advisable** for the chief internal auditor to receive a bonus based on the company's profit.

38 Preparation question: Part disposal

(a)   ANGEL GROUP
        CONSOLIDATED STATEMENT OF FINANCIAL POSITION AS AT 31 DECEMBER 20X8

	$'000
Non-current assets	
Property, plant and equipment	200.00
Investment in Shane (W3)	133.15
	333.15
Current assets (890 + 120 (cash on sale))	1,010.00
	1,343.15
Equity attributable to owners of the parent	
Share capital	500.00
Retained reserves (W4)	533.15
	1,033.15
Current liabilities	310.00
	1,343.15

ANGEL GROUP
CONSOLIDATED STATEMENT OF PROFIT OR LOSS AND OTHER COMPREHENSIVE INCOME
FOR THE YEAR ENDED 31 DECEMBER 20X8

	$'000
Profit before interest and tax [100 + (20 × 6/12)]	110.00
Profit on disposal of shares in subsidiary (W6)	80.30
Share of profit of associate (12 × 35% × 6/12)	2.10
Profit before tax	192.40
Income tax expense [40 + (8 × 6/12)]	(44.00)
Profit for the year	148.40
Other comprehensive income (not reclassified to P/L) net of tax [10 + (6 × 6/12)]	13.00
Share of other comprehensive income of associate (6 × 35% × 6/12)	1.05
Other comprehensive income for the year	14.05
Total comprehensive income for the year	162.45
Profit attributable to:	
Owners of the parent	146.60
Non-controlling interests (12 × 6/12 × 30%)	1.80
	148.40

	$'000
Total comprehensive income attributable to:	
Owners of the parents	159.75
Non controlling interests (18 × 6/12 × 30%)	2.70
	162.45

ANGEL GROUP
CONSOLIDATED RECONCILIATION OF MOVEMENT IN RETAINED RESERVES

	$'000
Balance at 31 December 20X7 (W5)	373.40
Total comprehensive income for the year	159.75
Balance at 31 December 20X8 (W4)	533.15

Workings

1   *Timeline*

1.1.X8	30.6.X8	31.12.X8
SOCI ←	→ ←	→
Subsidiary – 6/12	Associate – 6/12	
	↓	↓
	Group gain on disposal	Equity account in SOFP

2   *Goodwill - Shane*

	$'000	$'000
Consideration transferred		120.0
Non-controlling interests (FV)		51.4
Less:		
Share capital	100	
Retained reserves	10	
		(110.0)
		61.4

3   *Investment in associate*

	$'000
Fair value at date control lost	130.00
Share of post 'acquisition' retained reserves (W4)	3.15
	133.15

4   *Group retained reserves*

	Angel	Shane 70%	Shane 35% retained
Per qu/date of disposal (90 – (18 × 6/12))	400.00	81	90
Group profit on disposal (W4)	80.30		
Less retained reserves at acquisition/date of disposal		(10)	(81)
		71	9
Shane: 70% x 71	49.70		
Shane: 35% × 9	3.15		
	533.15		

5   *Retained reserves s b/f*

	Angel $'000	Shane $'000
Per Q	330.0	72
Less: Pre-acquisition retained reserves		(10)
	330.0	62
Shane – Share of post acquisition ret'd reserves (62 × 70%)	43.4	
	373.4	

6   *Group profit on disposal of Shane*

	$'000	$'000
Fair value of consideration received		120.0
Fair value of 35% investment retained		130.0
Less share of carrying value when control lost		
Net assets 190 – (18 × 6/12)	181.0	
Goodwill (W2)	61.4	
Less non-controlling interests (W7)	(72.7)	
		(169.7)
		80.3

7   *Non-controlling interests at date of disposal*

	$'000	$'000
Non-controlling interest at acquisition (FV)		51.4
NCI share of post-acqn retained earnings (30% × 71(W4))		21.3
		72.7

(b)   **Angel disposes of 10% of its holding**

If Angel disposes of 10% of its holding in Shane, Shane goes from being a 70% subsidiary to a 60% subsidiary. In other words **control is retained.** No accounting boundary has been crossed, and the event is treated as a transaction between owners.

The accounting treatment is as follows:

Statement of profit or loss and other comprehensive income

(i)   The subsidiary is **consolidated in full** for the whole period.

(ii)   The **non-controlling interest in the statement of profit or loss and other comprehensive income** will be based on percentage before and after disposal, ie time apportion.

(iii)   There is **no profit or loss on disposal.**

Statement of financial position

(i)   The **change (increase) in non-controlling interests** is shown as an **adjustment to the parent's equity.**

(ii)   **Goodwill** on acquisition **is unchanged** in the consolidated statement of financial position.

In the case of Angel and Shane you would time apportion the non-controlling interest in the statement of profit or loss and other comprehensive income, giving 30% for the first half the year and 40% for the second half. You would also calculate the adjustment to the parent's equity as follows:

	$'000
Fair value of consideration received	X
Increase in NCI in net assets and goodwill at disposal	(X)
Adjustment to parent's equity	X

39 Preparation question: Purchase of further interest

(a) **RBE already controls DCA** with its 70% investment, so **DCA is already a subsidiary** and would be fully consolidated. In substance, this is **not an acquisition**. Instead, it is treated in the group accounts as a **transaction between the group shareholders** ie the parent has purchased a 20% shareholding from NCI. No goodwill is calculated on the additional investment.

The value of the NCI needs to be worked out at the date of the additional investment (1 October 20X2), and the **proportion purchased by the parent needs to be removed from NCI**. The difference between the consideration transferred and the amount of the reduction in the NCI is included as an **adjustment to parent equity.**

(b) RBE GROUP CONSOLIDATED STATEMENT OF CHANGES IN EQUITY
FOR THE YEAR ENDED 31 DECEMBER 20X2

	Equity attributable to owners of the parent $'000	Non-controlling interest $'000	Total $'000
Balance at 1 January 20X2	3,350	650	4,000
Total comprehensive income for the year (W2)	1,350	150	1,500
Share issue (2m x $1.30)	2,600	-	2,600
Dividends paid (100 × 30%)	(200)	(30)	(230)
Adjustment to equity (on additional purchase of 20% of DCA's shares) (W3 and 4)	(37)	(503)	(540)
Balance at 31 December 20X2	7,063	267	7,330

Workings

1   *Group structure*

RBE

70%	originally
20%	1/10/X2
90%	

DCA

2   *Total comprehensive income*

NCI share:

	$'000
To 1 October 20X2 (30% × 600 × 9/12)	135
To 31 December 20X2 (10% × 600 × 9/12)	15
NCI share of TCI	150

Parent share:

	$'000
Parent share of TCI of DCA (600 – 150)	450
TCI of RBE	900
NCI share of TCI	1,350

3   *Decrease in NCI*

	$'000
NCI b/f 1 January 20X2	650

Share of TCI to 1 October 20X2 (W2)		135
Less: share of dividend paid (April 20X2) (30% × 100)		(30)
NCI at 1 October 20X2		755
Decrease in NCI on transfer of shares to parent (755× 20/30)		503

4   *Adjustment to equity*

	$000
Consideration transferred	(540)
Decrease in NCI on acquisition (W3)	503
Adjustment to parent's equity	(37)

In RBE's individual statement of financial position, the purchase of the 20% in DCA would have been recorded as follows:

	$'000	$'000
DEBIT Investment	540	
CREDIT Cash		540

Then in the group accounts, the adjustment to equity would be recorded as follows:

	$'000	$'000
DEBIT (reduce) NCI	503	
DEBIT (reduce) Parent's retained earnings	37	
CREDIT(cancel) Investment *		540

40 Ejoy

Text reference. Changes in group structure are covered in Chapter 14.

Top tips. This question required the production of a consolidated statement of profit or loss and other comprehensive income of a group. Candidates were expected to calculate and impairment test the investment in a subsidiary, to account for a joint venture, to deal with impairment and hedging of financial assets, and account for a discontinued operation.

Easy marks. Do not spend too long on the discontinued operation. You would not be penalised too heavily if you got this wrong and there are easy marks to be gained for adding across and other basic consolidation aspects.

Examiner's comment. Overall the question was quite well answered, with the majority of candidates achieving a pass mark. However, candidates answered the financial instruments part of the question quite poorly. The main problem seemed to be the application of knowledge; candidates could recite the principles of accounting for financial instruments but could not deal with the practical application thereof. The calculation of the goodwill was done well. However, the impairment testing of the investment in the subsidiary was poorly answered. Candidates need to understand this procedure as it will be a regular feature of future papers.

Marking scheme

	Marks
Goodwill	7
Joint venture	2
Financial assets	7
Statement of profit or loss and other comprehensive income	8
Tbay	4
Non-controlling interest	2
Maximum	30

EJOY: CONSOLIDATED STATEMENT OF PROFIT OR LOSS AND OTHER COMPREHENSIVE INCOME
FOR THE YEAR ENDED 31 MAY 20X6

	$m
Continuing operations	
Revenue (2,500 + 1,500)	4,000
Cost of sales (1,800 + 1,200 + 34 (W8))	(3,034)
Gross profit	966
Other income (70 + 10 – 3 (W11)	77
Distribution costs (130 + 120)	(250)
Administrative expenses (100 + 90)	(190)
Finance income (W6)	6
Finance costs (W7)	(134)
Profit before tax	475
Income tax expense (200 + 26)	(226)
Profit for period from continuing operations	249
Discontinued operations	
Profit for the year from discontinued operations ((30 × 6/12) – 2 (W8))	13
Profit for the year	262
Other comprehensive income for the year (not reclassified to P/L):	
Gain on property revaluation net of tax: 80 + 10 + (8 × 6/12)	94
Total comprehensive income for the year	356
Profit attributable to:	
Owners of the parent	257
Non-controlling interest (W2)	5
	262
Total comprehensive income for the year attributable to:	
Owners of the parent (bal. fig.)	348
Non-controlling interest (W2)	8
	356

Workings

1   Group structure

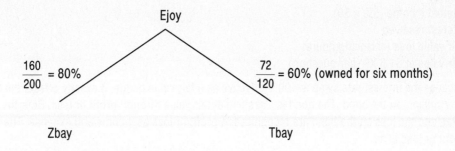

Tbay is a discontinued operation (IFRS 5).

Timeline

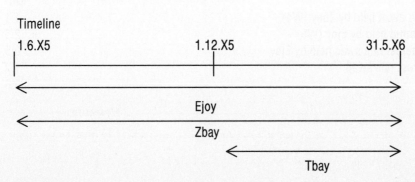

2   *Non-controlling interest*

	Profit for the year		Total comp income	
	Zbay $m	*Tbay* $m	*Zbay* $m	*Tbay* $m
PFY/TCI per question	34.0		44	
(30 × 6/12)/(38 × 6/12)		15		19
Less impairment loss on loan asset (W4)	(42.2)		(42.2)	
Interest income on loan asset (W4)	1.1		1.1	
	(7.1)	15	2.9	19
	× 20%	×40%	× 20%	× 40%
	(1.4)	6	0.6	7.6
	4.6		8.2	

3   *Goodwill*

		Zbay $m		*Tbay* $m
Consideration transferred		520		192
Non-controlling interests	(600 × 20%)	120	(310 × 40%)	124
Fair value of net assets at acquisition		(600)		(310)
		40		6

4   *Loan asset held by Zbay*

	$m
Carrying value of loan at 1.6.X5 (a financial asset)	60.0
Impairment loss (balancing figure)	(42.2)
Present value of expected future cash flows (20 × $\frac{1}{1.06^2}$ at 1.6.X5 (note)	17.8
Interest income (6% × 17.8)	1.1
At 31.5.X6	18.9

Note. The $20 million is expected to be received on 31 May 20X7, ie. in two years' time.

5   *Hedged bond (Ejoy)*

	$m
1.6.X5	50.0
Interest income (5% × 50)	2.5
Interest received	(2.5)
Fair value loss (balancing figure)	(1.7)
Fair value at 31.5.X6 (per question)	48.3

Because the interest rate swap is 100% effective as a fair value hedge, it exactly offsets the loss in value of $1.7 million on the bond. The bond is classified at fair value through profit or loss. Both the gain on the swap and the loss on the bond are recognised in profit or loss as income and expense. The net effect on profit or loss is nil.

6   *Finance income*

	$m
Interest income on loan asset held by Zbay (W4)	1.1
Interest receivable on bond held by Ejoy (W5)	2.5
Interest received on interest rate swap held by Ejoy	0.5
Fair value gain on interest rate swap	1.7
	5.8

7 Finance costs

	$m
Per draft statements of profit or loss and other comprehensive income (50 + 40)	90.0
Impairment loss (loan asset held by Zbay) (W4)	42.2
Fair value loss on hedged bond (W5)	1.7
	133.9

8 Impairment losses

	Zbay $m	Tbay $m
Notional goodwill (40 × 100%/80%) (6 × 100%/60%) (W3)	50.0	10.0
Carrying amount of net assets (W9)/(W10)	622.9	329.0
	672.9	339.0
Recoverable amount	(630.0)	
Fair value less costs of disposal (344 – (5 × 100%/60%))		(335.7)
Impairment loss: gross	42.9	3.3
Impairment loss recognised: all allocated to goodwill (80% × 42.9)/(60% × 3.3)	34.3	2.0

9 Carrying amount of net assets at 31 May 20X6 (Zbay)

	$m
Fair value of identifiable assets and liabilities acquired (1 June 20X4)	600.0
TCI for year to 31 May 20X5	20.0
TCI for year to 31 May 20X6 per draft statement of profit or loss and other comprehensive income	44.0
Less impairment loss (loan asset) (W4)	(42.2)
Interest income (loan asset) (W4)	1.1
	622.9

10 Carrying amount of net assets (Tbay)

	$m
Carrying value of investment in Tbay at 31 May 20X6:	
Fair value of net assets at acquisition (1 December 20X5)	310
Post acquisition TCI(38 × 6/12)	19
	329

11 Joint venture

	$m	$m
Elimination of Ejoy's share of gain on disposal (50% × 6)		3
DEBIT Other income	3	
CREDIT Investment in joint venture		3

41 Case study question: Traveler

Marking scheme

		Marks
(a)		
	Property, plant and equipment	4
	Goodwill	7
	Financial assets	4
	Defined benefit asset	4
	Current assets/total non-current liabilities	1
	Share capital	1
	Retained earnings	7
	Other components of equity	3
	Non-controlling interest	3
	Current liabilities	1
		35
(b)		
	Subjective assessment	7
	Up to 2 marks per element	
(c)		
	Subjective assessment	6
	Professional marks	2
		50

(a) TRAVELER GROUP
CONSOLIDATED STATEMENT OF FINANCIAL POSITION
AS AT 30 NOVEMBER 20X1

	$m
Non-current assets	
Property, plant and equipment: 439 + 810 + 620 + 10(W6) + 22(W6) − 56(W7) − 2.7(W9)	1,842.3
Goodwill (W2)	69.2
Financial assets: 108 + 10 + 20 − 7.9(W8)	130.1
Net defined benefit asset (W10): 72 − 22 − 55 + 45 − 22	18.0
	2,059.6
Current assets: 995 + 781 + 350	2,126.0
Total assets	4,185.6

Equity and liabilities	
Equity attributable to owners of the parent	
Share capital	1,120.0
Retained earnings (W3)	973.4
Other components of equity (W4)	66.7
	2,160.1
Non-controlling interests (W5)	343.5
	2,503.6
Non-current liabilities: 455 + 323 + 73	851.0
Current liabilities: 274 + 199 + 313 + 45 (W10)	831.0
Total equity and liabilities	4,185.6

Workings

1   *Group structure*

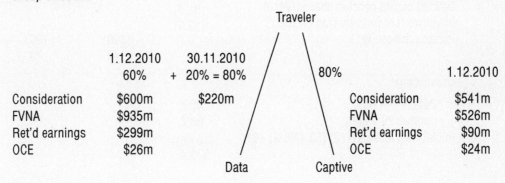

Traveler

	1.12.2010	30.11.2010			80%		1.12.2010
	60%	+ 20% = 80%					
Consideration	$600m	$220m		Consideration			$541m
FVNA	$935m			FVNA			$526m
Ret'd earnings	$299m			Ret'd earnings			$90m
OCE	$26m			OCE			$24m

Data   Captive

2 Goodwill

	Full method Data $m	Partial method Captive $m
Consideration transferred – for 60%	600	
Consideration transferred – for 80%		541.0
Non-controlling interests		
Fair value per qu	395	
526 × 20%		105.2
FV of identifiable net assets at acq'n:	(935)	526.0)
	60	120.2
Impairment losses (W12)	(50)	(61.0)
	10	59.2

69.2

3 Retained earnings

	Traveler $m	Data $m	Captive $m
Per question	1,066.0	442	169
Consideration (W7)	(56.0)		
Impairment of loan (W8)	(7.9)		
Depreciation of factory (W9)	(2.7)		
Defined benefit pension charge (W10)	(55.0)		
Impairment of pension plan (W10)	(19.0)		
Pre-acquisition (W1)		(299)	(90)
		143	79
Group share			
Data: 143 × 60%	85.8		
Captive: 79 × 80%	63.2		
Impairment losses(W12) (50 × 80%) +61	(101.0)		
	973.4		

4 Other components of equity

	Traveler $m	Data $m	Captive $m
Per question	60.0	37	45
Loss on remeasurement of defined benefit plan (W10)	(25.0)		
Pre-acquisition (W1)		(26)	(24)
		11	21
Group share post acqn:			
Data: 11 × 60 %	6.6		
Captive : 21 × 80%	16.8		
Adjustment to parent's equity (W11)	8.3		
	6 6.7		

5 Non-controlling interests

	Data $m	Captive $m
At acquisition (FV/W2)	395.0	105.2
Post acquisition share of retained earnings		
Data: 143 (W3) × 40%	57.2	
Captive: 79 (W3) × 20%		15.8
Post acquisition share of other components of equity		
Data: 11 (W4) × 40%	4.4	
Captive: 21 (W4) × 20%		4.2
	456.6	125.2
Acquisition of additional 20% of Data (W11)	(228.3)	-
	228.3	125.2
Impairment losses: 50(W12) × 20%	(10.0)	-
	218.3	125.2

343.5

6 Fair value adjustments

✓

Data:

	At acqn 1.10.20X0 $m	Movement $m	At year end 30.11.20X1 $m
Land: 935 – (600 + 299 + 26)	10	–	10

Captive:

	At acqn 1.10.20X0 $m	Movement $m	At year end 30.11.20X1 $m
Land: 526– (390 + 90+ 24)	22	-	22

7 Consideration transferred: Captive

This has been incorrectly treated as:

DEBIT	Cost of investment in Captive	$541m	
CREDIT	Profit or loss		$64m
CREDIT	Cash		$477m

The land transferred as part of the consideration needs to be removed from non-current assets, the $64m sales proceeds removed from profit or loss and a gain on disposal calculated. The gain is $64m sale consideration, less carrying value of $56m = $8m. The correct entries should have been:

DEBIT	Cost of investment in Captive	$541m	
CREDIT	Profit or loss (gain on disposal		$8m
CREDIT	Land		$56m
CREDIT	Cash		$477m

To correct, the entries are:

DEBIT	Profit or loss	$56m	
CREDIT	Land		$56m

8 Impairment of loan

The loan is a financial asset held at amortised cost under IFRS 9 *Financial instruments.* Traveler wishes to value the loan at fair value. However, IFRS 9 states that the classification of an instrument is determined on initial recognition and that reclassifications, which are not expected to occur frequently, are permitted only if the entity's business model changes.

Financial assets are subsequently measured at amortised cost if **both** of the following apply.

(i)   The asset is held within a business model whose objective is to hold the assets to collect the contractual cash flows.

(ii)   The contractual terms of the financial asset give rise, on specified dates, to cash flows that are solely payments of principal and interest on the principal outstanding.

All other financial assets are measured at fair value.

Traveler's objective for holding the debt instrument has not changed, and so it cannot measure it at fair value but must continue to measure it at amortised cost.

The impairment loss on the loan is calculated using the original effective interest rate as:

	$m	$m
Carrying value		29.00
Present value of future cash flows		
Year 1: $8m $\times \dfrac{1}{1.067}$	7.50	
Year 2: $8m $\times \dfrac{1}{1.0672^2}$	7.03	
Year 3: $8m $\times \dfrac{1}{1.0672^3}$	6.59	
	21.12	
	7.88	
	Round to $7.9m	

DEBIT	Profit or loss (and Traveler's retained earnings (W3)	$7.9m	
CREDIT	Financial assets		$7.9m

9   *Depreciation of factory*

Traveler wishes to account for the factory as a single asset. However, the roof and the building must be treated separately for the purposes of depreciation. The roof will be depreciated over five years and the remainder of the factory will be depreciated over 25 years taking into account the residual value of $2m:

	Building $m	Roof $m	Total $m
Cost	45.0	5	50.0
Depreciation:			
(45 – 2) ÷ 25years/ 5 ÷ 5years	(1.7)	(1)	(2.7)
	43.3	4	47.3

DEBIT	Profit or loss (and Traveler's retained earnings (W3))	$2.7m	
CREDIT	Property, plant and equipment		$2.7m

10   *Defined benefit pension plan*

According to IAS 19 *Employee benefits* (revised 2011), losses on remeasurement of the net defined benefit asset (previously called actuarial losses) must be recognised immediately in other comprehensive income. There will also be a ceiling placed on the amount to be recognised as an asset, which is the present value of available future refunds and reductions in future contributions of $18m. The adjustments are as follows:

	$m		$m
Net defined benefit asset b/d	72 Dr		
Charges to profit or loss			Dr Profit or loss (and
	(55) Cr	→	retained earnings)
Loss on remeasurement of defined benefit asset			Dr Other comprehensive income(and other components of equity)
	(25) Cr	→	
Contributions	45 Dr	→	Cr Current liabilities
	37 Dr		
Impairment loss (β)	(19) Cr	→	Dr Profit or loss
Asset ceiling (see above)	18 Dr		

11 *Adjustment to parent's equity on acquisition of additional 20% of Data*

This is an increase in the controlling interest and therefore a reduction in the non-controlling interest, of 20%/40%:

DEBIT	Non-controlling interest (W5) $456.6m × 20%/40%	$228.3m	
CREDIT	Investment		$220m
CREDIT	Parents equity (other components of equity (W4))		$8.3m

12 *Impairment of goodwill*

	Data $m	Captive $m
Net assets at year end per question	1,079	604.0
Fair value adjustments (W6)	10	22.0
	1,089	626.0
Goodwill (W2) Data 60, Captive 120.2 × 100%/80% (see note(i))	60	150.3
	1,149	776.3
Recoverable amount per question	(1,099)	(700.0)
Impairment loss gross	50	76.3
Impairment loss recognised (see note (ii)): 100%/80%	50	61.0

Notes

(i) Because the non-controlling interest in Data is at fair value, goodwill arises on this non-controlling interest, which bears its share of any impairment using the proportions in which profits and losses are shared at the year end when the impairment review arose, that is 20%. The gross impairment of $50m is taken to the goodwill working and the 20% ($10m) to the NCI working (W5). In the case of Captive, where the partial goodwill method is used, only 80% of the impairment is taken to the goodwill working.

(ii) Because the non-controlling interest in Data is at fair value, the goodwill is already grossed up, but Captive uses the partial goodwill method, so the goodwill needs to be grossed up for an unrecognised NCI of 20%.

(b) **Allocation of common costs under IFRS 8 *Operating segments***

If segment reporting is to fulfil a useful function, costs need to be appropriately assigned to segments. Centrally incurred expenses and central assets can be significant, and the basis chosen by an entity to allocate such costs **can therefore have a significant impact** on the financial statements. In the case of Traveler, head office management expenses, pension expenses, the cost of managing properties and interest and related interest bearing assets could be material amounts, whose misallocation could mislead users.

IFRS 8 *Operating segments* **does not prescribe a basis** on which to allocate common costs, but it does require that that basis should be **reasonable**. For example, it would not be reasonable to allocate the head office management expenses to the most profitable business segment to disguise a potential loss elsewhere. Nor would it be reasonable to allocate the pension expense to a segment with no pensionable employees.

A reasonable basis on which to allocate common costs for Traveler might be as follows:

(i)   **Head office management costs.** These could be allocated on the basis of turnover or net assets. Any allocation might be criticised as arbitrary – it is not necessarily the case that a segment with a higher turnover requires more administration from head office – but this is a fairer basis than most.

(ii)   **Pension expense.** A reasonable allocation might be on the basis of number of employees or salary expense of each segment.

(iii)   **Costs of managing properties.** These could be allocated on the basis of the value of the properties used by each business segment, or the type and age of the properties (older properties requiring more attention than newer ones).

(iv)   **Interest and interest-bearing assets.** These need not be allocated to the same segment – the interest receivable could be allocated to the profit or loss of one segment and the related interest bearing asset to the assets and liabilities of another.

The **amounts reported under IFRS 8 may differ from those reported in the consolidated financial statements** because IFRS 8 requires the information to be presented on the same basis as it is reported internally, even if the accounting policies are not the same as those of the consolidated financial statements. For example, segment information may be reported on a cash basis rather than an accruals basis. Such differences might include allocation of centrally incurred costs that are necessary for an understanding of the reported segment information.

IFRS 8 requires **reconciliations** between the segments' reported amounts and those in the consolidated financial statements. Entities must provide an explanation of such differences, and of the basis of accounting for transactions between reportable segments.

(c)   **Ethical issues and conflict of interest**

Increasingly businesses are expected to be **socially responsible as well as profitable**. Strategic decisions by businesses, particularly global businesses nearly always have wider social consequences. It could be argued, as Henry Mintzburg does, that a company produces two outputs: goods and services, and the social consequences of its activities, such as pollution.

The requirement to be a **good corporate citizen goes beyond the normal duty of ethical behaviour** in the preparation of financial statements. To act ethically, the directors must put the interests of the company and its shareholders first, for example they must not mislead users of financial statements and must exercise competence in their preparation. Corporate citizenship, on the other hand, is concerned with a company's **accountability to a wide range of stakeholders**, not just shareholders. There may well be a **conflict of interest between corporate social responsibility and maximising shareholder wealth**; for example it may be cheaper to outsource abroad, but doing so may have an adverse effect on the local economy.

In the context of **disclosure**, a company might prefer not to give information – for example segment information – away, as it could be useful to competitors and have a negative impact on profit and bonuses.

However, the two goals **need not conflict.** It is possible that being a good corporate citizen can **improve business performance. Customers may buy from a company that they perceive as environmentally friendly,** or which avoids animal testing, and **employees may remain loyal** to such a company, and both these factors are likely to increase shareholder wealth in the long term. If a company engages constructively with the country or community in which it is based, it may be seen by shareholders and potential shareholders as being a **good long- term investment** rather than in it for short-term profits. As regards disclosure, a company that makes **detailed disclosures,** particularly when these go beyond what is required by legislation or accounting standards, will be seen as **responsible and a good potential investment.**

42 Case study question: Robby

Text reference. Business combinations achieved in stages are covered in Chapter 14. Non-current assets are covered in Chapter 4. Joint operations are covered in Chapter 13 and financial instruments in Chapter 7.

Top tips. Part (a) required a consolidated statement of financial position with two subsidiaries, one of which was acquired in stages. Included in this part of the question was a joint operation, and there were adjustments for the revaluation of property, plant and equipment, impairment of receivables and sale and repurchase of land. The joint operation was fiddly and time-consuming, although not conceptually difficult as you are told what kind of joint arrangement it was. If you struggled with the details of the step acquisition of Zinc given in Note (b) of the question, look carefully at our goodwill calculation in (W3). The investment in Zinc was made up of the 55% investment at its cost and the 5% investment at its 31 May 20X2 fair value, with a gain on revaluation of the 5% taking place in the current year (to 31 May 20X3). Part (b)(i) was textbook knowledge of a topical issue. Note the examiner's comment for Part (b)(ii) on the ethical implications of the sale of land just before the year end. This type of question is in line with the examiner's pattern of applying ethical principles to transactions that might be designed to manipulate the financial statements. It is not enough just to discuss the accounting treatment without considering the ethical issues.

Easy marks. There are some standard consolidation workings here, and you could slot in the caption for, say, joint operation, even if you get the calculation wrong or do not have time to do it all. Leave enough time for Part (b) – the examiner has commented in the past that candidates often do not.

Examiner's comment. In Part 1(a), candidates showed themselves to be very good at preparing group accounts using the full goodwill method, and coped well with the impairment of the PPE. However, they had problems determining the fair value of the consideration as some candidates did not take into account the increase in the fair value of the equity interest. They also struggled with the joint operation. In Part 1(b), candidates did not seem to know the de-recognition rules of IFRS 9 and often described the nature of a financial instrument, when a financial instrument should be recognised and the valuation methods utilised, which was correct but did not answer the question. Answers to Part 1(b)(ii) were good, although many candidates spent a disproportionate amount of time discussing the accounting treatment with little time spent on the ethical aspect of the transaction.

ACCA Examiner's answer. The examiner's answer to this question is included at the back of this kit.

Marking scheme

		Marks
(a)		
	Property, plant and equipment	6
	Goodwill	6
	Non-controlling interest	4
	Financial assets	1
	Current assets	3
	Other components of equity	3
	Retained earnings	6
	Non-current liabilities	2
	Current liabilities	4
		35
(b)		
	(i) 1 mark per point up to max	9
	(ii) Manipulation	2
	Ethical discussion	4
		50

(a)   ROBBY GROUP
CONSOLIDATED STATEMENT OF FINANCIAL POSITION AS AT 31 MAY 20X3

	$m
Assets	
Non-current assets	
Property, plant and equipment: 112 + 60 + 26 + 24 (W8) + 3.6 (W9) + 6.12	
(W10) – 2.59 (W11) + 12 (W13)	241.13
Goodwill: 5 (W2) + 1 (W3)	6.00
Financial assets: 9 + 6 + 14	29.00
Jointly controlled operation: 6 – 6 (W10)	–
	276.13
Current assets:: 5 + 7 + 12 + 8 (W10) + 4 (W12)	36.00
Total assets	312.13
Equity and liabilities	
Equity attributable to owners of the parent	
Ordinary shares	25.00
Other components of equity (W4)	2.00
Retained earnings (W5)	81.45
	108.45
Non-controlling interests (W6)	27.64
	136.09
Non-current liabilities: 53 + 20 + 21 + 0.84 (W10)	94.84
Current liabilities: 47 + 6 + 2 +6.6 (W10) + 3.6 (W12) + 16 (W13)	81.20
Total equity and liabilities	312.13

Workings

1   *Group structure*

	1 June X1	Robby		1 June X0	1 Dec X2
	80% (sub)			5% (IEI) + 55% = 60%	
Pre-acquisition retained earnings	$16m	Hail Zinc	Pre-acquisition retained earnings	N/A	$15m

2   *Goodwill (Hail)*

	$m
Consideration transferred	50*
Non-controlling interest (fair value per question)	15
FV of identifiable net assets at acq'n	(60)
	5

*Note. Hail is valued at $55m as at 31 May 20X3, so there is a revaluation gain of $55m − $50m = $5m which needs to be reversed out in the calculation of consolidated other components of equity (W4).

3   *Goodwill (Zinc)*

	$m
Consideration transferred – for 55%	16
Non-controlling interest at fair value (per question)	9
Fair value of previously held interest (for 5% at 1 December 20X2)	5*
FV of identifiable net assets at acq'n: 26 + 3	(29)
	1

*Note. There will be a revaluation gain on the previously held interest, calculated as follows:

	$m
Fair value of 5% at date control achieved (1 December 20X2)	5
Fair value of 5% per SOFP, ie at 31 May 20X2: $19m per Robby's	
SOFP, less $16m consideration for 55%	(3)
Revaluation gain (1 June 20X2 to 1 December 20X2)	2

This gain on revaluation of the previously held interest is taken to profit or loss for the year, and hence to retained earnings (W5).

4   *Other components of equity*

	$m
Robby (per question)	11.00
Dividend income from Hail transferred to retained earnings (W7)	(2.00)
Reserve transfer on property, plant and equipment (W11)	(0.11)
Impairment loss on property, plant and equipment (W11)	(1.89)
Revaluation gain on investment in Hail (W2)	(5.00)
Pre-acquisition (W1)	2.00

5   *Retained earnings*

	Robby $m	Hail $m	Zinc $m
Per question	70.00	27.0	19.0
Gain on revaluation of 5% investment in Zinc (W3)	2.00		
Dividend income from Hail (W7)	2.00		
Fair value depreciation (W9)	-		(0.4)
Profit from joint operation (W10)	0.68		
Reserve transfer on PPE (W11)	0.11		
Impairment loss on PPE (W11)	(0.70)		
Reverse loss on debt factoring (W12)	0.40		
Reverse gain on sale and repurchase (W13)	(4.00)		
Pre-acquisition (W1)		(16.0)	(15.0)
		11.0	3.6

Group share of post-acquisition profits of:

	$m
Hail: 11 × 80%	8.80
Zinc: 3.6 × 60%	2.16
	81.45

6   *Non-controlling interests*

	Hail $m	Zinc $m
At acquisition (W2/W3)	15.0	9.00
Post acquisition share of retained earnings		
Hail: 11 (W5) × 20%	2.2	
Zinc: 3.6 (W5) × 40%		1.44
	17.2	10.44
	27.64	

7   *Dividend*

The $2m dividend income has been incorrectly recorded in other comprehensive income for the year, and therefore in other components of equity. It should have been recorded in profit or loss for the year, and therefore in retained earnings.

To correct, the entries are:

DEBIT Other components of equity $2m
CREDIT   Retained earnings $2m

8   *Fair value adjustment: Hail*

Hail:

	At acqn 1June 20X1 $m	Movement (2 years) $m	At year end 31 May 20X3 $m
Land: 60 – (20 + 16)	24	–	24
	Goodwill (FV of NA)	Retained	PPE in year end

9   *Fair value adjustment: Zinc*

Hail:

	At acqn 1 Dec 20X2 $m	Movement (6 months) $m	At year end 31 May 20X3 $m
PPE: (26 + 3) – (10 + 15)	4	(0.4)	3.6
	Goodwill (FV of NA)	Retained	PPE in year end

*Note. The fair value movement is the additional depreciation caused by the fair valuing for consolidation purposes: $4m × 1/5 × 6/12 = $0.4m

10   *Joint operation (in Robby's books)*

The treatment of the joint operation is set out in IFRS 11 *Joint arrangements*. Robby must recognise on a line-by-line basis its assets, liabilities, revenues and expenses plus its share (40%) of the joint assets, liabilities, revenue and expenses. The figures are calculated as follows:

Statement of financial position

	$m
Property, plant and equipment:	
1 June 20X2 cost: gas station (15 × 40%)	6.00
dismantling provision (2 × 40%)	0.80
	6.80
Accumulated depreciation: 6.8/10	(0.68)
31 May 20X3 NBV	6.12
Trade receivables (from other joint operator): 20 (revenue) × 40%	8.00
Trade payables (to other joint operator): 16 + 0.5 (costs) × 40%	6.60
Dismantling provision:	
At 1 June 20X2	0.80
Finance cost (unwinding of discount): 0.8 × 5%	0.04
At 31 May 20X3	0.84

Profit or loss for the year

	$m
Revenue: 20 × 40%	8.00
Cost of sales: 16 × 40%	(6.40)
Operating costs: 0.5 × 40%	(0.20)
Depreciation	(0.68)
Finance cost (unwinding of discount)	(0.04)
Profit from joint operation (to retained earnings (W10)	0.68

Robby has accounted only for its share of the construction cost of $6m. The journals to correct this are therefore as follows:

			$m	$m
DEBIT	Property, plant and equipment		6.12	
DEBIT	Trade receivables		8.00	
CREDIT	Joint operation	×		6.00
CREDIT	Trade payables			6.60
CREDIT	Provision			0.84
CREDIT	Retained earnings (Robby)			0.68

11   *Property, plant and equipment*

		Carrying amount $m	Revaluation surplus $m
1 June 20X0	Cost	10.00	
	Acc. depreciation $^2/_{10}$ × 10	(1.00)	
		9.00	
	Revaluation gain(bal. fig)	2.00	2.00
31 May 20X2	Revalued PPE c/d	11.00	
	Depreciation for year $^1/_{18}$ × 11	(0.61)	
	Transfer to retained earnings: 0.61 – 0.50		(0.11)
31 May 20X3	Balance	10.39	1.89
	Impairment loss (bal. fig.)	(2.59)	
	Recoverable amount	7.80	

The impairment loss is charged to other comprehensive income and therefore to other components of equity to the extent of the revaluation surplus. The remainder is taken to profit or loss and therefore to retained earnings. Thus $1.89 is taken to other components of equity and $2.59 – $1.89 = $0.7 to retained earnings.

Journals in Robby's books

Reserve transfer:

DEBIT	Other components of equity	$0.11m
CREDIT	Retained earnings	$0.11m

Impairment loss:

DEBIT	Other components of equity	$1.89m
DEBIT	Retained earnings	$0.70
CREDIT	Property, plant and equipment	$2.89m

12   *Debt factoring*

Robby should not have derecognised the receivables because the risks and rewards of ownership have not been transferred. The receivables must therefore be reinstated and the loss reversed:

DEBIT	Trade receivables	$4.0m	
CREDIT	Current liabilities		$3.6m
CREDIT	Retained earnings (to reverse loss)		$0.4m

13   *Sale and repurchase of land*

Robby should not have derecognised the land from the financial statements because the risks and rewards of ownership have not been transferred. The substance of the transaction is a loan of $16m, and the 5% 'premium' on repurchase is effectively an interest payment. This is an attempt to manipulate the financial statements in order to show a more favourable cash position. The sale must be reversed and the land reinstated at its carrying amount before the transaction. The repurchase, ie the repayment of the loan takes place one month after the year end, and so this is a current liability:

DEBIT	Property, plant and equipment	$12m	
DEBIT	Retained earnings (to reverse profit on disposal (16 – 12)	$4m	
CREDIT	Current liabilities		$16m

(b)   (i)   **Derecognition of a financial asset**

Derecognition is the removal of a previously recognised financial instrument from an entity's statement of financial position.

An entity should derecognise a **financial asset** when:

(1)   The **contractual rights** to the cash flows from the financial asset **expire**, or

(2)   The entity **transfers the financial asset or substantially all the risks and rewards of ownership** of the financial asset to another party.

IFRS 9 gives **examples of where an entity has transferred substantially all the risks and rewards of ownership**. These include:

(1)   An unconditional sale of a financial asset

(2)   A sale of a financial asset together with an option to repurchase the financial asset at its fair value   at the time of repurchase.

The standard also **provides examples of situations where the risks and rewards of ownership have not been transferred**:

(1)   A sale and repurchase transaction where the repurchase price is a fixed price or the sale price plus a lender's return

(2)   A sale of a financial asset together with a total return swap that transfers the market risk exposure back to the entity

(3)   A sale of short-term receivables in which the entity guarantees to compensate the transferee for credit losses that are likely to occur.

It is possible for only **part** of a financial asset or liability to be derecognised. This is allowed if the part comprises:

(1)   Only specifically identified cash flows, or

(2)   Only a fully proportionate (pro rata) share of the total cash flows

For example, if an entity holds a bond it has the right to two separate sets of cash inflows: those relating to the principal and those relating to the interest. It could sell the right to receive the interest to another party while retaining the right to receive the principal.

In the case of Robby, the substance of the transaction needs to be considered rather than its legal form. Robby has transferred the receivables to the factor in exchange for $3.6m cash, but it is liable for any shortfall between $3.6m and the amount collected. In principle, Robby is liable for the whole

$3.6m, although it is unlikely that the default would be as much as this. **Robby therefore retains the credit risk.** In addition, Robby is entitled to receive the benefit (less interest) of repayments in excess of $3.6m once the $3.6m has been collected. Therefore for amounts in excess of $3.6m Robby also retains the late payment risk. **Substantially all the risks and rewards** of the financial asset **therefore remain with Robby,** and the receivables should **continue to be recognised.**

(ii) **Sale of land**

Ethical behaviour in the preparation of financial statements, and in other areas, is of **paramount importance.** This applies equally to preparers of accounts, to auditors and to accountants giving advice to directors. Financial statements may be manipulated for all kinds of reasons, for example to enhance a profit-linked bonus. In this case, the purpose of the sale and repurchase is **to present a misleadingly favourable picture of the cash position,** which **hides** the fact that the Robby Group **has severe liquidity problems.** The extent of the liquidity problems can be seen in the current ratio of $36m/$81.2m = 0.44:1, and the gearing ratio of 0.83, calculated as follows:

$$\frac{53 + 20 + 21 \text{ (non-current liabilities)} + 3.6 \text{ (factored receivables)} + 16 \text{ (land option)}}{\text{Equity interest (including NCI)}} = \frac{113.60}{136.09} = 0.83$$

The effect of the sale just before the year end was to **eliminate the bank overdraft** and improve these ratios, although once the sale of land has been correctly accounted for as a loan, there is no improvement in gearing. The sale as originally accounted for might forestall proceedings by the bank, but as the substance of the transaction is a loan, it does not alter the true position and gives a **misleading impression** of it.

Company accountants act unethically if they use 'creative' accounting in accounts preparation to make the figures look better. To act ethically, the directors must put the interests of the company and its shareholders first, and must also have regard to other stakeholders such as potential investors or lenders. **If a treatment does not conform to acceptable accounting practice, it is not ethical.** Acceptable accounting practice includes conformity with the qualitative characteristics set out in the *Conceptual Framework* particularly fair presentation and verifiability. Conformity with the *Conceptual Framework* precludes **window-dressing transactions** such as this, and so the land needs to be reinstated in the accounts and a current liability set up for the repurchase.

43 Case study question: Bravado

Text reference. Business combinations achieved in stages are covered in Chapter 14. Ethics are covered in Chapter 2.

Top tips. This question required the preparation of a consolidated statement of financial position where the non-controlling interest on acquisition was at fair value. This is often called the full goodwill method. There was also a calculation and explanation of the impact on the calculation of goodwill if the non-controlling interest was calculated on a proportionate basis and a discussion of the ethics of showing a loan to a director as cash and cash equivalents. The main body of the question required candidates to deal with the calculation of goodwill in a simple situation, the calculation of goodwill where there was a prior holding in the subsidiary, an investment in an associate, a foreign currency transaction, deferred tax and impairment of inventory. Don't be put off by the fact that the goodwill on Message is negative (gain on a bargain purchase). This is unusual, and can sometimes mean your calculation is wrong, but you don't lose many marks for arithmetical mistakes

Easy marks. Part (b) is very generously marked, since the calculation is similar to that in part (a) – you just need the NCI share of the subsidiary's net assets. If you're pushed for time you should ignore the foreign currency investment, as it's fiddly and only carries 3 marks.

Examiner's comment. In general the basic calculation of goodwill under the full goodwill method was well done by candidates. However, they dealt less well with the business combination achieved in stages, the contingent consideration and the deferred tax. Many candidates did not complete the retained earnings calculation and often there was doubt over where the gain on bargain purchase should be recorded. (Group retained profits) The calculation of the impairment of inventories was dealt with quite well by candidates, as was the increase in the value of PPE and land. Often the increase in the depreciation charge as a result of the revaluation of PPE was not calculated correctly, nor was the deferred taxation effect. Many candidates got muddled with Part (b) and omitted Part (c) altogether, but those who attempted Part (c) did well on it.

Marking scheme

		Marks
(a)	Message	5
	Mixted	6
	Clarity	4
	Investment in equity instrument	4
	Retained earnings	3
	Post acquisition reserves	2
	Other components of equity	2
	Current liabilities	1
	NCI	2
	Inventories	2
	PPE	2
	Deferred tax	1
	Trade receivables	1
		35
(b)	Message	3
	Mixted	3
	Explanation	2
		8
(c)	Subjective	7
	Available	50

(a) BRAVADO GROUP
    CONSOLIDATED STATEMENT OF FINANCIAL POSITION AS AT 31 MAY 20X9

	$m
Non-current assets	
Property, plant and equipment: 265 + 230 + 161 + 40 (W7) + 12 (W7)	708.0
Goodwill (W2)	25.0
Investment in associate (W3)	22.5
Investment in equity instruments: 51 + 6 + 5 – 17.4 (W8)	44.6
	800.1
Current assets	
Inventories: 135 + 55 + 73 – 1.8 (W9)	261.2
Trade receivables: 91 + 45 + 32	168.0
Director's loan (W10)	1.0
Cash and cash equivalents: 102 + 100 + 8 – 1 (W10)	209.0
	639.2
	1,439.3
Equity attributable to owners of the parent	
Share capital	520.0
Retained earnings (W4)	282.3
Other components of equity (W5)	(0.4)
	801.9
Non-controlling interests (W6)	148.8
	950.7
Non-current liabilities	
Long-term borrowings: 120 + 15 + 5	140.0
Deferred tax: 25 + 9 + 3 + 2.6 (W7)	39.6
	179.6
Current liabilities	
Trade and other payables: 115 + 30 + 60 + 12 (W2)	217.0
Current tax payable: 60 + 8 + 24	92.0
	309.0
	1,439.3

Workings

1   *Group structure*

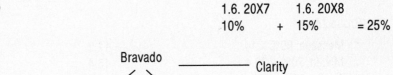

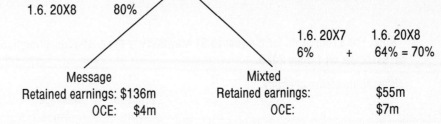

2   *Goodwill*

	Message $m	Message $m	Mixted $m	Mixted $m
Consideration transferred				
Cash		300		118
Contingent (at FV)		–		12
		300		130
Non-controlling interest (at fair value)		86		53
Fair value of previously held equity interest				15
Less fair value of net assets at acquisition				
Per question/170 + 6	400		176	
Deferred tax liability (W7)	–		(3)	
		(400)		(173)
(Gain on bargain purchase)/Goodwill		(14)*		25

***Note**. This is a gain on a bargain purchase and should be recorded in profit or loss for the year attributable to the parent (W4).

3   *Investment in associate*

	$m
Cost = fair value at date significant influence achieved: $9m + $11m	20.0
Share of post 'acquisition' retained earnings $10m* × 25%	2.5
	22.5

***Note**. The profit for the year to 31 May 20X9 is the relevant figure, as the investment only became an associate at the beginning of that year.

4   *Retained earnings*

	Bravado $m	Message $m	Mixted $m
Per question	240.0	150	80.0
Fair value movement (W7)			(1.6)
Loss on inventory (W10)	(1.8)		
Gain on bargain purchase (W2)	14.0		
Pre-acquisition		(136)	(55.0)
		14	23.4
Group share			
Message: 80% × 14	11.2		
Mixted: 70% × 23.4	16.4		
Clarity: 25% × 10*	2.5		
	282.3		

***Note**. The $10m profit for the year to 31 May 20X9 is the post-acquisition figure as Clarity became an associate on 1 June 20X8.

5   *Other components of equity*

	Bravado $m	Message $m	Mixted $m
Per question	17.0	4	7
Foreign IEI (W9)	(17.4)		
Pre-acquisition		(4)	(7)
Group share post acqn: Message	0.0	0	0
Mixted	0.0		
	(0.4)		

6   *Non-controlling interests*

	Message $m	Mixted $m
At date of control (FV/W2)	86.0	53
Post acquisition share of reserves		
Message: 14 (W4) × 20%	2.8	
Mixted: 23.4 (W4) × 30%		7
	88.8	60

148.8

7   *Fair value adjustments*

Message:

	At acqn 1.6.X8 $m	Movement $m	At year end 31.5 X9 $m
Land: 400 − (220 + 136 + 4)	40	–	40

Mixted:

	At acqn 1.6.X8 $m	Movement $m	At year end 31.5 X9 $m
		$\left(\dfrac{1}{7}\right)$	
Property, plant & equipment:170 + 6 − (100 + 55 + 7)	14	(2.0)	12.0
Deferred tax liability: (176 − 166) × 30%	(3)	0.4	(2.6)
	11	(1.6)	9.4

8   *Foreign currency investment in equity instrument*

	$m
Value on initial recognition: 11m dinars × 4.5 =	49.50
Value at 31 May 20X8: 10m dinars × 5.1 =	51.00
Gain	1.50

At 31 May 20X8, this gain would be recorded in other comprehensive income (not reclassified to profit or loss).

DEBIT	Investment in equity instrument	$1.5m	
CREDIT	Other components of equity (via OCI)		$1.5m

	$m
Value at 31 May 20X8	51.00
Value at 31 May 20X9: 7 × 4.8	(33.60)
Impairment	17.40

This is recorded as follows		$m	$m
DEBIT	Other components of equity (via OCI)	17.4	
CREDIT	Investment in equity instrument		17.4

9   *Inventories*

	$m	$m
Cost in financial statements		
1st stage (10,000 × 1,000)	10.0	
2nd stage (20,000 × 1,500)		30.0
Net realisable value		
1st stage (10,000 × (950 − 10))	(9.4)	
2nd stage (20,000 × (1,450 − 10))		(28.8)
	(0.6)	(1.2)

(1.8)

10   *Director's loan*

DEBIT	Loan receivable	$1m
CREDIT	Cash	$1m

(b)   **Goodwill if non-controlling interest is calculated on a proportionate basis**

	Message		*Mixted*	
	$m	$m	$m	$m
Consolidated transferred				
Cash		300		118.0
Contingent (at FV)		–		12.0
		300		130.0
Non-controlling interest (20% × 400)/(30% × 173)		80		51.9
Fair value of previously held equity interest				15.0
Less fair value of net assets at acquisition				
Per question	400		176	
Deferred tax liability (W7)	–		(3)	
	400		(173.0)	
(Gain on bargain purchase)/goodwill	(20)		23.9	

In the case of **Message**, if non-controlling interest is valued on a **proportionate basis**, the **gain on the bargain purchase is greater**. This is logical if the fair value of the non-controlling interest is seen as part of the cost of the acquisition, and the fair value of this NCI is greater than the NCI's proportionate share of the subsidiary's net assets.

In the case of **Mixted**, the **goodwill is less** because, as for Message, Bravado has 'paid' less. The non-controlling interest is, as for Message, seen as part of the cost of the acquisition.

(c)   **Treatment of loan to director**

Although there is no specific prohibition against this treatment in IFRS, there is a requirement not to be misleading. The treatment is in **breach of certain concepts** prescribed in the IASB's *Framework for the Preparation and Presentation of Financial Statements*, namely:

(i)   **Understandability.** If the loan is shown in cash, it hides the true nature of the practices of the company, making the financial statements less understandable to users.

(ii)   **Relevance.** The information should be disclosed separately as it is relevant to users.

(iii) **Reliability.** The reliability concept states that information must be free from bias and faithfully represent transactions. Clearly this is not the case if a loan to a director is shown in cash.

(iv)   **Comparability.** For financial statements to be comparable year-on-year and with other companies., transactions must be correctly classified, which is not the case here. If the cash balance one year includes a loan to a director and the next year it does not, then you are not comparing like with like.

In some countries, loans to directors are **illegal**, with directors being personally liable. Even if this is not the case, there is a potential **conflict of interest** between that of the director and that of the company, which is why separate disclosure is required as a minimum. Directors are responsible for the financial statements required by statute, and thus it is their responsibility to put right any errors that mean that the financial statements do not comply with IFRS. There is generally a legal requirement to maintain proper accounting records, and recording a loan as cash conflicts with this requirement.

There is, in addition, an **ethical aspect**. In obscuring the nature of the transaction, it is possible that the directors are **motivated by personal interest**, and are thus failing in their duty to act honestly and ethically. If one transaction is misleading, it casts doubt on the credibility of the financial statements as a whole.

In conclusion, the treatment is problematic and **should be rectified**.

44 Case study question: Grange

> **Text reference.** Changes in group structures are covered in Chapter 14 of your BPP Study Text. Foreign transactions are covered in Chapter 16. Ethics are covered in Chapter 2.
>
> **Top tips.** This question requires a thorough understanding of IFRS 3 revised and the importance of crossing – or not crossing – the 'control' boundary. There is a lot to do: you have a disposal where control is lost (subsidiary to associate), a disposal where control is retained (subsidiary to subsidiary) and a business combination in stages where the parent already has a controlling interest and is increasing its share. None of these should present problems if you have learned and practised this topic thoroughly. Remember that an increase or decrease in controlling interest that does not cross the control boundary goes to equity, not to profit or loss for the year, as it is a transaction between the owners.
>
> There are a few other adjustments too, including a foreign investment, a contingent liability and an investment property.
>
> **Easy marks.** Part (a) is very straightforward if you have learned the proforma for such calculations – and you should have. In Part (b) there are some easy marks for basic consolidation aspects. Part (c) is fairly open ended, and marks will be awarded for valid points.
>
> **Examiner's comments.** Candidates generally performed well in Part (a) of this question. The calculation of the loss arising on the disposal of the equity interest was extremely well answered with many candidates scoring full marks for that. The main issues that candidates had in part (b) were the calculations of the negative and positive movements in equity arising from the sale and purchase of equity holdings. Candidates also struggled with the calculation of post acquisition reserves, which was quite complex. Markers gave credit for the method and workings shown. The non-consolidation adjustments (investment property, provisions for environmental claims, restructuring provisions etc) were generally well tackled, although a major failing often involved the non-recognition of the restructuring provision, as a constructive obligation did not exist.
>
> Part (c) of the question required candidates to discuss the relationship between ethical behaviour and professional rules. The question required candidates to comment on the ethical behaviour of a director where the director possessed confidential information. The examiner was pleased with candidates' performance on this part, but emphasised that it is important to refer to the information in the question when writing the answer.

Marking scheme

		Marks
(a)	Fair value of consideration	1
	Fair value of residual interest	1
	Gain reported in comprehensive income	1
	Net assets	1
	Goodwill	2
		6
(b)	Property, plant and equipment	6
	Investment property	2
	Goodwill	3
	Retained earnings	7
	Other components of equity	5
	Non-controlling interest	2
	Non-current liabilities/trade and other payables	1
	Provisions for liabilities	3
	Intangible assets	2
	Current assets/investments in equity instruments	1
	Investment in associate	2
	Share capital	1
		35

(c)   Subjective up to   7
      Professional marks   2
                                                                                                            ──
                                                                                                            50

(a)   **Gain on disposal of equity interest in Sitin**

                                                                                              $m
      Fair value of consideration received   23
      Fair value of equity interest retained   13
      Less share of net assets and goodwill at date of disposal
              Net assets   (36)
              Goodwill (W2)   (7)
      Loss on disposal   (7)

(b)   GRANGE GROUP
      CONSOLIDATED STATEMENT OF FINANCIAL POSITION AS AT 30 NOVEMBER 20X9

      Non-current assets $m
      Property, plant and equipment
        257 + 311 + 238 + 5(W7) + 3.47(W7) − 6(W8) + 4(W10) − 28(W11)   784.47
      Investment property (W8): 6 + 2   8.00
      Goodwill (W2)   38.00
      Intangible assets (W7)   7.00
      Investment in associate (W3)   13.00
                                                                                             850.47
      Current assets: 475 + 304 + 141   920.00
                                                                                            1770.47

                                                                                              $m
      Equity attributable to owners of the parent
      Share capital   430.00
      Retained earnings (W4)   400.67
      Other components of equity (W5)   58 .98
                                                                                             889.65
      Non-controlling interests (W6)   140.82
      Non-current liabilities: 172 + 124 +38   1030.47
                                                                                             334.00

      Current liabilities
      Trade and other payables: 178 + 71 + 105   354.00
      Provisions: 10 + 6 + 4 + 25(W7) + 7(W9)   52.00
                                                                                             406.00
                                                                                            1770.47

Workings

1   *Group structure*

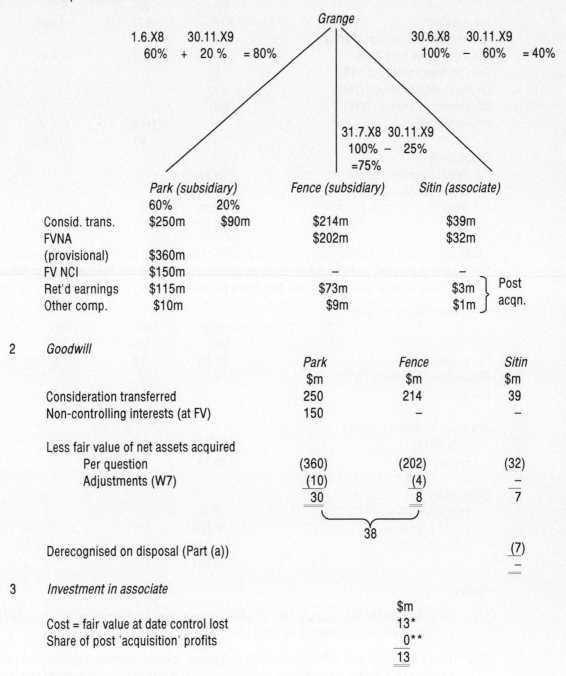

	Park (subsidiary)		Fence (subsidiary)	Sitin (associate)
	60%	20%		
Consid. trans.	$250m	$90m	$214m	$39m
FVNA			$202m	$32m
(provisional)	$360m			
FV NCI	$150m		–	–
Ret'd earnings	$115m		$73m	$3m } Post
Other comp.	$10m		$9m	$1m } acqn.

2   *Goodwill*

	Park	Fence	Sitin
	$m	$m	$m
Consideration transferred	250	214	39
Non-controlling interests (at FV)	150	–	–
Less fair value of net assets acquired			
Per question	(360)	(202)	(32)
Adjustments (W7)	(10)	(4)	–
	30	8	7

                38

Derecognised on disposal (Part (a))			(7)

3   *Investment in associate*

	$m
Cost = fair value at date control lost	13*
Share of post 'acquisition' profits	0**
	13

Notes

* The associate is held at $16m in the SOFP of Grange, therefore the effect of the part disposal and fair value exercise has been to impair the investment by $16m – $13m = $3m.

** The disposal was made at the year end so no post 'acquisition' reserves have arisen since it became an associate.

4   *Retained earnings*

	Grange $m	Park $m	Fence $m	Sitin $m
Per question	410	170	65.00	–
Loss on disposal of Sitin (Part (a))	(7)			
Fair value movement (W7)		(3)	4.47	
Gain on investment land (W8)	2			
Environmental provision (W9)	(7)			
Impairment of Grange (W11)	(28)			
Pre-acquisition		(115)	(73.00)	
		52	(3.53)	
Group share				
Park: 52 × 60%	31.20			
Fence: (3.53) × 100%	(3.53)			
Sitin: 3* × 100%	3.00			
	400.67			

*Note. There is no need for two columns here as Sitin changed from a subsidiary to an associate on the last day of the year, so there are no earnings arising after the change. The earnings for the period between the original acquisition and the date of the part disposal are given in the question as $3m.

5   *Other components of equity*

	Grange $m	Park $m	Fence $m	Sitin* $m
Per question	22.00	14	17	–
Revaluation of property (W10)	4.00			
Pre-acquisition		(10)	(9)	
		4	8	
Change in controlling interest				
Park (W12)	(3.80)			
Fence (W13)	25.38			
Group share				
Park: 4 × 60%	2.40			
Fence: 8 × 100%	8.00			
Sitin: 1 × 100%	1.00			
	58.98			

*Notes

1   ere is no need for two columns here as Sitin changed from a subsidiary to an associate on the last day of the year, so there is no other comprehensive income after the change.

2   The now realised gain of $1m, previously recognised in other comprehensive income (and therefore held in other components of equity), may be transferred to retained earnings as a reserves movement. This transfer is not required and not shown here.

6 Non-controlling interest

	Park $m	Fence $m	Sitin* $m
NCI at acquisition	150.0	–	–
NCI share of post-acquisition:			
Retained earnings: 52(W4) × 40%	20.8		
Other components: 4(W5) × 40%	1.6		
NCI at 30.11.X9 before changes	172.4		
Change in NCI on 30.11.X9			
Park (W12)	(86.2)		
Fence (W13)		54.62	
	86.2	54.62	–

140.82

*Note. There is no NCI in Sitin because it goes from being a 100% subsidiary to being an associate.

7 Fair value adjustments

Park

	At acqn (1.6.X8) $m	Movement $m	Year-end (30.11.X9) $m
Land*			
360 – (230 + 115 + 10)	5	–	5
Franchise: at 1.6.X8	10		
Depn. $10 \times 1\frac{1}{2}/5$	—	(3)	7
	15	(3)	12

*Note. For the purposes of the goodwill calculation, the fair value uplift is already included in the $360m given in the question for the fair value of the net assets of Park on acquisition.

Fence

	At acqn $m	Movement $m	Year-end (30.11.X9) $m
Contingent liability*			
at 31.7.X8	(30)	5	(25)
Property, plant and equipment			
excess at acquisition per qu.	4		
Depreciation 16 months ÷	–	–	–
120 months	–	(0.53)	3.47
	(26)	4.47	(21.53)

Note. For the purposes of the goodwill calculation, the contingent liability of $30 million is already included in the fair value of the net assets.

8 Investment land (Grange)

The land should be re-classified as investment property. IAS 40 states that land held for indeterminate use (Grange has not decided what to do with it) is investment property. The entries to re-classify are:

DEBIT	Investment property	$6m	
CREDIT	Property, plant and equipment		$6m

As Grange's policy is to maximise return on capital employed, it will use the fair value model, and the gain for the year end of $8m – $6m = $2m will be taken to profit or loss for the year shown in retained earnings.

DEBIT	Investment property	$2m	
CREDIT	Profit or loss (retained earnings)		$2m

The fall in value after the year end to $7m will be disclosed as a non-adjusting event after the reporting period.

9   *Provision for environmental claim*

The environmental obligations of $1m and $6m are a present obligation arising from past events and should be provided for:

DEBIT	Profit or loss (retained earnings)	$7m	
CREDIT	Provision		$7m

However, no provision should be made for the costs of changing the manufacturing process because the events to date do not provide sufficient detail to recognise a constructive obligation. Grange still has the option of making other changes such as buying a new machine, shutting down production or changing the product.

10 *Foreign property*

	$m
Value at 30 November 20X8 ($^{8m}/_2$)	4
Value at 30 November 20X9 ($^{12m}/_{1.5}$)	8
Gain	4

DEBIT	Property, plant and equipment	$4m	
CREDIT	Other comprehensive income (other components of equity)		$4m

11 *Restructuring*

No provision should be recognised for the restructuring because there is no constructive obligation. A constructive obligation arises when an entity:

(i)   Has a formal plan, and

(ii) Makes an announcement of the plan to those affected. There is insufficient detail to recognise a constructive obligation. However, there is evidence that Grange's property, plant and equipment (and Grange itself) is impaired. An impairment test should be performed on Grange.

	$m
Net assets per question	862
Revaluation of investment property (W8)	2
Provision (W9)	(7)
Revaluation of property (W10)	4
Impairment of Sitin (W3)	(3)
	858
Value in use at y/e if restructured	(830)
Impairment loss	28

All the loss of $28m is taken to profit or loss for the year (in retained earnings) as none of it relates to previously revalued assets.

12 *Decrease in controlling interest in Park*

	$m
Non-controlling interest at 30.11.X9 before changes*(W6)	172.4

Note. A 20% share owned by the non-controlling interest passes to the parent at that date.

Increase: $172.4m × 20%/40% = $86.2m

The gain is taken to equity (other components)

		$m	$m
DEBIT	NCI	86.2	
DEBIT	Parents' equity (bal. fig.)	3.8	
CREDIT	Cash		90

13   *Increase in controlling interest in Fence*

Non-controlling interest in Fence:

	$m
Net assets per question	232.00
Fair value adjustment (W7)	(21.53)
Goodwill (W2)	8.00
	218.47

The NCI arising on the part disposal is $218,470,000 \times 25\%$ - $54,620,000

The adjustment is taken to equity (other components)

		$m	$m
DEBIT	Cost of investment	80	
CREDIT	NCI		54.62
CREDIT	Parents' equity (other components of equity), balancing figure		25.38

(c)   **Ethical behaviour and rules**

The **compliance-based approach** to ethics requires companies and individuals to act within the **letter of the law,** or in conformity to the letter of a professional code of conduct. In essence, it says: follow the rules and that is enough. Certainly rules are an important part of ethics. A professional code of conduct such as the ACCA's is an effective and efficient way to communicate expectations as to what behaviour is expected and what is unacceptable.

The **advantages of rules-based approaches** can be summarised as follows:

(i)   They can be **enforced** through penalties for non-compliance, which makes compliance more likely.

(ii)   The rules are usually **clear and unambiguous**, and companies or individuals can generally provide evidence of compliance.

(iii)   They are usually **specific,** where a requirement for 'integrity' is too general.

There are disadvantages to rules-based approaches, the most important of which are:

(i)   **Rigidity.** The rules-based approach allows no leeway or deviation, irrespective of how illogical the situation is.

(ii)   **Limited scope.** Enforcement can be difficult in situations not covered explicitly by the rules. Accountants who view rules as the sole determinant of ethical behaviour will be unable to cope in situations where there is no rule.

(iii)   A director who lacks integrity may try to find **loopholes.**

(iv)   A **rule may be unfair or inappropriate** – even unethical. Ethical principles and values may be used to judge the appropriateness of a rule, and whether it should be changed.

(v)   Too much emphasis on rules, and on sanctions for non-compliance, means that ethics are perceived as **punitive.** A more positive view of ethics is required if public trust is to be maintained.

In deciding whether to disclose Brook's liquidity problems to Field, the finance director of Grange should consider more than simple compliance with rules. He needs to act ethically. However, even without confining himself to rules, he will be faced with a number of **conflicting demands** and questions to which there are no easy answers.

(i)   Should the finance director **betray his friend's confidence?** Does he have a duty to disclose, or is this '**inside information**' which should not be disclosed?

(ii)   What about the finance director's **duty to other stakeholders**, including the shareholders of Grange? Grange may not be paid if the poor liquidity position of Brook is disclosed, and the shareholders stand to lose.

(iii)   If he discloses the information, the finance director could be perceived as being **responsible** for Brook going into liquidation.

(iv)   Should the information passed to him by his friend be seen as an accurate assessment of Brook's creditworthiness, or is it a **subjective opinion?**

As can be seen, following rules is not the be all and end all of ethics, but even once it is accepted that integrity must play a role, the **questions are not always straightforward.**

45 Case study question: Ashanti

Text references. Complex groups are covered in Chapter 13 of your Study Text. Disposals are covered in Chapter 14. Financial instruments are covered in Chapter 7. Management of earnings is covered in Chapter 18 and also in Chapter 1 in the context of revenue recognition.

Top tips. This is an exceptionally demanding question, so don't worry too much if you didn't get it all. However, it is really important that you get the group structure. It is complicated. First you have a complex group. Then there are two disposals, one where control is lost (sub-subsidiary to sub-associate) and one where control is retained (70% to 60% subsidiary). In fact the adjustment on the disposal of the interest in Bochem does not belong in the statement of profit or loss and other comprehensive income, but we include it for completeness.

There are also a number of adjustments, some of which relate to financial instruments.

In Part (b), don't be tempted to waffle.

Easy marks. There are a surprising number of easy marks for such a complicated question. First there are the usual straightforward consolidation aspects – adding across, intragroup trading, setting up workings, revaluation of property. And part (c) is reasonably flexible, with credit available for sensible comments.

Examiner's comment. Candidates generally did well on this question. They showed a good understanding of the full goodwill method. Some made the mistake of showing a gain on disposal of the interest in Bochem in the statement of profit or loss and other comprehensive income, when it should be an adjustment to equity. The examiner stressed the importance of showing workings in a clear, concise manner, so that marks can be allocated for principles and method, even if mistakes are made in the calculations.

Marking scheme

		Marks
(a)	Consolidated statement of profit or loss and other comprehensive income	5
	Bochem	8
	Ceram	6
	Inventory	2
	Bond	4
	PPE	3
	Impairment of customer	2
	Employee benefits	2
	NCI	3
		35
(b)	1 mark per valid point, maximum	7
(c)	Description of management of earnings	3
	Moral/ethical considerations	3
		6
	Professional marks	2
		50

(a) ASHANTI GROUP
STATEMENT OF PROFIT OR LOSS AND OTHER COMPREHENSIVE INCOME
FOR THE YEAR ENDED 30 APRIL 20X5

	$m
Revenue: $810 + 235 + (142 \times \frac{6}{12}) - 15$ (W4) $- 5$ (W6)	1,096.00
Cost of sales: $686 + 137 + (84 \times \frac{6}{12}) - 15$ (W4) $+ 1$ (W4)	(851.00)
Gross profit	245.00
Other income: $31 + 17 + (12 \times \frac{6}{12}) + 3.8$ (W10)	57.80
Distribution costs: $30 + 21 + (26 \times \frac{6}{12})$	(64.00)
Administrative expenses: $55 + 29 + (12 \times \frac{6}{12}) + 2$ (W3)	
$\qquad + 1.6$ (W7) $+ 0.21$ (W8) $+ 2.2$ (W9)	(96.01)
Finance income: (W5) $0.842 + 0.836$	1.68
Finance costs: $8 + 6 + (8 \times \frac{6}{12}) + 11.699$ (W5) $+ 3$ (W6)	(32.70)
Share of profit of associate: $14 \times \frac{6}{12} \times 30\%$	2.10
Profit before tax	113.87
Income tax expense: $21 + 23 + (10 \times \frac{6}{12})$	(49.00)
Profit for the year	64.87
Other comprehensive income (items that will not be reclassified to profit or loss)	
Gain on investments in equity instruments: $20 + 9 + (6 \times \frac{6}{12})$	32.00
Gain/loss on property revaluation: $12 + 6 + 1.6$ (W7)	19.60
Actuarial loss on defined benefit plan: 14	(14.00)
Share of other comprehensive income of associate: $6 \times \frac{6}{12} \times 30\%$	0.90
Other comprehensive income for the year net of tax	38.5
Total comprehensive income for the year	103.37
Profit attributable to:	
$\quad$ Owners of the parent (bal. fig.)	50.48
$\quad$ Non-controlling interests (W2)	14.39
	64.87
Total comprehensive income attributable to:	
$\quad$ Owners of the parent	82.89
$\quad$ Non-controlling interests (W2)	20.48
	103.37

Workings

1   *Group structure*

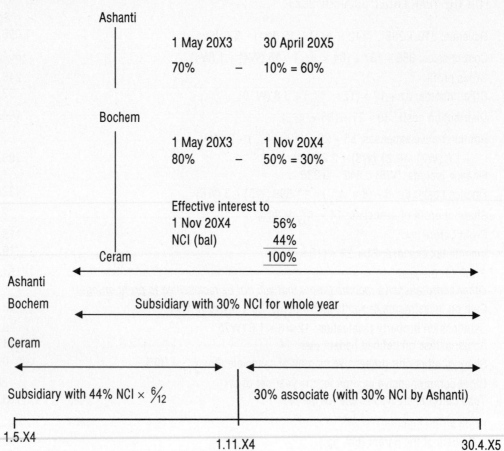

Ashanti

	1 May 20X3	30 April 20X5
	70%	–	10% = 60%

Bochem

	1 May 20X3	1 Nov 20X4
	80%	–	50% = 30%

Effective interest to
1 Nov 20X4   56%
NCI (bal)   44%

Ceram   100%

Ashanti

Bochem   Subsidiary with 30% NCI for whole year

Ceram

Subsidiary with 44% NCI × 6/12   30% associate (with 30% NCI by Ashanti)

1.5.X4   1.11.X4   30.4.X5

2   *Non-controlling interests*

| | Bochem | | Ceram | |
| | Profit for year | TCI | Profit for year | TCI |
	$m	$m	$m	$m
Per question	36.0	51.0		
14 × 6/12			7.0	
20 × 6/12				10
Depreciation of fair value adjustment (W3)	(2.0)	(2.0)		
Impairment of 'full' goodwill	(2.2)	(2.2)		
Profit on disposal of Ceram (W10)	3.8	3.8		
Share of profit of associate 14 × 6/12 × 30%	2.1			
Share of TCI of associate (6 × 6/12 × 30%) + 2.1		3.0		
	37.7	53.6	7.0	10
×	× 30%	× 30%	× 44%	× 44%

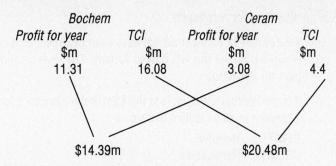

	Bochem		Ceram	
	Profit for year	TCI	Profit for year	TCI
	$m	$m	$m	$m
	11.31	16.08	3.08	4.4

$14.39m $20.48m

Note. There is no profit on the part disposal of Bochem because control is not lost.

3   *Fair value adjustments*

Bochem	At acquisition	Movement		At year end
	1 May 20X3	20X4	20X5	30 April 20X5
	$m	$m	$m	$m
Plant	10	¹⁰⁄₅ = (2)	(2)	6
(160 − (55 + 85 + 10))				

(4)

Ceram				
115 − 115	–	–		–

4   *Intragroup trading*

(i)   Cancel intra group sales/purchases:

DEBIT	Revenue ($10m + $5m)	$15m	
CREDIT	Cost of sales (purchases)		$15m

(ii)   Unrealised profit:

Note. The inventory sold to Ceram has been sold to third parties, so the unrealised profit arises only on the unsold inventory of Bochem.

DEBIT	Cost of sales (10 × ½ × 20%)	$1m	
CREDIT	Inventories (SOFP)		$1m

5   *Bond*

First calculate amortised cost using the original semi-annual effective interest of 4%, then compare with impaired value calculated using the original annual effective interest of 8%.

	$m
1 May 20X4 amortised cost	21.046
Effective interest @ 4%	0.842
31 October 20X4 cash received (20 × 5%)	(1.000)
	20.888
Effective interest @ 4%	0.836
30 April 20X5 cash received	(1.000)
30 April 20X5 c/d	20.724
Impairment loss (bal. fig.)	(11.699)
30 April 20X5 impaired value*	9.025

$$*2.34 \times \frac{1}{1.08} + 8 \times \frac{1}{(1.08)^2}$$

Double entries:

DEBIT	Profit or loss	$11.698m	
CREDIT	Bond		$11.698m

6   *Allowance for receivables*

The revenue of $5m should not have been recorded, as it is not probable that future economic benefits from the sale will flow to Ashanti. The revenue should only be recorded when the customer pays for the goods.

It is not appropriate to include the $5m in the allowance for doubtful debts of $8m, and so the allowance must be limited to $3m.

DEBIT	Revenue	$5m	
CREDIT	Receivables		$5m
DEBIT	Finance costs (impairment of receivable)	$3m	
CREDIT	Allowance for doubtful debts		$3m

7   *Property, plant and equipment*

		SOFP $m	Revaluation surplus $m	
1 May 20X3	Cost	12.000		
	Depreciation $^{12}\!/_{10}$	(1.200)		To OCI (not
	Revaluation (bal. fig)	2.200	2.2	re-classified
30 April 20X4	Revalued PPE c/d	13.000		on disposal)
	Depreciation for year $^{13}\!/_{9}$	(1.444)		
	Transfer to retained earnings: 1.444 – 1.2		(0.244)	
			1.956	and 1.6
	Revaluation loss (bal. fig.)	(3.556)	(1.956)	to P/L
30 April 20X5	Revalued PPE c/d	8.000	0.000	

Original entries:

DEBIT	Other comprehensive income	$3.56m	
CREDIT	Property, plant and equipment		$3.56m

Correct entries:

DEBIT	Other comprehensive income	$1.96m	
DEBIT	Profit or loss (bal. fig.)	$1.6m	
CREDIT	Property, plant and equipment		$3.56m

To correct:

DEBIT	Profit or loss	$1.6m	
CREDIT	Other comprehensive income		$1.6m

8   *Holiday pay accrual*

IAS 19 *Employee benefits* requires that an accrual be made for holiday entitlement carried forward to next year.

Number of days c/fwd: $900 \times 3 \times 95\% = 2,565$ days

Number of working days: $900 \times 255 = 229,500$

$$\text{Accrual} = \frac{2,565}{229,500} \times \$19m = \$0.21m$$

DEBIT	Administrative expenses	$0.21m	
CREDIT	Accruals		$0.21m

9 Goodwill

	Bochem	Ceram
	$m	$m
Consideration transferred: per question/136 × 70%	150.0	95.2
Fair value of non-controlling interest	54.0	26.0
Fair value of net assets	(160.0)	(115.0)
	44.0	6.2
Impairment loss to 30.4. 20X4: 44 × 15%	(6.6)	(−)
	37.4	
Impairment loss to 30.4.20X5: 44 × 5%	(2.2)	
	35.2	6.2

10 Profit on sale of Ceram

	$m	$m
Fair value of consideration received		90.0
Fair value of equity interest retained		45.0
Consolidated value of Ceram at date of disposal		
Net assets	160.0	
Goodwill	6.2	
	166.2	
Less NCI per question	(35.0)	
		(131.2)
		3.8

11 Sale of 10% of Bochem

As control is not lost, there is **no effect on the consolidated statement of profit or loss and other comprehensive income**. The sale is, in effect, a **transfer between owners** (Ashanti and the non-controlling interest). It is accounted for as an equity transaction directly in equity, and only reflected in the statement of changes in equity.

DEBIT	Cash	$34m	
CREDIT	Non-controlling interest (251.2 * × 10%)		$25.12m
CREDIT	Adjustment to parent's equity (not OCI)		$8.88m

* Net assets of Bochem at date of sale:

	$m
Net assets at 30 April 20X5	210.0
FV adjustments (W3)	6.0
	216.0
Goodwill (W9)	35.2
	251.2

BPP note. Because there is no effect on the consolidated statement of profit or loss and other comprehensive income, it was not necessary to do this working in order to obtain full marks. Nevertheless, it is good practice, so we have included it for completeness.

(b) Social and environmental information

There are a number of factors which encourage companies to disclose social and environmental information in their financial statements.

Public interest in corporate social responsibility is steadily increasing. Although financial statements are primarily intended for investors and their advisers, there is growing recognition that companies actually have **a number of different stakeholders**. These include **customers, employees and the general public,** all of whom are **potentially interested** in the way in which a company's operations affect the natural environment and the wider community. These stakeholders can have a **considerable effect on a company's**

performance. As a result many companies now deliberately attempt to build a **reputation for social and environmental responsibility.** Therefore the disclosure of environmental and social information is essential. There is also growing recognition that **corporate social responsibility is actually an important part of an entity's overall performance.** Responsible practice in areas such as reduction of damage to the environment and recruitment **increases shareholder value.** Companies that act responsibly and make social and environmental disclosures are **perceived as better investments** than those that do not.

Another factor is **growing interest by governments and professional bodies.** Although there are **no IFRSs** that specifically require environmental and social reporting, it may be required by **company legislation.** There are now a number of **awards for environmental and social reports** and high quality disclosure in financial statements. These provide further encouragement to disclose information.
At present companies are normally able to disclose **as much or as little information as they wish in whatever manner that they wish.** This causes a number of **problems.** Companies tend to disclose information **selectively** and it is difficult for users of the financial statements to **compare the performance of different companies.** However, there are **good arguments** for continuing to allow companies a certain amount of freedom to determine the information that they disclose. If detailed rules are imposed, **companies are likely to adopt a 'checklist' approach** and will **present information in a very general and standardised way,** so that it is of very little use to stakeholders.

(c)   **Management of earnings**

'Earnings management' involves exercising judgement with regard to financial reporting and structuring transactions so as to give a **misleadingly optimistic picture** of a company's performance. This is done with the intention, whether consciously or not, of **influencing outcomes that depend on stakeholders' assessments.** For example, a bank, or a supplier or customer may decide to do business with a company on the basis of a favourable performance or position. A director may wish to delay a hit to profit or loss for the year in order to secure a bonus that depends on profit. Indeed earnings management, sometimes called 'creative accounting' may be described as manipulation of the financial reporting process for private gain.

A director may also wish to present the company favourably in order to maintain a **strong position within the market.** The motive is not directly private gain - he or she may be thinking of the company's stakeholders, such as employees, suppliers or customers - but in the long term earnings management is not a substitute for sound and profitable business, and cannot be sustained.

'Aggressive' earnings management is a form of fraud and differs from reporting error. Nevertheless, all forms of earnings management may be **ethically questionable,** even if not illegal.

A more positive way of looking at earnings management is to consider the **benefits of not manipulating earnings:**

(I)   Stakeholders can rely on the data. Word gets around that the company 'tells it like it is' and does not try to bury bad news.

(ii)   It encourages management to safeguard the assets and exercise prudence.

(iii)   Management set an example to employees to work harder to make genuine profits, not arising from the manipulation of accruals.

(iv)   Focus on cash flow rather than accounting profits keeps management anchored in reality.

Earnings management goes against **the principle of corporate social responsibility.** Companies have duty not to mislead stakeholders, whether their own shareholders, suppliers, employees or the government. Because the temptation to indulge in earnings management may be strong, particularly in times of financial crisis, it is important to have **ethical frameworks and guidelines** in place. The letter of the law may not be enough.

46 Preparation question: Foreign operation

CONSOLIDATED STATEMENT OF FINANCIAL POSITION

	Standard $'000	Odense Kr'000	Rate	Odense $'000	Consol $'000
Property, plant and equipment	1,285	4,400	8.1	543	1,828
Inv in Odense	520	–		–	–
Goodwill (W2)	–	–		–	277
	1,805	4,400		543	2,105
Current assets	410	2,000	8.1	247	657
	2,215	6,400		790	2,762
Share capital	500	1,000	9.4	106	500
Retained earnings (W3)	1,115				1,395
Pre-acq'n		2,100	9.4	224	
Post acq'n	–	2,200	Bal fig	324	
	1,615	5,300		654	1,895
Non-controlling interest (W6)					131
					2,026
Loans	200	300	8.1	37	237
Current liabilities	400	800	8.1	99	499
	600	1,100		136	736
	2,215	6,400		790	2,762

CONSOLIDATED STATEMENT OF PROFIT OR LOSS AND OTHER COMPREHENSIVE INCOME

	Standard $'000	Odense Kr'000	Rate	Odense $'000	Consol $'000
Revenue	1,125	5,200	8.4	619	1,744
Cost of sales	(410)	(2,300)	8.4	(274)	(684)
Gross profit	715	2,900		345	1,060
Other expenses	(180)	(910)	8.4	(108)	(288)
Impairment loss (W2)					(21)
Dividend from Odense	40				–
Profit before tax	575	1,990		237	751
Income tax expense	(180)	(640)	8.4	(76)	(256)
Profit for the year	395	1,350		161	495

OTHER COMPREHENSIVE INCOME
Items that may subsequently be reclassified to profit or loss

	Standard $'000	Odense Kr'000	Rate	Odense $'000	Consol $'000
Exchange difference on translating foreign operations (W4)	–	–		–	72
TOTAL COMPREHENSIVE INCOME FOR THE YEAR	395	1,350		161	567

Profit attributable to:

Owners of the parent	463
Non-controlling interest (161 × 20%)	32
	495

Total comprehensive income for the year attributable to:

Owners of the parent	525
Non-controlling interest (161 + 48) × 20%	42
	567

CONSOLIDATED STATEMENT OF CHANGES IN EQUITY (EXTRACT)

	Retained earnings $'000
Balance at 20X5	1,065
Dividends paid	(195)
Total comprehensive income for the year (per SPLOCI)	525
Balance at 31/12/X6 (W3)/(W5)	1,395

Workings

1 Group structure

Standard

1.1.X4 | 80%

Pre-acquisition ret'd earnings 2,100,000 Krone

Odense

2 Goodwill

	Kr'000	Kr'000	Rate	$'000
Consideration transferred (520 × 9.4)		4,888		520
Non-controlling interests (3,100 × 20%)		620		66
Share capital	1,000		9.4	
Reserves	2,100			
		(3,100)		(330)
		2,408		256
Exchange differences 20X4-20X5		–	β	18
At 31.12.X5		2,408	8.8	274
Impairment losses 20X6		(168)	8.1	(21)
Exchange differences 20X6		–	β	24
At 31.12.X6		2,240	8.1	277

3 Consolidated retained earnings carried forward

	Standard $'000
Standard	1,115
Group share of post acquisition reserves at Odense (324 × 80%)	259
	1,374
Less goodwill impairment losses (W2)	(21)
Exchange on differences on goodwill (18 + 24)	42
	1,395

4 Consolidated retained earnings b/f proof

	$'000
Standard	915
Add post-acquisition retained earnings of Odense (4,355 @ 8.8 – 3,100 @ 9.4) × 80%	132
Less goodwill impairment losses (W2)	0
Exchange differences on goodwill (W2)	18
	1,065

5   *Exchange differences*

	$'000	$'000
On translation of net assets:		
Closing NA @ CR	654	
Opening NA @ OR (5,300 – 1,350 + 405 = 4,355 @ 8.8)	(495)	
Less retained profit as translated (161 (SOCI) – 405 @ 8.1)	(111)	
Exchange gain		48
On goodwill (W2)		24
		72

6   *Non-controlling interests (statement of financial position)*

	$'000
NCI at acquisition (W2)	66
NCI share of post acquisition reserves of Odense (324 × 20%)	65
	131

47 Memo

Text reference. Foreign currency is covered in Chapter 16.

Top tips. In this question, you had to produce a consolidated statement of profit or loss and other comprehensive income and statement of financial position for a parent company and its foreign subsidiary. Adjustments had to be made for intragroup items such as loans and inventory, and candidates had to deal with the treatment of goodwill as a foreign currency asset. Exchange gains and losses had to be recognised in the financial statements.

Easy marks. Just setting out the proforma and doing the mechanics of translation will earn you easy marks, even if you struggle with more difficult aspects.

Examiner's comment. This question was well answered. Candidates generally made good attempts at the translation of the foreign subsidiary, the calculation of goodwill, intragroup profit in inventory, and the gain on translation. At the same time, there were problems with the treatment of goodwill as a foreign currency asset, and the exchange gain on the intra group loan.

Marking scheme

	Marks
Consolidated statement of financial position	7
Translation of subsidiary's statement of financial position	5
Goodwill	1
Non-controlling interest	2
Post acquisition reserves	5
Consolidated statement of profit or loss and other comprehensive income	5
Unrealised profit	4
Loan	3
Available	32
Maximum	32

(Movement on reserves and exchange gain analysis not asked for)

MEMO
CONSOLIDATED STATEMENT OF FINANCIAL POSITION AT 30 APRIL 20X4

	$m
Assets	
Property, plant and equipment: 297 + 70(W5)	367
Goodwill (W2)	8
Current assets (355 + 48.6 – 0.6) (W7)	403
	778
Equity and liabilities	
Equity attributable to owners of the parent:	
Share capital	60
Share premium	50
Retained earnings (W3)	372
	482
Non-controlling interest (W4)	18
	500
Non-current liabilities (30 + 18.6 – 5)	44
Current liabilities: 6205 + 29 (W5)	234
	778

MEMO
CONSOLIDATED STATEMENT OF PROFIT OR LOSS AND OTHER COMPREHENSIVE INCOME
FOR THE YEAR ENDED 30 APRIL 20X4

	$m
Revenue (200 + 71 – 6)	265
Cost of sales (120 + 48 – 6 + 0.6 (W8)	(163)
Gross profit	102
Distribution costs and administrative expenses: 30 + 10 (W6)	(40)
Impairment of goodwill (W2)	(2)
Interest receivable	4
Finance costs (W6)	(1)
Exchange gains (W8)	1
Profit before tax	64
Income tax expense: 20 + 4.5 (W6)	(24)
Profit for the year	40
Other comprehensive income (items that may subsequently be reclassified to profit or loss)	
Exchange differences on foreign operations (W9) (9.7 + 1.6)	11
Total comprehensive income for the year	51
Profit attributable to	
Owners of the parent	38
Non-controlling interest (25% × 7.9) (W4)	2
	40
Total comprehensive income for the year attributable to	
Owners of the parent	47
Non-controlling interest (7.9 + 9.7) × 25%	4
	51

Workings

1   *Group structure*

Memo

1 May 20X3   75%

Random

Cost = 120m crowns
PAR = 80m crowns

2 Goodwill

	CRm	CRm	Rate	$m
Consideration transferred		120.0		48
Non-controlling interests (132 × 25%)		33.0		13.2
Less fair value of net assets at acq'n:				
Share capital	32		2.5	
Share premium	20			
Retained earnings	80			
		(132.0)		(52.8)
		21.0		8.4
Impairment losses		(4.2)	2.1	(2.0)
FX gain		–	β	1.6
At 30.4.X4		16.8	2.1	8.0

3 Retained earnings

	$m
Memo	360.0
Random (75% × 17.6 (W6))	13.2
Provision for unrealised profit (W7)	(0.6)
Impairment of goodwill (W2)	(2.0)
Exchange differences on goodwill (W2)	1.6
	372.2

4 Non-controlling interests

	$m
NCI at acquisition (W1)	13.2
NCI share of post acquisition reserves of Random ((W3) 17.6 × 25%)	4.4
	17.6

5 Translation of statement of financial position

	CRm	Rate	$m
Property, plant and equipment	146.0	2.1	69.5
Current assets	102.0	2.1	48.6
	248.0		118.1
Share capital	32.0	2.5	12.8
Share premium	20.0	2.5	8.0
Retained earnings:			
Pre-acquisition	80.0	2.5	32.0
	132.0		52.8

	CRm	Rate	$m
Post-acquisition: 15 + (2 – 1.2) (W8)	15.8	β	17.6
	147.8		70.4
Non-current liabilities (41 – 2 (W8))	39.0	2.1	18.6
Current liabilities (60 + 1.2 (W8))	61.2	2.1	29.1
	248.0		118.1

6 Translation of statement of profit or loss and other comprehensive income

	CRm	Rate	$m
Revenue	142	2	71
Cost of sales	(96)	2	(48)
Gross profit	46		23
Distribution and administrative expenses	(20)	2	(10)
Interest payable	(2)	2	(1)
Exchange gain (2 – 1.2) (W8)	0.8	2	0.4
Profit before tax	24.8		12.4
Income tax expense	(9)	2	(4.5)
Profit/total comprehensive income for the year	15.8		7.9

7   *Provision for unrealised profit*

		$m
Sale by parent to subsidiary (6 million × 20% × ½)		0.6

8   *Exchange gains and losses in the accounts of Random*

Loan to Random (non-current liabilities)

	CRm
At 1 May 20X3 ($5 million × 2.5)	12.5
At 30 April 20X4 ($5 million × 2.1)	(10.5)
Gain	2.0

Intro-group purchases (current liabilities)

	CRm
Purchase of goods from Memo ($6 million × 2)	12
Payment made ($6 million × 2.2)	(13.2)
Loss	(1.2)

Exchange differences in statement of profit or loss (retranslated to dollars)

	$m
Gain on loan (2 ÷ 2)	1.0
Loss on current liability/purchases (1.2 ÷ 2)	(0.6)
	0.4

(*Note.* This has been rounded up to $1 million.)

9   *Exchange differences arising during the year year to be recorded in other comprehensive income* (items that may subsequently be reclassified to profit or loss)

	$m	$m
Closing net assets at closing rate (W5)	70.4	
Less opening net assets at opening rate (W5)	(52.8)	
		17.6
Less retained profit as translated (W6)		(7.9)
		9.7
Exchange gain on retranslation of goodwill (W2)		1.6
		11.3

48 Case study question: Ribby

Text reference. Foreign currency transactions are covered in Chapter 16 of the text. Ethics is covered in Chapter 3.

Top tips. Part (a) of this question asked you to determine the functional currency of an overseas subsidiary. Make sure you produce arguments for and against your decision, as it is not clear cut. In Part (b), you were asked to prepare a consolidated statement of financial position for a simple group structure involving an overseas subsidiary and several adjustments for foreign currency loans, employee compensation, past service pension costs, inter company profit elimination, and early repayment of long term loans. It is important to grab the easy marks for basic consolidation workings, and not get bogged down in the adjustments. It is a good idea to provide a brief explanation of the adjustments, in case the figures are wrong. Part (c) required you to discuss the manipulation of financial statements and the nature of accountants responsibilities the profession and to society. Make sure you relate your answer to the information in Part (b), as you are asked to.

Easy marks. These are available for simply translating the statement of financial position at the correct rate, and setting out the proforma and the basic workings for group structure, non-controlling interest and retained earnings. If the share-based payment and the pensions adjustments worry you, ignore them and make a figure up – if you make a good attempt at the easy bits you will still pass comfortably.

Marking scheme

		Marks
(a)	Consideration of factors	6
	Conclusion	2
		8
(b)	Translation of Zian	6
	Loan	2
	Goodwill: Zian	4
	Non-controlling interest	4
	Building	3
	Early repayment of loan	1
	Pension	2
	Inventory	1
	Bonus	3
	Goodwill: Hall	2
	Retained earnings: Hall	2
	Zian	1
	Ribby	3
	Other components of equity	1
		35
(c)	Accounting	2
	Ethical discussion	3
	Quality of discussion	2
		7
	Maximum	50

(a) **Factors to consider in determining functional currency of Zian**

IAS 21 *The effects of changes in foreign exchange rates* defines functional currency as 'the currency of the primary economic environment in which the entity operates'. Each entity, whether an individual company, a parent of a group, or an operation within a group, should determine its functional currency and **measure its results and financial position in that currency**.

An entity should consider the following factors:

(i) Is it the currency that mainly **influences sales prices** for goods and services (this will often be the currency in which sales prices for its goods and services are denominated and settled)?

(ii) Is it the currency of the country whose **competitive forces and regulations** mainly determine the sales prices of its goods and services?

(iii) Is it the currency that **mainly influences labour, material and other costs** of providing goods or services? (This will often be the currency in which such costs are denominated and settled.)

Applying the first of these, it appears that **Zian's functional currency is the dinar**. Zian **sells its products locally** and its prices are determined by local competition. However, point (ii) on operating costs suggests that the **functional currency is the dollar**. Zen **imports goods which are paid for in dollars**, and while selling and operating costs are paid in dinars, it is the currency that determines the pricing of transactions that is important.

Other factors may also provide evidence of an entity's functional currency:

(i) It is the currency in which **funds from financing activities** are generated.
(ii) It is the currency in which **receipts from operating activities** are usually retained.

Zian finances its operations in part by means of a $4m loan from Hall. However, it **does not depend on Hall, or other group companies for finance**. Furthermore, Zian operates with a considerable degree of autonomy, and is not under the control of the parent as regards finance or management. It also generates sufficient cash lows to meet its cash needs. These aspects point away from the dollar as the functional currency.

The position is **not clear cut**, and there are arguments on both sides. However, **on balance it is the dinar** that should be considered as the functional currency, since this most faithfully represents the economic reality of the transactions, both operating and financing, and the autonomy of Zian in relation to the parent company.

(b) RIBBY GROUP
CONSOLIDATED STATEMENT OF FINANCIAL POSITION AS AT 31 MAY 20X8

	$m
Non-current assets	
Property, plant and equipment: 250 + 120 + 30 (W2) + 10 (W7) + 5.5 (W7) – 0.8 (W9)	414.7
Goodwill: 20 (W2) + 4.6 (W4)	24.6
Financial assets: 10 + 5 + 12.3 (W2) – 4 (W8)	23.3
	462.6
Current assets: 22 + 17 + 10 (W2) + 6 (W13) – 4 (W13)	51.0
	513.6
Equity	
Ordinary shares	60.0
Other components of equity*: 30 + 1.8	31.8
Retained earnings (W5)	122.6
	214.4
Non-controlling interests (W6)	67.7
	282.1
Non-current liabilities	
90 + 5 + 4 (W2) – 4 (W8) – 10 (W10) + 3.5 (W12)	88.5
Current liabilities	
110 + 7 + 6 (W2) + 10 (W10) + 1 (W10) + 3 (W11) + 6 (W13)	143.0
	513.6

*Note: Hall's 'other components of equity' are all pre-acquisition.

Workings

1   *Group structure*

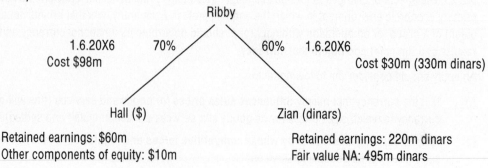

2   *Translation of SOFP of Zian at 31 May 20X8*

	Dinars (m)	Rate	$m
Property, plant and equipment	360	12	30.0
Financial assets	148	12	12.3
Current assets	120	12	10.0
	628		52.3
Share capital	209	11	19.0
Retained earnings			
Pre-acqn	220	11	20.0
	429		39.0
Post-acqn. (307 – 220 – 8 (W8)	79	ß	3.3
	508		42.3
Non-current liabilities 40 + 8 (W8)	48	12	4.0
Current liabilities	72	12	6.0
	628		52.3

3   *Goodwill: Hall*

	$m	$m
Consideration transferred		98
Fair value of non-controlling interests		42
Fair value of identifiable net assets at acq'n (per question)		(120)
		20

4   *Goodwill: Zian*

	Dinars (m)	Rate	$m
Consideration transferred (30 × 11)	330		30.0
Non-controlling interests	220		20.0
		11	
Less: fair value of net assets at acq'n per question	(495)		(45.0)
At 1 June 20X6	55		5.0
Impairment loss	(0)		(0.0)
Exchange loss	-		(0.4)
At 31 May 20X8	55	12	4.6

5   *Retained earnings*

	Ribby $m	Hall $m	Zian $m
Per question/as translated (W2)	120.0	80.0	23.3
Adjustments			
Fair value movement (W7)			(0.5)
Impairment (W9)	(0.8)		
Loan penalty (W10)	(1.0)		
Bonus/share options (W11)	(4.8)		
Past service cost (W12)	(3.5)		
Unrealised profit in inventory (W13)		(4)	
Pre-acquisition: per question		(60)	
as translated (W2)			(20.0)
		16	2.8
Group share: Hall: 16 × 70%	11.2		
Zian: 2.8 × 60%	1.7		
Exchange loss on goodwill ((W4) 0.4 × 60%)	(0.2)		
	122.6		

6   Non-controlling interests

	Hall $m	Zian $m
NCI at acquisition (W3)/(W4)	42.0	20.0
NCI share of post acquisition retained earnings:		
Hall ((W5) 16 × 30%)	4.8	
Zian ((W5) 2.8 × 40%)		1.1
Exchange loss on goodwill ((W4) 0.4 × 40%)		(0.2)
	46.8	20.9

67.7

7   Fair value adjustments

Hall:

	Acquisition 1 June 20X6 $m	Movement 2 years $m	Year end 31 May 20X8 $m
Land: 120 – 40 (SC) – 60 (RE) – 10 (other)	10	–	10

Zian:

	Acquisition 1 June 20X6	Movement (exchange diff)	Year-end 31 May 20X8 $m
Land (in dinars (m)) 495 – 209 (SC) – 220 (RE) = 66 In dollars: 66/11 (66/12)	6	(0.5)	5.5

Note: The land is non-depreciable so the movement for Zian is the change in exchange rate.

8   Intragroup loan

	Dinar
Initial value 1 June 20X7 ($4m × 10)	40
Year-end value 31 May 20X8 ($4m × 12)	48
Foreign exchange loss	8

Adjust in Zian's books (W6)

DEBIT Profit and loss (retained earnings)	8 dinars	
CREDIT Non-current liabilities		8 dinars

The intra-group loan will be eliminated from the consolidated SOFP.

DEBIT Non-current liabilities	$4m	
CREDIT Financial assets		$4m

9   Impairment loss on building

	$
Cost at 1 June 20X7: 40m dinar/10	4.0
Depreciation: 4m/20	(0.2)
	3.8
Impairment loss (bal. fig.)	(0.8)
Impaired value at 31 May 20X8: 36m dinar/12	3.0

10   *Early repayment of loan*

The decision to repay the loan early has two implications:

(i)   The loan must be transferred from non-current liabilities to current liabilities.

(ii)   A penalty for early re-payment. The double entries are:

DEBIT	Non-current liabilities	$10m	
CREDIT	Current liabilities		$10m

Being transfer to current liabilities

DEBIT	Profit or loss for the year	$1m	
CREDIT	Current liabilities		$1m

Being accrual of early repayment penalty

11   *Bonus and share options*

Half the bonus is to be paid in cash, so a liability of $(6m × ½) = $3m must be accrued.

The remainder of the bonus is to be paid in share options. The grant date will be 30 November 20X8, as this is when the terms of the share options become fixed. However, the services must be recognised as received, and so 12 months of the 18 month service period up to the grant date must be recognised.

The double entry is as follows:

DEBIT	Profit or loss (retained earnings)	$4.8m	
CREDIT	Current liabilities (cash bonus (6m × ½))		$3m
CREDIT	Other components of entity 90% × $6m × ½ × $\dfrac{12 \text{ months}}{18 \text{ months}}$		$1.8m

12   *Past service cost*

The past service cost of $3m relates to a benefit has already been vested, while the remaining $0.5m relates to an entitlement that has not yet fully vested, as it is given in return for services over the remaining two-year period. However, following the 2011 revision of IAS 19, all past service costs must be charge to profit or loss.

The double entry is as follows:

On 1 June 20X7:

DEBIT	Profit or loss (retained earnings)	$3.5m	
CREDIT	Present value of obligation (non-current liabilities)		$3.5m

13   *Sale of inventory*

This transaction is known as 'window dressing'. It should not be shown as a sale; the sale must be cancelled and the inventory re-instated at $2m (cost) rather than $6m sales price.

The entries for the cancellation of the sale are:

DEBIT	Sales	$6m	
CREDIT	Cash (current liabilities)		$6m

For the cancellation of the purchase:

DEBIT	Cash (current assets)	$6m	
CREDIT	Purchases		$6m

The above entries have no effect on retained earnings, but the elimination of unrealised profit, reducing inventory from $6m to $2m, will affect it.

DEBIT	Closing inventory/cost of sales (Hall's books): 6 − 2	$4m	
CREDIT	Inventory (current asset)		$4m

(c)   **Ethical implications of sale of inventory**

Members of the accounting profession enjoy a number of privileges. These include:

(i)   Special status and respect within the community.

(ii)   Self-regulation, that is regulation by the accountants' professional body

(iii)   An exclusive right to certain functions. For example, auditors must be members of certain professional bodies.

Like other professions, the accounting profession has **features that distinguish it** from non-professional jobs. The most important of these is specialist knowledge, but also recognition as being committed to the good of society, rather than just commercial gain.

To **earn this status and these privileges**, accountants should, as a minimum:

(a)   Be committed to the presentation of true, fair and accurate financial statements.

(b)   Show independence and objectivity in applying financial reporting standards.

(c)   Be committed to an ethical approach to business, and apply this in the preparation of financial statements.

Ethical behaviour in the preparation of financial statements, and in other areas, is of **paramount importance**. This applies equally to preparers of accounts, to auditors and to accountants giving advice to directors. Company accountants act unethically if they use 'creative' accounting in accounts preparation to make the figures look better.

In treating the inventory as sold, Ribby is indulging in '**window dressing**'. This is not a genuine sale; its purpose is purely **to show Ribby's subsidiary Hall in a better financial position** than is truly the case, in order to increase the likelihood of the sale of Hall. The 'sale' of inventory would increase cash and retained earnings by $4m, boosting the appearance of both profitability and liquidity. This would **mislead a potential buyer**. Nor would this manipulation be a 'one-off'; if the subsidiary is not sold, the transaction would be carried out again in the interim accounts. Neither the final accounts for 31 May 20X8, nor the interim accounts would give a fair presentation of the true picture.

The treatment of the inventory is therefore **unethical**, and should be reversed when preparing the consolidated financial statements.

49 Case study question: Rose

Text reference. Foreign currency transactions are covered in Chapter 16 of the text. Ethics is covered in Chapter 3.

Top tips. Part (a) of this question is similar to Ribby, earlier in this Kit. Part (a) (i) asked you to determine the functional currency of an overseas subsidiary. Make sure you produce arguments for and against your decision, as it is not clear cut. In Part (a)(ii), you were asked to prepare a consolidated statement of financial position for a simple group structure involving an overseas subsidiary and several adjustments for an additional interest acquired, a long-term bonus (current service cost), revaluation of a foreign property and change in residual value of plant. It is important to grab the easy marks for basic consolidation workings, and not get bogged down in the adjustments. It is a good idea to provide a brief explanation of the adjustments, in case the figures are wrong. **Note that although you are asked to show the exchange difference arising on the translation of Stem's net assets, the examiner has stated that it is acceptable to combine the translation reserve with retained earnings, as we do here.** Part (b) concerned fair values in a business combination and the ethical implications of the directors valuing customer relationships in a way that was not in accordance with IFRSs. Since this question was set, IFRS 13 *Fair value measurement* has been issued.

Easy marks. These are available for simply translating the statement of financial position at the correct rate, and setting out the proforma and the basic workings for group structure, non-controlling interest and retained earnings. If the bonus and foreign property revaluation adjustments worry you, ignore them and make some figures up – if you make a good attempt at the easy bits you will still pass comfortably.

Marking scheme

			Marks
(a)	(i)	1 mark per point up to maximum	7
	(ii)	Amortisation of patent	1
		Acquisition of further interest	5
		Stem – translation and calculation of goodwill	7
		Retained earnings and other equity	8
		Non-controlling interest	3
		Property, plant and equipment	6
		Non-current liabilities	1
		Employee bonus scheme	4
			35
(b)		Accounting treatment	4
		Ethical consideration	2
		Professional marks	2
		Maximum	50

(a)   (i)   **Factors to consider in determining functional currency of Stem**

IAS 21 *The effects of changes in foreign exchange rates* defines functional currency as 'the currency of the primary economic environment in which the entity operates'. Each entity, whether an individual company, a parent of a group, or an operation within a group, should determine its functional currency and **measure its results and financial position in that currency**.

An entity should consider the following factors:

(1)   What is the currency that mainly **influences sales prices** for goods and services (this will often be the currency in which sales prices for its goods and services are denominated and settled)?

(2)   What is the currency of the country whose **competitive forces and regulations** mainly determine the sales prices of its goods and services?

(3)   What is the currency that **mainly influences labour, material and other costs** of providing goods or services?(This will often be the currency in which such costs are denominated and settled.)

Applying the first of these, it appears that **Stem's functional currency is the dinar**. The price is denominated and settled in dinars and is determined by local supply and demand. However, when it comes to **costs and expenses**, Stem pays in a mixture of dollars, dinars and the local currency, so that aspect is less clear cut.

Other factors may also provide evidence of an entity's functional currency:

(1)   It is the currency in which **funds from financing activities** are generated.
(2)   It is the currency in which **receipts from operating activities** are usually retained.

Stem **does not depend on group companies for finance.** Furthermore, Stem operates with a considerable degree of autonomy, and is not under the control of the parent as regards finance or management. It also generates sufficient cash flows to meet its cash needs. These aspects point away from the dollar as the functional currency.

The position is **not clear cut**, and there are arguments on both sides. However, **on balance it is the dinar** that should be considered as the functional currency, since this most faithfully represents the economic reality of the transactions, both operating and financing, and the autonomy of Stem in relation to the parent company.

(ii) ROSE GROUP
CONSOLIDATED STATEMENT OF FINANCIAL POSITION AS AT 30 APRIL 20X8

	$m
Non-current assets	
Property, plant and equipment: 370 + 110 + 76 (W2) + 30 (W8) + 15 ((W8) 2.25 (W9) + 0.4 (W11)	603.65
Goodwill: 16 (W3) + 6.2 (W4)	22.20
Intangible assets (W8)	3.00
Financial assets: 15 + 7 + 10 (W2)	32.00
	660.85
Current assets: 118 + 100 + 66 (W2)	284.00
	944.85
Equity and liabilities	
Share capital	158.00
Retained earnings (W5)	277.39
Other components of equity (W6)	6.98
	442.37
Non-controlling interests (W7)	89.83
	532.20
Non-current liabilities: 56 + 42 + 32 (W2) + 0.65 (W10)	130.65
Current liabilities :185 + 77 + 20 (W2)	282.00
	412.65
	944.85

Workings

1 *Group structure*

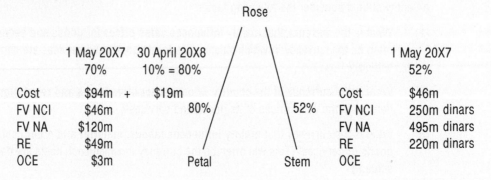

2   *Translation of SOFP of Stem at 30 April 20X8*

	Dinars (m)	Rate	$m
Property, plant and equipment	380	5	76.00
Financial assets	50	5	10.00
Current assets	330	5	66.00
	760		152.00
Share capital	200	6	33.33
Retained earnings			
Pre-acqn	220	6	36.67*
	420		70.00
Post-acqn. (300 – 220 (including FX differences	80	ß	30.00*
	500		100.00
Non-current liabilities	160	5	32.00
Current liabilities	100	5	20.00
	760		152.00

*$36.67m + *$30.00m = $66.67m total retained earnings.

3   *Goodwill: Petal*

	$m	$m
Consideration transferred		94
Fair value of non-controlling interests		46
Fair value of identifiable net assets at acq'n (120 + 4 (W8))		(124)
		16

4   *Goodwill: Stem*

	Dinars (m)	Rate	$m
Consideration transferred (46 × 6)	276	6	46.00
Non-controlling interests	250	6	41.67
Less fair value of net assets at acq'n per question	(495)	6	(82.50)
At 1 May 20X7	31		5.17
Exchange gain	-	ß	1.03
At 30 April 20X8	31	5	6.20

5   *Retained earnings*

	Rose $m	Petal $m	Stem $m
Per question/as translated (W2)	256.00	56	66.67
Adjustments			-
Fair value movement (W8)		(1)	
Exchange gain on fair values (W8)			2.5
Bonus (W10)	(0.65)		
Depreciation adjustment (W11)	0.40		
Pre-acquisition: per question		(49)	
as translated (W2)			(36.67)
		6	32.50

		Rose $m
Group share:	Petal: 6 × 70%	4.20
	Stem: 32.5 × 52%	16.90
Exchange gain on goodwill ((W4) 1.03 × 52%)		0.54
		277.39

6   *Other components of equity*

	Rose $m	Petal $m
Per question	7.00	4.00

Adjustments
    Revaluation of foreign property (W9)   2.25
    Pre acquisition   (3.00)
                                                                  1.00

    Group share: Petal: 1 × 70%   0.70
        Acquisition of 10% of NCI (W12)   (2.97)
                                                                  6.98

7   *Non-controlling interests*

	Petal $m	Stem $m
NCI at acquisition (W3)/(W4)	46.00	41.67
NCI share of post acquisition retained earnings:		
Petal ((W5) 6 × 30%)	1.80	
Stem ((W5) 32.5 × 48%)		15.60
NCI share of post-acquisition other components of equity (W6): 1 × 30%	0.3	
Exchange gain on goodwill ((W4) 1.03 × 48%)		0.49
	48.10	57.76
Acquisition of 10% of Petal	(16.03)	
	32.07	57.76

                                              89.83

8   *Fair value adjustments*

    Petal:

	Acquisition 1 May 20X7 $m	Movement 1 year $m	Year end 30 April 20X8 $m
Land: 120 – 38 (SC) –49 (RE) – 3 (OCE	30	–	30
Patent	4	(¼ ×4)=(1)	3
	34	(1)	33

    Stem:

	Acquisition 1 May 20X7	Movement (exchange diff)	Year-end 30 April 20X8 $m
Land (in dinars (m)) 495 – 200 (SC) – 220 (RE) = 75 In dollars: 75/6(75/5)	12.5	2.5 (ß)	15

    Note: The land is non-depreciable so the movement for Stem is the change in exchange rate.

9   *Foreign property revaluation (Rose)*

		$m
Cost at 1 May 20X7	30m dinars ÷ 6	5.00
Depreciation	5 ÷ 20	(0.25)
		4.75
Revaluation ß		2.25
Revalued amount at 30 April 20X8	35m dinars ÷ 5	7.00

    Note. The revaluation surplus goes to other components of equity (W6) and is added to property, plant and equipment.

10   *Long-term bonus scheme*

The cumulative bonus payable is $4.42m, calculated as follows, with a 5% annual increase:

Bonus as at:		$m
30 April 20X8	$40m × 2%	0.800
30 April 20X9	$0.8m × 1.05	0.840
30 April 20Y0	$0.8m × 1.05^2	0.882
30 April 20Y1	$0.8m × 1.05^3	0.926
30 April 20Y2	$0.8m × 1.05^4	0.972
		4.420

This is $884,000 ($4.42/5 years) per year. The current service cost is the present value of $884,000 at 30 April 20X8: $884,000 × $1/1.08^4$ = $0.65m

The double entry to record this is as follows.

DEBIT	Profit or loss/retained earnings (W5)	$0.65m	
CREDIT	Non-current liabilities		$0.65m

11   *Residual value of plant*

		$m	$m
Depreciation based on original residual value	(20 − 1.4) ÷ 6		3.10
Depreciation based on revised amount	(20 − (3.1 × 3 years) − 2.6) ÷ 3 years		2.70
Adjustment to depreciation in retained earnings and add back to PPE			0.40

12   *Acquisition of additional 10% interest in Petal*

Rose acquired an additional 10% interest on 30 April 20X8, going from 70% to 80%, so the non-controlling interests decreased by one third on that date, going from 30% to 20%. The amount of the decrease is calculated in W7 as $16.03m. The adjustment to parent's equity, which goes through other components of equity (W6), is calculated as follows.

DEBIT	Non-controlling interest (W7)	$16.03m
DEBIT	Other components of equity (ß)	$2.97m
CREDIT	Consideration transferred	$19m

(b)   **Acquisition of service company**

Rose's proposed valuation of the service company's assets (based on what it is prepared to pay for them, which is, in turn, influenced by future plans for the business) **does not comply with IFRS.**

Such a valuation needs to be based on the following IFRS:

(i)   IFRS 3 *Business combinations.* Under IFRS 3, an acquirer must allocate the cost of a business combination by recognising the acquiree's identifiable assets, liabilities and contingent liabilities that satisfy the recognition criteria at their **fair values** at the date of the acquisition.

(ii)   IFRS 13 *Fair value measurement,* published in May 2011, which defines fair value as as **'the price that would be received to sell an asset or paid to transfer a liability in an orderly transaction between market participants at the measurement date.'** This is also known as 'exit price'.

(iii) IAS 38 *Intangible assets,* which states that intangible assets acquired in business combinations can normally be measured sufficiently reliably to be **recognised separately from goodwill.**

Valuing the service company's assets on the basis of their value to Rose does not accord with the above standards. First, **the standards may recognise as assets items that Rose does not identify.** Secondly, there has been **no attempt to apply the IFRS 13 definition of fair value,** which specifies the price that would be paid by **market participants,** and implies that **Rose's judgement alone would not be sufficient.**

Turning to the **contract-based customer relationships** that the service company has, in proposing to value these at zero on the grounds that Rose already has good relationships with customers, Rose is **failing to apply IAS 38.** Under IAS 38, part of the cost of the acquisition should be allocated to these relationships, which will **have a value separate from goodwill** at the date of the acquisition. The fair value of the customer relationships should not be based on Rose's judgement of their worth but on that of a market participant such as a well informed buyer.

Ethical behaviour in the preparation of financial statements, and in other areas, is of **paramount importance**. Directors and company accountants act unethically if they use 'creative' accounting in accounts preparation to make the figures look better, in particular if their treatment would mislead users, as here. Motivation for misleading treatments can include market expectations, market position or expectation of a bonus.

To act ethically, the directors must put the interests of the company and its shareholders first, and must also have regard to other stakeholders such as potential investors or lenders. **If a treatment does not conform to acceptable accounting practice, it is not ethical.**

If the aim of the proposed treatment is to **deliberately** mislead users of financial statements, then it is **unethical**, and should not be put into practice. It is possible that non-compliance with IFRS 3, IFRS 13 and IAS 38 is a genuine **mistake**. If so, the mistake **needs to be corrected** in order to act ethically. There is, in any case a duty of professional competence in the preparation of financial statements, which would entail keeping up to date with IFRS and local legislation.

50 Preparation question: Consolidated statement of cash flows

STATEMENT OF CASH FLOWS FOR THE YEAR ENDED 31 DECEMBER 20X5

	$'000	$'000
Cash flows from operating activities		
Profit before tax	16,500	
Adjustments for:		
Depreciation	5,800	
Impairment losses (W2)	240	
	22,540	
Increase in trade receivables (9,800 – 7,500 – 600)	(1,700)	
Increase in inventories (16,000 – 10,000 – 1,600)	(4,400)	
Increase in trade payables (7,600 – 6,100 – 300)	1,200	
Cash generated from operations	17,640	
Income taxes paid (W1)	(4,200)	
Net cash from operating activities		13,440
Cash flows from investing activities		
Acquisition of subsidiary net of cash acquired	(600)	
Purchase of property, plant and equipment (W2)	(13,100)	
Net cash used in investing activities		(13,700)
Cash flows from financing activities		
Proceeds from issue of share capital		
(12,300 + 5,800 – 10,000 – 2,000 – (5,000 – 1,000))	2,100	
Dividends paid	(900)	
Dividends paid to non-controlling interest (W3)	(40)	
Net cash from financing activities		1,160
Net increase in cash and cash equivalents		900
Cash and cash equivalents at the beginning of the period		1,500
Cash and cash equivalents at the end of the period		2,400

Workings

1   *Additions to property, plant and equipment*

PROPERTY, PLANT AND EQUIPMENT

	$'000		$'000
b/d	25,000		
Revaluation surplus	500		
On acquisition	2,700	Depreciation	5,800
∴ Additions	13,100	c/d	35,500
	41,300		41,300

2   *Goodwill impairment losses*

GOODWILL

	$'000		$'000
b/d	0	∴ Impairment loss	240
On acquisition (5,000 +			
(4,800 × 30%) − 4,800)	1,640	c/d	1,400
	1,640		1,640

3   *Dividends paid to non-controlling interest*

NON-CONTROLLING INTEREST

	$'000		$'000
		b/d	0
∴ Dividends paid	40	Acquisition (4,800 × 30%)	1,440
c/d	1,750	TCI	350
	1,790		1,790

4   *Income taxes paid*

INCOME TAX PAYABLE

	$'000		$'000
		b/d	4,000
∴ Income taxes paid	4,200	Acquisition	200
c/d	5,200	I/S	5,200
	9,400		9,400

51 Case study question: Jocatt

Text reference. Group statements of cash flow are covered in Chapter 17. Ethical issues are covered in Chapter 2.

Top tips. In tackling part (a), remember that time management is the key to cash flow questions. Set out your proforma and workings and do not spend too long on the fiddly bits. The question also required candidates to understand how a business combination achieved in stages would work under the revised IFRS 3 – you need to know that the fair value of the previously held interest in Tigret, and the fair value of the non-controlling interest in Tigret as a subsidiary, go in the goodwill calculation. Other complications include a retirement benefit scheme, a rights issue and goodwill impairment (because the goodwill is more fiddly, being a piecemeal acquisition). Make sure you allow adequate time for Part (b)(i) and (ii). The examiner has recently stressed that students often don't – you can't hope to do well if you don't answer the whole question. There are 15 marks here for Part (b).

Easy marks. In Part (a) these are available for basic cash flow aspects – working capital calculations, non-controlling interest, tax and investment property additions. Follow our order for the workings – the easy ones come first. In Part (b), don't be tempted to write all you know about the direct method and how it works. The question is quite specific. Part (ii) follows on from Part (i), because one of the key problems with the indirect method is manipulation, and this has ethical implications.

Examiner's comment. Candidates generally performed well on this part of the question. The main areas where candidates found difficulties were:ensuring that the purchase of the subsidiary was dealt with in calculating cash flows across the range of assets and liabilities;the treatment of the past service costs relating to the defined benefit scheme; The calculation of the cash flow on taxation, although many candidates made a good attempt at this calculation

The first part of Part (b) on the indirect method of preparing cash flow statements was poorly answered. However, candidates performed well on the ethical aspects.

Marking scheme

	Marks
(a)	
Net profit before tax	1
Retirement benefit expense	2
Depreciation on PPE	1
Depreciation on investment property	1
Amortisation of intangible assets	1
Profit on exchange of land	1
Loss on replacement of investment property	1
Associate's profit	1
Impairment of goodwill	4
Gain on revaluation of investment in equity instruments (Tigret) prior to derecognition	1
Finance costs	1
Decrease in trade receivables	1
Decrease in inventories	1
Increase in trade payables	1
Cash paid to retirement benefit scheme	1
Finance costs paid	1
Income taxes paid	2
Purchase of associate	1
Purchase of PPE	2
Purchase of subsidiary	1
Additions – investment property	1
Proceeds from sale of land	1
Intangible assets	1
Purchase of investments in equity instruments	1
Repayment of long-term borrowings	1
Rights issue NCI	1
Non-controlling interest dividend	1
Dividends paid	1
Net increase in cash and cash equivalents	1
	35

(b)
(i)   Subjective   7

(ii)   Subjective   6

Professional   2

                                                            50

(a)   JOCATT GROUP
       STATEMENT OF CASH FLOWS FOR YEAR ENDED 30 NOVEMBER 20X2

	$m	$m
Cash flows from operating activities		
Profit before taxation	59.0	
Adjustments for:		
Depreciation	27.0	
Amortisation (W4)	17.0	
Impairment of goodwill (W3)	31.5	
Profit on exchange of land*: 15 + 4 − 10	(9.0)	
Gain on investment property* (W2)	(1.5)	
Loss on replacement of investment property (W2)	0.5	
Gain on revaluation of investment in equity instruments		
(Tigret - fair value on derecognition less fair value at 1 December		
20X1: 5 − 4)	(1.0)	
Retirement benefit expense: 10 − 8 + 2 (W9)	4.0	
Cash paid to defined benefit plan (W9)	(7.0)	
Share of profit of associate (W3)	(6.0)	
Interest expense paid (per question)	6.0	
	120.5	
Decrease in trade receivables: 62 − 113 − 5	56.0	
Decrease in inventories: 105 − 128	23.0	
Increase in trade payables: 144 − 55	89.0	
Cash generated from operations	288.5	
Interest paid	(6.0)	
Income taxes paid (W8)	(16.5)	
Net cash from operating activities		266
Cash flows from investing activities		
Acquisition of subsidiary, net of cash acquired: 15 − 7	(8.0)	
Acquisition of associate (W5)	(48.0)	
Purchase of property, plant and equipment (W1)	(98.0)	
Purchase of investment property (per question)	(1.0)	
Purchase of intangible assets (8 + 4)	(12.0)	
Purchase of investments in equity instruments (W6)	(5.0)	
Proceeds from sale of land	15.0	
Net cash used in investing activities		(157)
Cash flows used in financing activities		
Proceeds from issue of share capital: 290 − 275 − 15	0.0	
Repayment of long-term borrowings: 67 − 71	(4.0)	
Rights issue to non-controlling shareholders ((W7) and from SOCIE)	2.0	
Dividends paid (from SOCIE)	(5.0)	
Dividends paid to non-controlling interest shareholders (from SOCIE)	(13.0)	
Net cash used in financing activities		(20)
Net increase in cash and cash equivalents		89
Cash and cash equivalents at the beginning of the year		143
Cash and cash equivalents at the end of the year		232

*Note. The statement of profit or loss and other comprehensive income in the question shows 'gains on property' of $10.5m, which need to be added back to profit in arriving at cash generated from operations. This is made up of $1.5m gain on investment property (W2) and $9m gain on the exchange of surplus land for cash and plant (Note (vi) of the question. The double entry for the exchange is:

DEBIT   Cash $15m
DEBIT   Plant $4m
CREDIT   Land $10m
CREDIT   Profit or loss $9m

Separate from this, also shown in W2, is an impairment loss on the old heating system, for which the double entries are:

DEBIT   Profit or loss (old heating system) $0.5m
CREDIT   Investment property (old heating system) $0.5m

DEBIT   Investment property (new heating system) $1m
CREDIT   Cash   '$1m

Workings

1   *Purchase of property, plant and equipment*

PROPERTY, PLANT AND EQUIPMENT

	$m		$m
Balance b/d	254	Loss on reval'n to OCI	7
Acqn. of subsidiary	15	Depreciation	27
New plant exchange	4	Land exchanged (NBV)	10
Additions (bal. fig.)	98	Balance c/d	327
	371		371

2   *Investment property*

INVESTMENT PROPERTY

	$m		$m
Balance b/d	6.0	Disposal (see note above)	0.5
New system (cash paid)	1.0		
Gain (bal. fig.)	1.5	Balance c/d	8.0
	8.5		8.5

3   *Goodwill*

GOODWILL

	$m		$m
Balance b/d	68.0	Impairment loss (bal. fig.)	31.5
Acquisition of Tigret (W)	11.5	Balance c/d	48.0
	79.5		79.5

Working: Acquisition of Tigret

	$m	$m
Consideration transferred: $15m + $15m		30.0
Fair value of non-controlling interest		20.0
Fair value of previously held equity interest		5.0
		55.0
Identifiable net assets: 15 + 18 + 5 + 7	45.0	
Deferred tax: ($45m - $40m) × 30%	(1.5)	
		(43.5)
		11.5

4 Intangible assets

INTANGIBLE ASSETS

	$m		$m
Balance b/d	72	Amortisation (bal. fig.)	17
Acqn. of subsidiary	18		
Project (cash paid)	8		
Development (cash paid)	4	Balance c/d	85
	102		102

Note. The research costs of $2m and the marketing costs of $1m are charged to profit or loss for the year.

5 Acquisition of associate

INVESTMENT IN ASSOCIATE

	$m		$m
Balance b/d	–	Dividends received	–
Profit or loss	6	Balance c/d	54
Acquisition (bal. fig.)	48		
	54		54

6 Investments in equity instruments

INVESTMENTS IN EQUITY INSTRUMENTS

	$m		$m
Balance b/d	90		
Other comprehensive income*	3	Derecognition of investment in Tigret (now subsidiary)	5
Revaluation gain on investment in Tigret	1		
Additions (bal. fig.)	5	Balance c/d	94
	99		99

*Grossed up for related tax: $2m + $1m

7 Dividend paid to non-controlling interest

NON-CONTROLLING INTEREST

	$m		$m
Dividends paid (from SOCIE)	13	Balance b/d	36
Balance c/d	55	Total comprehensive income	10
		Fair value of NCI on acqn.	20
		Rights issue (note)	2
	68		68

Note. From SOCIE, also proceeds of $5m × NCI share of 40%. (This working duplicates the NCI column in the SOCIE.)

8 Tax paid

TAX PAYABLE

	$m		$m
		Balance b/d (deferred)	41.0
∴ Taxes paid	16.5	Balance b/d (current	30.0
		Profit or loss	11.0
Balance c/d (deferred)	35.0	OCI (on inv. in equity inst.)	1.0
Balance c/d (current)	33.0	Acquisition (W3)	1.5
	84.5		84.5

9   *Cash paid to defined benefit plan*

DEFINED BENEFIT LIABILITY

	$m		$m
Interest on plan assets (per qu)	8	Balance b/d	22
Contributions paid (bal. fig.)	7	OCI losses (per qu)	6
		Current service costs (per qu)	10
Balance c/d	25	Past service costs (W)	2
	40		40

Note. The enhanced benefits are past service costs, which need to be recognised immediately in profit or loss:

| DEBIT | Profit or loss for the year | $2m | |
| CREDIT | Defined benefit liability | | $2m |

(b)   (i)   **Use of the indirect method of preparing statements of cash flow**

The **direct method** of preparing cash flow statements discloses **major classes of gross cash receipts and gross cash payments**. It shows the items that affected cash flow and the size of those cash flows. Cash received from, and cash paid to, specific sources such as customers and suppliers are presented. This contrasts with the indirect method, where accrual-basis net income (loss) is converted to cash flow information by means of add-backs and deductions.

An important **advantage** of the direct method is that the users can see and understand the actual **cash flows,** and how they relate to items of income or expense. For example, payments of expenses are shown as cash disbursements and are deducted from cash receipts. In this way, the **user is able to recognise the cash receipts and payments** for the period.

From the point of view of the **user, the direct method is preferable**, because it discloses information, not available elsewhere in the financial statements, which could be of use in estimating future cash flow.

The **indirect method** involves **adjusting the net profit or loss** for the period for:

(1)   Changes during the period in inventories, operating receivables and payables

(2)   Non-cash items, eg depreciation, provisions, profits/losses on the sales of assets

(3)   Other items, the cash flows from which should be classified under investing or financing activities

From the point of view of the **preparer of accounts, the indirect method is easier to use,** and **nearly all companies use it in practice**. The main argument companies have for using the indirect method is that the **direct method is too costly. The disadvantage** of the indirect method is that **users find it difficult to understand** and it is therefore more **open to manipulation.** This is particularly true with regard to classification of cash flows. Companies may wish to classify cash inflows as operating cash flows and cash outflows as non-operating cash flows.

The directors' proposal to report the loan proceeds as operating cash flow may be an example of such manipulation. For Jocatt, the indirect method would **not,** as is claimed, **be more useful and informative to users** than the direct method. IAS 7 allows both methods, however, so the indirect method would still be permissible.

(ii)   **Reporting the loan proceeds as operating cash flow**

The directors of Jocatt have an **incentive to enhance operating cash flow,** because they receive extra income if operating cash flow exceeds a predetermined target. Accordingly, their proposal to classify the loan proceeds as operating cash flow should come under scrutiny.

Their proposal should first of all be considered in the light of their claim that the indirect method is more useful to users than the direct method. The opposite is the case, so while both methods are allowed, the directors' **motivation for wishing to use the method that is less clear to users** should be questioned.

The IAS 7 indirect method allows some leeway in classification of cash flows. For example, dividends paid by the entity can be shown as financing cash flows (showing the cost of obtaining financial resources) or operating cash flows (so that users can assess the entity's ability to pay dividends out of operating cash flows). However, the **purpose of such flexibility is to present the position as fairly as possible**. Classifying loan proceeds as operating cash flow does not do this.

Ethical behaviour in the preparation of financial statements, and in other areas, is of **paramount importance**. Directors act unethically if they use 'creative' accounting in accounts preparation to make the figures look better, in particular if their presentation is determined not by finding the best way to apply International Financial Reporting Standards, but, as here, by **self-interest.**

To act ethically, the directors must put the interests of the company and its shareholders first, and must also have regard to other stakeholders such as the loan provider. Accordingly, the **loan proceeds should be reported as cash inflows from financing activities,** not operating activities.

52 Case study question: Warrburt

Text reference. Group statements of cash flow are covered in Chapter 17 of the text. Foreign currency transactions are covered in Chapter 16. Ethics is covered in Chapter 3.

Top tips. This question has been amended from the original. There are many straightforward, non-group aspects to this group statement of cash flows, so make sure you don't get bogged down in the detailed adjustments at the expense of these. The adjustments to the net loss before tax include some more unusual ones, such as the profit on the investment in equity instruments and the exchange loss. (Note that the realised loss of $1.1m would not normally be adjusted, but it is here, because it is not an operating item and so must be transferred to the 'purchase of property, plant and equipment' caption.) We have set up workings for impairment on goodwill and intangibles, even though the amounts are given to you in the question. It is good practice to set up standard workings in case there is something missing from the information in the question, or you have to calculate the figures from scratch.

Don't skimp on Part (b) – it has ten marks.

Easy marks. These are available for setting out the proforma and workings, and also for valid points made in Part (b) on interpretation and Part (c) on ethical matters. Do not spend too much time on the fiddly foreign exchange working at the expense of these much easier marks.

Examiner's comments. Candidates generally performed well on Part (a) of the question producing good answers, which were rewarded with good marks on this part. The main issues, which caused problems, were the new IAS 1 format of the financial statements, which many candidates were not familiar with and the treatment of the benefits paid by the trustees of the defined benefit scheme, which had no cash flow effect. The calculation of the exchange loss on the PPE was problematical for some candidates from the viewpoint of how to treat it in the statement of cash flows. Also the calculation of trade payables often failed to take into account the creditor for the purchase of plant. In Part (b), Many candidates did not use the information in the first part of the question in answering this part but gave general advantages and disadvantages of statements of cash flows. Part (c) question was quite well answered. However, candidates should develop a greater understanding of ethical principles rather than simply the ability to reiterate the ethical codes.

Marking scheme

		Marks
(a)	Net loss before tax	1
	Investment in equity instruments	4
	Retirement benefit	3
	Property, plant and equipment	6
	Insurance proceeds	2
	Associate	4
	Goodwill and intangibles	1
	Finance costs	2

Taxation		4
Working capital		4
Proceeds of share issue		1
Repayment of borrowings		1
Dividends		1
Non-controlling interest		1
		35

(b)	Operating cash flow and discussion	10
(c)	Discussion including professional marks	5
	Available	50

(a) WARRBURT GROUP
STATEMENT OF CASH FLOWS FOR THE YEAR ENDED 30 NOVEMBER 20X8

	$m	$m
Operating activities		
Net loss before tax	(47)	
Adjustments for		
Gain on revaluation of investment in equity instruments		
(Alburt - fair value on disposal less fair value at 1 December 20X7: 45 – 38)	(7)	
Retirement benefit expense	10	
Depreciation	36	
Profit on sale of property plant and equipment: $63m – $56m	(7)	
Profit on insurance claim: $3m – $1m	(2)	
Foreign exchange loss (W9) $1.1m + $0.83m	2	
Share of profit of associate	(6)	
Impairment losses: $20m + $12m	32	
Interest expense	9	
	20	
Decrease in trade receivables: $92m – $163m	71	
Decrease in inventories: $135m – $198m	63	
Decrease in trade payables: $115m – $180m – $20.83m (W9)	(86)	
Cash generated from operations	68	
Retirement benefit contributions*	(10)	
Interest paid (W8)	(8)	
Income taxes paid (W7)	(39)	
Net cash from operating activities		11
Investing activities		
Purchase of property, plant and equipment: $56m (W1) + $1.1m (W9)	(57)	
Proceeds from sale of property, plant and equipment	63	
Proceeds from sale of investments in equity instruments	45	
Acquisition of associate (W4)	(96)	
Dividend received from associate: 25% × $8m	2	
Net cash used in investing activities		(43)
Financing activities		
Proceeds from issue of share capital: $650m – $595m	55	
Repayment of long-term borrowings: $20m – $64m	(44)	
Dividends paid	(9)	
Dividends paid to non-controlling shareholders (W6)	(5)	
Net cash used in financing activities		(3)
Net decrease in cash and cash equivalents		(35)
Cash and cash equivalents at beginning of year		323
Cash and cash equivalents at end of year		288

*Note.** Only the contributions paid are reported in the cash flow, because this is the only movement of cash. The amounts paid by the trustees are not included, because they are not paid by the company.

Workings

1   *Property plant and equipment*

PROPERTY, PLANT AND EQUIPMENT

	$m		$m
Balance b/fwd	360	Disposals	56
Gain on property revaluation	4	Depreciation	36
		Asset destroyed	1
Replacement asset from insurance		Balance c/fwd	350
company (at F V)	3		
Additions (on credit)*	20		
Additions (cash)*	56		
	443		443

*Note. The additions are translated at the historic rate. Adjustment for exchange rate differences are dealt with in (W9).

	$m
Additions (cash) $\dfrac{280}{5}$ =	56
Additions (credit) $\dfrac{100}{5}$	20
Total (excluding destroyed assets replaced): $78 - (3 - 1)$	76

2   *Impairment of goodwill*

GOODWILL

	$m		$m
Balance b/fwd	100	Impairment (Bal. fig.)	20
		Balance c/fwd	80
	100		100

3   *Impairment of other intangible assets*

OTHER INTANGIBLE ASSETS

	$m		$m
Balance b/fwd	240	Impairment (bal.fig.)	12
		Balance c/fwd	228
	240		240

4   *Purchase of associate*

INVESTMENT IN ASSOCIATE

	$m		$m
Balance b/fwd	Nil		
Statement of comprehensive income		Dividend received: $8m × 25%	2
(profit or loss)	6	Balance c/fwd	100
Purchase of associate (bal.fig.)	96		
	102		102

5   *Investments in equity instruments*

INVESTMENTS IN EQUITY INSTRUMENTS

	$m		$m
Balance b/fwd	150	Disposals at fair value	45
Fair value gain on investment in Alburt	7		
Other comprehensive income (reval'n*)	30	Balance c/fwd	142
	187		187

* Note: This is the gain on revaluation, which is shown in the statement of profit or loss and other comprehensive income net of deferred tax of $3m (W7), that is at $27m. The gross gain is therefore $30m and is the amount reflected in this working.

6   *Dividends paid to non-controlling interests*

NON-CONTROLLING INTERESTS

	$m		$m
Dividends paid (bal.fig.)	5	Balance b/fwd	53
Total comprehensive income	2		
Balance c/fwd	46		
	53		53

7   *Income taxes paid*

INCOME TAX PAYABLE

	$m		$m
Income taxes paid (bal. fig.)	39	Balance b/fwd (deferred)	26
		Balance b/fwd (current)	42
		Profit/loss for year	29
		Other comprehensive income for year (IEI) (W5)	3
Balance c/fwd (deferred)	28	Other comprehensive income for year (PPE) (W1)	2
Balance c/fwd (current)	35		
	102		102

8   *Interest paid*

INTEREST PAYABLE

	$m		$m
Interest paid (bal. fig.)	8	Balance b/fwd (short-term provisions)	4
Balance c/fwd (short-term provisions)	5	SPLOCI (profit or loss for year)	9
	13		13

9   *Exchange loss*

At 30 June 20X8:

DEBIT   Property, plant and equipment (W1) $\frac{380}{5}$ $76m

CREDIT   Payables $\frac{380}{5}$ $76m

To record purchase of property, plant and equipment

At 31 October 20X8;

DEBIT   Payables $\frac{280}{5}$ $56m

DEBIT   Profit/loss (loss) $1.1m

CREDIT   Cash $\frac{280}{4.9}$ $57.1m

Being payment of 280 million dinars

At 30 November 20X8:

DEBIT   P/L (loss) $0.83

CREDIT   Payables $\left(\frac{100}{4.8}=20.83\right)-\left(\frac{100}{5}=20\right)$ $0.83m

Being loss on re-translation of payable at the year end.

Notes

1   The $20.83m was wrongly included in trade payables, so must be removed from the decrease in trade payables in the SOCF.

2   The unrealised loss on retranslation of the payable ($0.83m) must always be adjusted. The realised loss on the cash payment of $1.1 would not normally be adjusted, but it relates to a non-operating item, so is transferred to 'purchase of PPE'.

(b)   **Key issues arising from the statement of cash flows**

The statement of financial position and the statement of profit or loss and other comprehensive income, and the ratios associated with these statements, can provide useful information to users, but it is the **statement of cash flows** which gives the **key insight** into a company's liquidity. Cash is the life-blood of business, and less able to be manipulated than profit. It is particularly important to look at where the cash has come from. If the cash is from trading activity, it is a healthy sign.

Although Warrburt has made a loss before tax of $23m, net cash from operating activities is a modest but healthy $11m. Before working capital changes, the cash generated is $20m. The question arises, however, as to **whether this cash generation can continue if profitability does not improve.**

Of some concern is the fact that **a large amount of cash has been generated by the sale of investments in equity instruments.** This source of cash generation is not sustainable in the long term.

Operating cash flow **does not compare favourably with liabilities** ($115m). In the long term, operating cash flow should finance the repayment of long-term debt, but in the case of Warrburt, working capital is being used to **for investing activities,** specifically the purchase of an associate and of property, plant and equipment. It remains to be seen whether these investments generate future profits that will sustain and increase the operating cash flow.

The company's **current ratio** (515/155 = 3.3) and **acid test ratio** (380/155 = 2.45) are **sound;** it appears that cash is tied up in long-term, rather than short-term investment. An encouraging sign, however, is that the cash used to repay long-term loans has been nearly replaced by cash raised from the issue of share capital. This means that **gearing will reduce**, which is particularly important in the light of possible problems sustaining profitability and cash flows from trading activities.

(c)   **Ethical responsibility of accountant**

Directors may, particularly in times of falling profit and cash flow, wish to **present a company's results in a favourable light.** This may involve manipulation by creative accounting techniques such as window dressing, or, as is proposed here, an **inaccurate classification.**

If the proceeds of the sale of investments in equity instruments and property, plant and equipment are presented in the cash flow statement as part of 'cash generated from operations', the picture is **misleading**. Operating cash flow is crucial, in the long term, for the survival of the company, because it derives from trading activities, which is what the company is there to do. **Sales of assets generate short term cash flow,** and cannot be repeated year-on-year, unless there are to be no assets left to generate trading profits with.

As **a professional, the accountant has a duty,** not only to the company he works for, but to his professional body, stakeholders in the company, and to **the principles of independence and fair presentation of financial statements.** It is essential that the accountant **tries to persuade the directors not to proceed with the adjustments**, which he or she must know violates IFRS 1, and may well go against the requirements of local legislation. If, despite his protests, the directors insist on the misleading presentation, then the accountant has a duty to **bring this to the attention of the auditors.**

53 Rockby and Bye

Text reference. Discontinued operations are covered in Chapter 15.

Top tips. This question required candidates to have knowledge of IFRS 5 and discontinued operations. The question has been amended to reflect the publication of a full IFRS, rather than the original exposure draft. In part (b), you had to discuss whether certain assets would be considered to be 'held for sale'.

Easy marks. The obvious easy marks are for Part (a), which is straight out of your Study Text. But as the examiner said, 'Often in questions of this nature, candidates assume certain facts about the scenario. If the assumptions are reasonable, due regard is taken and credit given.'

Examiner's comment. This question was well answered, though candidates did not use the facts of the question in formulating their answer as much as they should have done.

			Marks
(a)	Discussion – IFRS 5		3
	Impairment – IAS 36		5
(b)	(i)	Operating lease	4
		Plant	3
	(ii)	Property	6
		Available	21
		Maximum	19

(a) Sale of the subsidiary

IFRS 5 *Non-current assets held for sale and discontinued operations* requires an asset or disposal group to be classified as held for sale where it is **available for immediate sale** in its **present condition** subject only to **terms that are usual** and customary and the sale is **highly probable**. For a sale to be highly probable:

- Management must be **committed** to the sale.
- An **active programme to locate a buyer** must have been initiated.
- The **market price** must be **reasonable** in relation to the asset's current fair value.
- The sale must be **expected to be completed within one year** from the date of classification.

The proposed sale of Bye **appears to meet these conditions**. Although the sale had not taken place by the time that the 20X4 financial statements were approved, **negotiations were in progress** and the sale is expected to take place on 1 July 20X4, well **within a year** after the decision to sell. Rockby had **committed** itself to the sale **before its year-end of 31 March 20X4.**

Where a subsidiary is held for sale it **continues to be included** in the consolidated financial statements, but it is **presented separately** from other assets and liabilities in the statement of financial position and its assets and liabilities should not be offset. If Bye represents a **separate major line of business or geographical area** of operations it will also qualify as a **discontinued operation**, which means that on the **face of the statement of profit or loss** the group must disclose a single amount comprising the **total of its post-tax loss for the year** and **any post-tax gain or loss recognised on its remeasurement. Further analysis is required in the notes** and the notes must also disclose a description of the facts and circumstances leading to the expected disposal and the expected manner and timing of the disposal.

Bye must be **reviewed for** impairment immediately before its classification as 'held for sale'. The calculation is as follows:

	$'000
Net assets at 31 March 20X4	5,000
Goodwill	1,000
	6,000
Value in use at 15 May 20X4	3,900
Add losses incurred from 1 April 20X4 to 15 May 20X4	500
Value in use at 31 March 20X4	4,400
Fair value less costs to sell	4,500

Recoverable amount is the **higher of fair value less costs to sell** and **value in use**. In this case, recoverable amount **is fair value less costs to sell** and so there is an **impairment loss of $1.5 million.** IFRS 5 requires items held for sale to be measured at the **lower of carrying amount and fair value less costs to sell** and therefore Bye will be carried **at $4.5 million** in the statement of financial position and the loss of $1.5 million will be recognised in profit or loss.

(b)   **Items of plant**

If the items of plant are to be classified as 'held for sale', management must be **committed** to the sale and the sale must be **highly probable** and **expected to take place within one year**. The operating leases **do not appear to qualify** as the company is **undecided** as to whether to sell or lease the plant under finance leases. Therefore the company should **continue to treat them as non-current assets** and to depreciate them. The value in use of the items is greater than their carrying value and so they are **not impaired**.

The other items of plant will also **not be classified as 'held for sale'**. Although they were no longer in use at 31 March 20X4 and were sold subsequently, a **firm decision** to sell them **had not been made by the year-end**. IFRS 5 **prohibits retrospective use** of the 'held for sale' classification if, as in this case, assets are sold after the year end but before the financial statements are authorised for issue, although the sale should be **disclosed as an event after the reporting period**. IFRS 5 also requires **disclosure** of the **facts and circumstances** of the sale and a **description** of the items, together with the segment in which they are presented under IFRS 8 *Operating segments* (if applicable).

Head office land and buildings

In order to qualify as 'held for sale' an asset must be **available for immediate sale** in its **present condition**, subject to the usual terms. Although the company had taken the decision to sell the property at 31 March 20X3, the **subsidence** would have meant that a buyer was **unlikely to be found** for the property until the renovations had taken place. Therefore the property **did not qualify as 'held for sale' at 31 March 20X3**.

At 31 March 20X4 the property **had been on the market for nine months** at the price of $10 million. **No buyer** had yet been found. Despite the fact that the **market had deteriorated significantly** the company had **not reduced the price**. The property was eventually sold for $7.5 million on 1 June 20X4. To qualify as being held for sale at the year-end the **market price must be reasonable** in relation to the asset's current fair value. It appears that the market price of $10 million is **not reasonable when compared with the eventual selling price** of $7.5 million, the **offer** of $8.3 million received on 20 April or the **carrying value** of $7 million. Therefore the property **should not be classified as 'held for sale' at 31 March 20X4**.

54 Alexandra

Text reference. IAS 1 and IAS 8 are covered in Chapter 18 of your Study Text. Related parties are covered in Chapter 10. Pension plans are covered in Chapter 5.

Top tips. Part (a) was on reclassification of long-term debt as current. Part (b) had a correction of an error (IAS 8) arising from an incorrect application of IAS 18 *Revenue*. Thus you have the interaction of two standards, so don't just concentrate on one. Part (c) was on related party disclosures for key management personnel, which needed to be broken down by category, and part (d) required candidates to explain why a pension plan needed to be accounted for as a defined benefit plan. As this is a multi-topic standard question, you can always have a respectable go at the parts where your knowledge is strongest. As the examiner often says, all information in the question is included for a purpose, so there are plenty of pointers in Part (d).

Easy marks. Part (c) has some easy marks for reproducing definitions from IAS 24. Unusually, the employee benefits question (Part (d)) could be a source of easy marks, as it contains a number of hints, and gives you an opportunity to reproduce knowledge about the differences between the two types of plan without any complicated calculations.

Examiner's comment. In Part (a), only a few candidates mentioned that according to IAS 1 *Presentation of financial statements*, a liability should be classified as current if it is due to be settled within 12 months after the date of the statement of financial position. In Part (b), most candidates had a good understanding of the nature of IAS 18 *Revenue,* but few treated the change in accounting treatment as a correction of an error in accordance with IAS 8 *Accounting policies, changes in accounting estimates and errors.* The previous policy applied was not in accordance with IAS 18, which requires revenue arising from transactions involving the rendering of services to be recognised with reference to the stage of completion at the date of the statement of financial position. Most scored well on Part (c), realising that that the exclusion of the remuneration of the non-executive directors from key management personnel disclosures did not comply with the requirements of IAS 24 *Related party disclosures*. Part (d) was well answered, with most candidates coming to the right conclusion.

		Marks
(a)	1mark per question up to maximum	6
(b)	1mark per question up to maximum	5
(c)	1mark per question up to maximum	5
(d)	1mark per question up to maximum	7
Professional marks		2
Maximum		25

(a) **Default on loan**

Under IAS 1 *Presentation of financial statements,* a **long-term financial liability** due to be **settled within twelve months** of the year end date should be classified as a **current liability.** Furthermore, a **long-term financial liability** that is payable on **demand** because the entity **breached** a **condition** of its loan agreement should be classified as **current** at the year end even if the **lender** has agreed **after the year end**, and **before** the financial statements are **authorised for issue**, **not** to **demand payment** as a consequence of the breach.

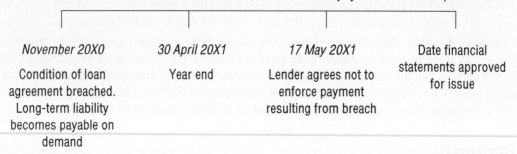

November 20X0	30 April 20X1	17 May 20X1	Date financial statements approved for issue
Condition of loan agreement breached. Long-term liability becomes payable on demand	Year end	Lender agrees not to enforce payment resulting from breach	

However, if the **lender** has **agreed** by the **year end** to provide a **period of grace** ending **at least twelve months after the year end** within which the entity can rectify the breach and during that time the lender cannot demand immediate repayment, the liability is classified as **non-current.**

In the case of Alexandra, the waiver was given before the year end, but only for the loan to be repaid a month after the year end, then a further waiver was agreed, but again only for a few weeks. It would **not therefore be appropriate for Alexandra to classify the bond as long-term debt** in the statement of financial position as at 30 April 20X1.

The fact that Alexandra has defaulted and sought two loan waivers may cast doubt on its ability to continue as a going concern, especially as the loan waivers may not be renewed. If there is uncertainty regarding Alexandra's going concern status, IAS 1 requires Alexandra to disclose these uncertainties. If Alexandra ceases to be a going concern, then the financial statements would need to be prepared on a break-up basis.

(b) **Maintenance contracts**

There are two aspects to consider:

(i) What is the correct way to recognise the revenue from the maintenance contracts?

(ii) What adjustments does Alexandra need to make, having changed its method of recognition?

Correct IAS 18 treatment

Under IAS 18 *Revenue,* when the outcome of a transaction involving the rendering of services can be estimated reliably, the associated revenue should be recognised by reference to the **stage of completion of the transaction** at the year end.

In uncertain situations, when the outcome of the transaction involving the rendering of services cannot be estimated reliably, the standard recommends a **no loss/no gain approach**. Revenue is recognised only to the extent of the expenses recognised that are recoverable.

For practical purposes, when services are performed by an indeterminate number of acts over a period of time, revenue should be recognised on a **straight line basis** over the period, unless there is evidence for the use of a more appropriate method.

Accordingly, **the new treatment**, and the one used to date by Xavier Co, is the **correct** accounting treatment under IAS 18 and the **previous treatment,** of recognising the revenue on invoicing at the beginning of the contract, was **incorrect.**

Adjustments under IAS 8

The accounting treatment previously used by Alexandra was incorrect because it did not comply with IAS 18. Consequently, the change to the new, correct policy is **the correction of an error rather than a change of accounting policy.**

IAS 8 *Accounting policies, changes in accounting estimates and errors* states that changes in accounting estimates result from changes in circumstances, new information or more experience, which is not the case here. This is a prior period error, which **must be corrected retrospectively**. This involves **restating the opening balances** for that period so that the financial statements are presented as if the error had never occurred.

In the opening balance of retained earnings, the maintenance contract income that was recognised in full in the year ended 30 April 20X0 must be split between the revenue due for that year (on an IAS 18 basis as described above) and that which should be deferred to subsequence periods. There will be less revenue recognised in the prior year, resulting in a **net debit to opening retained earnings.**

In the year ended 30 April 20X1, the correct accounting policy has been applied. Since the maintenance contracts typically run for two years, it is likely that most of the **income deferred from the prior year relating to this period will also be recognised** in the current period. The effect of this for the year ended 30 April 20X1 is that the reduction in profits of $6m will be mitigated by the recognition of income deferred from last year.

(c) **Directors' remuneration**

The disclosures that Alexandra has provided are insufficient to comply with IAS 24 *Related party disclosures* on two counts:

(i)   No breakdown of directors' remuneration

(ii)   Exclusion of remuneration of non-executive directors

Breakdown of directors' remuneration

IAS 24 *Related party disclosures* requires that entities should **disclose** key management personnel compensation **not only in total** but also **for each of the** following **categories:**

- Short-term employee benefits
- Post-employment benefits
- Other long-term benefits
- Termination benefits
- Share-based payment

The remuneration for the directors of Alexandra fits into the categories of 'short-term benefits' (ie salary and bonus) and 'share-based payment' (ie share options), and should be disclosed accordingly. Only totals for each category need to be disclosed, not the earnings of individual board members, so no cultural protocol will be breached by these disclosures. However, Alexandra is a public limited company, and so local legislation and corporate governance rules may require more detailed disclosure.

Non-executive directors

By excluding the non-executive directors from the remuneration disclosures, **Alexander is in breach of IAS 24.**

IAS 24 defines **key management personnel** as those persons having authority and responsibility for planning, directing and controlling the activities of the entity, directly or indirectly, including any director (**whether executive or otherwise**) of that entity.

Thus, the remuneration of the non-executive directors, who are key management personnel, should have been disclosed along with that of the executive directors.

(d)   **Pension plan**

Alexander wishes to account for its pension plan as a defined contribution scheme, probably because the accounting is more straightforward and the risk not reflected in the figures in the financial statements. These figures were material in the case of Alexandra. However, although the entity's plan has some features in common with a defined contribution plan, it needs to be considered whether this is really the case.

With **defined contribution** plans, the employer (and possibly, as here, current employees too) pay regular contributions into the plan of a given or 'defined' amount each year. The contributions are invested, and the size of the post-employment benefits paid to former employees depends on how well or how badly the plan's investments perform. If the investments perform well, the plan will be able to afford higher benefits than if the investments performed less well.

With **defined benefit** plans, the size of the post-employment benefits is determined in advance, ie the benefits are 'defined'. The employer (and possibly, as here, current employees too) pay contributions into the plan, and the contributions are invested. The size of the contributions is set at an amount that is expected to earn enough investment returns to meet the obligation to pay the post-employment benefits. If, however, it becomes apparent that the assets in the fund are insufficient, the employer will be required to make additional contributions into the plan to make up the expected shortfall. On the other hand, if the fund's assets appear to be larger than they need to be, and in excess of what is required to pay the post-employment benefits, the employer may be allowed to take a 'contribution holiday' (ie stop paying in contributions for a while).

The **main difference** between the two types of plans lies in **who bears the risk**: if the employer bears the risk, even in a small way by guaranteeing or specifying the return, the plan is a defined benefit plan. A defined contribution scheme must give a benefit formula based solely on the amount of the contributions.

Alexandra's is, in reality, a defined benefit plan. Alexandra, the employer, guarantees a pension based on the average pay of the employees in the scheme. The entity's liability is not limited to the amount of the contributions to the plan, but is supplemented by an insurance premium which the insurance company can increase if required in order to fulfil the plan obligations. The trust fund which the insurance company is building up, is in turn dependent on the yield on investments. If the insurer has insufficient funds to pay the guaranteed pension, Alexandra has to make good the deficit. Indirectly, through insurance premiums, the employer bears the investment risk. The employee's contribution, on the other hand is fixed.

A further indication that Alexander bears the risk is the provision that if an employee leaves Alexandra and transfers the pension to another fund, Alexandra is liable for, or is refunded the difference between the benefits the employee is entitled to and the insurance premiums paid. Alexandra thus **has a legal or constructive obligation** to make good the shortfall if the insurance company does not pay all future employee benefits relating to employee service in the current and prior periods.

In conclusion, even though the insurance company limits some of the risk, Alexandra, rather than its employees, bears the risk, so this is a **defined benefit plan.**

55 Carpart

Marking scheme

		Marks
Vehiclex	IAS 18	2
	IAS 11	1
	IAS 16	1
Sale of vehicles	IAS 18	3
	Repurchase four years	2
	Repurchase two years	3
	Demonstration	2
Professional marks		2
	Available	16

(a) **Vehiclex**

Generally, IAS 18 *Revenue* looks at each transaction **as a whole**. Sometimes, however, transactions are more complicated, and it is necessary to break a transaction down into its **component parts**. For example, a sale may include the transfer of goods and the provision of future servicing, the revenue for which should be deferred over the period the service is performed. The revenue for **each component part needs to be assessed separately** in applying the recognition criteria, and the transaction should be viewed from the customer's perspective, not that of the seller.

In this case, the construction of machinery needs to be considered separately from the sale of the car seats.

Machinery

No revenue should be recognised in respect of the machinery because:

(i)   There is no contract to sell the machinery to Vehiclex.
(ii)   The machinery is for the use of Carpart only, and will not be sold elsewhere.
(iii)   The contract with Vehiclex is not a construction contract under IAS 11 *Construction contracts.*

Accordingly, the machinery **must be accounted for under IAS 16** *Property, plant and equipment.* Assuming that the future economic benefits of the asset will flow to Carpart, and that the cost can be measured reliably, it should be recorded at cost and depreciated. The machinery should be **reviewed for impairment** so that it is not carried above its recoverable amount. For the purposes of an impairment review, the machinery would probably need to be treated as part of a cash generating unit. One indicator of impairment would be if seat orders are not at the minimum required to cover costs.

Sale of car seats

The contract to manufacture and sell seats is a **contract for the sale of goods**, not a service contract or a construction contract. Therefore, following IAS 18, revenue should be **recognised on sale**.

(b)   **Vehicle sales**

This is a **sale and repurchase** agreement. According to IAS 18, such agreements must be analysed to determine whether the seller has transferred the **significant risks and rewards** of ownership to the buyer. The transfer of risks and rewards can only be decided by examining each transaction. If the risks and rewards of ownership have been transferred, then revenue can be recognised.

If **significant risks and rewards remain with the seller**, then the transaction is *not* a sale and revenue cannot be recognised, even if legal title has been transferred. In such cases, the substance of the transaction is a **financing arrangement.**

In the case of the **vehicles sold without the option**, there is evidence that the **significant risks and rewards have been transferred.** Carpart's obligation to repurchase the vehicles at 20% of the original selling price is not retention of significant risks because this is considerably below the market price. In addition, this repurchase takes place four years into the vehicles economic life of five years, and the purchaser must maintain and service the vehicle and return it in good condition. Since the significant risks and rewards have been transferred, **Carpart should recognise revenue on the sale** of the vehicle.

The **vehicles sold with an option to repurchase** should be treated differently, as there is evidence that **Carpart has not transferred the risks and rewards of ownership**. The repurchase period is less than substantially all of the vehicles' economic life (only two years into the five year life), and the repurchase price is considerable, and also, at 70% of the original purchase price greater than the fair value, which is 55% of the original price. Importantly, the option is expected to be exercised, and so the transaction should be accounted for as if it will be.

Until the option expires, the vehicles must be accounted for as **operating leases**. They should be removed from inventories and debited to 'assets under operating leases'. They should be depreciated over the two year period of the option, with the depreciable amount being adjusted for the residual value. The cash received should not be recognised in the year as it would be for a proper sale, but should instead be split between rentals received in advance (30%) and long-term liabilities (70%). The **rental income will be recognised** in profit or loss over the two years.

Demonstration vehicles

These are not conventional inventory, but have the characteristics of **property, plant and equipment**, because they are held for use in the business (demonstrations) and are expected to be used in more than one accounting period. They should therefore be taken out of inventories, capitalised as property, plant and equipment and **depreciated** over the two year period during which they are being used as demonstration vehicles.

At the end of the two year period, the vehicles will be sold. They should therefore be **reclassified back** into **inventories** and no longer depreciated.

56 Ghorse

Text reference. Group re-organisations are covered in Chapter 14; deferred tax in Chapter 6; impairment in Chapter 4 and leases in Chapter 10.

Top tips. This is a 'mixed bag' question, dealing with a group re-organisation, deferred tax and revaluation, impairment and re-classification of a lease. These are all linked in with a calculation of the effect on return on capital employed. In Part (a) there is no need to spend time giving the IFRS 5 criteria for classification as held for sale, since we are told in the question that these criteria have been met.

Easy marks. None of this question is easy except for the calculation of ROCE; however, because it split equally across four topics, it is a good question to do. Do the parts you feel sure about, but have a go at all parts as the first few marks are the easiest to pick up.

Marking scheme

		Marks
(a)	Discontinuance	7
(b)	Deferred tax asset	6
(c)	Impairment	5
(d)	Lease	5
	Formation of opinion of impact on ROCE	2
	Maximum	25

(a)   The criteria in IFRS 5 *Non-current assets held for sale and discontinued operations* have been met for Cee and Gee. As the assets are to be disposed of in a single transaction, Cee and Gee together are deemed to be a **disposal group** under IFRS 5.

The disposal group as a whole is **measured on the basis required for non-current assets held for sale**. Any impairment loss reduces the carrying amount of the non-current assets in the disposal group, the loss being allocated in the order required by IAS 36 *Impairment of assets.* Before the manufacturing units are classified as held for sale, impairment is tested for on an individual cash generating unit basis. Once classified as held for sale, the impairment testing is done on a **disposal group basis.**

A disposal group that is held for sale should be measured at the **lower of** its **carrying amount** and **fair value less costs to sell.** Immediately before classification of a disposal group as held for sale, the entity must recognise impairment in accordance with applicable IFRS. Any impairment loss is generally recognised in profit or loss, but if the asset has been measured at a revalued amount under IAS 16 *Property, plant and equipment* or IAS 38 *Intangible assets,* the impairment will be treated as a revaluation decrease. **Once** the disposal group has been **classified as held for sale**, any **impairment loss** will be based on the **difference between the adjusted carrying amounts and the fair value less cost to sell.** The impairment loss (if any) will be **recognised in profit or loss**.

A **subsequent increase** in fair value less costs to sell may be **recognised** in profit or loss **only to the extent of any impairment previously recognised**. To summarise:

Step 1   Calculate carrying value under the individual standard, here given as $105m

Step 2   Classified as held for sale. Compare the carrying amount ($105m) with fair value less costs to sell ($125m). Measure at the lower of carrying value and fair value less costs to sell, here $105m.

Step 3 Determine fair value less costs to sell at the year end (see below) and compare with carrying value of $105m.

Ghorse has not taken account of the increase in fair value less cost to sell, but only part of this increase can be recognised, calculated as follows.

	$m
Fair value less costs to sell: Cee	40
Fair value less costs to sell: Gee	95
	135
Carrying value	(105)
Increase	30

Impairment previously recognised in Cee: $15m ($50m - $35m)

Step 4 The change in fair value less cost to sell is recognised but the gain recognised cannot exceed any impairment losses to date. Here the gain recognised is $50m – $35m = $15m

Therefore **carrying value can increase** by $15m to $120m as loss reversals are limited to impairment losses previously recognised (under IFRS 5 or IAS 36).

These adjustments **will affect ROCE**.

(b) IAS 12 *Income taxes* requires that deferred tax liabilities must be recognised for all taxable temporary differences. Deferred tax assets should be recognised for deductible temporary differences but only to the extent that taxable profits will be available against which the deductible temporary differences may be utilised.

The differences between the carrying amounts and the tax base represent temporary differences. These **temporary differences are revised** in the light of the revaluation for tax purposes to market value permitted by the government.

Deferred tax liability before revaluation

	Carrying amount $m	Tax base $m	Temporary difference $m
Property	50	48	2
Vehicles	30	28	2
			4
Other temporary differences			5
			9

Provision: 30% × $9m = $2.7m

Deferred tax asset after revaluation

	Carrying amount $m	Tax base $m	Temporary difference $m
Property	50	65	15
Vehicles	30	35	5
Other temporary differences			(5)
			15

Deferred tax asset: $15m × 30% = $4.5m

This will have a **considerable impact on ROCE.** While the release of the provision of $2.7m and the creation of the asset of $4.5m will not affect the numerator, profit before interest and tax (although it will affect profit or loss for the year), it will **significantly affect the capital employed figure**.

(c) IAS 36 *Impairment of assets* requires that no asset should be carried at more than its recoverable amount. At each reporting date, Ghorse must **review all assets for indications of impairment,** that is indications that the carrying value may be higher than the recoverable amount. Such indications include fall in the market value of an asset or adverse changes in the technological, economic or legal environment of the business.

(IAS 36 has an extensive list of criteria.) If **impairment is indicated**, then the asset's **recoverable amount** must be calculated. The manufacturer has reduced the selling price, but this does not automatically mean that the asset is impaired.

The **recoverable amount** is defined as the **higher of the asset's fair value less disposal of disposal and its value in use.** If the recoverable amount is less than the carrying amount, then the resulting impairment loss should be charged to profit or loss as an expense.

Value in use is the discounted present value of estimated future cash flows expected to arise from the continuing use of an asset and from its disposal at the end of its useful life. The value in use of the equipment is calculated as follows:

Year ended 31 October	Cash flows	Discounted (10%)
	$m	$m
20X8	1.3	1.2
20X9	2.2	1.8
20Y0	2.3	1.7
Value in use		4.7

The fair value less disposal costs of the asset is estimated at $2m. The recoverable amount must be the value in use of $4.7m, as this is higher. **Since the recoverable amount is higher than the carrying value of $3m, the asset is not impaired.** Consequently there will be no effect on ROCE.

(d) The manufacturing property was held under an operating lease. IAS 17 *Leases* requires that operating lease payments are charged to profit or loss over the term of the lease, generally on straight line basis.

The renegotiation of the lease means that its **terms have changed significantly**, and it now falls to be **classified as a finance lease**. Reasons for reclassification are as follows.

(i) The lease is for the major part of the economic life of the assets.

(ii) At the inception of the lease, the present value of the minimum lease payments is $5m × 6.8137 = $34.1m. The fair value of the asset is $35m. Thus the present value of the minimum lease payments is substantially all the fair value of the asset.

(iii) A finance lease does not require transfer of legal title.

Since the lease is now a finance lease, it will be shown in the statement of financial position at the **lower of fair value ($35m) and present value of the minimum lease payments ($34.1m)**, ie at $34.1m. However, since both assets and liabilities would increase, this reclassification would **not affect ROCE.**

Recalculation of ROCE

	$m
Profit before interest and tax	30.0
Add increase in value of disposal group	15.0
	45.0
Capital employed	220.0
Add increase in value of disposal group	15.0
Add release of deferred tax provision and	
deferred tax asset: 4.5 + 2.7	7.2
	242.2

∴ROCE is 45/242.2 = 13.6%

The directors were concerned that the above changes would adversely affect ROCE. In fact, the effect has been favourable, as **ROCE has risen from 13.6% to 18.6%,** so the **directors' fears were misplaced.**

57 Cate

Marking scheme

	Marks
Deferred tax	5
Investment in associate	5
IFRS 5 Discussion and conclusion	8
IAS 19 Discussion and conclusion	5
Professional marks	2
	25

(a) **Deferred tax**

In principle, IAS 12 *Income taxes* allows recognition of **deferred tax assets**, if material, for deductible temporary differences, unused tax losses and unused tax credits. However, IAS 12 states that **deferred tax assets should only be recognised to the extent that they are regarded as recoverable**. They should be regarded as recoverable to the extent that on the basis of all the evidence available it is **probable that there will be suitable taxable profits against which the losses can be recovered**. There is evidence that this is not the case for Cate:

(i)   While Cate has made a small profit before tax in the year to 31 May 20X6, this includes **significant non-operating gains**. In other words the profit is not due to ordinarly business activities.

(ii)   In contrast, **Cate's losses were due to ordinary business activities**, not from identifiable causes unlikely to recur (IAS 12).

(iii)   The fact that there are **unused tax losses** is strong evidence, according to IAS 12, that future taxable profits may not be available against which to offset the losses.

(iv)   When considering the likelihood of future taxable profits, Cate's forecast cannot be considered as sufficient evidence. These are **estimates which cannot be objectively verified**, and are based on possible customer interest rather than confirmed contracts or orders.

(v)   Cate **does not** have available any **tax planning opportunities** which might give rise to taxable profits.

In conclusion, **Cate should not recognise deferred tax assets on losses carried forward**, as there is insufficient evidence that future taxable profits can be generated against which to offset the losses.

(b)   **Investment in Bates**

Cate's approach to the valuation of the investment in Bates is open to question, and shows that Cate may **wish to avoid showing an impairment loss**.

There is an established principle that **an asset should not be carried at more than its recoverable amount**. If the carrying value is not recoverable in full, the asset must be written down to the recoverable amount. It is said to be impaired. The recoverable amount is the highest value to the business in terms of the cash flows that the asset can generate, and is the higher of:

(i)   The asset's fair value less costs of disposal, and

(ii)   The asset's value in use

Cate appears to be **raising difficulties** about both of these measures in respect of Bates.

(i)   **Fair value less costs of disposal**

An asset's fair value less costs of disposal is the amount net of incremental costs directly attributable to the disposal of an asset (excluding finance costs and income tax expense).. Costs of disposal include transaction costs such as legal expenses.

Cate argues that there is no binding sale agreement and that the quoted share price is not an appropriate measure of the fair value or its significant influence over Bates. IFRS 13 *Fair value measurement* defines fair value as 'the price that would be received to sell an asset.....in an orderly transaction between market participants'. Just because there is no binding sale agreement does not mean that Cate cannot measure fair value. IFRS 13 has a 3 level hierarchy in measuring fair value:

- Level 1 inputs = quoted prices (unadjusted) in active markets for identical assets

- Level 2 inputs = inputs other than quoted prices included within Level 1 that are observable for the asset or liability, either directly or indirectly (e.g. quoted prices for similar assets)

- Level 3 inputs = unobservable inputs for the asset

The measurement techniques proposed by Cate (earnings multiple and option-pricing model) are both Level 3 inputs. Therefore, if better Level 1 or 2 inputs are available, they should be used instead. A Level 1 input is available ie the quoted share price of Bates. Paragraph 69 of IFRS 13 requires a premium or discount to be considered when measuring fair value when it is a characteristic of the asset that market participants would take into account in a transaction. Therefore, the premium attributable to significant influence should be taken into account and this adjusted share price used as fair value (rather than the earnings multiple or option pricing model).,

Costs of disposal will be fairly easy to estimate. Accordingly, **it should be possible to arrive at a figure for fair value less costs of disposal.**

(ii)   **Value in use**

IAS 36 states that the value in use of an asset is measured as the present value of estimated future cash flows (inflows minus outflows) generated by the asset, including its estimated net disposal value (if any). IAS 28 *Investments in associates* gives some more specific guidance on investments where there is significant influence. In determining the value in use of these investments an entity should estimate:

(1)   Its share of the present value of the estimated future cash flows expected to be generated by the associate (including disposal proceeds)

(2)   The present value of future cash flows expected to arise from dividends to be received from the investment.

Cate has not produced any cash flow estimates, but it could, and should do so.

Conclusion

Cate is able to produce figures for fair value less cost to sell and for value in use, and it should do so. If the carrying amount exceeds the higher of these two, then the **asset is impaired** and must be written down to its recoverable amount.

(c) **IFRS 5 and investment in Date**

IFRS 10 *Consolidated financial statements* views a **group as an economic entity**. This means that it treats all providers of equity as shareholders in the group, even if they are not shareholders of the parent company. To be consistent with this, IFRS 5 *Non-current assets held for sale and discontinued operations* was amended: if a parent intends to dispose of a controlling interest in a subsidiary which meets the definition of 'held for sale', then the net assets are classified as 'held for sale', even if the parent retains an interest. Where there is a partial disposal, from subsidiary (control) to an associate (significant influence) or an investment in equity instruments (no significant influence), a gain arises on the both the part disposed of and the interest retained.

IFRS 5 *Non-current assets held for sale and discontinued operations* requires an asset or disposal group to be classified as held for sale where it is **available for immediate sale** in its **present condition** subject only to **terms that are usual** and customary and the sale is **highly probable**. For a sale to be highly probable:

- Management must be **committed** to the sale.
- An **active programme to locate a buyer** must have been initiated.
- The **market price** must be **reasonable** in relation to the asset's current fair value.
- The sale must be **expected to be completed within one year** from the date of classification.

While Date does not meet all the IFRS 5 criteria, it could still be argued that **Cate's presentation is correct** because:

(i) The issue of new shares to a new investor has **reduced Cate's holding** from 75% to 35%.

(ii) Cate **has agreed to this reduction** and decided not to subscribe to the issue of new shares, and to step down from the management of Date. This represents a change of strategy with regard to its investment.

(iii) The effect of (i) and (ii) is **equivalent to the sale of a controlling interest** and the retention of an investment that does not give control.

(iv) Date represents **a separate line of business** and information disclosed in accordance with IFRS 5 highlights the impact of Date on Cate's financial statements.

(v) IFRS 5 does not address the issue of dilution of control (a 'deemed disposal'). In the absence of direct guidance, IAS 8 *Accounting policies, changes in accounting estimates and errors* requires management **to use judgement** and apply other IFRSs and the *Conceptual Framework*.

In conclusion, while there is no specific guidance for this situation, the **principles of relevant standards are consistent with Cate's presentation.** The events should be treated as a partial disposal. Cate should **stop consolidating Date on a line-by-line basis f**rom the date that control was lost. The remaining holding should be treated as an **investment in equity instruments** (trade investment) rather than an associate, because although Cate has a holding of 35%, it no longer has significant influence over Date.

(d) **'Voluntary' post-retirement benefit plan**

Cate emphasises that the fund to provide post-retirement benefits is voluntary, and perhaps wishes to avoid accounting for the liability. However, there is evidence that in fact the **scheme should be accounted for as a defined benefit plan**:

(i) While the plan is voluntary, IAS 19 *Employee benefits* says that an entity must account for **constructive as well as legal obligations**. These may arise from informal practices, where an entity has no realistic alternative but to pay employee benefits, because employees have a valid expectation that they will be paid.

(ii) The plan is **not a defined contribution plan**, because if the fund does not have sufficient assets to pay employee benefits relating to service in the current or prior periods, Cate has a legal or constructive obligation to make good the deficit by paying further contributions.

(iii) The post-retirement benefit is based on final salaries and years of service. In other words it is **not linked solely to the amount that Cate agrees to contribute** to the fund. This is what 'defined benefit' means.

(iv) Should Cate decide to terminate its contributions to the plan, it **is contractually obliged to discharge the liability** created by the plan by purchasing lifetime annuities from an insurance company.

Cate must account for the scheme as a defined benefit plan and recognise, as a minimum, its net present obligation for the benefits to be paid.

58 Preparation question: Current issues

(a) (i) IFRS 10 states that an investor **controls** an investee if and only if it has all of the following.

Power over the investee

(1) Exposure, or rights, to **variable returns** from its involvement with the investee, and

(2) The **ability to use its power** over the investee to affect the amount of the investor's returns.

Power is defined as **existing rights that give the current ability to direct the relevant activities of the investee**. There is no requirement for that power to have been exercised.

Relevant activities may include:

- Selling and purchasing goods or services
- Managing financial assets
- Selecting, acquiring and disposing of assets
- Researching and developing new products and processes
- Determining a funding structure or obtaining funding.

In some cases assessing power is straightforward, for example, where power is obtained directly and solely from having the majority of voting rights or potential voting rights, and as a result the ability to direct relevant activities.

(ii) The absolute size of Twist's holding and the relative size of the other shareholdings alone are not conclusive in determining whether the investor has rights sufficient to give it power. However, the fact that Twist has **a contractual right to appoint, remove and set the remuneration of management** is sufficient to conclude that it **has power over Oliver.** The fact that Twist has not exercised this right is not a determining factor when assessing whether Twist has power. In conclusion, Twist does control Oliver, and should consolidate it.

(iii) In this case, the size of Copperfield's voting interest and its size relative to the other shareholdings are sufficient to conclude that Copperfield **does not have power**. Only two other investors, Murdstone and Steerforth would need to co-operate to be able to prevent Copperfield from directing the relevant activities of the Spenlow

(b) The requirement to consolidate an investment is determined by **control**, not merely by ownership. In most cases, this will involve the parent company owning a majority of the ordinary shares in the subsidiary (to which normal voting rights are attached). There are circumstances, however, when the parent may own only a minority of the voting power in the subsidiary, *but* the parent still has control.

IFRS 10 *Consolidated financial statements,* issued in 2011, retains **control** from its predecessor IAS 27 as the key concept underlying the parent/subsidiary relationship but it has broadened the definition and clarified its application.

IFRS 10 states that an investor **controls** an investee if and only if it has all of the following.

(i) **Power** over the investee

(ii) Exposure, or rights, to **variable returns** from its involvement with the investee, and

(iii) The **ability to use its power** over the investee to affect the amount of the investor's returns.

Power is defined as **existing rights that give the current ability to direct the relevant activities of the investee.** There is no requirement for that power to have been exercised.

Relevant activities may include:

- Selling and purchasing goods or services
- Managing financial assets
- Selecting, acquiring and disposing of assets
- Researching and developing new products and processes
- Determining a funding structure or obtaining funding.

In some cases assessing power is straightforward, for example, where power is obtained directly and solely from having the majority of voting rights or potential voting rights, and as a result the ability to direct relevant activities.

In other cases, assessment is more complex and more than one factor must be considered. IFRS 10 gives the following examples of **rights**, other than voting or potential voting rights, which individually, or alone, can give an investor power.

(i) Rights to appoint, reassign or remove key management personnel who can direct the relevant activities

(ii) Rights to appoint or remove another entity that directs the relevant activities

(iii) Rights to direct the investee to enter into, or veto changes to transactions for the benefit of the investor

(iv) Other rights, such as those specified in a management contract.

Applying the above criteria to Red's relationship with Blue:

Red has power to govern the financial and operating policies of Blue, through its **operating guidelines.** It also has the power to prohibit the investment manager from profiting personally from the investments. Red is exposed to and has rights to variable returns from its investment in Blue, as it receives 95% of the profits and 100% of the losses of Blue.

Red therefore **controls** Blue, and **Blue should be consolidated.**

(c) In order to meet the objective of IFRS 12 *Disclosure of interests in other entities*, entities are required to make the following disclosures.

(i) **Significant judgements and assumptions** made in determining control, joint control or significant influence and type of joint arrangement

(ii) Information on interests in subsidiaries such that the **composition of the group and non-controlling interest** is understood and restrictions, **risks and changes in ownership** can be evaluated

(iii) Information on interests in associates and joint arrangements such that the nature and extent of the interests, financial effects and associated risks can be evaluated.

(iv) Information on interests in **unconsolidated structured entities** such that the nature and extent of the interests and associated risks can be evaluated

(d)   (i)   **Problems with existing (IAS 39) hedging rules**

(1)   **The IAS 39 provisions are not based on consistent principles.** The provisions are rules based, which least to inconsistency and arbitrariness.

(2)   **Current rules do not provide sufficient information on risk management.** Increasingly users of financial statements have said that they wish to understand the risks that an entity faces, the   entity's strategy in managing those risks. Many believe that the IAS 39 requirements do not provide such an understanding.

(3)   **Current rules on hedging do not reflect risk management practice.** For example, there are instances where hedge accounting cannot be applied to groups of items, whereas for risk management purposes, items are often hedged on a group basis.

(4)   **Current rules are confusing and complex.** For example, many users believe that the distinction in IAS 39 between cash flow hedges and fair value hedges is unnecessarily complex and confusing.

(5)   **Current rules give insufficient disclosures** in the financial statements about an entity's risk management activities.

(ii)   **Proposals in the ED/Draft IFRS**

The proposed amendments are intended to 'improve the ability of investors to understand risk management activities and to assess the amounts, timing and uncertainty of future cash flows. The proposals will replace the 'rule-based' requirements for hedge accounting currently in IAS 39, and align the accounting more closely with risk management activities of an entity.

The ED proposed a new, principles-based model for hedge accounting that aims to align accounting with risk management activities. This will combine:

(1)   A management view, that aims to use information produced internally for risk management purposes, and

(2)   An accounting view that seeks to address the risk management issue of the timing of recognition of gains and losses.

(3)   The ED also proposes changes to:

(4)   Eligible hedging instruments and eligible hedged items

(5)   Hedge effectiveness

(6)   Accounting for qualifying fair value hedges. Under the ED proposals:

•   The gain or loss on the hedging instrument and the hedged item should be recognised in other comprehensive income.

•   The ineffective portion of the gain or loss is transferred to profit or loss.

(7)   Rebalancing of the hedging relationship

(8)   Discontinuing hedge accounting

(9)   Accounting for time value of purchased options

(10)   Improved disclosure requirements

(iii)   **Criticisms of the proposals**

The following concerns have been identified in connection with the proposals by Ernst & Young (*IFRS Outlook, March/April 2011*):

(1)   Some of the limitations proposed by the ED mean that entities will **not be able to fully reflect their risk management strategies for certain economic hedges** (such as those involving the use of internal derivatives).

(2) The **terminology has been criticised** as being either too precise or not precise enough, specifically the requirement that hedge relationships must be designated so that they produce an 'unbiased' result and 'minimise' ineffectiveness.

(3) The requirement to **adjust (re-balance) hedges** may be **applied inconsistently.**

(4) With regard to the extension of the ability to hedge risk components to **non-financial items,** it is felt that there is **insufficient guidance** on how risk components should be identified when they are not contractually specified.

(5) The proposals **on fair value hedges may be too complex** to implement. The primary financial

Statements would be cluttered and the presentation would result in the separate recognition of assets and liabilities that would not comply with the Conceptual Framework.

In his article *Hedge Accounting* for the April edition of *Accounting and Business* magazine, the P2 examiner Graham Holt also made the following points.

(1) The ED has been written on the assumption that risk management activities are undertaken at a micro level, when in fact risk management is usually applied at a **higher macro or portfolio level**.

(2) The separate **transfer** of hedging ineffectiveness **from other comprehensive income to profit or loss may present some operational challenges.**

(3) The ED introduces **new concepts and definitions** that may not be well understood.

(4) **Macro hedging is not addressed** in the ED, and it might make sense for the IASB to develop a model for macro hedging before finalising the standard on hedge accounting in general.

(5) The **piecemeal approach** to replacing IAS 39 may cause inconsistencies and operational difficulties.

59 Fair values and IFRS 13

Text reference. Current issues are covered in Chapter 19. Fair value is covered where relevant in Chapters 4, 5, 12 and elsewhere briefly.

Top tips. This question is very topical, as IFRS 13 was issued in 2011.

Easy marks. Part (a) is fairly open ended, and credit will be given for valid points if you back up your arguments.

(a) **Fair value measurement or historical cost**

The debate between historical cost accounting and fair value measurement centres on **reliability versus relevance**. Very broadly speaking, fair values are perceived as relevant but not reliable. Historical cost accounting is perceived as reliable but not relevant.

Fair value can be said to be more relevant than historical cost because it is based on current market values rather than a value that is in some cases many years out of date. Fair values for an entity's assets, it is argued, will be give a closer approximation to the value of the entity as a whole, and are more useful to a decision maker or an investor.

If there is **more standardisation in fair valuing** – IFRS 13 *Fair value measurement* is a step towards this – then in the future, if not immediately, fair value measurement will have the advantage of being both relevant and reliable.

Historical cost accounting traditionally matches cost and revenue. The objective has been to match the cost of the asset with the revenue it earns over its useful life. It has a number of **disadvantages.**

(i) If the historical cost differs from its fair value on initial recognition, the **matching process in future periods becomes arbitrary**.

(ii) Non-current asset **values are unrealistic**, particularly those of property.

(iii)   **Holding gains on inventory are included in profit.** During a period of high inflation the **monetary value of inventories held may increase significantly** while they are being processed. The conventions of historical cost accounting lead to the **realised part of this holding gain** (known as *inventory appreciation*) being **included** in **profit** for the year.

(iv)   **Comparisons over time are unrealistic**, because they do not take account of inflation.

(v)   **Costs incurred before an asset is recognised are not capitalised**. This is particularly true of development expenditure, and means that the historical cost does not represent the fair value of the consideration given to create the asset.

However, historical cost has a number of **advantages** over fair values, mainly as regards reliability.

(i)   It is **easy to understand**.

(ii)   It is grounded in **real transaction amounts**, and is therefore **objective** and objectively verifiable.

(iii)   There is **less scope for manipulation**.

Until there is **more uniformity and objectivity in fair valuing**, it is likely that historical cost accounting will continue to be used.

(b)   **IFRS 13 changes**

(i)   **Definition.** With the publication of IFRS 13, IFRS and US GAAP now have the same definition of fair value and the measurement and disclosure requirements are now aligned. IFRS 13 defines fair value as **'the price that would be received to sell an asset or paid to transfer a liability in an orderly transaction between market participants at the measurement date.'**

The previous definition used in IFRS was 'the amount for which an asset could be exchanged, or a liability settled, between knowledgeable, willing parties in an arm's length transaction'.

The price which would be received to sell the asset or paid to transfer (not settle) the liability is described as the 'exit price' and this is the definition used in US GAAP. Although the concept of the 'arm's length transaction' has now gone, the market-based current exit price retains the notion of an exchange between unrelated, knowledgeable and willing parties.

(ii)   **Measurement.** Fair value is a market-based measurement, not an entity-specific measurement. It focuses on assets and liabilities and on exit (selling) prices. It also takes into account market conditions at the measurement date. In other words, it looks at the amount for which the holder of an asset could sell it and the amount which the holder of a liability would have to pay to transfer it. It can also be used to value an entity's own equity instruments.

Because it is a market-based measurement, fair value is measured using the assumptions that market participants would use when pricing the asset, taking into account any relevant characteristics of the asset.

It is assumed that the transaction to sell the asset or transfer the liability takes place either:

(1)   In the **principal market** for the asset or liability; or

(2)   In the absence of a principal market, in the **most advantageous market** for the asset or liability. The principal market is the market which is the most liquid (has the greatest volume and level of activity) for that asset or liability. The most advantageous market is the market that maximises the amount that would be received to sell the asset or minimizes the amount that would be paid to transfer the liability (after taking into account transaction costs and transport costs). **In most cases the principal market and the most advantageous market will be the same.**

IFRS 13 acknowledges that when market activity declines an entity must use a valuation technique to measure fair value. In this case the emphasis must be on whether a transaction price is based on an orderly transaction, rather than a forced sale.

(iii)   **Non-financial assets.** For non-financial assets the fair value measurement looks at the use to which the asset can be put. It takes into account the ability of a market participant to generate economic benefits by using the asset in its highest and best use.

(iv)   **Valuation techniques.** IFRS 13 states that valuation techniques must be those which are appropriate and for which sufficient data are available. Entities should maximise the use of relevant **observable inputs** and minimise the use of **unobservable inputs**. The standard establishes a three-level hierarchy for the inputs that valuation techniques use to measure fair value:

Level 1 Quoted prices (unadjusted) in active markets for identical assets or liabilities that the reporting entity can access at the measurement date

Level 2 Inputs other than quoted prices included within Level 1 that are observable for the asset or liability, either directly or indirectly, eg quoted prices for similar assets in active markets or for identical or similar assets in non active markets or use of quoted interest rates for valuation purposes

Level 3 Unobservable inputs for the asset or liability, ie using the entity's own assumptions about market exit value

(v)   **Disclosure.** For assets and liabilities that are measured at fair value on a recurring or non-recurring basis, an entity must disclose the valuation techniques and inputs used to develop those measurements. For recurring fair value measurements using significant **unobservable inputs** (Level 3), it must disclose the effect of the measurements on profit or loss or other comprehensive income for the period.

(c)   **Investment in Greenfield**

The illustrative examples booklet accompanying IFRS 13 mentions the case of a financial asset for which sale is legally or contractually restricted for a specified period. The restriction is a characteristic of the instrument and, therefore, would be transferred to market participants. In this case the fair value of the instrument would be measured on the basis of the quoted price for an otherwise identical unrestricted equity instrument of the same issuer that trades in a public market, adjusted to reflect the effect of the restriction. The adjustment would reflect the amount market participants would demand because of the risk relating to the inability to access a public market for the instrument for the specified period. The adjustment will vary depending on:

(i)   The nature and duration of the restriction

(ii)   The extent to which buyers are limited by the restriction (eg there might be a large number of qualifying investors)

(iii)   Qualitative and quantitative factors specific to both the instrument and the issuer

60 Jones and Cousin

> **Text reference.** This topic is covered in Chapter 19 of the text.
>
> **Top tips.** In part (b), make full use of the information in the question, but do not simply regurgitate it.
>
> **Easy marks.** Part (a) is very straightforward book work. Part (b) also has easy marks for style and layout.

		Marks
(a)	Principle	6
	Mandatory discussion	7
	Available/ maximum	13
(b)	Principal risks	9
	Treasury policies	3
	Available/ maximum	12
	Style and presentation	2
	Available	27
	Maximum	25

(a) In December 2010, the IASB issued an IFRS Practice Statement *Management Commentary*, which is the international equivalent of the UK's Operating and Financial Review. The purpose of the commentary is to provide a context for interpreting a company's **financial position, performance and cash flows**. The principles and objectives of a Management Commentary (MC) are as follows:

   (i) To provide **management's view** of the entity's performance, position and progress;

   (ii) To **supplement and complement** information presented in the financial statements;

   (iii) To include **forward-looking information**; and

   (iv) To include information that possesses the **qualitative characteristics** described in the *Conceptual Framework* (see Chapter 1).

The Practice Statement says that to meet the objective of management commentary, an entity should include information that is essential to an understanding of:

   (i) The **nature of the business**

   (ii) Management's **objectives and its strategies** for meeting those objectives

   (iii) The entity's most significant **resources, risks and relationships**

   (iv) The **results** of operations and **prospects**

   (v) The critical **performance measures and indicators** that management uses to evaluate the entity's performance against stated objectives

The arguments for a mandatory MC are largely to do with content and comparability. It is argued that a mandatory MC will make it easier for companies themselves to judge what is required in such a report and the required standard of reporting, thereby making such reports more **robust, transparent and comparable**. If an MC is not mandatory then there may be **uncertainty** as to content and the possibility of **misinformation**. There is also the risk that without a mandatory MC directors may take a **minimalist approach** to disclosure which will make the MC less useful and the information to be disclosed will be in hands of senior executives and directors.

However, the **arguments against** a mandatory MC are that it could **stifle the development of the MC as a tool** for communication and may lead to a **checklist approach** to producing it. It is argued that a mandatory

MC is not required as market forces and the needs of investors should lead to companies feeling the pressure to provide a useful and reliable report. The IASB decided to issue a Practice Statement rather than an IFRS and to leave it to regulators to decide who would be required to publish a management commentary. This approach avoids the **adoption hurdle**, ie that the perceived cost of applying IFRSs might increase, which could otherwise dissuade jurisdictions/ countries not having adopted IFRSs from requiring its adoption, especially where requirements differ significantly from existing national requirements.

(b)

Jones and Cousin
Annual Report 20X6
Management Commentary

Introduction

Jones and Cousin is a public quoted company and the group develops, manufactures and markets products in the medical sector. This report is designed to assist members of the group in understanding and assessing the strategies of the group and the potential success of these strategies.

Risks

The group faces a number of risks which will be considered under the headings of:

- Market risk
- Product risk
- Currency risk

Market risk

The market in which the group operates is quite fiercely competitive and contains a number of different competitors including specialised and large international corporations. There is the risk that any technical advances or product innovations by these competitors could adversely affect the group's profits. Also this element of competition also means that there is a risk of loss of market share or lower than expected sales growth which could affect the share price.

The sector in which the group operates is heavily monitored by local governments and the group's share of revenue in a market sector is often determined by government policy. The group is therefore heavily dependent upon governments providing the funds for health care. Any reduction in funds by governments would almost certainly lead to a fall in revenue for the group.

Product risk

The products of the group are essentially a low health risk. However, there is always the possibility of a problem with products which may lead to legal action which would be costly and damage the group's reputation and goodwill. The industry is highly regulated in terms of both medical and environmental laws. Any such claims would have an adverse effect on sales, profit and share price.

There will always be innovations in this market sector and the group is careful to protect its products with patents and will enter into legal proceedings where necessary to protect those patents. There is also the problem of infringing the patents of others. If claims were brought for infringement of patents of other companies this would be costly and damaging and alternative products would have to be found.

There are constantly new products being developed by the group which is costly in terms of research and development expenditure. Product innovation may not always be successful and this highly regulated market may not always gain the regulatory approval required.

Currency risk

The group operates in twenty-seven different countries and earns revenue and incurs costs in several different currencies. Although the dollar is the group's functional currency only 5% of its business is in the country of incorporation. Therefore exchange fluctuations in the main currencies in which it trades may have a material effect on the group's profits and cash flows.

Relationships

The group has a positive ethical programme. It sources its products from a wide range of suppliers largely in the form of long term contracts for the supply of goods. The group has a policy of ensuring that such suppliers are suitable from both qualitative and ethical perspectives.

The group has a set of corporate and social responsibility principles for which the Board of Directors is responsible. The risks that the group bears from these responsibilities are managed by the Managing Director. The group operates in many geographical areas and encourages its subsidiaries to help local communities to reinvest in local educational projects. Great care is taken by the group to ensure that obsolete products are disposed of responsibly and safely. Wherever possible reusable materials are used.

Group policy is to attract and retain employees and to maintain an equal opportunities policy for all employees. To this end employees regularly receive in-house training and are kept informed of management policies.

Treasury policies

The group uses derivative products to protect against both currency risk and interest rate risk. This is done by the used of fixed rate currency swaps and using floating to fixed rate interest rate swaps. All financial instruments are accounted for as cash flow hedges which means that gains and losses are recognised initially in reserves and are only released to profit or loss when the hedged item also affects profit or loss.

61 Lockfine

Text reference. IFRS 1 and IFRS 13 are covered in Chapter 19 of your Study Text. IFRS 3 is covered in Chapter 12.

Top tips. This was a specialised industry question, set in the fishing industry. As the examiner has stated, no specialist knowledge of the industry was required. The question was broken down into four almost equal parts. Parts (a) and (b) covered IFRS 1 *First time adoption of International Financial Reporting Standards* in respect of fair value measurement and transition to IFRS 3 *Business combinations.* Part (c) was on intangible assets, and part (d) covered restructuring plans and provisions.

Easy marks. There are some relatively easy marks in Part (d) for listing out the IAS 37 criteria for a constructive obligation to restructure.

Examiner's comment. In Part (a), the treatment of deemed cost was not well answered by candidates. Fair value becomes the 'deemed cost' going forward under the IFRS cost model. In Part (b) candidates recognised that if an entity during the transition process to IFRS, decides to retrospectively apply IFRS3 to a certain business combination then it must apply that decision consistently to all business combinations. However the key point often missed was that the decision to apply IFRS 3 cannot be made selectively. Part (c) was very well answered, with the main omission being the fact that under IAS 1 *Presentation of financial statements* an entity should disclose accounting policies relevant to an understanding of its financial statements. Part (d) was also answered well. Candidates were well versed in the principles behind how a constructive obligation to restructure arises under. IAS 37, *Provisions, contingent liabilities and contingent assets.*

Marking scheme

		Marks
(a)	1mark per question up to maximum	6
(b)	1mark per question up to maximum	6
(c)	1mark per question up to maximum	6
(d)	1mark per question up to maximum	5
Professional marks		2
Maximum		25

(a) **IFRS 1 and deemed cost**

IFRS 1 *First time adoption of International Financial Reporting Standards* states that an entity may elect to measure an item of property, plant and equipment at the **date of transition to IFRS** at fair value and **use that fair value as its deemed cost at that date**. Fair value is defined in IFRS 1 as amended by IFRS 13 *Fair value measurement* as:

'the price that would be received to sell an asset or paid to transfer a liability in an orderly transaction between market participants at the measurement date.'

An entity adopting IFRS for the first-time may, under IFRS 1 as amended by IFRS 13, elect **to use a previous GAAP revaluation** of an item of property, plant and equipment at or before the date of transition to IFRS as deemed cost at the date of the revaluation under the following conditions.

(i)   The revaluation was broadly comparable to fair value.

(ii)   The revaluation was broadly comparable to cost or depreciated cost in accordance with IFRS, adjusted to reflect, for example, changes in a general or specific price index.

In addition, IFRS 1 does not give detailed rules about determining fair value, and first-time adopters who use fair value as deemed cost **must only provide limited disclosures**, not a full description of the methods and assumptions used.

In the case of Lockfine, the question to be decided is whether the selling agents' estimates can be used as the fair value to be used, in turn, as deemed cost under IFRS 1.

The selling agents' estimates provide only limited information about the valuation methods and assumptions, and it is doubtful that they can be relied upon for determining fair value in accordance with IAS 16 *Property, plant and equipment* and IFRS 13 *Fair value measurement*. Under IAS 16 measurement of fair value must be **reliable.** While it is correct to use independent valuers, IAS 16 requires that the reporting entity know the **assumptions** that have been made in assessing reliability. In addition, using the average of the highest amounts may not be prudent.

IFRS 1 allows more latitude than IAS 16. Lockfine is **not in breach of IFRS 1 which does not specify detailed rules for this particular case**, and allows fair value as determined on the basis of selling agents' estimates. This is a cost effective approach for entities that do not perform a full retrospective application of the requirements of IAS 16.

(b) **Fishing rights**

IFRS 1 requires that if an entity which is in the process of adopting IFRS decides to apply IFRS 3 retrospectively to a business combination, it **cannot do so selectively,** but must apply IFRS 3 **consistently to all business combinations** that occur between the date on which it decides to adopt

IFRS 3 and the date of transition. An entity must have regard to **similar transactions in the period.** When allocating values to the assets and liabilities of the acquired company, the entity needs to have documentation to support its purchase price allocation. Without this, use of other methods of price allocation is not permitted unless the methods are strictly in accordance with IFRS.

Lockfine was **unable to recognise** the fishing rights of the business combination as separately identifiable because it **could not obtain a reliable value** for the rights, so it included the rights within goodwill.

IAS 38 has two criteria, both of which must be met for an entity to recognise an intangible asset, whether purchased or internally generated:

(i)   It is probably that the future economic benefits attributable to the asset will flow to the entity.

(ii)   The cost of the asset can be measured reliably.

The fishing rights **satisfy the first, but not the second of these criteria**. Accordingly the fishing rights were **correctly subsumed within goodwill.** As long as the goodwill presented under the first IFRS financial statements did not require a write down for impairment, it should be the net carrying amount at the date of transition.

Although the fishing rights have a finite life, **they will not be amortised over the period** specified by the rights, because they are included within goodwill. Instead, **the goodwill is reviewed annually for impairment** in accordance with IAS 36 *Impairment of assets*.

(c)   **Electronic map data**

The standard that applies here is IAS 38 *Intangible assets*. Under IAS 38, an intangible asset is an asset with the following characteristics.

(i)   It meets the standard's **identifiability criteria.** This means it must be separable or must arise from contractual or other legal rights

(ii)   It is probable that **future economic benefits** attributable to the asset will flow to the entity. These could be in the form of increased revenues or cost savings.

(iii)   The entity has **control**, that is the power to obtain benefits from the asset.

(iv)   Its cost can be **measured reliably.**

It appears that the capitalised expenses of the acquisition and production of the electronic map data **meet these criteria.**

(i)   The electronic maps are identifiable because they are capable of being separated from the entity as a whole and sold (or transferred or licensed), regardless of whether the entity intends to do this.

(ii)   They are controlled by Lockfine.

(iii)   It is probable that benefits attributable to the maps will flow to the entity because the electronic maps will generate revenue when used by the fishing fleet.

(iv)   Their value can be measured reliably – Lockfine has a record of the costs.

The **electronic maps** will therefore be **recognised as an intangible asset at cost**. Generally they will subsequently be carried at cost less any amortisation and impairment losses.

Regarding the **database**, Lockfine believes that this has an indefinite useful life and, by implication, should not be amortised but should be tested annually for impairment. IAS 38 regards an intangible asset as having an indefinite useful life when, based on analysis of all the relevant factors, there is no foreseeable limit to the period over which the asset is expected to generate net cash inflows for the entity.

Indefinite does not mean the same as infinite and in the context of IAS 38 has specific implications. In particular, the indefinite useful life should not depend on future planned expenditure in excess of that required to maintain the asset. In this respect, **Lockfine complies with IAS 38.**

In addition, IAS 38 identifies certain factors that may affect the useful life, changing it in this instance from indefinite to finite. These include technological or commercial obsolescence and actions by competitors.

There is no specific requirement for an entity to disclose the IAS 38 criteria for recognition of an intangible asset arising from development, although it does require disclosure of assets which have an indefinite useful life (the carrying amount and reasons for assessing the useful life as indefinite(. However, under IAS 1 *Presentation of financial statements,* entities **must disclose accounting policies that are relevant for an understanding of their financial statements.** The electronic maps and the data base constitute a material amount of total assets, so the accounting policies, including the IAS 38 criteria for development expenditure, need to be disclosed.

(d)   **Restructuring plans**

IAS 37 criteria

IAS 37 *Provisions, contingent liabilities and contingent assets* **contains specific requirements** relating to **restructuring provisions**. The general recognition criteria apply and IAS 37 also states that **a provision should be recognised** if an entity has a **constructive obligation** to carry out a restructuring. A constructive obligation exists where **management has a detailed formal plan** for the restructuring, identifying **as a minimum:**

(i)   The business or part of the business being restructured

(ii)   The principal locations affected by the restructuring

(iii) The location, function and approximate number of employees who will be compensated for the termination of their employment

(iv) The date of implementation of the plan

(v) The expenditure that will be undertaken.

In addition, the plan must have raised a **valid expectation** in those affected that the entity will carry out the restructuring. To give rise to such an expectation and therefore a constructive obligation, the **implementation must be planned to take place as soon as possible**, and the timeframe must be such as to make changes to the plan unlikely.

Plan A

Lockfine proposes recognising a provision in respect of the plan to sell 50% of its off-shore fleet in a year's time and to make 40% of the seamen redundant. However, although the plan has been communicated to the public, the above criteria are not met. **The plan is insufficiently detailed**, and various aspects are not finalised. The figure of 40% is tentative as yet, the **fleets and employees affected have not been identified**, and a decision has not been made on whether the off-shore fleet will be restructured in the future. Some of these issues await further analysis.

The proposal does not, therefore, meet the IAS 37 criteria for a detailed formal plan and an announcement of the plan to those affected by it. Lockfine cannot be said to be committed to this restructuring and so **a provision should not be recognised**.

Plan B

Lockfine has not proposed recognising a provision for the plan to reorganise its headquarters and make 20% of the headquarters' workforce redundant. However, it is likely that this treatment is incorrect, because the plan appears to meet the IAS 37 criteria above:

(i) The locations and employees affected have been **identified.**

(ii) An **announcement** has been made and employee representatives notified – it is not necessary to notify individual employees as their representatives have been told.

(iii) The conclusion of the three month consultation period indicates that the above announcement is sufficiently detailed to give rise to a **valid expectation** that the restructuring will take place, particularly if the discussions have been about the terms of the redundancy.

It will be necessary to **consider the above negotiations** – provided these are about details such as the terms of redundancy rather than about changing the plan, then the IAS 37 criteria have been met. Accordingly, a provision needs to be recognised.

62 Burley

Marking scheme

		Marks
(a)	Revenue recognition	3
	Inventory	3
	Events after reporting period	3
		9
(b)	Jointly controlled	3
	Accounting for entity	2
	Decommissioning	5
		10
(c)	Asset definition/IAS 38/IAS 36	4
	Professional marks	2
		25

(a) Revenue from the sale of goods should only be recognised when **all the following conditions** are satisfied.

   (i) The entity has transferred the **significant risks and rewards** of ownership of the goods to the buyer

   (ii) The entity has **no continuing managerial involvement** to the degree usually associated with ownership, and no longer has effective control over the goods sold

   (iii) The amount of revenue can be **measured reliably**

   (iv) It is probable that the **economic benefits** associated with the transaction will flow to the enterprise

   (v) The **costs incurred** in respect of the transaction can be measured reliably

   The transfer of risks and rewards can only be decided by examining each transaction. In the case of the oil sold to third parties, all the revenue should be recognised as all the criteria have been met.

Revenue up to 1 October 20X9

The arrangement between Burley and Slite is a **joint arrangement** under IFRS 11 *Joint arrangements*, since both entities jointly control an asset – the oilfield. However, the arrangement is not structured as a separate entity, so it is a **joint operation not a joint venture**. This means that **each company accounts for its share of revenue** in respect of oil produced up to 1 October 20X9, calculated, using the selling price to third parties of $100 per barrel, as:

Burley: 60%
Slite: 40%

Excess oil extracted

Burley has over-extracted and Slite under-extracted by 10,000 barrels of oil. The **substance** of the transaction is that **Burley has purchased the oil from Slite** at the point of production at the market value ruling at that point, namely $100 per barrel. Burley should therefore **recognise a purchase** from Slite in the amount of 10,000 × $100 = $1m.

The accounting entries would be:

DEBIT	Purchases	$1m	
CREDIT	Slite – financial liability		$1m

The **amount payable to Slite at the year end** will **change with the movement in the price of oil** and therefore the financial liability recorded at the year end should reflect the best estimate of the cash payable. By the year end the price of oil has risen to $105 per barrel, so the financial liability will be 10,000 × $105 = $1,050,000, an **increase of $50,000**. The accounting entries to reflect this increase in liability and expense to profit or loss at the year end will be:

DEBIT	Expense (P/L)	$50,000	
CREDIT	Slite – financial liability		$50,000

After the year end the price of oil changes again, and the transaction is settled at $95 per barrel. The cash paid by Burley to Slite on 12 December 20X9 is 10,000 × $95 = $950,000. This means that a **gain arises after the year end** of $1,050,000 - $950,000 = $100,000. This gain will be **taken to profit or loss** in the **following accounting period**:

DEBIT	Slite – financial liability	$100,000	
CREDIT	Profit or loss		$100,000

The gain arising is an **event after the reporting period.** These are defined by IAS 10 *Events after the reporting period* as events, both favourable and unfavourable, that occur between the end of the reporting period and the date that the financial statements are authorised for issue.

The question arises of whether this is an **adjusting or non-adjusting** event. An adjusting event is an event after the reporting period that provides further evidence of conditions that existed at the end of the reporting period. A non-adjusting event is an event after the reporting period that is indicative of a **condition that arose after the end of the reporting period**. The price of oil changes frequently in response to a number of factors, reflecting events that arose after the year end. It would therefore not be appropriate to adjust the financial statements in response to the decline in the price of oil. The gain is therefore a **non-adjusting** event after the reporting period.

Inventory

IAS 2 *Inventories* requires that inventories should be stated at the **lower of cost and net realisable value.** Net realisable value (NRV) is the estimated selling price in the ordinary course of business less the estimated cost of completion and the estimated costs of making the sale.

In estimating NRV, entities must use reliable evidence of the **market price** available at the time. Such evidence includes any movements in price that reflect conditions at the year end, including prices recorded after the year end to the extent that they confirm these conditions. In the case of Burley, the appropriate market price to use is that recorded at the year end, namely **$105 per barrel**, since the decline to $95 results from conditions arising after the year end. Selling costs are $2 per barrel, so the amount to be used for NRV in valuing the inventory is $105 - $2 = $103 per barrel.

Net realisable value, in this instance, is higher than cost, which was $98 per barrel. The inventory should be stated at the lower of the two, that is at $98 per barrel, giving a total inventory value of $98 × 5,000 = $490,000. No loss is recorded as no write-down to NRV has been made.

(b) **Arrangement with Jorge**

Burley wishes to account for its arrangement with Jorge using the equity method. It can only do so if the arrangement meets the criteria in IFRS 11 *Joint arrangements* for a **joint venture.**

A **joint arrangement** is an arrangement, as here, of which two or more parties have joint control. A **joint venture** is a joint arrangement whereby the parties that have control of the arrangement have **rights to the net assets** of the arrangement.

Wells is a **separate vehicle**. As such, it could be either a joint operation or joint venture, so other facts must be considered.

There are no facts that suggest that Burley and Jorge have rights to substantially all the benefits of the assets of Wells nor an obligation for its liabilities.

Each party's liability is limited to any unpaid capital contribution.

As a result, each party has an interest in the **net assets** of Wells and should account for it as a **joint venture** using the **equity method.**

Decommissioning costs

Decommissioning costs are not payable until some future date, therefore the **amount of costs** that will be incurred is generally **uncertain**. IAS 16 *Property, plant and equipment* requires that management should record **its best estimate** of the entity's obligations. Since the cash flows are delayed, **discounting is used.** The estimate of the amount payable is discounted to the date of initial recognition and the discounted amount is capitalised. A corresponding credit is recorded in provisions. Changes in the liability and resulting from changes in the discount rate adjust the cost of the related asset in the current period.

The decommissioning costs of Wells are accounted for as follows:

	$m
Cost ten years ago	240.0
Depreciation: 240 ×10/40	(60.0)
Decrease in decommissioning costs: 32.6 – 18.5	(14.1)
Carrying value at 1 December 20X8	165.9
Less depreciation: 165.9 ÷ 30 years	(5.5)
Carrying amount at 30 November 20X9	160.4

The provision as restated at 1 December 20X8 would be increased at 30 November 20X9 by the unwinding of the discount of the new rate of 7%.

	$m
Decommissioning liability: 32.6 – 14.1	18.5
Finance costs: 18.5 × 7%	1.3
Decommissioning liability at 30 November 20X9	19.8

Pipeline

Since Burley has joint control over the pipeline, even though its interest is only 10%, it would not be appropriate to show the pipeline as an investment. This is a **joint arrangement** under IFRS 11.

The pipeline is a **jointly controlled asset,** and it is **not structured through a separate vehicle.** Accordingly, the arrangement is a **joint operation.**

IFRS 11 *Joint arrangements* requires that a joint operator **recognises line-by-line the following** in relation to its interest in a joint operation:

(i) Its **assets**, including its share of any jointly held assets
(ii) Its **liabilities**, including its share of any jointly incurred liabilities
(iii) Its **revenue** from the sale of its share of the output arising from the joint operation
(iv) Its **share of the revenue from the sale of the output** by the joint operation, and
(v) Its **expenses**, including its share of any expenses incurred jointly.

This treatment is applicable in both the separate and consolidated financial statements of the joint operator.

(c) **Intangible asset**

The relevant standard here is IAS 38 *Intangible assets.* An intangible asset may be recognised if it meets the **identifiability criteria** in IAS 38, if it is probable that **future economic benefits** attributable to the asset will flow to the entity and if its **fair value can be measured reliably.** For an intangible asset to be identifiable, the asset must be separable, or it must arise from contractual or other legal rights.

It appears that these **criteria have been met.** The licence has been acquired separately, and its value can be measured reliably at the purchase price.

Burley does not yet know if the extraction of oil is commercially viable, and does not know for sure whether oil will be discovered in the region. If, on further exploration, some or all activities must be discontinued, then the licence must be **tested for impairment** following IAS 36 *Impairment of assets.* (IAS 36 has a number of impairment indicators, both internal and external.)

It is possible that the licence may **increase in value** if commercial viability is proven. However, IAS 38 does not allow revaluation unless there is an **active market** for the asset.

63 Seltec

Text references. Financial instruments are covered in Chapter 7, brands in Chapter 4, and business combinations in Chapters 12 to 17. This is a specialised industry question – other specialised industries are covered in Chapter 20 of your text.

Top tips. Note that IFRS 9 simplifies the treatment of embedded derivatives that are financial assets within the scope of the standard - these no longer need to be separated from their host contract. However, the more complex rules still apply to embedded derivatives that are not assets. In Part (b), you need to think carefully about what constitutes a business combination – substance is more important than form.

Easy marks. These are available for the definition of embedded derivatives and basic principles of intangible assets.

Examiner's comment. The examiner was satisfied in the main with candidates' answers, but disappointed that few recognised the embedded derivative. Answers to the final part of the question, on business combinations, were disappointing, the main weakness being the application of the knowledge and the understanding of the nature of the purchase of the entities.

Marking scheme

	Marks
Hedge accounting	5
Futures	5
Embedded derivative	4
Brands	5
Business combinations	4
Professional marks	2
	25

(a)   **Financial instruments**

Derivatives

IAS 32 *Financial instruments: presentation* and IFRS 9 *Financial instruments* define a **derivative** as a financial instrument or other contract that has all three of the following characteristics.

(i)   Its value changes in response to the change in a specified interest rate, financial instrument price, commodity price, foreign exchange rate, index of prices or rates, credit rating or credit index, or other variable (sometimes called the 'underlying').

(ii)   It requires no initial net investment or an initial net investment that is smaller than would be required for other types of contracts that would be expected to have a similar response to changes in market factors.

(iii) It is settled at a future date.

A contract is **not considered to be a derivative where its purpose is to take physical delivery** in the normal course of business, unless the entity has a practice of settling the contracts on a net basis.

In the case of Seltec, while the company often takes physical delivery of the edible oil, it does so only to sell shortly afterwards, and usually settles on a net basis. Thus the **contracts will be considered to be derivative** contracts rather than contracts for purchase of inventory. Derivatives are accounted for at fair value through profit or loss, unless hedge accounting applies.

Hedge accounting

The rules on hedge accounting are currently set out in IAS 39 – this part of IFRS 9 has not been completed. Hedge accounting is permitted only in certain circumstances:

(i)   The hedging relationship must be **designated at its inception as a hedge** based on the entity's risk management objective and strategy. There must be formal documentation

(ii)   The hedge is expected to be **highly effective** in achieving offsetting changes in fair value or cash flows attributable to the hedged risk. This means that the ratio of the gain or loss on the hedging instrument compared to the loss or gain on item being hedged is within the ratio 80% to 125%. (Note: the hedge need not necessarily be *fully* effective.)

(iii) For **cash flow hedges**, a **forecast transaction** that is the subject of the hedge must be **highly probable** and must present an exposure to variations in cash flows that could ultimately affect profit or loss.

(iv)   The effectiveness of the hedge can be **measured reliably**.

(v)   The hedge is **assessed** on an ongoing basis (annually) and has been **effective during the reporting period**.

There are two kinds of hedging that Seltec may consider: fair value hedging and cash flow hedging.

A **fair value hedge** is a hedge of the exposure to changes in the fair value of a recognised asset or liability, or an identified portion of such an asset or liability, that is attributable to a particular risk and could affect profit or loss. The **gain or loss** resulting from **re-measuring** the hedging instrument at fair value is **recognised in profit or loss**. The gain or loss on the hedged item attributable to the **hedged risk** should **adjust the carrying amount** of the hedged item and be **recognised in profit or loss**.

A **cash flow hedge**: a hedge of the exposure to variability in cash flows that:

(i)   Is attributable to a particular risk associated with a recognised asset or liability (such as all or some future interest payments on variable rate debt) or a highly probable forecast transaction (such as an anticipated purchase or sale), and that

(ii)   Could affect profit or loss

The portion of the gain or loss on the hedging instrument that is determined to be an **effective** hedge must be **recognised in other comprehensive income(items that may subsequently be reclassified to profit or**

loss) and transferred to profit or loss when the hedged item is recognised in profit or loss. The **ineffective portion** of the gain or loss on the hedging instrument must be **recognised in profit or loss**.

The rules for cash flow hedges are particularly restrictive because it is difficult to isolate and measure the cash flows attributable to the specific risks for the non-financial items. Cash flow hedging results in higher volatility in earnings, so, provided the documentation and other requirements are met, **Seltec may prefer to use fair value hedging.** Seltec must take into account all changes in the price of edible oil of all types and geographical locations that it processes and sells and these must be compared with the changes in the value of the future. The hedge will be ineffective if the contracts have different prices. However, a hedge does not need to be fully effective, and hedge accounting may still be used provided the effectiveness is in the range 80% to 125%.

Embedded derivative

Certain contracts that are not themselves derivatives (and may not be financial instruments) include derivative contracts that are 'embedded' within them. These non-derivatives are called **host contracts** IFRS 9 defines an embedded derivative as a derivative instrument that is combined with a non-derivative host contract to form a single hybrid instrument. Some of the cash flows of the instrument vary in a way that is similar to a stand-alone derivative.

Ordinary derivatives must be accounted for at fair value in the statement of financial position with changes recognised through profit or loss.

IFRS 9 treatment

Where the host contract is a financial asset within the scope of the IFRS 9, the classification and **measurement rules of the standard are applied to the entire hybrid contract**. However, in this case the contract is a financial liability, not a financial asset within the scope of IFRS 9. Accordingly, the following rules apply:

The embedded derivative must be **separated from its host contract** and accounted for as a derivative, provided the following conditions are met.

(i)   The economic characteristics and risks of the embedded derivative are not closely related to the economic characteristics and risks of the host contract.

(ii)   A separate instrument with the same terms as the embedded derivative would meet the definition of a derivative.

(iii)   The hybrid (combined) instrument is not measured at fair value with changes in fair value recognised in the profit or loss (a derivative embedded in a financial asset or financial liability need not be separated out if the entity holds the combined instrument at fair value through profit or loss).

If the embedded derivative is separated from its host contract, the **host contract is accounted for under the applicable IFRS.** A contract denominated in a foreign currency contains an embedded derivative unless:

(i)   The foreign currency denominated in the contract is the currency of one of the parties to the contract.

(ii)   The foreign currency is that commonly used in the market in which such transactions take place.

(iii)   The foreign currency is that in which the related goods or services are denominated in routine commercial transactions.

In the case of Seltec, **none of the above three exceptions apply**. Seltec's trade in edible oil is generally in dollars, not pound sterling, the pound is not the functional currency of either party, and it is not the currency normally used in transactions in the business environment in which Seltec operates. Finally, the economic characteristics and risks of the embedded derivative are not closely related to the economic characteristics and risks of the host contract, since changes in the price of oil and currency fluctuations have different risks.

In conclusion, IFRS 9 would treat Seltec's contracts as containing an embedded derivative. The currency derivative must be accounted for at fair value through profit or loss.

(b)   **Intangible assets**

An entity should **assess** the useful life of an intangible asset, which may be **finite or indefinite**. An intangible asset has an indefinite useful life when there is **no foreseeable limit** to the period over which the asset is expected to generate net cash inflows for the entity.

Seltec wishes to treat both brands as having indefinite useful lives. However, this may not be appropriate, and there are certain factors that need to be considered:

(i)   Does the brand have long-term potential? The first brand has a proven track record, but the second, named after a famous film star, may last only as long as the film star's popularity, which will not be indefinite.

(ii)   Is Seltec committed to supporting the brand? In the case of the first, it is, but the second is a relatively new product, and it is not clear that Seltec is in for the long haul.

If, as is likely, the **useful life of the second brand is considered to be finite**, its cost less residual should be amortised on a systematic basis over its useful life, using the straight-line method as an approximation if the pattern of benefits cannot be determined reliably.

The **first brand**, which is correctly said to have an **indefinite useful life**, should not be amortised. Its useful life should be reviewed at each reporting period to determine whether the assessment of the useful life as indefinite is still applicable. If not, the change, from indefinite to finite would be accounted for as a change in accounting estimate as per IAS 8. It should also be assessed for impairment in accordance with IAS 36, and otherwise accounted for like the second brand.

Purchase of entities

IFRS 3 *Business combinations* defines a business combination as 'a transaction or event in which an acquirer obtains control of one or more businesses. A business is defined as an integrated set of activities and assets that is capable of being conducted and managed for the purpose of providing a return directly to investors or other owners, members or participants'. Such a return may be in the form of cash, dividends or lower costs.

The two limited liability **companies do not meet the IFRS 3 definition of a business** because they are not self-sustaining and do not generate revenue independently of Seltec. The acquisition **should be treated as a purchase of property.**

64 Ethan

Marking scheme

	Marks
Impairment testing	5
Deferred taxation	6
Fair value option – IFRS 9	7
Financial liability	5
Communication skills	2
	25

(a) **Fair value**

The **fair value** of an asset is the price that would be received to sell an asset or paid to transfer a liability in an orderly transaction between market participants at the measurement date (IFRS 13 *Fair value measurement*). IFRS 13 states that valuation techniques must be those which are appropriate and for which sufficient data are available. Entities should maximise the use of relevant **observable inputs** and minimise the use of **unobservable inputs**. The standard establishes a three-level hierarchy for the inputs that valuation techniques use to measure fair value.

Level 1 Quoted prices (unadjusted) in active markets for identical assets or liabilities that the reporting entity can access at the measurement date

Level 2 Inputs other than quoted prices included within Level 1 that are observable for the asset or liability, either directly or indirectly, eg quoted prices for similar assets in active markets or for identical or similar assets in non-active markets or use of quoted interest rates for valuation purposes

Level 3 Unobservable inputs for the asset or liability, ie using the entity's own assumptions about market exit value

Although an active market exists for Ethan's investment properties, Ethan uses a discounted cash flow model to measure fair value. This is **not in accordance with IFRS 13**. As the fair value hierarchy suggests,

IFRS 13 favours Level 1 inputs, that is market-based measures, over unobservable (Level 3) inputs such as discounted cash flows.

Goodwill and deferred tax

If the **fair value** of the investment properties **is not measured correctly** in accordance with IFRS 13, this means that the **deferred tax liability** on investment properties **may also be incorrect.** In addition, as goodwill is calculated as consideration transferred less fair value of net assets, **goodwill may be incorrect**. This is because deferred tax is calculated on the difference between the carrying amount of the asset and its tax base. So if the carrying amount is incorrect, the deferred tax will be incorrect. The goodwill calculation uses the fair value of **all** net assets, not just the investment properties and the related deferred tax liability, so it is **incorrect to use an increase in the deferred tax liability** as the **basis** for assessing whether goodwill is impaired.

The reasoning behind Ethan's approach is that as the deferred tax liability decreases, the fair value of net assets increases, thereby decreasing goodwill. However, this method of determining whether goodwill is impaired **does not accord with IAS 36** *Impairment of assets.* IAS 36 requires that goodwill should be **reviewed for impairment annually** for any indicators of impairment, which may be internal or external, and are not confined to changes in the deferred tax liability. Where it is not possible to measure impairment for individual assets, the loss should be measured for a **cash generating unit.**

The **recoverable amount** is **defined** as the **higher** of:

(i) The **asset's fair value less costs to sell.** This is the price that would be received to sell the asset in an orderly transaction between market participants at the measurement date under current market conditions, net of costs of disposal.

(ii) The asset's **value in use.** This is the present value of estimated future cash flows (inflows minus outflows) generated by the asset, including its estimated net disposal value (if any) at the end of its useful life.

If an **asset's carrying amount** is **higher than its recoverable amount**, an **impairment loss** has occurred. The impairment loss should be **written off against profit or loss** for the year, and the corresponding credit (write-off) applied first to goodwill, then to the investment properties, then to other assets pro-rata .

Deferred tax assets on losses

In theory, unused tax losses give rise to a deferred tax asset. However, IAS 12 *Income taxes* states that **deferred tax assets should only be recognised to the extent that they are regarded as recoverable.** They should be regarded as recoverable to the extent that on the basis of all the evidence available it is **probable that there will be suitable taxable profits against which the losses can be recovered**. It is unlikely that future taxable profits of Ethan will be sufficient to realise all of the tax loss because of:

(i) The announcement that a substantial loss will be incurred this year instead of the expected profit

(ii) Considerable negative variances against budgets in the past

Consequently, **Ethan should not recognise the deferred tax asset.**

(b) **IFRS 9 fair value option**

Generally under IFRS 9 *Financial instruments*, the debt issued to finance its investment properties would be accounted for using **amortised cost,** while the properties themselves are at fair value. This is an **accounting mismatch,** that is a recognition or measurement inconsistency between the debt liability and the asset to which it relates. The asset and liability, and the gains and losses arising on them, would be measured on different bases.

The IFRS 9 **fair value option** allows an entity to **designate a liability at initial recognition as being at fair value through profit or loss** if using this option would **eliminate or significantly reduce** an accounting mismatch. Ethan has argued that the basis of measurement of the debt and the investment properties is **similar**, particularly as regards **interest rates**. This argument holds good in respect of the interest, and so the **fair value option would be allowed.**

However, IFRS 9 stipulates that if a liability is designated as being at fair value through profit or loss, **changes in the fair value that are due to changes in the liability's credit risk must be recognised directly** in other comprehensive income rather than profit or loss. Such **changes may not be re-classified** to profit or loss in subsequent years, although a **reserves transfer** is permitted from other components of equity to retained earnings. On the other hand, **if changes in the fair value attributable to the credit risk** of the liability **create or enlarge an accounting mismatch in profit or loss**, then all fair value movements are **recognised in profit or loss.**

(c) **B shares of subsidiary**

Ethan's accounting treatment of the B shares (as equity instruments) does not comply with IAS 32 *Financial instruments: presentation.* The IAS 32 definition of a financial liability includes any liability that is **a contractual obligation to deliver cash or another financial asset to another entity.** A financial instrument may only be classified as an equity instrument rather than a liability if the instrument does not include an obligation to deliver cash or other financial asset to another entity, or to exchange financial instruments with another entity under conditions that are potentially unfavourable.

In the **subsidiary's books,** the B shares would be treated as a **financial liability.** They contain an **obligation** to deliver cash in the form of a fixed dividend. The dividend is cumulative and must be paid whether or not the subsidiary has sufficient legally distributable profits when it is due, and so **the subsidiary cannot avoid this obligation.**

In the **consolidated financial statements,** the B shares would also be treated as a financial liability, **the intragroup element of this liability (70%) would cancel against the investment in B shares in the parent's (Ethan's) statement of financial position.** The shares **owned by external parties would not cancel;** they would remain **a financial liability.** It **is incorrect to treat them as non-controlling interest** because they are **not equity.**

65 Norman

> **Text reference.** Segment reporting is covered in Chapter 18 of the Study Text. Revenue recognition is covered in Chapter 1.
>
> **Top tips.** This question deals with segmental reporting and the application of the principles to a given scenario. The second part of the question dealt with income recognition in three different scenarios. Revenue recognition has been specifically flagged by this examiner as being important.
>
> **Easy marks.** In effect, this question is in five parts. Part (a) has easy marks for bookwork, application being more difficult, and Part (b) has two scenarios. Thus, if you are not sure of one aspect, you can pick up marks on the other.
>
> **Examiner's comment.** Part (a) was quite well answered. However, some candidates confused IFRS 8 with its predecessor, IAS 14, although there are differences in how a segment is determined. Candidates were good at applying the principles to the scenario. Part (b) was also answered well, with candidates applying their knowledge of IAS 18.

		Marks
(a)	Identification of segments	2
	Definition	2
	Reporting information	2
	Normal applicability	5
		11
(b)	Sale of businesses	4
	Vouchers	4
	Grant income	4
	Quality of discussion	2
		14
	Maximum	25

(a) **Determining operating segments**

IFRS 8 *Operating segments* states that an operating segment is a reported **separately** if:

(i) It **meets the definition of an operating segment**, ie:

    (1) It engages in business activities from which it may **earn revenues** and **incur expenses**,

    (2) Its operating results are **regularly reviewed by the entity's chief operating decision maker** to make decisions about resources to be allocated to the segment and assess its performance, and

    (3) **Discrete financial information** is available for the segment,

and

(ii) It exceeds **at least one** of the following quantitative thresholds:

    (1) Reported revenue is **10% or more the combined revenue** of all operating segments (external and intersegment), or

    (2) The absolute amount of its reported profit or loss is **10% or more of the greater of,** in absolute amount, **all operating segments not reporting a loss, and all operating segments reporting a loss**, or

    (3) Its assets are **10% or more of the total assets** of all operating segments.

At least **75% of total external revenue** must be reported by operating segments. Where this is not the case, additional segments must be identified (even if they do not meet the 10% thresholds).

Two or more operating segments **below** the thresholds may be aggregated to produce a reportable segment if the segments have similar economic characteristics, and the segments are similar in a **majority** of the following aggregation criteria:

(1) The nature of the products and services
(2) The nature of the production process
(3) The type or class of customer for their products or services
(4) The methods used to distribute their products or provide their services
(5) If applicable, the nature of the regulatory environment

Operating segments that do not meet **any of the quantitative thresholds** may be reported separately if management believes that information about the segment would be useful to users of the financial statements.

For Norman, **the thresholds are as follows.**

(i)   Combined revenue is $1,010 million, so 10% is $101 million.
(ii)   Combined reported profit is $165 million, so 10% is $16.5 million.
(iii) Combined reported loss is $10 million, so 10% is $1 million.
(iv) Total assets are $3,100 million, so 10% is $310 million.

The **South East Asia segment** meets the criteria, passing all three tests. Its combined revenue is $302 million; its reported profit is $60 million, and its assets are $800 million.

The **European segment** also meets the criteria, but only marginally. Its reported revenue, at $203 million is greater than 10% of combined revenue, and only one of the tests must be satisfied. However, its loss of $10 million is less than the greater of 10% of combined profit and 10% of combined loss, so it fails this test. It also fails the assets test, as its assets, at $300 million are less than 10% of combined assets ($310 million).

IFRS 8 requires further that at least 75% of total external revenue must be reported by operating segments. Currently, only 50% is so reported. Additional operating segments (the 'other regions') must be identified until this 75% threshold is reached.

IFRS 8 may result in a **change** to the way Norman's operating segments are reported, depending on how segments were previously identified.

(b)   **Sale of hotel complex**

The issue here is one of **revenue recognition**, and the accounting treatment is governed by IAS 18 *Revenue*. It can be argued in some cases where property is sold that the seller, by continuing to be involved, has **not transferred the risks and rewards of ownership**. In such cases, the sale is not genuine, but is often in substance a **financing arrangement**. IAS 18 requires that the substance of a transaction is determined by looking at the transaction as a whole. If two or more transactions are linked, they should be treated as one transaction to better reflect the commercial substance.

Norman continues to operate and manage the hotel complex, receiving the bulk (75%) of the profits, and the residual interest reverts back to Norman; effectively, Norman retains the risks and rewards of ownership. Conquest does not bear any risk: its minimum annual income is guaranteed at $15m. The sale should not be recognised. In substance it is a financing transaction. The **proceeds** should be treated as a **loan**, and the payment of **profits** as **interest**.

Discount vouchers

The treatment of the vouchers is governed by IAS 18 *Revenue* . The principles of the standard require that

(i)   The voucher should be accounted for as a **separate component** of the sale
(ii)   The amount of the proceeds allocated to such vouchers should be measured at **fair value**.

The vouchers are issued as part of the sale of the room and redeemable against future bookings. The substance of the transaction is that **the customer is purchasing both a room and a voucher**. This means that revenue should be reported as the amount of consideration received less the fair value of the voucher. In determining the fair value, the following considerations apply:

(i)   The value to the holder, not the seller
(ii)   The discount the customer obtains
(iii) The percentage of vouchers that will be redeemed
(iv) The time value of money

Vouchers worth $20 million are eligible for discount as at 31 May 20X8. However, based on past experience, it is likely that only one in five vouchers will be redeemed, that is vouchers worth $4 million. Room sales are $300 million, **so effectively, the company has made sales worth $(300m + 4m) = $304 million in exchange for $300 million**. The proceeds need to be split proportionally, that is the discount of $4 million needs to be allocated between the room sales and the vouchers, as follows:

Room sales: $\dfrac{300}{304} \times \$300m = \$296.1m$

Vouchers (balance) = $3.9m

The $3.9 million attributable to the vouchers is only recognised when the obligations are fulfilled, that is when the vouchers are redeemed.

Government grant

The applicable standard relating to this transaction is IAS 20 *Accounting for government grants and disclosure of government assistance.* The principle behind the standard is that of accruals or matching: the **grant received must be matched with the related costs**.

Government grants are assistance by government in the form of transfers of resources to an entity in return for past or future compliance with certain conditions relating to the operating activities of the entity. There are two main types of grants:

(i)   **Grants related to assets**: grants whose primary condition is that an entity qualifying for them should purchase, construct or otherwise acquire long-term assets. Subsidiary conditions may also be attached restricting the type or location of the assets or the periods during which they are to be acquired or held. In this case the condition relates to the cost of building the hotels, which must be $500m or more.

(ii)   **Grants related to income**: These are government grants other than grants related to assets.

It is not always easy to match costs and revenues if the terms of the grant are not explicit about the expense to which the grant is meant to contribute. In the case of Norman, the intention of the grant is to create employment in the area, and the building of hotels is for that purpose. However, on balance, the grant can be seen as **capital based,** because the amount is not tied into payroll expenditure or numbers of jobs created, and the repayment clause is related to the cost of the asset (building of hotels). Accordingly, IAS 20 allows two possible approaches:

(i)   Match the grant against the depreciation of the hotels using a deferred income approach.
(ii)   Deduct the grant from the carrying value of the asset.

66 Preparation question: Reconstruction scheme

Text reference. This topic is covered in Chapter 20 of the Study Text.

Top tips. In part (b), the changes to be considered are in the *market* value (or income stream) rather than the *nominal* value of each investor class. You only have sufficient information to look at future income (which will anyway have a considerable influence on market value) so you should look at that. It is also essential to recognise that the ordinary shareholders stand to lose control of the company under the current proposals.

(a)   STATEMENT OF FINANCIAL POSITION OF CONTEMPLATION GROUP
        AS AT 1 JULY 20X2 AFTER RECONSTRUCTION

	$'000
Non-current assets	3,600
Current assets	4,775
	8,375
Ordinary 25c shares (W3)	1,875
8% preference shares of $1 each, fully paid ($3.3m - $0.8m dividend in arrears)	2,500
Reserves (W1)	-
14% 20Y5 loan notes	3,000
Current liabilities	1,000
	8,375

Workings

1   *Reserves*

	$'000
Reserves at 30 June 20X2	(9,425)
Cancellation of previous ordinary shares	10,000
Net effect of issue of ordinary shares to preference shareholders in lieu of accrued arrears of dividend (W2)	300
Issue of new ordinary shares to holders of previous ordinary shares	(875)
	Nil

2   *Net effect of elimination of accrued preference dividend arrears*

	$'000
Cancellation of dividend arrears (8% × 4 × $2.5m)	800
Issue of new shares	500
Net effect: loss in nominal value of holding	300

3   *Ordinary shares*

	No	$'000
Issued to loan note holders	2,000,000	500
Issued to preference shareholders	2,000,000	500
Issued to existing ordinary shareholders	3,500,000	875
	7,500,000	1,875

Note. The purpose of the reconstruction is to eliminate the negative reserves and allow the company to start again. The table below shows the effect of each of the four adjustments ((a) to (d) in the question) in achieving this.

Ref	Item	Debit	Credit
		$'000	$'000
(a)	Ordinary share capital cancelled	10,000	
(b)	11% loan notes retired	3,500	
	14% loan notes issued		3,000
	2,000,000 25c shares issued		500
(c)	Cancellation of dividend arrears (8% × 4 × $2.5m)	800	
	Issue of new shares		500
(d)	Issue of shares to existing shareholders 3.5m × 25c		875
	Elimination of negative reserves balance		9,425
		14,300	14,300

(b)   (i)   **Loan note holders**

	$'000
Cancellation of previous loan notes	3,500
Issue of new loan notes	3,000
Issue of new shares	500
Net effect on nominal value of holding	Nil

Loan note interest (before tax is paid by the recipient) would be $385,000 pa ($3.5m x 11%) if no reconstruction was effected and $420,000 ($3m x 14%) if the scheme is agreed. In addition, the loan note holders would be entitled to a share of earnings from their ordinary shares. (Maximum $273,867: see below).

Loan note holders as fixed chargeholders would be repaid in full in the event of a liquidation and must therefore balance the risk of the company's failure in the future, when its assets may have declined in value, thus reducing their usefulness as security, against the forecast increase in return. They must also assess the effect of an extra few years' delay in redemption, which increases the risk. If loan note holders have confidence in the new strategy, then they are better off under the reconstruction.

(ii) Preference shareholders

	$'000
Cancellation of dividend arrears (8% × 4 × $2.5m)	800
Issue of new shares	500
Net effect: loss in nominal value of holding	300

No preference dividend could be paid if the reconstruction scheme does not go ahead as all profits for the foreseeable future would be applied in reducing retained losses. If the scheme is agreed, the annual dividend could be restored immediately and, as above, there would be an equity interest with a maximum dividend of $273,867 (see below).

Preference shareholders are assured of repayment of their capital at the moment but may not be in the future if losses are made again. If they are prepared to accept the risk that the new strategy may fail, then they are better off under the reconstruction.

(iii) Existing ordinary shareholders

	$'000
Cancellation of previous shares	(10,000)
Cancellation of previous negative reserves: 9,425 – 800*	8,625
Issue of new shares	875
Net effect: loss of nominal value of equity	(500)

Note. The $800,000 accrued arrears of preference dividends has been excluded from the figure for negative reserves because they are dealt with in (ii) above and do not affect the ordinary shareholders.

Ordinary shareholders will receive no dividend for many years if the scheme is not accepted. If it is accepted, then for the first few years, earnings will be as follows.

	$
Post-tax profits before interest	1,500,000
Loan note interest (less tax relief) 14% × 65% × $3m	273,000
	1,227,000
Preference dividend	200,000
Earnings	1,027,000

However, of this 1,000/(1,000 + 875) (part (a) (W3)) will be attributable to the new shares issued to loan note holders and preference shareholders (500/1,875 × $1,027,000 = $273,867 each). Therefore, the existing shareholders will receive a maximum dividend of 875/(1,875) × $1,027,000 = $479,267. It is, of course, exceedingly unlikely that the company will distribute its entire post-tax profit, and so the actual dividend would probably be lower.

(c)
To:	A Grieved
From:	Financial Adviser
Date:	28 June 20X2
Subject:	*Proposed scheme of reconstruction*

You have commented that you feel the proposed scheme is 'unfair': presumably you mean to the existing ordinary shareholders. This claim can be examined by looking at the outcome for you as an ordinary shareholder in each of the three options open to the directors:

(i) To liquidate the company;
(ii) To continue without reconstructing;
(iii) To adopt the proposed reconstruction.

(i) If the company is liquidated, the net assets would amount to the following.

	$'000
Realisation of assets (gross) ($3.1m + $3.5m)	6,600
Less loan notes	3,500
Less arrears of preference dividends	800
Net assets	2,300

This would be entirely absorbed by the claims of the preference shareholders ($2.5m). Thus there would be nothing left over for distribution to ordinary shareholders.

(ii) If no reconstruction takes place the profits after tax and interest will amount to approximately $1.25m ($1.5m profit before interest – [65% x 11% x $3.5m] interest) per annum. Thus it will be some seven years before the deficit on the profit and loss account is cleared and a further year to clear the arrears of preference dividends. Thus, the ordinary shareholders cannot expect a dividend for over eight years. The present value of such a dividend stream is minimal.

(iii) The net interest of the original ordinary shareholders in the reconstructed company is: 3,500,000 shares × 25c = $875,000.

There are no reserves.

In addition, the original shareholders can expect to receive dividends or a share in retained earnings from the time of the reconstruction.

So, while the original ordinary shareholders have given up more than the preference shareholders and the loan note holders (who have lost nothing) the reconstruction offers more than the possible alternative options.

Thus, from the point of view of income, the proposed scheme seems the best option under discussion.

However, you should also consider the fact that your control over the company has been seriously diluted. Over half the equity after the reconstruction ie 54% (4m shares/7.5m shares (W3)) would be owned by the loan note holders and preference shareholders, who would also still own their loan notes and preference shares. The scheme could be amended so that control remains in the hands of the existing shareholders, who are, after all, not cushioned by holding loan notes or preference shares. If preference shareholders were given fewer ordinary shares, the scheme would be more equitable. The loan note holders would be unlikely to agree to any scaling down of their share allocation.

Nevertheless, with this proviso, it seems that the scheme is fair to ordinary shareholders who otherwise have no hope of dividends or repayment of capital in the event of a liquidation.

Please let me have your comments on the attached draft letter to the directors of Swanee as soon as possible. If they can be persuaded to agree to the suggested scaling down of new equity, then I would advise you to accede to the proposal.

(d) The Directors
Contemplation Limited
Anytown   28 June 20X2

Dear Sirs,

We are acting for A Grieved, the holder of 10% of the ordinary capital of Contemplation Limited, and refer to the proposals for reconstructing the company.

We consider that this proposal is unfairly advantageous to the existing shareholders. The loan note holders would increase their return from their investment from $385,000 pa (interest only) to $693,867 ($420,000 interest plus $273,867 share of the projected earnings).

The preference shareholders' return will also increase dramatically from a notional $200,000 pa (unlikely to be paid in the foreseeable future) to $473,867 pa ($200,000 preference dividend and $273,867 share of earnings).

This seems excessive in view of the reduced financial and business risk which would result from the reconstruction. We would suggest that an increase in return of 50% to $577,500 would adequately compensate the loan note holders for the additional risk of holding equity rather than loans. Consequently we would suggest that, in addition to the new 14% loan notes an issue of 1,150,193 shares would be more appropriate.

In view of the power of loan note holders, we accept that they may not accept a revision to the scheme that reduces the total nominal value of their investment in the company. The preference shareholders, however, are in a different category. There seems no justification for issuing to them such a high proportion of the new 25c shares. If they were to be given 730,282 shares (assuming the above scaling down was not accepted), their projected return would still increase by 50% and the existing ordinary shareholders would retain control of the company.

We look forward to your comments on the above suggestions.

Yours faithfully,

F Adviser & Co

67 Plans

Text reference. This topic is covered in Chapter 20 of the Study Text.

Top tip. The Examiner has mentioned internal reconstructions as an area he may test.

Key considerations and accounting impacts

There are a number of reasons why a group may re-organise, for example:

- Companies may be transferred to another business during a **divisionalisation process**
- To **create efficiencies** of group structure for **tax purposes**

The impact of each of the proposed structures is discussed below.

Plan 1: share for share exchange

If the purchase consideration is in the form of shares, then a share premium account will need to be set up in the books of Y. This share premium account must comprise the minimum premium value, which is the excess of the book value of the investment over the nominal value of the shares issued: $70m – $50m = $20m.

The impact on the individual company accounts and on the group accounts is as follows:

	Note	X $m	Y $m	Z $m	Group $m
Property, plant and equipment		600	200	45	845
Goodwill					10
Cost of investment in Y	1	130			
Cost of investment in Z	2		70		
Net current assets		160	100	20	280
		890	370	65	1,135

	Note	X	Y	Z	Group
Share capital	3	120	110	40	120
Share premium	4		20		
Retained earnings	5	770	240	25	1,015
		890	370	65	1,135

Notes

1   *Cost of investment in Y*

   This is increased by the total value of the shares issued: $50m + $20m = $70m.

2   *Cost of investment in Z*

   Transferred to Y. The book value of the investment is preserved.

3   *Share capital*

   Y's share capital is increased by the nominal value of the shares issued, $50m.

4   *Share premium*

   This is as discussed above.

5   *Retained earnings*

Goodwill arising on the purchase of Z is $10m ($70m − ($40m + $20m)). The group retained earnings are calculated as follows.

	X $m	Y $m	Z $m
Per question	770	240	25
Retained earnings at acquisition		−	(20)
	770	240	5
Share of post-acquisition retained earnings of Y (240 x 100%)	240		
Share of post-acquisition retained earnings of Z (5 x 100%)	5		
	1,015		

Plan 2: cash purchase

The group accounts are not affected by the change as the reorganisation is internal. It has no impact on the group as a single entity.

If the purchase consideration is in the form of cash, a gain or loss on the sale of Z will arise in the books of X. This does not count as a distribution as the cash price of $75m is not in excess of the fair value of the net assets of Z, $80m. The effect on the accounts would be as follows:

	Note	X $m	Y $m	Z $m	Group $m
Property, plant and equipment		600	200	45	845
Goodwill					10
Cost of investment in Y		60			
Cost of investment in Z	1		75		
Net current assets	2	235	25	20	280
		895	300	65	1,135
Share capital		120	60	40	120
Retained earnings	3	775	240	25	1,015
		895	300	65	1,135

Notes

1   *Cost of investment in Z*

This is the cash consideration of $75m.

2   *Net current assets*

X's cash increases by $75m and Y's cash decreases by $75m.

3   *Retained earnings*

X's retained earnings have been increased by $5m, being the profit on the sale of the investment in Z. This is eliminated on consolidation as it is an intragroup transaction. The consolidated retained earnings are calculated in exactly the same way as in the share for share exchange.

Summary and conclusion

There are advantages and disadvantages to each of the two plans. Before we could make a recommendation we would need more information about *why* the group wishes to restructure.

Neither plan changes the group financial statements. From an internal point of view it results in a closer relationship between Y and Z. This may be advantageous if Y and Z are close geographically or in terms of similarity of business activities. Alternatively, it might be advantageous for tax reasons.

68 Decany

Marking scheme

			Marks
(a)	(i)	Decany	5
		Ceed	5
		Rant	3
			13
	(ii)	IAS 27	5
(b)		Discussion - subjective	5
		Professional marks	2
			25

(a) (i) **Individual entity statements of financial position after the restructuring plan**

	Note	Decany $m	Ceed $m	Rant $m
Non-current assets				
Property, plant and equipment at depreciated cost/valuation		600	170 + 15 = 185.0	45 – 10 = 35
Cost of investment in Ceed		130		11
Cost of investment in Rant	1		98.0	
Loan receivable	2	98		
Current assets	2	155 + 25 = 180	130 – 98 = 32.0	20 + 98 = 118
		1,008	315.0	164
Equity and reserves				
Share capital			70 + 5 =	

		140	75.0	35
Share premium	3		6.0	
Retained earnings	5	776	185.5	10
		916	266.5	45
Non-current liabilities				
Long-term loan	6	5	4.0	106
Provisions	7	2	9.5	
Current liabilities				
Dividend payable			25.0	
Trade payables		85	10.0	13
		1,008	315.0	164

Notes

1   *Sale of shares in Rant*

In Creed's books:

DEBIT	Investment in Rant	$98m	
CREDIT	Cash		$98

This is the cash consideration of $98m.

Decany has made a profit on the sale of rant of $98m – $95m = $3m, which is added to Decany's retained earnings. In Decany's books:

DEBIT	Cash	$98m	
CREDIT	Investment in Rant		$95m
CREDIT	Profit or loss (and retained earnings)		$3m

2   *Loan receivable*

Decany now has a loan receivable of $98m and Ceed's cash decreases by $98m. In Decany's books:

DEBIT	Loan receivable	$98m	
CREDIT	Cash (current assets)		$98m

In Rant's books:

DEBIT	Cash (current assets)	$98m	
CREDIT	Loan payable		$98m

3   *Sale of land by Rant to Creed/calculation of share premium*

The value of the shares issued to Decany is the land less the mortgage, ie $11m. The difference between this and the nominal value is the share premium.

In Ceed's books:

DEBIT	Land	$15m	
CREDIT	Mortgage liability (long-term loan)		$4m
CREDIT	Share capital		$6m
CREDIT	Share premium (balancing figure)		$5m

In Rant's books:

DEBIT	Investment in Ceed	$11m	
DEBIT	Mortgage liability (long-term loan)	$4m	
CREDIT	Land		$10m
CREDIT	Profit or loss (and retained earnings)		$5m

4   *Dividend payable by Ceed to Decany*

In Creed's books:

DEBIT	Retained earnings	$25m	
CREDIT	Dividend payable		$25m

In Creed's books:

DEBIT	Dividend receivable (current assets)	$25m	
CREDIT	Retained earnings		$25m

5   *Retained earnings*

	Decany $m	Ceed $m	Rant $m
Per question	750	220.0	5
Dividend from Ceed to Decany	25	(25.0)	-
Profit on sale of Rant	3	-	-
Profit on sale or land			5
Provision for restructuring (note 6)	(2)	(9.5)	-
	776	185.5	10

6   *Long-term loan (Rant)*

	$m
Per question	12
Loan payable (note 2)	98
Mortgage liability (note 3)	(4)
	106

7   *Redundancy costs and provision for restructuring*

The fact that there is a detailed plan for restructuring with employees identified for redundancy creates a constructive obligation under IAS 37 *Provisions, contingent liabilities and contingent assets*, and accordingly a provision should be made for redundancy costs and restructuring. Creed will incur the redundancy costs, which should be recognised in its financial statements at the present value of the future cash flows:

	$m
$4m \times 1/1.03$	3.9
$6m \times 1/1.03^2$	5.6
	9.5

The provision of $9.5m will be shown in Creed's financial statements, and the overall restructuring provision of $2m in the financial statements of Decany.

(ii)   **IAS 27 rules on reorganisation and payment of dividends between group companies**

IAS 27 *Separate financial statements* was issued in 2011 and carries forward a change made to IAS 27 *Consolidated and separate financial statements* in 2008 in respect of group reorganisations. In limited reorganisations IAS 27 effectively allows the **cost of an investment in a subsidiary to be based on the previous carrying amount of the subsidiary rather than on its fair value**. This is only allowed when a new parent (Ceed) is inserted above an existing parent of a group or entity (Rant), and where the following **criteria** are satisfied.

(1)   The new parent (Ceed) obtains control of the original parent or entity (Rant) by issuing equity instruments in exchange for existing equity instruments of the original parent or entity.

(2)   The assets and liabilities of the new group and the original group are the same immediately before and after the reorganisation.

(3)   The owners of the original parent or entity (Decany) before the reorganisation have the same absolute and relative interests in the net assets of the original group and the new group immediately before and after the reorganisation,

The reorganisation of the Decany group appears to meet all the above criteria. (In respect of (3), Rant has not acquired a further interest in Ceed as a result of the transfer of land because the shares in Ceed issued to Rant are non-voting.)

A further amendment carried forward in the revised IAS 27 was the removal of the 'cost method'. This required an entity to recognise distributions as income only if they came from post-acquisition retained earnings. Distributions received in excess of such retained earnings were regarded as a recovery of investment and were recognised as a reduction in the cost of the investment. Now, however, IAS 27 requires all dividends **in profit or loss in its separate financial statements when its right to receive the dividend is established.** The distinction between pre- and post-acquisition profits, which had been problematic, is no longer required.

If such dividends are paid, the entity is required to consider whether there is has been an **impairment.** Applying IAS 36 *Impairment of assets,* impairment is indicated in the following cases.

(1)   The dividend exceeds the total comprehensive income of the subsidiary, jointly controlled entity or associate in the period the dividend is declared.

(2)   The carrying amount of the investment in the separate financial statements exceeds the carrying amounts in the consolidated financial statements of the investee's net assets, including associated goodwill.

Neither of these apply in the case of Creed, and so there is no indication that Creed is impaired.

(b)   **Impact of reconstruction plan**

The reconstruction plan has no impact on the group financial statements as all the intra-group transactions will be eliminated on consolidation. From an internal point of view it results in **a closer relationship between Creed and Rant.** This may be advantageous if Creed and Rant are close geographically or in terms of similarity of business activities. Alternatively, it might be advantageous for tax reasons.

Regarding the restructuring plan, IAS 37 *Provisions, contingent liabilities and contingent assets* **contains specific requirements** relating to **restructuring provisions**. The general recognition criteria apply and IAS 37 also states that **a provision should be recognised** if an entity has a **constructive obligation** to carry out a restructuring. A constructive obligation exists where **management has a detailed formal plan** for the restructuring, identifying **as a minimum:**

(i)   The business or part of the business being restructured

(ii)   The principal locations affected by the restructuring

(iii)   The location, function and approximate number of employees who will be compensated for the termination of their employment

(iv)   The date of implementation of the plan

(v)   The expenditure that will be undertaken.

It appears that these criteria have been met. However, the amount of $2m in Decany's financial statements seems rather large, considering that the redundancy is provided separately in the accounts of Ceed, and the restructuring does not involve any relocation.

The plan shows the companies in a **more favourable light** in that Rant's **short-term cash flow problem is eliminated**. Rant now has cash available. However, it is showing a much increased long-term loan. In the financial statements of Rant, the investment in Ceed must be accounted as a financial asset under IFRS 9 *Financial instruments.*

It is possible that the purchase consideration for rant of $98m could be seen as **a transaction at an overvalue.** It creates a profit of $3m, which could be seen as artificial. The question also arises as to whether this $3m should be recognised, and of whether it should be viewed as a distribution. Should problems arise in connection with local legislation, a share exchange might be a less problematic plan than a cash purchase.

The question may also arise as to whether Ceed has effectively **made a distribution**. This could happen where the purchase consideration was well in excess of the fair value of Rant. An alternative to a cash purchase would be a share exchange. In this case, local legislation would need to be reviewed in order to determine the requirements for the setting up of any share premium account.

69 IFRSs and SMEs

> **Text reference.** SMEs are covered in Chapter 21 of your Study Text.
>
> **Top tips.** This question required candidates to discuss the need to develop a set of IFRSs especially for small to medium-sized enterprises (SMEs). Do not be tempted to waffle or repeat yourself. Since this question was set, the IASB has published an IFRS for SMEs.
>
> **Easy marks.** This is a knowledge-based question, so all marks are easy if you know it.
>
> **Examiner's comment.** This question was generally well answered and the topic will feature in future exams.

Marking scheme

		Marks
(a)	Subjective	7
(b)	Purpose	3
	Definition of entity	4
	How to modify	6
	Items not dealt with	3
	Full IFRS	3
	Available	26
	Maximum	25

(a) Originally, International Accounting Standards (IASs) issued by the International Accounting Standards Committee (IASC) were **designed to be suitable for all types of entity**, including small and medium entities (SMEs) and entities in developing countries. Large listed entities based their financial statements on national GAAP which normally **automatically complied** with those IASs due to choices permitted in the past. In recent years, IASs and IFRSs have become **increasingly complex and prescriptive**. They are now designed **primarily** to meet the information needs of **institutional investors in large listed entities** and their advisers. In many countries, IFRSs are **used mainly by listed companies**.

There is a case for continued use of full IFRSs by SMEs. It can be argued that the **main objectives** of general purpose financial statements **are the same for all types of company**, of whatever size. Compliance with full IFRSs ensures that the financial statements of SMEs **present their financial performance fairly** and gives them greater **credibility**. It also ensures their **comparability** with those of other entities.

There were also many arguments for developing a separate set of standards for SMEs, and these have been taken into account (see below) Full IFRSs have become very **detailed and onerous** to follow. The **cost** of complying may **exceed the benefits** to the entity and the users of its financial statements. At present, an entity cannot describe their financial statements as IFRS financial statements unless they have complied with every single requirement.

SME financial statements are normally **used by a relatively small number of people**. Often, the **investors** are also **involved in day to day management**. The **main external users** of SME financial statements tend to be **lenders and the tax authorities**, rather than institutional investors and their advisers. These users have **different information needs** from those of investors. For these users, the accounting treatments and the detailed disclosures required may sometimes **obscure the picture** given by the financial statements. In some cases, **different, or more detailed information may be needed.** For example, related party transactions are often very significant in the context of SME activities and expanded disclosure may be appropriate.

The *IFRS for Small and Medium-Sized Entities* (IFRS for SMEs) was published in July 2009, and therefore falls to be examinable in 2010. It is only 230 pages, and has **simplifications** that reflect the needs of users of SMEs' financial statements and cost-benefit considerations. It is designed to facilitate financial reporting by small and medium-sized entities in a number of ways:

(i)   It provides significantly **less guidance** than full IFRS.

(ii) Many of the **principles** for recognising and measuring assets, liabilities, income and expenses in full IFRSs are **simplified**.

(iii) Where full IFRSs allow accounting policy choices, the IFRS for SMEs **allows only the easier** option.

(iv) **Topics not relevant** to SMEs are **omitted**.

(v)   Significantly **fewer disclosures** are required.

(vi) The standard has been written in **clear language** that can easily be translated.

(b)   **Issues in developing IFRSs for SMEs**

(i)   **The purpose of the standards and type of entity to which they should apply**

The main objective of accounting standards for SMEs is that they should provide the users of SME financial statements with **relevant, reliable and understandable information**. The standards should be **suitable for SMEs globally** and should **reduce the financial reporting burden** on SMEs. It is generally accepted that SME standards should be built on the **same conceptual framework** as full IFRSs.

It could also be argued that SME standards should **allow for easy transition** to full IFRS as some SMEs will become listed entities or need to change for other reasons. This would mean that SME standards **could not be separately developed from first principles** (as many would prefer) but instead would be a **modified version of full IFRS**. Some argue that ease of transition is not important as relatively few SMEs will need to change to IFRS in practice.

The **definition** of an SME could be based on **size** or on **public accountability** or on a combination of the two. There are several disadvantages of basing the definition on size limits alone. Size limits are **arbitrary** and **different limits are likely to be appropriate in different countries.** Most people believe that SMEs are **not simply smaller versions of listed entities**, but differ from them in more fundamental ways.

The most important way in which SMEs differ from other entities is that they are **not usually publicly accountable**. Using this as the basis of a definition raises other issues: which types of company are publicly accountable? Obviously the **definition would include** companies which have **issued shares** or other instruments **to the public**. It has been suggested that this category should also include companies **holding assets in a fiduciary capacity** (such as banks or providers of pensions), companies that provide **essential public services** (utility companies) and any entity with **economic significance in its country** (which in turn would have to be defined). This would mean that SME standards could potentially be used by a very large number of entities covering a very large range in terms of size.

There is a case for allowing **national standard setters** to **impose size limits** or otherwise **restrict** the types of entities that could use SME standards. There is also a case for allowing national standard setters to **define 'publicly accountable'** in a way that is appropriate for their particular jurisdiction.

The *IFRS for SMEs* published in July 2009 does not use size or quantitative thresholds, but qualification is determined by public accountability. It is up to legislative and regulatory authorities and standard-setters in individual jurisdictions to decide who may or must use the IFRS for SMEs.

(ii) **How existing standards could be modified to meet the needs of SMEs**

The starting point for modifying existing standards should be the most likely **users** of SME financial statements and their **information needs**. SME financial statements are mainly used by **lenders** and **potential lenders, the tax authorities** and **suppliers**. In addition, the **owners and management** (who are often the same people) may be dependent on the information in the financial statements. SME financial statements must **meet the needs** of their users, but the **costs** of providing the information **should not outweigh the benefits.**

There is considerable scope for **simplifying disclosure and presentation requirements**. Many of the existing requirements, for example those related to financial instruments, discontinued operations and earnings per share, are **not really relevant** to the users of SME financial statements. In any case, lenders and potential lenders are normally able to ask for additional information (including forecasts) if they need it.

The SME standards are a **simplified version of existing standards**, using only those principles that are likely to be relevant to SMEs. The IASB has proposed that the **recognition and measurement principles** in full IFRSs should **remain unchanged** unless there is a good argument for modifying them. Clearly the SME standards will have to be sufficiently rigorous to produce information that is relevant and reliable. However, many believe that there is a **case for simplifying** at least some of the more **complicated measurement requirements** and that it will be difficult to reduce the financial reporting burden placed on SMEs otherwise.

(iii) **How items not dealt with by SME standards should be treated**

Because SME standards **do not cover all possible transactions** and events, there will be occasions where an SME has to **account for an item that the standards do not deal with**. There are several alternatives.

(a) The entity is **required to apply the relevant full IFRS**, while still following SME standards otherwise.

(b) Management can **use its judgement** to develop an accounting policy based on the relevant full IFRS, or the *Framework*, or other IFRSs for SMEs and the other sources of potential guidance cited in IAS 8.

(c) The entity could continue to follow its **existing practice**.

In theory, the **first alternative is the most appropriate** as this is the most likely to result in relevant, reliable and comparable information. The argument against it is that SMEs may then effectively have to comply with **two sets of standards**.

Another issue is whether an SME should be able to **opt to comply** with a specific full IFRS or IFRSs while still following SME standards otherwise. There is an argument that SMEs should be able to, for example, make the additional disclosures required by a full IFRS if there is a good reason to do so. The argument against optional reversion to full IFRSs is that it would lead to **lack of comparability**. There would also need to be safeguards against entities attempting to 'pick and mix' accounting standards.

70 Whitebirk

Text reference. Small and medium-sized entities are covered in Chapter 21 of your Study Text.

Top tips. This is a topical issue and was the subject of a March 2010 *Student Accountant* article by the examiner. Part (a) on the different approaches which could have been used and the main differences between the *IFRS for SMEs* and full IFRS, was reasonably straightforward. Part (b) required you to apply the standard to specific areas: goodwill and research and development expenditure.

Easy marks. This was a rich source of easy marks for the well-prepared candidate. Make sure your arguments are well-structured in order to earn those two marks for clarity and quality of discussion.

Examiner's comment. Part (a) was very well answered. Answers to Part (b) were more variable. Some were unclear about how to account for the transactions and used full IFRS.

			Marks
(a)	(i)/(ii)	Subjective assessment including professional	16
(b)	(i)	Business combination	4
	(iii)	Research and development expenditure	2
			22

(a)   (i)   **Approaches which the IASB could have taken in developing the IFRS for SMEs**

There were three main approaches which the IASB could have taken in developing the *IFRS for Small and Medium-sized Entities (IFRS for SMEs)*.

(1)   **National GAAP for SMEs and IFRS for listed companies**

It could be argued that small and medium-sized entities have little in common with larger listed entities and that listed entities have more in common with listed entities in other developed countries. It would therefore be appropriate for listed companies to use IFRS and for smaller entities to have their own national 'little GAAP'.

The **disadvantage** of this approach is the **inconsistency** within countries between 'big GAAP' and 'little GAAP'. This would make comparability difficult. Further, if an SME, having applied national GAAP for SMEs for some time, then wished to list its shares on a capital market, the **transition to IFRS** would be even more **onerous** than it is currently.

(2)   **Exemptions for SMEs within existing standards**

Another approach would be exemptions for smaller companies from some of the requirements of existing standards, and for these exemptions to be contained within IFRS, probably as an appendix.

This approach has the **disadvantage** that preparers of small company financial statements would still need to look through mainstream IFRS to determine what they did not need to do. Arguably this is **far less convenient** than having a 'stand-alone' standard designed for SMEs.

(3)   **A separate set of standards only relevant for SMEs**

This is closest to what actually happened, but it is not as convenient as having one standard as a one-stop shop. It would have resulted in a proliferation of accounting standards, adding to a already complex picture.

In the event, none of the above approaches was followed. Instead the *IFRS for SMEs*, published in July 2009, is a self-contained document. It is the first set of international accounting requirements developed specifically for small and medium-sized entities. Although it has been **prepared on a similar basis to IFRS**, it is a **stand-alone product** and will be updated on its own timescale.

(ii)   **Modifications to reduce the burden of reporting for SMEs**

The *IFRS for SMEs* is only 230 pages, and has **simplifications** that reflect the needs of users of SMEs' financial statements and cost-benefit considerations. It is designed to facilitate financial reporting by small and medium-sized entities in a number of ways:

(1)   It provides significantly **less guidance** than full IFRS. A great deal of the guidance in full IFRS would not be relevant to the needs of smaller entities.

(2)   Many of the **principles** for recognising and measuring assets, liabilities, income and expenses in full IFRSs are **simplified**. For example, goodwill and intangibles are always amortised over their estimated useful life (or ten years if it cannot be estimated). Research and development costs must be expensed. With defined benefit pension plans, all actuarial gains and losses are to be recognised immediately in other comprehensive income. All past service costs are to be recognised immediately in profit or loss. To measure the defined benefit obligation, the projected unit credit method must be used.

(3)   Where full IFRSs allow accounting policy choices, the *IFRS for SMEs* **allows only the easier option**. Examples of alternatives not allowed in the *IFRS for SMEs* include: revaluation model for intangible assets and property, plant and equipment, proportionate consolidation for investments in jointly-controlled entities and choice between cost and fair value models for investment property (measurement depends on the circumstances).

(4)   **Topics not relevant** to SMEs are **omitted**: earnings per share, interim financial reporting, segment reporting, insurance and assets held for sale.

(5)   Significantly **fewer disclosures** are required.

(6)   The standard has been written in **clear language** that can easily be translated.

The above represents a considerable reduction in reporting requirements - perhaps as much as 90% – compared with listed entities. Entities will naturally wish to use the *IFRS for SMEs* if they can, but **its use is restricted**.

The restrictions are **not related to size**. There are several disadvantages of basing the definition on size limits alone. Size limits are **arbitrary** and **different limits are likely to be appropriate in different** countries. Most people believe that SMEs are **not simply smaller versions of listed entities**, but differ from them in more fundamental ways.

The most important way in which SMEs differ from other entities is that they are **not usually publicly accountable**. Accordingly, there are **no quantitative thresholds** for qualification as a SME; instead, the scope of the IFRS is determined by a **test of public accountability**. The IFRS is suitable for all entities except those whose securities are publicly traded and financial institutions such as banks and insurance companies.

Another way in which the use of the *IFRS for SMEs* is restricted is that **users cannot cherry pick** from this IFRS and full IFRS. If an entity adopts the *IFRS for SMEs,* it **must adopt it in its entirety**.

(b)   (i)   **Business combination**

IFRS 3 *Business combinations* allows an entity to adopt the full or partial goodwill method in its consolidated financial statements. The *IFRS for SMEs* **only allows the partial goodwill method**. This avoids the need for SMEs to determine the fair value of the non-controlling interests not purchased when undertaking a business combination.

In addition, IFRS 3 *Business combinations* requires goodwill to be tested annually for impairment. The *IFRS for SMEs* **requires goodwill to be amortised instead**. This is a much simpler approach and the *IFRS for SMEs* specifies that if an entity is unable to make a reliable estimate of the useful life, it is presumed to be ten years, simplifying things even further.

Goodwill on Whitebirk's acquisition of Close will be calculated as:

	$'000
Consideration transferred	5,700
Non-controlling interest: 10% × $6m	600
	6,300
Less fair value of identifiable net assets acquired	(6,000)
Goodwill	300

This goodwill of $0.3m will be amortised over ten years, that is $30,000 per annum.

(ii)   **Research and development expenditure**

The *IFRS for SMEs* requires all internally generated research and development expenditure to be **expensed through profit or loss.** This is simpler than full IFRS - IAS 38 *Intangible Assets* requires internally generated assets to be capitalised if certain criteria (proving future economic benefits) are met, and it is often difficult to determine whether or not they have been met.

Whitebirk's total expenditure on research ($0.5m) and development ($1m) must be written off to profit or loss for the year, giving a charge of $1.5m.

Mock exams

ACCA

Paper P2

Corporate Reporting (International)

Mock Examination 1

Question Paper	
Time allowed	
Reading and planning	**15 minutes**
Writing	**3 hours**
This paper is divided into two sections	
Section A	This ONE question is compulsory and MUST be attempted
Section B	TWO questions ONLY to be answered

DO NOT OPEN THIS PAPER UNTIL YOU ARE READY TO START UNDER EXAMINATION CONDITIONS

SECTION A – This ONE question is compulsory and MUST be attempted

Question 1

(a) Jay, a public limited company, has acquired the following shareholdings in Gee and Hem, both public limited companies.

Date of Acquisition	Holding acquired	Fair value of net assets	Purchase consideration
		$m	$m
Gee			
1 June 20X3	30%	40	15
1 June 20X4	50%	50	30
Hem			
1 June 20X4	25%	32	12

The following statements of financial position relate to Jay, Gee and Hem at 31 May 20X5.

	Jay	Gee	Hem
	$m	$m	$m
Property, plant and equipment	300	40	30
Investment in Gee	52		
Investment in Hem	22		
Current assets	100	20	15
Total assets	474	60	45
Share capital of $1	100	10	6
Share premium account	50	20	14
Revaluation surplus	15		
Retained earnings	139	16	10
Total equity	304	46	30
Non-current liabilities	60	4	3
Current liabilities	110	10	12
Total equity and liabilities	474	60	45

The following information is relevant to the preparation of the group financial statements of the Jay Group.

(i) Gee and Hem have not issued any new share capital since the acquisition of the shareholdings by Jay. The excess of the fair value of the net assets of Gee and Hem over their carrying amounts at the dates of acquisition is due to an increase in the value of Gee's non-depreciable land of $10 million at 1 June 20X3 and a further increase of $4 million at 1 June 20X4, and Hem's non-depreciable land of $6 million at 1 June 20X4. There has been no change in the value of non-depreciable land since 1 June 20X4. Before obtaining control of Gee, Jay did not have significant influence over Gee but has significant influence over Hem. Jay has accounted for the investment in Gee at fair value with changes being recorded in profit or loss. The market price of the shares of Gee at 31 May 20X5 had risen to $6.50 per share as there was speculation regarding a takeover bid.

(ii) On 1 June 20X4, Jay sold goods costing $13 million to Gee for $19 million. Gee has used the goods in constructing a machine which began service on 1 December 20X4. Additionally, on 31 May 20X5, Jay purchased a portfolio of investments from Hem at a cost of $10 million on which Hem had made a profit of $2 million. These investments have been incorrectly included in Jay's statement of financial position under the heading 'Investment in Hem'.

(iii) Jay sold some machinery with a carrying value of $5 million on 28 February 20X5 for $8 million. The terms of the contract, which was legally binding from 28 February 20X5, was that the purchaser would pay a non-refundable initial deposit of $2 million followed by two instalments of $3·5 million (including total interest of $1 million) payable on 31 May 20X5 and 20X6. The purchaser was in financial difficulties at the year end and subsequently went into liquidation on 10 June 20X5. No payment is expected from the liquidator. The deposit had been received on 28 February 20X5 but the first instalment was not received. The terms of the agreement were such that Jay maintained title to the machinery until the first instalment was paid. The machinery was still physically held by Jay and the machinery had been treated as sold in the financial statements. The amount outstanding of $6 million is included in current assets and no interest has been accrued in the financial statements.

(iv) Group policy on depreciation of plant and equipment is that depreciation of 10% is charged on a reducing balance basis.

(v) There are no intra-group amounts outstanding at 31 May 20X5.

(vi) It is the group's policy to value the non-controlling interest on acquisition at fair value. The fair value at the non-controlling interest in Gee on 1 July 20X4 was $12m.

Required

Prepare the consolidated statement of financial position of the Jay Group as at 31 May 20X5 in accordance with International Financial Reporting Standards.

(Candidates should calculate figures to one decimal place of $ million.) **(35 marks)**

(b) In the year ended 31 May 20X6 Jay purchased goods from a foreign supplier for 8 million euros on 28 February 20X6. At 31 May 20X6, the trade payable was still outstanding and the goods were still held by Jay. Similarly Jay has sold goods to a foreign customer for 4 million euros on 28 February 20X6 and it received payment for the goods in euros on 31 May 20X6. additionally Jay had purchased an investment property on 1 June 20X5 for 28 million euros. At 31 May 20X6, the investment property had a fair value of 24 million euros. The company uses the fair value model in accounting for investment properties.

Jay would like advice on how to treat this transaction in the financial statements for the year ended 31 May 20X6. Its functional and presentation currency is the dollar.

Exchange rates	Euro: $	Average rate (Euro: $) for year to
1 June 20X5	1.4	
28 February 20X6	1.6	
31 May 20X6	1.3	1.5

(8 marks)

(c) Jay has a reputation for responsible corporate behaviour and sees the workforce as the key factor in the profitable growth of the business. The company is also keen to provide detailed disclosures relating to environmental matters and sustainability.

Discuss what matters should be disclosed in Jay's annual report in relation to the nature of corporate citizenship, in order that there might be a better assessment of the performance of the company. **(7 marks)**

(Total = 50 marks)

SECTION B – TWO questions ONLY to be attempted

Question 2

6/08

Sirus is a large national public limited company (plc). The directors' service agreements require each director to purchase 'B' ordinary shares on becoming a director and this capital is returned to the director on leaving the company. Any decision to pay a dividend on the 'B' shares must be approved in a general meeting by a majority of all of the shareholders in the company. Directors are the only holders of 'B' shares.

Sirus would like advice on how to account under International Financial Reporting Standards (IFRSs) for the following events in its financial statements for the year ended 30 April 20X8.

(a) The capital subscribed to Sirus by the directors and shareholders is shown as follows in the statement of financial position as at 30 April 20X8:

Equity

	$m
Ordinary 'A' shares	100
Ordinary 'B' shares	20
Retained earnings	30
Total equity	150

On 30 April 20X8 the directors had recommended that $3 million of the profits should be paid to the holders of the ordinary 'B' shares, in addition to the $10 million paid to directors under their employment contracts. The payment of $3 million had not been approved in a general meeting. The directors would like advice as to whether the capital subscribed by the directors (the ordinary 'B' shares) is equity or a liability and how to treat the payments out of profits to them. **(6 marks)**

(b) When a director retires, amounts become payable to the director as a form of retirement benefit as an annuity. These amounts are not based on salaries paid to the director under an employment contract. Sirus has contractual or constructive obligations to make payments to former directors as at 30 April 20X8 as follows.

    (i) Certain former directors are paid a fixed annual amount for a fixed term beginning on the first anniversary of the director's retirement. If the director dies, an amount representing the present value of the future payment is paid to the director's estate.

    (ii) In the case of other former directors, they are paid a fixed annual amount which ceases on death.

The rights to the annuities are determined by the length of service of the former directors and are set out in the former directors' service contracts. **(6 marks)**

(c) On 1 May 20X7 Sirus acquired another company, Marne plc. The directors of Marne, who were the only shareholders, were offered an increased profit share in the enlarged business for a period of two years after the date of acquisition as an incentive to accept the purchase offer. After this period, normal remuneration levels will be resumed. Sirus estimated that this would cost them $5 million at 30 April 20X8, and a further $6 million at 30 April 20X9. These amounts will be paid in cash shortly after the respective year ends. **(5 marks)**

(d) Sirus raised a loan with a bank of $2 million on 1 May 20X7. The market interest rate of 8% per annum is to be paid annually in arrears and the principal is to be repaid in 10 years time. The terms of the loan allow Sirus to redeem the loan after seven years by paying the interest to be charged over the seven year period, plus a penalty of $200,000 and the principal of $2 million. The effective interest rate of the repayment option is 9.1%. The directors of Sirus are currently restructuring the funding of the company and are in initial discussions with the bank about the possibility of repaying the loan within the next financial year. Sirus is uncertain about the accounting treatment for the current loan agreement and whether the loan can be shown as a current liability because of the discussions with the bank. **(6 marks)**

Appropriateness of the format and presentation of the report and quality of discussion **(2 marks)**

Draft a report to the directors of Sirus which discusses the principles and nature of the accounting treatment of the above elements under International Financial Reporting Standards in the financial statements for the year ended 30 April 20X8.

(Total = 25 marks)

Question 3

ACR, 6/07

(a) Router, a public limited company, operates in the entertainment industry. It recently agreed with a television company to make a film which will be broadcast on the television company's network. The fee agreed for the film was $5 million with a further $100,000 to be paid every time the film is shown on the television company's channels. It is hoped that it will be shown on four occasions. The film was completed at a cost of $4 million and delivered to the television company on 1 April 20X7. The television company paid the fee of $5 million on 30 April 20X7 but indicated that the film needed substantial editing before they were prepared to broadcast it, the costs of which would be deducted from any future payments to Router. The Directors of Router wish to recognise the anticipated future income of $400,000 in the financial statements for the year ended 31 May 20X7. **(5 marks)**

(b) Router has a number of film studios and office buildings. The office buildings are in prestigious areas whereas the film studios are in 'out of town' locations. The management of Router wish to apply the 'revaluation model' to the office buildings and the 'cost model' to the film studios in the year ended 31 May 20X7. At present both types of building are valued using the 'revaluation model'. One of the film studios has been converted to a theme park. In this case only, the land and buildings on the park are leased on a simple lease from a third party. The lease term was thirty years seventeen years ago. The lease of the land and buildings was classified as a finance lease even though the financial statements purport to comply with IAS 17 *Leases*.

The terms of the lease were changed on 31 May 20X7. Router is now going to terminate the lease early in eight years' time in exchange for a payment of $10 million on 31 May 20X7 and a reduction in the monthly lease payments. Router intends to move from the site in eight years' time. The revised lease terms have not resulted in a change of classification of the lease in the financial statements of Router. **(10 marks)**

(c) At 1 June 20X6, Router held a 25% shareholding in a film distribution company, Wireless, a public limited company, which it had purchased for $50m, when Wireless's reserves were $40m. On 1 January 20X7, Router sold a 15% holding in Wireless thus reducing its investment to a 10% holding. Router no longer exercises significant influence over Wireless. Before the sale of the shares the reserves of Wireless on 1 January 20X7 were $60m and the goodwill relating to the acquisition of Wireless was $5 million. Router received $40 million for its sale of the 15% holding in Wireless. At 1 January 20X7, the fair value of the remaining investment in Wireless was $23 million and at 31 May 20X7 the fair value was $26 million **(6 marks)**

(d) Additionally Router purchased 60% of the ordinary shares of a radio station, Playtime, a public limited company, on 31 May 20X7. The remaining 40% of the ordinary shares are owned by a competitor company who owns a substantial number of warrants issued by Playtime which are currently exercisable. If these warrants are exercised, they will result in Router only owning 35% of the voting shares of Playtime. **(4 marks)**

Required

Discuss how the above items should be dealt in with the group financial statements of Router for the year ended 31 May 20X7. **(Total = 25 marks)**

Question 4

Handrew, a public limited company, is adopting International Financial Reporting Standards (IFRS) in its financial statements for the year ended 31 May 20X5. The directors of the company are worried about the effect of the move to IFRS on their financial performance and the views of analysts. The directors have highlighted some 'headline' differences between IFRS and their current local equivalent standards and require a report on the impact of a move to IFRS on the key financial ratios for the current period.

Differences between local Generally Accepted Accounting Practice (GAAP) and IFRS

Leases

Local GAAP does not require property leases to be separated into land and building components. Long-term property leases are accounted for as operating leases in the financial statements of Handrew under local GAAP. Under the terms of the contract, the title to the land does not pass to Handrew but the title to the building passes to the company.

The company has produced a schedule of future minimum operating lease rentals and allocated these rentals between land and buildings based on their relative fair value at the start of the lease period. The operating leases commenced on 1 June 20X4 when the value of the land was $270 million and the building was $90 million. Annual operating lease rentals paid in arrears commencing on 31 May 20X5 are land $30 million and buildings $10 million. These amounts are payable for the first five years of the lease term after which the payments diminish. The minimum lease term is 40 years.

The net present value of the future minimum operating lease payments as at 1 June 20X4 was land $198 million and buildings $86 million. The interest rate used for discounting cash flows is 6%. Buildings are depreciated on a straight line basis over 20 years and at the end of this period, the building's economic life will be over. The lessor intends to redevelop the land at some stage in the future. Assume that the tax allowances on buildings are given to the lessee on the same basis as the depreciation charge based on the net present value at the start of the lease, and that operating lease payments are fully allowable for taxation.

Plant and equipment

Local GAAP requires the residual value of a non-current asset to be measured at the date of acquisition or latest valuation. The residual value of much of the plant and equipment is deemed to be negligible. However, certain plant (cost $20 million and carrying value $16 million at 31 May 20X5) has a high residual value. At the time of purchasing this plant (June 20X3), the residual value was thought to be approximately $4 million. However the value of an item of an identical piece of plant already of the age and in the condition expected at the end of its useful life is $8 million at 31 May 20X5 ($11 million at 1 June 20X4). Plant is depreciated on a straight line basis over eight years.

Investment properties

Local GAAP requires investment property to be measured at market value and gains and losses reported in equity. The company owns a hotel which consists of land and buildings and it has been designated as an investment property. The property was purchased on 1 June 20X4. The hotel has been included in the statement of financial position at 31 May 20X5 at its market value on an existing use basis at $40 million (land valuation $30 million, building $10 million). A revaluation gain of $5 million has been recognised in equity. The company could sell the land for redevelopment for $50 million although it has no intention of doing so at the present time. The company wants to recognise holding gains/losses in profit and loss. Local GAAP does not require deferred tax to be provided on revaluation gains and losses.

The directors have calculated the following ratios based on the local GAAP financial statements for the year ended 31 May 20X5.

Return on capital employed

$$\frac{\text{Profit before interest and tax}}{\text{Share capital, reserves and non-current liabilities}} \quad \frac{\$130m}{\$520m} \times 100\% \text{ ie } 25\%$$

Gearing ratio

$$\frac{\text{Non - current liabilities}}{\text{Share capital and reserves}} \qquad \frac{\$40m}{\$480m} \times 100\% \text{ ie } 8.3\%$$

Price Earnings ratio

$$\frac{\text{Market price per share}}{\text{Earnings per share}} \qquad \frac{\$6 \text{ per share}}{\$0.5 \text{ per share}} \text{ ie } 12$$

The issued share capital of Handrew is 200 million ordinary shares of $1. There is no preference capital. The interest charge and tax charge in the statements of profit or loss are $5 million and $25 million respectively. Interest and rental payments attract tax allowances in this jurisdiction when paid. Assume taxation is 30%.

Required

Write a report to the directors of Handrew:

(a)   Discussing the impact of the change to IFRS on the reported profit and statement of financial position of Handrew at 31 May 20X5.   **(18 marks)**

(b)   Calculate and briefly discuss the impact of the change to IFRS on the three performance ratios.

(7 marks)

(Candidates should show in an appendix calculations of the impact of the move to IFRS on profits, taxation and the statement of financial position. Candidates should not take into account IFRS 1 *First time adoption of International Financial Reporting Standards* when answering this question.)

(Total = 25 marks)

Answers

DO NOT TURN THIS PAGE UNTIL YOU HAVE
COMPLETED THE MOCK EXAM

A PLAN OF ATTACK

If this were the real Corporate Reporting exam and you had been told to turn over and begin, what would be going through your mind?

The answer may be 'I can't do this to save my life'! You've spent most of your study time on groups and current issues (because that's what your tutor/BPP Study Text told you to do), plus a selection of other topics, and you're really not sure that you know enough. The good news is that this may get you through. The first question, in Section A, is very likely to be on groups. In Section B you have to choose three out of four questions, and at least one of those is likely to be on current issues – a new IFRS, ED or discussion paper. So there's no need to panic. First spend **five minutes or so looking at the paper**, and develop a **plan of attack**.

Looking through the paper

The compulsory question in Section A is, as a case study on groups, in this case a complex group. You also have a fairly easy bit on corporate citizenship. In **Section B** you have **four questions on a variety of topics:**

- Question 2 is a mixed bag question, covering financial instruments, retirement benefits, business combinations and a loan agreement
- Question 3 requires a discussion about issues concerning a change in a accounting policy.
- Question 4 is about the implications of a move to IFRS.

You **only have to answer three out of these four questions.** You don't have to pick your optional questions right now, but this brief overview should have convinced you that you have enough **choice** and variety to have a respectable go at Section B. So let's go back to the compulsory question in Section A.

Compulsory question

Question 1 requires you to **prepare a consolidated statement of financial position for a complex group**. This question looks daunting, partly because of the piecemeal acquisition aspects. However, there are easy marks to be gained for basic consolidation techniques such as intragroup trading. Part (c) is a good source of easy marks too.

Optional questions

Deciding between the optional questions is obviously a personal matter – it depends how you have spent your study time. However, here are a few pointers.

Question2 is a multi-standard question covering financial instruments, employee benefits and business combinations. You should be able to answer parts of this, if not the whole question.

Question 3 is about a specialised entity. However, it uses knowledge from standards you have covered, so you should be able to find a way in.

Question 4 is fairly straight forward if you know the topic. In our opinion, everyone should do this question.

Allocating your time

BPP's advice is always allocate your time **according to the marks for the question** in total and for the parts of the question. But **use common sense.** If you're doing Question 1 but have no idea about fair value, jot down something (anything!) and move onto Part (b), where most of the easy marks are to be gained.

Forget about it!

And don't worry if you found the paper difficult. More than likely other candidates will too. The paper is marked fairly leniently and always has a good pass rate. If this were the real thing, you would need to **forget** the exam the minute you left the exam hall and **think about the next one**. Or, if it's the last one, **celebrate**!

Question 1

Marking scheme

			Marks
(a)	Property, plant and equipment		4
	Goodwill		5
	Associate		4
	Investment		1
	Current assets		1
	Share capital		1
	Revaluation surplus		2
	Retained earnings		7
	Non-controlling interest		6
	Non-current liabilities		4
	Current liabilities		
(b)	Inventory, goods sold		8
(c)	Corporate citizenship:		
	Corporate governance		2
	Ethics		2
	Employee reports		2
	Environment		1
		Maximum	50

(a) JAY GROUP
     CONSOLIDATED STATEMENT OF FINANCIAL POSITION AT 31 MAY 20X5

	$m
Assets	
Property, plant and equipment (W9) 300 + 40 + 14 + (5 – 0.1) – 5.7 (W9)	353.2
Goodwill (W2)	10.0
Investment in associate (W3)	13.0
Investment (10 – 0.5) (W6)	9.5
Current assets (120 – 6) (W7)	114.0
	499.7
Equity and liabilities	
Share capital	100.0
Share premium	50.0
Revaluation surplus (W8)	15.0
Retained earnings (W4)	136.7
	301.7
Non-controlling interest (W5)	14.0
	315.7
Non-current liabilities	64.0
Current liabilities	120.0
	499.7

Workings

1   *Group structure*

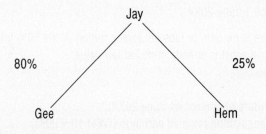

2   *Goodwill: Gee (on acquiring control)*

	$m
Consideration transferred	30
Non-controlling interests	12
Fair value of previously held equity interest	
($30m consideration transferred × 30%/50%)	18
Fair value of identifiable net assets at acq'n	(50)
	10

3   *Investment in associate*

	$m
Cost of investment	12
Share of profit for year ended 31 May 20X5 (W5)	1
	13

4   Retained earnings

	Jay	Gee	Hem
	$m	$m	$m
Per question	139.00	16	10
PUP on machinery (W6)	(5.70)		
PUP on investment (associate) (W6)	(0.5)		
Impairment loss on receivable	(1.10)		
Pre-acquisition (NA excl FV adjustments, SC and SP):			
50 – 14 – 10 – 20		(6)	
32 – 6 – 6 – 14			(6)
		10	4
Group share			
Gee: 80% × 10	8.0		
Hem: 25% × 4	1		
Less fair value gain recognised in Jay's separate			
FS since Gee has been a sub *:	(4.0)		
	136.7		

	$m
* Fair value gain in Jay's separate FS since Gee has been a sub (from 1 June 20X4)	
Fair value of 80% at 31 May 20X5	52
Less: Fair value of 40% at 1 June 20X4	(30)
Less: Fair value of 30% at 1 June 20X4 (30 x 30%/50%)	(18)
Fair value gain since 1 June 20X4	4

Tutorial note. There is no gain or loss on derecognition of the 30% financial asset at 1 June 20X4 because the financial asset is already stated at fair value.

5   Non-controlling interests

	$m
NCI at acquisition (date of control ie1 June 20X4)	12
NCI share of post acquisition retained earnings ((W4) 10 × 20%)	2
	14

6   Provision for unrealised profit
Sales from Jay to Gee

	$m
Profit (19 – 13)	6.0
Less depreciation on machine constructed with goods: (6 × 10% × 6/12)	(0.3)
	5.7

Sale of investments from Hem to Jay

	$m
Group share of profit (25% × 2)	0.5

7   Impairment of receivable

	$m
Cost of machinery	8.0
Less deposit received	(2.0)
Bad debt written off	6.0
Less net book value of machine (included in tangible assets) (W9)	(4.9)
Impairment loss deducted from retained earnings	1.1

8   Revaluation surplus

	$m
Jay	15.00
Gee: at date control acquired (80% × 14 – 14)	0.00
	15.00

9 *Property, plant and equipment*

	$m	$m
Jay		300.0
Gee		40.0
Fair value adjustment (land)		14.0
Machine		
Cost	5.0	
Less depreciation (3/12 × 10% × 5)	(0.1)	
		4.9
Provision for unrealised profit (W6)		(5.7)
		353.2

Note that Jay has retained title to the machinery because the first instalment has not been paid.

(b) The initial transaction of the purchase of goods from the foreign supplier would be **recorded in the ledger accounts at $5 million (€8/1.6)**. Therefore both the purchase and the payables balance would be recorded at this amount. At the **year end** the payables balance is **restated to the closing rate** but the **inventories remain at $5 million**. Therefore the payable is restated to $6.2 million (€8m/1.3) and an **exchange loss** is taken to profit or loss of $1.2 million ($6.2 – 5m).

On the **sale**, the original transaction is recorded at $2.5 million (€4m/1.6) as both a sale and a receivable. When payment is made the amount actually received is $3.1 million (€4m/1.3) and an **exchange gain** is recognised in profit or loss of $0.6 million ($3.1 – 2.5m).

When the investment property was first purchased it should have been recognised in the statement of financial position at $20 million (€28m/1.4). At the year end the investment property has fallen in value to €24 million and the exchange rate has changed to 1.3. Therefore at 31 May 20X6 the property would be valued at $18.5 million (€24m/1.3).

The **fall in value** of $1.5 million ($20 – 18.5m) is recognised in **profit or loss**. The loss is a mixture of a fall in value of the property and a gain due to the exchange rate movement. However, as the investment property is a **non-monetary asset the foreign currency element is not recognised separately**.

(c) **Nature of corporate citizenship**

Increasingly businesses are expected to be **socially responsible as well as profitable**. Strategic decisions by businesses, particularly global businesses nearly always have wider social consequences. It could be argued, as Henry Mintzburg does, that a company produces two outputs: goods and services, and the social consequences of its activities, such as pollution.

One major development in the area of corporate citizenship is the **environmental report.** While this is not a legal requirement, a large number of major companies produce them. Worldwide there are around 20 award schemes for environmental reporting, notably the ACCA's.

Jay might be advised to adopt the guidelines on sustainability given in the **Global Reporting Initiative**. These guidelines cover a number of areas (economic, environmental and social). The GRI specifies key performance indicators for each area. For environmental reporting, the indicators are:

(i)   Energy
(ii)   Water
(iii)   Biodiversity
(iv)   Emissions
(v)   Energy and waste
(vi)   Products and services
(vii)   Compliance
(viii) Transport

Another environmental issue which the company could consider is **emission levels** from factories. Many companies now include details of this in their environmental report.

The other main aspect of corporate citizenship where Jay scores highly is in its **treatment of its workforce.** The company sees the workforce as the key factor in the growth of its business. The car industry had a reputation in the past for **restrictive practices,** and the annual report could usefully discuss the extent to which these have been eliminated.

Employees of a businesses are **stakeholders** in that business, along with shareholders and customers. A company wishing to demonstrate good corporate citizenship will therefore be concerned with **employee welfare**. Accordingly, the annual report might usefully contain information on details of working hours, industrial accidents and sickness of employees.

In conclusion, it can be seen that the annual report can, and should go **far beyond the financial statements** and traditional ratio analysis.

Question 2

Text reference. Chapter 7 of the Study Text deals with financial instruments. Chapter 5 covers employee benefits. Business combinations are covered in Chapters 12 to 17, with this topic mainly being covered in Chapter 12.

Top tips. This is a 'mixed bag' question, dealing with aspects of financial instruments, retirement benefits, business combinations and a loan agreement. Part (a) requires a clear understanding of the distinction between liability and equity. Part (b), on retirement benefits needed you to understand the principles behind the creation of a provision and present value techniques, taking into account actuarial considerations in determining the liability. Part (c) dealt with the acquisition of a subsidiary and a contingent payment. (Bear in mind that the treatment of contingent consideration changed with the revision of IFRS 3.) Part (d) involved the early repayment of the loan.

Easy marks. These are available for stating the principles governing the accounting treatment, even if you make mistakes with the figures.

Examiner's comment. The examiner was reasonably satisfied with answers to Parts (b), (c) and (d). However, he was disappointed that, in Part (a), many did not seem to know the definitions of equity and liability. Lack of technical knowledge was a weakness in this question, as was time management.

Marking scheme

		Marks
(a)	Definition of financial liability and equity	3
	Principle in IAS 32	1
	Discussion	2
(b)	IAS 19	1
	Financial liability	2
	Provision	1
	Build up over service period	1
	Recalculate annually	1
(c)	Purchase method	1
	Cost of business combinations	1
	Future payment	1
	Remuneration versus cost of acquisition	2
(d)	Not exercised	2
	Expected exercise	1
	IFRS 9	1
	Current v non-current	2
Communication in report		2
	Maximum	25

Report

To: The Directors, Sirus
From: Accountant
Date: 15 June 20X8

Accounting treatment of items in the financial statements

(a)   **Directors' ordinary 'B' shares**

The capital of Sirus must be shown **either as a liability or as equity**. The criteria for distinguishing between financial liabilities and equity are found in IAS 32 *Financial instruments: presentation.* Equity and liabilities must be classified **according to their substance, not just their legal form,**

A **financial liability** is defined as any liability that is:

(i)   A contractual obligation:

–   To deliver cash or another financial asset to another entity, or

–   To exchange financial instruments with another entity under conditions that are potentially unfavourable; or

(ii)   a contract that will or may be settled in the entity's own equity instruments.

An **equity instrument** is any contract that evidences a **residual interest** in the assets of an entity after deducting all of its liabilities

The **ordinary 'B' shares,** the capital subscribed by the directors must, according to the directors' service agreements, be returned to any director on leaving the company. There is thus a **contractual obligation** to deliver cash. The redemption **is not discretionary,** and Sirus has no right to avoid it. The mandatory nature of the repayment makes this capital a **liability** (if it were discretionary, it would be equity). On initial recognition, that is when the 'B' shares are purchased, the financial liability must be stated at the **present value of the amount due on redemption,** discounted over the life of the service contract. In subsequent periods, the financial liability may be carried at fair value through profit or loss, or at amortised cost under IFRS 9.

In contrast, the **payment of \$3 million** to holders of 'B' shares, is discretionary in that it must be approved in a general meeting by a majority of all shareholders. This approval may be refused, and so it would not be correct to show the \$3 million as a liability in the statement of financial position at 30 April 20X8. Instead, it should be recognised when approved. The dividend when recognised will be treated as **interest expense**. This is because IAS 32 (para 35-36) requires the treatment of dividends to follow the treatment of the instrument, ie because the instrument is treated as a liability, the dividends are treated as an expense.

(b)   **Directors' retirement benefits**

These are unfunded defined benefit plans, which are likely to be governed by IAS 19 *Employee benefits,* but IAS 32 and IFRS 9 on financial instruments, and IAS 37 *Provisions, contingent liabilities and contingent assets* also apply.

Sirus has contractual or constructive obligations to make payments to former directors. The treatment and applicable standard depends on the obligation.

(i)   **Fixed annuity with payment to director's estate on death**. This **meets the definition of a financial liability under IAS 32**, because there is a contractual obligation to deliver cash or a financial asset. The firm does not have the option to withhold the payment. The rights to these annuities are earned over the directors' period of service, so it follows that the costs should also be recognised over this service period.

(ii)   **Fixed annuity ceasing on death**

The timing of the death is clearly uncertain, which means that the annuities have a **contingent element** with a mortality risk to be calculated by an actuary. It meets the definition of an insurance contract, which is outside the scope of IFRS 9, as are employers' obligations under IAS 19. However, insofar as there is a constructive obligation, these annuities fall within the scope of IAS 37, because these are liabilities of uncertain timing or amount. The amount of the obligation should be measured

in a manner similar to a warranty provision: that is the **probability of the future cash outflow** of the present obligation should be measured for the class of all such obligations. An estimate of the costs should include any liability for post retirement payments that directors have earned so far. The liability should **be built up over the service period** and will in practice be calculated on an actuarial basis as under IAS 19 *Employee benefits*. If the effect is material, the liability will be discounted. It should be **re-calculated every year** to take account of directors joining or leaving, or any other changes.

(c) **Acquisition of Marne**

An increased profit share is payable to the directors of Marne if the purchase offer is accepted. The question arises of whether this additional payment constitutes **remuneration or consideration** for the business acquired. Because the payment is for two years only, after which time remuneration falls back to normal levels, the payment should be seen as part of the **purchase consideration.**

The second issue is the treatment of this consideration. IFRS 3 (revised January 2008) *Business combinations* requires that an acquirer must be identified for all business combinations. In this case Sirus is the acquirer. The cost of the combination must be measured as the sum of the fair values, at the date of exchange, of assets given or liabilities assumed in exchange for control.

IFRS 3 recognises that, by entering into an acquisition, the acquirer becomes obliged to make additional payments. Not recognising that obligation means that the consideration recognised at the acquisition date is not fairly stated.

The revised IFRS 3 **requires recognition of contingent consideration, measured at fair value, at the acquisition date.** This is, arguably, consistent with how other forms of consideration are fair valued.

The acquirer may be required to pay contingent consideration in the form of equity or of a debt instrument or cash. In this case, it is in the form of cash, or increased remuneration.

Accordingly, the **cost of the combination must include the full $11m,** measured at net present value at 1 May 20X7. The payment of $5 million would be discounted for one year and the payment of $6 million for two years.

(d) **Repayment of bank loan**

The bank loan is to be repaid in ten years' time, but the terms of the loan state that Syrus can pay it off in seven years. The issue arises as to **whether the early repayment option is likely to be exercised.**

If, when the loan was taken out on 1 May 20X7 the option **of early repayment was not expected to be exercised, t**hen at 30 April 20X8 the normal terms apply. The loan would be stated at $2 million in the statement of financial position, and the effective interest would be 8% × $2 million = $160,000, the interest paid.

If at 1 May 20X7 it was expected that the **early repayment option would be exercised**, then the **effective interest rate would be 9.1%,** and the effective interest 9.1% × $2 million = $182,000. The cash paid would still be $160,000, and the difference of $22,000 would be added to the carrying amount of the financial liability in the statement of financial position, giving $2,022,000.

IFRS 9 *Financial instruments* requires that the carrying amount of a financial asset or liability should be adjusted to reflect actual cash flows or revised estimates of cash flows. This means that, even if it was thought at the outset that early repayment would not take place, if **expectations then change, the carrying amount must be revised** to reflect future estimated cash flows using the effective interest rate.

The directors of Sirus are currently in discussion with the bank regarding repayment in the next financial year. However, these discussions do not create a legal obligation to repay the loan in twelve months, and Sirus has an unconditional right to defer settlement for longer than twelve months. Accordingly, **it would not be correct to show the loan as a current liability on the basis of the discussions with the bank.**

I hope that this report is helpful to you.

Signed, Accountant

Question 3

Marking scheme

		Marks
(a)	Revenue recognition	5
(b)	Studios and offices	10
(c)	Film distribution company	7
(d)	Playtime	4
	Available	26
	Maximum	25

(a) **Recognition of income from the film**

IAS 18 *Revenue* states that **revenue** on a service contract may **only be recognised** when the outcome of the transaction can be **measured reliably**. If **certain criteria** are met, the stage of completion method may be used, that is revenue should be recognised by reference to the stage of completion of the transaction at the reporting date. The criteria are as follows.

(i) The amount of revenue can be measured reliably.
(ii) It is probable that economic benefits will flow to the seller.
(iii) The stage of completion at the reporting date can be measured reliably.
(iv) The costs incurred, or costs to be incurred, can be measured reliably.

If these criteria are not met, revenue arising from the rendering of services should be recognised **only to the extent that that expenses recognised are recoverable**.

In the case of Router, the **fee for making the film of $5m can** be measured reliably, has been paid and **can therefore be recognised** and matched against the costs incurred of $4m. However, the **anticipated future income of $400,000 should not be recognised**. The $100,000 will only be received when the film is shown, which is expected to be four times. However, the revenue should not be recognised before then because there is a **'performance' condition**, namely the substantial editing that is required before the film can be shown.

The **costs of editing need to be assessed** and matched against any revenue in future years. However, costs incurred to date **cannot be carried forward** and matched against future income unless they meet the IAS 38 definition of an intangible asset, and this does not appear to be the case.

(b) **Land and buildings**

IAS 16 *Property, plant and equipment* allows assets to be revalued, provided all assets within one class are treated in the same way. While the Router's buildings (office buildings and film studios) have different characteristics and could be **classified differently under IAS 16**, to change from the revaluation model to the cost model for the film studios involves a change in accounting policy, and may conflict with IAS 8 *Accounting policies, changes in accounting estimates and errors.*

The **general rule** under IAS 8 is that an entity should apply accounting policies **consistently** from year to year. Accounting policies may be changed only in two specific cases:

(i)   There has been a **new accounting standard** or interpretation or changes to an accounting standard.

(ii) The change results in the financial statements providing **more reliable and more relevant information** about the effects of transactions, other events or conditions on the entity's financial position, financial performance or cash flows.

The first criterion does not apply here, and Routers will have to ascertain whether the second is appropriate. If the 'cost model' is adopted, the following **adjustments** will need to be made:

(i)   Calculate depreciated historical cost at the beginning of the period.

(ii) Adjust the opening balance on the revaluation surplus and any other component of equity affected.

(iii) Present comparative amounts, as if the accounting policy had always been applied.

Currently the theme park land and buildings are classified as a **finance lease**. This is unusual. Land is normally classified as an **operating lease** because it is considered to have an **indefinite life**, the exception being when ownership passes to the lessee during the lease term. The policy is not appropriate and **adjustments** need to be made:

(i)   Separate the land out from the lease.

(ii) Remove the asset and liability relating to the land from the statement of financial position.

(iii) Treat the lease payments as rentals in the income statement

(iv) Make a prior period adjustment to reflect this change.

The **buildings may continue to be treated as property, plant and equipment**, and no adjustment needs to be made to the carrying value. However, in future years the carrying value will be **depreciated over a shorter period**, reflecting the decrease in the remaining useful life of the building, following the **change in the lease terms** on 31 May 20X7.

The change in the lease term will also require the lease liability to be **assessed for derecognition** IFRS 9 *Financial instruments.* This would be appropriate if the new lease terms are **substantially different** from the current terms, but that **does not appear to the case here**. The change appears to be a **modification, not an extinguishment**. After separating out the land, the lease liability will then be amended further by **deducting the one off payment of $10m** from the carrying amount, together with any transaction costs. The **liability will be remeasured** (taking any difference on remeasurement to profit or loss) to the present value of revised future cash flows discounted using the original effective interest rate.

(c) **Sale of 15% holding in Wirerles**

Wireless is **currently an associate** and is accounted for under the equity method in accordance with IAS 28 *Investments in associates.* The reduction from a 25% holding to a 10% holding and the loss of significant influence means that, **after the sale**, it must be accounted for in **accordance with IFRS 9**. Router must recognise in profit or loss a gain on disposal, calculated as follows:

	$m
Fair value of consideration received	40
Fair value of interest retained	23
Equity valuation at disposal:	
Cost	(50)
Share of post acquisition reserves 25% × ($60m -- $40m)	(5)
	8

The gain to be recognised is therefore $8m.

At 1 January 20X7, after the disposal, the 10% financial asset remaining is held at its fair value of $23m.

Under IFRS 9, the remaining investment will be classified as **an investment in equity instruments or a financial asset at fair value through profit and loss**. The asset will be **recorded at fair value**. If an irrecoverable election has been made in accordance with IFRS 9, changes in fair value will be reported in other comprehensive income (items that will not be reclassified to profit or loss).

At 31 May 20X7, the asset will be remeasured and a **gain** of $26m – $23m = $3m **reported in other comprehensive income or in profit or loss, depending on whether the irrevocable election has been made.**

(d) **Investment in Playtime**

Although Router owns 60% of the shares of Playtime, which would normally give it control, the warrants held by the competitor company, currently exercisable, mean that this **control is in doubt.** Unlike its predecessor, IAS 2, IFRS 10 *Consolidated financial statements* does not specifically mention warrants. However, it states that an investor controls an investee if it has power over the investee, and defines power as 'existing rights that give the investor the ability to direct the activities of the investee. Voting power is the most obvious of these, and so warrants with the potential to give the holder voting power or reduce another party's voting power should be taken into account when assessing control. The **competitor would gain control** over Playtime if it exercised the warrants, and should therefore **consolidate Playtime**. Playtime cannot be controlled by both Router and the competitor, so it is probably more appropriate for **Router** to account for its investment in Playtime **under IAS 28, or even IFRS 9** if significant influence is reduced. All circumstances that affect voting rights, and not just share ownership, will need to be considered in reaching a decision.

Question 4

Text reference. International issues are covered in Chapter 19.

Top tips. This question dealt with the implications of a move to IFRS by a company. It is likely to become less frequent, though topical at the moment. Additionally, the impact of the changes of accounting policy on three key performance ratios had to be calculated and discussed. The question dealt with leases, plant and equipment, and investment properties, and the ratios to be adjusted were ROCE, gearing, and the PE ratio.

Easy marks. Marks were allocated for general principles, which candidates can easily score highly on. Additionally, marks were allocated for a report format. Marks are only given for the report if candidates set out the report in a formal way, with appendices for detailed calculations, but this is easy to do.

Examiner's comment. The question was quite well-answered although frequently the adjustments to the profit for the year and statement of financial position were inaccurate, and candidates could not deal with the deferred tax implications.

Marking scheme

		Marks
Report		4
(a)	Discussion	18
(b)	Discussion and calculation	7
	Available	29
	Maximum	25

REPORT

To: Directors of Handrew
From:
Subject: Impact of the move to International Financial Reporting Standards (IFRS)
Date: June 20X5

This report discusses the impact of the change to IFRS on the financial statements for the year ended 31 May 20X5, including the effect of the change on three key performance ratios. Calculations are included in an Appendix.

Leases

IAS 17 *Leases* classifies leases into finance leases and operating leases. A finance lease **transfers substantially all the risks and benefits of ownership** to the lessee while an operating lease does not. Unlike local GAAP, IAS 17 requires leases to be **separated** into **land and buildings components**. A lease of **land** is **normally classified as an operating lease**; a lease of **buildings** may be **either a finance lease or an operating lease.**

There are several indications that the company's **leases of land** *are* operating leases. **Title does not pass** at the end of the lease term. In addition, at 1 June 20X4 the **present value of the lease commitments was only 73% of the fair value of the land** (for a lease to be a finance lease the present value of the lease commitments must normally be 'substantially all' of the fair value of the leased asset). The **lessor intends to redevelop the land**, which also suggests that Handrew does not enjoy the benefits of ownership. In contrast, **title to the buildings does pass** to the company at the end of the lease term; the **present value of the lease commitments is 96%** (substantially all) **of the fair value of the buildings**; and the buildings are **leased for a period equal to their economic life**. The substance of the agreement appears to be that Handrew **has purchased the buildings** and the leases are financing arrangements, rather than rental agreements. The **leases of the buildings are finance leases.**

The buildings must be treated as assets of the company and **recognised on the statement of financial position**. **Non-current assets will increase by $86 million at 1 June 20X4** (the inception of the lease). The buildings should be **depreciated** over 20 years and therefore there will be an **expense of $4.3 million** and the **carrying value of the buildings will be $81.7 million** at 31 May 20X5. The company should also **recognise a corresponding liability for the lease rentals**. At 31 May 20X5 this is **$81.2 million** (see Appendix). **Current liabilities will increase by $5.1 million** (the amount due on 31 May 20X6) and **non-current liabilities will increase by $76.1 million. Interest of $5.2 million will be recognised** in profit or loss. The **tax charge for the year will also be affected**, as lease rentals on the buildings will no longer be included in the income statement as a taxable expense.

Leases of land **will continue to be treated as operating leases** and lease rentals of $30 million will be recognised in profit or loss.

Plant and equipment

IAS 16 *Property, plant and equipment* requires **residual values** of non-current assets **to be reviewed at each year end**. Residual value is defined as the **estimated amount** that the company **would currently obtain** from the disposal of the asset, if it were **already of the age** and **in the condition expected** at the **end of its useful life**. Any **changes in residual value** are **reflected in the depreciation charge** and are accounted for **prospectively,** as a change in accounting estimate. Depreciation is **reduced to zero** if the **residual value is equal to or greater than the asset's carrying value.**

Therefore under IAS 16 the residual value of the asset would be **$8 million** rather than $4 million. This means that the **depreciation charge** for the year ended 31 May 20X5 will be **$1 million**, rather than $2 million as at present (see Appendix).

Investment properties

IAS 40 *Investment property* allows investment properties to be measured **either at cost or at fair value**. If a property is **measured at fair value, gains and losses** on remeasurement **must be recognised in profit or loss**. As **the company wishes to do this**, it will **adopt the fair value model.** Under IFRS, fair value is normally taken to be **market value, rather than existing use value**. Therefore the hotel should be valued at **$50 million**. Because **the market price is obtainable** if the land is sold for redevelopment the land **should be valued at $50 million** and the **building at nil**.

Profit for the year is increased by the **revaluation gain of $15 million**. Of this amount, **$5 million has been previously recognised in equity** and would be **transferred to profit or loss**. IAS 12 *Income taxes* **requires deferred tax to be provided on revaluation gains**, regardless of whether there is an actual intention to sell the property.

Impact on performance ratios

Three key performance ratios have been calculated as follows:

	Local GAAP	IFRS
Return on capital employed	$\dfrac{130}{520} \times 100\% = 25\%$	$\dfrac{151.7}{607.45} \times 100\% = 24.9\%$
Gearing ratio	$\dfrac{40}{480} \times 100\% = 8.3\%$	$\dfrac{120.9}{486.55} \times 100\% = 24.8\%$
Price earnings ratio	$\dfrac{\$6}{\$0.5} = 12$	$\dfrac{\$6}{\$0.558} = 10.8$

There is very **little effect on return on capital employed. Profit has increased** by $21.7 million, mainly because the operating lease rentals have been excluded and the gain on revaluation has been included. However, **capital employed has also increased**, due to the recognition of the finance lease liability.

Gearing has increased significantly, mainly because of the recognition of the finance lease liability.

As a consequence of the increase in profits, **earnings per share has risen** and therefore the **price earnings ratio has fallen.**

Appendix: impact of the change to IFRS on profit, taxation and the statement of financial position

1   *Effect on profit*

	$m	$m
Profit before interest and tax under local GAAP		130.00
Add back operating lease rentals		10.00
Less: depreciation on building (86 ÷ 20)		(4.30)
Effect of increase in residual value: add back excess depreciation (W2)		1.00
Investment property: revaluation gain (5 + 10)		15.00
Profit before interest and tax under IFRS		151.70
Interest:		
Under local GAAP	5.0	
Add interest on finance leases (W1)	5.2	
		(10.20)
Taxation:		
Under local GAAP	25.00	
Add increase in charge under IFRS (Appendix 2)	4.95	
		(29.95)
Profit for the year under IFRS		111.55

Earnings per share under IFRS: $\dfrac{111.58}{200} = 55.8\text{c}$

2   *Effect on taxation*

	Current tax $m	Deferred tax $m	Total $m
Operating lease rentals (increase in profit)	10		
Interest expense on finance lease (decrease in profit)	(5.2)		
Tax deductible depreciation on plant (decrease in profit)	(4.3)		
Reduction of depreciation on plant (increase in profit)		1	
Gain on investment property (increase in profit)		15	
	0.5	16	16.5
Increase in tax charge at 30%	0.15	4.8	4.95

3   *Effect on statement of financial position amounts*

	Equity $m	Non-current liabilities $m	Net assets $m
At 31 May 20X5 under local GAAP	480.00	40.0	520.0
Lease (W1):			
Liability		86.0	86.0
Operating lease rentals	10.00	(10.0)	
Depreciation	(4.30)		(4.3)
Interest	(5.20)	5.2	
Current liability		(5.1)	(5.1)
Plant: depreciation (W2)	1.00		1.0
Investment property: gain	10.00		10.0
Tax (Appendix 2)	(4.95)	4.8	(0.15)
At 31 May 20X5 under IFRS	486.55	120.9	607.45

Workings

1   *Finance lease*

	$m
Net present value of future lease commitments	86.0
Interest at 6%	5.2
Repayment	(10.0)
Total liability at 31 May 20X5	81.2
Interest at 6%	4.9
Repayment	(10.0)
Total liability at 31 May 20X6	76.1

Therefore $5.1 million (10 – 4.9) is included in current liabilities.

2   *Excess depreciation*

	$m
Cost	20
Depreciation for year ended 31 May 20X4 (20 – 4 ÷ 8)	(2)
Carrying value at 1 June 20X4	18
Residual value at 1 June 20X4	(11)
Depreciable amount	7
Annual depreciation charge (7 ÷ 7)	1

ACCA

Paper P2

Corporate Reporting (International)

Mock Examination 2

Question Paper	
Time allowed	
Reading and planning	**15 minutes**
Writing	**3 hours**
This paper is divided into two sections	
Section A	This ONE question is compulsory and MUST be attempted
Section B	TWO questions ONLY to be answered

DO NOT OPEN THIS PAPER UNTIL YOU ARE READY TO START UNDER EXAMINATION CONDITIONS

ACCA

Paper P2

Corporate Reporting (International)

Mock Examination 2

Time allowed	
Reading and planning	15 minutes
Writing	3 hours

This paper is divided into two sections:

Section A   This ONE question is compulsory and MUST be attempted

Section B   TWO questions ONLY to be answered

DO NOT OPEN THIS PAPER UNTIL YOU ARE READY TO START UNDER EXAMINATION CONDITIONS

SECTION A – This ONE question is compulsory and MUST be attempted

Question 1

Beth, a public limited company, has produced the following draft statements of financial position as at 30 November 20X7. Lose and Gain are both public limited companies:

	Beth $m	Lose $m	Gain $m
Assets			
Non current assets			
Property, plant and equipment	1,700	200	300
Intangible assets	300		
Investment in Lose (at cost)	200		
Investment in Gain	180		
	2,380	200	300
Current assets			
Inventories	800	100	150
Trade receivables	600	60	80
Cash	500	40	20
	1,900	200	250
Total assets	4,280	400	550
Share capital of $1	1,500	100	200
Other reserves	300		
Retained earnings	400	200	300
Total equity	2,200	300	500
Non-current liabilities	700		
Current liabilities	1,380	100	50
Total liabilities	2,080	100	50
Total equity and liabilities	4,280	400	550

The following information is relevant to the preparation of the group financial statements of the Beth Group.

(i)	Date of acquisition	Holding acquired %	Retained earnings at acquisition $m	Purchase consideration $m
Lose:	1 December 20X5	20	80	40
	1 December 20X6	60	150	160
Gain:	1 December 20X6	30	260	180

Lose and Gain have not issued any share capital since the acquisition of the shareholdings by Beth. The fair values of the net assets of Lose and Gain were the same as their carrying amounts at the date of the acquisitions.

Beth did not have significant influence over Lose at any time before gaining control of Lose, but does have significant influence over Gain. There has been no impairment of goodwill on the acquisition of Lose since its acquisition, but the recoverable amount of the net assets of Gain has been deemed to be $610 million at 30 November 20X7.

It is the group's policy to value its non-controlling interests at fair value. The fair value of the non-controlling interest in Lose at 1 December 20X6 was $53.33m.

The fair value of the 20% holding in Lose on 30th November 20X6 was also $53.33m.

(ii) Lose entered into an operating lease for a building on 1 December 20X6. The building was converted into office space during the year at a cost to Lose of $10 million. The operating lease is for a period of six years, at the end of which the building must be returned to the lessor in its original condition. Lose thinks that it would cost $2 million to convert the building back to its original condition at prices at 30 November 20X7.

The entries that had been made in the financial statements of Lose were the charge for operating lease rentals ($4 million per annum) and the improvements to the building. Both items had been charged to the profit or loss. The improvements were completed during the financial year.

(iii)   On 1 October 20X7, Beth sold inventory costing $18 million to Gain for $28 million. At 30 November 20X7, the inventory was still held by Gain. The inventory was sold to a third party on 15 December 20X7 for $35 million.

(iv)   Beth had contracted to purchase an item of plant and equipment for 12 million euros on the following terms:

Payable on signing contract (1 September 20X7)	50%
Payable on delivery and installation (11 December 20X7)	50%

The amount payable on signing the contract (the deposit) was paid on the due date and is refundable. The following exchange rates are relevant:

20X7	Euros to 1 dollar
1 September	0.75
30 November	0.85
11 December	0.79

The deposit is included in trade receivables at the rate of exchange on 1 September 20X7. A full year's charge for depreciation of property, plant and equipment is made in the year of acquisition using the straight line method over six years.

(v)   Beth sold some trade receivables which arose during November 20X7 to a factoring company on 30 November 20X7. The trade receivables sold are unlikely to default in payment based on past experience but they are long dated with payment not due until 1 June 20X8. Beth has given the factor a guarantee that it will reimburse any amounts not received by the factor. Beth received $45 million from the factor being 90% of the trade receivables sold. The trade receivables are not included in the statement of financial position of Beth and the balance not received from the factor (10% of the trade receivables factored) of $5 million has been written off against retained earnings.

(vi)   Beth granted 200 share options to each of its 10,000 employees on 1 December 20X6. The shares vest if the employees work for the Group for the next two years. On 1 December 20X6, Beth estimated that there would be 1,000 eligible employees leaving in each year up to the vesting date. At 30 November 20X7, 600 eligible employees had left the company. The estimate of the number of employees leaving in the year to 30 November 20X8 was 500 at 30 November 20X7. The fair value of each share option at the grant date (1 December 20X6) was $10. The share options have not been accounted for in the financial statements.

(vii)   The Beth Group operates in the oil industry and contamination of land occurs including the pollution of seas and rivers. The Group only cleans up the contamination if it is a legal requirement in the country where it operates. The following information has been produced for Beth by a group of environmental consultants for the year ended 30 November 20X7:

Cost to clean up contamination	Law existing in country
$m	
5	No
7	To come into force in December 20X7
4	Yes

The directors of Beth have a widely publicised environmental attitude which shows little regard for the effects on the environment of their business. The Group does not currently produce a separate environmental report and no provision for environmental costs has been made in the financial statements. Any provisions would be shown as non-current liabilities. Beth is likely to operate in these countries for several years.

Other information

Beth is currently suffering a degree of stagnation in its business development. Its domestic and international markets are being maintained but it is not attracting new customers. Its share price has not increased whilst that of its competitors has seen a rise of between 10% and 20%. Additionally it has recently received a significant amount of adverse publicity because of its poor environmental record and is to be investigated by regulators in several countries. Although Beth is a leading supplier of oil products, it has never felt the need to promote socially responsible policies and practices or make positive contributions to society because it has always maintained its market share. It is renowned for poor customer support, bearing little regard for the customs and cultures in the

communities where it does business. It had recently made a decision not to pay the amounts owing to certain small and medium entities (SMEs) as the directors feel that SMEs do not have sufficient resources to challenge the non-payment in a court of law. The management of the company is quite authoritarian and tends not to value employees' ideas and contributions.

Required

(a) Prepare the consolidated statement of financial position of the Beth Group as at 30 November 20X7 in accordance with International Financial Reporting Standards. **(35 marks)**

(b) Describe to the Beth Group the possible advantages of producing a separate environmental report.

(8 marks)

(c) Discuss the ethical and social responsibilities of the Beth Group and whether a change in the ethical and social attitudes of the management could improve business performance. **(7 marks)**

Note. Requirement (c) includes 2 professional marks for development of the discussion of the ethical and social responsibilities of the Beth Group. **(Total = 50 marks)**

SECTION B – TWO questions ONLY to be attempted

Question 2

Enterprise, a public limited company, has four business segments which are reported separately in its internal accounts. The segments are vehicle leasing, vehicle sales, property letting, and insurance. Each business segment constituted a 100% owned subsidiary of the group except for the vehicle leasing and sales segments which comprised two subsidiaries each. The results of these segments for the year ended 30 April 20X4 before taking account of the information below are as follows.

SEGMENT INFORMATION AS AT 30 APRIL 20X4 BEFORE THE SALE OF CARP

		Revenue		Segment results (profit/(loss))	Segment assets	Segment liabilities
		External	Internal			
		$m	$m	$m	$m	$m
Vehicle leasing:	Carp	40	2	9	39	17
	Far	5	3	(1)	8	3
Vehicle sales:	Fish	30	5	(8)	35	12
	Near	25	0	(4)	12	4
Property letting		60	65	15	96	32
Insurance		40	4	(4)	58	47
		200	79	7	248	115

There were no significant intragroup balances in the segment assets and liabilities. Carp and Far, both public limited companies, formed the leasing segment and Carp was 80% and Far is 100% owned by Enterprise. Carp had been originally formed by the Enterprise Group. Enterprise decided to sell Carp and the sale was completed on 30 April 20X4. On the same date the group acquired a radio station. The fair values of the assets and liabilities of the radio station were respectively $30 million and $13 million. The purpose of the purchase of the radio station was to use it as a medium for advertising the group's services and products. The radio station is to be included within the 'Insurance' segment as it is principally this product that it will advertise.

The remainder of the share capital of Carp is owned by a director of Carp who is not a director of Enterprise. During the current financial year this director had leased a number of vehicles from Carp for his family members. The lease payments were agreed at a discount of 20% to the market rate.

The group operates a defined benefit pension scheme for its employees. During the year, the directors of Enterprise sold a property to the pension fund and entered into a leaseback agreement for the same property. The directors and some employees constitute the board of the pension fund and the fund is managed by a merchant bank. Before the sale of Carp, the group had a defined benefit obligation with a net present value of $50 million and plan assets with a fair value of $23 million. The sale of the subsidiary had reduced the net present value of the obligation at 30 April 20X4 to $37 million. No transfer of assets was made to the purchasing company's pension scheme.

Fish and Near, public limited companies, constitute the vehicle sales segment. They were wholly acquired on 1 May 20X1 from Motors, a public limited company, for $30 million when the fair value of their net assets was $22 million. At 30 April 20X2, when the carrying value of the net assets of Fish and Near were respectively $20 million and $5 million, an impairment review was carried out because of the impact of a new tax law on the goodwill and an impairment loss recognised. However, the actual net cash flows for the years 20X3 and 20X4 were higher than forecast, because of the pessimistic nature of the original forecasts and a change in economic conditions. The group revised the calculation of the recoverable amount of the segment based on a revision of all future cash flows from 1 May 20X4. The recoverable amount of Fish and Near at the respective dates is set out below:

	Recoverable amount at 30 April 20X2 (original cash flows)	Recoverable amount at 30 April 20X4 (revised cash flows)
	$m	$m
Fish	16	29
Near	8	10

The depreciated historical cost of Fish and Near's net assets at 30 April 20X4 was $26 million and $8 million. The assets had not previously been revalued.

The tax law is still in place at 30 April 20X4.

Required

(a) Discuss by specific reference to the information above:

    (i) Which segments of Enterprise would constitute a 'reportable' segment under IFRS 8 *Operating segments* as at 30 April 20X4, after the sale of Carp and the purchase of the radio station. **(7 marks)**

    (ii) Which parties would be deemed to be related parties under IAS 24 *Related party disclosures* for disclosure purposes in the financial statements of Carp and Enterprise as at 30 April 20X4. **(5 marks)**

(b) Calculate the financial effect of the sale of Carp on the pension scheme, showing the gain or loss resulting from the curtailment of the pension obligation and the net pension liability after the sale of Carp. **(6 marks)**

(c) Describe with suitable calculations, the nature of any impairment reviews that would have been carried out on the net assets of Fish and Near at 30 April 20X2 and 30 April 20X4. **(7 marks)**

(Total = 25 marks)

Question 3

The Gow Group, a public limited company, and Glass, a public limited company, have agreed to create a new entity, York, a limited liability company on 31 October 20X6. the companies' line of business is the generation, distribution, and supply of energy. Gow supplies electricity and Glass supplies gas to customers. Each company has agreed to subscribe net assets for a 50% share in the equity capital of York. York is to issue 30 million ordinary shares of $1. There was no written agreement signed by Gow and Glass but the minutes of the meeting where the creation of the new company was discussed have been formally approved by both companies. Each company provides equal numbers of directors to the Board of Directors. The net assets of York were initially shown at amounts agreed between Gow and Glass, but their values are to be adjusted so that the carrying amounts at 31 October 20X6 are based on International Financial Reporting Standards.

Gow had contributed the following assets to the new company in exchange for its share of the equity:

	$m
Cash	1
Trade receivables – Race	7
Intangible assets – contract with Race	3
Property, plant and equipment	9
	20

The above assets form a cash generating unit (an electricity power station) in its own right. The unit provided power to a single customer, Race. On 31 October 20X6 Race went into administration and the contract to provide power to Race was cancelled. On 1 December 20X6, the administrators of the customer provisionally agreed to pay a final settlement figure of $5 million on 31 October 20X7, including any compensation for the loss of the contract. Gow expects York will receive 80% of the provisional amount. On hearing of the cancelled contract, an offer was received for the power station of $16 million. York would be required to pay the disposal costs estimated at $1 million.

The power station has an estimated remaining useful life of four years at 31 October 20X6. it has been agreed with the government that it will be dismantled on 31 October 20Y0. The cost at 31 October 20Y0 of dismantling the power station is estimated to be $5 million.

The directors of Gow and York are currently in the final stages of negotiating a contract to supply electricity to another customer. As a result the future net cash inflows (undiscounted) expected to arise from the cash generating unit (power station) are as follows:

	$m
31 October 20X7	6
31 October 20X8	7
31 October 20X9	8
31 October 20Y0	8
	29

The dismantling cost has not been provided for, and future cash flows are discounted at 6 per cent by the companies.

Glass had agreed to contribute the following net assets to the new company in exchange for its share of the equity:

	$m
Cash	10
Intangible asset	2
Inventory at cost	6
Property at carrying value	4
Lease receivable	1
Lease payable	(3)
	20

The property contributed by Glass is held on a 10 year finance lease which was entered into on 31 October 20X0. The property is being depreciated over the life of the lease on the straight line basis. As from 31 October 20X6, the terms of the lease have been changed and the lease will be terminated early on 31 October 20X8 in exchange for a payment of $1 million on 31 October 20X6 and a further two annual payments of $600,000. The first annual payment under the revised terms will be on 31 October 20X7. York will vacate the property on 31 October 20X8 and the revised lease qualifies as a finance lease. The cash paid on 31 October 20X6 is shown as a lease receivable and the change in the lease terms is not reflected in the values placed on the net assets above. The effective interest rate of the lease is 7%.

Glass had entered into a contract with an agency whereby for every new domestic customer that the agency gained, the agency received a fixed fee. On the formation of York, the contract was terminated and the agency received $500,000 as compensation for the termination of the contract. This cost is shown as an intangible asset above as the directors feel that it represents the economic benefits related to the future reduced cost of gaining retail customers. Additionally, on 31 October 20X6, a contract was signed whereby York was to supply gas at fair value to a major retailer situated overseas over a four year period. On signing the contract, the retailer paid a non refundable cash deposit of $1.5 million which is included in the cash contributed by Glass. The retailer is under no obligation to buy gas from York but York cannot supply gas to any other company in that country. The directors intend to show this deposit in profit or loss when the first financial statements of York are produced. At present, the deposit is shown as a deduction from intangible assets in the above statement of net assets contributed by Glass.

(All calculations should be made to one decimal place and assume the cash flows relating to the cash generating unit (electricity power station) arise at the year end.)

Required

(a)   Discuss the nature and accounting treatment of the relationship between Gow, Glass and York.   **(5 marks)**

(b)   Prepare the statement of financial position of York at 31 October 20X6, using International Financial Reporting Standards, discussing the nature of the accounting treatments selected, the adjustments made and the values placed on the items in the statement of financial position.   **(20 marks)**

(Total = 25 marks)

Question 4

The transition to International Financial Reporting Standards (IFRSs) involves major change for companies as IFRSs introduce significant changes in accounting practices that were often not required by national generally accepted accounting practice. It is important that the interpretation and application of IFRSs is consistent from country to country. IFRSs are partly based on rules, and partly on principles and management's judgement. Judgement is more likely to be better used when it is based on experience of IFRSs within a sound financial reporting infrastructure. It is hoped that national differences in accounting will be eliminated and financial statements will be consistent and comparable worldwide.

Required

(a)   Discuss how the changes in accounting practices on transition to IFRSs and choice in the application of individual IFRSs could lead to inconsistency between the financial statements of companies.   **(17 marks)**

(b)   Discuss how management's judgement and the financial reporting infrastructure of a country can have a significant impact on financial statements prepared under IFRS.   **(6 marks)**

Appropriateness and quality of discussion.   **(2 marks)**

(Total = 25 marks)

Answers

DO NOT TURN THIS PAGE UNTIL YOU HAVE
COMPLETED THE MOCK EXAM

A PLAN OF ATTACK

Managing your nerves

As you turn the pages to start this exam a number of thoughts are likely to cross your mind. At best, examinations cause anxiety so it is important to stay focused on your task for the next three hours! Developing an awareness of what is going on emotionally within you may help you manage your nerves. Remember, you are unlikely to banish the flow of adrenaline, but the key is to harness it to help you work steadily and quickly through your answers.

Working through this mock exam will help you develop the exam stamina you will need to keep going for three hours.

Managing your time

Planning and time management are two of the key skills which complement the technical knowledge you need to succeed. To keep yourself on time, do not be afraid to jot down your target completion times for each question, perhaps next to the title of the question on the paper.

Focusing on scoring marks

When completing written answers, remember to communicate the critical points, which represent marks, and avoid padding and waffle. Sometimes it is possible to analyse a long sentence into more than one point. Always try to maximise the mark potential of what you write.

As you read through the questions, jot down on the question paper, any points you think you might forget. There is nothing more upsetting than coming out of an exam having forgotten to write a point you knew!

Also remember you can only score marks for what is on paper; you must write down enough to help the examiner to give you marks!

Structure and signpost your answers

To help you answer the examiner's requirements, highlight as you read through the paper the key words and phrases in the examiner's requirements.

Also, where possible try to use headings and subheadings, to give a logical and easy-to-follow structure to your response. A well structured and signposted answer is more likely to convince the examiner that you know your subject.

Your approach

This paper has two sections. The first section contains one question which is compulsory. The second has three questions and you must answer two of them.

You have a choice.

- Read through and answer the Section A question before moving on to Section B
- Go through Section B and select the two questions you will attempt. Then go back and answer the question in Section A first
- Select the two questions in Section B, answer them and then go back to Section A

You will have fifteen minutes before the start of the exam to go through the questions you are going to do.

Time spent at the start of each question confirming the requirements and producing a plan for the answers is time well spent.

Question selection

When selecting the two questions from Section B make sure that you read through all of the requirements. It is painful to answer part (a) of a question and then realise that parts (b) and (c) are beyond you, by then it is too late to change your mind and do another question.

When reviewing the requirements look at how many marks have been allocated to each part. This will give you an idea of how detailed your answer must be.

Generally, you need to be aware of your strengths and weaknesses and select accordingly.

Doing the exam

Actually doing the exam is a personal experience. There is not a single *right way*. As long as you submit complete answers to question 1 and any two from questions 2 to 4 after the three hours are up, then your approach obviously works.

Looking through the paper

The compulsory case study question is, as will always be the case, on groups, in this case a business combination achieved in stages. You also have an associate, some foreign currency, debt factoring and ethical issues. In Section B you have three questions on a variety of topics:

- Question 2 covers segment reporting and related parties. The segment reporting part, at least, is fairly straightforward.
- Question 3 is a multi-standard question, covering leasing, financial instruments, impairment and revenue recognition.
- Question 4 is on the challenges of a move to IFRS.

You only have to answer three out of these four questions. You don't have to pick your optional questions right now, but this brief overview should have convinced you that you have enough choice and variety to have a respectable go at Section B. So let's go back to the compulsory question in Section A.

Compulsory question

Question 1 requires you to prepare a consolidated statement of financial position for a group in which there has been a business combination achieved in stages. Additional adjustments include debt factoring, a provision, capitalisation of leasehold expenses and a foreign currency contract. The key with this question, which you cannot avoid doing, is not to panic. There is a lot of number crunching, and you might not be able to complete the question. The thing to do is to set out your proformas and then patiently, but briskly, work through the workings, doing as much as you can. By using a strategy of picking the low hanging 'fruit' you could get 80% of the group aspects right which enables you to put 22 marks in the bank!

Optional questions

Deciding between the optional questions is obviously a personal matter – it depends how you have spent your study time.

One thing is clear – the optional questions all contain a discursive element and are all based around a scenario. The Examiner has said that the emphasis in this paper is on giving advice in a practical situation.

The secret is to plan your answer; break it down into bite sized subsections, clearly labelled to help your examiner to quickly conclude you understand the problem and have a logical answer.

Allocating your time

The golden rule is always allocate your time according to the marks for the question in total and for the parts of the question. But be sensible. If (for example) you have committed yourself to answering Question 5, but can think of nothing to say about fair value, you may be better off trying to pick up some extra marks on the questions you can do.

Afterwards

Don't be tempted to do a post mortem on the paper with your colleagues. It will only worry you and them and it's unlikely you'll be able to remember exactly what you wrote anyway. If you really can't resist going over the topics covered in the paper, allow yourself a maximum of half an hour's 'worry time', then put it out of your head! Relax as it's all out of your hands now!

Question 1

Marking scheme

		Marks
(a)	Goodwill – Lose	5
	Non-controlling interest	1
	Group reserves	2
	Associate and impairment	5
	Intra-group profit	2
	Foreign currency	4
	Debt factoring	4
	Share options	4
	Provision	3
	Operating lease	3
	Other statement of financial position items	2
	Maximum	35
(b)	Benefits of environmental report – Maximum	8
(c)	Discussion of ethical and social responsibility – subjective	5
	Professional marks	2
	Maximum	7
	Maximum	50

(a) BETH GROUP
CONSOLIDATED STATEMENT OF FINANCIAL POSITION
AS AT 30 NOVEMBER 20X7

	$m
Non-current assets	
Property, plant and equipment: 1,700 + 200 + (W6) 10 + 2 – 2	1,910
Goodwill (W2)	17
Other intangible assets	300
Investment in associate (W3)	183
	2,410
Current assets	
Inventories: 800 + 100	900
Trade receivables: 600 + 60 – 1 (W8) + 50 (W9)	709
Cash: 500 + 40	540
	2,149
Total assets	4,559
Equity and liabilities	
Equity attributable to owners of the parent	
Share capital	1,500
Retained earnings (W4)	447
Other reserves: 300 + 9 (W10)	309
	2,256
Non-controlling interests (W5)	65
	2,321
Non-current liabilities: 700 + 2 (W7) + 11 (W11)	713
Current liabilities: 1,380 + 100 + 45 (W9)	1,525
Total equity and liabilities	4,559

Workings

1   *Group structure*

	1 Dec X5		1 Dec X6	Beth			1 Dec X6
	20%	+	60% = 80%				30%
Pre-acquisition retained earnings	$80m		$150m			Pre-acquisition retained earnings	$260m

Lose   Gain

2   *Goodwill: Lose (at date control obtained)*

	$m	$m
Consideration transferred		160.00
Non-controlling interests		53.33
Fair value of previously held equity interest		53.33
Fair value of identifiable assets acquired and liabilities assumed		
Share capital	100	
Retained earnings	150	
		(250.00)
		16.66

3   *Investment in associate*

	$m
Cost	180
Share of post acquisition retained earnings (W4)	12
Unrealised profit in inventories (W6)	(3)
Impairment loss (to profit or loss/retained earnings) (bal fig)	(6)
Recoverable amount: $610 × 30%	183

4   *Retained earnings*

	Beth	Lose 80%	Gain
	$m	$m	$m
Per question	400.00	200	300
Profit on derecognition of investment*	13.33		
Unrealised profit (W6)	(3.00)		
Operating lease (W7): 10 - 2		8	
Foreign currency (W8)	(1.00)		
Debt factoring reversal (W9)	5.00		
Share-based payment (W10)	(9.00)		
Provision (W11)	(11.00)		
Pre-acquisition		(150)	(260)
		58	40
Group share			
Lose: 58 × 80%	46.40		
Gain: 40 × 30%	12.00		
Impairment (W3)	(6.00)		
	446.73	rounded up to 447	

*Profit on derecognition of investment:

	$m
Fair value at date control obtained	53.33
Cost	(40.00)
	13.33

5   *Non-controlling interests: Lose*

	$m
NCI at acquisition	53.33
NCI share of post acquisition retained earnings ((W4) 58 × 20%)	11.60
	64.93

Non-controlling interest: $64.93m rounded up to $65m.

6   *Unrealised profit on intra-group trading with associate (Gain)*

	$m
Inventories: selling price	28
Cost	(18)
Profit	10

IAS 28 requires that Beth's share of this profit should be eliminated. Beth's share is 30% × $10m = $3m.

| DEBIT | Cost of sales/retained earnings (Beth) | $3m | |
| CREDIT | Investment in associate | | $3m |

Note. The unrealised profit is eliminated from retained earnings in the books of the seller (Beth) and from inventories in the books of the holder (Gain), ie the investment in associate.

7   *Lease*

IAS 16 *Property, plant and equipment* requires that Lose should capitalise the leasehold improvements of $10m and depreciate them over the term of the lease. The requirement in the lease to return the building in its original condition is an obligation arising from past events, so a provision of $2m should be made for the estimated costs.

Capitalise leasehold improvements

DEBIT	Property, plant and equipment	$10m	
CREDIT	Cost of sales /retained earnings		$10m

Provide for conversion costs

DEBIT	Property, plant and equipment	$2m	
CREDIT	Non-current liability		$2m

Adjust for depreciation

DEBIT	Cost of sales/retained earnings	$2m	
	(10 + 2) ÷6		
CREDIT	Property, plant and equipment		$2m

Note. The PPE adjustment will affect non-controlling interest in Lose.

8   *Foreign currency contract*

The payment to the supplier is a refundable deposit. It is deemed to be a monetary amount and is re-translated at the year end.

At 1 September 20X7	$m
€12m × 50% ÷ 0.75	= 8.00

At y/e (30 November 20X7)	
€12m × 50% ÷ 0.85	= 7.06
Loss	= 0.94 (rounded to $1m)

DEBIT	Retained earnings	$1m	
CREDIT	Receivables		$1m

9   *Debt factoring*

Under IFRS 9 *Financial instruments* a financial asset must be de-recognised:

(i)   If the contractual rights to the cash flows have expired

(ii)   If the financial asset has been transferred, together with the risks and rewards

Condition (ii) has not been met. Beth still bears the risks and rewards of ownership . Accordingly, the receivable must be reinstated.

DEBIT	Receivables	$50m	
CREDIT	Retained earnings		$5m
CREDIT	Loan (current liabilities)		$45m

10   *Share options*

Following IFRS 2, a charge must be made to profit or loss and a corresponding credit to equity, as follows.

200 options × (10,000 − (600+500)) × ½ × $10
= $8.9m, rounded to $9m

DEBIT	Retained earnings	$9m	
CREDIT	Equity (Share-based payment reserve/other reserves)		$9m

11   *Provision for contamination clear up*

Following IAS 37, a provision must be recognised if and only if:

(i)   A present obligation (legal or constructive) has arisen as a result of a past event

(ii)   Payment is probable

(iii)   The amount can be measured reliably

In this case, a provision must be made for the costs of contamination only where there is a legal obligation to clean it up. A moral obligation does not justify a provision. $4m relates to costs where there is an existing law. $7m relates to a law that will come in December 20X7, but it is assumed that the law will apply retrospectively. The total provision that must be made is $(7+4)m = $11m.

DEBIT	Profit and loss/retained earnings	$11m	
CREDIT	Non-current liability		$11m

(b) **Advantages of a separate environmental report**

Most countries do not have any legal requirements to produce an environmental report, and until fairly recently, environmental reporting was not seen as important. However, there would be a number of advantages for Beth in producing an environmental report.

(i) Producing a separate report will force Beth to **improve its practices** on environmental matters, an area the group has neglected.

(ii) Customers will see the efforts the group is making, and this will **increase customer confidence** in the group and its products.

(iii) The oil industry has a negative image when it comes to environmental matters. If Beth can be shown to be making an effort, and giving a detailed report on the changes made, this will **give the group an edge over its competitors.**

(iv) Beth has a **poor reputation as a good corporate citizen**. This needs to be put right and **be seen to be put right.**

(v) The group is facing potential litigation. If it takes steps to improving environmental performance and reporting on this, it can **improve relationships with regulators,** and therefore reduce the potential threat.

(vi) Beth operates in a number of different countries, and so needs to **improve its international reputation.** The international trend is towards improving environmental performance and increased provision of environmental information. Sustained efforts in this area will enhance the group's standing in the international arena.

(vii) Environmental performance covers areas such as waste management, resources and costs. Improvements in these areas will bring **economies and efficiencies** which will improve the group's profitability.

(viii) **Management information systems will be enhanced** in order to provide environmental information.

(ix) A good quality environmental report will make Beth **attractive to investors** and financial analysts, who are keen to see evidence of sustainability.

(x) Companies Beth supplies and contracts with may have to demonstrate to their own investors that they are dealing with reputable suppliers and contractors. Good environmental practices and reporting will **make Beth a more attractive supplier and contractor** to deal with.

A separate environmental report on its own is clearly not enough to give these benefits – the report must be underpinned by **sustained action**.

(c) **Ethical and social responsibilities**

Ethics and corporate social responsibility are important in themselves, but also because they can improve business performance. At present the company is stagnating, because it has focused on maintaining market share and on its own shareholders at the expense of other stakeholders. Corporate social responsibility is concerned with a company's **accountability to a wide range of stakeholders**, not just shareholders. For Beth, the most significant of these include:

(i) Regulators
(ii) Customers
(iii) Creditors
(iv) Employees

Regulators

The relationship with regulators is not good, mainly because of a poor reputation on environmental matters. Beth just does the bare minimum, for example cleaning up contamination only when legally obliged to do so. Adopting **environmentally friendly policies** and reporting in detail on these in an environmental report will go some way towards mending the relationship. **Litigation costs**, which have a direct impact on profit, can be **avoided.**

Customers

Currently Beth provides poor customer support, and makes no effort to understand the customs and cultures of the countries in which it operates. Moreover, it makes no positive contributions and does not promote socially responsible policies. This attitude could easily **alienate its present customers and deter new ones**. A **competitor** who does make positive contributions to the community, for example in sponsoring education or environmental programmes, will be **seen as having the edge** and could take customers away from Beth. Corporate social responsibility involves **thinking long-term** about the community rather than about short-term profits, but in the long term, profits could suffer if socially responsible attitudes are not adopted.

Creditors

Suppliers are key stakeholders, who must be handled responsibly if a reputation in the wider business community is not to suffer. **Beth's policy of not paying small and medium-sized companies is very short-sighted**. While such companies may not be in a position to sue for payment, the effect on goodwill and reputation will be very damaging in the long term. Suppliers may be put off doing business with Beth. Perhaps a key component can only be sourced from a small supplier, who will not sell to Beth if word gets around that it does not pay. This **unethical and damaging policy must be discontinued** and relationships with all suppliers fostered.

Employees

Employees are very important stakeholders. Beth's authoritarian approach to management and its refusal to value employees or listen to their ideas, is **potentially damaging to business performance**. High staff turnover is costly as new staff must be recruited and trained. Employees who do not feel valued will not work as hard as those who do. In addition, **employees may have some good ideas** to contribute that would benefit performance; at the moment Beth is missing out on these ideas.

Acting responsibly and ethically is not just right; it is also profitable.

Question 2

Marking scheme

			Marks
(a)	(i)	Segment reporting	6
	(ii)	Related parties	5
(b)		Pension fund	7
(c)		Impairment	7
		Available/Maximum	25

(a) (i) **Segment reporting**

IFRS 8 *Operating segments* states that an operating segment is a reported **separately** if:

1 **It meets the definition of an operating segment**, ie:

- It engages in business activities from which it may **earn revenues** and **incur expenses**,

- Its operating results are **regularly reviewed by the entity's chief operating decision maker** to make decisions about resources to be allocated to the segment and assess its performance, and

- **Discrete financial information** is available for the segment,

and

2 It exceeds **at least one** of the following quantitative thresholds:

- Reported revenue is **10% or more the combined revenue** of all operating segments (external and intersegment), or

- The absolute amount of its reported profit or loss is **10% or more of the greater of,** in absolute amount, **all operating segments not reporting a loss, and all operating segments reporting a loss**, or

- Its assets are **10% or more of the total assets** of all operating segments.

At 30 April 20X4 **all four** operating segments are **reportable segments,** assuming the segment information is regularly reviewed by the entity's chief operating decision maker. IFRS 8 states that total external revenue reported by operating segments **should be at least 75% of total external revenue** and this **condition will only be met** if at least the **property letting, vehicle sales and one other segment** are reported separately.

After the sale of Carp, the vehicle leasing segment represents only 3% of total revenue, 5% of total segment losses (1/17) and 4% of total assets. Although it falls below the 10% thresholds it **can still be reported as a separate operating segment** provided it meets the operating segment definition

BPP
LEARNING MEDIA

and management believes that **information about the segment would be useful** to users of the financial statements. Alternatively the group could consider **amalgamating it with vehicle sales** as long as the segments have **similar economic characteristics**, and the segments are **similar in each of the following respects**:

- The nature of the products and services;
- The nature of the production process;
- The type or class of customer;
- The methods used to distribution the products or provide the services; and
- If applicable, the nature of the regulatory environment.

The radio station may be reported as a separate segment, rather than combining it with the insurance segment, as it passes the 10% threshold test for segment assets (30/239), but only if its separate operating results will be **regularly reviewed by the entity's chief operating decision maker**.

(ii) **Related parties**

IAS 24 *Related party disclosures* defines a **related party** as a party that **controls**, or **is controlled** by the entity or has **significant influence** or **joint control** over the entity. **Directors** are **key management personnel** and therefore are **related parties**. The director of Carp has leased a number of vehicles from Carp for his family's use and therefore **the transaction must be disclosed** in the financial statements of Carp. However, he is not a director of Enterprise and the directors of Carp and Enterprise are **not related parties simply by virtue of their investment in Carp**. Whether director is a related party of Enterprise (and therefore whether the leasing transaction is disclosed in the financial statements of Enterprise) will depend on **whether the director is key management of the Enterprise group**. In reaching a conclusion the directors of Enterprise will need to consider a number of factors, including whether the director had a significant amount of authority in relation to Enterprise. On balance, the transaction probably need not be disclosed.

Carp was a related party of Enterprise (a subsidiary) for the year ended 30 April 20X4 and therefore **any transactions between the two companies must be disclosed** in the financial statements of **both**.

Under the revised IAS 24 (revised December 2003) a pension scheme is automatically considered a related party. The fact that the directors are Board members is no longer relevant to this.

(b) **Effect of the sale of Carp on the pension scheme**

There has been a **curtailment** of the scheme. The effect of the sale is to **reduce the net present value of the obligation by $13 million**.

	Before sale $m	Reduction $m	After sale $m
Net present value of obligation	50.0	(13.0)	37.0
Fair value of plan assets	(23.0)	–	(23.0)
	27.0	(13.0)	14.0

There is a **gain on sale of $13 million** and the net **pension fund liability is reduced to $14 million**.

(c) **Nature of impairment reviews**

An impairment review took place **at 30 April 20X2**. Goodwill arising on the acquisition of Fish and Near **cannot be allocated** between the two subsidiaries, so the impairment review takes place in two stages:

	Fish $m	Near $m
Carrying value of net assets	20	5
Recoverable amount	16	8
Impairment	4	Nil

The **impairment loss on Fish is recognised** and then the **two subsidiaries are combined** in order to carry out the impairment review on the goodwill:

	$m
Fish	16
Near	5
	21
Goodwill (30 – 22)	8
	29
Total recoverable amount (16 + 8)	24
Additional impairment loss (goodwill)	5

There are two reasons why a further impairment review needs to be carried out at 30 April 20X4: both Fish and Near are **making losses**; and it now appears that the **original impairment review was inaccurate.**

	Fish $m	Near $m	Goodwill $m	Total $m
Carrying value of net assets (per segment information)	23	8	3	34
Recoverable amount	29	10		39

Neither company is impaired at 30 April 20X4, nor is the goodwill impaired. Because the actual cash flows were better than forecast, it is possible that the original impairment loss may have **reversed**. The carrying value of the assets is compared with depreciated historic cost:

	Fish $m	Near $m
Carrying value of net assets (per segment information)	23	8
Depreciated historic cost	26	8
Reversal	3	–

Under IAS 36 *Impairment of assets*, an impairment loss **can be reversed** where there has been a **favourable change in estimates**. The carrying value of the net assets can be increased up to the **lower of recoverable amount ($29 million) and depreciated historical cost ($26 million)**. Therefore a **gain of $3 million is recognised** in profit or loss. The impairment loss on goodwill is **not reversed** as IAS 36 now **prohibits** this.

Question 3

> **Text reference.** Impairment is covered in Chapter 4; IAS 39 (impairment of financial instruments) in Chapter 7; leasing in Chapter 10; revenue in Chapter 1.
>
> **Top tips.** As this is a multi-issue question, it is important to allocate your time sensibly between the different aspects. Do not spend too long on Gow's net assets at the expense of Glass's.
>
> **Easy marks.** Part (a) is straightforward. Marks can be gained for backing up your arguments even if you come to the wrong conclusion.

Marking scheme

		Marks
(a)	Nature of relationship and accounting treatment	5
(b)	Impairment and calculation	7
	IAS 39	3
	Lease	5
	Revenue	4
	Issues with values contributed	2
	Available	26
	Maximum	25

(a) IFRS 11 *Joint arrangements* defines a joint arrangement as an arrangement of which two or more parties have joint control. Joint control is the contractually agreed sharing of control of an arrangement, which exists only when decisions about the relevant activities require the unanimous consent of the parties sharing control.

On the face of it, it would appear that York is a joint arrangement jointly controlled by Gow and Glass. Both venturers appear to have joint control and have contributed assets and other resources to the joint venture. The only issue however is that there is **no written contract** and the definition of a joint venture is that it is a contractual arrangement. However, the **substance of the arrangement** should be considered and with the **minutes** of the discussions about the setting up of the venture being formally approved by both companies this would certainly **imply a contractual arrangement**.

In terms of the accounting for such a joint arrangement, this depends on whether it is classified under IFRS 11 as a **joint operation** or a **joint venture.** A joint operation is a joint arrangement whereby the parties that have joint control of the arrangement have rights to the assets and obligations for the liabilities relating to the arrangement. A joint venture is a joint arrangement whereby the parties that have joint control of the arrangement have rights to the net assets of the arrangement.

The arrangement is **structured through a separate entity** – as such it could be either. However, there are no facts to suggest that Gow and Glass have rights to substantially all the benefits of the assets of York, nor an obligation for its liabilities. It appears rather that each company has an interest in the **net assets** of York and should account for it as a joint venture using the **equity method** in the group accounts of both Gow and Glass.

(b) **Gow's net assets**

The loss of the only customer of the power station (a cash generating unit) would be an **indicator** of a possible impairment of that cash generating unit. Therefore according to IAS 36 *Impairment of assets* an **impairment test** must be carried out on the power station. The power station has a current carrying value of $20 million. This must be **compared to the recoverable amount** of the power station which is the higher of the power station's fair value less costs of disposal and its value in use.

The fair value less costs of disposal is the potential sale proceeds (offer of $16m) less the disposal costs ($1m). The value in use is the discounted value of the expected future cash flows from the power station.

The future dismantling costs of $5 million must also be included in this calculation as it has been agreed with the government that this will take place therefore it is a liability.

Carrying value = $20 million
Fair value less costs of disposal = $16 million – $1 million = $15 million
Value in use (W1) = $21 million

Therefore the recoverable amount is the higher of $21 million and $15 million. As this recoverable amount of $21 million is actually higher than the carrying value of the power station ($20 million) then there is **no impairment**. The discounted present value must be shown as a long term provision and as part of the cost of land and buildings.

There is however a further issue with Gow's assets and that is the debt from Race. IAS 39 *Financial instruments: recognition and measurement* states that **financial assets must be assessed at each reporting date for impairment**. (Note that IFRS 9 does not yet cover impairment.)It is highly likely that the **debt from Race is impaired** as Race has gone into receivership. The value of the amount to be received is the anticipated cash from the final settlement. As the cash is not likely to be received for a year then it should be discounted.

Value of receivable (W2) = $3.8 million

A further factor here is that the **value of the contract with Race** shown as an intangible asset will now be **zero**.

Glass's net assets

The building **remains an asset** of the joint venture and there is no reason to alter its carrying value. However, its **remaining useful life will change** and the future depreciation charges will be $2 million each year for the next two years. As this is a change in estimate it is accounted for **prospectively not retrospectively**. Therefore this **does not affect the current statement of financial position**.

The lease liability must be assessed under IFRS 9 *Financial instruments* to determine whether it is to be derecognised. In this case there is a change to the lease term but it **will not be derecognised**. The lease liability, however, will change and will be measured at the **present value of the future cash payments**.

Value of lease liability (W3) = $1.1 million

The **lease receivable is also extinguished** as this is the payment of $1 million on 31 October 20X6.

IAS 38 states that if intangible non-current assets are to be recognised in the statement of financial position they must give a right to future economic benefits, be capable of being disposed of separately from the business and have a readily ascertainable market value. The **payment to the agency of $0.5 million** does not meet any of these criteria and **cannot be recognised as an intangible asset** and must be removed from the statement of financial position.

The terms of the contract with the overseas retailer can in fact be split into **two separate contracts** in accordance with IAS 18 *Revenue*. There is one contract to provide gas to the overseas retailer and the income from this will be accounted for in the normal way when gas is supplied. The other element of the contract is not to supply gas to any other company in that country over the four year period. Therefore the **$1.5 million deposit** received should not be taken to profit or loss immediately but spread over the four year period. The deposit should not have been deducted from intangible assets but instead should be shown as **deferred income**.

Intangible assets (W4) = $3m
Deferred income (W5) = $1.5m

STATEMENT OF FINANCIAL POSITION OF YORK AS AT 31 OCTOBER 20X6

	$m	$m
Land and buildings (9 + 4 + 4) (W1)		17.0
Intangible assets (W4)		3.0
		20.0
Current assets		
Inventory		
Receivables (W2)	6.0	
Cash (1 + 10)	3.8	
	11.0	
Total assets		20.8
		40.8
Share capital		
Reserves (bal fig)		30.0
		4.2
Lease liability (W3)		1.1
Long-term provision (W1)		4.0
Deferred income (W5)		1.5
		40.8

Workings

1 Value in use – power station

	$m
Cash flow	
31 Oct 20X7 $\left(6 \times \dfrac{1}{1.06}\right)$	5.7
31 Oct 20X8 $\left(7 \times \dfrac{1}{1.06^2}\right)$	6.2
31 Oct 20X9 $\left(8 \times \dfrac{1}{1.06^3}\right)$	6.7
31 Oct 20Y0 $\left((8-5) \times \dfrac{1}{1.06^4}\right)$	2.4
	21.0

The dismantling costs must also be discounted and added into the value of property, plant and equipment $5 million $\times \dfrac{1}{1.06^4}$ 0.792 = $4 million

2 Value of receivable – Race

Discounted present value = $5 million × 80% × 1/1.06
= $3.8 million

3 Value of lease payable

$0.6 million × 1/1.07   = $0.56 million
$0.6 million × 1/(1.07 × 1.07) = $0.52 million
                             $1.08 rounded to $1.1 million

4 Intangible assets in Glass

	$m
Per statement of financial position	2.0
Less agency fee	(0.5)
Add value of overseas deposit	1.5
	3.0

5 Deferred income

Deposit from overseas retailer = $1.5 million

Question 4

Marking scheme

		Marks
(a)	Changes from national GAAP	2
	Complexity	1
	Recognition, measurement, disclosure	2
	Alternative forms of presentation	1
	Inconsistent principles	2
	Alternative accounting treatments	3
	Little industry related guidance	1
	IFRS I	2
	Interpretation of IFRS	2
	Adoption date	1
		17
(b)	Management judgements	2
	Disclosure of sensitivity	1
	Regulatory infrastructure	2
	Training/markets	1
	Communication	2
		8
	Maximum	25

(a) **The challenge**

Implementation of International Financial Reporting Standards entails **a great deal of work** for many companies, particularly those in countries where local GAAP has not been so onerous. For example, many jurisdictions will not have had such detailed rules about recognition, measurement and presentation of financial instruments, and many will have had no rules at all about share-based payment.

A challenge for preparers of financial statements is also **a challenge for users**. When financial statements become far more complex under IFRS than they were under local GAAP, users may find them hard to understand, and consequently of little relevance.

Presentation

Many developed countries have legislation requiring set formats and layouts for financial statements. For example, in the UK there is the Companies Act 2006. IFRS demands that presentation is in accordance with IAS 1 *Presentation of financial statements,* but this standard allows alternative forms of presentation. In choosing between alternatives, **countries tend to adopt the format that is closest to local GAAP**, even if this is not necessarily the best format. For example, UK companies are likely to adopt the two-statement format for the statement of profit or loss and other comprehensive income, because this is closest to the old profit and loss account and statement of total recognised gains and losses.

Concepts and interpretation

Although later IAS and IFRS are based to an extent on the IASB *Conceptual Framework,* there is **no consistent set of principles** underlying them. The *Conceptual Framework* itself is being revised, and there is controversy over the direction the revision should take. Consequently, preparers of accounts are likely to think in terms of the conceptual frameworks – if any – that they have used in developing local GAAP, and these may be different from that of the IASB. German accounts, for example, have traditionally been aimed at the tax authorities.

Where IFRS themselves give clear guidance, this may not matter, but where there is uncertainty, preparers of accounts will fall back on their traditional conceptual thinking.

Choice of accounting treatment

Although many so-called 'allowed alternatives' have been eliminated from IFRS in recent years, choice of treatment remains. For example, IAS 16 *Property, plant and equipment* gives a choice of either the cost model or the revaluation model for a class of property, plant or equipment.

It could be argued that choice is a good thing, as companies should be able to select the treatment that most fairly reflects the underlying reality. However, in the context of change to IFRS, there is a danger that companies **will choose the alternative that closely matches the approach followed under local GAAP, or the one that is easier to implement**, regardless of whether this is the best choice.

Choice of recognition or measurement method

An example of **potential inconsistency** is IAS 21 *The effects of changes in foreign exchange rates.* The identification of the functional currency under this standard can be a subjective process, with arguments on either side. Revenue recognition is also an aspect of accounting that can cause considerable variation between companies and between countries, even if they all adopt IAS 18 *Revenue,* because this standard allows variations in recognition methods. For example some companies with customer loyalty programmes may defer part of the revenue received.

Inconsistency of timing and exemptions taken

IFRSs have provision for early adoption, and this can affect comparability, although impact of a new standard must be disclosed under IAS 8 *Accounting policies, changes in accounting estimates and errors.* Further, IFRS 1 *First time adoption of International Financial Reporting Standards* permits a number of exemptions during the periods of transition to IFRS. This gives scope for manipulation, if **exemptions are 'cherry-picked'** to produce a favourable picture.

(b)   **Impact of management judgement on IFRS financial statements**

The extent of the impact will vary, depending on how developed local GAAP was before the transition. However, in general it is likely that **management judgement will have a greater impact** on financial statements prepared under IFRS than under local GAAP. The main reasons for this are as follows.

(i)   The **volume** of rules and number of areas addressed by IFRS is likely to be greater than that under local GAAP.

(ii)   Many issues are perhaps **addressed for the first time**, for example share-based payment.

(iii)   IFRSs are likely to be **more complex** than local standards.

(iv)   IFRSs allow **choice** in many cases, which leads to subjectivity.

(v)   Selection of **valuation method** requires judgement, and many IFRS leave the choice of method open. This affects areas such as pensions, impairment, intangible assets acquired in business combinations, onerous contracts and share-based payment.

Financial reporting infrastructure

As well as sound management judgement, implementation of IFRS requires a sound financial reporting infrastructure. Key aspects of this include the following.

(i) **A robust regulatory framework**. For IFRS to be successful, they must be rigorously enforced.

(ii) **Trained and qualified staff**. Many preparers of financial statements will have been trained in local GAAP and not be familiar with the principles underlying IFRS, let alone the detail. Some professional bodies provide conversion qualifications – for example, the ACCA's Diploma in International Financial Reporting – but the availability of such qualifications and courses may vary from country to country.

(iii) **Availability and transparency of market information**. This is particularly important in the determination of fair values, which are such a key component of many IFRSs.

(iv) **High standards of corporate governance and audit**. This is all the more important in the transition period, especially where there is resistance to change.

Overall, there are significant advantages to the widespread adoption of IFRS, but if the transition is to go well, there must be a realistic assessment of potential challenges.

ACCA

Paper P2

Corporate Reporting (International)

Mock Examination 3

December 2012

Question Paper	
Time allowed	
Reading and planning	**15 minutes**
Writing	**3 hours**
This paper is divided into two sections	
Section A	**This ONE question is compulsory and MUST be attempted**
Section B	**TWO questions ONLY to be answered**

DO NOT OPEN THIS PAPER UNTIL YOU ARE READY TO START UNDER EXAMINATION CONDITIONS

ACCA

Paper P2

Corporate Reporting
(International)

Mock Examination 3

December 2012

Question paper		
Time allowed		
Reading and planning		15 minutes
Writing		3 hours
This paper is divided into two sections		
Section A	This ONE question is compulsory and MUST be attempted	
Section B	TWO questions ONLY to be attempted	

DO NOT OPEN THIS PAPER UNTIL YOU ARE READY TO START UNDER EXAMINATION CONDITIONS

SECTION A – This ONE question is compulsory and MUST be attempted

Question 1

Minny is a company which operates in the service sector. Minny has business relationships with Bower and Heeny. All three entities are public limited companies. The draft statements of financial position of these entities are as follows at 30 November 20X2.

	Minny $m	Bower $m	Heeny $m
Assets			
Non-current assets			
Property, plant and equipment	920	300	310
Investment in subsidiaries:			
Bower	730		
Heeny		320	
Investment in Puttin	48		
Intangible assets	198	30	35
	1,896	650	345
Current assets	895	480	250
Total assets	2,791	1,130	595
Equity and liabilities			
Share capital	920	400	200
Other components of equity	73	37	25
Retained earnings	895	442	139
Total equity	1,888	879	364
Non-current liabilities	495	123	93
Current liabilities	408	128	138
Total liabilities	903	251	231
Total equity and liabilities	2,791	1,130	595

The following information is relevant to the preparation of the group financial statements.

(i) On 1 December 20X0, Minny acquired 70% of the equity interests of Bower. The purchase consideration comprised cash of $730 million. At acquisition, the fair value of the non-controlling interest in Bower was $295 million. On 1 December 20X0, the fair value of the identifiable net assets acquired was $835 million and retained earnings of Bower were $319 million and other components of equity were $27 million. The excess in fair value is due to non-depreciable land.

(ii) On 1 December 20X1, Bower acquired 80% of the equity interests of Heeny for a cash consideration of $320 million. The fair value of a 20% holding of the non-controlling interest was $72 million; a 30% holding was $108 million and a 44% holding was $161 million. At the date of acquisition, the identifiable net assets of Heeny had a fair value of $362 million, retained earnings were $106 million and other components of equity were $20 million. The excess in fair value is due to non-depreciable land.

It is the group's policy to measure the non-controlling interest at fair value at the date of acquisition.

(iii) Both Bower and Heeny were impairment tested at 30 November 20X2. The recoverable amounts of both cash generating units as stated in the individual financial statements at 30 November 20X2 were Bower, $1,425 million, and Heeny, $604 million, respectively. The directors of Minny felt that any impairment of assets was due to the poor performance of the intangible assets. The recoverable amount has been determined without consideration of liabilities which all relate to the financing of operations.

(iv) Minny acquired a 14% interest in Puttin, a public limited company, on 1 December 20X0 for a cash consideration of $18 million. The investment was accounted for under IFRS 9 Financial instruments and was designated as at fair value through other comprehensive income. On 1 June 20X2, Minny acquired an additional 16% interest in Puttin for a cash consideration of $27 million and achieved significant influence. The value of the original 14% investment on 1 June 20X2 was $21 million. Puttin made profits after tax of $20 million and $30 million for the years to 30 November 20X1 and 30 November 20X2 respectively. On 30 November 20X2, Minny received a dividend from Puttin of $2 million, which has been credited to other components of equity.

(v) Minny purchased patents of $10 million to use in a project to develop new products on 1 December 20X1. Minny has completed the investigative phase of the project, incurring an additional cost of $7 million and has determined that the product can be developed profitably. An effective and working prototype was created at a cost of $4 million and in order to put the product into a condition for sale, a further $3 million was spent. Finally, marketing costs of $2 million were incurred. All of the above costs are included in the intangible assets of Minny.

(vi) Minny intends to dispose of a major line of the parent's business operations. At the date the held for sale criteria were met, the carrying amount of the assets and liabilities comprising the line of business were:

	$m
Property, plant and equipment (PPE)	49
Inventory	18
Current liabilities	3

It is anticipated that Minny will realise $30 million for the business. No adjustments have been made in the financial statements in relation to the above decision.

Required

(a) Prepare the consolidated statement of financial position for the Minny Group as at 30 November 20X2

(35 marks)

(b) Minny intends to dispose of a major line of business in the above scenario and the entity has stated that the held for sale criteria were met under IFRS 5 *Non-current assets held for sale and discontinued operations*. The criteria in IFRS 5 are very strict and regulators have been known to question entities on the application of the standard. The two criteria which must be met before an asset or disposal group will be defined as recovered principally through sale are: that it must be available for immediate sale in its present condition and the sale mustbe highly probable.

Required

Discuss what is meant in IFRS 5 by 'available for immediate sale in its present condition' and 'the sale must be highly probable', setting out briefly why regulators may question entities on the application of the standard. **(7 marks)**

(c) Bower has a property which has a carrying value of $2 million at 30 November 20X2. This property had been revalued at the year end and a revaluation surplus of $400,000 had been recorded in other components of equity. The directors were intending to sell the property to Minny for $1 million shortly after the year end. Bower previously used the historical cost basis for valuing property.

Required

Without adjusting your answer to Part (a), discuss the ethical and accounting implications of the above intended sale of assets to Minny by Bower. **(8 marks)**

(Total = 50 marks)

Section B – TWO questions ONLY to be attempted

Question 2

Coate, a public limited company, is a producer of ecologically friendly electrical power (green electricity).

(a) Coate's revenue comprises mainly the sale of electricity and green certificates. Coate obtains green certificates under a national government scheme. Green certificates represent the environmental value of green electricity. The national government requires suppliers who do not produce green electricity to purchase a certain number of green certificates. Suppliers who do not produce green electricity can buy green certificates either on the market on which they are traded or directly from a producer such as Coate. The national government wishes to give incentives to producers such as Coate by allowing them to gain extra income in this way.

Coate obtains the certificates from the national government on satisfactory completion of an audit by an independent organisation, which confirms the origin of production. Coate then receives a certain number of green certificates from the national government depending on the volume of green electricity generated. The green certificates are allocated to Coate on a quarterly basis by the national government and Coate can trade the green certificates.

Coate is uncertain as to the accounting treatment of the green certificates in its financial statements for the period ended 30 November 20X2 and how to treat the green certificates which were not sold at the end of the reporting period. **(7 marks)**

(b) During the year ended 30 November 20X2, Coate acquired an overseas subsidiary whose financial statements are prepared in a different currency to Coate. The amounts reported in the consolidated statement of cash flows included the effect of changes in foreign exchange rates arising on the retranslation of its overseas operations. Additionally, the group's consolidated statement of cash flows reported as a loss the effect of foreign exchange rate changes on cash and cash equivalents as Coate held some foreign currency of its own denominated in cash. **(5 marks)**

(c) Coate also sold 50% of a previously wholly owned subsidiary, Patten, to a third party, Manis. Manis is in the same industry as Coate. Coate has continued to account for the investment in Patten as a subsidiary in its consolidated financial statements. The main reason for this accounting treatment was the agreement that had been made with Manis, under which Coate would exercise general control over Patten's operating and financial policies. Coate has appointed three out of four directors to the board. The agreement also stated that certain decisions required consensus by the two shareholders.

Under the shareholder agreement, consensus is required with respect to:

(i) Significant changes in the company's activities
(ii) Plans or budgets that deviate from the business plan
(iii) Accounting policies; acquisition of assets above a certain value; employment or dismissal of senior employees; distribution of dividends or establishment of loan facilities

Coate feels that the consensus required above does not constitute a hindrance to the power to control Patten, as it is customary within the industry to require shareholder consensus for decisions of the types listed in the shareholders' agreement. **(6 marks)**

(d) In the notes to Coate's financial statements for the year ended 30 November 20X2, the tax expense included an amount in respect of 'Adjustments to current tax in respect of prior years' and this expense had been treated as a prior year adjustment. These items related to adjustments arising from tax audits by the authorities in relation to previous reporting periods.

The issues that resulted in the tax audit adjustment were not a breach of tax law but related predominantly to transfer pricing issues, for which there was a range of possible outcomes that were negotiated during 20X2 with the taxation authorities. Further at 30 November 20X1, Coate had accounted for all known issues arising from the audits to that date and the tax adjustment could not have been foreseen as at 30 November 20X1, as the audit authorities changed the scope of the audit. No penalties were expected to be applied by the taxation authorities. **(5 marks)**

Required

Discuss how the above events should be accounted for in the individual or, as appropriate, the consolidated financial statements of Coate.

Note. The mark allocation is shown against each of the four events above.

Professional marks will be awarded in question 2 for the clarity and quality of the presentation and discussion.

(2 marks)

(Total = 25 marks)

Question 3

Blackcutt is a local government organisation whose financial statements are prepared using International Financial Reporting Standards.

(a)   Blackcutt wishes to create a credible investment property portfolio with a view to determining if any property may be considered surplus to the functional objectives and requirements of the local government organisation. The following portfolio of property is owned by Blackcutt.

Blackcutt owns several plots of land. Some of the land is owned by Blackcutt for capital appreciation and this may be sold at any time in the future. Other plots of land have no current purpose as Blackcutt has not determined whether it will use the land to provide services such as those provided by national parks or for short-term sale in the ordinary course of operations.

The local government organisation supplements its income by buying and selling property. The housing department regularly sells part of its housing inventory in the ordinary course of its operations as a result of changing demographics. Part of the inventory, which is not held for sale, is to provide housing to low-income employees at below market rental. The rent paid by employees covers the cost of maintenance of the property. **(7 marks)**

(b)   Blackcutt has outsourced its waste collection to a private sector provider called Waste and Co and pays an annual amount to Waste and Co for its services. Waste and Co purchases the vehicles and uses them exclusively for Blackcutt's waste collection. The vehicles are painted with the Blackcutt local government organisation name and colours. Blackcutt can use the vehicles and the vehicles are used for waste collection for nearly all of the asset's life. In the event of Waste and Co's business ceasing, Blackcutt can obtain legal title to the vehicles and carry on the waste collection service. **(6 marks)**

(c)   Blackcutt owns a warehouse. Chemco has leased the warehouse from Blackcutt and is using it as a storage facility for chemicals. The national government has announced its intention to enact environmental legislation requiring property owners to accept liability for environmental pollution. As a result, Blackcutt has introduced a hazardous chemical policy and has begun to apply the policy to its properties. Blackcutt has had a report that the chemicals have contaminated the land surrounding the warehouse. Blackcutt has no recourse against Chemco or its insurance company for the clean-up costs of the pollution. At 30 November 20X6, it is virtually certain that draft legislation requiring a clean up of land already contaminated will be enacted shortly after the year end. **(4 marks)**

(d)   On 1 December 20X0, Blackcutt opened a school at a cost of $5 million. The estimated useful life of the school was 25 years. On 30 November 20X6, the school was closed because numbers using the school

declined unexpectedly due to a population shift caused by the closure of a major employer in the area. The school is to be converted for use as a library, and there is no expectation that numbers using the school will increase in the future and thus the building will not be reopened for use as a school. The current replacement cost for a library of equivalent size to the school is $2·1 million. Because of the nature of the non-current asset, value-in-use and net selling price are unrealistic estimates of the value of the school. The change in use would have no effect on the estimated life of the building. **(6 marks)**

Required

Discuss how the above events should be accounted for in the financial statements of Blackcutt.

Note. The mark allocation is shown against each of the four events above.

Professional marks will be awarded in question 3 for the clarity and quality of the presentation and discussion.

(2 marks)

(Total = 25 marks)

Question 4

The International Accounting Standards Board has recently completed a joint project with the Financial Accounting Standards Board (FASB) on fair value measurement by issuing IFRS 13 *Fair value measurement.* IFRS 13 defines fair value, establishes a framework for measuring fair value and requires significant disclosures relating to fair value measurement.

The IASB wanted to enhance the guidance available for assessing fair value in order that users could better gauge the valuation techniques and inputs used to measure fair value. There are no new requirements as to when fair value accounting is required, but the IFRS gives guidance regarding fair value measurements in existing standards. Fair value measurements are categorised into a three-level hierarchy, based on the type of inputs to the valuation techniques used. However, the guidance in IFRS 13 does not apply to transactions dealt with by certain specific standards.

Required

(a)   (i)   Discuss the main principles of fair value measurement as set out in IFRS 13. **(7 marks)**

     (ii)   Describe the three-level hierarchy for fair value measurements used in IFRS 13. **(6 marks)**

(b)   Jayach, a public limited company, is reviewing the fair valuation of certain assets and liabilities in light of the introduction of IFRS 13.

    It carries an asset that is traded in different markets and is uncertain as to which valuation to use. The asset has to be valued at fair value under International Financial Reporting Standards. Jayach currently only buys and sells the asset in the Australasian market. The data relating to the asset are set out below.

Year to 30 November 20X2	Asian market	European market	Australasian market
Volume of market - units	4 million	2 million	1 million
Price	$19	$16	$22
Costs of entering the market	$2	$2	$3
Transaction costs	$1	$2	$2

    Additionally, Jayach had acquired an entity on 30 November 20X2 and is required to fair value a decommissioning liability. The entity has to decommission a mine at the end of its useful life, which is in three years' time. Jayach has determined that it will use a valuation technique to measure the fair value of the liability. If Jayach were allowed to transfer the liability to another market participant, then the following data would be used.

Input	Amount
Labour and material cost	$2 million
Overhead	30% of labour and material cost
Third party mark-up – industry average	20%
Annual inflation rate	5%
Risk adjustment – uncertainty relating to cash flows	6%
Risk-free rate of government bonds	4%
Entity's non-performance risk	2%

Jayach needs advice on how to fair value the liability.

Required

Discuss, with relevant computations, how Jayach should fair value the above asset and liability under IFRS 13.   **(10 marks)**

Professional marks will be awarded in question 4 for the clarity and quality of the presentation and discussion.

(2 marks)

(Total = 25 marks)

Answers

**DO NOT TURN THIS PAGE UNTIL YOU HAVE
COMPLETED THE MOCK EXAM**

A PLAN OF ATTACK

Managing your nerves

As you turn the pages to start this exam a number of thoughts are likely to cross your mind. At best, examinations cause anxiety so it is important to stay focused on your task for the next three hours! Developing an awareness of what is going on emotionally within you may help you manage your nerves. Remember, you are unlikely to banish the flow of adrenaline, but the key is to harness it to help you work steadily and quickly through your answers.

Working through this mock exam will help you develop the exam stamina you will need to keep going for three hours.

Managing your time

Planning and time management are two of the key skills which complement the technical knowledge you need to succeed. To keep yourself on time, do not be afraid to jot down your target completion times for each question, perhaps next to the title of the question on the paper.

Focusing on scoring marks

When completing written answers, remember to communicate the critical points, which represent marks, and avoid padding and waffle. Sometimes it is possible to analyse a long sentence into more than one point. Always try to maximise the mark potential of what you write.

As you read through the questions, jot down on the question paper, any points you think you might forget. There is nothing more upsetting than coming out of an exam having forgotten to write a point you knew!

Also remember you can only score marks for what is on paper; you must write down enough to help the examiner to give you marks!

Don't write in the answer booklet during the 15 minutes reading time!

Structure and signpost your answers

To help you answer the examiner's requirements, highlight as you read through the paper the key words and phrases in the examiner's requirements.

Also, where possible try to use headings and subheadings, to give a logical and easy-to-follow structure to your response. A well structured and signposted answer is more likely to convince the examiner that you know your subject.

Your approach

This paper has two sections. The first section contains one long case study question which is compulsory. The second has three questions and you must answer two of them.

You have a choice.

- Read through and answer the Section A question before moving on to Section B
- Go through Section B and select the two questions you will attempt. Then go back and answer the question in Section A first
- Select the two questions in Section B, answer them and then go back to Section A

You are allowed 15 minutes before the start of the exam to go through the questions you are going to do.

Time spent at the start of each question confirming the requirements and producing a plan for the answers is time well spent.

Question selection

When selecting the two questions from Section B make sure that you read through all of the requirements. It is painful to answer part (a) of a question and then realise that parts (b) and (c) are beyond you, by then it is too late to change your mind and do another question.

When reviewing the requirements look at how many marks have been allocated to each part. This will give you an idea of how detailed your answer must be.

Generally, you need to be aware of your strengths and weaknesses and select accordingly.

Doing the exam

Actually doing the exam is a personal experience. There is not a single *right way*. As long as you submit complete answers to question 1 and any two from questions 2 to 4 after the three hours are up, then your approach obviously works.

Looking through the paper

The compulsory question is a case study. It has a consolidated statement of financial position with a sub-subsidiary, an associate, a disposal group and various adjustments (intangible asset, impairment, dividends) plus a written part on IFRS 5. In Section B you have three questions on a variety of topics:

- Question 2 is a scenario question covering IAS 20, IAS 7, IFRS 10 definition of control and adjustment for tax liability
- Question 3 is a specialised industry question covering Investment property, leasing, provisions and impairment
- Question 4 is on the topical issue of fair value measurement under IFRS 13

You only have to answer two out of these three questions. You don't have to pick your optional questions right now, but this brief overview should have convinced you that you have enough choice and variety to have a respectable go at Section B. So let's go back to the compulsory question in Section A.

Compulsory question

Part (a) requires a consolidated statement of financial position, with plenty of opportunity to pass, even if you don't get all the complexities such as the disposal group. Don't be intimidated by the fact that there is a complex group – a lot of the consolidation adjustments are the same as for a simple group. Just keep going, set out your workings clearly, and above all make sure you complete the question. Don't get bogged down in the bond or pension scheme stages. Part (b) is a relatively straightforward discussion question on IFRS 5, with marks available for sensible points. Part (c) is subjective and credit will be given for valid arguments.

Optional questions

Deciding between the optional questions is obviously a personal matter – it depends how you have spent your study time.

In our opinion, questions 3 and 4 are more straightforward than question 2. Question 4 allows plenty of scope for earning marks through textbook knowledge of principles, and question 3 has the advantage over question 2 covering more mainstream topics. Question 2 has a rather obscure Part (b), although you could make up the marks elsewhere. The secret is to plan your answer; break it down into bite sized subsections, clearly labelled to help your marker to quickly conclude you understand the problem and have a logical answer.

Use the information in the scenario

It is there for a purpose! Many students lose marks because they do not do this.

Allocating your time

The golden rule is always allocate your time according to the marks for the question in total and for the parts of the question. But be sensible. If, for example, you have committed yourself to answering Question 2, but are stuck on the foreign exchange, you may be better off trying to pick up some extra marks on the questions you can do.

Afterwards

Don't be tempted to do a post mortem on the paper with your colleagues. It will only worry you and them and it's unlikely you'll be able to remember exactly what you wrote anyway. If you really can't resist going over the topics covered in the paper, allow yourself a maximum of half an hour's 'worry time', then put it out of your head! Relax as it's all out of your hands now!

Question 1

Marking scheme

		Marks
(a)		
	Property, plant and equipment	5
	Goodwill	5
	Intangible assets	1
	Investment in Puttin	4
	Current assets	1
	Disposal group	5
	Retained earnings	6
	Other components of equity	4
	Non-controlling interest	3
	Current liabilities	1
		35
(b)		
	Definition – 1 mark per point up to maximum	4
	Discussion	3
(c)		
	Accounting treatment	4
	Ethical considerations	4
		50

(a) MINNY GROUP
CONSOLIDATED STATEMENT OF FINANCIAL POSITION
AS AT 30 NOVEMBER 20X2

	$m
Non-current assets	
Property, plant and equipment: 920 + 300 + 310 + 89(W7) + 36(W7) − 49(W10)	1,606.0
Goodwill (W2)	190.0
Intangible assets: 198 + 30 + 35 − 27(W8) − 9(W9)	227.0
Investment in associate (W3)	50.5
	2,073.5
Current assets: 895 + 480 + 250 − 18(W10)	1,607.0
Disposal group held for sale (W10): 49 + 18 − 34	33.0
Total assets	3,713.5
Equity and liabilities	
Equity attributable to owners of the parent	
Share capital	920.00
Retained earnings (W4)	936.08
Other components of equity (W5)	77.80
	1,933.88
Non-controlling interests (W6)	394.62
	2,328.50
Non-current liabilities: 495 + 123 + 93	711.00
Current liabilities: 408 + 128 + 138 − 3 (W10)	671.00
Current liabilities associated with disposal group (W10)	3.00
Total equity and liabilities	3,713.50

Workings

1   *Group structure*

Minny			
1 Dec 20X0	70% (Consideration = $730m)	FV NA	$835m
		Retained earnings	$319m
		OCE	$27m
		FV NCI	$295m
Bower			
1 Dec 20X1	80% (Consideration = $320m)	FV NA	$362m
		Retained earnings	$106m
		OCE	$20m
		FV NCI	$161m

Heeny

	%
Effective interest: 70% × 80%	56
∴ Non-controlling interest	44
	100

2   *Goodwill*

	Bower $m		*Heeny* $m
Consideration transferred	730	320 × 70%	224
Non-controlling interests	295		161
FV of identifiable net assets at acq'n:	(835)		(362)
	190		23
Impairment losses (W8)	-		(23)
	190		-
		190	

3   *Investment in associate*

	$m	$m
'Cost' at 1 June 20X2:		
Fair value of 14% holding per qu	21	
Cost of additional 16%	27	
		48.0
Share of profit for 6 months to 30 Nov 20X2: 30 ×		4.5
6/12 × 30%		
Dividends paid		(2.0)
		50.5

{ $2.5m post sig. inf.

Notes

(i)   The investment had been designated per IFRS 9 *Financial instruments* as being at fair value through other comprehensive income. The gain of $21m – $18m = $3m now realised is not reclassified to profit or loss for the year, but may be transferred as a reserve movement from other components of equity (W5) to retained earnings (W4).

(ii)   The dividend should have been credited to Minny's profit or loss for the year rather than to other comprehensive income. The associate is not impaired as the carrying amount in the separate financial statements of Minny does not exceed the carrying amount in the consolidated financial statement, and the dividend does not exceed the total comprehensive income of the associate in the period in which it is declared.

4   *Retained earnings*

	Minny $m	*Bower* $m	*Heeny* $m
Per question	895.00	442	139
Reclassification of gain on Puttin (W3)	3.00		
Reclassification of dividend from Puttin* (W5)	2.00		
Investigation and marketing of intangible (W10)	(9.00)		
Impairment loss on disposal group (W10)	(34.00)		
Pre-acquisition (W1)		(319)	(106)
		123	33
Group share			
Bower: 123 × 70%	86.10		
Heeny: 33 × 56%	18.48		
Share of post-acqn. profit of Puttin (W3)	2.50		
Impairment loss on Heeny (W8) (50 × 56%)	(28.00)		
	936.08		

5   Other components of equity

	Minny $m	Bower $m	Heeny $m
Per question	73.0	37	25
Reclassification of gain on Puttin (W3)	(3.0)		
Reclassification of dividend from Puttin (W4)	(2.0)		
Pre-acquisition (W1)		(27)	(20)
		10	5
Group share post acqn:			
Bower: 10 × 70 %	7.0		
Heeny: 5 × 56%	2.8		
	77.8		

6   Non-controlling interests

	Bower $m	Heeny $m
At acquisition (FV per qu (W2))	295.0	161.00
Post acquisition share of retained earnings		
Bower: 123 (W4) × 30%	36.9	
Heeny: 33 (W4) × 44%		14.52
Post acquisition share of other components of equity		
Bower: 10 (W5) × 30%	3.0	
Heeny: 5 (W5) × 44%		2.20
NCI share of investment in Heeney: 320 × 30%	(96.0)	-
Heeny impairment losses: 50 (W8) × 44%	-	(22.00)
	238.9	155.72

394.62

7   Fair value adjustments

Bower:

	At acqn 1.12..20X0 $m	Movement $m	At year end 30.11.20X2 $m
Land: 835 − (400 + 319 + 27)	89	–	89

Heeny:

	At acqn 1.12.20X1 $m	Movement $m	At year end 30.11.20X2 $m
Land: 362− (200 + 106+ 20)	36	-	36

8   *Impairment test*

	Bower $m	Heeny $m
Carrying amount		
Assets	1,130	595
Fair value adjustments (W7)	89	36
Goodwill (W2)	190	23
	1,409	654
Recoverable amount	(1,425)	(604)
Impairment loss	-	50
Allocated to: goodwill		23
intangible assets (bal. fig.)		27
		50

Note. Bower is not impaired as the carrying amount is below the recoverable amount, but Heeny's assets are impaired. The impairment loss is allocated first to goodwill and then to the intangible assets, because the directors believe that it is the poor performance of the intangible assets which is responsible for the reduction in the recoverable amount.

9   *Development costs*

	$m	
Patent	10	Intangible asset
Investigation phase	7	Profit or loss
Prototype	4	} Intangible asset:
Preparation for sale	3	development costs
Marketing	2	Profit or loss

The adjustment required to eliminate the items which should be expensed to profit or loss is:

DEBIT	Profit or loss (retained earnings)	$9m	
CREDIT	Intangible assets		$9m

10   *Disposal group held for sale*

Assets and liabilities of the disposal group are re-classified as current and shown as separate line items in the statement of financial position. The disposal group is impaired, and the impairment loss is calculated as follows.

	$m
Property, plant and equipment	49
Inventory	18
Current liabilities	(3)
Carrying value	64
Anticipated proceeds (FV less costs to sell)	30
Impairment loss	34

(Deduct from assets and retained earnings

(b)   **Held for sale criteria under IFRS 5 *Non-current assets held for sale and discontinued operations***

The held for sale criteria in IFRS 5 *Non-current assets held for sale and discontinued operations* are very strict, and often decision to sell an asset or disposal group is made well before they are met. It may be difficult for regulators, auditors or users of accounts to determine whether an entity **genuinely intends to dispose** of the asset or group of assets.

IFRS requires an asset or disposal group to be classified as held for sale where it is **available for immediate sale** in its **present condition** subject only to **terms that are usual** and customary and the sale is **highly probable**.

The standard does not give guidance on **terms that are usual and customary** but the guidance notes give examples. Such terms may include, for example, a specified period of time for the seller to vacate a headquarters building that is to be sold, or it may include contracts or surveys. However, they would not include terms imposed by the seller that are not customary, for example, a seller could not continue to use its headquarters building until construction of a new headquarters building had taken place.

For a sale to be **highly probable:**

- Management must be **committed** to the sale.
- An **active programme to locate a buyer** must have been initiated.
- The asset must be **marketed at a price** that is **reasonable in relation to its own fair value**
- The sale must be **expected to be completed within one year** from the date of classification.

- It is **unlikely** that **significant changes** will be made to the plan **or the plan withdrawn.**

Regulators may question entities' application of this standard because the definition of highly probable as 'significantly more likely than probable' is **subjective**. Entities may wish to separate out an unprofitable/impaired part of the business in order to **show a more favourable view of continuing operations,** and so regulators have reason look very closely at whether the classification as held for sale is genuine.

(c) **Transfer of property**

The proposed transfer of property from Bower to its parent Minny is not a normal sale. The property's carrying value of $2m probably reflects the current value as it was revalued at the year end, but the 'sale' price is only $1m. In effect, this is a distribution of profits of $1m, the shortfall on the transfer.

Distributions of this kind are not necessarily wrong or illegal. Bower's retained earnings of $442m, plus the 'realised' revaluation surplus of $400,000 more than cover the distribution, so, depending on the distributable profits rules in the jurisdiction in which it operates, it is likely to be legal.

Certain IFRS may apply to the transfer.

(i) If the asset **meets the held for sale** criteria under IFRS 5 *Non-current assets held for sale and discontinued operations,* it will **continue to be included** in the consolidated financial statements, but it will be **presented separately** from other assets in the statement of financial position. An asset that is held for sale should be measured at the **lower of** its **carrying amount** and **fair value less costs to sell.** Immediately before classification of the asset as held for sale, the entity must update any impairment test carried out.

(ii) As the transfer is from a subsidiary to its parent, **IAS 24 *Related party disclosures*** will apply and in the **individual financial statements of Bower and Minny, although it would be eliminated on consolidation.** Knowledge of related party relationships and transactions affects the way in which users assess a company's operations and the risks and opportunities that it faces. Even if the company's transactions and operations have not been affected by a related party relationship, disclosure puts users on notice that they may be affected in future, but in this case the related party relationship clearly has affected the price of the transfer.

Even though the transfer is likely to be legal, and even if it is correctly accounted for and disclosed in accordance with IAS 24 and IFRS 5 (or IAS 16 if the IFRS 5 criteria are not met) the transaction raises ethical issues. **Ethical behaviour** in the preparation of financial statements, is of **paramount importance**. This applies equally to preparers of accounts, to auditors and to accountants giving advice to directors.

Financial statements may be manipulated for all kinds of reasons, for example to enhance a profit-linked bonus or to disguise an unfavourable liquidity position. In this case, suspicion might be aroused by the fact that **the transfer of the property between group companies at half the current value has no obvious logical purpose**, and looks like a cosmetic exercise of some kind, although its motives are unclear. Accounting information should be truthful and neutral, and while the transaction is probably permissible, the **directors need to explain** why they are doing it.

Question 2

Marking scheme

	Marks
(a) 1 mark per point up to maximum	7
(b) 1 mark per point up to maximum	5
(c) 1 mark per point up to maximum	6
(d) 1 mark per point up to maximum	5
Professional marks	2
	25

(a)   Green certificates

The applicable standard relating to the green certificates is IAS 20 *Accounting for government grants and disclosure of government assistance.*

The principle behind the standard is that of accruals or matching: the **grant received must be matched with the related costs**.

Government grants are assistance by government in the form of transfers of resources to an entity in return for past or future compliance with certain conditions relating to the operating activities of the entity. A government grant is recognised only when there is reasonable assurance that the entity will comply with the conditions attaching to it and the grants will be received. In the case of the green certificates, the condition that must be complied with is the environmentally friendly production of electricity, as verified by the an independent audit.

There are two main types of grants:

(i)   **Grants related to assets.** These are grants whose primary condition is that an entity qualifying for them should purchase, construct or otherwise acquire long-term assets. Subsidiary conditions may also be attached restricting the type or location of the assets or the periods during which they are to be acquired or held.

(ii)   **Grants related to income.** These are government grants other than grants related to assets.

Since Coate can trade the green certificates, they are not long-term assets, and therefore fall into the category of **grants related to income.** They must be matched against the related costs of production of 'green electricity', as they are a form of government compensation for these costs.

There are two possible ways of presenting the grants (green certificates).

(i)   As a credit in profit or loss, either separately or under a general heading such as 'other income', or

(ii)   As a deduction from the related expense.

The **green certificates** are items held for sale in the ordinary course of business, and therefore should be recognised as **inventories** in accordance with IAS 2 *Inventories.* Green certificates that are unsold at the end of the reporting period are included in inventory and charged to production as **part of the cost of sales.**

A **deferred income approach** is used to match the grant to the related cost as follows.

To record the quarterly receipt of the grant

| DEBIT | Certificate (SOFP) | $ Fair value of certificate at receipt |
| CREDIT | Deferred income (SOFP) | $ Fair value of certificate at receipt |

On the sale of a certificate: contribution to cost of production

When the certificate is sold its fair value may be recognised in profit or loss. It is treated as a deduction from cost of sales because it is a contribution to the cost of generating the 'green electricity'.

| DEBIT | Deferred income (SOFP) | $ Fair value of certificate at receipt |
| CREDIT | Cost of sales (SPLOCI) | $ Fair value of certificate at receipt |

On the sale of a certificate: surplus/deficit

The certificate may be sold for more or less than its fair value at the time it was received from the government. This surplus/deficit is taken to/deducted from revenue in the SPLOCI.

DEBIT	Bank/receivable (SOFP)	$ Fair value of trade
CREDIT	Certificate (SOFP)	$ Fair value of certificate at receipt
DEBIT/CREDIT	Revenue (SPLOCI)	$ Balance (deficit/surplus)

Following IAS 1 *Presentation of financial statements,* Coates is required to **disclose its accounting policy** in relation to government grants. IAS 20 specifically requires disclosure of **the nature and extent of the government assistance given and any conditions not yet fulfilled or related contingencies.** The disclosures of unfulfilled conditions are unlikely to be extensive because an audit must be completed to show that the conditions have been fulfilled.

(b)   **Foreign exchange and cash flows**

According to IAS 7 *Statement of cash flows,* **unrealised foreign exchange gains and losses are not cash flows.** However, IAS 7 requires that the components making up the total opening and closing balances of cash and cash equivalents in the statement of cash flows should be disclosed in order to **reconcile cash and cash equivalents at the beginning and end of the period.**

Individual accounts (foreign cash balances)

Coates holds **foreign currency cash and cash equivalent** balances. As these are **monetary items**, IAS 21 *The effects of changes in foreign exchange rates* requires them to be **retranslated at the closing rate** at the reporting date. Exchange **gains and losses are recorded in profit or loss** in Coates's **individual** financial statements

In the **consolidated statement of cash flows,** if the **indirect method** is adopted, these exchange differences are **removed from profit before tax** as an adjustment within 'operating activities' . Instead they are shown at the foot of the consolidated statement of cash flows (as a separate heading from operating, investing and financing activities) as **part of the reconciliation** between opening and closing cash and cash equivalent balances.

Group accounts (overseas subsidiary)

IAS 21 requires the **assets and liabilities** (both monetary and non-monetary) of the overseas subsidiary to be **translated at the closing rate in the consolidated financial statements. Income and expenses** are

translated at the rate ruling at the date of the transaction or the **average rate** as a close approximation. **Exchange differences** arising on retranslation of opening net assets and profit are recorded in **other comprehensive income** and then held as a separate component of equity. **On disposal** of the subsidiary, the gains or losses are **reclassified from other comprehensive income to profit or loss for the year.**

As the subsidiary was acquired during the current year, its cash and cash equivalents at the date of acquisition would have been recorded as a **cash flow within 'investing activities'.** As its year end cash and cash equivalents balance would have also been included in the closing cash and cash equivalents balance at the foot of the group statement of cash flows translated at the closing rate, the exchange difference arising from the **movement in exchange rates** between the acquisition date and the year-end will have to be shown **separately at the foot of the statement of cash flows** as part of the movement in cash and cash equivalents.

(c)   **Treatment of former subsidiary**

Coate wishes to continue to consolidate its investment in Patten, of which it has sold 50% to Manis. The requirement (or in this case permission) to consolidate an investment is determined by **control**, not merely by ownership. In most cases, this will involve the parent company owning a majority of the ordinary shares in the subsidiary (to which normal voting rights are attached). There are circumstances, however, when the parent may own an equal share or only a minority of the voting power in the subsidiary, *but* the parent still has control. Coate is arguing that it still has control over Patten because of the agreement made with Manis that Coate would exercise general control over Patten's operating and financial policies. Whether this is the case will be determined in accordance with IRS 10 *Consolidated financial statements.*

IFRS 10 states that an investor **controls** an investee if and only if it has all of the following.

(i)   **Power** over the investee

(ii)   Exposure, or rights, to **variable returns** from its involvement with the investee, and

(iii)   The **ability to use its power** over the investee to affect the amount of the investor's returns.

Power is defined as **existing rights that give the current ability to direct the relevant activities of the investee**. In some cases assessing power is straightforward, for example, where power is obtained directly and solely from having the majority of voting rights or potential voting rights, and as a result the ability to direct relevant activities. In other cases, assessment is more complex and more than one factor must be considered. Coate has only 50% of the voting rights of Patten, and so other factors come into play here.

IFRS 10 gives the following examples of **rights**, other than voting or potential voting rights, which individually, or alone, can give an investor power.

(i)   Rights to appoint, reassign or remove key management personnel who can direct the relevant activities

(ii)   Rights to appoint or remove another entity that directs the relevant activities

(iii)   Rights to direct the investee to enter into, or veto changes to transactions for the benefit of the investor

(iv)   Other rights, such as those specified in a management contract.

Coates does not appear to have these rights over Patten. While the shareholder agreement gives Coates influence over Patten, the requirement for consensus with Manis relates to **decisions made in the ordinary course of business,** such as significant changes in the company's activities or budgets, appointment and dismissal of senior employees. Coates argues that it is customary within the industry to require shareholder consensus for such decisions, but the **extent of the restrictions precludes control by Coates**. Rather, the consensus requirements suggest **joint control,** and indicate that this is a joint arrangement, as per IFRS 11 *Joint arrangements.* IFRS 11 defines joint control as:

> The contractually agreed sharing of control of an arrangement, which exists only when decisions about the relevant activities require the unanimous consent of the parties sharing control

There are two types of joint arrangements: joint ventures and jointly controlled entities. Patten is a **separate vehicle**. As such, it could be either a joint operation or joint venture, so other facts must be considered.

There are no facts that suggest that Coates and Manis have rights to the assets of Patten in the consolidated financial statements nor an obligation for its liabilities. Therefore, as each party has an interest in the **net assets** of Patten, Patten should be treated as a **joint venture** (rather than a joint operation). Manis must be **de-consolidated from the Coates group,** and **equity accounted for** as a **joint venture** instead.

(d)   **Tax adjustment**
According to IAS 12 *Income taxes* the tax expense in the statement of profit or loss and other comprehensive income includes the tax charge for the year, any under or overprovision of income tax from the previous year and any increase or decrease in the deferred tax provision:

	$
Current tax expense	X
Under/overprovisions relating to prior periods	X/(X)
Increases/decreases in the deferred tax balance	X/(X)
	X

While the correction of an over or under provision relates to a prior period, this is **not a prior period adjustment** as defined in IAS 8 *Accounting policies, changes in accounting estimates and errors* and as assumed by Coates. Rather, it is a **change in accounting estimate.**

Changes in accounting estimates result from new information or new developments and, accordingly, are **not corrections of errors.** A prior period error, which would require a prior period adjustment is **an omission or misstatement arising form failure to use reliable information** that was available or could have been obtained at the time of the authorisation of the financial statements. This is **not the case here.** Coates had accounted for all known issues at the previous year end (30 November 20X1), and could not have foreseen that the tax adjustment would be required. No penalties were applied by the taxation authorities, indicating that there were no fundamental errors in the information provided to them. Correction of an over- or under-provision for taxation is routine, since taxation liabilities are difficult to estimate.

The effect of a change in accounting estimate must be **applied by the company prospectively** by including it in profit or loss in the period of change, with separate disclosure of the adjustment in the financial statements.

Question 3

> **Text reference.** Specialised industries are covered in general terms in Chapter 20 of your Study Text. Investment property and impairment are covered in Chapter 4, leases are covered in Chapter 11 and provisions in Chapter 9.
>
> **Top tips.** As usual, this specialised industry question does not require knowledge the sector concerned. However, the fact that this is a local government organisation partly affects the use to which the properties are put in Parts (a) and (d). Part (a) requires application rather than just knowledge, but the issues are uncontroversial. Part (b) was tricky as the detailed guidance on whether an arrangement is a lease is covered by a document not examinable. However, you should have been able to make a reasonable argument from the *Conceptual Framework* and IAS 17 *Leases*.
>
> **Easy marks.** Part (a) on investment property should be familiar to you from your F7 studies, and Part (c) is a very straightforward test of IAS 37.
>
> **ACCA Examiner's answer.** The Examiner's answer to this question is included at the back of this Kit.

	Marks
(a) 1 mark per point up to maximum	7
(b) 1 mark per point up to maximum	6
(c) 1 mark per point up to maximum	4
(d) 1 mark per point up to maximum	6
Professional marks	2
	25

(a) **Investment property**

IAS 40 *Investment property* applies to the accounting for property (land and/or buildings) **held to earn rentals or for capital appreciation or both.** Examples of investment property given in the standard include, but are not limited to:

(i) Land held for **long-term capital appreciation**

(ii) Land held for **undetermined future use**

Assets which IAS 40 states are not investment property, and which are therefore **not covered** by the standard include:

(i) Property held for use in the **production or supply of goods or services** or for administrative purposes

(ii) Property held for **sale in the ordinary course of business** or in the process of construction of development for such sale

Owner-occupied property, property being **constructed on behalf of third parties** and property leased to a third party **under a finance lease** are also specifically **excluded** by the IAS 40 definition.

If the entity provides **ancillary services** to the occupants of a property held by the entity, the appropriateness of classification as investment property is determined by the significance of the services provided. If those services are a relatively insignificant component of the arrangement as a whole (for instance, the building owner supplies security and maintenance services to the lessees), then the entity may treat the property as investment property. **Where the services provided are more significant** (such as in the case of an owner-managed hotel), the property should be classified as **owner-occupied.**

Applying IAS 40 to Blackcutt's properties, **the land owned for capital appreciation** and which may be sold any time in the future **will qualify as investment property.** Likewise, the **land whose use has not yet been determined** is also covered by the IAS 40 definition of investment property: as it has no current purpose it is deemed to be held for capital appreciation.

Investment property should be recognised as an asset where it is probable that the future economic benefits associated with the property will flow to the entity and the value can be measured reliably. IAS 40 permits an entity to choose between the cost model and the fair value model. Where the fair value model applies, the property is valued in accordance with IFRS 13 *Fair value measurement.* Gains or losses arising from changes in the fair value of investment property are recognised in profit or loss for the year.

The **houses routinely bought and sold** by Blackcutt in the ordinary course of its operations will **not qualify as investment property**, but will be treated under IAS 2 *Inventories.*

The **part of the housing inventory** not held for sale but **used to provide housing to low-income employees does not qualify as investment property** either. The properties are **not held for capital appreciation**, and because the rent is **below market rate** and only covers the maintenance costs, **they cannot be said to be held for rentals.** The **rental income is incidental** to the purposes for which the property is held, which is to provide housing services. As with the example of the owner-managed hotel above, the services are significant, and the property should be classified as **owner occupied.** Further indication that it is owner occupied is provided by the fact that it is rented out to **employees of the organisation.** It will be accounted for under IAS 16 *Property, plant and equipment.*

(b)   **Lease**

The issue here is whether the arrangement with the private sector provider Waste and Co is, or contains, a lease, even if it does not take the legal form of a lease. The **substance of the arrangement should be considered** in connection with the *Conceptual Framework for Financial Reporting* and IAS 17 *Leases*. Key factors to consider are as follows.

(i)   Who obtains most of the **benefit** from the asset?

(ii)   Who **controls** the asset by operating it or directing others to do so?

(iii)   Who has the **right to use** the asset or to direct others to do so?

(iv)   Who has the **risks and rewards** associated with the asset?

The answer in each case is **Blackcutt.**

(i)   Waste and Co purchases the vehicles and uses them exclusively for Blackcutt. If Waste and Co goes out of business, Blackcutt can re-possess the vehicles and continue to use them for waste collection.

(ii)   Blackcutt controls the vehicles, since it stipulates how they are painted, and ostensibly owns them because they must be painted with Blackcutt's name.

(iii)   Blackcutt can use the vehicles and uses them exclusively for waste collection for nearly all their life.

(iv)   Following on from this, Blackcutt has the risks and rewards associated with the asset.

The arrangement is in substance **a lease**. As Blackcutt has **substantially all the risks and rewards of ownership,** the arrangement should be treated as a **finance lease.** The vehicles should be recorded in assets in Blackcutt's statement of financial position, with a corresponding lease liability. The value of the lease may be determined by considering the fair value of acquiring the vehicle. The service element relating to the waste collection may be considered separately.

(c)   **Provision**

Under IAS 37 *Provisions, contingent liabilities and contingent assets,* provisions must be recognised in the following circumstances, and must not be recognised if they do not apply.

(i)   There is a **legal** or **constructive obligation** to transfer benefits as a result of **past events**.
(ii)   It is probably that **an outflow of economic resources** will be required to **settle** the **obligation.**
(iii)   A **reliable estimate** of the amount required to settle the obligation can be made.

A legal or constructive obligation is one created by an **obligating event.** Here the obligating event is the **contamination of the land**, because of the virtual certainty of legislation requiring the clean-up. As Blackcutt has no recourse against Chemco or its insurance company this past event will certainly give rise to a **transfer of economic benefits from** Blackcutt.

Consequently, Blackcutt **must recognise a provision** for the best estimate of the clean-up costs. It should **not set up a corresponding receivable**, since no reimbursement may be obtained from Chemco or its insurance company.

(d)   **Impairment of building**

The basic principle of IAS 36 *Impairment of assets* is that an asset should be carried at no more than its recoverable amount, that is the amount to be recovered through use or sale of the asset. If an **asset's value** is **higher than its recoverable amount**, an **impairment loss** has occurred. The impairment loss should be **written off** against profit or loss for the year.

Entities must determine, at each reporting date, whether there are any indications that impairment has occurred. In this case, **impairment is indicated** because the use to which the building is to be put has changed significantly (from a school to a library), a situation which will continue for the foreseeable future.

The **recoverable amount** is **defined** as the **higher** of the **asset's fair value less costs to sell** and the asset's **value in use.** However, these values are unavailable because of the specialised nature of the asset, and the only information available is depreciated replacement cost. Using a **depreciated replacement cost approach**, the impairment loss would be calculated as follows.

Asset	Cost/replacement cost $'000	Accumulated depreciation 6/25 $'000	Carrying amount/ replacement cost $'000
School	5,000	(1,200)	3,800
Library	2,100	(504)	(1,596)
Impairment loss			2,204

Blackcutt should therefore recognise an **impairment loss of $2.204m** in profit or loss for the year.

Question 4

Text reference. Fair value measurement under IFRS 13 is covered in Chapter 7 of your Study Text with more detail on business combination aspects in Chapter 12. The IFRS 13 definition of fair value occurs throughout the text and is relevant to many topics.

Top tips. Fair value measurement is a topical issue and the subject of a recent standard. In recent sittings there has been a computational element in the current issues question. This time it is more detailed and technical than in previous settings. However, students would do well to apply common sense to the information in the scenario, even if not confident in their knowledge, bearing in mind the examiner's comment to a previous paper: 'often the content of the scenario will help students answer the question as the scenario gives candidates direction in terms of their answers.'

Easy marks. Credit will be given for textbook knowledge in Part (a) of the principles of IFRS 13 *Fair value measurement* and its three-level hierarchy, which candidates should have found straightforward.

ACCA Examiner's answer. The examiner's answer to this question is included at the back of this kit.

Marking scheme

		Marks
(a)	(i) 1 mark per point up to maximum	7
	(ii) IFRS 13 hierarchy	6
(b)	1 mark per point up to maximum	6
	Calculations	4
Professional marks		2
		25

(a) (i) **IFRS 13 principles of fair value measurement**

IFRS 13 *Fair value measurement* defines fair value as **'the price that would be received to sell an asset or paid to transfer a liability in an orderly transaction between market participants at the measurement date.'**

The previous definition used in IFRS was 'the amount for which an asset could be exchanged, or a liability settled, between knowledgeable, willing parties in an arm's length transaction'.

The price which would be received to sell the asset or paid to transfer (not settle) the liability is described as the 'exit price', the definition also used in US GAAP. Although the concept of the 'arm's length transaction' has now gone, the market-based current exit price retains the notion of an exchange between unrelated, knowledgeable and willing parties.

Fair value is a **market-based measurement,** not an entity-specific measurement. It **focuses on assets and liabilities and on exit (selling) prices.** It also takes into account market conditions at the measurement date. In other words, it looks at the amount for which the holder of an asset could sell it and the amount which the holder of a liability would have to pay to transfer it. It can also be used to value an entity's own equity instruments.

Because it is a market-based measurement, fair value is measured using the assumptions that market participants would use when pricing the asset, taking into account any relevant characteristics of the asset.

It is assumed that the transaction to sell the asset or transfer the liability takes place either:

(1) In the **principal market** for the asset or liability; or

(2) In the absence of a principal market, in the **most advantageous market** for the asset or liability.

The **principal market** is the market which is the **most liquid** (has the greatest volume and level of activity for that asset or liability). In most cases the principal market and the most advantageous market will be the same.

Fair value is **not adjusted for transaction costs.** Under IFRS 13, these are **not a feature of the asset or liability,** but may be taken into account when **determining the most advantageous market.**

Fair value measurements are based on an asset or a liability's **unit of account**, which is specified not by IFRS 13, but by each IFRS where a fair value measurement is required. For most assets and liabilities, the unit of account is the individual asset or liability, but in some instances may be a group of assets or liabilities.

IFRS 13 acknowledges that when **market activity declines**, an entity must use a **valuation technique** to measure fair value. In this case the emphasis must be on whether a transaction price is based on an orderly transaction, rather than a forced sale.

The IFRS identifies **three valuation approaches.**

(1) **Market approach.** A valuation technique that uses prices and other relevant information generated by market transactions involving identical or comparable (ie similar) assets, liabilities or a group of assets and liabilities, such as a business.

(2) **Cost approach.** A valuation technique that reflects the amount that would be required currently to replace the service capacity of an asset (often referred to as current replacement cost).

(3) **Income approach.** Valuation techniques that convert future amounts (eg cash flows or income and expenses) to a single current (ie discounted) amount. The fair value measurement is determined on the basis of the value indicated by current market expectations about those future amounts.

For **non-financial assets** the fair value measurement looks at the use to which the asset can be put. It takes into account the ability of a market participant to generate economic benefits by using the asset in its **highest and best use.**

(ii)   **IFRS 13 three-level hierarchy for fair value measurement**

IFRS 13 states that valuation techniques must be those which are appropriate and for which sufficient data are available. Entities should maximise the use of relevant **observable inputs** and minimise the use of **unobservable inputs**. The standard establishes a three-level hierarchy for the inputs that valuation techniques use to measure fair value:

Level 1	**Quoted prices** (unadjusted) in active markets for identical assets or liabilities that the reporting entity can access at the measurement date. If there is a quoted price in an active market, an entity uses that rice without adjustment to measure fair value. An example is prices on a stock exchange. Active markets are ones where transactions take place with sufficient frequency and volume for pricing information to be provided.	
Level 2	**Inputs other than quoted prices** included within Level 1 that are observable for the asset or liability, either directly or indirectly, eg quoted prices for similar assets in active markets or for identical or similar assets in non-active markets or use of quoted interest rates for valuation purposes	
Level 3	**Unobservable inputs** for the asset or liability, ie using the entity's own assumptions about market exit value. For example, cash flow forecasts may be used to value an entity that is not listed.	

Each fair value measurement is categorized based on the lowest level input that is significant to it.

Entities may use more than one valuation technique to measure fair value in a given situation. A **change of valuation technique** is **considered to be a change of accounting estimate** in accordance with IAS 8. However, the disclosures in IAS 8 for a change in accounting estimate are **not required** for revisions resulting from a change in valuation technique or its application.

(b)   (i)   **Fair value of asset**

Year to 30 November 20X2	Asian market	European market	Australasian market
Volume of market - units	4m	2m	1m
	$		$
Price	19	16	22
Costs of entering the market	(2)	(2)	n/a*
Potential fair value	17	14	22
Transaction costs	(1)	(2)	(2)
Net profit	16	12	20

*Notes

(1)   Because Jayach currently buys and sells the asset in the Australasian market, the **costs of entering that market** are not incurred and therefore **not relevant.**

(2)   Fair value is **not adjusted for transaction costs.** Under IFRS 13, these are not a feature of the asset or liability, but may be taken into account when determining the most advantageous market.

(3)   The **Asian market is the principal market** for the asset because it is the market with the greatest volume and level of activity for the asset. If information about the Asian market is available and Jayach can access the market, then Jayach should base its fair value on this market. Based on the Asian market, the **fair value of the asset would be $17**, measured as the price that would be received in that market ($19) less costs of entering the market ($2) and ignoring transaction costs.

(4)   If **information** about the Asian market is **not available**, or if Jayach **cannot access the market**, Jayach must measure the fair value of the asset using the price in the **most advantageous market.** The most advantageous market is the market that maximises the amount that would be received to sell the asset, after taking into account both transaction costs and usually also costs of entry, that is the net amount that would be received in the respective markets. The most advantageous market here is therefore the **Australasian market.** As explained above, costs of entry are not relevant here, and so, based on this market, the **fair value would be $22.**

It is assumed that market participants are independent of each other and knowledgeable, and able and willing to enter into transactions.

(ii) **Fair value of decommissioning liability**

Because this is a business combination, Jayach must measure the liability at fair value in accordance with IFRS 13, rather than using the best estimate measurement required by IAS 37 *Provisions, contingent liabilities and contingent assets*. In most cases there will be no observable market to provide pricing information. If this is the case here, Jayach will use **the expected present value technique** to measure the fair value of the decommissioning liability. If Jayach were contractually committed to transfer its decommissioning liability to a market participant, it would conclude that a market participant would use the inputs as follows, arriving at a **fair value of $3,215,000.**

Input	Amount
	$'000
Labour and material cost	2,000
Overhead: 30% × 2,000	600
Third party mark-up – industry average: 2,600 × 20%	520
	3120
Inflation adjusted total (5% compounded over three years): 3,120 × 1.05³	3,612
Risk adjustment – uncertainty relating to cash flows: 3,612 × 6%	217
	3,829
Discount at risk-free rate plus entity's non-performance risk (4% + 2% = 6%): 3,829 ÷ 1.06³	3,215

ACCA examiner's answers: June and December 2012 papers

> **Note:** The ACCA examiner's answers are correct at the time of going to press but may be subject to some amendments before the final versions are published.

1 **(a)** Robby Consolidated Statement of Financial Position at 31 May 2012

	$m
Assets	
Non-current assets:	
Property, plant and equipment (W8)	241·13
Goodwill (5 + 1) (W1 and W2)	6·00
Financial assets	29·00
Current assets (W9)	36·00
Total assets	312·13
Equity and Liabilities	
Ordinary shares	25·00
Other components of equity (W3)	2·00
Retained earnings (W3)	81·45
Total equity	108·45
Non-controlling interest (W4)	27·64
Total equity	136·09
Non-current liabilities including provision (W11)	94·84
Current liabilities (W10)	81·20
Total equity and liabilities	312·13

Working 1

Hail

	$m
Fair value of consideration for 80% interest	50·00
Fair value of non-controlling interest	15·00
	65·00
Fair value of identifiable net assets acquired	(60·00)
Goodwill	5·00

On consolidation, there will be a reversal of the fair value adjustments to the investment held at fair value through profit and loss. Further, the dividend income on investment should be taken to profit or loss and not other comprehensive income. Therefore the adjustments required are:

Dr Other comprehensive income	5·00
Cr Investment in Hail	5·00
Dr Other comprehensive income	2·00
Cr Retained earnings	2·00

Working 2

Zinc

	$m
Consideration: at 1 June 2009	2·00
at 1 June 2011	16·00
Increase in fair value to 31 May 2011	1·00
Investment in Zinc in Robby's financial statements	19·00
Increase in fair value of equity interest (5·00 – 2·00 – 1·00)	2·00
Fair value of consideration	21·00
Fair value of non-controlling interest	9·00
	30·00
Fair value of identifiable net assets	(26·00)
Increase in value	(3·00)
Goodwill	1·00

Working 3

Retained earnings

	$m
Robby:	
Balance at 31 May 2012	70·00
Dividend from Hail	2·00
Increase in fair value of equity interest – Zinc	2·00
Post-acquisition reserves: Hail	8·80
Zinc	2·16
Joint operation	0·68
Impairment loss	(0·70)
Transfer from OCE	0·11
Factoring trade receivables	0·40
Reversal of disposal profit on land under option	(4·00)
	81·45

Hail:	
Group reserves – 80% of 11	8·80
NCI – 20% of 11	2·20
Post-acquisition reserves (27 – 16)	11·00

Zinc:	
Post-acquisition reserves (19 – 15)	4·00
Less increase in depreciation (W2)	(0·40)
	3·60
Group reserves – 60% of 3·60	2·16
NCI – 40% of 3·60	1·44
	3·60

Other components of equity

	$m
Robby:	
Balance at 31 May 2012	11·00
Dividend to retained earnings	(2·00)
Profit on revaluation of investment in Hail	(5·00)
Impairment loss	(1·89)
Transfer to retained earnings	(0·11)
	2·00

Working 4

Non-controlling interest

	$m
Hail:	
At acquisition	15·00
Post-acquisition share	2·20
	17·20
Zinc:	
At acquisition	9·00
Post-acquisition share	1·44
	10·44
Total	27·64

Working 5

Trade receivables

The correcting double entry is:

	$m
DR Trade receivables	4·00
CR Secured borrowings	3·60
CR Retained earnings	0·40

Working 6

Impairment of PPE

Any impairment loss on a revalued asset is charged to other comprehensive income to the extent of the amount relating to that asset in the revaluation surplus and thereafter in profit or loss.

PPE	Depreciated historical cost $m	Revalued carrying amount $m
31 May 2011	9·00	9·00
Revaluation		2·00
Total	9·00	11·00
Depreciation to 31 May 2012	(0·50)	(0·61)
Balance 31 May 2012	8·50	10·39
Impairment loss	(0·70)	(2·59)
31 May 2012 after impairment loss	7·80	7·80

There will have been a transfer of $0·11 (0·61 – 0·50) million from the revaluation surplus to retained earnings for the excess depreciation charged in the year so the remaining amount in the revaluation surplus is $1·89m (2·00 – 0·11). $1·89m of the impairment will be recognised in other comprehensive income and the remaining $0·7m in profit or loss.

Working 7

Joint operation

SOFP	1 June 2011 $m	Dismantling cost $m	Depreciation $m	Unwinding of discount $m	31 May 2012 $m
PPE	6	2 x 40%	(6·8 x 1/10)		6·12
Trade receivables					8
Trade payables (0·2 + 6·4)					6·6
Provision		0·8		0·04	0·84

Income statement	
Revenue (20·00 x 40%)	8
Cost of sales (16·00 x 40%)	(6·4)
Operating cost (0·50 x 40%)	(0·2)
Depreciation	(0·68)
Finance expense	(0·04)
Net profit	0·68

Working 8

Property, plant and equipment

	$m	$m
Robby	112·00	
Hail	60·00	
Zinc	26·00	
		198·00
Increase in value of land – Hail (60 – 20 – 16)		24·00
Increase in value of PPE – Zinc (26 – 10 – 15)		1·00
Further increase in value of PPE at acquisition		3·00
Less: increased depreciation (1 + 3)/5 x 6/12		(0·40)
Impairment loss		(2·59)
Joint operation (W7)		6·12
Land – option to repurchase		12·00
		241·13

The sale of land should not be recognised in the financial statements as the risks and rewards of ownership have not been transferred. The land can be repurchased at the sale price plus a premium, which represents effectively an interest payment. It is effectively manipulating the financial statements in order to show a better cash position. The land should be reinstated at its carrying amount before the transaction, so $12 million, a current liability recognised of $16 million and the profit on disposal of $4 million that was recorded reversed.

Working 9

Current assets

	$m	$m
Robby	5·00	
Hail	7·00	
Zinc	12·00	
		24·00
Factoring trade receivables		4·00
Joint operation (W7)		8·00
		36·00

Working 10

Current liabilities

	$m
Robby	47·00
Hail	6·00
Zinc	2·00
Secured borrowings	3·60
Joint operation (W7) (6·40 trade payable + 0·20 operating costs)	6·60
Land sale	16·00
	81·20

Working 11

Non-current liabilities

	$m
Robby	53·00
Hail	20·00
Zinc	21·00
Joint operation (0·80 provision + unwinding of discount 0·04) (W7)	0·84
	94·84

(b) **(i)** The basic rules for the derecognition model in IFRS 9 *Financial Instruments* is to determine whether the asset under consideration for derecognition is:

(i) an asset in its entirety, or

(ii) specifically identified cash flows from an asset (or a group of similar financial assets), or

(iii) a fully proportionate (pro rata) share of the cash flows from an asset (or a group of similar financial assets), or

(iv) a fully proportionate (pro rata) share of specifically identified cash flows from a financial asset (or a group of similar financial assets).

Once the asset under consideration for de-recognition has been determined, an assessment is made as to whether the asset should be derecognised. Derecognition is required if either:

(i) the contractual rights to the cash flows from the financial asset have expired, or

(ii) financial asset has been transferred, and if so, whether the transfer of that asset is subsequently eligible for derecognition.

An asset is transferred if either the entity has transferred the contractual rights to receive the cash flows, or the entity has retained the contractual rights to receive the cash flows from the asset, but has assumed a contractual obligation to pass those cash flows on under an arrangement that meets the following three conditions:

(i) the entity has no obligation to pay amounts to the eventual recipient unless it collects equivalent amounts on the original asset;

(ii) the entity is prohibited from selling or pledging the original asset (other than as security to the eventual recipient);

(iii) the entity has an obligation to remit those cash flows without material delay.

Once an entity has determined that the asset has been transferred, it then determines whether or not it has transferred substantially all of the risks and rewards of ownership of the asset. If substantially all the risks and rewards have been transferred, the asset is derecognised. If substantially all the risks and rewards have been retained, derecognition of the asset is precluded. If the entity has neither retained nor transferred substantially all of the risks and rewards of the asset, then the entity must assess whether it has relinquished control of the asset or not. If the entity does not control the asset then derecognition is appropriate; however, if the entity has retained control of the asset, then the entity continues to

recognise the asset to the extent to which it has a continuing involvement in the asset. Robby has transferred its rights to receive cash flows and its maximum exposure is to repay $3·6 million. This is unlikely, but Robby has guaranteed that it will compensate the bank for all credit losses. Additionally, Robby receives the benefit of amounts received above $3·6 million and therefore retains both the credit risk and late payment risk. Substantially, all the risks and rewards remain with Robby and therefore the receivables should still be recognised.

(ii) Manipulation of financial statements often does not involve breaking rules, but the purpose of financial statements is to present a fair representation of the company's or group's position, and if the financial statements are misrepresented on purpose then this could be deemed unethical. The financial statements in this case are being manipulated to hide the fact that the group has liquidity problems. The Robby Group has severe problems with a current ratio of 0·44 ($36m/$81·2m) and a gearing ratio of 0·83 ($53 + 20 + 21 + factored receivables 3·6 + land option 16 = 113·6/equity interest including NCI $136·09m). The sale and repurchase of the land would make little difference to the overall position of the company, but would maybe stave off proceedings by the bank if the overdraft were eliminated. Robby has considerable PPE, which may be undervalued if the sale of the land is indicative of the value of all of the PPE.

Accountants have the responsibility to issue financial statements that do not mislead users as they assume that such professionals are acting in an ethical capacity, thus giving the financial statements credibility. Accountants should seek to promote or preserve the public interest. If the idea of a profession is to have any significance, then it must have the trust of users. Accountants should present financial statements that meet the qualitative characteristics set out in the Framework. Faithful representation and verifiability are two such concepts and it is critical that these concepts are applied in the preparation and disclosure of financial information.

2 (a) A lease is classified as a finance lease if it transfers substantially the entire risks and rewards incident to ownership. All other leases are classified as operating leases. Classification is made at the inception of the lease. Whether a lease is a finance lease or an operating lease depends on the substance of the transaction rather than the form. Situations that would normally lead to a lease being classified as a finance lease include the following:

– the lease transfers ownership of the asset to the lessee by the end of the lease term;

– the lessee has the option to purchase the asset at a price which is expected to be sufficiently lower than fair value at the date the option becomes exercisable that, at the inception of the lease, it is reasonably certain that the option will be exercised;

– the lease term is for the major part of the economic life of the asset, even if title is not transferred;

– at the inception of the lease, the present value of the minimum lease payments amounts to at least substantially all of the fair value of the leased asset;

– the lease assets are of a specialised nature such that only the lessee can use them without major modifications being made.

In this case the lease back of the building is for the major part of the building's economic life and the present value of the minimum lease payments amounts to all of the fair value of the leased asset. Therefore the lease should be recorded as a finance lease.

The building is derecognised at its carrying amount and then reinstated at its fair value with any disposal gain, in this instance $1·5 million ($5m – $3·5m) being deferred over the new lease term. The building is depreciated over the shorter of the lease term and useful economic life, so 20 years. Finance lease accounting results in a liability being created, finance charge accruing at the implicit rate within the lease, in this case 7%, and the payment reducing the lease liability in arriving at the year-end balance. The associated double entry for the lease is as follows:

	$000	$000
Sale of building		
Dr cash	5,000	
Cr building		3,500
deferred income		1,500
Leased asset and liability		
Dr asset – finance lease	5,000	
Cr finance lease creditor		5,000
Deferred income release		
Dr deferred income	75	
Cr profit or loss		75
Depreciation of asset		
Dr depreciation	250	
Cr assets under finance lease		250
Rentals paid		
Dr interest	350	
finance lease creditor	91	
Cr cash		441

(b) Under IAS 19 *Employee Benefits*, the accounting procedures would be:

Recognition of actuarial gains and losses (remeasurements):

Actuarial gains and losses are renamed 'remeasurements' and will be recognised immediately in 'other comprehensive income' (OCI). Actuarial gains and losses cannot be deferred or recognised in profit or loss; this is likely to increase volatility in the statement of financial position and OCI. Remeasurements recognised in OCI cannot be recycled through profit or loss in subsequent periods. Thus William will not be able to spread these gains and losses over the remaining working life of the employees.

Recognition of past service cost:

Past-service costs are recognised in the period of a plan amendment; unvested benefits cannot be spread over a future-service period. The plan benefits which were enhanced on 1 June 2011 would have to be immediately recognised and the unvested benefits would not be spread over five years from that date. A curtailment occurs only when an entity reduces significantly the number of employees. Curtailment gains/losses are accounted for as past-service costs. Thus William will need to realise that any curtailment is only recognised in these circumstances and will result in immediate recognition of any gain or loss.

Measurement of pension expense:

Annual expense for a funded benefit plan will include net interest expense or income, calculated by applying the discount rate to the net defined benefit asset or liability. The discount rate used is a high-quality corporate bond rate where there is a deep market in such bonds, and a government bond rate in other markets.

Presentation in the income statement:

The benefit cost will be split between (i) the cost of benefits accrued in the current period (service cost) and benefit changes (past-service cost, settlements and curtailments); and (ii) finance expense or income. This analysis can be in the income statement or in the notes.

(c) Expenses in respect of cash-settled share-based payment transactions should be recognised over the period during which goods are received or services are rendered, and measured at the fair value of the liability. The fair value of the liability should be remeasured at each reporting date until settled. Changes in fair value are recognised in the statement of comprehensive income.

The credit entry in respect of a cash-settled share-based payment transaction is presented as a liability. The fair value of each share appreciation right (SAR) is made up of an intrinsic value and its time value. The time value reflects the fact that the holders of each SAR have the right to participate in future gains. At 31 May 2012, the expense will comprise any increase in the liability plus the cash paid based on the intrinsic value of the SAR.

Liability 31 May 2012 (10 x 500 x $24)	$120,000
Liability 31 May 2011 (17 x 500 x $14)	($119,000)
Cash paid (7 x 500 x $21)	$73,500
Expense year ending 31 May 2012	$74,500

Therefore the expense for the year is $74,500 and the liability at the year end is $120,000.

(d) IAS 37 *Provisions, Contingent Liabilities and Contingent Assets* describes contingent liabilities in two ways. Firstly, as reliably possible obligations whose existence will be confirmed only on the occurrence or non-occurrence of uncertain future events outside the entity's control, or secondly, as present obligations that are not recognised because: (a) it is not probable that an outflow of economic benefits will be required to settle the obligation; or (b) the amount cannot be measured reliably.

In Chrissy's financial statements contingent liabilities are not recognised but are disclosed and described in the notes to the financial statements, including an estimate of their potential financial effect and uncertainties relating to the amount or timing of any outflow, unless the possibility of settlement is remote.

However, in a business combination, a contingent liability is recognised if it meets the definition of a liability and if it can be measured. The first type of contingent liability above under IAS 37 is not recognised in a business combination. However, the second type of contingency is recognised whether or not it is probable that an outflow of economic benefits takes place but only if it can be measured reliably. This means William would recognise a liability of $4 million in the consolidated accounts. Contingent liabilities are an exception to the recognition principle because of the reliable measurement criteria.

3 **(a)** The fair value model in IAS 40 *Investment Property* defines fair value as the amount for which an asset could be exchanged between knowledgeable, willing parties in an arm's length transaction. Fair value should reflect market conditions at the date of the statement of financial position. The standard gives a considerable amount of guidance on determining fair value; in particular, that the best evidence of fair value is given by current prices on an active market for similar property in the same location and condition and subject to similar lease and other constraints. Therefore investment properties are not being valued in accordance with the best possible method. This means that goodwill recognised on the acquisition of an investment property through a business combination of real estate investment companies is different as compared to what it should be under IFRS 3 *Business Combination* valuation principles. In reality, the fair value of both the property and the deferred tax liability are reflected in the purchase price of the business combination. The difference between this purchase price and the

net assets recognised according to IFRS 3, upon which deferred tax is based, is recognised as goodwill in the consolidated statement of financial position.

Ethan's methods for determining whether goodwill is impaired, and the amount it is impaired by, are not in accordance with IAS 36 *Impairment of Assets*. The standard requires assets (or cash generating units (CGU) if not possible to conduct the review on an asset by asset basis) to be stated at the lower of carrying amount and recoverable amount. The recoverable amount is the higher of fair value less costs to sell and value in use. Fair value less costs to sell is a post-tax valuation taking account of deferred taxes. According to IAS 36, the deferred tax liability should be included in calculating the carrying amount of the CGU, since the transaction price also includes the effect of the deferred tax and the purchaser assumes the tax risk. Therefore, the impairment testing of goodwill should be based on recoverable amount, rather than on the relationship between the goodwill and the deferred tax liability as assessed by Ethan.

Ethan should disclose both the methodology by which the recoverable amount of the CGU, and therefore goodwill, is determined and the assumptions underlying that methodology under the requirements of IAS 36. The standard requires Ethan to state the basis on which recoverable amount has been determined and to disclose the key assumptions on which it is based.

In accordance with IAS 36, where impairment testing takes place, goodwill is allocated to each individual real estate investment identified as a cash-generating unit (CGU). Periodically, but at least annually, the recoverable amount of the CGU is compared with its carrying amount. If this comparison results in the carrying amount being greater than the recoverable amount, the impairment is first allocated to the goodwill. Any further difference is subsequently allocated against the value of the investment property.

The recognition of deferred tax assets on losses carried forward is not in accordance with IAS 12 *Income Taxes*. Ethan is not able to provide convincing evidence to ensure that Ethan would be able to generate sufficient taxable profits against which the unused tax losses could be offset. Historically, Ethan's activities have generated either significant losses or very minimal profits; they have never produced large pre-tax profits. Therefore, in accordance with IAS 12, there is a need to produce convincing evidence from Ethan that it would be able to generate future taxable profits equivalent to the value of the deferred tax asset recognised.

Any decision would be based mainly on the following:

–   history of Ethan's pre-tax profits;

–   previously published budget expectations and realised results in the past;

–   Ethan's expectations for the next few years; and

–   announcements of new contracts.

There have been substantial negative variances arising between Ethan's budgeted and realised results. Also, Ethan has announced that it would not achieve the expected profit, but rather would record a substantial loss. Additionally, there is no indication that the losses were not of a type that could clearly be attributed to external events that might not be expected to recur. Thus the deferred tax asset should not be recognised or at the very least reduced.

(b)   Normally debt issued to finance Ethan's investment properties would be accounted for using amortised cost model. However, Ethan may apply the fair value option in IFRS 9 *Finanical Instruments* as such application would eliminate or significantly reduce a measurement or recognition inconsistency between the debt liabilities and the investment properties to which they are related. The provision requires there to be a measurement or recognition inconsistency that would otherwise arise from measuring assets or liabilities or recognising the gains and losses on them on different bases. The option is not restricted to financial assets and financial liabilities. The IASB concludes that accounting mismatches may occur in a wide variety of circumstances and that financial reporting is best served by providing entities with the opportunity of eliminating such mismatches where that results in more relevant information. Ethan supported the application of the fair value option with the argument that there is a specific financial correlation between the factors that form the basis of the measurement of the fair value of the investment properties and the related debt. Particular importance was placed on the role played by interest rates, although it is acknowledged that the value of investment properties will also depend, to some extent, on rent, location and maintenance and other factors. For some investment properties, however, the value of the properties will be dependent on the movement in interest rates.

Under IFRS 9, entities with financial liabilities designated as FVTPL recognise changes in the fair value due to changes in the liability's credit risk directly in other comprehensive income (OCI). There is no subsequent recycling of the amounts in OCI to profit or loss, but accumulated gains or losses may be transferred within equity. The movement in fair value due to other factors would be recognised within profit or loss. However, if presenting the change in fair value attributable to the credit risk of the liability in OCI would create or enlarge an accounting mismatch in profit or loss, all fair value movements are recognised in profit or loss. An entity is required to determine whether an accounting mismatch is created when the financial liability is first recognised, and this determination is not reassessed. The mismatch must arise due to an economic relationship between the financial liability and the associated asset that results in the liability's credit risk being offset by a change in the fair value of the asset. Financial liabilities that are required to be measured at FVTPL (as distinct from those that the entity has designated at FVTPL), including financial guarantees and loan commitments measured at FVTPL, have all fair value movement recognised in profit or loss. IFRS 9 retains the flexibility that existed in IFRS 7 *Financial Instruments: Disclosures* to determine the amount of fair value change that relates to changes in the credit risk of the liability.

(c) Ethan's classification of the B shares as equity instruments does not comply with IAS 32 *Financial Instruments: Presentation*. IAS 32 paragraph 11, defines a financial liability to include, amongst others, any liability that includes a contractual obligation to deliver cash or financial assets to another entity. The criteria for classification of a financial instrument as equity rather than liability are provided in IAS 32 paragraph 16. This states that the instrument is an equity instrument rather than a financial liability if, and only if, the instrument does not include a contractual obligation either to deliver cash or another financial asset to the entity or to exchange financial assets or liabilities with another entity under conditions that are potentially unfavourable to Ethan. IAS 32 paragraph AG29 explains that when classifying a financial instrument in consolidated financial statements, an entity should consider all the terms and conditions agreed between members of a group and holders of the instrument, in determining whether the group as a whole has an obligation to deliver cash or another financial instrument in respect of the instrument or to settle it in a manner that results in classification as a liability. Therefore, since the operating subsidiary is obliged to pay an annual cumulative dividend on the B shares and does not have discretion over the distribution of such dividend, the shares held by Ethan's external shareholders should be classified as a financial liability in Ethan's consolidated financial statements and not non-controlling interest. The shares being held by Ethan will be eliminated on consolidation as intercompany.

4 (a) (i) The existing guidance requires a provision to be recognised when: (a) it is probable that an obligation exists; (b) it is probable that an outflow of resources will be required to settle that obligation; and (c) the obligation can be measured reliably. The amount recognised as a provision should be the best estimate of the expenditure required to settle the present obligation at the balance sheet date, that is, the amount that an entity would rationally pay to settle the obligation at the balance sheet date or to transfer it to a third party. This guidance, when applied consistently, provides useful, predictive information about non-financial liabilities and the expected future cash flows, and is consistent with the recognition criteria in the Framework. The IASB has initiated a project to replace IAS 37 for three main reasons:

1. To address inconsistencies with other IFRSs. IAS 37 requires an entity to record an obligation as a liability only if it is probable (i.e. more than 50% likely) that the obligation will result in an outflow of cash or other resources from the entity. Other standards, such as IFRS 3 *Business Combinations* and IFRS 9 *Financial Instruments*, do not apply this 'probability of outflows' criterion to liabilities.

2. To achieve global convergence of accounting standards. The IASB is seeking to eliminate differences between IFRSs and US generally accepted accounting principles (US GAAP). At present, IFRSs and US GAAP differ in how they treat the costs of restructuring a business. IAS 37 requires an entity to record a liability for the total costs of restructuring a business when it announces or starts to implement a restructuring plan. In contrast, US GAAP requires an entity to record a liability for individual costs of a restructuring only when the entity has incurred that particular cost.

3. To improve measurement of liabilities in IAS 37. The requirements in IAS 37 for measuring liabilities are unclear. As a result, entities use different measures, making it difficult for analysts and investors to compare their financial statements. Two aspects of IAS 37 are particularly unclear. IAS 37 requires entities to measure liabilities at the 'best estimate' of the expenditure required to settle the obligation. In practice, there are different interpretations of what 'best estimate' means: the most likely outcome, the weighted average of all possible outcomes or even the minimum or maximum amount in the range of possible outcomes. IAS 37 does not specify the costs that entities should include in the measurement of a liability. In practice, entities include different costs. Some entities include only incremental costs while others include all direct costs, plus indirect costs and overheads, or use the prices they would pay contractors to fulfil the obligation on their behalf.

(ii) The IASB has decided that the new IFRS will not include the 'probability of outflows' criterion. Instead, an entity should account for uncertainty about the amount and timing of outflows by using a measurement that reflects their expected value, i.e. the probability-weighted average of the outflows for the range of possible outcomes. Removal of this criterion focuses attention on the definition of a liability in the Framework, which is a present obligation of an entity arising from past events, the settlement of which is expected to result in an outflow from the entity of resources embodying economic benefits. Furthermore, the new IFRS will require an entity to record a liability for each individual cost of a restructuring only when the entity incurs that particular cost.

The exposure draft proposes that the measurement should be the amount that the entity would rationally pay at the measurement date to be relieved of the liability. Normally, this amount would be an estimate of the present value of the resources required to fulfil the liability. It could also be the amount that the entity would pay to cancel or fulfil the obligation, whichever is the lowest. The estimate would take into account the expected outflows of resources, the time value of money and the risk that the actual outflows might ultimately differ from the expected outflows.

If the liability is to pay cash to a counterparty (for example to settle a legal dispute), the outflows would be the expected cash payments plus any associated costs, such as legal fees. If the liability is to undertake a service, for example to decommission plant at a future date, the outflows would be the amounts that the entity estimates it would pay a contractor at the future date to undertake the service on its behalf. Obligations involving services are to be measured by reference to the price that a contractor would charge to undertake the service, irrespective of whether the entity is carrying out the work internally or externally.

(b) Under IAS 37, a provision of $105 million would be recognised since this is the estimate of the present obligation. There will be no profit or loss impact other than the adjustment of the present value of the obligation to reflect the time value of money by unwinding the discount.

Under the proposed approach there are a number of different outcomes:

–   with no risk and probability adjustment, the initial liability would be recognised at $129 million which is the present value of the resources required to fulfil the obligation based upon third-party prices. This means that in 10 years the provision would have unwound to $180 million, the entity will spend $150 million in decommission costs and a profit of $30 million would be recognised. If there were no market for the dismantling of the platform, then Royan would recognise a liability by estimating the price that it would charge another party to carry out the service.

–   With risk and probability being taken into account, then the expected value would be (40% x $129m + 60% x $140m), i.e. $135·6m plus the risk adjustment of $5 million, which totals $140·6 million.

– $105 million being the present value of the future cashflows discounted.

The ED suggests that the entity should take the lower of:

(a)   the present value of the resources required to fulfil the obligation, i.e. $105 million;

(b)   the amount that the entity would have to pay to cancel the obligation, for which information is not available here; and

(c)   the amount that the entity would have to pay to transfer the obligation to a third party, i.e. $140·6 million incorporating the administrative costs.

Therefore $105 million should be provided.

The ED makes specific reference to provisions relating to services such as decommissioning where it suggests that the amount to transfer to a third party would be the required liability, so $140·6 million would be provided.

Marks

1 **(a)** Property, plant and equipment   6
Goodwill   6
NCI   4
Financial asset   1
Current asset   3
OCE   3
Retained earnings   6
Non-current liabilities   2
Current liabilities   4
    ──
    35
    ──

(b) **(i)** 1 mark per point up to max   9

(ii) Manipulation   2
Ethical discussion   4
    ──
    6
    ──
    50
    ──

2 **(a)** Definition of lease   3
Leaseback principle   1
Accounting   3

(b) Accounting treatment   7

(c) Cash-based payments   2
Calculation   3

(d) Contingent liability – discussion   4

Communication skills   2
    ──
    25
    ──

3 Impairment testing   5
Deferred taxation   6
Fair value option – IFRS 9   7
Financial liability   5
Communication skills   2
    ──
    25
    ──

4 Existing guidance and critique   9
New proposals   7
IAS 37 and ED   7
Communication skills   2
    ──
    25
    ──

1 Minny Group

(a) Consolidated Statement of Financial Position at 30 November 2012

	$m
Assets:	
Non-current assets:	
Property, plant and equipment (W9)	1,606·00
Goodwill (W2)	190·00
Intangible assets (W4)	227·00
Investment in Puttin (W3)	50·50
	2,073·50
Current assets (W10)	1,607·00
Disposal group (W11)	33·00
Total assets	3,713·50
Equity and liabilities	
Equity attributable to owners of parent	
Share capital	920·00
Retained earnings (W5)	936·08
Other components of equity (W5)	77·80
	1,933·88
Non-controlling interest (W7)	394·62
	2,328·50
Total non-current liabilities (W10)	711·00
Disposal group (W11)	3·00
Current liabilities (W6)	671·00
Total liabilities	1,385·00
Total equity and liabilities	3,713·50

Working 1

Bower

	$m	$m
Purchase consideration		730
Fair value of non-controlling interest		295
Fair value of identifiable net assets acquired:		
Share capital	400	
Retained earnings	319	
OCE	27	
FV adjustment – land	89	
		(835)
Goodwill		190

Working 2

Heeny

	$m	$m
Purchase consideration –		320
Less consideration belonging to NCI – (30% of $320)		(96)
NCI fair value of 44% holding		161
Fair value of identifiable net assets:		
Share capital	200	
Retained earnings	106	
OCE	20	
FV adjustment – land	36	
		(362)
Goodwill		23

Impairment test of Bower and Heeny

	Bower $m	Heeny $m
Goodwill	190	23
Assets	1,130	595
Fair value adjustment	89	36
Total asset value	1,409	654
Recoverable amount	(1,425)	(604)
Impairment	n/a	50

There is no impairment in the case of Bower but Heeny's assets are impaired. Goodwill of $23 million plus $27 million of the intangible assets will be written off. The reason for the latter write down is because the directors feel that the reason for the reduction in the recoverable amount is due to the intangible assets' poor performance.

Group reserves will be debited with $28 million and NCI with $22 million, being the loss in value of the assets split according to the profit sharing ratio.

Total goodwill is therefore ($190m + $23m − $23m impairment), i.e. $190 million

Working 3

Puttin

The gain of $3 million ($21m − $18m) recorded within OCE up to 1 June 2012 would not be transferred to profit or loss for the year but can be transferred within equity and hence to retained earnings under IFRS 9 *Financial Instruments*.

The amount included in the consolidated statement of financial position would be:

	$m
Cost ($21 million + $27 million)	48
Share of post-acquisition profits ($30 million x 0·5 x 30%)	4·5
Less dividend received	(2·0)
	50·5

The dividend should have been credited to Minny's profit or loss and not OCI. Dividend income as an investment and as an associate is treated in the same way as a credit to profit or loss. There is no impairment as the carrying amount of the investment in the separate financial statements does not exceed the carrying amount in the consolidated financial statements nor does the dividend exceed the total comprehensive income of the associate in the period in which the dividend is declared.

Working 4

Intangible assets

Minny should recognise the $10 million as an intangible asset plus the cost of the prototype of $4 million and the $3 million to get it into condition for sale. The remainder of the costs should be expensed including the marketing costs. This totals $9 million, which should be taken out of intangibles and expensed.

Dr Retained earnings $9 million
Cr Intangible assets $9 million

Working 5

Retained earnings

	$m
Balance at 30 November 2012: Minny	895·00
Post-acquisition reserves: Bower (70% of (442 − 319))	86·10
Heeny (56% of (139 − 106))	18·48
Puttin: fair value of investment at acquisition from OCE	3·00
Puttin: share of post-acquisition retained profits (W3) (4·5 − 2)	2·50
Dividend income from OCE	2·00
Intangible assets	(9·00)
Impairment loss on goodwill of Heeny (W2)	(28·00)
Impairment loss on disposal group (W11)	(34·00)
Total	936·08

Other components of equity

	$m
Balance at 30 November 2012: Minny	73
Post-acquisition reserves: Bower (70% of (37 – 27))	7
Heeny (56% of (25 – 20))	2·8
Dividend income to retained earnings	(2)
Transfer to retained earnings	(3)
	77·8

Working 6

Current liabilities

	$m
Balance at 30 November 2012	
Minny	408
Bower	128
Heeny	138
	674
Disposal group	(3)
	671

Working 7

Non-controlling interest

	$m
Bower (W1)	295
Heeny (W2) – purchase consideration	(96)
Fair value	161
Post-acquisition reserves – Bower	
Retained earnings (30% of (442 – 319))	36·9
OCE (30% of (37 – 27))	3
Heeny	
Retained earnings (44% of (139 – 106))	14·52
OCE (44% of (25 – 20))	2·2
Impairment loss (W2)	(22)
	394·62

Working 8

Intangibles

	$m	$m
Minny	198	
Bower	30	
Heeny	35	
Intangible expensed	(9)	
Impairment of intangible	(27)	
		227

Working 9

Property, plant and equipment

	$m	$m
Minny	920	
Bower	300	
Heeny	310	
		1,530
Increase in value of land – Bower (W1)		89
Increase in value of land – Heeny (W2)		36
		1,655
Disposal group		(49)
		1,606

Working 10

Non-current liabilities

	$m	$m
Minny	495	
Bower	123	
Heeny	93	
		711

Current assets

	$m	$m
Minny	895	
Bower	480	
Heeny	250	
		1,625
Disposal group		(18)
		1,607

Working 11

Disposal group

	$m
PPE	49
Inventory	18
Current liabilities	(3)
Proceeds	(30)
Impairment loss	34

The assets and liabilities will be shown as single line items in the statement of financial position. Assets at ($67 – 34 m), i.e. $33 million and liabilities at $3 million. A plan to dispose of net assets is an impairment indicator.

(b) An asset or disposal group is available for immediate sale in its present condition, if the entity has the intention and ability to transfer the asset or disposal group to a buyer. There is no guidance in the standard on what constitutes available for immediate sale but the guidance notes set out various examples. Customary terms of sale such as surveys and searches of property do not preclude the classification as held for sale. However, present conditions do not include any conditions that have been imposed by the seller of the asset or disposal group, such as if planning permission is required before sale. In this case, the asset is not held for sale. The problem is determining whether the entity truly intends to dispose of the group of assets.

A sale is 'highly probable' where it is significantly more likely than probable that the sale will occur and probable is defined as 'more likely than not'. IFRS 5 attempts to clarify what this means by setting out the criteria for a sale to be highly probable. These criteria are: there is evidence of management commitment; there is an active programme to locate a buyer and complete the plan; the asset is actively marketed for sale at a reasonable price compared to its fair value; the sale is expected to be completed within 12 months of the date of classification; and actions required to complete the plan indicate that it is unlikely that there will be significant changes to the plan or that it will be withdrawn.

Because the standard defines 'highly probable' as 'significantly more likely than probable', this creates a high threshold of certainty before recognition as held-for-sale. IFRS 5 expands on this requirement with some specific conditions but the uncertainty still remains. Thus, a number of issues has arisen over the implementation of the standard, mainly due to the fact that there is subjectivity over the requirements of the standard.

(c) A company may distribute non-cash assets. The transfer of the asset from Bower to Minny amounts to a distribution of profits rather than a loss on disposal. The shortfall between the sale proceeds and the carrying amount is $1 million and this will be treated as a distribution. Bower has retained earnings of $442 million available at the year end plus the sale of the non-current asset will 'realise' an additional amount of $400,000 from the revaluation reserve. It is likely that the sale will be legal, depending upon the jurisdiction concerned. If the transaction meets the criteria of IFRS 5 *Non-current Assets Held for Sale and Discontinued Operations* paragraphs 6 to 8, then the asset would be held in the financial statements of Bower in a separate category from plant, property and equipment and would be measured at the lower of carrying amount at held-for-sale date and fair value less costs to sell. If the asset is held for sale, IAS 16 *Property, Plant and Equipment* does not apply.

The boundary between ethical practices and legality is sometimes blurred. Questions would be asked of the directors as to why they would want to sell an asset at half of its current value, assuming that $2 million is the current value and that $1 million is not a fair approximation of fair value. It may raise suspicion. Corporate reporting involves the development and disclosure of information, which should be truthful and neutral. Both Bower and Minny would need to make related party disclosures so that the transaction is understood by stakeholders.

The nature of the responsibility of the directors requires a high level of ethical behaviour. Shareholders, potential shareholders, and other users of the financial statements rely heavily on the financial statements of a company as they can use this information to make an informed decision about investment. They rely on the directors to present a true and fair view of the company. Unethical behaviour is difficult to control or define. However, it is likely that this action will cause a degree of mistrust between the directors and shareholders unless there is a logical business reason for their actions. Shareholders in most jurisdictions who receive an unlawful dividend are liable to repay it to the company.

2 **(a)** Coate should determine, apply and disclose appropriate policies covering the acquisition, the presentation and measurement of the certificates in its financial statements. The green certificates should be accounted for as government grants in accordance with IAS 20 *Accounting for Government Grants and Disclosure of Government Assistance*. The green certificates qualify as government grants in accordance with IAS 20, as they represent assistance by government in the form of resources provided to an entity in return for past compliance with certain conditions relating to its operating activities. A government grant is recognised only when there is reasonable assurance that the entity will comply with any conditions attached to the grant and the grant will be received.

A grant is recognised as income over the period necessary to match it with the related costs, for which they are intended to compensate, on a systematic basis.

The certificates are income-related grants according to the standard as the certificates are not long-term assets. The qualification of the green certificates as income-related grants has implications for the financial statements. In accordance with IAS 20, the green certificates must be shown as a credit in profit or loss, either separately or under a general heading such as 'Other income'. Alternatively, they must be deducted in reporting the related expense. Additionally, Coate should disclose an accounting policy for government grants and provide the additional disclosures required in respect of the nature and extent of the government assistance given and any unfulfilled conditions or other contingencies attaching.

To the extent that the certificates were not sold by the end of the accounting period, Coate should recognise them under inventories in accordance with IAS 2 *Inventories*, as they are held for sale in the ordinary course of business within the meaning of the standard. On sale, the income from green certificates is shown as 'Sale of green certificates' in accordance with IAS 18 *Revenue* and the related green certificates, included in inventory, are charged to production as part of the cost of sales.

The journal entry to record the quarterly receipt of the grant is:

DR	Certificate (SOFP)	$fair value of certificate at receipt
CR	Deferred revenue (SOFP)	$fair value of certificate at receipt

On the sale of a certificate – this is when its value is realised and the following entries will be posted:

DR	Deferred revenue (SOFP)	$fair value of certificate at receipt
CR	Cost of sale (SOCI)	$fair value of certificate at receipt

Being a contribution to the cost of generating electricity.

DR	Bank/Receivable (SOFP)	$fair value of trade
CR	Certificate (SOFP)	$fair value of certificate at receipt
DR/CR	Revenue (SOCI)	$balance

Being the surplus or deficit as compared to the proceeds received from the national government and hence the true value of the sale of the certificate.

The accounting policies relating to the accounting treatment of the green certificates should be disclosed in the financial statements as required by IAS 1 *Presentation of Financial Statements*.

(b) IAS 7 *Statement of Cash Flows* states that unrealised gains and losses arising from changes in foreign exchange rates are not cash flows. However, the effect of exchange rate changes on cash and cash equivalents held or due in a foreign currency is reported in the statement of cash flows in order to reconcile cash and cash equivalents at the beginning and the end of the period. This amount is presented separately from cash flows from operating, investing and financing activities and includes the differences had those cash flows been reported at the end of period exchange rates.

The method of translation for foreign operations in IAS 21 *The Effects of Changes in Foreign Exchange Rates* requires monetary and non-monetary assets and liabilities to be translated at the closing rate, and income and expense items to be translated at the rate ruling at the date of the transaction or an average rate that approximates to the actual exchange rates. All exchange differences are taken to a separate component of equity, until disposal of the foreign operation when they are classified from equity to profit or loss.

All exchange differences relating to the retranslation of a foreign operation's opening net assets to the closing rate will have been recognised in other comprehensive income and presented in a separate component of equity. As such exchange differences have no cash flow effect, they will not be included in the consolidated statement of cash flows. However, the opening net assets of Coate include foreign currency cash and cash equivalents; therefore the exchange difference arising on their retranslation at the closing rate for the current period will have been reflected in the closing balances in the financial statements. Such translation differences should be reported in the cash flow statement to determine the total movement in cash and cash equivalents in the period.

(c) In accordance with IFRS 10 *Consolidated Financial Statements*, an investor considers all relevant facts and circumstances when assessing whether it controls an investee. An investor controls an investee when it is exposed, or has rights, to variable returns from its involvement with the investee and has the ability to affect those returns through its power over the investee.

An investor controls an investee if and only if the investor has all of the following elements:

- power over the investee, that is the investor has existing rights that give it the ability to direct the relevant activities (the activities that significantly affect the investee's returns)
- exposure, or rights, to variable returns from its involvement with the investee
- the ability to use its power over the investee to affect the amount of the investor's returns.

Power arises from rights which may be obvious through voting rights or be complex because of contractual arrangements. An investor that holds only protective rights cannot have power over an investee and so cannot control an investee. A parent must also have the ability to use its power over the investee to affect its returns from its involvement with the investee.

The shareholder agreement shows that Coate has influence over the company but the restrictions in the agreement with regards to decisions to be made in the ordinary course of business, such as consensus between shareholders required for acquisition of assets above a certain value, employment or dismissal of senior employees, distribution of dividends or establishment of loan facilities, indicates that Coate does not control Patten. Such terms of the agreement indicate the existence of a joint arrangement in accordance with IFRS 11 *Joint Arrangements*, that is a joint venture, as decisions are made at entity level operations and not regarding individual assets and liabilities.

Coate argued that the restrictions do not constitute a hindrance to the power to control, as it is customary within the industry to require shareholder consensus for decisions of the types listed in the shareholders' agreement.

However, the agreement contains so many significant restrictions with respect to operating and financial decisions that it does not entail control of Patten. As shareholder consensus is required in respect of many significant decisions, Coate is unable to utilise the position it has at board level where it has the power to cast the majority of votes.

As such, Coate is required to deconsolidate Patten as a subsidiary from its group accounts as it does not control the entity. Further, Coate should account for Patten in accordance with IAS 28 *Associates and Joint Ventures*. This will require Coate to equity account for Patten within the consolidated financial statements.

(d) The tax adjustments resulting from the taxation authority audits should be treated as a change in an accounting estimate and not as a prior period adjustment. Tax expenses are difficult to estimate correctly and tax computations are open for review or audit by taxation authorities for a number of years after the end of the reporting period. IAS 8 *Accounting Policies, Changes in Accounting Estimates and Errors* provides that the effect of a change in an accounting estimate should be recognised prospectively by including it in profit or loss in the period of the change. It also states that an entity should correct material prior period errors retrospectively in the first set of financial statements authorised for issue after their discovery by restating the comparative amounts. A prior period error is an omission from or misstatement in the entity's financial statements arising from a failure to use or misuse of reliable information that was available at the time of authorisation of the financial statements and could reasonably be expected to have been obtained and taken into account at the time of their preparation and presentation.

IAS 12 *Income Taxes* requires separate disclosure of the major components of the tax expense. It states that such components may include any adjustments recognised in the period for current tax of prior periods and the deferred tax expense. Thus, separate disclosure of these elements of the tax adjustments is required. The audit adjustments did not arise from a failure to use reliable information, which was available during previous reporting periods, as Coate correctly applied the provisions of tax law. The issues that the adjustments related to were transfer pricing issues for which there was a range of possible outcomes that were negotiated during 2012 with the taxation authorities. This indicates that these adjustments were effectively a change in an accounting estimate. Further at 31 May 2011, Coate had accounted for all known issues arising from the audits to that date and the adjustment could not have been foreseen as at 31 May 2011, as the audit authorities changed the scope of the audit. Thus, the adjustments could not have been made at 31 May 2011 as the information and conditions did not exist at that date. Further, no penalties were expected to be applied by the taxation authorities, which indicates that there were no errors in the provision of information to the authorities, which again points to a change in accounting estimate and not a prior period error.

3 (a) IAS 40 *Investment Property* sets out the accounting treatment for investment property and the related disclosure requirements. It deals with the recognition, measurement and disclosure of investment property. The scope includes property held for capital appreciation or to earn rentals. Investment property is defined as property held by the owner or held on a finance lease to earn rentals or for capital appreciation or both, rather than for:

- use in producing or supplying goods or services or for administrative purposes; or
- sale in the ordinary course of business.

The definition excludes owner-occupied property, property intended for sale in the ordinary course of business, property being constructed on behalf of third parties and property that is leased to a third party under a finance lease.

Where the fair value model under IAS 40 is applied, such a property is measured at fair value. Where an entity provides ancillary services to occupants of a property owned by the entity, the property is an investment property if such ancillary services are a relatively insignificant portion of the arrangement as a whole. Where, however, such services are a more significant portion, such as in a hotel, the property is treated not as investment property, but as an owner-occupied property.

Investment property should be recognised as an asset when it is probable that the future economic benefits associated with the property will flow to the entity and the cost of the property can be reliably measured.

Thus, the land that is owned by Blackcutt for capital appreciation which may be sold at any time in the future and the land that has no current purpose are both considered to be investment property under IAS 40. If the land has no current purpose, it is considered to be held for capital appreciation.

Blackcutt supplements its income by buying and selling property, and the housing department regularly sells part of its housing inventory. As these sales are in the ordinary course of its operations and are routinely occurring, then the housing stock held for sale will be classified as inventory. The part of the inventory which is not held for sale, held to provide housing to low-income employees at below market rental will not be treated as investment property as the property is not held for capital appreciation and the income just covers the cost of maintaining the properties and thus is not for profit. The property is held to provide housing services rather than rentals. The rental revenue is incidental to the purposes for which the property is held. This property will be accounted for under IAS 16 *Property, Plant and Equipment*. The property is treated as owner occupied as set out above.

(b) An entity may enter into an arrangement that does not take the legal form of a lease but conveys a right to use an asset. An entity should use the Conceptual Framework for Financial Reporting in conjunction with IAS 17 *Leases* to determine whether such arrangements are, or contain, leases that should be accounted for in accordance with the standard. Determining whether an arrangement is, or contains, a lease is based on the substance of the arrangement and requires an assessment of:

(i)   the risks and rewards of the arrangement and how best to recognise them;
(ii) the right to use the asset or direct others to use the asset;
(iii) the right to control the use of the underlying asset by operating the asset or directing others to operate the asset;
(iv) who obtains much of the benefit from the asset.

In this case, the private sector provider purchases the vehicles and uses them exclusively for the local government organisation. The vehicles are ostensibly those of Blackcutt as they are painted with the local government name and colours. Blackcutt can use the vehicles and the vehicles are used in this connection for nearly all of the asset's life. In the event of the private sector provider's business ceasing, Blackcutt can re-possess the vehicles and carry on the refuse collection service. Thus, the arrangement fits the terms of a lease and Blackcutt should account for the vehicles as a finance lease.

The value associated with the lease can be obtained by considering the fair value of acquiring the vehicle. This will also be the initial lease obligation. The payment made by Blackcutt to the leasing company may be two-fold, representing the cost of the lease obligation and the service element relating to the cost of the collection of the waste.

(c) A provision shall be recognised under IAS 37 *Provisions, Contingent Liabilities and Contingent Assets* when there is a present obligation (legal or constructive) as a result of a past event, it is probable that an outflow of resources embodying economic benefits or service potential will be required to settle the obligation, and a reliable estimate can be made of the amount of the obligation. If the above conditions are not met, no provision shall be recognised. In this case, the obligating event is the contamination of the land because of the virtual certainty of legislation requiring the clean up. Additionally, there is probably going to be an outflow of resources embodying economic benefits, because Blackcutt has no recourse against the entity or its insurance company. Therefore a provision is recognised for the best estimate of the costs of the clean up. As Blackcutt has no recourse against Chemco, recovery of the costs of clean up is not likely and hence no corresponding receivable should be recorded.

(d) An asset is carried at more than its recoverable amount if its carrying amount exceeds the amount to be recovered through use or sale of the asset. If this is the case, the asset is described as impaired and IAS 36 *Impairment of Assets* requires the recognition of an impairment loss. At the end of each reporting period, an assessment should take place as to whether there is any indication that an asset may be impaired. If any indication exists, the recoverable amount should be estimated taking into account the concept of materiality in identifying whether the recoverable amount of an asset needs to be estimated. If no indication of an impairment loss is present, IAS 36 does not require a formal estimate of the recoverable amount, with the exception of intangible assets.

Impairment in this case is indicated because the purpose for which the building is used has changed significantly from a place for educating students to a library and this is not anticipated to change for the foreseeable future. There is insufficient information to determine value in use and net selling price (fair value less selling costs); as such, depreciated replacement cost should be used as an approximation of the recoverable amount. An impairment loss using a depreciated replacement cost approach would be determined as follows:

Asset	Cost/replacement cost $000	Accumulated depreciation $000 – 6/25	Carrying amount/ replacement cost $000 30 November 2012
School	5,000	(1,200)	3,800
Library	2,100	504	(1,596)
Impairment loss			2,204

Thus Blackcutt would record the impairment loss of $2·204m.

4 (a) (i) Fair value has had a different meaning depending on the context and usage. The IASB's definition is the price that would be received to sell an asset or paid to transfer a liability in an orderly transaction between market participants at the measurement date. Basically it is an exit price. Fair value is focused on the assumptions of the market place and is not entity specific. It therefore takes into account any assumptions about risk. Fair value is measured using the same assumptions and taking into account the same characteristics of the asset or liability as market participants would. Such conditions would include the condition and location of the asset and any restrictions on its sale or use. Further, it is not relevant if the entity insists that prices are too low relative to its own valuation of the asset and that it would be unwilling to sell at low prices. Prices to be used are those in 'an orderly transaction'. An orderly transaction is one that assumes exposure to the market for a period before the date of measurement to allow for normal marketing activities and to ensure that it is not a forced transaction. If the transaction is not 'orderly', then there will not have been enough time to create competition and potential buyers may reduce the price that they are willing to pay. Similarly, if a seller is forced to accept a price in a short period of time, the price may not be representative. It does not follow that a market in which there are few transactions is not orderly. If there has been competitive tension, sufficient time and information about the asset, then this may result in a fair value for the asset.

IFRS 13 does not specify the unit of account for measuring fair value. This means that it is left to the individual standard to determine the unit of account for fair value measurement. A unit of account is the single asset or liability or group of assets or liabilities. The characteristic of an asset or liability must be distinguished from a characteristic arising from the holding of an asset or liability by an entity. An example of this is that if an entity sold a large block of shares, it may have to do so at a discount to the market price. This is a characteristic of holding the asset rather than of the asset itself and should not be taken into account when fair valuing the asset.

Fair value measurement assumes that the transaction to sell the asset or transfer the liability takes place in the principal market for the asset or liability or, in the absence of a principal market, in the most advantageous market for the asset or liability. The principal market is the one with the greatest volume and level of activity for the asset or liability that can be accessed by the entity.

The most advantageous market is the one which maximises the amount that would be received for the asset or minimises the amount that would be paid to transfer the liability after transport and transaction costs.

An entity does not have to carry out an exhaustive search to identify either market but should take into account all available information. Although transaction costs are taken into account when identifying the most advantageous market, the fair value is not after adjustment for transaction costs because these costs are characteristics of the transaction and not the asset or liability. If location is a factor, then the market price is adjusted for the costs incurred to transport the asset to that market. Market participants must be independent of each other and knowledgeable, and able and willing to enter into transactions.

IFRS 13 sets out a valuation approach, which refers to a broad range of techniques, which can be used. These techniques are threefold. The market, income and cost approaches.

(ii) When measuring fair value, the entity is required to maximise the use of observable inputs and minimise the use of unobservable inputs. To this end, the standard introduces a fair value hierarchy, which prioritises the inputs into the fair value measurement process.

Level 1 inputs are quoted prices (unadjusted) in active markets for items identical to the asset or liability being measured. As with current IFRS, if there is a quoted price in an active market, an entity uses that price without adjustment when measuring fair value. An example of this would be prices quoted on a stock exchange. The entity needs to be able to access the market at the measurement date. Active markets are ones where transactions take place with sufficient frequency and volume for pricing information to be provided. An alternative method may be used where it is expedient. The standard sets out certain criteria where this may be applicable. For example, where the price quoted in an active market does not represent fair value at the measurement date. An example of this may be where a significant event takes place after the close of the market such as a business reorganisation or combination.

The determination of whether a fair value measurement is level 2 or level 3 inputs depends on whether the inputs are observable inputs or unobservable inputs and their significance.

Level 2 inputs are inputs other than the quoted prices in level 1 that are directly or indirectly observable for that asset or liability. They are quoted assets or liabilities for similar items in active markets or supported by market data. For example, interest rates, credit spreads or yield curves. Adjustments may be needed to level 2 inputs and if this adjustment is significant, then it may require the fair value to be classified as level 3.

Level 3 inputs are unobservable inputs. The use of these inputs should be kept to a minimum. However, situations may occur where relevant inputs are not observable and therefore these inputs must be developed to reflect the assumptions that market participants would use when determining an appropriate price for the asset or liability. The entity should maximise the use of relevant observable inputs and minimise the use of unobservable inputs. The general principle of using an exit price remains and IFRS 13 does not preclude an entity from using its own data. For example, cash flow forecasts may be used to value an entity that is not listed. Each fair value measurement is categorised based on the lowest level input that is significant to it.

(b)

Year to 31 December 2012	Asian Market	European Market	Australasian Market
Volume of market – units	4 million	2 million	1 million
Price	$19	$16	$22
Costs of entering the market	($2)	($2)	(n/a) see note
Potential fair value	$17	$14	$22
Transaction costs	($1)	($2)	($2)
Net profit	$16	$14	$20

Note: As Jayach buys and sells in Australasia, the costs of entering the market are not relevant as these would not be incurred. Further transaction costs are not considered as these are not included as part of the valuation.

The principal market for the asset is the Asian market because of the fact that it has the highest level of activity due to the highest volume of units sold. The most advantageous market is the Australasian market because it returns the best profit per unit. If the information about the markets is reasonably available, then Jayach should base its fair value on prices in the Asian market due to it being the principal market, assuming that Jayach can access the market. The pricing is taken from this market even though the entity does not currently transact in the market and is not the most advantageous. The fair value would be $17, as transport costs would be taken into account but not transaction costs.

If the entity cannot access the Asian or European market, or reliable information about the markets is not available, Jayach would use the data from the Australasian market and the fair value would be $22. The principal market is not always the market in which the entity transacts. Market participants must be independent of each other and knowledgeable, and able and willing to enter into transactions.

Input	Amount ($ 000)
Labour and material cost	2,000
Overhead (30%)	600
Third party mark-up – industry average (20% of 2,600)	520
Total	3,120
Annual inflation rate (3,120 x 5% compounded for three years)	492
Total	3,612
Risk adjustment – 6%	217
Total	3,829
Discounted at risk free rate of government bonds plus entity's non-performance risk – 6%	3,215

The fair value of a liability assumes that it is transferred to a market participant at the measurement date. In many cases there is no observable market to provide pricing information. In this case, the fair value is based on the perspective of a market participant who holds the identical instrument as an asset. If there is no corresponding asset, then a valuation technique is used. This would be the case with the decommissioning activity. The fair value of a liability reflects any compensation for risk and profit margin that a market participant might require to undertake the activity plus the non-performance risk based on the entity's own credit standing. Thus the fair value of the decommissioning liability would be $3,215,000.

			Marks
1	**(a)**	Property, plant and equipment	5
		Goodwill	5
		Intangible assets	1
		Investment in Puttin	4
		Current assets	1
		Disposal group	5
		Retained earnings	6
		Other components of equity	4
		Non-controlling interest	3
		Current liabilities	1
			35
	(b)	1 mark per point up to maximum – definition	4
		Discussion	3
	(c)	Accounting treatment	4
		Ethical considerations	4
			50
2	**(a)**	1 mark per point up to maximum	7
	(b)	1 mark per point up to maximum	5
	(c)	1 mark per point up to maximum	6
	(d)	1 mark per point up to maximum	5
		Professional marks	2
			25
3	**(a)**	1 mark per point up to maximum	7
	(b)	1 mark per point up to maximum	6
	(c)	1 mark per point up to maximum	4
	(d)	1 mark per point up to maximum	6
		Professional marks	2
			25
4	**(a)** **(i)**	1 mark per point up to maximum	9
	(ii)	IFRS 13 hierarchy	4
	(b)	1 mark per point up to maximum	6
		Calculations	4
		Professional marks	2
			25

Mathematical tables

Present value table

Present value of $1 = (1+r)^{-n}$ where r = discount rate, n = number of periods until payment.

This table shows the present value of £1 per annum, receivable or payable at the end of n years.

Periods (n)	Discount rates (r)									
	1%	2%	3%	4%	5%	6%	7%	8%	9%	10%
1	0.990	0.980	0.971	0.962	0.952	0.943	0.935	0.926	0.917	0.909
2	0.980	0.961	0.943	0.925	0.907	0.890	0.873	0.857	0.842	0.826
3	0.971	0.942	0.915	0.889	0.864	0.840	0.816	0.794	0.772	0.751
4	0.961	0.924	0.888	0.855	0.823	0.792	0.763	0.735	0.708	0.683
5	0.951	0.906	0.863	0.822	0.784	0.747	0.713	0.681	0.650	0.621
6	0.942	0.888	0.837	0.790	0.746	0.705	0.666	0.630	0.596	0.564
7	0.933	0.871	0.813	0.760	0.711	0.665	0.623	0.583	0.547	0.513
8	0.923	0.853	0.789	0.731	0.677	0.627	0.582	0.540	0.502	0.467
9	0.914	0.837	0.766	0.703	0.645	0.592	0.544	0.500	0.460	0.424
10	0.905	0.820	0.744	0.676	0.614	0.558	0.508	0.463	0.422	0.386
11	0.896	0.804	0.722	0.650	0.585	0.527	0.475	0.429	0.388	0.350
12	0.887	0.788	0.701	0.625	0.557	0.497	0.444	0.397	0.356	0.319
13	0.879	0.773	0.681	0.601	0.530	0.469	0.415	0.368	0.326	0.290
14	0.870	0.758	0.661	0.577	0.505	0.442	0.388	0.340	0.299	0.263
15	0.861	0.743	0.642	0.555	0.481	0.417	0.362	0.315	0.275	0.239
16	0.853	0.728	0.623	0.534	0.458	0.394	0.339	0.292	0.252	0.218
17	0.844	0.714	0.605	0.513	0.436	0.371	0.317	0.270	0.231	0.198
18	0.836	0.700	0.587	0.494	0.416	0.350	0.296	0.250	0.212	0.180
19	0.828	0.686	0.570	0.475	0.396	0.331	0.277	0.232	0.194	0.164
20	0.820	0.673	0.554	0.456	0.377	0.312	0.258	0.215	0.178	0.149

Periods (n)	Discount rates (r)									
	11%	12%	13%	14%	15%	16%	17%	18%	19%	20%
1	0.901	0.893	0.885	0.877	0.870	0.862	0.855	0.847	0.840	0.833
2	0.812	0.797	0.783	0.769	0.756	0.743	0.731	0.718	0.706	0.694
3	0.731	0.712	0.693	0.675	0.658	0.641	0.624	0.609	0.593	0.579
4	0.659	0.636	0.613	0.592	0.572	0.552	0.534	0.516	0.499	0.482
5	0.593	0.567	0.543	0.519	0.497	0.476	0.456	0.437	0.419	0.402
6	0.535	0.507	0.480	0.456	0.432	0.410	0.390	0.370	0.352	0.335
7	0.482	0.452	0.425	0.400	0.376	0.354	0.333	0.314	0.296	0.279
8	0.434	0.404	0.376	0.351	0.327	0.305	0.285	0.266	0.249	0.233
9	0.391	0.361	0.333	0.308	0.284	0.263	0.243	0.225	0.209	0.194
10	0.352	0.322	0.295	0.270	0.247	0.227	0.208	0.191	0.176	0.162
11	0.317	0.287	0.261	0.237	0.215	0.195	0.178	0.162	0.148	0.135
12	0.286	0.257	0.231	0.208	0.187	0.168	0.152	0.137	0.124	0.112
13	0.258	0.229	0.204	0.182	0.163	0.145	0.130	0.116	0.104	0.093
14	0.232	0.205	0.181	0.160	0.141	0.125	0.111	0.099	0.088	0.078
15	0.209	0.183	0.160	0.140	0.123	0.108	0.095	0.084	0.074	0.065
16	0.188	0.163	0.141	0.123	0.107	0.093	0.081	0.071	0.062	0.054
17	0.170	0.146	0.125	0.108	0.093	0.080	0.069	0.060	0.052	0.045
18	0.153	0.130	0.111	0.095	0.081	0.069	0.059	0.051	0.044	0.038
19	0.138	0.116	0.098	0.083	0.070	0.060	0.051	0.043	0.037	0.031
20	0.124	0.104	0.087	0.073	0.061	0.051	0.043	0.037	0.031	0.026

Cumulative present value table

This table shows the present value of £1 per annum, receivable or payable at the end of each year for *n* years.

Periods					Discount rates (r)					
(n)	1%	2%	3%	4%	5%	6%	7%	8%	9%	10%
1	0.990	0.980	0.971	0.962	0.952	0.943	0.935	0.926	0.917	0.909
2	1.970	1.942	1.913	1.886	1.859	1.833	1.808	1.783	1.759	1.736
3	2.941	2.884	2.829	2.775	2.723	2.673	2.624	2.577	2.531	2.487
4	3.902	3.808	3.717	3.630	3.546	3.465	3.387	3.312	3.240	3.170
5	4.853	4.713	4.580	4.452	4.329	4.212	4.100	3.993	3.890	3.791
6	5.795	5.601	5.417	5.242	5.076	4.917	4.767	4.623	4.486	4.355
7	6.728	6.472	6.230	6.002	5.786	5.582	5.389	5.206	5.033	4.868
8	7.652	7.325	7.020	6.733	6.463	6.210	5.971	5.747	5.535	5.335
9	8.566	8.162	7.786	7.435	7.108	6.802	6.515	6.247	5.995	5.759
10	9.471	8.983	8.530	8.111	7.722	7.360	7.024	6.710	6.418	6.145
11	10.37	9.787	9.253	8.760	8.306	7.887	7.499	7.139	6.805	6.495
12	11.26	10.58	9.954	9.385	8.863	8.384	7.943	7.536	7.161	6.814
13	12.13	11.35	10.63	9.986	9.394	8.853	8.358	7.904	7.487	7.103
14	13.00	12.11	11.30	10.56	9.899	9.295	8.745	8.244	7.786	7.367
15	13.87	12.85	11.94	11.12	10.38	9.712	9.108	8.559	8.061	7.606
16	14.718	13.578	12.561	11.652	10.838	10.106	9.447	8.851	8.313	7.824
17	15.562	14.292	13.166	12.166	11.274	10.477	9.763	9.122	8.544	8.022
18	16.398	14.992	13.754	12.659	11.690	10.828	10.059	9.372	8.756	8.201
19	17.226	15.678	14.324	13.134	12.085	11.158	10.336	9.604	8.950	8.365
20	18.046	16.351	14.877	13.590	12.462	11.470	10.594	9.818	9.129	8.514

Periods					Discount rates (r)					
(n)	11%	12%	13%	14%	15%	16%	17%	18%	19%	20%
1	0.901	0.893	0.885	0.877	0.870	0.862	0.855	0.847	0.840	0.833
2	1.713	1.690	1.668	1.647	1.626	1.605	1.585	1.566	1.547	1.528
3	2.444	2.402	2.361	2.322	2.283	2.246	2.210	2.174	2.140	2.106
4	3.102	3.037	2.974	2.914	2.855	2.798	2.743	2.690	2.639	2.589
5	3.696	3.605	3.517	3.433	3.352	3.274	3.199	3.127	3.058	2.991
6	4.231	4.111	3.998	3.889	3.784	3.685	3.589	3.498	3.410	3.326
7	4.712	4.564	4.423	4.288	4.160	4.039	3.922	3.812	3.706	3.605
8	5.146	4.968	4.799	4.639	4.487	4.344	4.207	4.078	3.954	3.837
9	5.537	5.328	5.132	4.946	4.772	4.607	4.451	4.303	4.163	4.031
10	5.889	5.650	5.426	5.216	5.019	4.833	4.659	4.494	4.339	4.192
11	6.207	5.938	5.687	5.453	5.234	5.029	4.836	4.656	4.486	4.327
12	6.492	6.194	5.918	5.660	5.421	5.197	4.988	4.793	4.611	4.439
13	6.750	6.424	6.122	5.842	5.583	5.342	5.118	4.910	4.715	4.533
14	6.982	6.628	6.302	6.002	5.724	5.468	5.229	5.008	4.802	4.611
15	7.191	6.811	6.462	6.142	5.847	5.575	5.324	5.092	4.876	4.675
16	7.379	6.974	6.604	6.265	5.954	5.668	5.405	5.162	4.938	4.730
17	7.549	7.120	6.729	6.373	6.047	5.749	5.475	5.222	4.990	4.775
18	7.702	7.250	6.840	6.467	6.128	5.818	5.534	5.273	5.033	4.812
19	7.839	7.366	6.938	6.550	6.198	5.877	5.584	5.316	5.070	4.843
20	7.963	7.469	7.025	6.623	6.259	5.929	5.628	5.353	5.101	4.870

Review Form – Paper P2 Corporate Reporting (International and UK) (1/13)

Name: _____   Address: _____

_____

_____

How have you used this Kit?
(Tick one box only)

☐ Home study (book only)

☐ On a course: college _____

☐ With 'correspondence' package

☐ Other _____

Why did you decide to purchase this Kit?
(Tick one box only)

☐ Have used the complementary Study text

☐ Have used other BPP products in the past

☐ Recommendation by friend/colleague

☐ Recommendation by a lecturer at college

☐ Saw advertising

☐ Other _____

Which BPP products have you used?

Text	☐	Success CD	☐	Interactive Passcards	☐
Kit	☑	i-Pass	☐	Home Study Package	☐
Passcards	☐				

Which BPP products have you used?

During the past six months do you recall seeing/receiving any of the following?
(Tick as many boxes as are relevant)

☐ Our advertisement in *Student Accountant*

☐ Our advertisement in *Pass*

☐ Our advertisement in *PQ*

☐ Our brochure with a letter through the post

☐ Our website www.bpp.com

Which (if any) aspects of our advertising do you find useful?
(Tick as many boxes as are relevant)

☐ Prices and publication dates of new editions

☐ Information on product content

☐ Facility to order books off-the-page

☐ None of the above

Your ratings, comments and suggestions would be appreciated on the following areas.

	Very useful	Useful	Not useful
Passing ACCA exams	☐	☐	☐
Passing P2	☐	☐	☐
Planning your question practice	☐	☐	☐
Questions	☐	☐	☐
Top Tips etc in answers	☐	☐	☐
Content and structure of answers	☐	☐	☐
'Plan of attack' in mock exams	☐	☐	☐
Mock exam answers	☐	☐	☐

Overall opinion of this Kit	Excellent ☐	Good ☐	Adequate ☐	Poor ☐

Do you intend to continue using BPP products?   Yes ☐   No ☐

The BPP author of this edition can be e-mailed at: katyhibbert@bpp.com

Please return this form to: Nick Weller, ACCA Publishing Manager, BPP Learning Media Ltd, FREEPOST, London, W12 8BR

Review Form (continued)

TELL US WHAT YOU THINK

Please note any further comments and suggestions/errors below.